Z80 MICROPROCESSOR TECHNOLOGY

HARDWARE, SOFTWARE AND INTERFACI

James Bignell
Robert Donovan
MANATEE COMMUNITY COLLEGE
BRADENTON, FLORIDA

Delmar Publishers Inc.®

NOTICE TO THE READER

Publisher does not warrant or guarantee any of the products described herein or perform any independent analysis in connection with any of the product information contained herein. Publisher does not assume, and expressly disclaims, any obligation to obtain and include information other than that provided to it by the manufacturer.

The reader is expressly warned to consider and adopt all safety precautions that might be indicated by the activities described herein and to avoid all potential hazards. By following the instructions contained herein, the reader willingly assumes all risks in connection with such instructions.

The publisher makes no representations or warranties of any kind, including but not limited to, the warranties of fitness for particular purpose or merchantability, nor are any such representations implied with respect to the material set forth herein, and the publisher takes no responsibility with respect to such material. The publisher shall not be liable for any special, consequential or exemplary damages resulting, in whole or in part, from the readers' use of, or reliance upon, this material.

COVER PHOTO: Reproduced by permission of Zilog, Inc.

Delmar Staff
Administrative Editor: Mark W. Huth
Associate Editor: Jonathan Plant
Production Editor: Eleanor Isenhart
Art Director: Ronald Blackman
Design Coordinator: John Orozco

Delmar Publishers' Online Services
To access Delmar on the World Wide Web, point your browser to:
http://www.delmar.com/delmar.html
To access through Gopher: gopher://gopher.delmar.com
(Delmar Online is part of "thomson.com", an Internet site with information on more than 30 publishers of the International Thomson Publishing organization.)
For information on our products and services:
email: info@delmar.com
or call 800-347-7707

For information, address Delmar Publishers Inc.,
2 Computer Drive West, Box 15-015,
Albany, New York 12212-5015

Printed in the United States of America
Published simultaneously in Canada
by Nelson Canada,
A Division of International Thomson Limited

10 9 8 7 6 5 4

Library of Congress Cataloging in Publication Data

Bignell, James.
Z80 microprocessor technology.

Includes index.
1. Zilog Z80 (Microprocessor) I. Donovan, Robert.
II. Title.
QA76.8.Z54B54 1986 004.165 85-25302
ISBN 0-8273-2492-8

Contents

Preface

Z80® *Microprocessor Technology* was written to be the primary text for a systematic and sequential course in microprocessors. It is assumed that the student has had a good course in basic digital electronics and will be able to use typical electronic tools such as oscilloscopes, voltmeters, and signal generators. Although it is not necessary, a knowledge of programming in some higher languages will be quite helpful for the student who is to read the material presented in this text.

The material is divided into 14 chapters and is intended to be covered in a typical one-semester course. The authors have tried to write the material clearly and systematically. The Z 80 microprocessor was chosen to revolve the subject material around because the authors feel that it offers a good representation of the subject material and is not so complex as to be difficult for the student to comprehend. The Z 80 is widely used and easier to understand than a 16-bit processor, such as the 68000. The choice of typical LSI interface chips such as the 8255, 8253, and the 8251 were chosen because they are typical of LSI ICs used by many companies and are straightforward and easily understood. It is the opinion of the authors that after the completion of the material presented in this textbook a student could easily transfer the knowledge learned to another processor or LSI interface IC as needed.

Programming is stressed throughout the text and Chapters 4–8 are on the Z 80 instruction set and programming. Both authors strongly feel that the student must master the programming of a microprocessor to fully understand the hardware associated with the processor.

A simple but efficient Z 80 microtrainer was designed to be used in the labs of this text. The Biggy trainer, as it is called, can be constructed by the students in the course, or the instructor could adapt another trainer for the lab portion of the course. Each chapter except the last one has lab exercises that reinforce the material presented in the chapter. These labs refer to and use the Z 80 Biggy trainer as the base of operation, but almost any Z 80 trainer could be adapted to run the labs.

The course was first envisioned as having each student or lab group build the Z 80 Biggy trainer during the labs of the first three chapters. This would cost about $100.00 per trainer and take the students between 12 and 20 hours to complete.

Because most institutions who would be teaching a micro course cannot afford the $100.00 per student price tag, it was decided that the course should also be able to use preconstructed trainers. Therefore, there are labs at the end of the first three chapters for students to complete on an up-and-running trainer. The authors had the first class of students to use the Biggy trainer build those trainers, and we have used them each semester ever since. It is hard to match the degree of skill and knowledge acquired by students who build their own trainers with any other teaching method.

The appendixes have a complete set of schematics and parts list for the Biggy trainer, and the Instructor's Guide gives further guidance as to how to manage a group of students while building the trainers.

Programs presented in this text are written in assembly language and have been assembled with a Z 80 assembler. It is recommended that the students use a small microcomputer, or other computer, to assemble the program used in the lab. There are many microcomputers that are Z 80 based and have editor assemblers available for them. If it is impossible to find such a computer, the programs can be hand assembled but it is best if the students get used to using an assembler, because that is what they will see in industry.

To ease the students' learning of the Z 80 instruction set, we have provided two complete tables of the instruction set in the appendixes. One is listed alphabetically by mnemonic, and other numerically by op code. Each instruction has a short explanation, flag code, and number of clock cycles used. The authors have found that a complete list of the instruction set is easier for the beginning student to use than a short and incomplete table, as is often used in many other texts. Such a table is presented in this text for students to use after they have acquired a good understanding of the Z 80 instructor set.

ACKNOWLEDGMENTS

The authors would like to thank the reviewers for their help in developing this text. These reviewers include Ernest Arney, ITT Technical Institute; Robert D. Carpenter, Wake Technical College; Ray Dong, Foothill College; Ronald C. Emery, Indiana University–Purdue University; and Frank T. Gergelyi, Metropolitan Technical Institute.

We would like to thank the following companies for permission to use the illustrations listed.

Bobbs-Merrill Educational Publishing: 11-13. From TV TYPEWRITER COOKBOOK, © copyright 1976, by Don Lancaster, used with permission of the publisher, Howard W. Sams & Co., Inc.

Intel Corporation: 2-8, 2-9, 2-10, 9-3, 9-5, 9-6, 9-7, 9-8, 9-9, 9-10, 10-3, 10-5, 10-6, 11-5. From MEMORY COMPONENTS HANDBOOK 1983 and COMPONENT DATA CATALOG, January 1981. "Reprinted by permission in Intel Corporation, copyright 1981 and 1983." Intel Corporation assumes no responsibility for any errors that may appear in this document, nor for any error introduced in its reproduction."

Motorola Semiconductor Products: A-24, A-25, A-26, A-27, A-28, A-29. From MOTOROLA POWER DATA BOOK, Third Edition 1982 and SMALL SIGNAL TRANSISTOR DATA 1983. Reprinted by permission of Motorola Semiconductor Products.

National Semiconductor Corp.: 12-18, 12-19, A-13, A-14, A-15, A-16, A-17, A-18, A-19, A-20, A-21, A-22, A-23. From LINEAR DATA BOOK 1980. Reprinted by permission of National Semiconductor Corp.

Zilog, Inc.: 4-8, 4-9, 4-10, 5-2, 5-4, 5-5, 5-7, 5-11, 5-14, 6-3, 6-4, 6-8, 6-9, 6-10, 6-11, 7-1, 7-2, 7-4, A-30, A-31, A-32, A-33. From Z 80 CPU Z 80A CPU TECHNICAL

MANUAL, September 1978. "Reproduced by permission. © 1978 Zilog, Inc. This material shall not be reproduced without the written consent of Zilog, Inc."

We would also like to thank Naomi Ford and Freda Welty for their invaluable help and patience in the production of this text.

If readers wish to further their study in the electronics technology field, Delmar Publishers Inc. also has available the following titles:

Bignell and Donovan, DIGITAL ELECTRONICS, 2307-7

Gulledge, BASIC FOR TECHNICIANS, 2310-7

PASCAL FOR TECHNICIANS, 2620-3

Hansen, CAD APPLICATIONS: ELECTRONICS, 2546-0

Kirkpatrick, ELECTRONIC DRAFTING AND PRINTED CIRCUIT BOARD DESIGN, 2315-8

Pallas, ELECTRONIC DEVICES AND CIRCUIT ANALYSIS, 2318-2

Perozzo, PRACTICAL ELECTRONICS TROUBLESHOOTING, 2433-2

MICROCOMPUTER TROUBLESHOOTING, 2500-2

Power, ELECTRONICS MATHEMATICS, 2410-3

Rader, FUNDAMENTALS OF ELECTRONICS MATHEMATICS, 2321-2

Shimizu, ELECTRONIC FABRICATION, 2450-2

Silva, BASIC FOR ELECTRONICS, 2467-7

Stein, INTRODUCTION TO DIGITAL DATA COMMUNICATIONS, 2436-7

Sullivan, MODERN ELECTRONICS MATHEMATICS, 2088-4

Chapter 1

MICROCOMPUTER STRUCTURE AND THE CENTRAL PROCESSING UNIT

OBJECTIVES

After completing this chapter, you should be able to

- explain the four basic parts of a microcomputer.
- explain the operation of the basic Z 80 control signals.
- explain and use the basic machine cycles of the Z 80 CPU.

1.1 THE FOUR BASIC PARTS OF A TYPICAL MICROCOMPUTER

Figure 1–1 shows the arrangement of the four basic parts of any computer system. In this text we will concentrate on the Z 80 central processor, but these four basic parts are common to any microsystem. The first three parts—memory, input/output, and central processor—are hardware and are actual electronic parts. The fourth part—the program—is the fuel that runs the other three parts. Programs are called software because they are not electronic parts but rather binary numbers stored in the memory. Without the program, the other three parts are about as useful as a boat anchor without a boat.

1.2 THE PROGRAM

A program is a sequential list of instructions stored as binary numbers in memory and designed to accomplish some task. The central processor can read the binary numbers and, based on their value, do one part of the task for each stored instruction. The Z 80 stores its instructions as 8-bit binary numbers. As you should remember, an 8-bit binary number is called a *byte*. Each central processor has a predefined set of responses to various values of bytes. This is called the *instruction set* of the central processor. Starting in Chapter 4, we will study the Z 80 instruction set in depth.

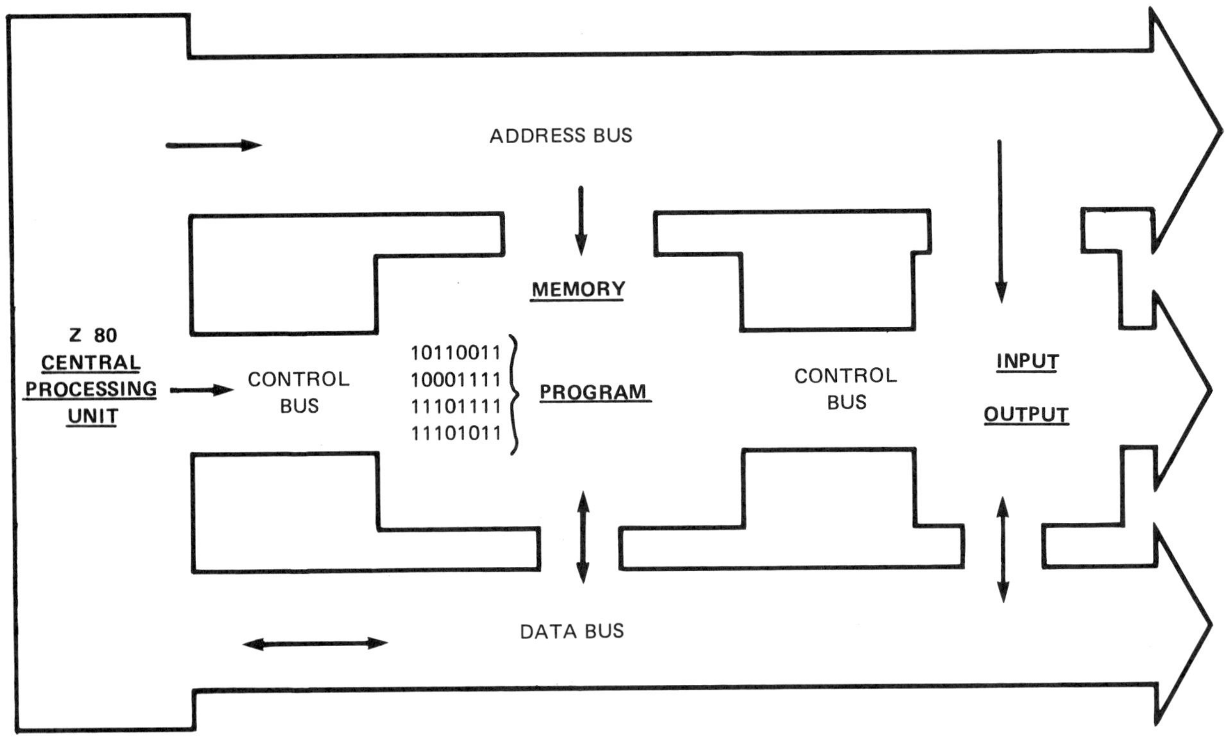

FIGURE 1–1 Basic layout of the four parts of a microcomputer

1.3 THE MEMORY

The memory of a microcomputer is an array of memory cells that can store binary numbers. The memory of the Z 80 system is designed to store 8-bit binary numbers or bytes. The size of the memory is measured by the total number of bytes that the memory can store.

Figure 1–2 shows the block drawing for a typical 64K Z 80 memory. The address input lines are used to select the memory location that is to be read or written to in the memory. The data lines are used to transfer the selected byte to the central processor or to store a byte from the central processor in the memory. The operation (read or write) is accomplished by strobing the appropriate control line low at the time the data is needed or is present on the data line to be stored.

It must be emphasized here that the block drawing in Figure 1–2 is just that—a block drawing which represents many ICs and gates designed to accomplish the job of the computer's memory. In Chapter 2 we will discuss in depth the actual makeup of this important part of the computer. Notice that the memory in Figure 1–2 has 16 address lines (A_0 to A_{15}). This means that there are 2^{16} possible binary numbers or memory locations in this memory. That works out to 65 536 memory locations, not 64 000. The discrepancy comes about because of the way computer people define 1K of memory. 1K

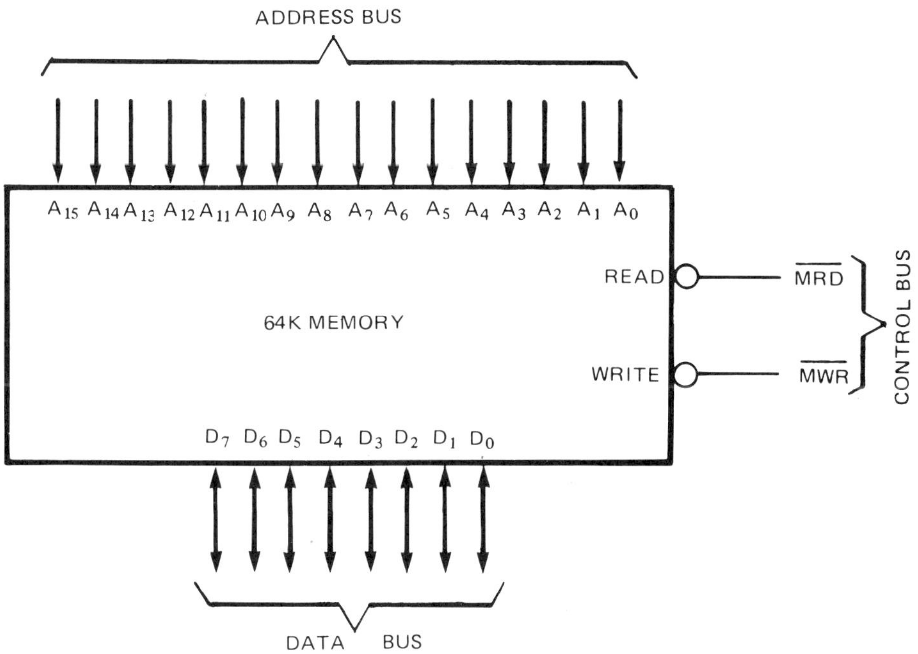

FIGURE 1–2 Block drawing of a 64K memory

of memory is defined as 2^{10}, which is 1024 not 1000. Therefore, 64 × 1024 = 65 536 memory locations. But we don't say 65K, we say 64K because 1K is defined as 1024, not 1000. This all came about because 10 address lines (A_0 to A_9) can address 1024 memory locations.

1.4 THE INPUT AND OUTPUT OF THE COMPUTER

Input and output (I/O) devices are the way the computer communicates with the outside world. Typical I/O devices you might be familiar with are CRT terminals, tape recorders, disk drives, and printers. All of these I/O devices just mentioned are complex devices, but an output port can be as simple as a set of D latches, and an input port can be as simple as a set of tri-state gates. Figure 1–3 shows a simple input and output port of the type just described.

When the central processor wishes to output a byte to the output port, it first places the byte on the data bus and then pulses the $\overline{\text{IOWR}}$ control line low. This causes the byte present on the data bus to be latched on the Q and $\overline{\text{Q}}$ output of the eight D latches, thus storing the byte and displaying it.

To input the binary number that the switches are set to, the computer first brings the $\overline{\text{IORD}}$ control line low. This causes the output of the tri-state gate to raise or lower the lines of the data bus to the value of their associated switch. The central processor

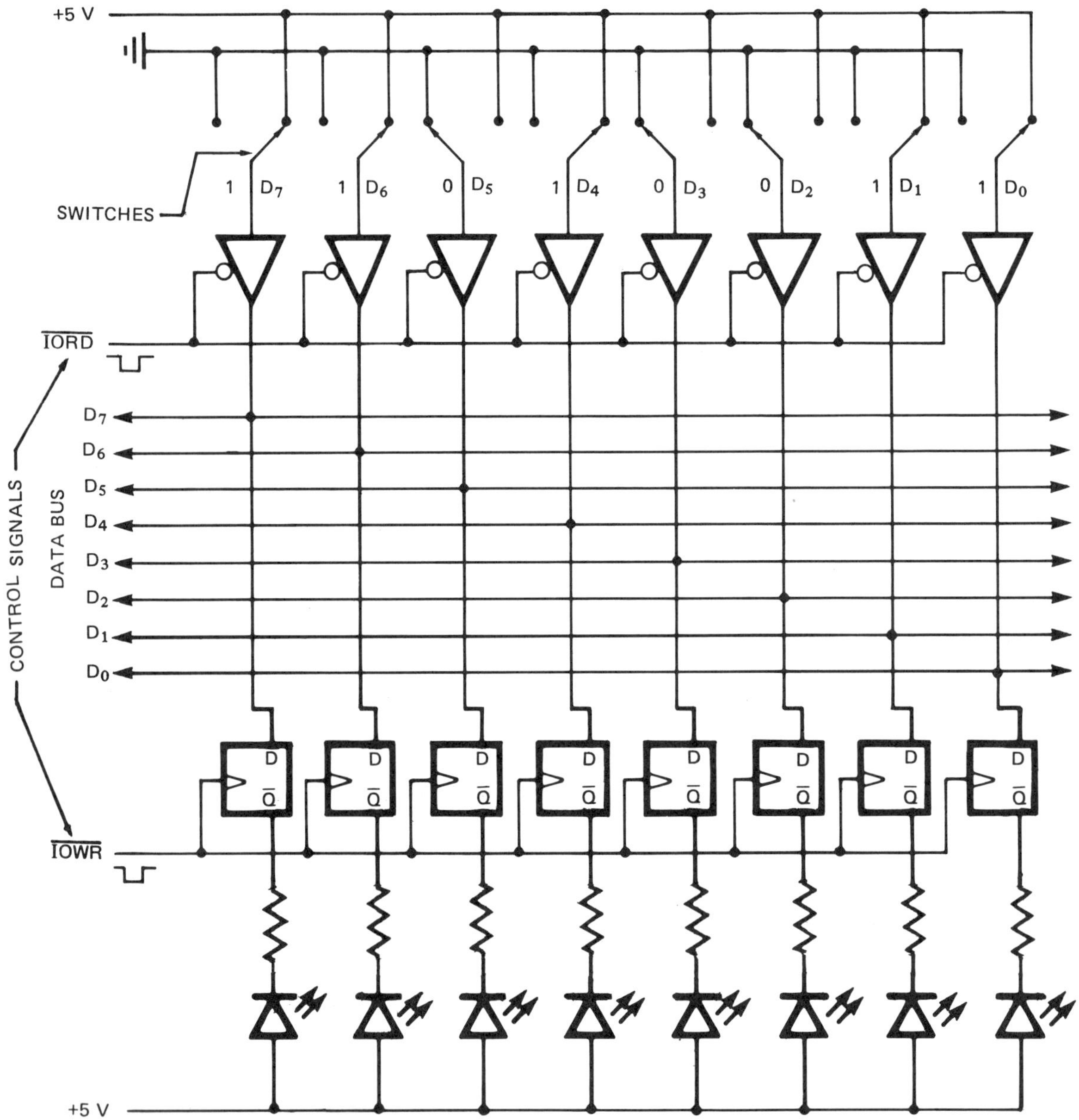

FIGURE 1–3 Input/output port

then latches the byte present on the data bus into an internal register. After the byte has been latched into the central processor, the $\overline{\text{IORD}}$ line is raised to a 1 value, causing the tri-state gate outputs to once again go into their high-impedance states. The example just described is very simple and lacks some of the finer points, but we will look into the subject of input and output in depth in Chapter 3.

1.5 THE ADDRESS BUS, DATA BUS, AND CONTROL BUS

As you probably have figured out by now, the central processor controls memory and the I/O devices with four basic control lines which are memory read ($\overline{MRD}$), memory write ($\overline{MWR}$), input/output read ($\overline{IORD}$), and input/output write ($\overline{IOWR}$). Not all central processors use these four lines, but they all have control lines that can do the same thing and control the memory and I/O devices.

The trainer in this text uses these four basic control lines and a few more that are used to control other processes in the computer. Other systems of memory and input/output control will be explained at appropriate times throughout the text, but for now we will concentrate on these four. These four control signals make up the major part of the control bus on the Biggy trainer. The control bus and the address bus are unidirectional or one way. They carry information from the central processor to other parts of the computer and never in reverse. The data bus on the other hand carries information in both directions, from the central processor to the computer and from the computer parts to the central processor. This type of bus is called a bidirectional bus. The data bus is the highway on which the central processor does business with the other parts of the computer. Because it is connected to all the other parts of the computer and must be able to transfer data in both directions it must be buffered with a bidirectional bus driver such as a 74LS245. We will discuss this bus at a later time.

1.6 THE Z 80 CENTRAL PROCESSOR

The letters CPU stand for central processing unit and it is the brain of the computer. The CPU controls all the other parts of the computer and it interprets and executes the program.

Before the advent of single-chip CPUs, central processors were made from many chips and placed on printed circuit boards. They were large and power hungry. Large-scale integration of the CPU has produced a great number of single-chip central processors, such as the 6800, 6502, 8080, 8085, and Z 80. Because all of these CPUs are in a single 40-pin package, they are called *microprocessors*. The term "micro" seems to infer that the computing power is somewhat less than a minicomputer or mainframe CPU, and that is true of most of the 8-bit CPUs. An 8-bit CPU has an 8-bit data bus. Today's new 16-bit single-chip CPUs, such as the 68000 and Z8000, are quite powerful and can no longer be thought of as being small. Because the Z 80 CPU is one of, if not, the most powerful and widely used 8-bit CPU in production today, we will use it as a typical example in this text.

Figure 1-4 shows the pinout and pin grouping for the Z 80 CPU. The Z 80 CPU is made from MOS technology, has a single power supply of +5 V, and can handle a 1-TTL load on any of its outputs. The address bus has 16 lines or pins; therefore, the Z 80 CPU can directly address up to 2^{16}, 65 536 or 64K memory locations. The data bus is eight bits wide, bidirectional, and used to transfer instruction or data to and from the CPU and the rest of the computer system.

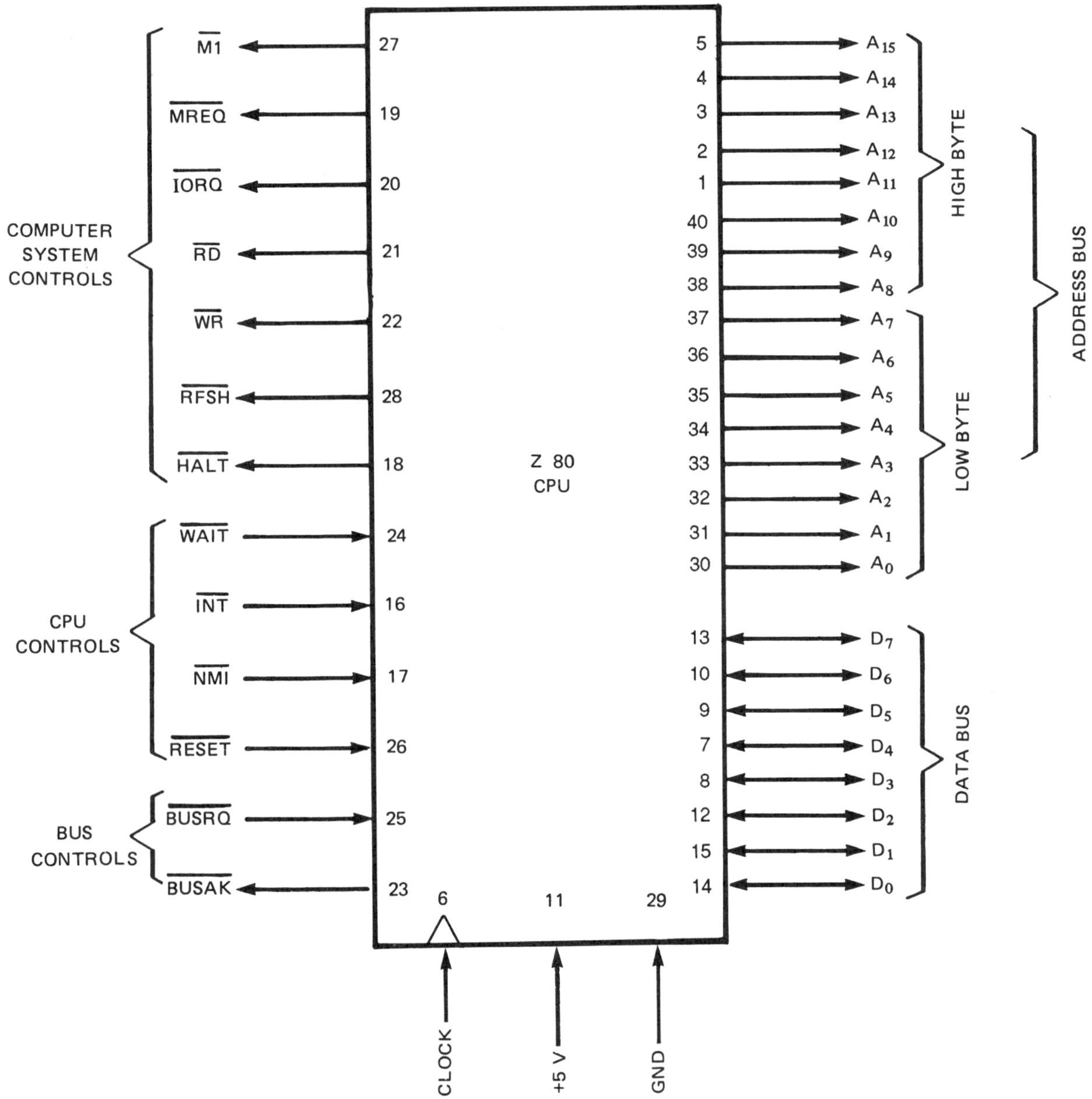

FIGURE 1–4 The Z 80 pinout and function

1.7 THE CLOCK

The clock (pin 6) is connected to an external clock of no greater than 2 MHz for the Z 80 or 4 MHz for Z 80A. This clock is used by the CPU to synchronize the operation of the CPU and all other operations of the computer system. A crystal oscillator is usually used, and the duty cycle of its output must be even. The clock's output voltages must not be greater than 0.45 V for a logic 0 and no less than 4.4 V for a logic 1. The specifications and characteristics of the Z 80 can be confirmed by consulting the Z 80 DC and AC specifications sheets in the Appendix. Figure 1–5 shows the schematic of the clock used in the Biggy trainer. The basic frequency of 4 MHz is obtained by a crystal oscillator made from a pair of 74LS04 inverters, two resistors, and a feedback capacitor. The output of this oscillator is a good stable 4 MHz, but it is not an even duty cycle and does not reach a voltage of 4.4 V which the Z 80 needs. To correct these things, the 4-MHz clock is divided by 2, using a 74LS74 D flip-flop. The frequency is now an even duty cycle of 2 MHz and is used to turn on and off a PNP transistor. This will pull up the clock input of the Z 80 to +5 V very quickly. The $\overline{Q}$ of the 74LS74 D flip-flop is also connected to the emitter of the PNP transistor. This will bring the clock input low when the pull-up transistor is off. The pull-up transistor will pull up

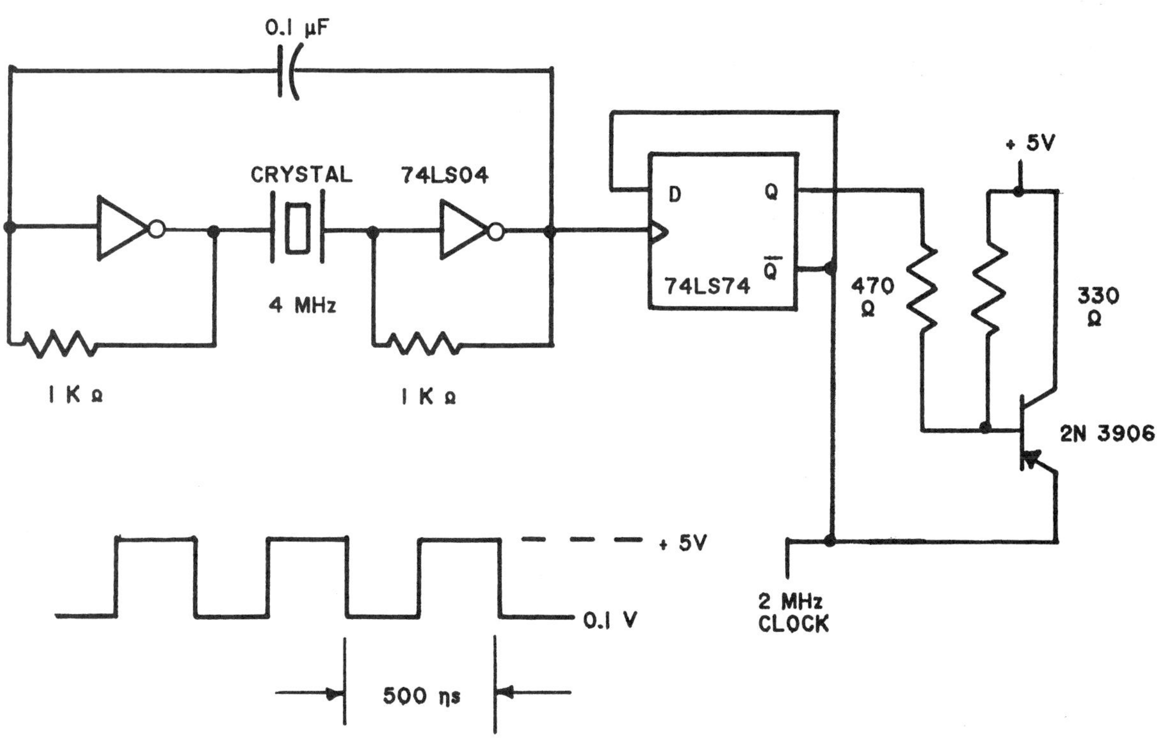

FIGURE 1–5 The Biggy trainer clock circuit

the clock input and the $\overline{Q}$ of the 74LS74 will pull it down to logic 0. This circuitry gives the Z 80 used in the Biggy trainer an even-duty-cycle, 2-MHz, and a fast rising and falling clock signal to use.

1.8 $\overline{MREQ}$, $\overline{IORQ}$, $\overline{RD}$, $\overline{WR}$, AND OTHER CONTROL SIGNALS

The $\overline{MREQ}$, $\overline{IORQ}$, $\overline{RD}$, and $\overline{WR}$ control signals are used by the Z 80 to control access to memory and input/output devices on the computer's data bus.

$\overline{MREQ}$ (memory request) is an active low signal that goes low when the CPU has a valid and stable address on the address bus for a memory location in the computer's memory. This signal indicates that a memory read or write is to take place.

$\overline{IORQ}$ (input/output request) is an active low signal that goes low when the CPU has a valid and stable 8-bit I/O device address on the least significant byte of the address bus. This signal is used to indicate that an input/output device is to be accessed on the CPU's data bus.

$\overline{RD}$ (read) is an active low signal used to signal any device or memory to place data on the data bus for the CPU to latch into its internal registers. The $\overline{RD}$ signal is used in conjunction with the $\overline{MREQ}$ and $\overline{IORQ}$ to produce an $\overline{MRD}$ (memory read) and an $\overline{IORD}$ (input/output read) signal, as we will see later.

$\overline{WR}$ (write) is also an active low signal, but it is used to indicate that data is stable and present on the data bus for any external input/output device or memory to latch. The $\overline{WR}$ signal is also used in conjunction with $\overline{MREQ}$ and $\overline{IORQ}$ to produce $\overline{MWR}$ and $\overline{IOWR}$ control signals.

$\overline{M1}$ is a special, active low control signal that indicates the CPU is in an instruction fetch machine cycle. An instruction machine cycle is when the CPU is addressing the memory and reading a byte from the memory that will be its next instruction. All instructions are stored in the memories and are part of the program except for one. This exception is an interrupt instruction. An interrupt instruction comes from a special input device called an interrupt input port. When the CPU wants an instruction from an interrupt input port, the $\overline{IORQ}$ and $\overline{M1}$ will both go low. These two low signals are used to produce a signal called $\overline{INTACK}$ (interrupt acknowledge). Interrupts are a method of interrupting the flow of a program from outside the computer and will be studied in depth later.

$\overline{RFSH}$ (refresh) is a signal that goes low when the lower seven bits of the address bus contain the refresh number for refreshing the dynamic RAM of the computer. This ability to automatically refresh dynamic RAM is one of the major reasons that designers like the Z 80 CPU. The use of this signal will be studied later in Chapter 2.

$\overline{BUSRQ}$ and $\overline{BUSAK}$ (bus request and bus acknowledge) The $\overline{BUSRQ}$ is an active low input used by external devices to gain control of the computer's address and data bus. When brought low, the CPU will put its address and data bus in high impedance and produce a low on $\overline{BUSAK}$ to indicate that it has done so. This is used in direct memory addressing and will also be studied later.

$\overline{\text{HALT}}$ (halt) When this signal goes low, it indicates that the CPU has executed a halt instruction and is doing nothing except refreshing the dynamic RAM if dynamic RAM is used. An interrupt or reset operation will take the CPU out of the halt state.

$\overline{\text{WAIT}}$ (wait) This active low input tells the CPU to hold the address on the address bus while the memory or input/output device finishes using it. While the $\overline{\text{WAIT}}$ is low, the address bus will not change and the CPU will do nothing, not even refresh any dynamic RAM.

$\overline{\text{RESET}}$, $\overline{\text{INT}}$, and $\overline{\text{NMI}}$ (reset, interrupt, and nonmaskable interrupt) $\overline{\text{INT}}$ and $\overline{\text{NMI}}$ are active low input signals used to interrupt the flow of a program and will be studied in depth in later chapters. $\overline{\text{RESET}}$ is a special type of interrupt used to start the computer. When $\overline{\text{RESET}}$ is brought low, the computer will fetch the next instruction at address 0000 Hex. When $\overline{\text{RESET}}$ again goes high, the computer will start at 0000 Hex. $\overline{\text{RESET}}$ is used to start the computer at the beginning of the program.

1.9 INSTRUCTION FETCH MACHINE CYCLES

The CPU executes all instructions by executing one or more predefined machine cycles. There are three types of machine cycles: memory read or write, input/output device read or write, and interrupt acknowledge. Machine cycles are from three to six clock periods long. One clock period is called a *T state* and is the time from the rising edge of the clock to the rising edge of the next clock. In the Biggy trainer the clock frequency is 2 MHz and the period is

$$P = \frac{1}{f} = \frac{1}{2\ \text{MHz}} = 500\ \text{ns}$$

Figure 1–6 shows the machine cycles used to execute a load instruction. This instruction reads the next two memory locations and puts their content into a pair of registers

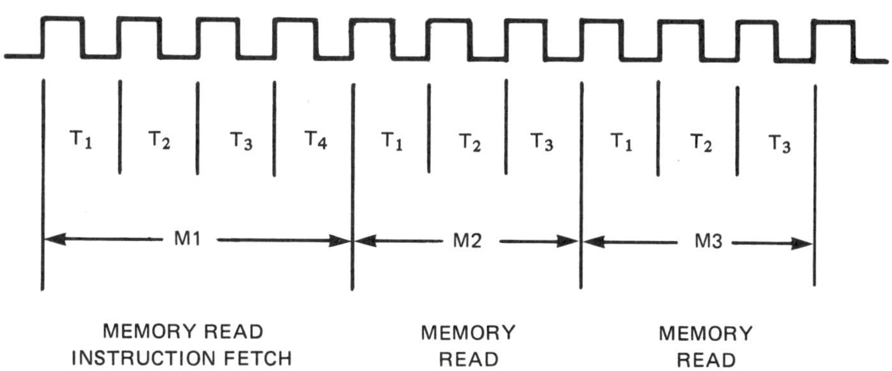

FIGURE 1–6 Machine cycles for a typical load instruction

inside the CPU. To do this, the CPU must first fetch the instruction from the memory, decode it to determine which instruction it is, and then read the next two memory locations.

All three of the machine cycles in Figure 1–6 are memory read machine cycles, but the first machine cycle is a special memory read machine cycle. Every instruction starts with this machine cycle because the machine cycle fetches or reads the instruction from the memory. Because it always is the first machine cycle in an instruction, we call it the M1 cycle.

Figure 1–7 shows the waveforms for the M1 machine cycle, which is always at least four T-state or clock cycles long. This machine cycle latches the instruction byte into the instruction decoder inside the CPU, decodes it, produces the refresh cycle, and, in some cases, executes the instruction. As can be seen shortly after the first T state, the address bus is set to the memory address of the next instruction, and the $\overline{M1}$ control signal from the CPU goes low, indicating that this machine cycle is an M1 or instruction fetch machine cycle.

About halfway through the T_1 state, the $\overline{MREQ}$ and $\overline{RD}$ go low, indicating that this is a memory read machine cycle also. These two signals are ORed together to produce an $\overline{MRD}$ control signal that is used to select the memory and allow it to dump the contents of the addressed memory location onto the data bus. The circuit that produces the $\overline{MRD}$ control signal for the Biggy trainer can be seen in Figure 1–8.

The time between $\overline{MRD}$ going low and the contents of the addressed memory location becoming stable on the data bus is a function of the propagation delay of the computer's memory and is typically between 100 ns to 400 ns. The data or instruction is latched into the CPU's instruction decoder on the rising edge of the T_3 state, and shortly thereafter the $\overline{MREQ}$ and $\overline{RD}$ control signals return high, causing $\overline{MRD}$ to also return to an inactive state. This deselects the memory, and the data bus goes to its high impedance state or not used state.

During the T_3 and T_4 states the CPU is decoding the just-acquired instruction and setting itself up for any other needed machine cycle or is just executing the instruction if no other machine cycles are needed. Some instructions will cause the CPU to add a fifth or sixth T state to the M1 machine cycle to complete the internal execution of an instruction. While all this is taking place, the data bus is not in use, and the Z 80 takes advantage of this to produce a memory refresh cycle for dynamic RAM. This process of the M1 machine cycle will be discussed in more detail in Chapter 2.

1.10 THE MEMORY READ MACHINE CYCLE

As shown in Figure 1–9, the memory read machine cycle is very similar to the M1 machine cycle except it lacks the $\overline{M1}$ signal and the refresh part of the M1 machine cycle. The memory read machine cycle is only three T-state or clock cycles long and is used by the CPU to bring data from a memory location into the internal registers in the CPU. Note that data is latched on the falling edge of T_3 and not on the rising edge, as in the M1 machine cycle.

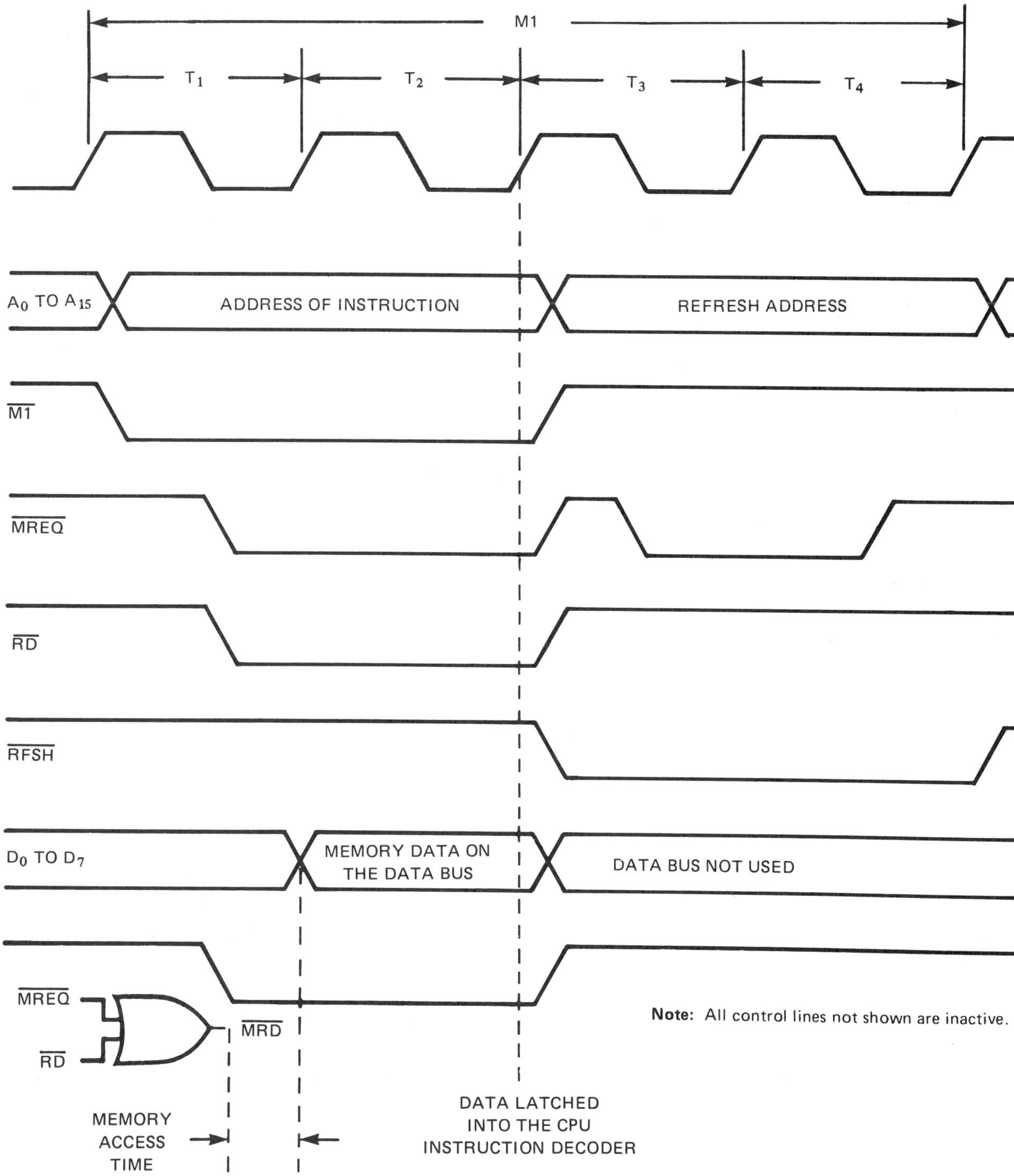

FIGURE 1–7 M1 machine cycle

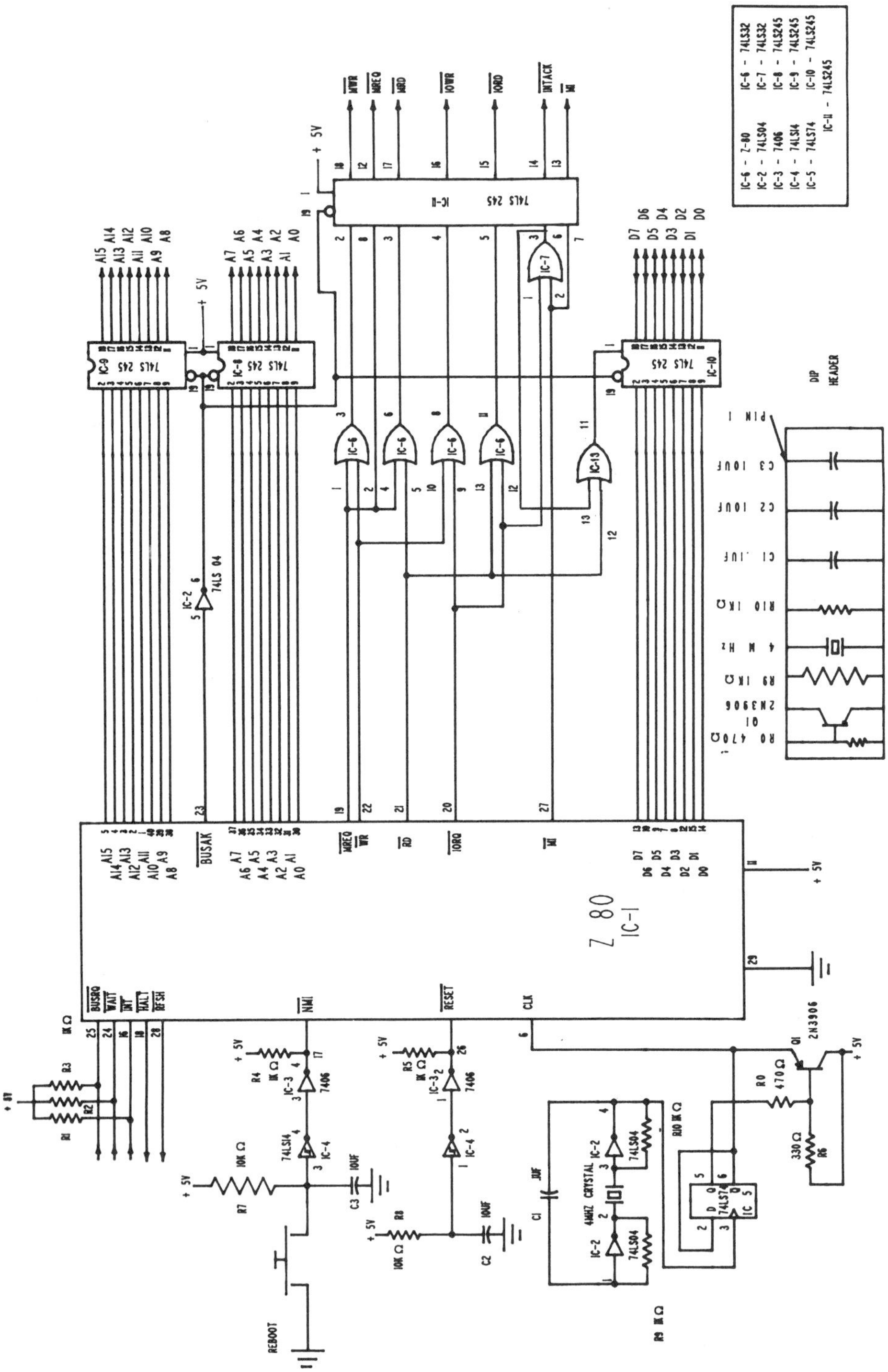

IC-1 - Z-80
IC-2 - 74LS04
IC-3 - 7406
IC-4 - 74LS14
IC-5 - 74LS74
IC-6 - 74LS32
IC-7 - 74LS32
IC-8 - 74LS245
IC-9 - 74LS245
IC-10 - 74LS245
IC-11 - 74LS245
Z 80
IC-1
DIP
HEADER
PIN 1
REBOOT
4MHZ CRYSTAL
2N3906

FIGURE 1–8

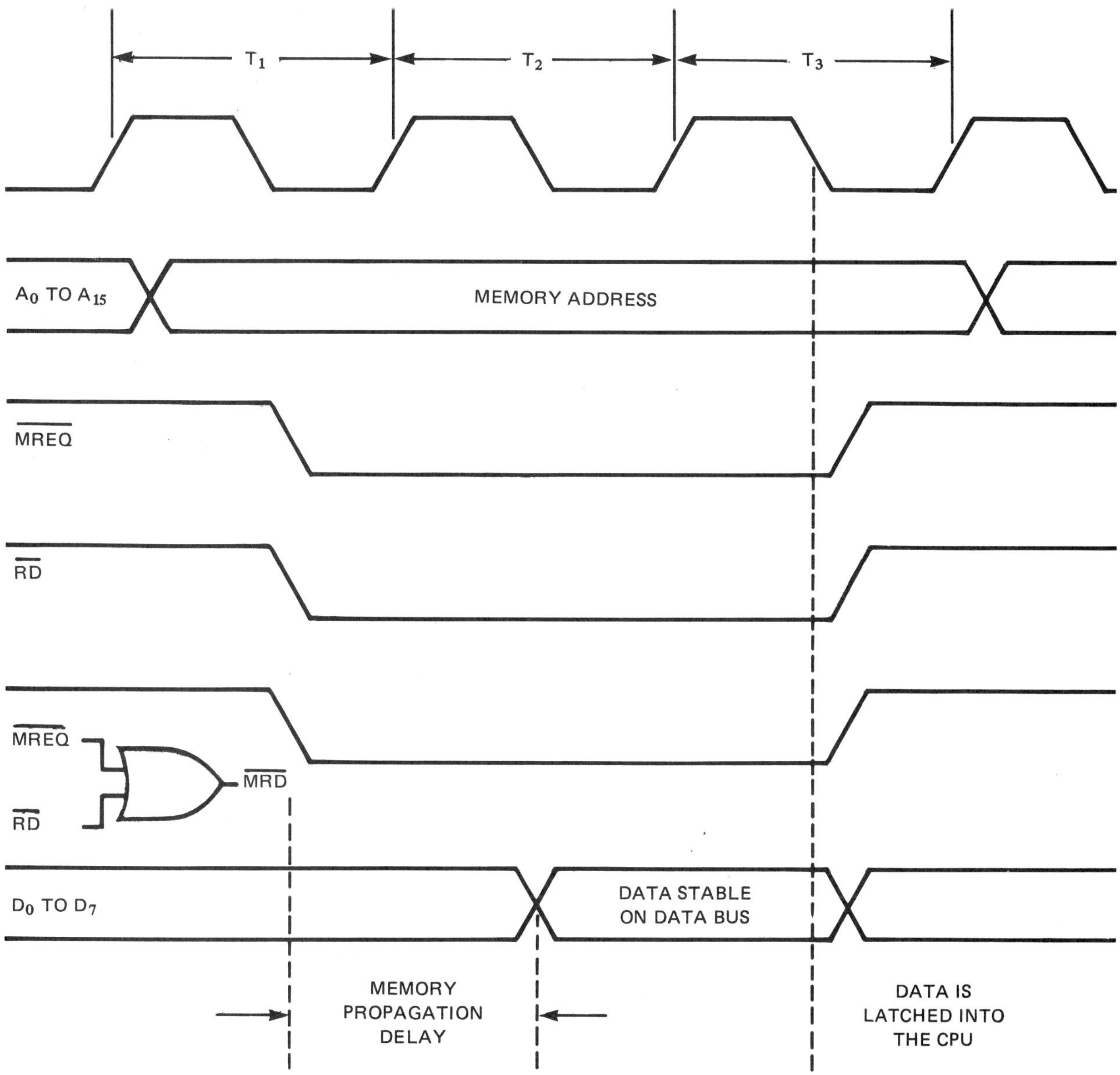

Note: All control signals not shown are inactive.

FIGURE 1–9 Memory read machine cycle

1.11 THE MEMORY WRITE MACHINE CYCLE

The memory write machine cycle shown in Figure 1–10 is used by the CPU to store a byte of data in a memory location whose address is placed on the address bus shortly after the rising edge of the T_1 state of this machine cycle. Again, the $\overline{MREQ}$ control signal goes low about halfway through the first T state. The data to be stored is placed on the data bus at this time and is held stable until shortly after the rising edge of the next T_1 state of the next machine cycle. The $\overline{WR}$ control signal goes low shortly after the falling edge of the T_2 state and returns high shortly after the falling edge of the T_3 state. The $\overline{MREQ}$ and $\overline{WR}$ are ORed together to produce a $\overline{MWR}$ control signal to latch the data present on the data bus into the memory location whose address is on the address

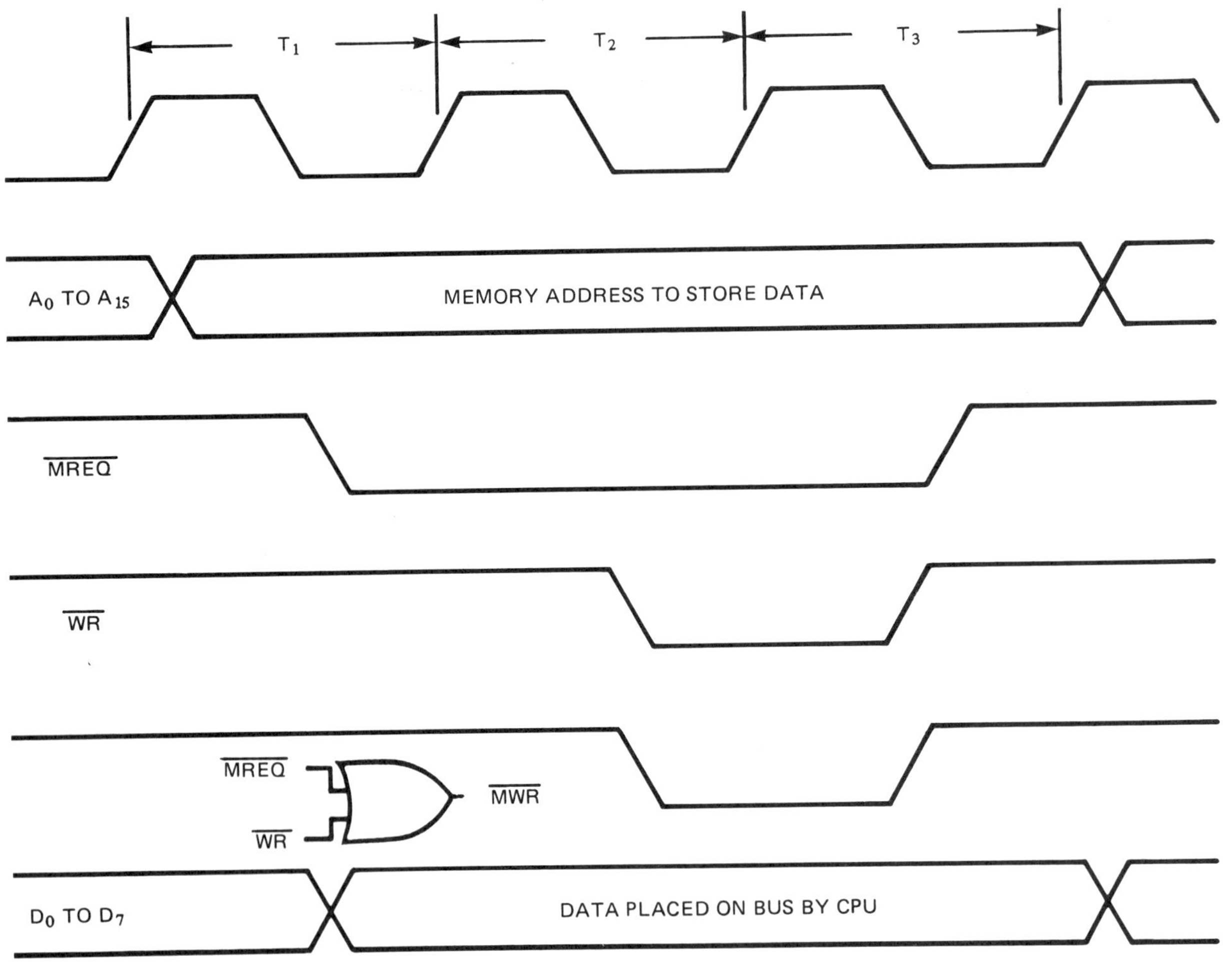

Note: All control signals not shown are inactive.

FIGURE 1–10 Memory write machine cycle

bus. The digital circuitry to produce the $\overline{MWR}$ control signal on the Biggy trainer is shown in Figure 1–8.

1.12 THE INPUT/OUTPUT READ AND WRITE MACHINE CYCLES

As can be seen in Figures 1–11 and 1–12, the input/output machine cycles are almost exactly like the memory read and memory write machine cycles, except that $\overline{IORQ}$ is

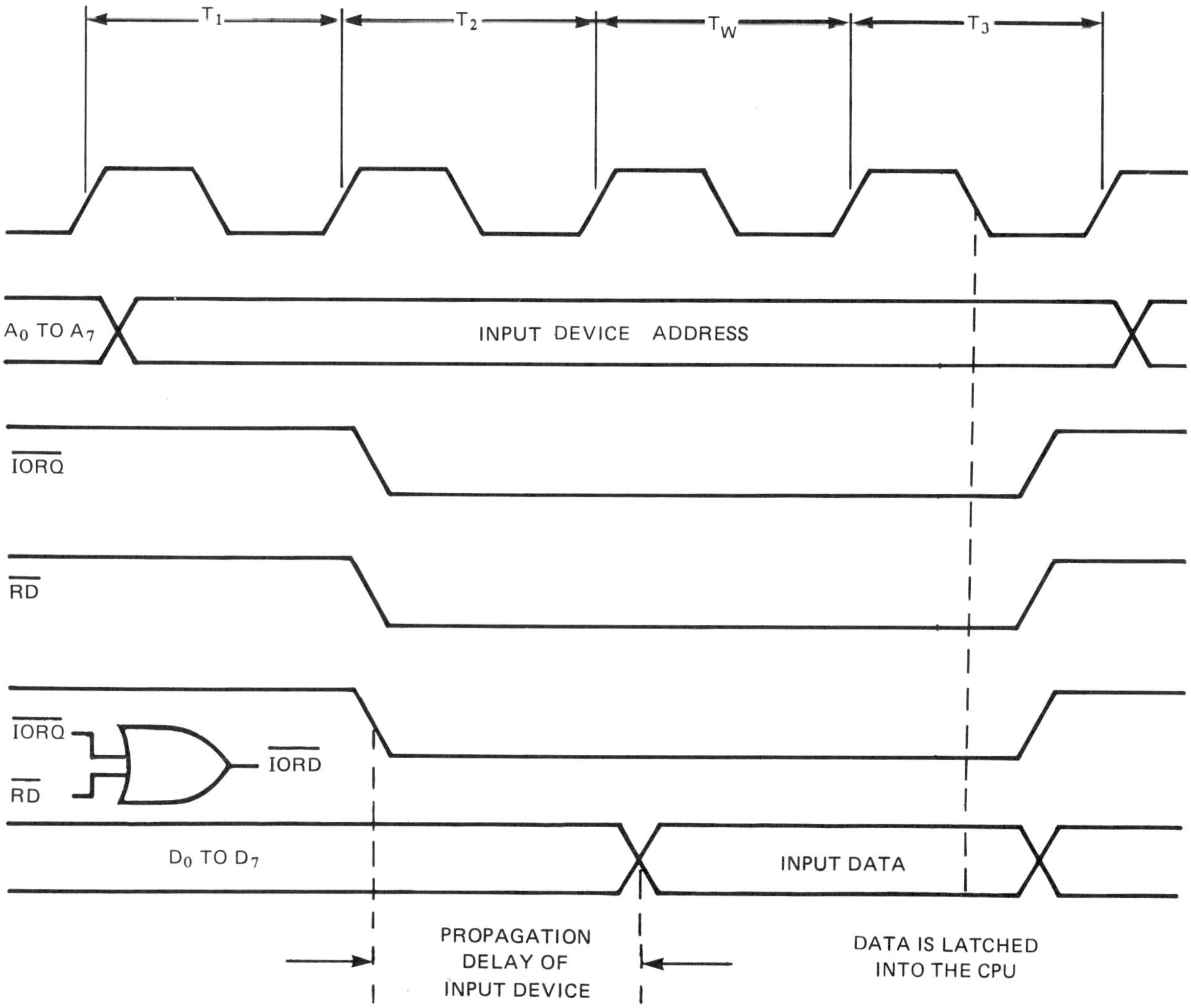

Note: All control signals not shown are inactive.

FIGURE 1–11 Input/output read machine cycle

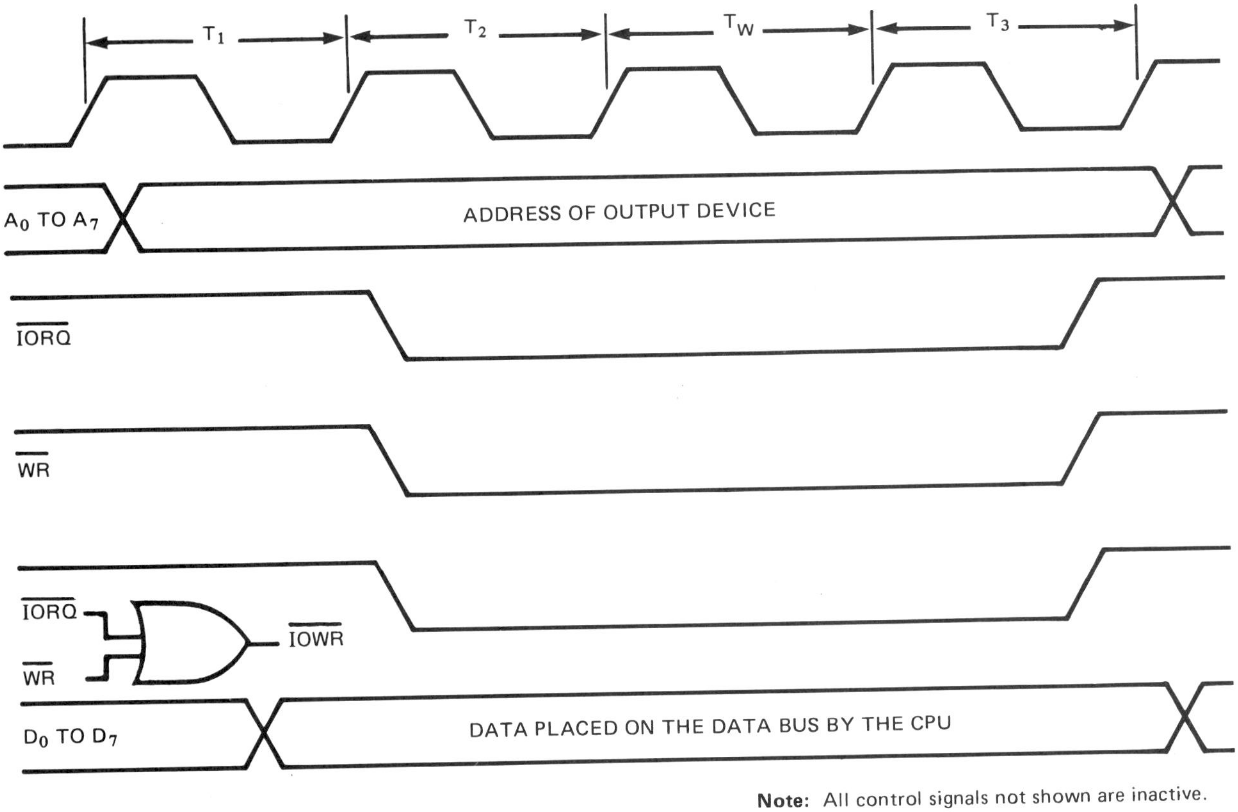

FIGURE 1–12 Input/output write machine cycle

active while $\overline{MREQ}$ is inactive or high and there is an extra T_W or wait T state between the T_2 and T_3 states. This produces an $\overline{IORD}$ or $\overline{IOWR}$ instead of an $\overline{MRD}$ or $\overline{MWR}$ control signal. The address of an input/output device is only 8 bits wide; therefore, only A_0 to A_7 are used to select the input/output device. The extra T_W state is used to lengthen the T_2 state so that the CPU has more time to test the state of inputs to the CPU such as $\overline{WAIT}$. The OR gates used to produce the $\overline{IORD}$ and $\overline{IOWR}$ control signals are shown in Figure 1–8.

1.13 THE INTERRUPT ACKNOWLEDGE MACHINE CYCLE

On the rising edge of the last T state of every instruction, the state (high or low) of the interrupt input $\overline{INT}$ is tested. If the $\overline{INT}$ is low, then the CPU executes a special type of M1 machine cycle called an interrupt acknowledge cycle. This machine cycle makes

$\overline{IORQ}$ and $\overline{M1}$ low, which indicates that the next instruction should come from a special type of input port, called an interrupt input port.

Figure 1–13 shows the waveforms for the interrupt acknowledge machine cycle. Notice that $\overline{IORQ}$ and $\overline{M1}$ are ORed together to produce a new control signal called $\overline{INTACK}$ (interrupt acknowledge). Interrupts are a method of interrupting the program flow by an external device, such as a printer or keyboard, which may need attention from the CPU. We will discuss the whole subject of interrupts in great detail in later chapters.

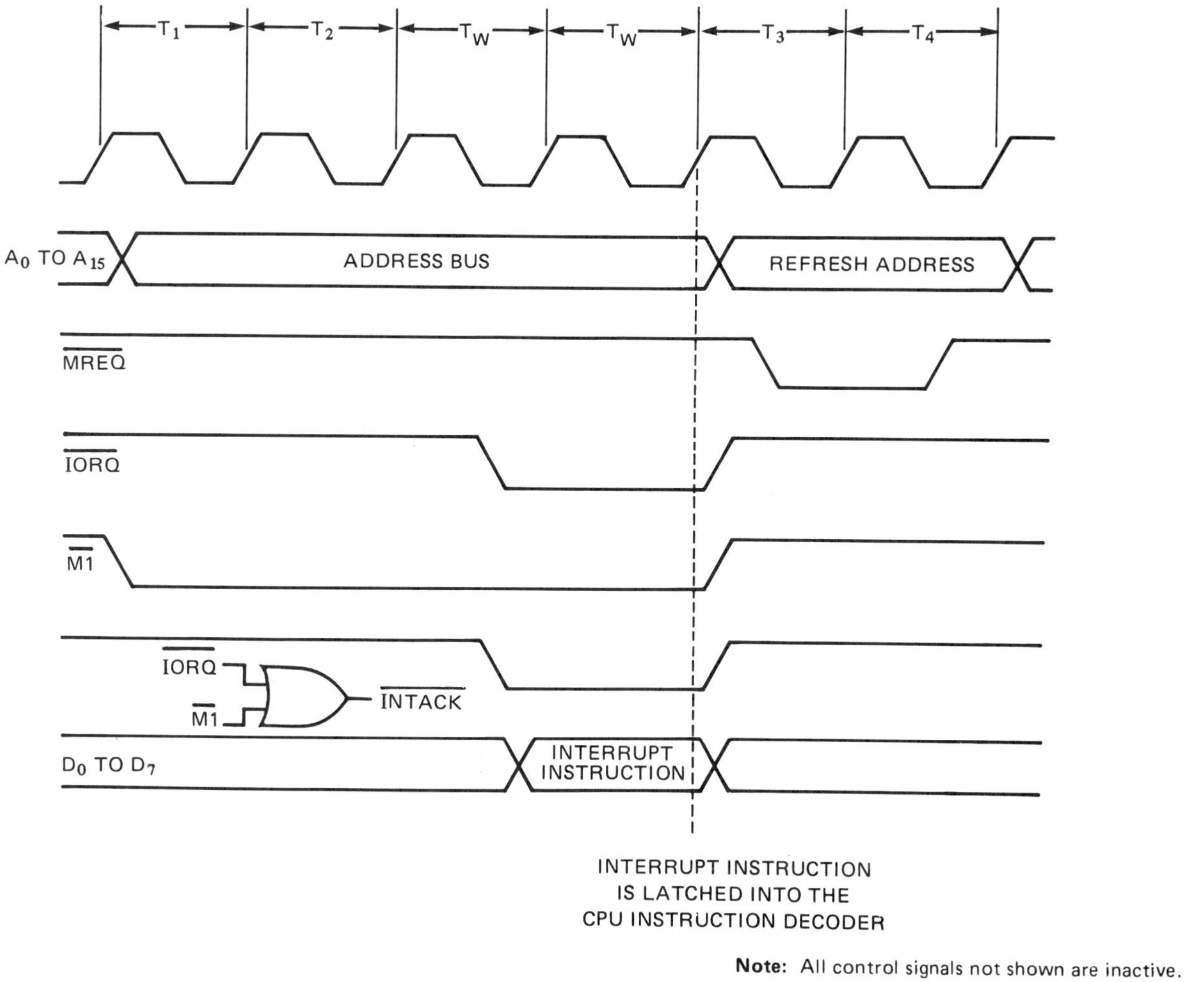

FIGURE 1–13 Interrupt acknowledge machine cycle

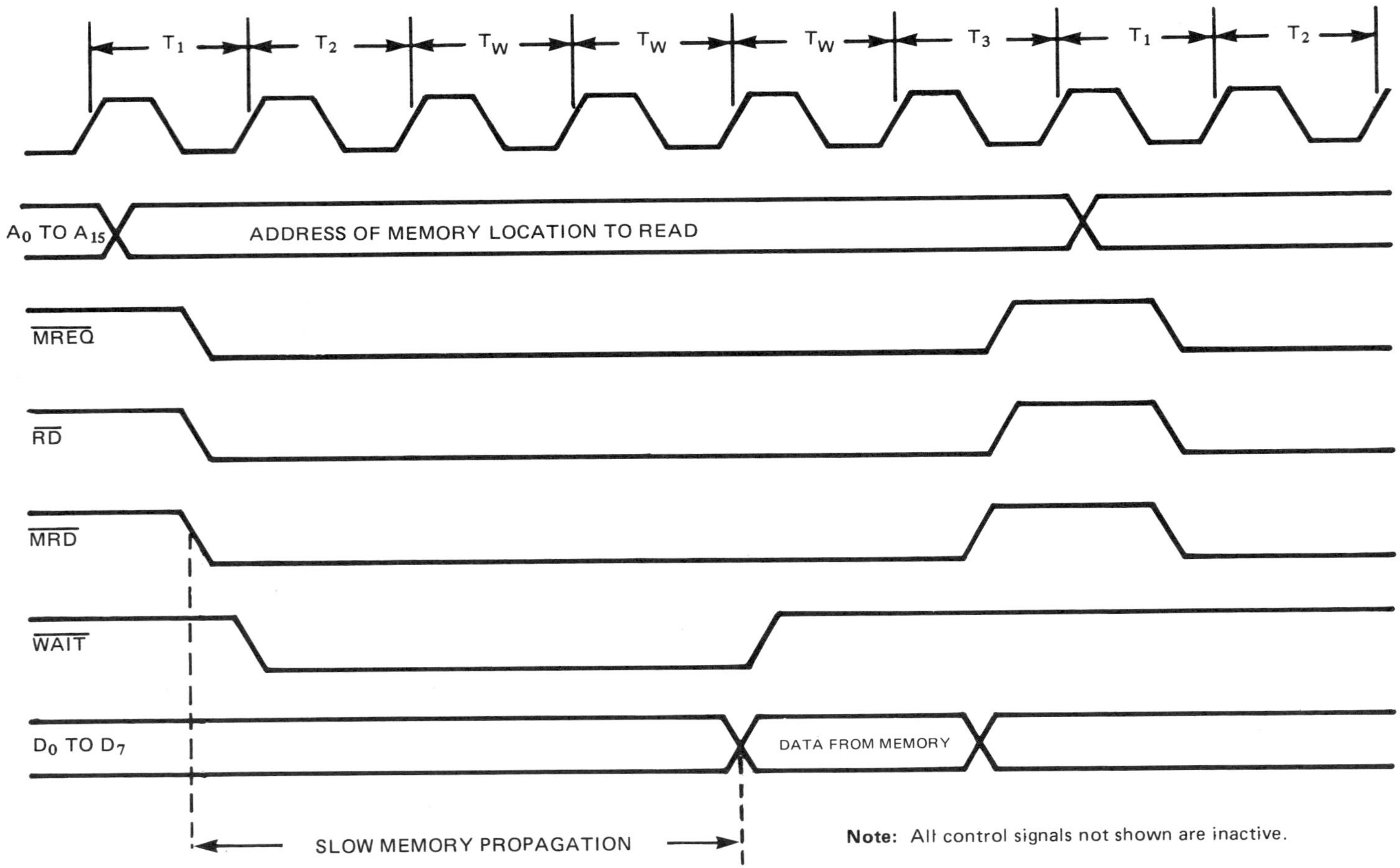

Note: All control signals not shown are inactive.

FIGURE 1–14 The $\overline{\text{WAIT}}$ control signal used to stretch a memory read machine cycle for a slow memory

The Z 80 CPU adds two T_W states or wait states between T_2 and T_3 of the interrupt acknowledge machine cycle in order to give external circuitry, such as a ripple priority decoder, time to select the interrupt input port to be used in the interrupt process. Notice that the refresh procedure is also present in this machine cycle.

1.14 THE $\overline{WAIT}$ INPUT TO THE CPU

During the T_2 state of every machine cycle, the CPU samples the $\overline{WAIT}$ input control signal for an active low state. When a low state is detected, the CPU executes T_W states which changes nothing on the address bus, data bus, or control bus. The CPU will stay this way until the $\overline{WAIT}$ again goes high and the CPU will then enter the T_3 state of the machine cycle. The whole purpose of this procedure is to allow slow memory or input/output devices to slow up the CPU's machine cycle long enough to react to the control signals. Figure 1–14 shows a memory read machine cycle that has used the $\overline{WAIT}$ input to stretch the machine cycle to give the memory time to dump its contents on the data bus.

1.15 $\overline{BUSRQ}$ AND $\overline{BUSAK}$ CONTROL SIGNALS

On the rising edge of the last T state of every machine cycle, the CPU samples the $\overline{BUSRQ}$ (bus request) input for a low or active state. If an active $\overline{BUSRQ}$ is found, the CPU will, on the next rising edge of the clock, place the address bus, data bus, and all control lines in high-impedance state. The $\overline{BUSAK}$ control output signal will go low at the same time, indicating that the buses are in the HiZ or high-impedance state. The $\overline{BUSAK}$ (bus acknowledge) signal is used to control the bus driver and to allow other devices access to the bus system of the computer. This is called direct memory access.

The Biggy trainer does not use the $\overline{INT}$, $\overline{WAIT}$, or $\overline{BUSRQ}$ inputs. It uses a pull-up resister to +5 V to keep them inactive. The three inputs are placed on the breadboard for future use.

1.16 BUFFERING THE ADDRESS BUS, DATA BUS, AND CONTROL BUS

Because the Z 80 is made from MOS (metal-oxide semiconductor) technology, it has only a 1-TTL load capability on its output. Therefore, the chip output must be buffered with some chip which is capable of supplying the current necessary to drive all the inputs that will be placed on the data bus, address bus and control bus. Most computer designs today use the 74LS240 or 74LS245 octal bus driver or similar chip. We chose to use the 74LS245 bidirectional bus driver because it is 8 bits wide and can sink up to 24 mA of current. Figure 1–15 shows the logic drawing of the chip. The 74LS245 has eight sets of back-to-back tri-state gates that are controlled by two control signals, $\overline{CS}$ (chip select) and DIR (direction).

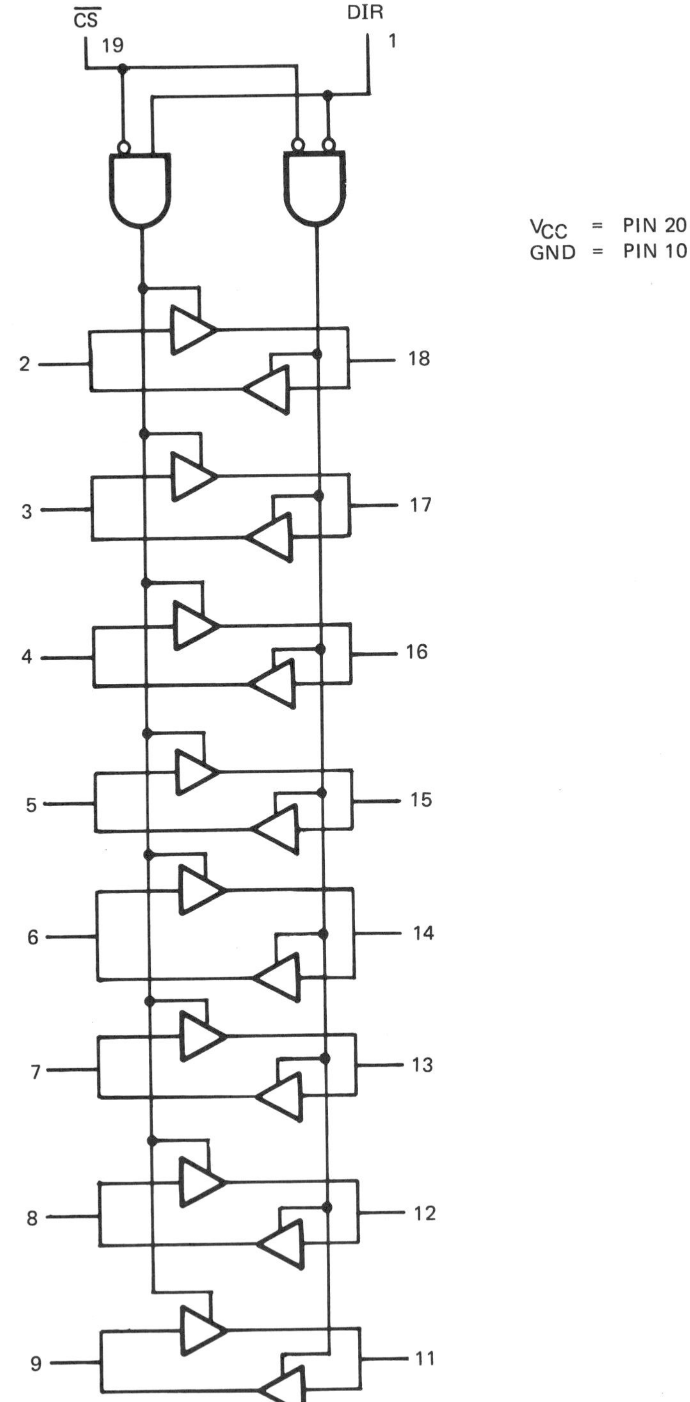

FIGURE 1–15 The 74LS245 bidirectional bus driver

When the $\overline{\text{CS}}$ input is high, all the tri-state gates are in their high-impedance state, and no data can pass through the 74LS245. A low on the $\overline{\text{CS}}$ (chip select) will enable the chip and pass data through it. The direction of the data flow will depend on the logic state of the DIR (direction) input. A low on the DIR will pass data from pin 18 to pin 2 and a high on the DIR will pass data the other way, from pin 2 to pin 18. Because this chip can pass data in both directions, it is called a bidirectional bus driver.

Two 74LS245 ICs are used to buffer the address bus. Because the address bus is a one way or unidirectional bus, the (direction) DIR input was tied high to force the data to flow from pin 2 to pin 18 or from the CPU to the computer. This is also true of the 74LS245 used to buffer the CPU control bus. The $\overline{\text{CS}}$ (chip select) input for these two buffering chips is tied to the $\overline{\text{BUSAK}}$ through a 74LS04 inverter. When the $\overline{\text{BUSAK}}$ becomes active, the inverter will produce a high output to the 74LS245's $\overline{\text{CS}}$ input, thus placing the two buses in their high-impedance states.

The 74LS245 that buffers the data bus also has its $\overline{\text{CS}}$ tied to the same inverter. Therefore, it will also go into high impedance when the $\overline{\text{BUSAK}}$ goes low. The main difference with the data bus drive is that direction of data flow is controlled by the logic state of the $\overline{\text{RD}}$ signal from the CPU. As you remember from the previous discussion of the Z 80 machine cycles, whenever the CPU is transferring data on the data bus from the computer's parts into the CPU, the $\overline{\text{RD}}$ control signal goes low. Therefore, when the CPU is reading data into itself, the $\overline{\text{RD}}$ is low, causing the data to flow from pin 18 to pin 2 or from the computer to the CPU. All other bus transfers are write transfers, where data is going from the CPU to other parts of the computer, and in these cases the $\overline{\text{RD}}$ control signal will be high. The logic schematic for the Biggy trainer shows this buffering method in Figure 1–8.

1.17 THE $\overline{\text{RESET}}$ INPUT

When the $\overline{\text{RESET}}$ input is brought low, the computer stops executing the program and when the $\overline{\text{RESET}}$ comes back high, the next instruction is fetched from memory location 0000 Hex (hexidecimal). This is a method of forcing the CPU to start at the beginning of a program called the operating system. All CPUs have some type of reset that starts the operation of the CPU at a fixed known memory location.

The Biggy trainer uses a power-on one-shot made from a resistor, capacitor, and a Schmitt trigger inverter input. This one-shot produces a high pulse for a short time until the capacitor charges above the upper threshold of the Schmitt trigger. When the upper threshold is reached, the output of the 74LS14 goes low and stays low. This short power-on high-going pulse is inverted and buffered by a 7406 open collector and is used to reset the Z 80 CPU. In most computers, the power on $\overline{\text{RESET}}$ pulse is used to reset other LSI chips to begin the computer's setup programming.

1.18 THE $\overline{\text{NMI}}$ (NONMASKABLE INTERRUPT)

The use of the $\overline{\text{RESET}}$ input is one method of forcing the CPU to start the program at a fixed address and the $\overline{\text{NMI}}$ (nonmaskable interrupt) is another. The difference between the $\overline{\text{RESET}}$ and $\overline{\text{NMI}}$ is the address the CPU is forced to fetch the next instruction from (0066 Hex) and that the $\overline{\text{NMI}}$ is a call to subroutine and not a forced jump. These terms (subroutine and jump) may not mean too much at this point, but they will later.

The Biggy trainer uses the $\overline{\text{NMI}}$ to reboot the computer. This is done by using a circuit very similar to the power-on reset, except that the resistor in the RC timing part is smaller, thus causing the pulse to be shorter on power-up. After the capacitor is fully charged, it can be discharged by the REBOOT button, thus causing the $\overline{\text{NMI}}$ to reboot the computer.

The term *boot* is a part of computer history. It refers to a short program, which was usually hand entered through a front panel, that ran another input device, such as a paper-tape reader. The main program was then loaded into memory from the paper-tape reader by the boot program. It was said that the computer pulled itself up by the "bootstraps," thus the term REBOOT means to start over and boot in the program again.

EXERCISE 1

1. What are the four main parts of the computer?
2. How many bits are in a byte?
3. How many bytes are in 1K of computer memory that is 8 bits wide?
4. What is the purpose of the data bus in a computer?
5. What is the purpose of the address bus in a computer?
6. How many address lines does the Z 80 CPU have?
7. Which of the three bus systems discussed is bidirectional?
8. Which pin is the clock input of the Z 80 CPU?
9. Explain the operation of the $\overline{\text{MREQ}}$ control signal of the Z 80 CPU.
10. What is happening when the $\overline{\text{M1}}$ control signal is low?
11. What is the purpose of the $\overline{\text{IORQ}}$ Z 80 control signal?
12. What are the minimum and maximum numbers of clock cycles for a machine cycle?
13. Draw the waveforms for the address bus, data bus, $\overline{\text{MREQ}}$, $\overline{\text{RD}}$, $\overline{\text{M1}}$, and $\overline{\text{RFSH}}$ signals of the Z 80 CPU for the load instruction of Figure 1–6.
14. Which output control signal of the Z 80 will place the bus driver of the Biggy trainer in the HiZ state?
15. Draw the pinout of the 74LS245 IC and describe its operation.
16. What is an interrupt signal? What is it used for?
17. What two Z 80 CPU control signals are used to make the $\overline{\text{MRD}}$ control signal used in the Biggy trainer?
18. How long is one T state in the Biggy trainer?
19. Explain what happens when the $\overline{\text{WAIT}}$ Z 80 input control signal goes low.
20. What does the Z 80 $\overline{\text{RESET}}$ input control signal do?

Lab 1

OBJECTIVE

After completing this lab, you should be able to

- observe the waveforms of the $\overline{\text{M1}}$ machine cycle on the scope.

Procedure

1. Read Appendix B to familiarize yourself with the use of the Biggy trainer operating commands.
2. Enter the HALT instruction (76 Hex) into memory location 0800 Hex, reboot the computer, and run the HALT instruction at 0800 Hex. When the HALT instruction is executed, the Z 80 will do M1 machine cycles one after the other until the Z 80 is reset or interrupted.
3. After you have run the HALT instruction, use one channel of the scope to display the $\overline{\text{MREQ}}$ control signal and use the other to display the following control signals with respect to the $\overline{\text{MREQ}}$ signal.

   $\overline{\text{M1}}$, $\overline{\text{RD}}$, $\overline{\text{WR}}$, $\overline{\text{MRD}}$, $\overline{\text{MWR}}$, $\overline{\text{IORQ}}$, $\overline{\text{RFSH}}$, AND $\overline{\text{HALT}}$

4. Using a sheet of graph paper, graph the signals listed in step 3 and have the instructor check the graphed signals.

Chapter 2

COMPUTER MEMORY AND ADDRESS DECODERS

OBJECTIVES

After completing this chapter, you should be able to

- describe the difference between ROM, PROM, EPROM, EEPROM, and RAM.
- describe the methods of programming and erasing an EPROM.
- describe the refreshing of dynamic RAM.
- construct address decoder and decipher memory location from the schematic of a computer's address decoder.

2.1 COMPUTER MEMORY

The memory of a computer is a device that can store binary numbers. The address bus supplies a binary number to the memory, which selects the memory location; the control bus strobes the memory's chip select; and the data bus supplies the data to the memory for storage or takes the data from the memory on a read operation.

You might think of a computer memory as a man standing in front of a conveyor belt with a cabinet of pigeon holes behind it. The pigeon holes are memory locations; the data bus is the conveyor belt; and the man who is sorting mail is the control bus, see Figure 2–1. The letter that the mail sorter is storing or removing from the pigeon holes could be analogous to the binary number in the computer's memory. Of course this analogy is rather far fetched, but it represents the basic ideas around which a computer memory is designed.

Before the advent of good IC memory circuits in the early 1970s, the basic memory used for computer memories was the core type. Core memory stored a bit of information by magnetizing a small donut-shaped piece of magnetic material. The magnetic donuts were strung in a memory matrix with small insulated wires through them, as shown in Figure 2–2.

When a magnetic donut was to be magnetized, a current of one-half the amperage to magnetize it was sent through the column wire, and a current of one-half the amperage to do the job was sent through the row wire. At the intersection of the row and column

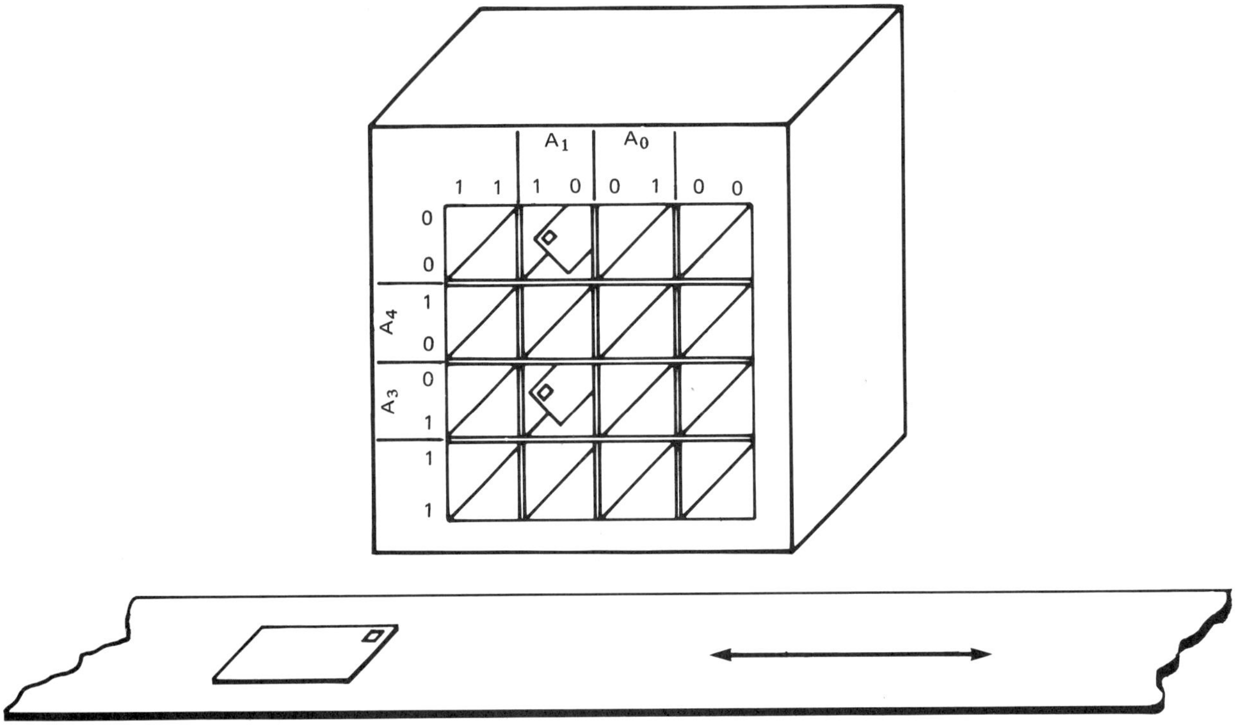

FIGURE 2–1 Analogy to a computer memory

wires, the magnetizing force was enough to magnetize the donut at that intersection but no other.

Once magnetized, the donut would stay magnetized until a current in the opposite direction through the row and column wires reversed its magnetic polarity. A sense wire was strung through all the donuts, so that if the donut at the intersection of the row and column did reverse its magnetic polarity, a small current would be induced in the sense wire. The current would only be induced if the donut selected did reverse its magnetic polarity, thus causing the lines of magnetic flux to cut the sense wire.

If the sense amplifier connected to the sense wire sensed a current, then the bit was a 0 value but if no current was sensed, the bit was a 1. Of course, reading the memory location destroyed the 0 value. Therefore, after reading the memory, if a 0 was detected, the currents of the row and column were reversed to restore the 0 magnetism to the donut that was storing that bit.

These core memories were large, power-hungry, and expensive, but were also nonvolatile. Nonvolatile means that after the power was turned off the memory would retain its memory bit pattern for the next time the power was turned back on. All IC RAM memories are volatile and lose their bit pattern when the power is lost.

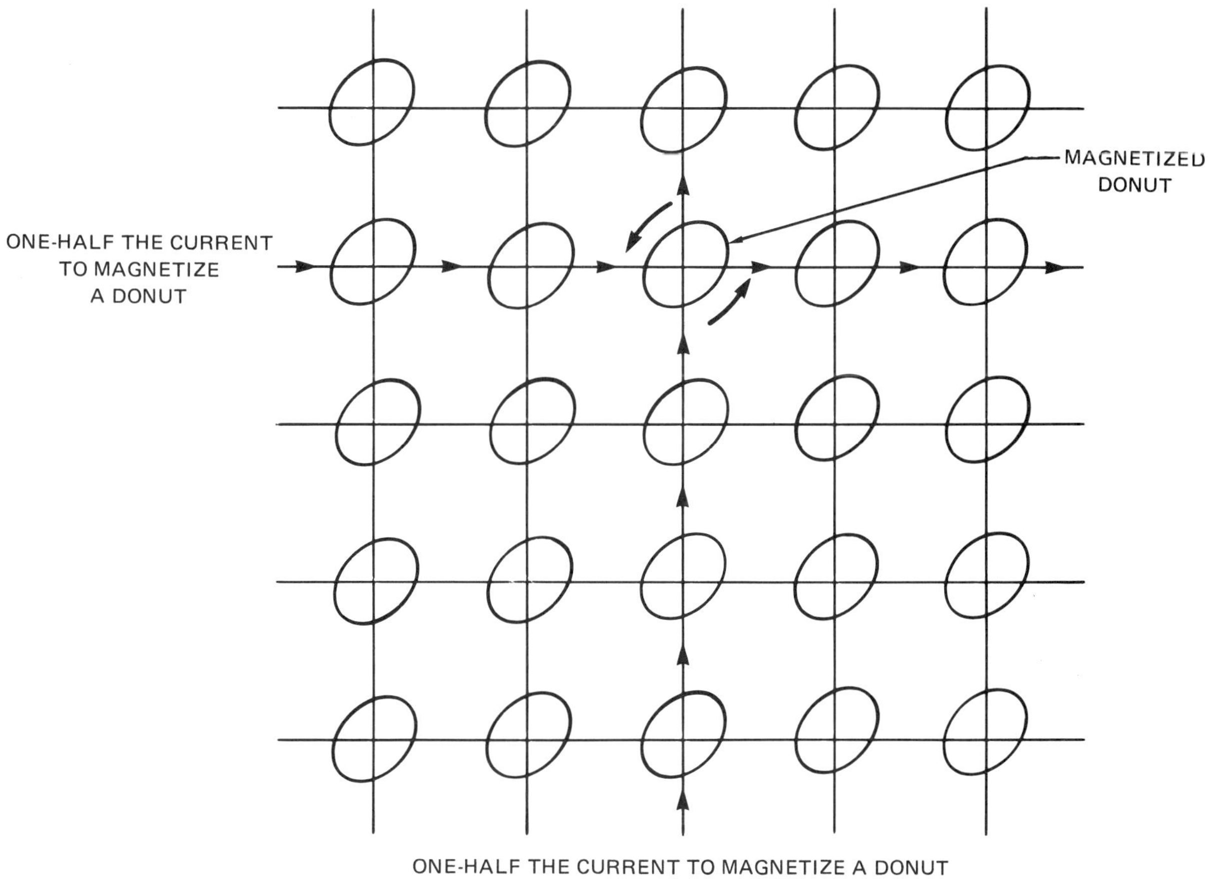

FIGURE 2–2 Magnetic core memory array

2.2 ROM

Because of the problem of RAM memories losing their stored bit patterns when the power is removed, a new type of IC memory was developed to hold boot programs or small operating systems called ROM (read only memory). The ROM has a permanently stored bit pattern and cannot be changed. When power is reapplied, this permanently stored bit pattern or program will be there. ROMs are manufactured with predefined programs for computers and are quite inexpensive after the development cost is met. Because of the high cost of developing the ROM, most ROMs are made for large computer manufacturers for mass production purposes.

Figure 2–3 shows a ROM made from a diode matrix, decoder, and some tri-state gates. The ROM has four memory locations that store 4-bit binary numbers. This is called

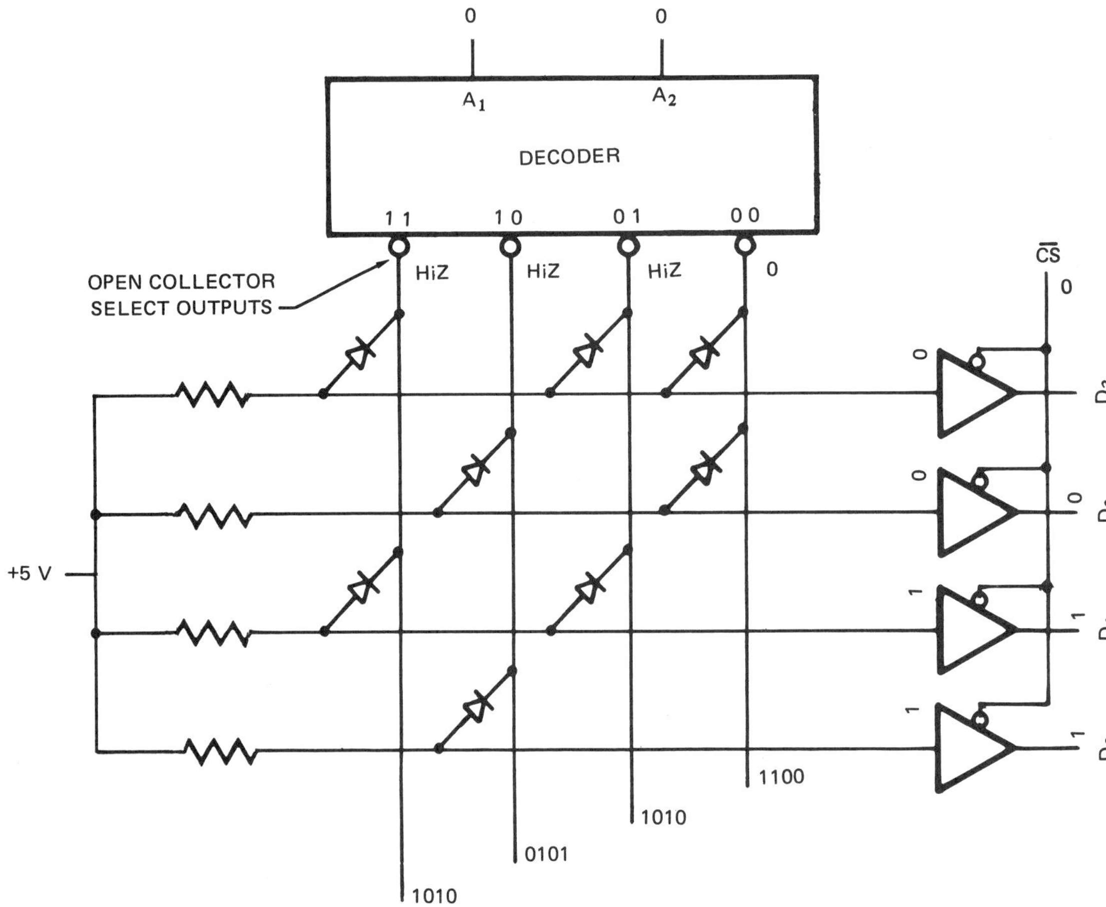

FIGURE 2–3 A 4 by 4 ROM made from diodes, resistors, tri-state gates, and a decoder

a 4 by 4 ROM. A ROM with 2K memory locations of 8 bits each would be a 2048 by 8 ROM. This is the way memory ICs are measured for size (number of memory locations by bit size of each location.)

A binary number placed into the address inputs of the decoder in Figure 2–3 will cause one of the select outputs to go low, thus forward biasing any of the diodes connected to it. This pulls the input of the corresponding tri-state gate low (actually 0.7 V). All the other select output lines from the decoder will be HiZ or high impedance, which causes their corresponding tri-state gate inputs to be pulled high by the pull-up resistor connected to it. The output of the selected 4-bit binary number is placed on the data outputs when the chip select $\overline{CS}$ is low. The chip select $\overline{CS}$ is used by the CPU to turn on or off the ROM.

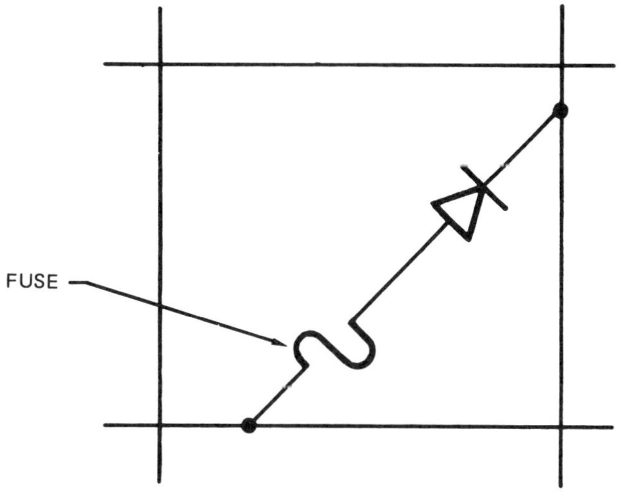

FIGURE 2–4 A PROM memory cell

2.3 PROM

The problem with ROM memory is that once the chip is made the bit pattern stored in it cannot change, and to have a new chip manufactured is quite expensive. The PROM was introduced to help alleviate this problem. PROM stands for programmable read only memory and can have the bit pattern set by the user to his or her desired pattern. The programming is done by blowing a small semiconductor fuse in the memory cell that you wish to make a 1. This is shown in Figure 2–4.

To program a typical PROM the address of the memory location is placed on the address lines of the PROM, the data to be stored is placed on the data output lines, $\overline{CS}$ is held high and the program input PM is pulsed high for a few milliseconds. This will blow the fuse on each diode where a 1 was placed and not on the diode where a 0 was placed. When a fuse is blown, the memory cell will from that time on, read as a 1 because the diode has effectively been disconnected.

2.4 THE EPROM

After a PROM was programmed, its bit pattern was fixed except for unprogrammed 0s which could be changed to 1s but once a 1 value always a 1 value. The EPROM uses a light-sensitive memory cell that can have the 1 value change in it to a 0 value, but unlike the PROM its memory cells can be erased or all changed back to 1 values by the exposure of the IC to ultraviolet light.

The memory cell of an EPROM (erasable programmable read only memory) has a floating gate to the field-effect transistor that can be charged by placing a high voltage of about 25 V on it. Charging this floating gate causes the memory cell to become a 0. Because the electrons are forced across a very thin barrier of silicon dioxide (an insulator) to charge the floating gate, they will not cross back unless their energy level is increased artificially. The exposure of ultraviolet light will do just that, causing the floating gate to lose its charge thus, making the memory cell regain its 1 value. Most EPROMs will be completely erased with exposure to an ultraviolet light with a wavelength of 2500 angstroms or shorter and an intensity of 15 W-s/cm for 15–20 minutes. Standard fluorescent germicidal lamps of 15 W work quite well for erasing EPROMs. The IC should be placed about 1 inch below the lamp. Actual erasing begins about 4000 angstroms in wavelength. This means that a standard fluorescent light used for visual lighting can in about 3 to 4 years erase an EPROM. Direct sunlight can do the job in as little as one week. Therefore, the EPROM should have the optical window covering the chip itself, covered to prevent external light from entering the chip.

The 2716 is a 2K by 8 EPROM, which is typical of the EPROMs used today. We will study its operation and programming methods because it is typical and the Biggy trainer also uses it for its read only memory. It should be noted here that the 2708, which was a very early EPROM, is somewhat different in its programming methods. It is still found in older equipment.

Figure 2–5 shows the pinout of the 2716 EPROM. There are 11 address lines (A_0 to A_{10}), which select the memory location to read or program, and eight data lines (D_0 to D_7), which are used to output data or place data into memory. The IC has one +5-V power supply and +25 V on the V_{pp} input for programming of memory. The $\overline{OE}$ (output enable) controls the internal tri-state gates on the D_0 to D_7 output pins. The $\overline{CE}$

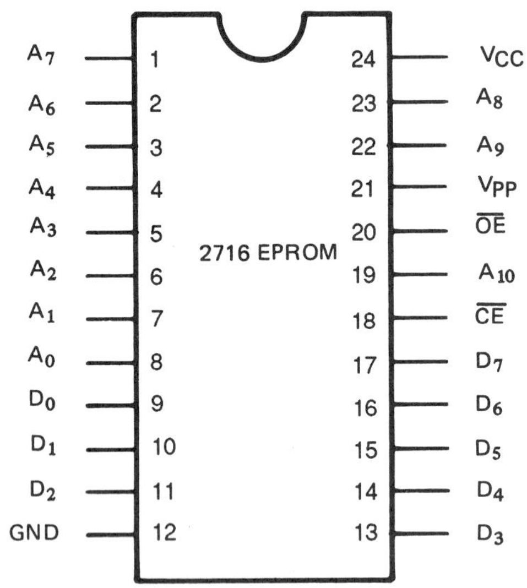

FIGURE 2–5 2716 EPROM

2716 — (2K BY 8)
2732 — (4K BY 8)
2764 — (8K BY 8)
27128 — (16K BY 8)
27256 — (32K BY 8)

FIGURE 2–6 Typical EPROMs

(chip enable) also controls the output tri-states gates, the difference is that when $\overline{CE}$ returns to the inactive state (high) the 2716 goes into its standby mode, which causes it to draw about 75% less power.

Using the $\overline{CE}$ to select the chip costs the designer access time. *Access time* is the time from when the IC memory is selected ($\overline{CE}$ goes low) to when the output lines have a stable output value. If the $\overline{CE}$ is used, the access time is about 450 ns as compared to 120 ns for the $\overline{OE}$ on a standard 2716 EPROM. During normal reading operation the V_{PP} (voltage program power) pin is held at +5 V and $\overline{CE}$ or $\overline{OE}$ are used to gate the output onto the computer's data bus.

To program the 2716 EPROM, the V_{PP} pin is brought up to +25 V, the $\overline{OE}$ is made high, and the $\overline{CE}$ is used to control programming. The byte to store in the memory is placed on the output lines (D_0–D_7), and the $\overline{CE}$ pin is pulsed high from a low state for 50 ms. You can randomly program the memory locations or do them sequentially. Once programmed, a 0 will remain a 0 until it is erased by exposure to ultraviolet light.

EPROMS have fast become the major IC used for storage of boot programs and operating systems in computers today. Some typical chips used today are listed in Figure 2–6.

2.5 THE EEPROM (ELECTRICALLY ERASABLE PROGRAMMABLE READ ONLY MEMORY)

EPROMs cannot be selectively cleared, nor can they be cleared very fast. The EEPROM (or E^2PROM) is an improvement over the basic EPROM technology. Figure 2–7 shows the basic EPROM and EEPROM memory transistors and their floating gates. In the EPROM the electrons were forced across the silicon dioxide insulation by placing a high voltage across the P substrata and the normal gates. The electrons then collected on the floating gate and were trapped, thus charging the gate. When the gate is charged, the field-effect transistor will not conduct.

In the E^2PROM the floating gate and normal gate have a protruding portion that comes very close to the drain of the transistor. Electrons are forced onto the floating gate by producing a high voltage of − to + from drain to normal gate and just as in the EPROM transistor, the electrons collect on the floating gate, thus charging it negatively. By reversing the voltage polarity the electrons can be removed and the charge reversed. This gives the E^2PROM the ability to be cleared and then reprogrammed quickly, with voltage of about 21 V.

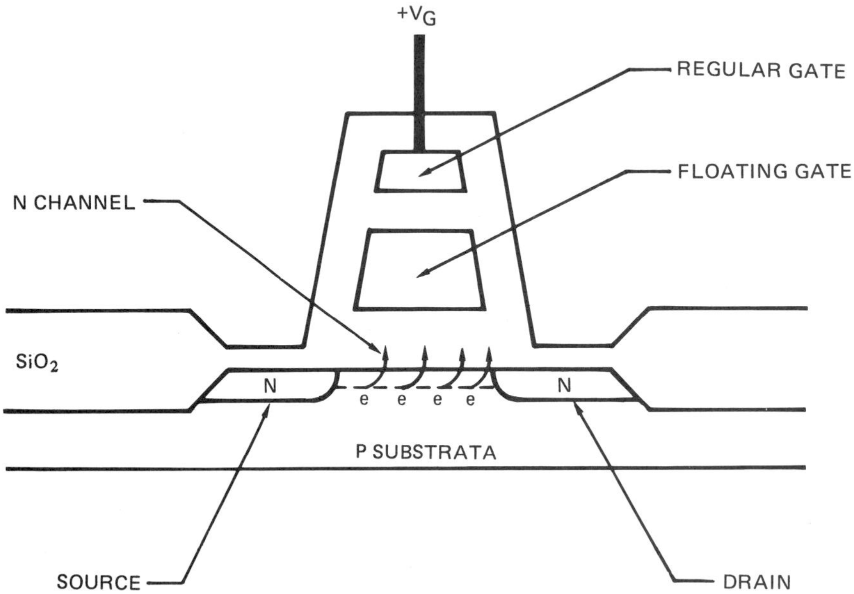

(A) The EPROM FET transistor

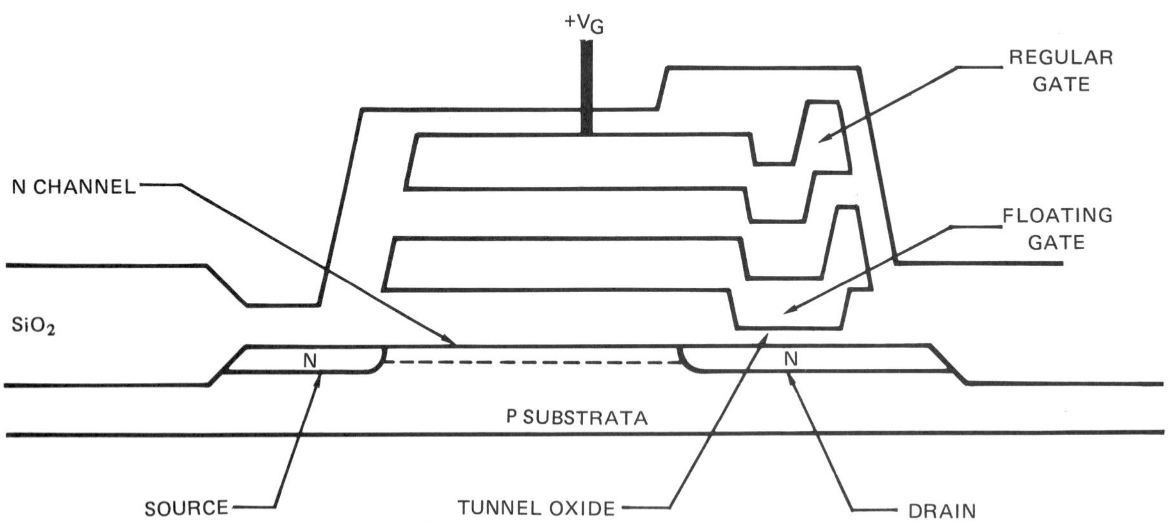

(B) EEPROM transistor

FIGURE 2–7 The EPROM and EEPROM transistors

E^2PROM technology has not produced the ultimate read/write memory yet. The number of storages is not unlimited, it stands at above 10^4, writes, at this time, and it still takes about 50 ms to program a byte into the memory. Because of these limitations, the E^2PROM will not be used as a RAM memory, but it is being used to store terminal setup characteristics, printer setup characteristics, and short programs that need quick changing from time to time. Figure 2–8 shows Intel's 2815 E^2PROM. Notice the similarity of pinout with the 2716 EPROM.

2.6 STATIC RAM (RANDOM ACCESS MEMORY)

Random access memory is really read/write memory. The term "random access" means that the memory will access or read/write to any memory location that the address input indicates. The static RAM IC memory uses a simple set/reset flip-flop made from cross-coupled transistors as a memory cell. This memory cell can be either set or reset and will hold the set or reset value until the power is turned off. Typical read/write speed for MOS (metal-oxide semiconductor) RAMS range from 55 ns to 450 ns. This is quite fast enough for almost all computer operations today. All static RAM ICs are volatile and lose memory patterns with the loss of power. The old core memory and bubble memory do not have this problem.

Static RAM is made with four basic technologies: MOS (metal-oxide semiconductor), CMOS (complementary metal-oxide semiconductor), TTL (transistor-transistor logic), and ECL (emitter-coupled logic). TTL RAM is much faster than MOS RAM but is not as dense. A typical TTL RAM like Motorola's MCM93415 is a 1K by 1 RAM with an access time of 45 ns. CMOS RAM is slower than TTL RAM, somewhat denser, and uses much less power. When a CMOS RAM is not being read from or written to, it usually uses no power at all. This means that a small long-life battery, such as a silver-oxide cell, can be used as a backup power supply for the RAM when the main power is turned off. This makes the CMOS RAM appear to be nonvolatile, and it is used in many applications, such as portable computers. A typical CMOS RAM is Motorola's MCM61L16P20, which is a 2K by 8 CMOS RAM with an access time of 200 ns.

ECL is the fastest of the four basic technologies. It uses more power but is much faster. A typical ECL RAM, such as Motorola's MCM10474-15, is a 1K by 4 ECL RAM with a 15-ns access time.

The RAMs used in the Biggy trainer are 2114A 1K by 4 static MOS RAMs. Figure 2–9 shows the pinout of the RAM. This RAM has four data lines that are used to transfer data to and from the memory. A_0 to A_9 are the address inputs that select the memory location that is to be read from or written to. The $\overline{CS}$ (chip select) is used to gate information into or out of the RAM while the $\overline{WE}$ (write enable) is used to determine a read or write operation. Figure 2–10 shows the read and write waveforms for the 2114A RAM.

When $\overline{WE}$ is high and $\overline{CS}$ goes low, the RAM puts the contents of the selected address on the data outputs. When the $\overline{CS}$ and $\overline{WE}$ both go low, the data present on the data line is stored into the memory location selected by the binary number on the address inputs (A_0 to A_9).

intel®

2815
16K (2K X 8) ELECTRICALLY ERASABLE PROM

- **Reliable Floating Gate Technology**
- **Cost-Effective Non-Volatile Memory Alternative**
- **Erase/Write Specifications Guaranteed 0–70°C**
- **Very Fast Access Times**
  —2815, 250 ns Max.
  —2815-3, 350 ns
  —2815-4, 450 ns
- **Two-Line Control**
- **Low Power Dissipation**
  —Active Current, 110 mA
  —Standby Current, 50 mA
- **Compatible with 2716 EPROM**
- **Simple 21V Programming Interface**

The Intel 2815 is a 2048-word by 8-bit Electrically Eraseable Programmable Read Only Memory (E^2PROM). It is fabricated using Intel's FLOTOX cell design and powerful HMOS-E* technology. The 2815's E^2 functionality enables in-circuit reprogrammable memory flexibility, while maintaining the non-volatility of the data stored.

The Intel 2815 is erased and written in-circuit. Byte and chip erasure are accomplished with a single 50 mS pulse after which data can be written a byte at a time. Because of its unique architecture, selection of the chip to be erased or written is performed with the same address control circuitry as that used for read operations.

Read operations with the 2815 are performed at standard 5V TTL levels. The 250 ns access time is fast enough so that the 2815 can be interfaced to processor system busses with no wait states. The microprocessor to 2815 interface is achieved with a minimum of external circuitry.

The 2815 was designed in accordance with Intel's byte-wide pinout philosophy and therefore conforms to the JEDEC approved byte-wide family standard. The two-line control architecture of this standard ensures elimination of bus contention in high-speed microprocessor systems. The 2815 is pin-for-pin compatible with the Intel 2816 E^2PROM and it is therefore directly upgradable for those systems requiring faster write times in the future.

Application of the 2815 for program storage, error logging, or prototyping memory maximizes the user potential to reduce service costs. As a program storage medium, users are able to update firmware remotely, saving the costs of increased parts inventories and more frequent service calls. Revision levels, service call logs, and system configuration parameters can also be stored non-volatilely, so that they can be easily accessed or updated on a service call. The 2815 is also an excellent alternative to CMOS RAMs and batteries in systems requiring non-volatile parameter storage. The 2815's many features, wide temperature range, extremely reliable operation, and design-in ease combine to give you a powerful tool for adding dramatically increased functionality to your systems.

*HMOS-E is a patented process of Intel Corporation.

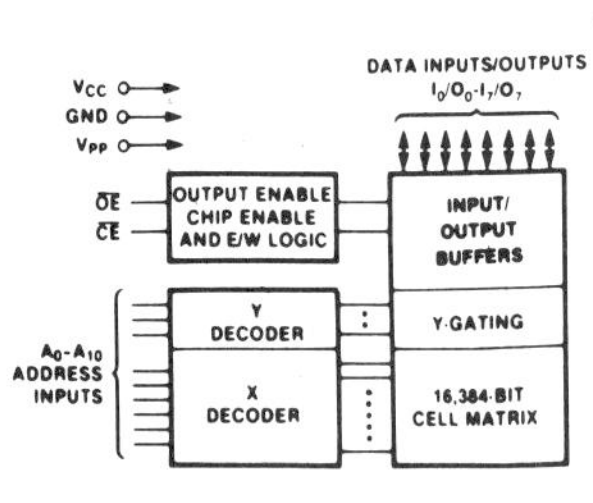

2815 Functional Block Diagram

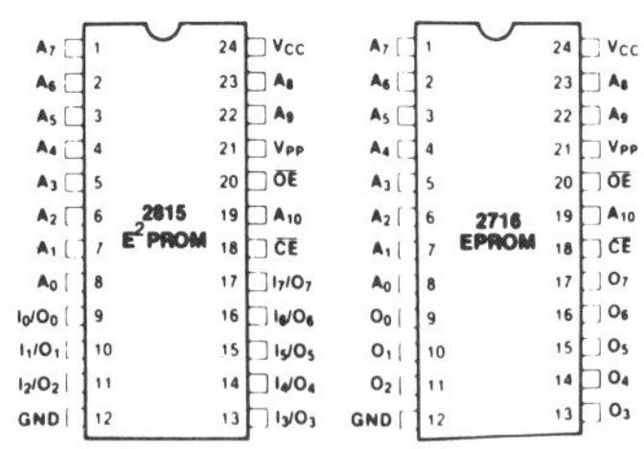

PIN NAMES

A_0-A_{10}	ADDRESSES
$\overline{CE}$	CHIP ENABLE
$\overline{OE}$	OUTPUT ENABLE
O_0-O_7	DATA OUTPUTS
I_0-I_7	DATA INPUTS
V_{PP}	PROGRAM VOLTAGE

Pin Configuration

OCTOBER 1982
AFN-02025A

FIGURE 2–8 The 2815 EEPROM

intel®

2114A
1024 X 4 BIT STATIC RAM

	2114AL-1	2114AL-2	2114AL-3	2114AL-4	2114A-4	2114A-5
Max. Access Time (ns)	100	120	150	200	200	250
Max. Current (mA)	40	40	40	40	70	70

- **HMOS Technology**
- **Low Power, High Speed**
- **Identical Cycle and Access Times**
- **Single +5V Supply ±10%**
- **High Density 18 Pin Package**
- **Completely Static Memory - No Clock or Timing Strobe Required**
- **Directly TTL Compatible: All Inputs and Outputs**
- **Common Data Input and Output Using Three-State Outputs**
- **2114 Upgrade**

The Intel® 2114A is a 4096-bit static Random Access Memory organized as 1024 words by 4-bits using HMOS, a high performance MOS technology. It uses fully DC stable (static) circuitry throughout, in both the array and the decoding, therefore it requires no clocks or refreshing to operate. Data access is particularly simple since address setup times are not required. The data is read out nondestructively and has the same polarity as the input data. Common input/output pins are provided.

The 2114A is designed for memory applications where the high performance and high reliability of HMOS, low cost, large bit storage, and simple interfacing are important design objectives. The 2114A is placed in an 18-pin package for the highest possible density.

It is directly TTL compatible in all respects: inputs, outputs, and a single +5V supply. A separate Chip Select ($\overline{CS}$) lead allows easy selection of an individual package when outputs are or-tied.

PIN CONFIGURATION

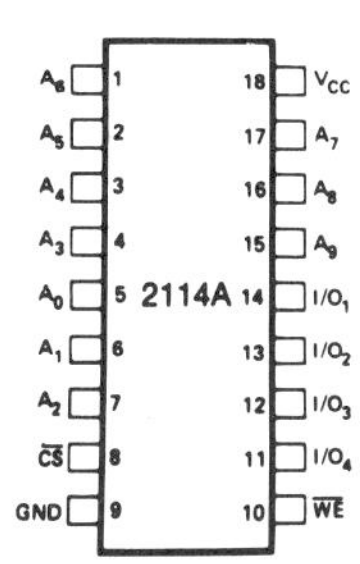

LOGIC SYMBOL

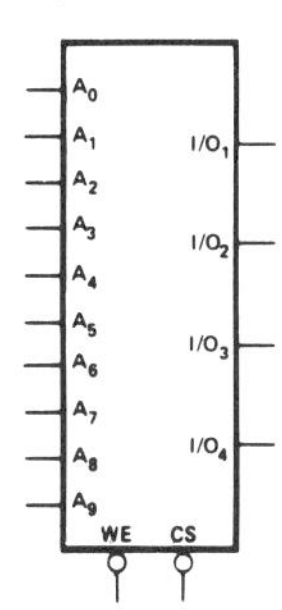

BLOCK DIAGRAM

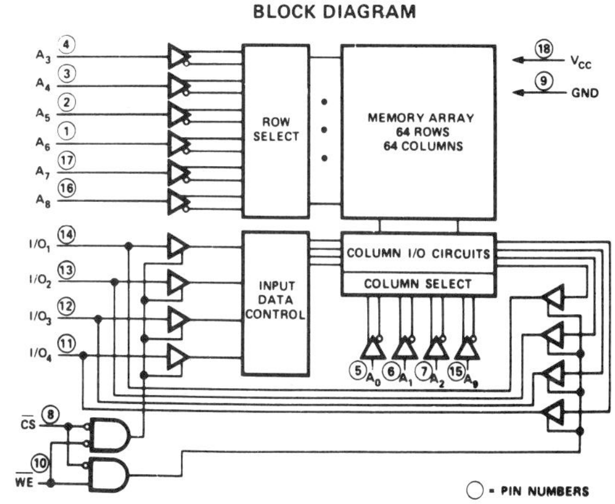

PIN NAMES

A_0–A_9	ADDRESS INPUTS	V_{CC}	POWER (+5V)
$\overline{WE}$	WRITE ENABLE	GND	GROUND
$\overline{CS}$	CHIP SELECT		
I/O_1–I/O_4	DATA INPUT/OUTPUT		

FIGURE 2–9 The 2114A static RAM

2114A FAMILY

A.C. CHARACTERISTICS $T_A = 0°C$ to $70°C$, $V_{CC} = 5V \pm 10\%$, unless otherwise noted.

READ CYCLE [1]

SYMBOL	PARAMETER	2114AL-1 Min.	Max.	2114AL-2 Min.	Max.	2114AL-3 Min.	Max.	2114A-4/L-4 Min.	Max.	2114A-5 Min.	Max.	UNIT
t_{RC}	Read Cycle Time	100		120		150		200		250		ns
t_A	Access Time		100		120		150		200		250	ns
t_{CO}	Chip Selection to Output Valid		70		70		70		70		85	ns
t_{CX}	Chip Selection to Output Active	10		10		10		10		10		ns
t_{OTD}	Output 3-state from Deselection		30		35		40		50		60	ns
t_{OHA}	Output Hold from Address Change	15		15		15		15		15		ns

WRITE CYCLE [2]

SYMBOL	PARAMETER	2114AL-1 Min.	Max.	2114AL-2 Min.	Max.	2114AL-3 Min.	Max.	2114A-4/L-4 Min.	Max.	2114A-5 Min.	Max.	UNIT
t_{WC}	Write Cycle Time	100		120		150		200		250		ns
t_W	Write Time	75		75		90		120		135		ns
t_{WR}	Write Release Time	0		0		0		0		0		ns
t_{OTW}	Output 3-state from Write		30		35		40		50		60	ns
t_{DW}	Data to Write Time Overlap	70		70		90		120		135		ns
t_{DH}	Data Hold from Write Time	0		0		0		0		0		ns

NOTES:
1. A Read occurs during the overlap of a low $\overline{CS}$ and a high $\overline{WE}$.
2. A Write occurs during the overlap of a low $\overline{CS}$ and a low $\overline{WE}$. t_W is measured from the latter of $\overline{CS}$ or $\overline{WE}$ going low to the earlier of $\overline{CS}$ or $\overline{WE}$ going high.

WAVEFORMS

READ CYCLE ③

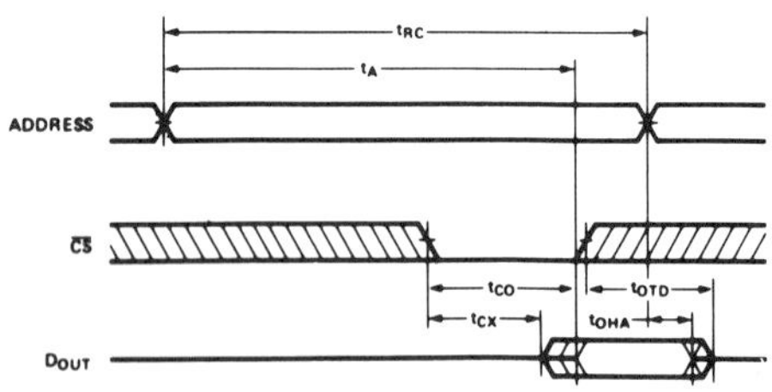

NOTES:
3. $\overline{WE}$ is high for a Read Cycle.
4. If the $\overline{CS}$ low transition occurs simultaneously with the $\overline{WE}$ low transition, the output buffers remain in a high impedance state.
5. $\overline{WE}$ must be high during all address transitions.

WRITE CYCLE

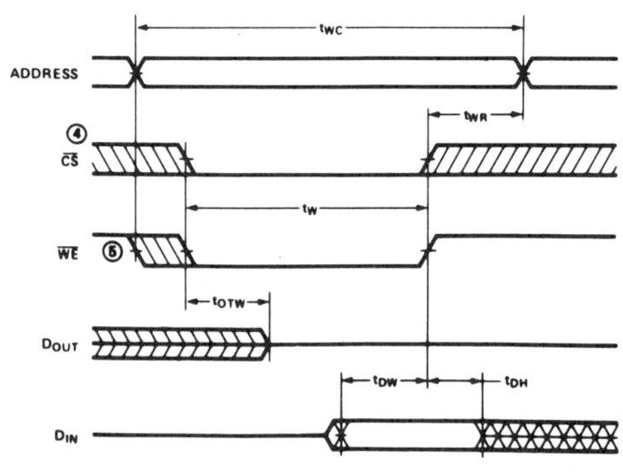

FIGURE 2–10 The read/write waveforms and timing for the 2114A static RAM

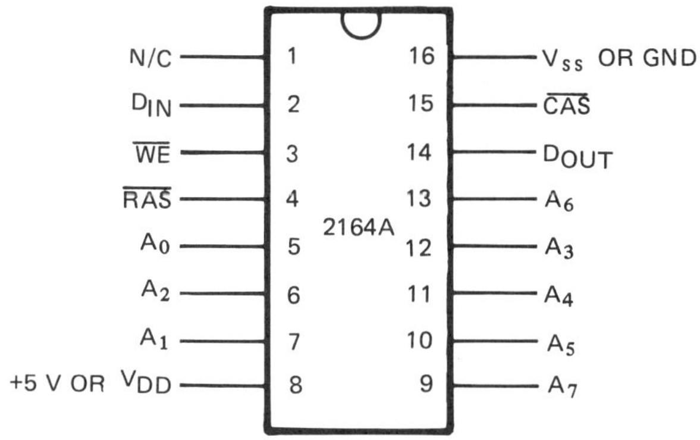

FIGURE 2–11 The industrial standard 16-pin package pinout for dynamic RAMs

2.7 *DYNAMIC RAM*

Dynamic RAM uses a single transistor and a small capacitor for a memory storage cell. Because of the few components used per memory cell, the dynamic RAM is very dense. At present the dynamic RAM can hold more memory cells per IC than any other type of RAM. Bubble memories, which use magnetic domains to store data, can store more data, but they are slow and are not truly random access memory.

Because of the high density and relatively low power consumption, the dynamic RAM has fast become the major computer memory used today. The only problem with dynamic RAM is that it must have every memory cell read or written to every 2 ms or the small capacitor in the memory cell will discharge and the RAM will lose the stored bit pattern. This refresh operation takes computer time and other circuits to accomplish. The Z 80 CPU has a built-in transparent refreshing system for dynamic RAM that does not waste any CPU time. This makes the Z 80 CPU very attractive to designers.

The 2164A dynamic RAM is a 64K by 1 NMOS (N-channel metal-oxide semiconductor) made by Intel. It has a single +5-V power supply, and its outputs can handle two TTL loads. Figure 2–11 shows the pinout of the RAM.

The RAM comes in a 16-pin package. To address 64K of memory, you need 16 address pins (A_0 to A_{15}). To get all 16 address inputs, one data input, V_{CC} ground, and the control inputs into one 16-pin package, the address inputs were cut in half and multiplexed into the chip. This means that only eight pins are used to supply the RAM IC with 16 address inputs. To do this, two new control lines were added: $\overline{RAS}$ (row address strobe) and $\overline{CAS}$ (column address strobe). These two strobes latch address information into the row and column of the memory cell matrix used by the RAM. Figure 2–12 shows the memory cell array and the row and column address latches.

To read or write to the RAM, the least significant byte (LSB) of the address is placed on the A_0 to A_7 address inputs, and then the $\overline{RAS}$ (row address strobe) is brought low which latches the LSB of the address bus into the row latches of the memory array. Then the most significant byte (MSB) of the address is placed on the A_0 to A_7 address inputs

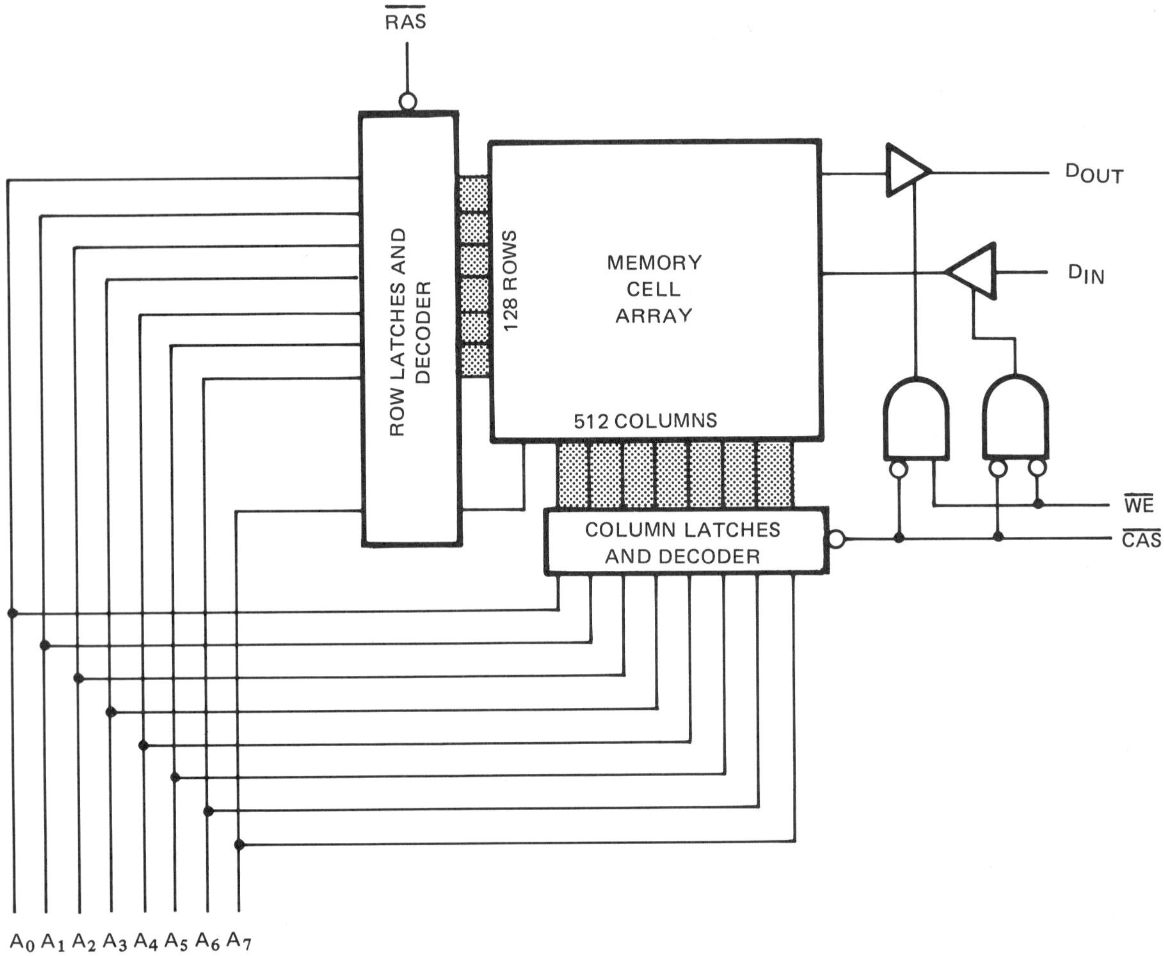

FIGURE 2–12 2164 RAM block drawing

and latched into the column latches of the memory array when $\overline{CAS}$ goes low. Shortly after the low-going $\overline{CAS}$ signal, the data is put on the D_{OUT} pin, or the data on the D_{IN} pin is stored. The type of operation (read or write) is controlled by the $\overline{WE}$ signal.

To refresh the memory cells in the array, it is only necessary to latch in a new row address, because each time a new row is selected all the memory cells on that row are refreshed. Notice that the row address is actually only 7 bits wide, and the column address is 9 bits wide. Therefore, only a 7-bit refresh address is needed to refresh the entire dynamic memory.

During the M1 machine cycle of the Z 80 CPU, the internal refresh register is incremented and placed on the lower seven bits of the address bus. Then the $\overline{MREQ}$ and $\overline{RFSH}$ go low. By ORing these two signals a dynamic refresh signal can be produced. This is shown with an address multiplexing method in Figure 2–13.

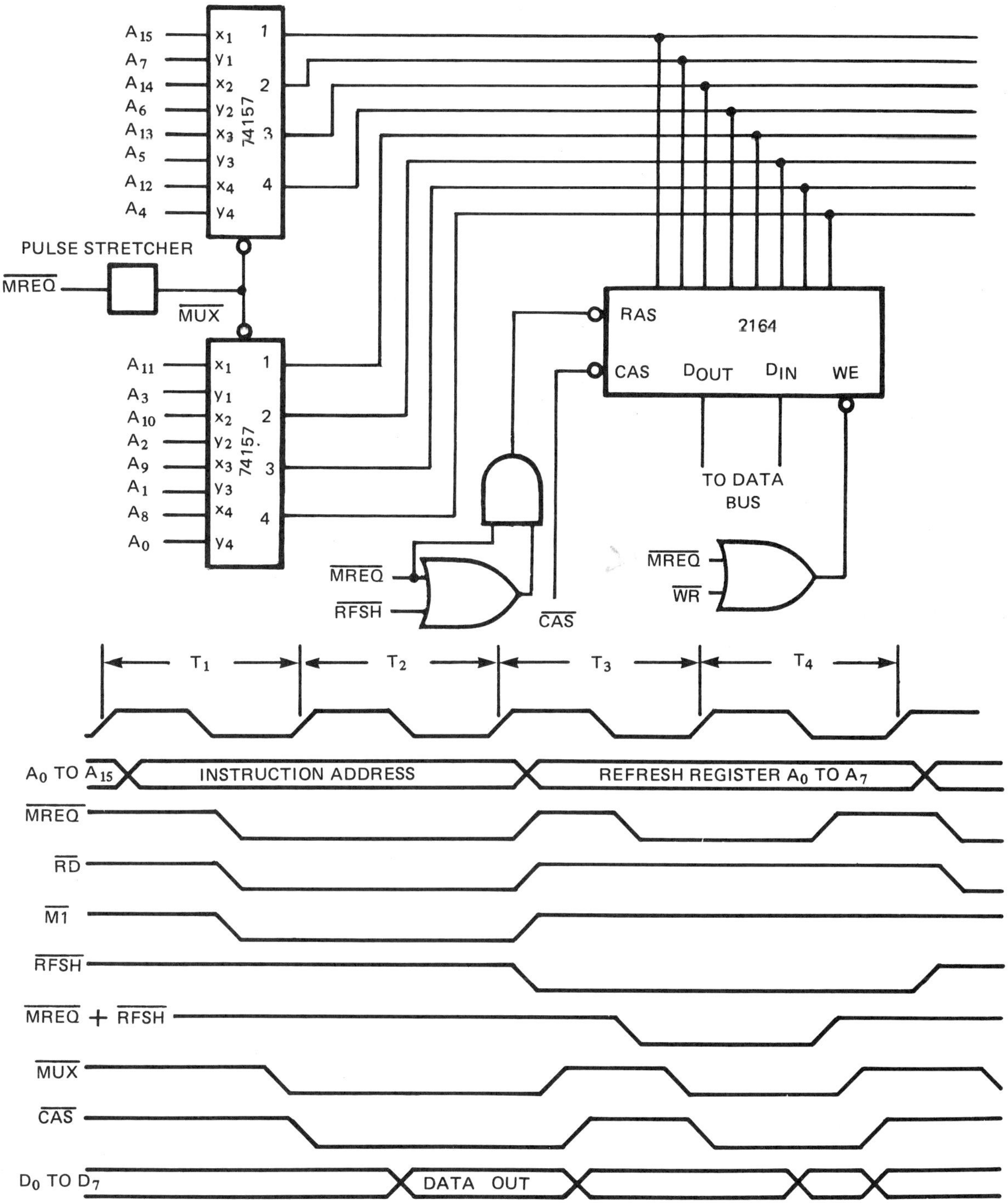

FIGURE 2–13 2164 RAM with waveforms

Shortly after the rising edge of the T_1 state, the address bus becomes stable with the address of the next instruction to fetch from memory. Shortly after the falling edge of the T_1 state, the $\overline{MREQ}$ and $\overline{RD}$ go low. The $\overline{MREQ}$ going low strobes the $\overline{RAS}$ of the 2164 dynamic RAM and latches the low byte (A_0 to A_7) of the address into the row address latches inside the RAM. Very quickly after the $\overline{MREQ}$ goes low, a new control signal called $\overline{MUX}$ (multiplex) goes low. This signal can be derived by using a short one-shot pulse stretcher, triggered on the falling edge of $\overline{MREQ}$, or by other methods. When the $\overline{MUX}$ goes low, the address fed to the 2164 RAM is changed to the high byte of the instruction address. Very shortly after the low-going $\overline{MUX}$ changes the address feed to the dynamic RAM, the $\overline{CAS}$ goes low. Again the new signal can be derived by using a one-shot pulse stretcher that is triggered on the falling edge of $\overline{MUX}$, or by other methods. The sequence of low-going $\overline{MREQ}$, $\overline{MUX}$, and final $\overline{CAS}$ loads the 2164 dynamic RAM with the address, and the RAM will give up its data from the addressed memory cell. The whole process is repeated again when the $\overline{RFSH}$ control line and $\overline{MREQ}$ go low. But this time the lower seven bits of the address bus contain the just-incremented refresh register. Every time an M1 machine cycle takes place, the refresh register is incremented by 1. Thus, every 128 M1 machine cycles the total dynamic memory is refreshed. If the longest instruction was 15 T states or clock cycles long, then the time to refresh the whole 64K of dynamic memory would be 500 ns times 15 times 128 which is 0.96 ms. This is well within the 2 ms needed for refreshing the RAM. When the CPU runs the HALT instruction, the CPU does M1 machine cycles but does not decode the fetched instruction. This is to maintain the refreshing of the dynamic memory.

2.8 THE MEMORY DECODER

The memory decoder selects the memory ICs that are to be used. Because the central or core memory of a computer is usually made up of some ROM and some RAM, it is necessary to decode the address bus to select different sets of IC memories. The address decoder for the Biggy trainer is shown in Figure 2–14.

The decoder chip used is a 74LS138, which is a full 3-bit decoder with three enable inputs, two active low and one active high. A_{15} is inverted and fed to the active high enable (pin 6 of the 74LS138). A_{14} and A_{13} are fed to the two active low enables (pins 4 and 5 of the 74LS138). This means that the top or most significant three bits of a memory address must be low to enable any of the 74LS138 outputs. Therefore, only addresses from

0000 0000 0000 0000 or 0000 Hex to 0001 1111 1111 1111 or 1FFF Hex

will enable any of the 74LS138 outputs, because any 1 on any of the three most significant bits will disable the 74LS138 outputs.

A_{12}, A_{11}, and A_{10} are fed to the select inputs of the 74LS138 to select one of the eight outputs when A_{15}, A_{14}, and A_{13} are low. If A_{15}, A_{14}, A_{13}, A_{12}, A_{11}, and A_{10} are low or 0, then the 0 output of the 74LS138 will be active, which means it will go low. Any address from

0000 0000 0000 0000 or 0000 Hex to 0000 0011 1111 1111 or 03FF Hex

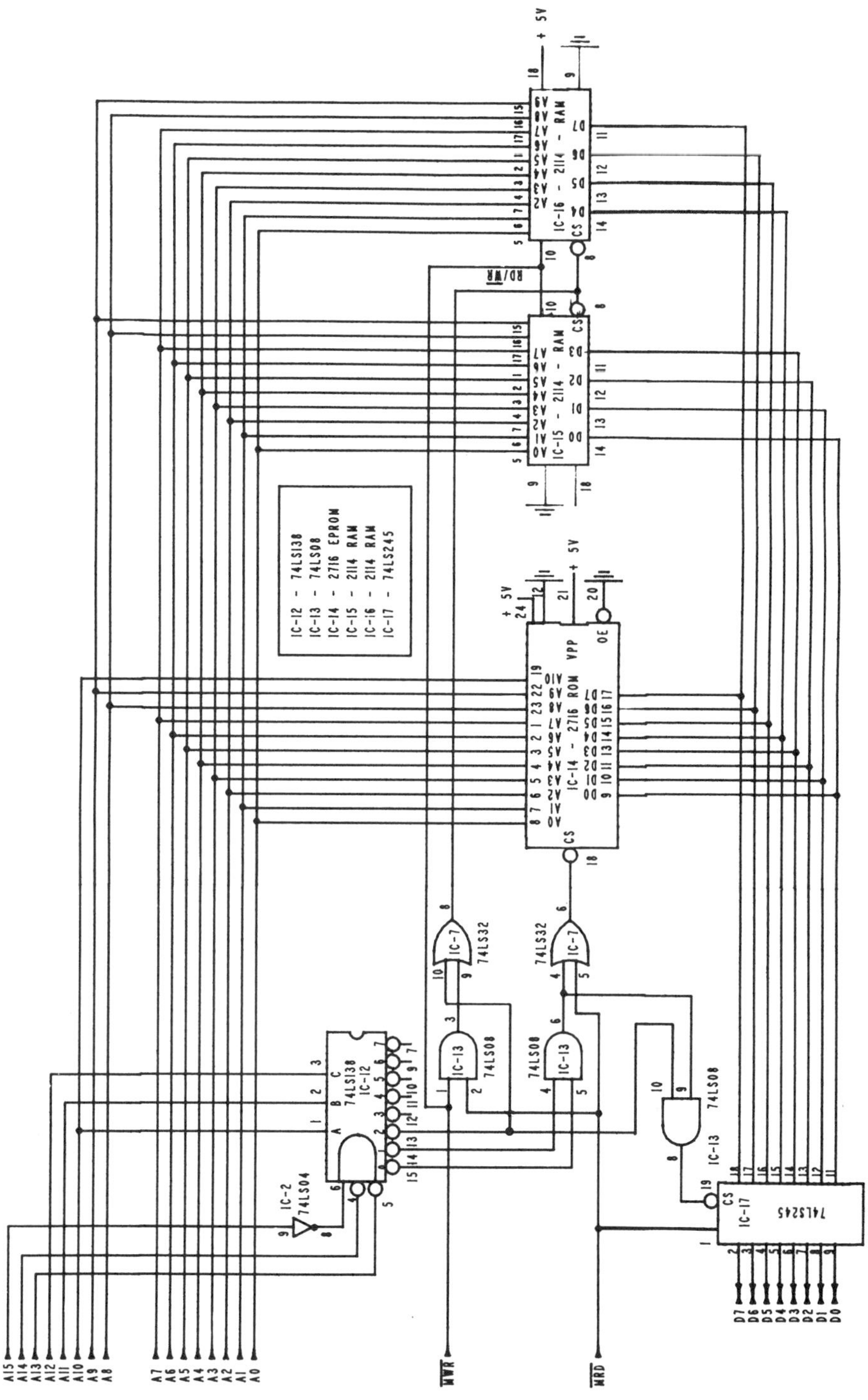
IC-12 - 74LS138
IC-13 - 74LS08
IC-14 - 2716 EPROM
IC-15 - 2114 RAM
IC-16 - 2114 RAM
IC-17 - 74LS245

FIGURE 2–14

will make the 0 output of the 74LS138 go low or active. This is 2^{10} (1024 or 1K) possible addresses. If the next output (the 1 output of the 74LS138) goes low, then the address must lie between

0000 0100 0000 0000 or 0400 Hex and 0000 0111 1111 1111 or 07FF Hex

This is the next 1K of memory after the 0 1K block. The 74LS138 will divide the address into 1K blocks that start with address 0000 Hex and go to 1FFF Hex.

This was done because the memory ICs to be used are 1K static RAMs (2114). Therefore, the IC memory will decode the low address line (A_0 to A_9) to select the unique memory location, and the address decoder will select the proper block of 1K memory chips to find the byte in for the given address placed on the address bus.

The output of the 74LS138 address decoder will be active or inactive as the address bus changes in value. To select or turn on the memory at the proper time when the CPU is ready for the memory to be selected, the 74LS138 outputs are ORed with $\overline{MRD}$ and $\overline{MWR}$. This means that $\overline{MRD}$ or $\overline{MWR}$ must go low (any 0 into an AND gate will produce a 0 out), and the number 2 output of the 74LS138 must go low to produce a low signal to the $\overline{CS}$ of the 2114 RAM ICs.

Therefore, the CPU can place the address of the memory location it wishes to read or write to on the address bus and strobe the appropriate control signal ($\overline{MRD}$ or $\overline{MWR}$) low to activate the memory chip. The memory chip has tri-state output, so it can be wired directly to the buffered data bus. The memory IC will only input from or output to the data bus when it has been selected by a low $\overline{CS}$ (pin 8). Whether the memory operation is to be an $\overline{MRD}$ or $\overline{MWR}$ operation is determined by the RD/$\overline{WR}$ input (pin 10) of the 2114 RAM. This pin is connected to the $\overline{MWR}$ control signal. When the RD/$\overline{WR}$ input is low, the CPU is going to store or write data to the RAM.

The 2716 EPROM is a 2K by 8 memory IC. Therefore, outputs 0 and 1 of the 74LS138 address decoder were fed into an AND gate to produce an active low output for a 2K block of memory. This 2K memory select was ORed with only the $\overline{MRD}$ because the 2716 EPROM is read only memory, and we want to prevent any possibility of writing to a read only memory. It can be seen that the first 2K of the Biggy trainer's memory is read only memory and the next 1K is RAM memory. An additional 5K of memory could be added to the Biggy trainer without adding another 74LS138 address decoder, if desired.

Most memory ICs do not have enough power to directly drive the data bus when they are being read, so a bidirectional data bus driver is used to drive the bus. A 74LS245 was used in the Biggy trainer. The three outputs of the 74LS138 that select memory blocks in the Biggy trainer were fed to AND gates to produce an active low $\overline{CS}$ to select or enable the 74LS245 bus driver when any of the 3K blocks of memory were addressed. If more memory were to be added, the extra outputs of the 74LS138 that select the new 1K blocks of memory would have to be fed to more AND gates, so they could also enable the 74LS245 bus driver.

The direction of data flow through the 74LS245 bus driver is controlled by the $\overline{MRD}$ control signal. When the $\overline{MRD}$ is low or active, data is fed from the memory to the data bus. When the $\overline{MRD}$ is inactive or high, the data is fed from the data bus to the memory.

EXERCISE 2

1. What is a ROM?
2. What is the difference between a PROM and an EPROM?
3. How is an EPROM cleared?
4. What is an EEPROM?
5. What are the most dense types of IC RAM used today?
6. Which type of RAM uses very little power?
7. Draw the industrial pinout standard for a 16-pin dynamic RAM.
8. Which type of RAM is fastest (TTL, MOS, CMOS, or ECL)?
9. What is meant when an EPROM is said to be a 2K by 8 EPROM?
10. What would be the output of the ROM circuit in Figure 2–3 if A_1 and A_2 were high and the $\overline{CS}$ was low?
11. Draw the pinout of the 2716 EPROM.
12. Why can a 64K dynamic RAM be refreshed with only a 7-bit refresh register?
13. During which machine cycle does the Z 80 refresh the dynamic RAM?
14. How many more K of RAM could be added to the Biggy trainer without adding another 74LS138 address decoder?
15. Design an address decoder that would decode the first 16 1K blocks of memory for a computer with 16 address lines, (use a 74LS154 and a 74LS05).
16. What is the highest RAM address in the Biggy trainer?
17. What is the highest ROM address in the Biggy trainer?
18. What type of RAMs were used in the Biggy trainer?
19. Which type of RAM is nonvolatile?
20. What was the purpose of the $\overline{MUX}$ signal in Figure 2–13?

Lab 2

OBJECTIVES

After completing this lab, you should be able to

- describe the operation of a memory decoder.
- explain how to buffer the input/output of a static memory.
- use some typical debugging methods to troubleshoot computers.

Procedure

1. Construct the circuit shown on the wireless breadboard of the Biggy trainer.
2. Try to read and write to the 1K nibble of memory you just wired. If it is working, then proceed to part 3 of the procedure. If it is not working then go through the following debug procedure.
   A. If the Biggy trainer is not operating then remove the data, address, and control lines that are connected to the Biggy trainer one at a time to find the one that is holding down the computer.
   B. When you have the computer up and operating, if the new memory is still not operating then enter and run the following short program.

ADDRESS	OPCODE	MNEMONIC
0800	32 00 20	LD (2000H), A
0803	C3 00 08	JP 0800H

   This program will output the A register to the first memory location in the new memory just wired to the computer and jump back to do it again. This will produce a continuous low-going $\overline{CS}$ signal at the 74LS245 and 2114 ICs. Use the scope to look for these signals and the $\overline{MWR}$ signal also. If they are not present, then use the scope to trace back the signal to find the fault.
3. Applying the knowledge learned in this chapter, use another 2114 RAM and the rest of the 74LS245 bidirectional bus driver to add the most significant four bits to the new memory. Have your instructor check its operation.

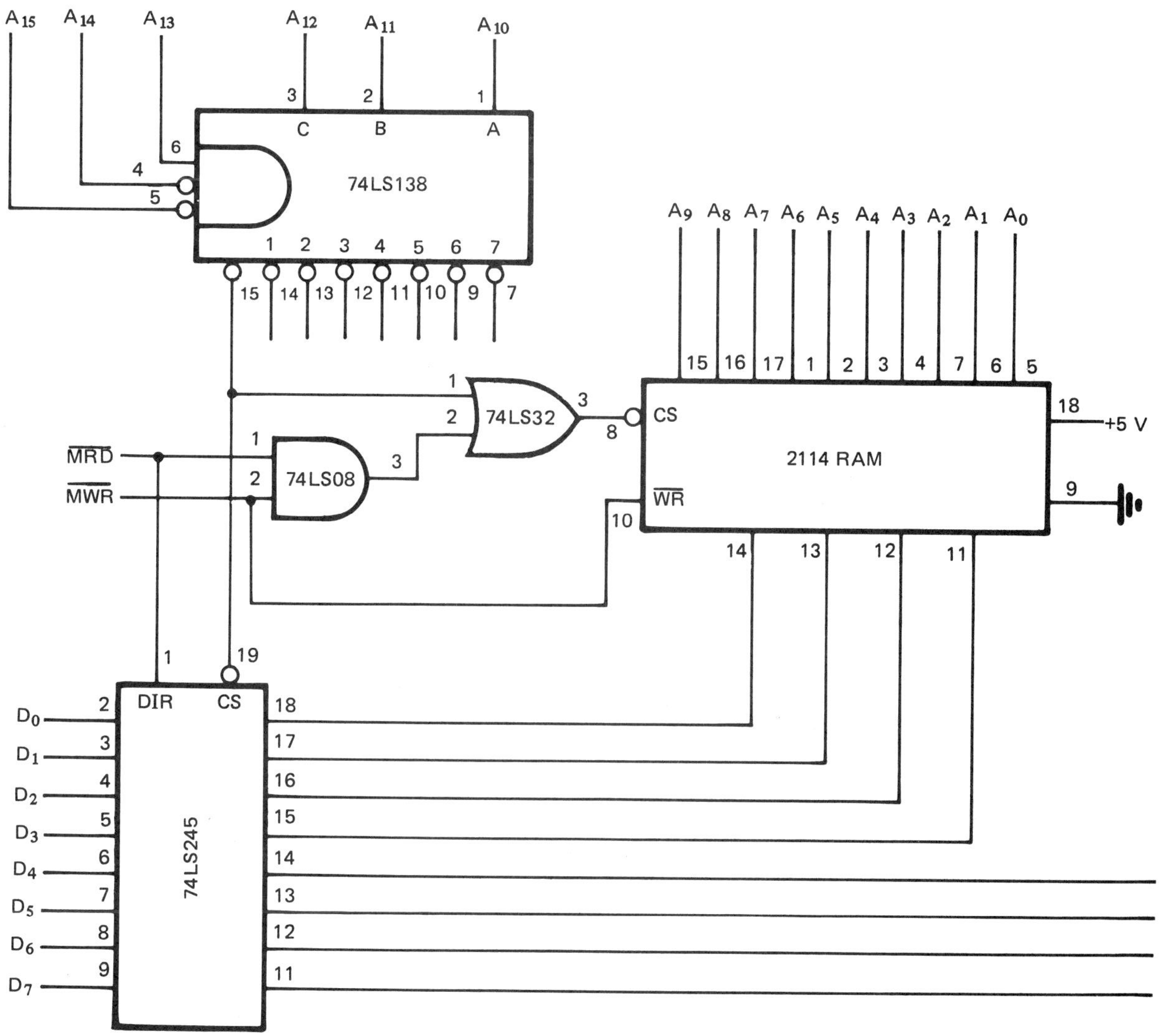
A15
A14
A13
A12
A11
A10
74LS138
C
B
A
A9 A8 A7 A6 A5 A4 A3 A2 A1 A0
74LS32
74LS08
CS
2114 RAM
WR
+5 V
MRD
MWR
DIR
CS
74LS245
D0
D1
D2
D3
D4
D5
D6
D7

Chapter 3

COMPUTER INPUT/OUTPUT

OBJECTIVES

After completing this chapter, you should be able to

- describe the operation of a simple output port that uses D latches.
- describe the operation of the input/output read and write machine cycles of the Z 80 CPU.
- describe the operation of an input port constructed with tri-state gates.
- explain the difference between memory mapped input/output and direct input/output.
- describe the operation of a typical input/output address decoder.
- explain the operation of the Biggy trainer input/output system.

3.1 THE Z 80 INPUT/OUTPUT MACHINE CYCLES

The 8080A, 8085, and Z 80 CPUs all have direct input/output addressing capabilities. That means that they can directly address input/output devices separate from RAM and ROM memories. The 8080A and 8085 can generate an 8-bit address for input/output devices. This means they can directly address up to 2^8 or 256 separate input/output devices or ports. The Z 80 can generate a 16-bit address for an input or output port. Thus the Z 80 can directly address 64K input/output ports.

Outputting a byte to an output port is accomplished by using the input/output write machine cycle described in Chapter 1. Figure 3–1 shows the waveforms for the input/output write machine cycle. Shortly after the rising edge of the T_1 state, the address bus changes to the address of the output port to be written to. Shortly after the falling edge of the T_1 state, the CPU places the byte to be written to the output port on the data bus and shortly after the rising edge of the T_2 state, both $\overline{IORQ}$ and $\overline{WR}$ go low. When the $\overline{IORQ}$ and $\overline{WR}$ both go low, this produces a control signal called $\overline{IOWR}$ as can be seen in Figure 3–1. This control signal will be low only when an output port is being written to and is used to strobe the output port that is being addressed by the address bus. The extra T_W state is added to lengthen the T_2 state because many output ports are slow and need more time to produce a low $\overline{WAIT}$ input. A low $\overline{WAIT}$ input will cause the CPU

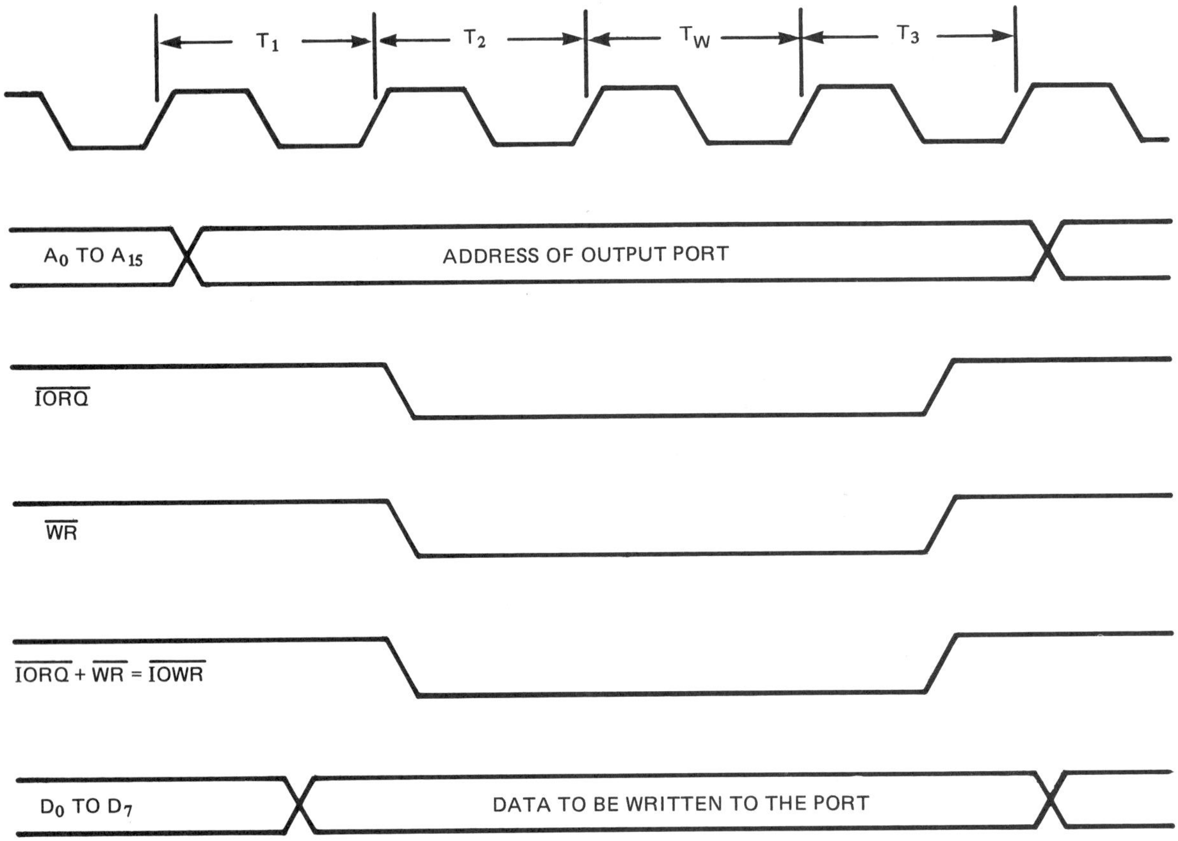

Note: All control signals not shown are inactive.

FIGURE 3–1 Input/output write machine cycle

to generate an indefinite number of T_W states. The $\overline{WAIT}$ is used only by output ports which must have a longer input/output write machine cycle. Notice that the data is stable on the data bus long before and after the $\overline{IOWR}$ is active. This means that the output port could latch the data on the data bus at the rising edge or falling edge of the $\overline{IOWR}$ control signal.

Figure 3–2 shows the input/output read machine cycle. It is very similar to the input/output write machine cycle except that the $\overline{RD}$ goes low instead of the $\overline{WR}$, which produces an $\overline{IORD}$ control signal instead of an $\overline{IOWR}$. The data placed in the data bus shortly after the $\overline{IORD}$ goes low is latched into a CPU internal register on the falling edge of the T_3 state.

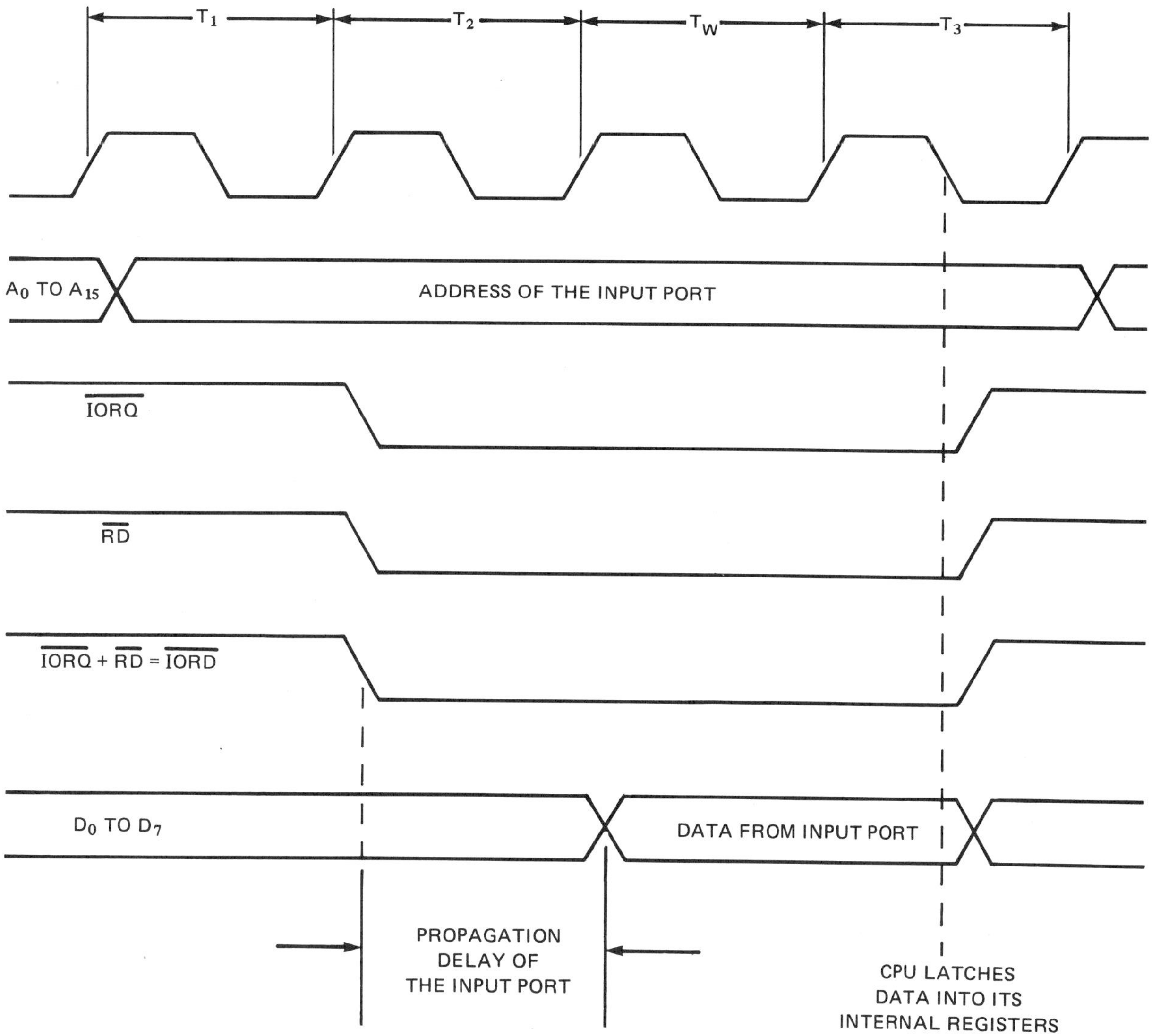

FIGURE 3–2 Input/output read machine cycle

3.2 THE ADDRESS DECODER FOR AN INPUT OR OUTPUT PORT

If the CPU is to read or write to a specific input/output port, then the binary number placed on the address bus during the input/output machine cycle must select one port and only one for a given binary address number. This is done with an address decoder very similar to the memory address decoder discussed in Chapter 2. The main difference is that the I/O decoder will decode the address to a single active output for a unique address input to the decoder.

Because very few computers need more than five or six input/output ports, it is not necessary to build a full decoder. Also, even though the Z 80 can produce a full 16-bit address for its input/output ports, an 8-bit address is all that is usually used. Figure 3–3 shows a partial decoder that will decode an 8-bit address and produce an active low output for address inputs 0 to 7.

The 74138 IC is a 3-bit full decoder with three enables and active low outputs. Two of the enable inputs are active low while the other is active high. A 7406 open-collector inverter IC is used to make a wired NOR gate that will enable or disable the 74138

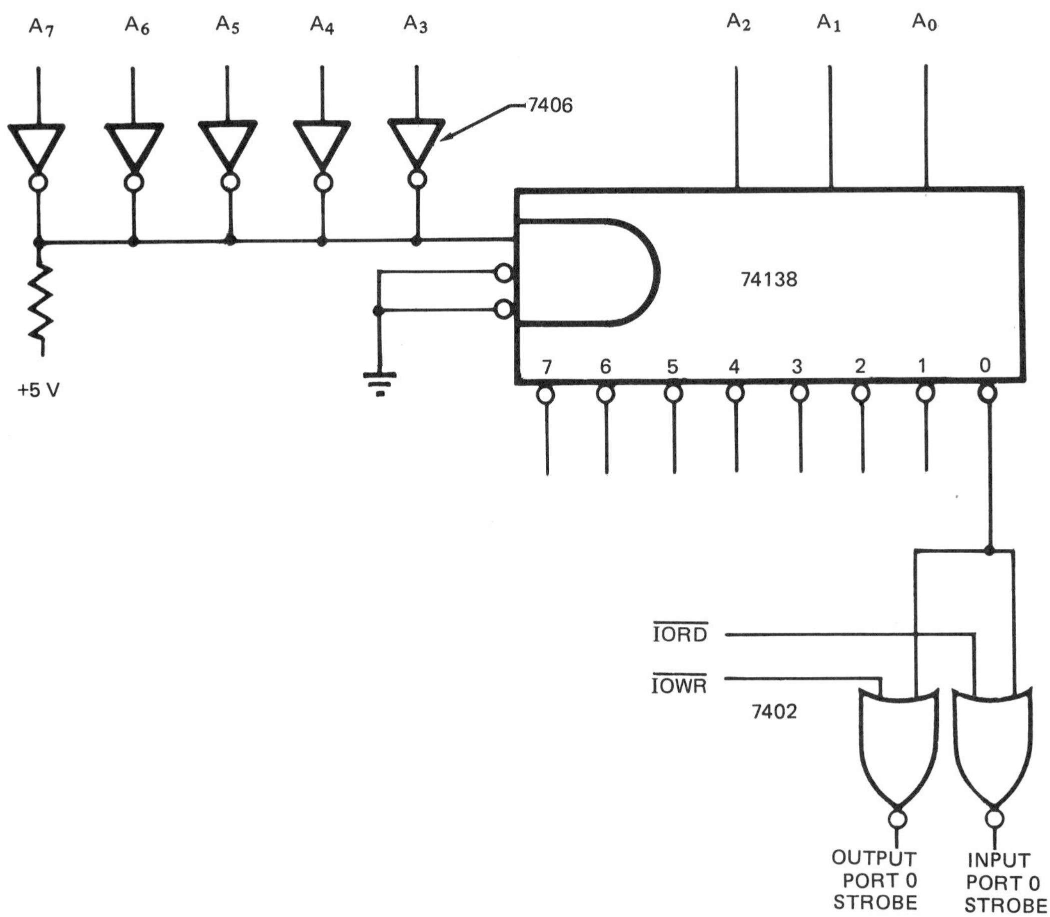

FIGURE 3–3 Partial input/output address decoder

decoder when any one of the address lines above A_2 goes high. Therefore, the decoder will only produce active low outputs for addresses 00000000 binary to 00000111 binary. By feeding the active low output of the 74138 and an I/O control signal such as $\overline{IORD}$ or $\overline{IOWR}$ into a NOR gate, an input/output control strobe can be produced, as shown in Figure 3–3. The active high input or output port strobe will be active only when its address is present on the address bus and when the associated control signal ($\overline{IORD}$ or $\overline{IOWR}$) is active. This type of decoder was used for the input/output decoder in the Biggy trainer. Figure 3–4 shows the complete input/output circuitry for the Biggy trainer. The only difference in the two decoders of Figures 3–3 and 3–4 is that the two active low enables on the 74138 were used to substitute for two of the 7406 inverters, thus allowing those inverters to be used elsewhere.

A full decoder can be made if needed for computers with large I/O needs by cascading decoder chips such as the 74138 or 74154. Figure 3–5 shows a split schematic of a full 8-bit decoder that will produce 256 active low outputs, one output for each possible binary number that could be input to the decoder.

Decoders of this size are not often needed, but decoders that decode in blocks of four or eight are often used because many LSI ICs use the first two address lines (A_0 and A_1) internally to select an internal register when the IC is selected. An example of this is a programmable input/output LSI IC such as the 8255, which we will study later.

Sometimes the control signals for the input or output ports are $\overline{MRD}$ and $\overline{MWR}$. This makes the I/O port a part of the contiguous RAM or ROM memory spaces. This is a necessity on some CPUs such as the 6800 and 6502 because these do not have any control signals just for input/output operations. This is called memory mapped input/output and has the advantage of being able to use all the instructions for memory control on the input/output ports. The disadvantage is that the input ports take up part of the space for memory.

3.3 THE OUTPUT PORT

Basically an output port is a set of D latches that have their D inputs connected to the data bus and their clocks connected to an output strobe from an I/O decoder. Figure 3–6 shows an output port that a computer can use to display a byte of information to its user. It is constructed from two 7475 ICs which contain four transparent D latches each. When the output strobe 0 goes high, the $\overline{Q}$ outputs take on the complemented values of their associated data bus lines and will change as they change; but when the output strobe 0 returns low or inactive, the value of the $\overline{Q}$ will not change any more and will reflect the complemented value of its associated data bus line at the instant the output strobe 0 went inactive or low. This will store or latch the complemented value of the byte that the CPU wished to display in the D latches. $\overline{Q}$ was used rather than Q because a TTL IC can sink more current in a low state than a high state. When $\overline{Q}$ goes low, the LED attached to it through the current-limiting resistor will light, indicating that a 1 was present on the data bus for that particular bit of the byte that was just latched. The word "port" is used to describe this circuit because it is a hole or port through which the CPU can push data to the outside world.

The Biggy trainer uses three output ports similar to the one in Figure 3–6 to display

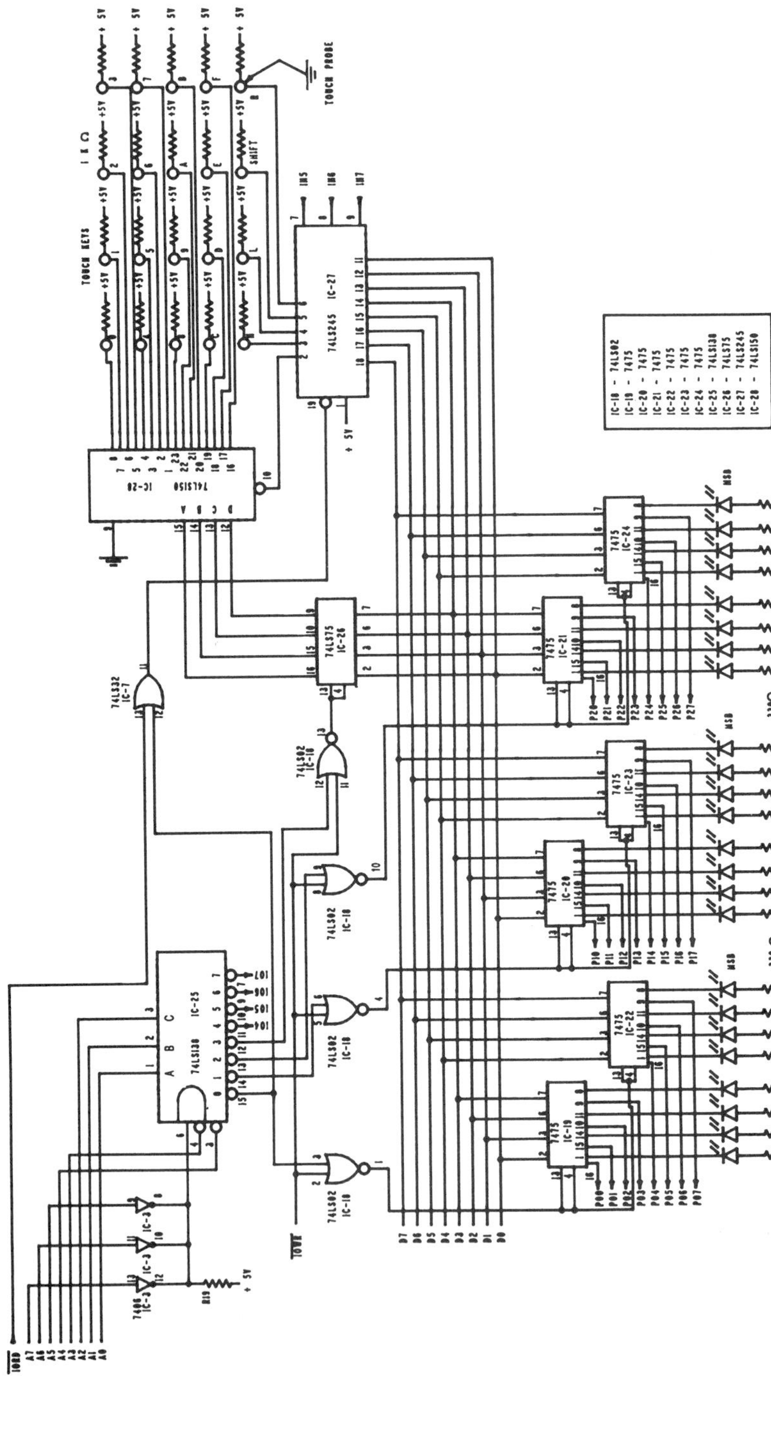

FIGURE 3–4

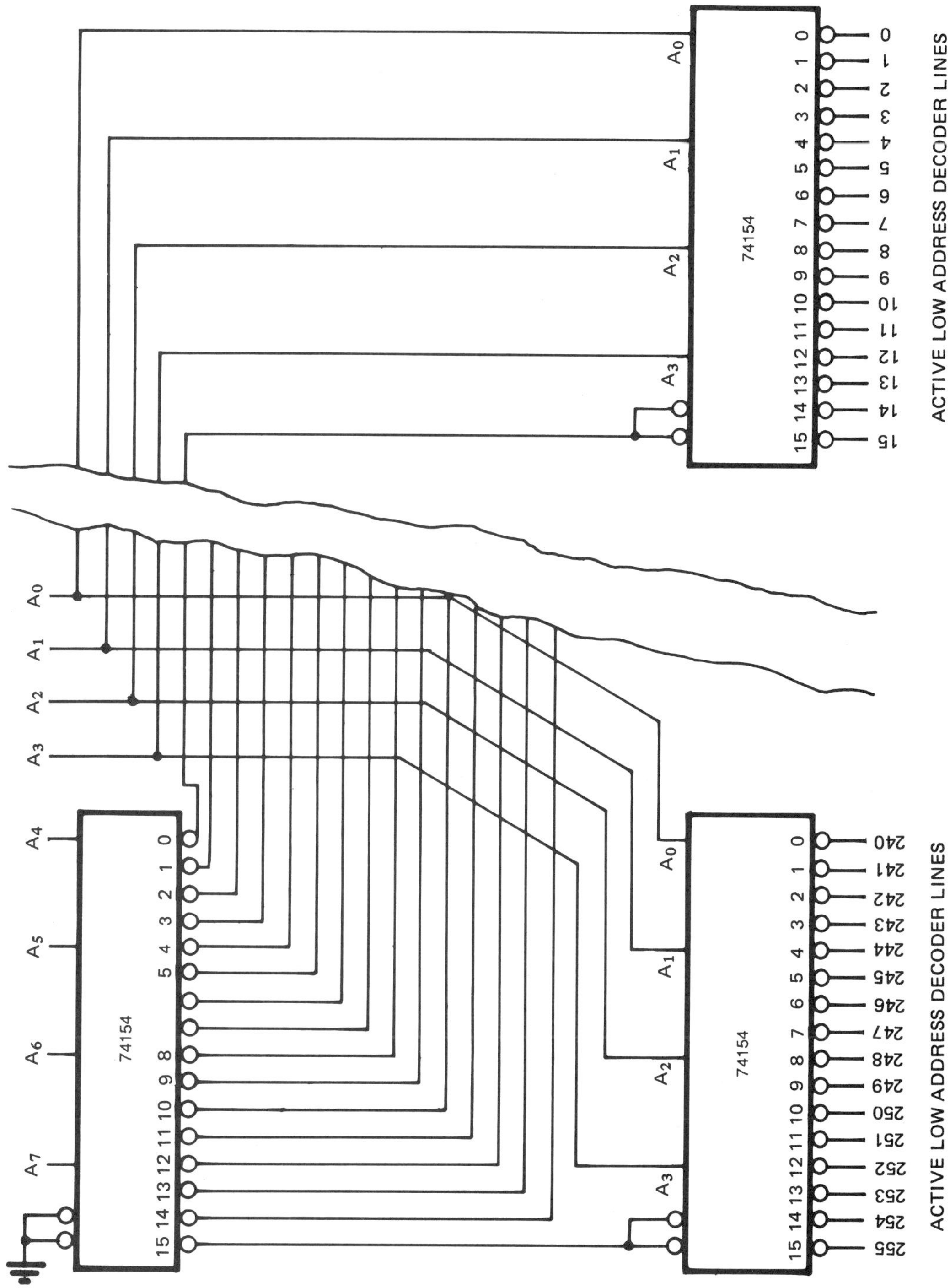

FIGURE 3–5 256 I/O decoder

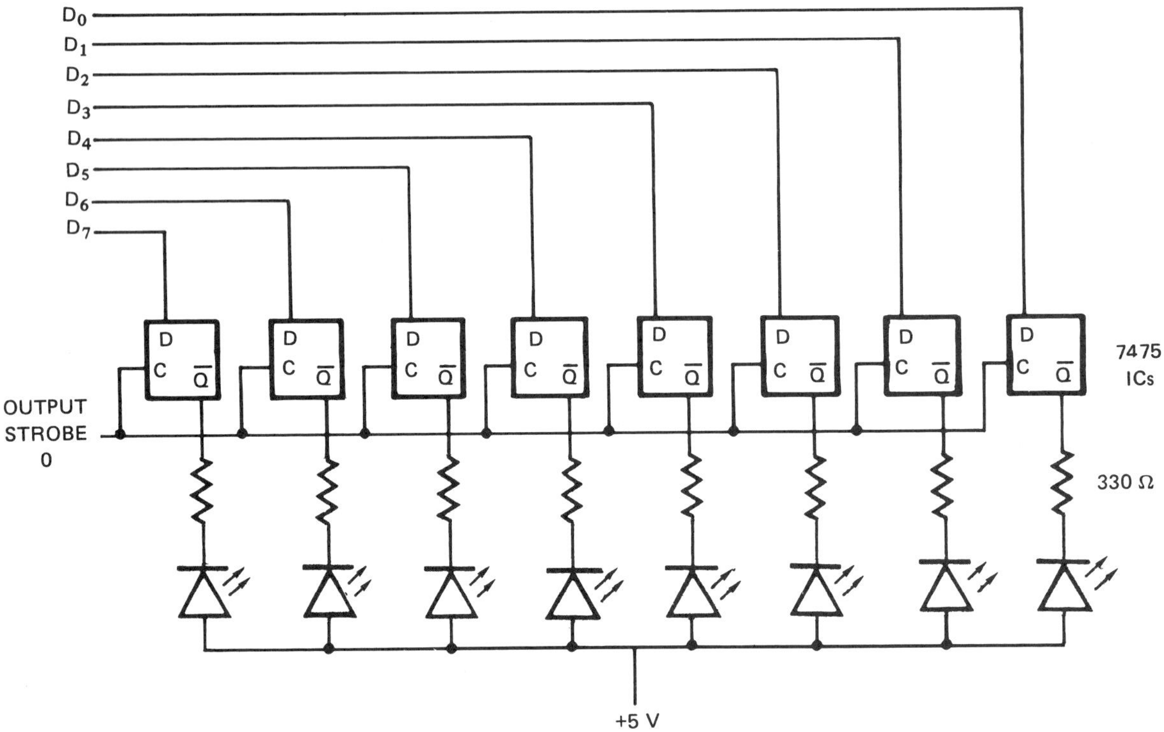

FIGURE 3–6 Output port 0

the current memory address and its contents to the computer user. The Q outputs are also placed on the wireless breadboard or proto board for future use by the student. This is shown in Figure 3–4.

3.4 THE INPUT PORT

An input port uses a set of tri-state gates to gate data onto the data bus when the CPU is ready for it. Figure 3–7 shows a typical input port used by many computers to obtain the necessary information needed to program other LSI ICs for proper operation of the computer.

When the CPU does not desire any information from the input port, the input strobe 0 control line is low, which places the tri-state gates attached to it in their HiZ (high-

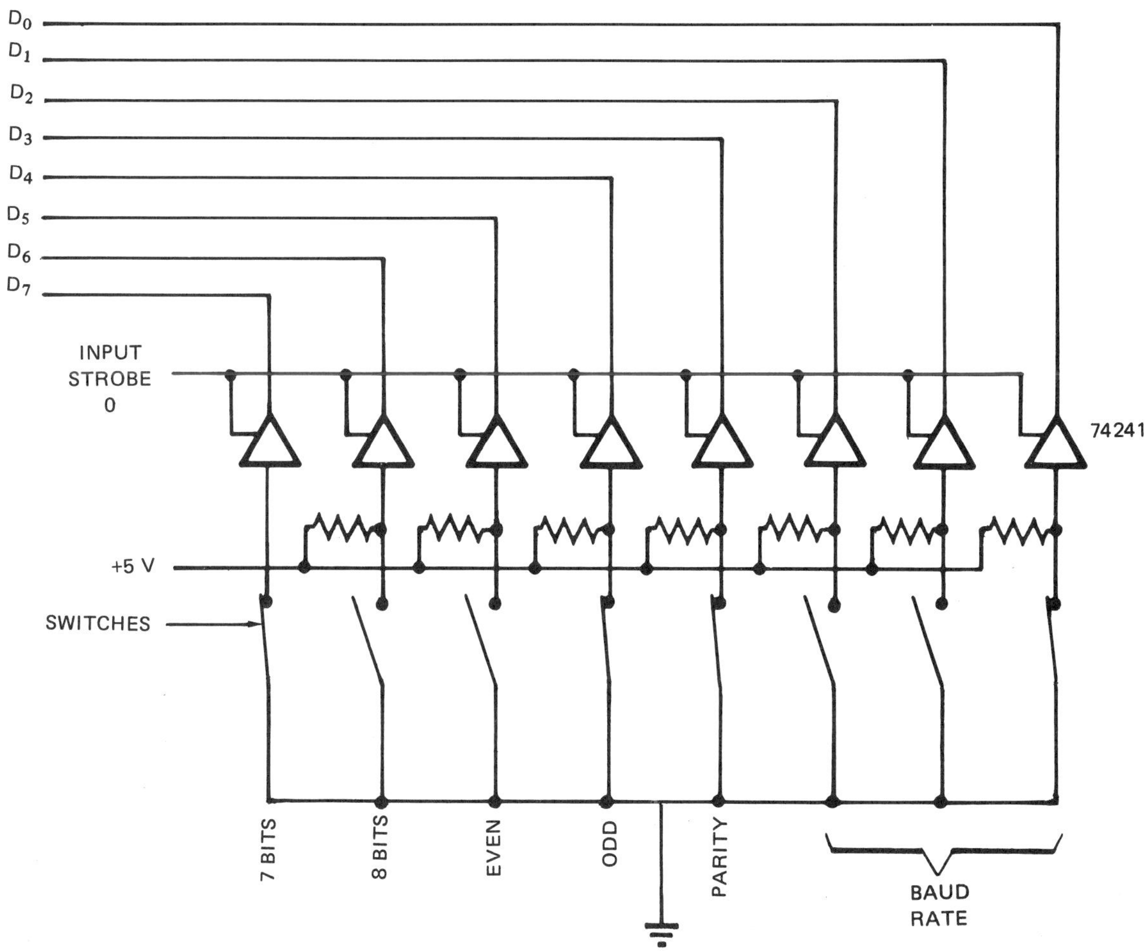

FIGURE 3–7 Configuration input port

impedance) state. This keeps them from loading down the data bus with a 1 or 0 value so that other parts of the computer can use the data bus.

If the CPU wants to input the value shown on the switches into one of its internal registers, then it executes an input/output read machine cycle that would bring the input strobe 0 high or active, causing the logic values of the tri-state gates inputs to be transferred to the data bus where the CPU can latch it into its internal register.

The bits of input port 0 in Figure 3–7 indicate to the computer the configuration it is to use for an RS-232C serial communication system. We will study this type of communication in Chapter 11.

3.5 THE BIGGY TRAINER KEYBOARD INPUT

The keyboard input for the Biggy trainer is shown in Figure 3–4. The input port is made from a 74LS245 bidirectional bus drive that is hard-wired to transfer data from the keyboard to the data bus. This is done by making pin 1 (the direction control) high. Pin 19 is the $\overline{CS}$, which enables or disables the tri-state gates of the 74LS245. Pin 19 is connected to the input port strobe 0. When the computer wishes to read the keyboard, it executes an input/output read machine cycle to input port 0.

The H, L, SHIFT, and RUN keys are tied high through pull-up resistors and are tied to pins 3, 4, 5, and 6, respectively. This corresponds to D_6, D_5, D_4, and D_3 of the data bus when the input port is read. This keyboard is designed to be made using bolts for keys and a grounded probe to touch the bolts with. Thus, when one of the keys, such as the RUN key is touched by the grounded probe, its logic value becomes 0 for as long as the probe is in contact with the bolt head. Therefore, by reading the input port in rapid succession, the computer can determine when the probe has touched one of the four keys just mentioned. The remaining 16 keys are multiplexed into an input line which is connected to D_7 through the tri-state gate of the 74LS245. The key that is selected to be multiplexed onto the input port is selected by the binary number placed on the 74150 multiplexer select inputs.

The 74150 select inputs are connected to the outputs of a 4-bit output port that the computer can control. Therefore, the computer can select the key to be read by first outputting the binary number that will select it through the 74150 to the input port and then reading the input port.

The computer starts by outputting 0 to the select inputs of the 74150 and then reading the input port. It then repeats this for the next key. This continues until a key is detected as being low or active, at which time the computer will take the appropriate action indicated by that key. The program for this scanned keyboard will be studied in Chapter 8.

EXERCISE 3

1. List two microprocessors that do not have direct input/output ports separate from their central memory.
2. Draw the waveforms for the Z 80 input/output read machine cycle.
3. If the Z 80 CPU had a clock frequency of 2 MHz, how long would it take to execute an input/output read machine cycle?
4. Draw the circuit for a decoder that will decode eight blocks, each with four addresses, from an 8-bit address.
5. How many output ports are in the Biggy trainer?
6. How many input ports are in the Biggy trainer?
7. How many extra input ports could be added to the Biggy trainer without adding another 74LS138 decoder?

8. How many extra output ports could be added to the Biggy trainer without adding another 74LS138 decoder?
9. What is the port address of the one 4-bit output port in the Biggy trainer?
10. What is meant by memory mapped input/output?
11. Draw the circuit for an 8-bit input port using a 74LS245 IC and a set of eight switches. (Use the address decoder in Figure 3–3 to supply the port strobe.)
12. What would be the value of the 74LS138 IC outputs if the number F4 Hex was input to the address inputs of Figure 3–3?
13. Which T state and which edge (rising or falling) does the data on the data bus get latched into the Z 80 CPU in an input/output read machine cycle?
14. How many 74154 ICs are needed to complete the full 8-bit address decoder in Figure 3–5?
15. Why was the $\overline{Q}$ output used to drive the LEDs in Figure 3–6?
16. What would be the value of the select inputs of the 74150 in the Biggy trainer if D_7 of input port 0 was high and key A was being touched by the probe?
17. Can an input port and an output port have the same port address?
18. Why does the Z 80 CPU add an extra T_W state to all the input/output machine cycles?
19. What is a partial decoder?
20. What are the three output ports in the Biggy trainer used for?

Lab 3

OBJECTIVES

After completing this lab, you should be able to
- construct an output port for the Biggy trainer.
- construct an input port for the Biggy trainer.
- use the Biggy trainer's operating system to load a program and execute it.

Equipment needed:

A fully operational Biggy trainer
One 74LS245 IC
One 74LS138 IC
One 7406 IC
Nine 1-kΩ, ¼-W resistors
Three 330-Ω, ¼-W resistors
One FND 510 common anode seven-segment LED
One 8-switch dip switch

Procedure

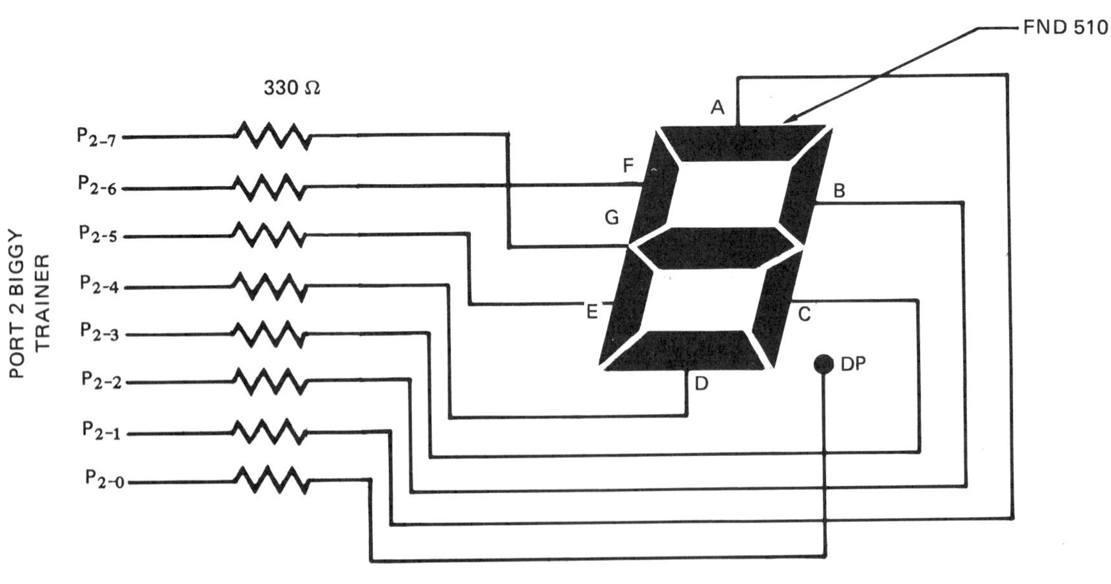

1. Determine the pin configuration of the FND 510 common anode seven-segment display by using the following procedure:
   A. Connect one pin of the FND 510 to +5 V and use a 330-Ω resistor connected to ground as a probe.
   B. Probe all the other pins of the LED to light a segment. If no segment will light, then move the +5 V to another pin. Continue this until you find the common anode of the FND 510.
   C. After the common anode is located, then determine the A, B, C, D, E, F, G and decimal point segments of the display.
2. After determining the pinout of the FND 510 display, wire the circuit shown in the figure and then read Appendix B to familiarize yourself with the operation of the Biggy trainer operating system.
3. Notice that the seven-segment display changes its configuration when a hex key is pressed on the Biggy Trainer. This is because the display is connected to port 2, which the Biggy trainer uses to display the contents of memory and new entries to be entered into memory.

   A 0 on one pin of port 2 will cause a segment to light on the FND 510. Determine the binary number that will produce a 0 on the display and test it. Then complete the following table and use the Biggy trainer's keyboard to verify it.

Character Displayed	$P_{2\text{-}7}$	$P_{2\text{-}6}$	$P_{2\text{-}5}$	$P_{2\text{-}4}$	$P_{2\text{-}3}$	$P_{2\text{-}2}$	$P_{2\text{-}1}$	$P_{2\text{-}0}$
0	1	0	0	0	0	0	0	1
1								
2								
3								
4								
5								
6								
7								
8								
9								
A								
B								
C								
D								
E								
F								

4. Do not disconnect the seven-segment display just built but construct the 8-bit input port shown in the figure beside it.

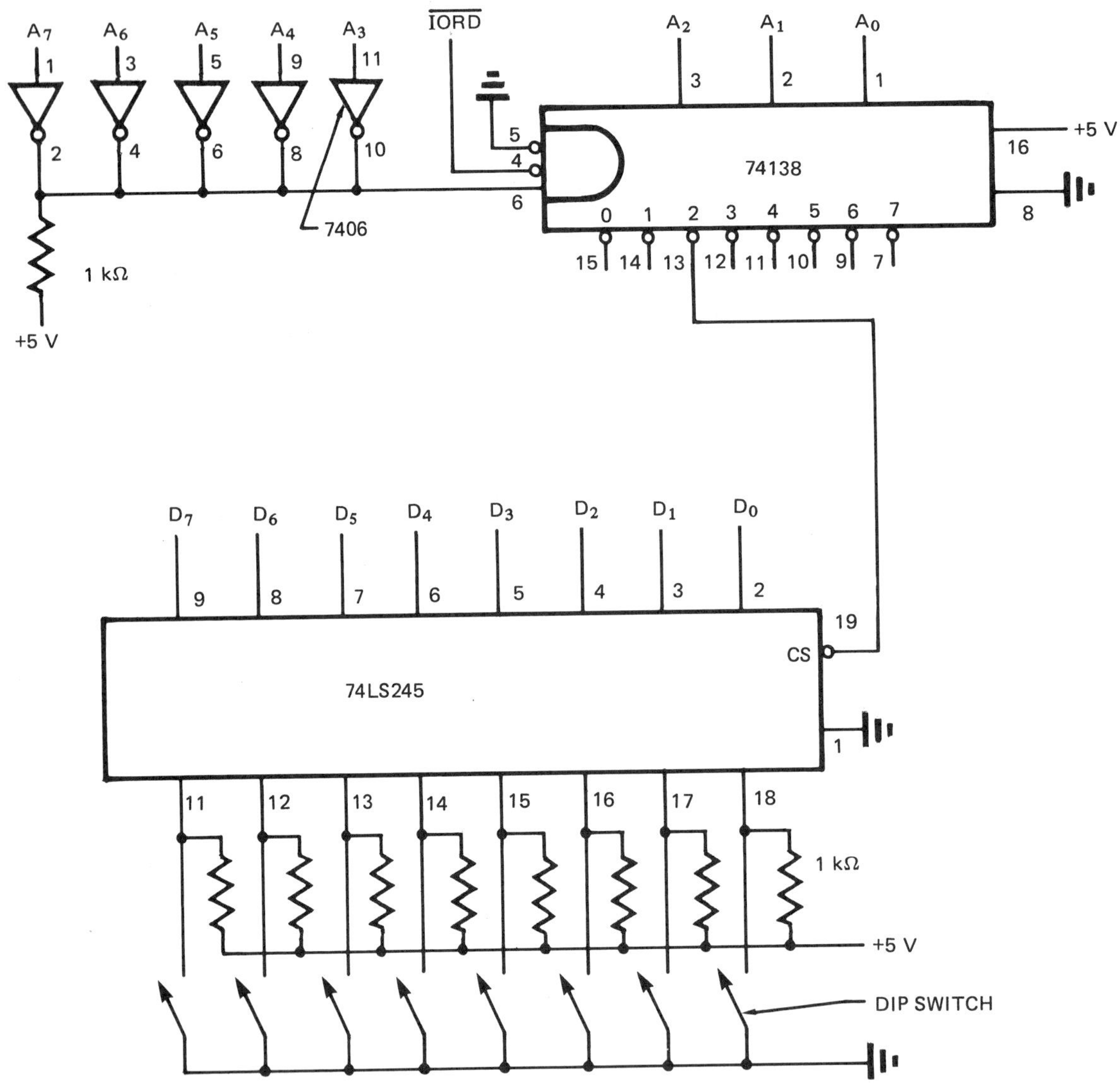

5. After constructing the input port, enter the following program and run it. You do not have to understand how the program works at this time, but you may want to come back to it and analyze it after you have studied Chapters 4–7.

```
0800                    ORG     0800H           ;PROGRAM START
0800 210009     START:  LD      HL,0900H        ;LOCATION OF TABLE
0803 0E02               LD      C,02H           ;ADDRESS OF PORTS
0805 ED68               IN      L,(C)           ;GET LOW BYTE OF ADDRESS
0807 7E                 LD      A,(HL)          ;GET BYTE FOR DISPLAY
0808 ED79               OUT     (C),A           ;PUT BYTE OUT TO DISPLAY
080A C30008             JP      0800H           ;DO AGAIN
                ;****** BYTE TABLE FOR GENERATION OF THE CHAR.*******
                ;
0900                    ORG     0900H           ;START OF TABLE
0900 81         TABLE:  DB      81H             ;BYTE FOR NO. 0
                ;       YOU MUST SUPPLY THE REST OF THIS TABLE
                ;       FROM PART 3 OF THIS LAB.
                ;
                ;
0000                    END
```

6. Place the upper or most significant four bits of the input port at ground or 0 by closing the dip switch associated with them. Now enter a binary number on the lower four bits of the input port. What is the program doing and how?

Chapter 4

THE Z 80 INTERNAL REGISTERS AND LOAD INSTRUCTIONS

OBJECTIVES

After completing this chapter, you should be able to

- describe the general-purpose and special-purpose registers in the Z 80.
- describe the function of the program counter, stack pointer, index registers, accumulator, and flags register.
- use the EXCHANGE instructions in programming.
- use the INPUT and OUTPUT instructions.
- transfer data using 8-bit and 16-bit loads.
- calculate the displacement byte to be used in indexed addressing.
- use block LOAD instructions to transfer a block of data.

4.1 CPU REGISTERS

A register is a set of read/write memory bits that work together as a unit. The Z 80 CPU contains eighteen 8-bit registers and four 16-bit registers. The 8-bit registers are grouped together in pairs and may be used as individual 8-bit registers or together as a 16-bit register. Twelve of the 8-bit registers are general-purpose registers that may be used by the programmer as needed. They are grouped into two sets. The main register set, grouped in pairs, is shown in Figure 4–1.

B, C, D, E, H, and L are general-purpose 8-bit registers that may be used as needed by the programmer. B and C work together as a pair, as do D and E, and H and L. B, D, and H are used as the HIGH byte and C, E, and L are used as the LOW byte. Register A is an 8-bit accumulator register that contains the results of arithmetic and logical operations. The flags register, F, is an 8-bit register. Six of the bits are set or reset by the operations that are carried out by the CPU. The six flags indicate various conditions that result from operations such as whether a carry from the highest-order bit occurred or whether or not the result of an operation was zero. The flags will be discussed in detail as they are used. The A and F registers are sometimes used as a 16-bit register, with A as the HIGH byte and F as the LOW byte.

The CPU contains an alternate register set (Figure 4–2) that parallels the main register

MAIN REG SET		
ACCUMULATOR A	FLAGS F	
B	C	GENERAL-PURPOSE REGISTERS
D	E	GENERAL-PURPOSE REGISTERS
H	L	GENERAL-PURPOSE REGISTERS

FIGURE 4–1 Main register set

set (Figure 4–1). These registers are also 8-bit registers matched in pairs to be used as 16-bit registers. B′ is paired with C′, D′ with E′, H′ with L′, and A′ with F′. The programmer works with the main register set but can swap data between the main register set and alternate register set as needed by using the EXCHANGE instruction that will be studied in this chapter.

The other registers in the CPU are the special-purpose registers shown in Figure 4–3. The program counter PC is a 16-bit register that keeps track of the location in memory that contains the next program instruction to be implemented. The stack pointer SP is a 16-bit register. The stack is a memory section in which data in the general-purpose registers can be stored or stacked until needed, when it is restored from the stack. The stack pointer keeps track or "points" to the location in memory to be used next as part of the stack. The PUSH instruction transfers 16 bits of data from a register pair onto the stack, and the POP instruction removes it from the stack into a register pair. The stack will be discussed in detail as it is used. The index registers IX and IY are used with instructions that incorporate the indexed addressing mode. They will be discussed in detail when used. The interrupt vector register I is an 8-bit register that contains the high byte of an address in memory that contains the next instruction to be used if the main program is interrupted by an external device. The device that interrupts the program provides the low byte of the address of the next instruction. When the interrupt routine is completed, the computer returns to the main program and continues from where it

ALTERNATE REG SET		
ACCUMULATOR A′	FLAGS F′	
B′	C′	GENERAL-PURPOSE REGISTERS
D′	E′	GENERAL-PURPOSE REGISTERS
H′	L′	GENERAL-PURPOSE REGISTERS

FIGURE 4–2 Alternate register set

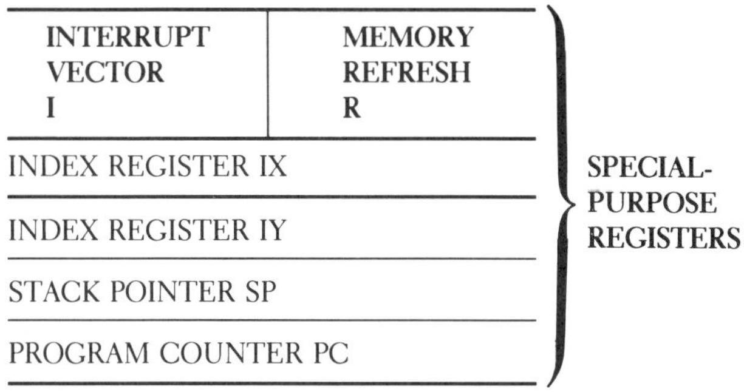

FIGURE 4–3 Special-purpose registers

was. The memory refresh register R is an 8-bit register that is used to refresh dynamic memories. The refresh counter provides seven bits of the address to be refreshed.

When a program is run, instructions are transferred (fetched) from memory into the instruction register inside the CPU. The instruction is decoded, and the proper control signals are generated to implement the instruction. The set of instructions or operation codes (op codes) that are recognized by the CPU is called the *instruction set*. We now begin a study of the Z 80 instruction set. A summary of the instructions discussed in this chapter is contained in Appendix C. Refer to it often as you read the chapter, and it will become a valuable reference sheet.

4.2 EXCHANGE INSTRUCTIONS

The programmer can switch between the main register set and the alternate register set by using an EXCHANGE instruction. The operation code 08H (H indicates a hexadecimal number) instructs the Z 80 to switch the contents of the AF register pair with the contents of the AF′ register pair. The other registers remain unaffected by this operation. This exchange instruction is given the op code 08H and a mnemonic code of EX AF,AF′. Mnemonic means "intended to assist memory," (in this case, the programmer's). It is easier to remember what EX AF,AF′ means than 08H. When a programmer writes a program using mnemonic codes instead of op codes, the programmer is writing in assembly language. The assembly language program must be transferred into op codes either by a program called an *assembler* or by hand. In the mnemonic code EX AF,AF′, EX describes the operation, and AF and AF′ are called *operands*. When 08H is transferred from memory into the instruction decoder of the Z 80 during an M1 cycle and decoded, AF and AF′ are implied as the operands or registers to be used. 08H is the only byte needed to describe the operation. This method of specifying the operands is called *implied addressing*. This instruction uses one machine cycle, the M1 cycle, which consists of four T states. D9H is the op code for an exchange instruction that switches the contents of register pairs BC, DE, and HL with BC′, DE′, HL′, respectively. The mnemonic code assigned is EXX. This instruction uses only the M1 machine cycle with four T states. It also is an example of implied addressing.

EXAMPLE: Suppose

	AF	contains	3712 Hex
	AF′	contains	0040 Hex
	BC	contains	A943 Hex
	BC′	contains	0629 Hex
	DE	contains	1463 Hex
	DE′	contains	0000 Hex
	HL	contains	7325 Hex
and	HL′	contains	0326 Hex

What will be the contents of the registers after the instruction EX AF,AF′ (op code 08H) is run?

SOLUTION: 08 Hex switches the contents of AF and AF′. AF will contain 0040 Hex and AF′ will contain 3712 Hex. The other registers remain the same.

EXAMPLE: If the data in the previous example is kept, what will be the contents of each register after EXX (op code D9H) is run?

SOLUTION: D9 does not affect the AF register pair. The contents of BC, DE, and HL will be switched with BC′, DE′, and HL′, respectively.

BC	will contain	0629 Hex
BC′	will contain	A943 Hex
DE	will contain	0000 Hex
DE′	will contain	1463 Hex
HL	will contain	0326 Hex
HL′	will contain	7325 Hex

EXAMPLE: If the Z 80 is operating at 2 MHz, how long will it take to fetch the instruction EXX and complete the exchanges?

SOLUTION: The time required for one T state is the reciprocal of the frequency.

$$\text{Time of one T state} = 1/(2 \times 10^6) = 0.5\ \mu s$$

This instruction requires four T states:

$$4 \times 0.5\ \mu s = 2\ \mu s$$

There are four other exchange instructions. EBH exchanges the contents of HL with the contents of DE. Its mnemonic code is EX DE,HL. It uses one machine cycle and four T states and is an example of implied addressing. The other three involve the stack pointer and will be discussed later.

4.3 INPUT/OUTPUT INSTRUCTIONS

Microprocessors are often used to control a process or a system. To do so, information from the outside needs to be brought into the computer. That data must be massaged by the computer according to the program being run, and the result or answer must be output to the outside world to adjust the system or process. One way to bring information into the computer is through our input port with an IN instruction. The result can be output with an OUT instruction.

One way to output the contents of the accumulator to an output port is with the instruction OUT (n),A. OUT represents the operation. A represents the source of the data to be used, and (n) is an 8-bit value that names the outport port to be used. (n) can range from 0 to 255. This is a 2-byte instruction, with the second byte naming the output port to be used in binary. The op code is D3H. The instruction is fetched and decoded during the M1 cycle. A memory read machine cycle fetches the second byte of the instruction, which names the port to be used. An output machine cycle transfers the data from A to the output port. The contents of A remains unchanged. These three machine cycles use four, three, and four T states, respectively, for a total of 11 states. During the input/output write machine cycle, the Z 80 places the address of the output port to be used on address lines A_0–A_7. Decoders enable the proper output port, and the contents of the accumulator is latched via the data bus. In this case the second byte of the instruction contained the address. This is called the *immediate mode* of addressing because the address follows immediately after the first byte.

EXAMPLE: What op code would output the contents of the accumulator to output port number 04?

SOLUTION: The first byte must be D3, and the second byte names the port 04.

EXAMPLE: What will happen when the op codes D3FFH are executed?

SOLUTION: The contents of the accumulator will be output to port FF. The data in the accumulator will not change.

By using another OUTPUT instruction, the user can output the contents of A, B, C, D, E, H, or L to a port. The first byte is always EDH. The second byte of the instruction specifies the register to be output, the source. The second byte follows the format 01rrr001, where rrr is the register to be output according to the code in Figure 4–4. This is called *register addressing* because the register contains the operand.

The port to be used must be loaded into the C register before the instruction is executed. The mnemonic for this instruction is OUT (C),r, where r represents the source register to be output. (C) represents the contents of register C, which is the destination output port. This method of addressing is called *register indirect*. The contents of the C register are read to find the address of the port to be used. Out (C),r uses mixed addressing: register addressing for the source, and register indirect addressing for the destination.

EXAMPLE: If the C register contains 35H, the D register contains EFH, and the op code ED51 is performed, what will happen?

SOLUTION: ED51 specifies that the contents of one of the registers are to be output to the output port whose address is contained in register C, in this case 35H. The contents of the register specified by byte two of the instruction will be output to port 35H. Byte two is 51H or 01010001(2). Bits 5, 4, 3 specify register 010, which is the D register. D contains EFH. EFH is output to port 35H.

CODE	REGISTER
000	B
001	C
010	D
011	E
100	H
101	L
110	External Memory
111	Accumulator

FIGURE 4–4 3-bit register code

EXAMPLE: Write the op code to output the contents of the H register to output port number 1.

SOLUTION: The first byte must be EDH. The second byte is of the form 01rrr001. The code for the H register is 100. The second byte becomes 01100001(2) or 61H. The C register must be loaded with the address of the output port to be used, in this case 01H.

The second byte of the instruction for each register is listed in Figure 4–5. Each of these instructions uses three machine cycles and 12 T states. We will study LOAD instructions in this chapter that will enable us to load register C with the address of the desired port.

Two INPUT instructions parallel the OUTPUT instructions discussed so far. The op code DBH instructs the Z 80 to input eight bits of data into the accumulator from the input port called out in the second byte of the instruction. Its mnemonic code is IN A,(n). Like OUT (n),A the instruction requires three machine cycles and 11 T states and uses the immediate mode of addressing. The op code EDH is the first byte of an INPUT instruction, just as it was for an OUTPUT instruction. The second byte specifies which operation is to be performed. The second byte of the INPUT instruction follows the format 01rrr000, whereas the second byte of OUT (C),r follows the format 01rrr001. Only the least significant bit of the second byte differs. ED followed by an odd number specifies OUT (C),r; ED followed by an even number specifies IN r,(C), the mnemonic for this INPUT command. Once again the port is specified by the contents of register C, which is register indirect addressing, and the register to be used is specified by bits 5, 4, 3 of byte 2. The 3-bit code listed in Figure 4–4 is used. IN r,(C) consumes three machine cycles and 12 T states.

EXAMPLE: What op code will input a byte from input port 36H into the accumulator?

SOLUTION: DB36.

A	B	C	D	E	H	L
79	41	49	51	59	61	69

FIGURE 4–5 Second byte of OUT (C),r instruction

EXAMPLE: What does the 2-byte op code ED50 mean? The C register contains E9H.

SOLUTION: ED signifies either the IN r,(C) or the OUT (C),r instruction. The second byte is 50H or 01010000. Bits 4, 5, and 6 specify register D. Since bit 0 equals 0, this is an IN r,(C) instruction. The byte of data at input port E9 will be transferred into the D register.

4.4 REGISTER TO REGISTER LOADS

An op code of the format 01rrrr'r'r' loads eight bits of data from register r', specified by bits 2, 1, 0, to register r, specified by bits 5, 4, 3. The mnemonic code is LD r,r'. The 3-bit register code listed in Figure 4–4 is used to specify the register. This is another example of register addressing. This instruction uses only the M1 machine cycle with four T states.

EXAMPLE: What does the op code 54H instruct the Z 80 to do?

SOLUTION:

54H = 01010100

This is the proper format for an LD r,r' instruction. The source register is register 100, and the destination register is register 010. Figure 4–4 shows that 100 represents register H and 010 represents register D. 54 loads the contents of H into D or LD D,H. The contents of H remain unchanged.

EXAMPLE: What op code would load register L into register B?

SOLUTION: The op code would be of the format 01rrrr'r'r', where r' is the source and r is the destination. L is represented by 101 and B by 000. The op code would be 01000101(2) or 45H.

The register to register loads are summarized in Figure 4–6. All of these loads are represented symbolically by r←r'. Data can be loaded into registers B, C, D, E, H, L, A by using the LOAD IMMEDIATE instruction. The first byte of this 2-byte instruction follows the format 00rrr110, where bits 5, 4, 3 specify the register to be loaded, following

		LD r,r' SOURCE REGISTER						
		B	C	D	E	H	L	A
DESTINATION REGISTER	B	40	41	42	43	44	45	47
	C	48	49	4A	4B	4C	4D	4F
	D	50	51	52	53	54	55	57
	E	58	59	5A	5B	5C	5D	5F
	H	60	61	62	63	64	65	67
	L	68	69	6A	6B	6C	6D	6F
	A	78	79	7A	7B	7C	7D	7F

FIGURE 4–6 8-bit register to register loads, LD r,r'

REGISTER	B	C	D	E	H	L	A
OP CODE	06 n	0E n	16 n	1E n	26 n	2E n	3E n

FIGURE 4–7 LD r,n LOAD IMMEDIATE op codes

the code in Figure 4–4. The second byte of the instruction is the eight bits of data to be loaded. The mnemonic code for this instruction is LD r,n, where n represents one byte of data. The symbolic representation is r←n. This instruction uses two machine cycles: an M1 cycle to fetch, and a memory read machine cycle to read the data contained in the second byte of the instruction. A total of seven T states is required. The destination is addressed by register addressing, and the source, the data, by immediate addressing.

EXAMPLE: What does the op code 160FH do?

SOLUTION: 16H = 00010110(2). This is the proper format for a LOAD IMMEDIATE instruction with register 010 or D specified. The data 0F will be loaded into the D register.

The 8-bit LOAD IMMEDIATE instructions are summarized in Figure 4–7.

EXAMPLE: Write a program that will load F0 into register H then output the contents of H to output port 0 to verify its contents.

SOLUTION: In order to use the OUT (C),r command the C register must contain the address of the output port, 00. First, load C using the LD r,n instruction, whose op code is 0E (Figure 4–7). The second byte contains the data 00. Next, load H with the data F0 by using LD r,n. The op code is 26, as shown in Figure 4–7, followed by the data F0. Finally, to output H to port 00, use the OUT (C),r instruction. The op code is ED61 (Figure 4–5). The program will be loaded into RAM at address 0800. The mnemonic listing called the source code, will be

```
 LD   C,00H
 LD   H,F0H
OUT   (C),H
HLT
```

The op-codes must now be obtained. If done by hand, the process is called *hand assembling*, which can be quite tedious for a long program. The alternative is to enter the mnemonic codes into a program called an assembler, which lists the op codes for you. Most of the programs in this book were assembled on a Kaypro computer using a Z 80 assembler from Avocet systems. The mnemonic codes are entered in a column. The programmer can enter remarks for his or her own use following a ;. They do not affect the program. An origin command is used first to tell the editor assembler where the program is to be located in memory. ORG 0800H means place the first op code at address 0800H. When entered into the assembler, this program would appear as

```
ORG    800H
LD     C,00H    ;LOAD C for OUT
LD     H,F0H    ;Initialize H
OUT    (C),H    ;OUT H
HLT             ;HALT
END
```

The END command is for the assembler and not the Z 80.

The assembled program would look like this:

```
0800                ORG    0800H
0800 0E00           LD     C,00H        ;Load C for OUT
0802 26F0           LD     H,0F0H       ;Initialize H
0804 ED61           OUT    (C),H        ;OUTPUT H
0806 76             HALT
0000                END
```

The list of op codes created in the second column is called the object code. After execution of 76H, HALT, the Z 80 executes NO OPERATION, NOP, commands until an interrupt or reset is received. It prevents the Z 80 from continuing after the OUT instruction and using whatever happens to be next as an instruction. Run the program to verify the results.

EXAMPLE: Output the contents of register B′ to output port 2.

SOLUTION: B′ cannot be output directly. The exchange EXX instruction must be used. The desired data will then be in register B. Register C needs to be loaded with 02, the intended port. Then OUT (C),r can be used. Finally, EXX will be executed a second time to restore the data to their original registers.

```
0800           ORG    0800H
0800 D9        EXX
0801 0E02      LD     C,02H
0803 ED41      OUT    (C),B
0805 D9        EXX
0806 76        HALT
0000           END
```

The accumulator can be loaded with data from memory by using the instruction LD A,(nn). This is a 3-byte instruction. nn represents the 16-bit address in memory that will be specified in the second and third bytes of the command. The LOW byte is first, followed by the HIGH. The parentheses indicate that (nn) is the address of a memory location that contains the data to be used; that is, (nn) “points to” memory. (nn) is not the data to be used. The first byte is always 3A. Specifying a LOW byte and a HIGH byte as a pointer is called *extended addressing*. An M1 cycle fetches the instruction. Two memory read cycles must be performed to obtain the LOW and HIGH bytes of the address to be used. A fourth machine cycle transfers the data from memory to the accumulator. This instruction requires four machine cycles and 13 T states.

EXAMPLE: What op code will load the contents of memory location 0BFF into the accumulator?

SOLUTION: 3A must be the first byte followed by LOW byte, HIGH byte: 3AFF0B.

In a similar command, the contents of A can be loaded into memory. Extended addressing is again used, this time to specify the destination. The mnemonic code is LD (nn),A. The first byte is always 32H, followed by the LOW byte and then the HIGH byte of the address.

EXAMPLE: What op code would load the contents of the accumulator into 0AA0?

SOLUTION: The first byte would be 32 followed by LOW byte and HIGH byte of the address to be used: 32A00A.

4.5 INDEXED ADDRESSING

So far we have used implied, immediate, register, register indirect, and extended addressing. The indexed mode of addressing involves one of the two special-purpose, 16-bit index registers IX or IY. The op code specifies which will be used. The index register is used as a starting point. The op code also specifies a displacement, d, which is added to the contents of the index register to form a pointer to memory. The address formed points to the data to be used or is the address at which data will be stored. If the IX register is to be used, the first byte of the op code is DDH; for IY it is FDH.

Registers B, C, D, E, H, L, and A can be loaded by using indexed addressing. The first byte specifies IX or IY. The second specifies the register to be loaded by using the register addressing and the 3-bit code in Figure 4–4. The second byte follows the format 01rrr110. The third byte is the displacement d, the offset from the address in the index register. The mnemonic code is LD r,(IX+d) or LD r,(IY+d).

EXAMPLE: Suppose IX contains 0900. What would the op code DD4E08 do?

SOLUTION: DD specifies that IX is to be used. 4EH is 01001110. Register 001, C, is specified. d = 08. 08 is added to 0900. The address of the data is 0908. The contents of that location will be moved into the C register.

Indexed addressing can be used to load data from a register to a location in memory. The mnemonic code is LD (IX+d),r or LD (IY+d),r. The first byte is again DDH for IX and FDH for IY. The second byte follows the format 01 110 rrr. The third byte is again d.

EXAMPLE: What will the op code FD72FE do? Suppose that IY contains 0A09.

SOLUTION: FD specifies the IY index register. 72H = 01110010. The source register is 010 or D. The destination is 110 or external memory. The displacement d is FE, a signed 2's complement number. FEH = 11111110. The true magnitude of this number is found by taking the 2's complement: 2's complement = 00000010 or 2. FE means −2. This byte must be added to a 16-bit address contained in the IY index register. When −2 is written as a 16-bit number, it becomes FFFEH.

0A09	=	0000	1010	0000	1001
FFFE	=	1111	1111	1111	1110
1		0000	1010	0000	0111

The overflow is ignored. The resulting address is 0A07. The contents of the D register will be stored at 0A07. The address used is two bytes lower than that in the index register.

EXAMPLE: What will the op code DD72EE do? Suppose that IX contains 0900.

SOLUTION: DD72 specifies that the contents of the D register be stored at the address pointed to by the sum of IX and d.

0900H	=	0000	1001	0000	0000
FFEEH	=	1111	1111	1110	1110
1		0000	1000	1110	1110

The resulting address in 08EEH. The contents of D will be stored at location 08EEH. Note that the HIGH byte decremented from 09 to 08 as required.

EXAMPLE: If the IX register contains 0920H, what displacement byte should be used to point to 08FE?

SOLUTION:

0920H	=	0000	1001	0010	0000
-08FEH	=	0000	1000	1111	1110

This subtraction can be done by adding the 2's complement of 08FE.

0920H	=	0000	1001	0010	0000
2's complement of 08FE	=	1111	0111	0000	0010
1		0000	0000	0010	0010

The result is 22H. $-22H$ must be added to the contents of IY to obtain the address to be used. To form the displacement byte, write -22 as an 8-bit signed 2's complement number.

22H	=	0010	0010		
signed 2's complement	=	1101	1110	=	DEH

Check: 0920	=	0000	1001	0010	0000
+ FFDE	=	1111	1111	1101	1110
		0000	1000	1111	1110
		08FEH			

The 8-bit LOAD instructions that use indexed addressing are summarized in Figure 4–8, along with all 8-bit loads. The shaded blocks contain instructions that can be run on the 8080, 8085, or Z 80. The nonshaded blocks apply only to the Z 80.

SOURCE

DESTINATION		IMPLIED		REGISTER							REG INDIRECT			INDEXED		EXT. ADDR.	IMME.
		I	R	A	B	C	D	E	H	L	(HL)	(BC)	(DE)	(IX + d)	(IY + d)	(nn)	n
REGISTER	A	ED 57	ED 5F	7F	78	79	7A	7B	7C	7D	7E	0A	1A	DD 7E d	FD 7E d	3A n n	3E n
	B			47	40	41	42	43	44	45	46			DD 46 d	FD 46 d		06 n
	C			4F	48	49	4A	4B	4C	4D	4E			DD 4E d	FD 4E d		0E n
	D			57	50	51	52	53	54	55	56			DD 56 d	FD 56 d		16 n
	E			5F	58	59	5A	5B	5C	5D	5E			DD 5E d	FD 5E d		1E n
	H			67	60	61	62	63	64	65	66			DD 66 d	FD 66 d		26 n
	L			6F	68	69	6A	6B	6C	6D	6E			DD 6E d	FD 6E d		2E n
REG INDIRECT	(HL)			77	70	71	72	73	74	75							36 n
	(BC)			02													
	(DE)			12													
INDEXED	(IX+d)			DD 77 d	DD 70 d	DD 71 d	DD 72 d	DD 73 d	DD 74 d	DD 75 d							DD 36 d n
	(IY+d)			FD 77 d	FD 70 d	FD 71 d	FD 72 d	FD 73 d	FD 74 d	FD 75 d							FD 36 d n
EXT. ADDR	(nn)			32 n n													
IMPLIED	I			ED 47													
	R			ED 4F													

FIGURE 4–8 8-bit loads

The sources are listed across the top with the mode of addressing used indicated. The destination registers are listed down the side with mode of addressing indicated.

EXAMPLE: What does FD6E09 do?

SOLUTION: FD6E falls in the (IY + d) indexed mode column for the source of data and in the L row, register addressing, for the destination. FD6E09 loads the contents of memory location IY+09 into register L. The contents of IY+09 do not change.

EXAMPLE: What does FD70F7 do?

SOLUTION: The contents of the B register are loaded into memory address IY+F7.

4.6 16-BIT LOAD INSTRUCTIONS

Figure 4–9 summarizes the 16-bit LOAD instructions. Using the immediate mode of addressing allows 16 bits of data to be loaded into the BC, DE, or HL pair, the SP, IX, or IY. The data in byte 2 is loaded into the LOW byte of the register, and the data in byte 3 is loaded into the HIGH byte. For example, 013355 would load 33 into the C register and 55 into the B register. FD210009 would load 0900 into the IY register.

Using extended addressing allows the 16-bit registers BC, DE, HL, SP, IX, IY to be loaded from a specified location in memory, or their contents can be stored in a specified location in memory. Remember that the LOW byte is listed first.

DESTINATION \ SOURCE		REGISTER AF	REGISTER BC	REGISTER DE	REGISTER HL	REGISTER SP	REGISTER IX	REGISTER IY	IMM. EXT. nn	EXT. ADDR. (nn)	REG. INDIR. (SP)
REGISTER	AF										F1
REGISTER	BC								01 n n	ED 4B n n	C1
REGISTER	DE								11 n n	ED 5B n n	D1
REGISTER	HL								21 n n	2A n n	E1
REGISTER	SP				F9		DD F9	FD F9	31 n n	ED 7B n n	
REGISTER	IX								DD 21 n n	DD 2A n n	DD E1
REGISTER	IY								FD 21 n n	FD 2A n n	FD E1
EXT. ADDR.	(nn)		ED 43 n n	ED 53 n n	22 n n	ED 73 n n	DD 22 n n	FD 22 n n			
REG. IND. (PUSH INSTRUCTIONS →)	(SP)	F5	C5	D5	E5		DD E5	FD E5			

POP INSTRUCTIONS ↑

NOTE: The Push & Pop Instructions adjust the SP after every execution

FIGURE 4–9 16-bit loads

EXAMPLE: What will the op code ED530009 do?

SOLUTION: ED53 specifies that the contents of register E be stored at address 0900 and the contents of D be stored at 0901.

EXAMPLE: What will the op code 2ADD08 do?

SOLUTION: 2A specifies that the contents of the address specified in bytes 2 and 3 be loaded into the L register. The following byte of data will be loaded into the H register.

EXAMPLE: Suppose the registers and memory contain the following data:

Address	Data	
0900	A9	BC contains 3456
0901	B2	DE contains 789A
0902	57	HL contains 0904
0903	49	IX contains 0900
0904	62	IY contains 0903
0905	74	
0906	89	

```
0800                          ORG     0800H
0800 ED430509                 LD      (0905H),BC
0804 ED5B0209                 LD      DE,(0902H)
0808 DD6603                   LD      H,(IX+03H)
080B FD6E00                   LD      L,(IY+00H)
080E 76                       HALT
0000                          END
```

What will be contained in each of the registers after the program has run?

SOLUTION: ED43 specifies that the contents of the BC register pair be loaded into memory pointed to by bytes 4 and 3 and the following address. The contents of C are loaded into 0905 and the contents of B are loaded into 0906. ED5B specifies that the contents of memory pointed to by bytes 4 and 3 be loaded into the E register and that the following byte be loaded into the D register. The contents of 0902 are loaded into E, and the contents of 0903 are loaded into D.

DE contains 4957

DD6603 specifies that the H register be loaded from (IX+03).

H contains 49

FD6E00 specifies that L be loaded from the contents of IY+00.

L contains 49.

4.7 BLOCK TRANSFER INSTRUCTIONS

A program in memory or a block of data can be loaded from one section of memory into another by using one of the block transfer instructions. In the block transfer instructions HL points to the source location, DE points to the destination location, and BC is a byte counter.

The op code EDB0 specifies that the contents of memory pointed to by HL be loaded into memory pointed to by DE. The HL pair is incremented, the DE register pair is incremented, and the BC pair is decremented. This is repeated until BC = 0. The mnemonic code for this instruction is LDIR (load, increment, repeat).

EDA0 is similar, but only one byte is transferred each time the instruction is used. The mnemomic is LDI (load, increment).

EDA8 has the mnemonic code LDD (load, decrement). HL, DE, and BC are decremented each time a byte is transferred. It does not repeat the process automatically.

EDB8 has the mnemonic LDDR (load, decrement, repeat). After each transfer HL, DE, and BC are decremented, and the process repeats until BC = 0.

EXAMPLE: Suppose HL contains 09D0, DE contains 0800, and BC contains 0F. What will happen if the op code EDBϕ is run?

SOLUTION: EDBϕ is the LOAD, INCREMENT, REPEAT instruction. Fifteen bytes of data will be transferred from 09D0, 09D1, 09D2, . . ., 09DE to 0800, 0801, 0802, . . ., 080E.

INPUT GROUP

INPUT DESTINATION			SOURCE PORT ADDRESS: IMMED. (n)	SOURCE PORT ADDRESS: REG. INDIR. (C)	
INPUT 'IN'	REG ADDRESSING	A	DB n	ED 78	
		B		ED 40	
		C		ED 48	
		D		ED 50	
		E		ED 58	
		H		ED 60	
		L		ED 68	
'INI' – INPUT & Inc HL, Dec B	REG, INDIR	(HL)		ED A2	BLOCK INPUT COMMANDS
'INIR' – INP, Inc HL, Dec B, REPEAT IF B≠0	REG, INDIR	(HL)		ED B2	BLOCK INPUT COMMANDS
'IND' – INPUT & Dec HL, Dec B	REG, INDIR	(HL)		ED AA	BLOCK INPUT COMMANDS
'INDR' – INPUT, Dec HL, Dec B, REPEAT IF B≠0	REG, INDIR	(HL)		ED BA	BLOCK INPUT COMMANDS

OUTPUT GROUP

	PORT DESTINATION ADDRESS		SOURCE: REGISTER A	B	C	D	E	H	L	REG. IND. (HL)	
'OUT'	IMMED.	(n)	DB n								
'OUT'	REG. IND.	(C)	ED 79	ED 41	ED 49	ED 51	ED 59	ED 61	ED 69		
'OUTI' – OUTPUT Inc HL, Dec b	REG. IND.	(C)								ED A3	BLOCK OUTPUT COMMANDS
'OTIR' – OUTPUT, Inc HL, Dec B, REPEAT IF B≠0	REG. IND.	(C)								ED B3	BLOCK OUTPUT COMMANDS
'OUTD' – OUTPUT Dec HL & B	REG. IND.	(C)								ED AB	BLOCK OUTPUT COMMANDS
'OTDR' – OUTPUT, Dec HL & B, REPEAT IF B≠0	REG. IND.	(C)								ED BB	BLOCK OUTPUT COMMANDS

FIGURE 4–10 Input/output op codes

A block of data can be input through an input port into memory by using a similar process. Register pair HL is loaded with the address of the first memory location to be used (destination of first byte). Register C is loaded with the address of the port to be used. Register B is used as a byte counter. Since B is 8 bits wide, up to 256 bytes can be input with each block input. INIR (input, increment, repeat) inputs a byte of data, increments HL, decrements B, and repeats the process until B is 00H. The op code is EDB2H. An external circuit must be able to supply the bytes of data as needed. INI (input, increment) is similar, except that one byte is entered each time the instruction is implemented. It does not repeat automatically. B is decremented each time. INDR (input, decrement, repeat) is the same as INIR, except that the HL register is decremented each time a byte is input. Its op code is EDBA. IND (input, decrement) inputs one byte, decrements HL, and decrements the counter B. Its op code is EDAAH.

Four block output instructions parallel these four input instructions. Register pair HL is used to point to the source of data, register C contains the address of the output port to be used, and B is used as a byte counter. These input and output op codes are summarized in Figure 4–10.

EXERCISE 4

1. What is the function of the program counter (PC)?
2. What is the function of the stack pointer (SP)?
3. What is the function of the index registers IX and IY?
4. Name the 8-bit general-purpose registers.
5. Name the 16-bit general-purpose register pairs.
6. Which exchange instruction switches the contents of AF with AF′?
7. Which exchange instruction switches the contents of BC, DE, HL with BC′, DE′, and HL′, respectively?
8. How many input ports can the Z 80 address? How many output ports?
9. Can the contents of the L register be output directly to port 2? How?
10. Can data be input directly into register B? How?
11. What are the functions of the instructions INIR and INDR?
12. What are the functions of the instructions OTIR and OTDR?
13. Discuss the difference between a register load and a load immediate instruction.
14. Which registers can be loaded directly from memory?
15. What will the op code DD4EA0 do?
16. What will the op code DD4EF0 do?
17. If IX contains 0956H, what displacement byte should be used to point to 0978H? To 0912H?
18. If IY contains 09A0H, what displacement byte should be used to point to 09BBH? To 09A7?

Lab 4

OBJECTIVES

After completing this lab, you should be able to

- write and implement programs using the exchange instructions.
- write and implement programs using 8-bit loads and output instructions.
- write and implement programs using block load instructions.

Procedure

1. Write a program that will
   a. Load the data shown in the first example in Section 4.2 into the registers listed in that example.
   b. Run the first example in Section 4.2.
   c. Output the contents of registers A,B, and D to output ports 0,1, and 2, respectively.
   d. Halt.
2. Modify the program to run the second example in Section 4.2.
3. Write and run a program that will load F0AA into BC, output B to port 0, and C to port 1.
4. Write and run a program that will transfer 20 bytes of data from 0950, 0951, and so on, to 0900,0901, and so on.

Chapter 5

THE ARITHMETIC AND LOGIC INSTRUCTIONS

OBJECTIVES

After completing this chapter, you should be able to

- name the flags and describe how they are set or reset.
- predict the contents of the flags register after a program has run.
- use 8-bit arithmetic and logic instructions.
- describe the difference between ADD and ADC instructions.
- describe the difference between SUB and SBC instructions.
- describe the difference between SUB and CP instructions.
- mask data by using logic instructions.
- use 16-bit arithmetic instructions.
- describe the difference in the way that 8-bit and 16-bit increment and decrement instructions affect the flags.

5.1 FLAGS

The main register set and the alternate register set each have an 8-bit flags register: F and F′. Six of the eight bits are set or reset by various operations that are performed by the CPU. In this chapter several operations that affect the flags will be studied. In the following chapters the flags will be used to enable the CPU to make decisions. The format of the flags register is shown in Figure 5–1. The two bits labeled X are not used. The sign flag, S, is used with signed numbers. If the result of an operation that affects the sign flag is negative, the sign flag is set (1); if positive, the flag is reset (0). The sign flag follows the most significant bit (MSB) of the result.

If the result of an operation that affects the zero flag is zero, the zero flag, Z, is set (1). Otherwise Z is reset (0).

The H and N flags are used in binary coded decimal (BCD) arithmetic. In BCD math four bits represent one decimal digit. If a carry occurs as a result of an addition or subtraction, or if a non-BCD number results, the result must be corrected. The half-carry flag, H, indicates whether there was a carry from the least significant BCD digit to the most significant BCD digit (bit 3 to bit 4). The subtract flag, N, indicates whether

S	Z	X	H	X	P/V	N	C

FIGURE 5–1 Flags register

the operation was addition or subtraction. The results are corrected when a decimal adjust the accumulator (DAA) is performed. This is the main use of the H and N flags.

The parity/overflow flag (P/V) serves a dual function. In 2's complement arithmetic it indicates that the result in the accumulator is incorrect. The magnitude of the answer is too great to be represented as a signed 2's complement number (greater than +127 or less than −128). In this mode it is checking for overflow, which is represented by V. In logical operations such as ANDing or ORing, or Exclusive-ORing, the flag is set if the number of 1's in the accumulator is even. In this mode it is checking parity, which is represented by P.

The result of addition problems always appears in the accumulator. If a carry from the most significant bit occurs, the carry flag (C) is set. If the operation is subtraction, the flag is set if a borrow for the MSB occurs. We will use these flags as we work with the arithmetic and logic operations.

5.2 8-BIT ADD INSTRUCTIONS

The ADD instruction adds the contents of the source location to the contents of the accumulator. The result appears in the accumulator. The contents of the source register remain unchanged. The ADD instructions are listed in Figure 5–2 with the mode of addressing indicated.

Using register addressing allows the contents of any of the general-purpose registers in the main register set to be added to the accumulator. The mnemonic code for this instruction is ADD A,r, where r represents the source register. The op code follows the format 10000rrr, where rrr is the 3-bit register code listed in Figure 4–4.

EXAMPLE: What op code will add the contents of the H register to the accumulator?

SOLUTION: The code for register H is 100. The op code is 10000100 or 84H. This result agrees with Figure 5–2.

SOURCE

	REGISTER ADDRESSING							REG. INDIR.	INDEXED		IMMED.
	A	B	C	D	E	H	L	(HL)	(IX+d)	(IY+d)	n
'ADD'	87	80	81	82	83	84	85	86	DD 86 d	FD 86 d	C6 n

FIGURE 5–2 8-bit ADD instructions

EXAMPLE: What will be displayed at output ports 0, 1, and 2 after the following program has run?

```
0800                    ORG     0800H
0800 3E00               LD      A,00H       ;INITIALIZE A
0802 0631               LD      B,31H       ;INITIALIZE B
0804 0E02               LD      C,02H       ;INITIALIZE C
0806 1607               LD      D,07H       ;INITIALIZE D
0808 1E23               LD      E,23H       ;INITIALIZE E
080A 261F               LD      H,1FH       ;INITIALIZE H
080C 2EFF               LD      L,0FFH      ;INITIALIZE L
080E 83                 ADD     A,E         ;ADD E
080F 82                 ADD     A,D         ;SUM 1
0810 D300               OUT     (00H),A     ;OUT SUM 1 TO 0
0812 80                 ADD     A,B         ;ADD B
0813 84                 ADD     A,H         ;SUM 2
0814 D301               OUT     (01H),A     ;OUT SUM 2 TO 1
0816 ED61               OUT     (C),H       ;OUT H TO 2
0818 76                 HALT
0000                    END
```

SOLUTION:

```
0800     ACC  =  00
0802       B  =  31
0804       C  =  02
0806       D  =  07
0808       E  =  23
080A       H  =  1F
080C       L  =  FF
080E     ACC  =  00 + 23 = 23
080F     ACC  =  23 + 07 = 2A
0810  PORT 0  =  2A
0812     ACC  =  2A + 31 = 5B
0813     ACC  =  5B + 1F = 7A
0814  PORT 1  =  7A
0816  H is output to port specified by register C
      C = 02        H = 1F
      PORT 2  =  1F
```

Confirm these results by loading this program into your trainer.

All of the flags are affected by the ADD A, r instruction. The N flag is reset (0), indicating an ADD operation. The P/V flag will monitor the carry from bit 6 into the sign bit. If there is a carry from bit 6 but not from bit 7, or vice versa, the result is incorrect and the P/V flag will be set. The other flags will be set or reset according to the result of the operations. The effect of the ADD instructions on the flags is summarized in Figure 5–3.

S	Z	X	H	X	P/V	N	C
$\updownarrow$	$\updownarrow$	–	$\updownarrow$	–	V	0	$\updownarrow$

where $\updownarrow$ indicates that the flag is set or reset according to the results of the operation; V indicates that the flag monitors overflow, as opposed to parity.

FIGURE 5–3 Effect of 8-bit ADD on flags

EXAMPLE: Suppose that the accumulator contains 99H and that the B register contains 88H. What will be the contents of the accumulator, flags, and B register after the ADD A, B instruction is run?

SOLUTION:

```
99H = 1001    1001
88H = 1000    1000
     -------------
     10010    0001
```

After the addition the accumulator will contain 00100001 or 21H. The B register will still contain 88H. The flags register is of the form S Z X H X P/V N C. The sign flag, S, is reset (0) because the MSB, 7, of the result is 0. The result in the accumulator is not zero, so the zero flag, Z, is reset (0). There was a carry from the least significant four bits, so the half-carry flag, H, is set (1). There is no carry from bit 6 into the sign bit, but there is a carry from bit 7. Since these differ, the result is incorrect, and the P/V flag is set (1). The answer is too large to be expressed as an 8-bit signed 2's complement number. The subtract flag, N, is reset, and the carry flag, C, is set because there was a carry from the MSB. The flags register is 00X1X101. The X's represent the two bits that were not used and are indeterminate.

In another ADD instruction the HL register pair contains the address of the data to be added to the accumulator. The mnemonic is ADD A,(HL). The op code is 86H. This is an example of register indirect addressing. We have to "look in" a register to get the address of the data to be used.

EXAMPLE: What will be the contents of the accumulator after the following program has run? Suppose that address 0900H contains 3EH.

```
0800                ORG     0800H
0800 210009         LD      HL,0900H
0803 3E10           LD      A,10H
0805 86             ADD     A,(HL)
0806 D300           OUT     (00H),A
0808 76             HALT
0000                END
```

SOLUTION:

0800	HL is loaded with 0900
0803	10H is loaded into accumulator
0805	The contents of memory pointed to by HL are added to the accumulator. 0900 contains 3EH, so 3EH is added to the 10H already in the accumulator. The result is 4EH.
0806	4EH is output to port 00H.

Data stored in memory can also be added to the accumulator by using indexed addressing. The instruction specifies which index register is to be used (IX or IY) and specifies a displacement byte d. When using the IX register, the mnemonic code is ADD A,(IX+d). The parentheses mean "contents of." The op code is DD86d. All flags are affected. When using the IY register, the mnemonic code is ADD A,(IY+d) and the op code is FD86d.

EXAMPLE: Suppose these numbers are stored in memory:

Address	Data
09E5	F0
09E6	AB
09E7	96
09E8	53
09E9	64

What will be the contents of the accumulator after the following program has run?

```
0800                      ORG    0800H
0800 3AE809               LD     A,(09E8H)      ;INITIALIZE A
0803 DD21E509             LD     IX,09E5H       ;INITIALIZE IX
0807 DD8604               ADD    A,(IX+04H)     ;SUM
080A D300                 OUT    (00H),A        ;SUM TO OUT 0
080C 76                   HALT
0000                      END
```

SOLUTION:

Address	Description		
0800	A is loaded with contents of 09E8: ACC = 53H		
0803	IX is loaded with 09E5 as a pointer		
0807	d = 04. The contents of 09E5+04 are added to the accumulator: ACC = 53H + 64H = B7H	0101	0011
080A	B7H is output to port 00	0110	0100
080C	HALT	1011	0111

EXAMPLE: Using this data stored in memory and the IY register, write a program that will initialize the accumulator with the contents of 0987, initialize the IY register to 0987, add the contents of 0981 to the accumulator, output the result to output port 2, and HALT.

0981	04
0982	05
0983	06
0984	07
0985	08
0986	09
0987	0A

SOLUTION:

Address	Op code	Mnemonic	Comments
0800	3A8709	LD A,(0987H)	;Initialize A
0803	FD218709	LD IY,0987H	;Initialize IY

IY contains 0987. To add the contents of 0981 to the accumulator, the displacement byte, d, must be −6. 6 in binary is 00000110. The 2's complement is 11111010 or FAH. If an assembler is to be used, the mnemonic code ADD A, (IY − 6) can be entered, and the assembler will calculate the displacement FAH.

0807	FD86FA	ADD A,(IY-6)	;IY-6
080A	D302	OUT (02H),A	;SUM to OUT 2
080C	76	HLT	

The assembled program is listed.

```
0800                    ORG     0800H
0800 3A8709             LD      A,(0987H)        ;INITIALIZE A
0803 FD218709           LD      IY,0987H         ;INITIALIZE IY
0807 FD86FA             ADD     A,(IY-06H)       ;SUM
080A D302               OUT     (02H),A          ;SUM TO OUT 2
080C 76                 HALT
0000                    END
```

By using the immediate mode of addressing, one can specify the byte to be added to the accumulator in the second byte of the instruction. The mnemonic code is ADD A,n, where n represents one byte of data. The op code is C6n. All flags are affected.

EXAMPLE: What will C60F do?

SOLUTION: 0FH will be added to the accumulator.

5.3 8-BIT ADD WITH CARRY INSTRUCTIONS

These 11 ADD instructions are paralleled by a set of ADD WITH CARRY (ADC) instructions. The ADC instructions are listed in Figure 5–4. In an ADC instruction the contents of the source and the carry flag are added to the contents of the accumulator. This is useful in addition problems involving numbers that are more than one byte long

SOURCE

	REGISTER ADDRESSING							REG. INDIR.	INDEXED		IMMED.
	A	B	C	D	E	H	L	(HL)	(IX+d)	(IY+d)	n
ADD w CARRY 'ADC'	8F	88	89	8A	8B	8C	8D	8E	DD 8E d	FD 8E d	CE n

FIGURE 5–4 ADD WITH CARRY (ADC)

(multiple-precision addition). The least significant bytes can be added, and the carry flag will be set if a carry occurs. The next bytes can be added by using ADC, and the carry from the first bytes will be added in.

EXAMPLE: A 3-byte number is stored at memory locations 0900, 0901, and 0902. 0900 contains the least significant byte and 0902 the most significant byte. It is to be added to a 3-byte number stored at 0903, 0904, 0905. 0903 contains the least significant byte. Write a program that will add these two numbers and store the results at 0906, 0907, 0908, least significant byte first. Output the result to ports 0, 1, and 2.

Address	Data
0900	7F
0901	A3
0902	04
0903	63
0904	04
0905	92

SOLUTION: The data at 0900 will be moved into the accumulator, and the data at 0903 will be added to it. The result will be stored at 0906. The process will be repeated by using the other bytes and the ADC instruction. ADD is used the first time to keep a carry bit from being added to the least significant byte if the carry flag is set. IX+d will point to the bytes to be loaded into the accumulator, IY+d to the bytes to be added to the accumulator.

```
0800                   ORG    0800H
0800 DD210009          LD     IX,0900H       ;INITIALIZE IX
0804 FD210309          LD     IY,0903H       ;INITIALIZE IY
0808 DD7E00            LD     A,(IX+00H)     ;LSB
080B FD8600            ADD    A,(IY+00H)     ;SUM LSB
080E 320609            LD     (0906H),A      ;STORE LSB
0811 D302              OUT    (002H),A       ;LSB TO OUT 2
0813 DD7E01            LD     A,(IX+01H)     ;MIDDLE BYTE
0816 FD8E01            ADC    A,(IY+01H)     ;SUM MIDDLE
0819 320709            LD     (0907H),A      ;STORE MIDDLE
081C D301              OUT    (01H),A        ;MIDDLE TO 01
081E DD7E02            LD     A,(IX+02H)     ;MSB
0821 FD8E02            ADC    A,(IY+02H)     ;SUM MSB
0824 320809            LD     (0908H),A      ;STORE MSB
0827 D300              OUT    (00H),A        ;MSB TO OUT 00
0829 76                HALT
0000                   END
```

SOURCE

	REGISTER ADDRESSING							REG. INDIR.	INDEXED		IMMED.
	A	B	C	D	E	H	L	(HL)	(IX+d)	(IY+d)	n
'ADD'	87	80	81	82	83	84	85	86	DD 86 d	FD 86 d	C6 n
ADD w CARRY 'ADC'	8F	88	89	8A	8B	8C	8D	8E	DD 8E d	FD 8E d	CE n
SUBTRACT 'SUB'	97	90	91	92	93	94	95	96	DD 96 d	FD 96 d	D6 n
SUB w CARRY 'SBC'	9F	98	99	9A	9B	9C	9D	9E	DD 9E d	FD 9E d	DE n

FIGURE 5–5 8-bit SUBTRACT instructions

The ADC instructions affect the flags in the same manner that the ADD instructions do. The flags are summarized in Figure 5–3.

5.4 *8-BIT SUBTRACT INSTRUCTIONS*

A byte of data can be subtracted from the accumulator by using the SUBTRACT instruction SUB. These instructions follow the same format as the ADD instructions and are listed in Figure 5–5.

The source of data to be subtracted can be specified by using register, register indirect, indexed, or immediate addressing. As noted in Figure 5–6, the C, Z, S, and H flags are set or reset according to the result. The P/V flag monitors for overflow. The flag is set if the result is incorrect. The N flag is set.

S	Z	X	H	X	P/V	N	C
↕	↕	–	↕	–	V	1	↕

where V indicates that the flag monitors overflow.

FIGURE 5–6 Effect of SUBTRACT instruction on the flags

EXAMPLE: What will be the contents of the accumulator and flag register after the following program has run? Suppose that address 0905 contains A2H.

```
0800                ORG     0800H
0800 210509         LD      HL,0905H
0803 3EE9           LD      A,0E9H
0805 96             SUB     (HL)
0806 76             HALT
0000                END
```

SOLUTION:

0800	HL is loaded with 0905H
0802	A is loaded with E9H
0806	The contents of 0905 are subtracted from A

Data in accumulator	1110	1001
Data in 0905	1010	0010

The subtraction is handled by the 2's complement method. The problem becomes

```
    1110   1001
  + 0101   1110
  1 0100   0111
```

There was carry from bit 6 into the sign bit, and a carry generated out of the sign bit. Since both occurred, the result is correct, and the P/V flag is reset. The sign bit is reset because bit 7 is zero. The carry flag is set because a carry occurred. There was a carry from bit 3 to bit 4, so the half-carry flag, H, is set. N is set because this problem is subtraction. The result is not zero, so Z is reset. The flags are

S	Z	X	H	X	P/V	N	C
0	0	–	1	–	0	1	1

Check:

Data in accumulator	1110	1001
2's complement	0001	0111
Decimal equivalent	-23	
Data to be subtracted	1010	0010
2's complement	0101	1110
Decimal equivalent	-94	

-23 − (-94) = -23 + 94 = 71
71 in binary is 01000111
This matches the result in the accumulator.

5.5 8-BIT SUBTRACT WITH CARRY INSTRUCTIONS

In a SUBTRACT WITH CARRY instruction (SBC) the contents of the source register and the carry flag are subtracted from the accumulator. SBC has the same affect on the flags as the SUBTRACT instructions did. See Figure 5–6.

SBC (Figure 5–5) enables the programmer to implement multiple-precision subtraction. The least significant byte is subtracted by using the SUB instruction, and SBC is used on the more significant bytes.

EXAMPLE: Write a program that will subtract the 3-byte number stored at 0950, 51, and 52 from the 3-byte numbers at 0953, 54, 55. Store the results at 0956, 57, 58. 0952, 55, and 58 are the least significant bytes. Output the results to output ports 0, 1, and 2, so that port 2 is the least significant byte.

SOLUTION: The same approach can be used that was used for multiple-precision addition. IX+d will be used to point to the minuend, IY+d to the subtrahend.

```
LD IX,0953H
LD IY,0950H
LD A,(IX+02H)
SUB (IY+02H)
LD (0958),A
OUT (02H),A
LD A,(IX+01H)
SBC A,(IY+01H)
LD (0957),A
OUT (01H),A
LD A,(IX+00H)
SBC A,(IY+00H)
LD (0956H),A
OUT (00H),A
```

The assembled program is shown.

```
0800                ORG     0800H
0800 DD215309       LD      IX,0953H
0804 FD215009       LD      IY,0950H
0808 DD7E02         LD      A,(IX+02H)
080B FD9602         SUB     (IY+02H)
080E 325809         LD      (0958H),A
0811 D302           OUT     (02H),A
0813 DD7E01         LD      A,(IX+01H)
0816 FD9E01         SBC     A,(IY+01H)
0819 325709         LD      (0957H),A
081C D301           OUT     (01H),A
081E DD7E00         LD      A,(IX+00H)
0821 FD9E00         SBC     A,(IY+00H)
0824 325609         LD      (0956H),A
0827 D300           OUT     (00H),A
0829 76             HALT
0000                END
```

5.6 8-BIT LOGICAL OPERATIONS

AND, OR, and Exclusive-OR operations can be performed between the data in the accumulator and the source data. These op codes are summarized in Figure 5–7.

SOURCE

	REGISTER ADDRESSING							REG. INDIR.	INDEXED		IMMED.
	A	B	C	D	E	H	L	(HL)	(IX+d)	(IY+d)	n
'AND'	A7	A0	A1	A2	A3	A4	A5	A6	DD A6 d	FD A6 d	E6 n
'XOR'	AF	A8	A9	AA	AB	AC	AD	AE	DD AE d	FD AE d	EE n
'OR'	B7	B0	B1	B2	B3	B4	B5	B6	DD B6 d	FD B6 d	F6 n

FIGURE 5–7 Logic operations

The mnemonic codes for AND instructions follow the same format as the LOAD instructions. AND A,B means AND the contents of B with the accumulator. AND A,(IX+d) means AND the contents of memory pointed to by IX plus the displacement byte d with the accumulator. When a byte of data is ANDed with the accumulator, corresponding bits are ANDed and the result appears in the accumulator.

EXAMPLE: Suppose the accumulator contains A9H. What would be in the accumulator after the op code E6F0 is run?

SOLUTION: E6 specifies that the immediately following byte be ANDed with the accumulator.

Contents of accumulator - A9	= 1010		1001
Byte 2 - F0	= 1111		0000
Result in accumulator	= 1010		0000

The accumulator will contain AOH.

The upper four bits (most significant nibble) were ANDed with 1's and the data did not change. A 1 enables the AND gate, and the data passes unaltered. The lower four bits (least significant nibble) were ANDed with 0's, and 0's resulted. A zero inhibits the AND, and the output is zero. The AND instruction is used in this way to eliminate data from the byte, or "mask out" data that is not needed in the operation. The process is called "masking."

EXAMPLE: Suppose the accumulator contains 8CH. Mask the data in the accumulator so that only the least significant and most significant bits remain.

SOLUTION: The contents of the accumulator must be masked with 10000001 or 81H. The op code E681 will AND 81H with the contents of the accumulator. The result will be

Data in accumulator	=	1000	1100
Data in byte 2	=	1000	0001
Result in accumulator	=	1000	0000

The accumulator will contain 80H.

As shown in Figure 5–8, the flags are affected by the AND instruction. The carry flag is reset; the zero flag and sign flag are set or reset according to the result. The P/V flag indicates the parity of the result (set if the total number of 1's in the result is even). The N flag, subtraction, is reset, and the H flag, half-carry, is set.

S	Z	X	H	X	P/V	N	C
↕	↕	–	1	–	P	0	0

where P indicates that the P/V flag monitors the parity.

FIGURE 5–8 Effect of AND on the flags

EXAMPLE: What will be the contents of the accumulator and flags register after the following program has run?

```
0800                  ORG    0800H
0800 3E77             LD     A,77H
0802 0625             LD     B,25H
0804 A0               AND    B
0805 76               HALT
0000                  END
```

SOLUTION: The LOAD IMMEDIATE instruction is used to load A and B. A contains 77H, and B contains 25H. As shown in Figure 5–7, A0 specifies that B be ANDed with the accumulator.

Contents of accumulator	=	0111	0111
Contents of B register	=	0010	0101
Result in accumulator	=	0010	0101

The accumulator will contain 25H.

On an AND instruction the carry flag is always reset. The result is not zero, so the zero flag is reset. The result contains three 1's, which is an odd number, so the parity flag is reset. The sign flag follows the most significant bit of the results, in this case 0. N is reset, and H is set. The flags register is of the format

S	Z	X	H	X	P/V	N	C
0	0	X	1	X	0	0	0

The Exclusive-OR op codes are listed in Figure 5-7. Various bits of the accumulator can be toggled (changed) by using the XOR, Exclusive-OR, instruction. Figure 5–9 shows the truth table of an Exclusive-OR.

To leave the data unaltered, Exclusive-OR the bit with a 0; to invert, Exclusive-OR it with a 1.

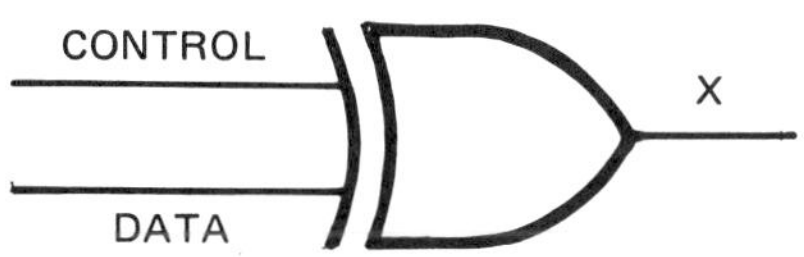

INPUTS		OUTPUT
CONTROL	DATA	X
0	0	0
0	1	1
1	0	1
1	1	0

FIGURE 5–9 Exclusive-OR truth table

EXAMPLE: Suppose the accumulator contains 5EH. Invert the most significant nibble and leave the least significant nibble unaltered.

SOLUTION: Op code EEn specifies that byte 2 be Exclusive-ORed with the accumulator. 11110000 would invert the most significant nibble and leave the least significant unaltered. EEF0 is the desired op code.

The mnemonic code for Exclusive-OR is XOR. XOR A,(HL) means Exclusive-OR the contents of memory pointed to by HL with the accumulator. As shown in Figure 5–10, the flags behave the same as for the AND instruction, except that the H flag is always reset.

The third logical operation is OR. All bits ORed with 1 become 1. All bits ORed with 0 remain unchanged. The op codes are listed in Figure 5–7. As a result of an OR instruction, the C, N, and H flags are reset. The P flag indicates the parity of the result. The Z and S flags are set or reset according to the result. The OR instruction affects the flags in the same way that XOR did. See Figure 5–10.

S	Z	X	H	X	P/V	N	C
↕	↕	–	0	–	P	0	0

FIGURE 5–10 Effect of XOR on the flags

EXAMPLE: What will be the contents of the accumulator and flags after the following program is run?

Address	Data
08FC	F0
08FD	A9
08FE	28
08FF	35
0900	47
0901	86
0902	00
0903	09

```
0800                     ORG    0800H
0800 DD2A0209            LD     IX,(0902H)
0804 DD7E01              LD     A,(IX+01H)
0807 DDB6FD              OR     (IX-03H)
080A 76                  HALT
0000                     END
```

SOLUTION:

0800 The LOW byte of IX is loaded with the contents of 0902. The HIGH byte is loaded with the contents of 0903. IX will contain 0900H.

0803 Accumulator is loaded with contents of address pointed to by IX+01 = 0900+01=0901H. The accumulator will contain 86H.

0806 The accumulator is ORed with the contents of IX+FD.

Contents of IX = 0900H	=	0000	1001	0000	0000
d = FDH	=	1111	1111	1111	1101
Address of source	=	0000	1000	1111	1101
	=	08FDH			

The contents of 08FD is A9

A9H is ORed with 86H

Contents of accumulator	=	86H	=	10000110
Contents of source	=	A9H	=	10101001
Results in accumulator			=	10101111
	=	AFH		

The flags C, N, and H are all reset. The result has six 1's, which is even, so the parity flag is set. The result is not zero, so the zero flag is reset. Bit 7 is set, so the sign flag is also set. The flags are

S	Z	X	H	X	P/V	N	C
1	0	–	0	X	1	0	0

5.7 8-BIT COMPARE, INCREMENT, DECREMENT

The COMPARE instruction, CP, is similar to the SUBTRACT instruction, except that the accumulator remains unchanged. The op codes are shown in Figure 5–11. The effect of the COMPARE instruction on the flags is summarized in Figure 5–12.

	SOURCE										
	REGISTER ADDRESSING							REG. INDIR.	INDEXED		IMMED.
	A	B	C	D	E	H	L	(HL)	(IX+d)	(IY+d)	n
COMPARE 'CP'	BF	B8	B9	BA	BB	BC	BD	BE	DD BE d	FD BE d	FE n
INCREMENT 'INC'	3C	04	0C	14	1C	24	2C	34	DD 34 d	FD 34 d	
DECREMENT 'DEC'	3D	05	0D	15	1D	25	2D	35	DD 35 d	FD 35 d	

FIGURE 5–11 CP, INC, DEC op codes

S	Z	X	H	X	P/V	N	C
↕	↕	–	↕	–	V	1	↕

FIGURE 5–12 Effect of COMPARE on flags

EXAMPLE: Suppose the accumulator contains 26H and the B register contains 39H. What will be the contents of the accumulator and flags register after the op code B8 is implemented?

SOLUTION: B8 specifies the instruction CP A,B.

Contents of accumulator	= 26H	=	0010	0110
Contents of B register	= 39H	=	0011	1001
2's complement of B register		=	1100	0111

		Decimal				
0010	0110	38				
1100	0111	−57				
1110	1101	−19	Check: 19	=	0011	0011
			2's comp	=	1110	1101

The accumulator remains unchanged (26H). The N flag, subtract, will be set. The P/V flag monitors overflow. There was no carry from bit 6 into the sign bit and no carry from the sign bit. The result is correct, and the V flag will be reset. No carry was generated, so C is 0. The result is not equal to zero, so Z is 0. Bit 7 of the result is 1, so the sign bit is set. There was no carry from bit 3 to bit 4, so H is reset. The flags are

C	Z	P/V	S	N	H
0	0	0	1	1	0

After the COMPARE instruction is completed, the zero flag indicates whether the accumulator and source were equal. If equal, Z = 1; if not, Z = 0.

Using the 8-bit INCREMENT instructions, INC, allows the contents of any of the general-purpose registers to be increased by 1. See Figure 5–11 for the op codes. Also, the contents of the address pointed to by the HL register pair IX+d or IY+d can be incremented.

The effect of the 8-bit INC instruction on the flags is summarized in Figure 5–13.

S	Z	X	H	X	P/V	N	C
↕	↕	–	↕	–	V	0	·

where · indicates that no change will occur in the status of the flag.

FIGURE 5–13 Effect of 8-bit INCREMENT on flags

The carry flag is not affected by the INC instruction. The P/V flag monitors overflow. The subtract flag, N, is reset. Z, S, and H are set or reset according to the result in the accumulator.

The 8-bit registers and memory locations can be decremented, decreased by 1, by using the DECREMENT instruction DEC. The flags are affected in the same manner as with INC, except that the N flag is set. The op codes are shown in Figure 5-11.

5.8 16-BIT ARITHMETIC INSTRUCTIONS

The instructions studied thus far in this chapter have operated on 8-bit registers. Several of the instructions have a 16-bit counterpart. As we discuss these 16-bit instructions, note that the flags behave differently than they did for the 8-bit instructions. The op codes for the 16-bit arithmetic instructions are shown in Figure 5–14.

DESTINATION		SOURCE: BC	DE	HL	SP	IX	IY
'ADD'	HL	09	19	29	39		
'ADD'	IX	DD 09	DD 19		DD 39	DD 29	
'ADD'	IY	FD 09	FD 19		FD 39		FD 29
ADD WITH CARRY AND SET FLAGS 'ADC'	HL	ED 4A	ED 5A	ED 6A	ED 7A		
SUB WITH CARRY AND SET FLAGS 'SBC'	HL	ED 42	ED 52	ED 62	ED 72		
INCREMENT 'INC'		03	13	23	33	DD 23	FD 23
DECREMENT 'DEC'		0B	1B	2B	3B	DD 2B	FD 2B

FIGURE 5–14 16-bit arithmetic op codes

Sixteen bits of data can be added to the contents of the HL register pair, the IX register, or the IY register. These operations affect the flags, as shown in Figure 5–15.

S	Z	X	H	X	P/V	N	C
·	·	–	X	–	·	0	↕

where X indicates that the result is unknown and · indicates no change to the flag.

FIGURE 5–15 Effect of 16-bit ADD on the flags

EXAMPLE: What will be the contents of the HL, IX, and IY registers and the contents of the flags register after the following is run?

```
0800                        ORG     0800H
0800 97                     SUB     A
0801 2A5009                 LD      HL,(0950H)
0804 DD2A5209               LD      IX,(0952H)
0808 FD2A5409               LD      IY,(0954H)
080C ED4B5609               LD      BC,(0956H)
0810 ED5B5809               LD      DE,(0958H)
0814 19                     ADD     HL,DE
0815 DD19                   ADD     IX,DE
0817 FD09                   ADD     IY,BC
0819 FD29                   ADD     IY,IY
081B 76                     HALT
0000                        END
```

Address	Data
0950	F0
0951	0F
0952	AA
0953	64
0954	53
0955	42
0956	31
0957	20
0958	1F
0959	0E

SOLUTION:

0800	ACC = 0 Flags: S=0, Z=1, H=0, P/V=0, N=1, C=0
0801	L Loaded with contents of 0950, H with 0951 HL contains 0FF0
0804	LOW byte of IX loaded with contents of 0952. HIGH byte with 0953. IX contains 64AA
0808	LOW byte of IY loaded with contents of 0954. HIGH byte with 0955. IY contains 4253
080C	C loaded with contents of 0956, B with 0957. BC contains 2031H
0810D	E loaded with contents of 0958, D with 0959. DE contains 0E1F

0814	HL = HL+DE =	0FF0 + 0E1F			
		0000	1111	1111	0000
		0000	1110	0001	1111
		0001	1110	0000	1111
	HL = 1E0F				
0815	IX = IX + DE =	64AA + 0E1F			
	=	0110	0100	1010	1010
		0000	1110	0001	1111
		0111	0010	1100	1001
	IX = 72C9				
0817	IY = IY + BC =	4253 + 2031			
	IY =	6284			
0819	IY = IY + IY =	6284 + 6284			
	=	0110	0010	1000	0100
		0110	0010	1000	0100
		1100	0101	0000	1000
	IY = C508				

At the completion of this program, HL contains 1E0FH, IX contains 72C9, and IY contains C508. The Z, P/V, and S flags are not affected by these 16-bit instructions. They were determined by SUB A in the first operation; Z = 1, P/V = 0, S = 0. As a result of the last operation, ADDing IY to IY, the C flag = 0, N = 0, and H is undetermined, The flags are

S	Z	X	H	X	P/V	N	C
0	1	–	X	–	0	0	0

In the 16-bit ADC instruction, the contents of BC, DE, HL, or SP can be added to HL along with the carry flag. The flags are affected as shown in Figure 5–16.

S	Z	X	H	X	P/V	N	C
↕	↕	–	H	–	V	0	↕

FIGURE 5–16 Effect of 16-bit ADC on the flags

In the 8-bit ADC the H flag was determined by the result of the operation. In the 16-bit operation the half-carries from each 8-bit register could conflict, and the flag is not definite. The other flags are affected in the same way.

The op codes for the 16-bit increments and decrements are shown in Figure 5–14. BC, DE, HL, SP, IX, or IY can be incremented or decremented. None of the 16-bit increments or decrements affect the flags, as shown in Figure 5–17. Note that the 8-bit

S	Z	X	H	X	P/V	N	C
·	·	–	·	–	·	·	·

where · indicates flag is not affected.

FIGURE 5–17 Effect of 16-bit increment and decrement on the flags increment and decrement affect the flags in a different manner.

The BC, DE, HL, or SP registers can be added with carry or subtracted with carry to the HL register pair. There is no 16-bit subtract instruction. The flags are affected in the same way for these ADC and SBC instructions, except for N. N is set by the SBC instruction and reset by the ADC instruction. The flags are summarized in Figure 5–18. With the exception of H, the flags are affected in the same manner as for the 8-bit ADC and SBC instructions.

S	Z	X	H	X	P/V	N	C
↕	↕	–	X	–	V	*	↕

* N = 0 for ADC HL
N = 1 for SBC HL

FIGURE 5–18 Effect of 16-bit ADC and SBC on the flags

5.9 BLOCK SEARCHES

The COMPARE, INCREMENT, and DECREMENT functions are combined into single instructions that can be used to search a block of memory for a particular byte of data. In order to use the instruction CPI, compare and increment, the accumulator, the HL register pair, and the BC register pair must first be initialized. The accumulator must contain the data to be searched for, the HL register pair must point to the beginning address of the block, and the BC register pair must contain the number of memory locations to be searched. Each time the instruction is implemented, the contents of memory pointed to by HL are compared to the accumulator. If they are equal, the zero flag is set. Otherwise it is reset. HL is incremented, and BC is decremented. If BC becomes zero, the P/V flag is reset. Otherwise P/V = 1. This sequence occurs each time the instruction is implemented.

CPIR (compare, increment, repeat) is the same, except that it repeats until either the contents of memory pointed to by HL equal A, or until BC = 0. The flags indicate which happens first.

CPD (compare, decrement) is the same as CPI, except that HL is decremented each time instead of incremented. HL would be initialized to point to the bottom of the block instead of the top.

CPDR (compare, decrement, repeat) is the same as CPIR, except that HL is decremented each time. The op codes for the search instructions are shown in Figure 5–19.

	Mnemonic	Op Code
Compare, Increment	CPI	EDA1
Compare, Increment, Repeat	CPIR	EDB1
Compare, Decrement	CPD	EDA9
Compare, Decrement, Repeat	CPDR	EDB9

FIGURE 5–19 Block search instructions

EXAMPLE: Write a program that will search a block of memory 128 bytes long beginning at 0900H to find CCH. If CCH is found, output its location to ports 00 and 01, and output the contents of that location to port 02H. If the byte is not found, output FFH to all three ports.

SOLUTION: BC must be initialized to the hexadecimal equivalent of 128.

$$128 = 1000 \quad 0000 = 80H.$$

```
        ORG     0800H
        LD      A,0CCH          ;SEARCH FOR CC
        LD      HL,0900H        ;BEGINNING AT 0900H
        LD      BC,80H          ;128 BYTES
        CPIR                    ;SEARCH
        LD      C,00H           ;LOAD C FOR OUT
        JR      NZ,NOTF         ;IF NOT FOUND JUMP
        OUT     (C),H
        INC     C
        OUT     (C),L
        INC     C
        OUT     (C),A
        HALT
NOTF:   LD      D,0FFH
        OUT     (C),D           ;NOT FOUND
        INC     C               ;SO OUTPUT
        OUT     (C),D           ;FF'S
        INC     C
        OUT     (C),D
        HALT
        END
```

The assembled program is shown.

```
0800                   ORG    0800H
0800 3ECC              LD     A,0CCH       ;SEARCH FOR CC
0802 210009            LD     HL,0900H     ;BEGINNING AT 0900H
0805 018000            LD     BC,80H       ;128 BYTES
0808 EDB1              CPIR                ;SEARCH
080A 0E00              LD     C,00H        ;LOAD FOR OUT
080C 2009              JR     NZ,NOTF      ;IF NOT FOUND JUMP
080E ED61              OUT    (C),H
0810 0C                INC    C
0811 ED69              OUT    (C),L
0813 0C                INC    C
0814 ED79              OUT    (C),A
0816 76                HALT
0817 16FF      NOTF:   LD     D,0FFH
0819 ED51              OUT    (C),D        ;NOT FOUND
081B 0C                INC    C            ;SO OUTPUT
081C ED51              OUT    (C),D        ;FF´S
081E 0C                INC    C
081F ED51              OUT    (C),D
0821 76                HALT
0000                   END
```

EXERCISE 5

1. Describe how the dual-purpose P/V flag is set or reset.
2. Describe how the Z flag is set or reset.
3. Describe how the S flag is set or reset.
4. Describe how the H flag is set or reset.
5. Describe how the N flag is set or reset.
6. Describe how the C flag is set or reset.
7. Describe the difference between the ADD and ADC instructions.
8. Describe the difference between the SUB and SBC instructions.
9. Describe the difference between the SUB and CP instructions.
10. Describe the difference in the way the 8-bit and 16-bit INCREMENT instructions affect the flags.
11. Describe the difference in the way that 8-bit and 16-bit DECREMENT instructions affect the flags.
12. Which registers can be ADDed to the HL register pair?
13. Can IY be ADDed to IX?
14. Can IY be ADDed to IY?
15. What is the mnemonic code and op code for each of the following operations:
    a. Add the contents of H to A.
    b. Add byte 2 of the instruction to A.
    c. Subtract from A the contents of the memory location pointed to by HL and the carry flag.
    d. Exclusive-OR the contents of memory location pointed to by the IX index register with a displacement byte of 8H.
    e. Decrement the IY register.
    f. Add the carry flag and the contents of BC to HC.
16. Write a program that will initialize the B register with 1FH and the D register with 30H, add the two registers, and compare the result with 4FH.
17. Write a program that will clear A, initialize the IY register with 0950H, and use indexed addressing to add the contents of 0956H to A and then subtract the contents of 094AH from A.
18. Write a program that will clear the accumulator, add the contents of memory location 0950H to it, and mask out bits 5, 6, and 7.
19. What will be the contents of the accumulator and flags register after the program of Problem 17 has run?
20. What will be the contents of the accumulator and flags register after the program of Problem 18 has run?

Lab 5

OBJECTIVES

After completing this lab, you should be able to
- write programs using arithmetic and logic instructions.
- execute programs using arithmetic and logic instructions.

Procedure

1. Predict the contents of output ports 0, 1, and 2 after the program in the second example of Section 5.2 has run. Enter and run the program.
2. Enter the data shown in the fifth example of Section 5.2. Predict the contents of output port 00H after the program has run. Enter and run the program.
3. Enter the data and the triple-precision addition program shown in the example in Section 5.3. Run the program and check the results. Change the data and rerun the program. Verify the results.
4. Write a program that will clear the accumulator, add data stored at location 0950H to the accumulator, subtract data contained at 0960H from the accumulator, mask out the least significant four bits, and output the result to port 01H.
5. Write a program that will Exclusive-OR the contents of the L register with the contents of the D register and output the results to port 02H.
6. Add to the program in the first example in Section 5.8 so that the contents of HL are output to ports 00 and 01. Predict the results of the program and verify.

Chapter 6

THE BRANCH AND ROTATE INSTRUCTIONS

OBJECTIVES

After completing this chapter, you should be able to

- describe the difference between ROTATE instructions and SHIFT instructions.
- describe the effect of each ROTATE or SHIFT instruction on the source register and carry flag.
- use ROTATE or SHIFT instructions in programs.
- predict the effect of each instruction on the flags.
- describe the difference between the 1-byte ROTATE instructions and their counterparts.
- list the eight conditions upon which jumps can be based.
- describe the relationship of the Z, P, C, and S flags to the conditional jumps.
- predict the address of the next instruction after a relative jump has been performed.
- calculate the displacement byte, e, for a desired relative jump.
- use unconditional, conditional, and relative jumps in programs.
- use the DJNZ to control loops.

6.1 ROTATES AND SHIFTS

Data in the accumulator, a general-purpose register, or any memory location can be rotated or shifted. A SHIFT instruction causes the register or memory location together with the carry flag to function as a shift register. For example, SHIFT LEFT ARITHMETIC (SLA) causes each bit in the source location to shift left. Bit 7 is shifted into the carry flag. A zero is shifted into bit 0. The operation is represented symbolically in Figure 6–1.

A ROTATE instruction causes the source location and carry flag to function as a ring counter. For example, ROTATE LEFT causes each bit in the source location to shift left. Bit 7 shifts into the carry flag, and the carry flag shifts into bit 0. The operation is represented symbolically in Figure 6–2.

FIGURE 6-1 SHIFT LEFT ARITHMETIC (SLA)

FIGURE 6-2 ROTATE LEFT (RL)

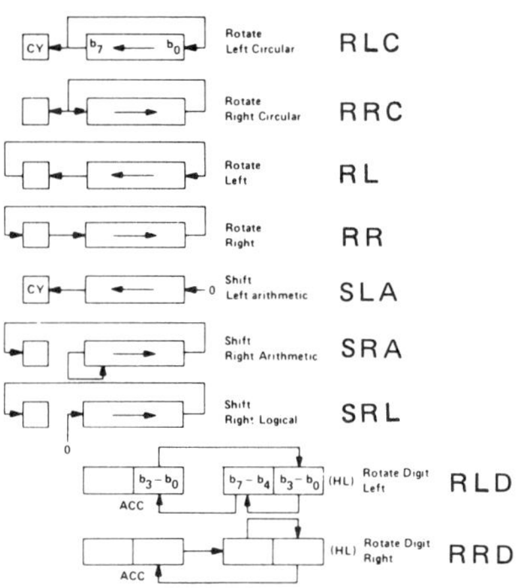

FIGURE 6–3 ROTATE and SHIFT instructions

Source and Destination

TYPE OF ROTATE OR SHIFT	A	B	C	D	E	H	L	(HL)	(IX + d)	(IY + d)
'RLC'	CB 07	CB 00	CB 01	CB 02	CB 03	CB 04	CB 05	CB 06	DD CB d 06	FD CB d 06
'RRC'	CB 0F	CB 08	CB 09	CB 0A	CB 0B	CB 0C	CB 0D	CB 0E	DD CB d 0E	FD CB d 0E
'RL'	CB 17	CB 10	CB 11	CB 12	CB 13	CB 14	CB 15	CB 16	DD CB d 16	FD CB d 16
'RR'	CB 1F	CB 18	CB 19	CB 1A	CB 1B	CB 1C	CB 1D	CB 1E	DD CB d 1E	FD CB d 1E
'SLA'	CB 27	CB 20	CB 21	CB 22	CB 23	CB 24	CB 25	CB 26	DD CB d 26	FD CB d 26
'SRA'	CB 2F	CB 28	CB 29	CB 2A	CB 2B	CB 2C	CB 2D	CB 2E	DD CB d 2E	FD CB d 2E
'SRL'	CB 3F	CB 38	CB 39	CB 3A	CB 3B	CB 3C	CB 3D	CB 3E	DD CB d 3E	FD CB d 3E
'RLD'								ED 6F		
'RRD'								ED 67		

	A
RLCA	07
RRCA	0F
RLA	17
RRA	1F

FIGURE 6-4 ROTATE and SHIFT op codes

Each of the nine rotate and shift instructions is represented symbolically in Figure 6–3.

In the SHIFT RIGHT ARITHMETIC instruction (SRA) the contents of the source location is shifted right. Bit 7 shifts into bit 6 but remains unchanged.

ROTATE DIGIT LEFT (RLD) and ROTATE DIGIT RIGHT (RRD) are used in BCD operations. Bits are rotated in groups of four as data are rotated between the address pointed to by the HL register pair and the accumulator.

The op codes for all nine operations are summarized in Figure 6–4.

EXAMPLE: After the following program has run, what will be the contents of the accumulator and carry flag?

```
0800                    ORG     0800H
0800 97                 SUB     A
0801 0696               LD      B,96H
0803 CB18               RR      B
0805 0E00               LD      C,00H
0807 ED41               OUT     (C),B
0809 76                 HALT
0000                    END
```

SOLUTION:

0800 Subtracting A from A clears the accumulator and affects the flags. The carry flag is reset.

0801 Register B is loaded with 96H or 10010110.

0803 B is rotated right through the carry flag.

	Cy	B
Before RR B	0	10010110
After RR B	0	01001011

0804 C is loaded with 00H for a register indirect output.

0806 B is output to port 00.

EXAMPLE: Suppose that address 0950H contains E4H. What will be displayed at output ports 00 and 01 after the following program has run?

```
0800                ORG     0800H
0800 3E87           LD      A,87H
0802 215009         LD      HL,0950H
0805 ED67           RRD
0807 D300           OUT     (00H),A
0809 7E             LD      A,(HL)
080A D301           OUT     (01H),A
080C 76             HALT
0000                END
```

SOLUTION:

0800 A is loaded with 87
0802 HL is loaded with 0950
0805

	Accumulator	(HL)
Before RRD	87	E4
After RRD	84	7E

0807 84H is output to port 00
0809 7EH is loaded into accumulator
080A 7E is output to port 01

EXAMPLE: What will be the contents of the H register and carry flag after the following program has run? Suppose 09E3 contains 88H.

```
0800                ORG    0800H
0800 21E309         LD     HL,09E3H       ;INITIALIZE HL
0803 66             LD     H,(HL)         ;INITIALIZE H
0804 CB2C           SRA    H              ;SHIFT RIGHT ARITH
0806 CB2C           SRA    H
0808 CB2C           SRA    H
080A CB2C           SRA    H
080C 76             HALT
0000                END
```

SOLUTION:

0800 HL is loaded with 09E3
0803 H is loaded with contents of 09E3
which is 88H = 1000 1000

	Carry Flag	H Register
	Unknown	10001000
0804	0	11000100
0806	0	11100010
0808	0	11110001
080A	1	11111000

The carry flag will be set, and the H register will contain F8H.

The time required to execute the ROTATE and SHIFT instructions ranges from two machine cycles, eight T states to RLC one of the registers to six machine cycles, 23 T states to RLC using indexed addressing. The time required to execute each instruction is listed in Appendix C.

On the ROTATE and SHIFT instructions the N and H flags are reset. The P/V flag monitors parity. C, Z, and S are set or reset according to the result of the shift. The effects on the flags are summarized in Figure 6–5.

S	Z	X	H	X	P/V	N	C
↕	↕	–	0	–	P	0	↕

FIGURE 6–5 Effect of rotate and shift on flags register

Single-byte instructions can be used to rotate the accumulator. They are rotate the accumulator left circular (RLCA), rotate the accumulator right circular (RRCA), rotate the accumulator left (RLA), and rotate the accumulator right (RRA). They are distinguished from their counterparts by the absence of a space between the operation and the source register. The op codes are 07, 0F, 17, 1F, respectively. Note that these are the second bytes of the op codes for the RLC A, RRC A, RL A, and RR A op codes listed in Figure 6–4.

These 1-byte instructions require one machine cycle and four T states for execution. These instructions have no effect on the Z, P/V, and S flags. N and H are reset, and C is set or reset according to the result. The effects of the single-byte ROTATE instructions are summarized in Figure 6–6.

S	Z	X	H	X	P/V	N	C
·	·	–	0	–	·	0	↕

FIGURE 6–6 Effect of single-byte ROTATE instructions on the flags

EXAMPLE: Two programs are listed. Discuss any differences in the results.

```
0800                    ORG     0800H
0800 97                 SUB     A
0801 3EE7               LD      A,0E7H
0803 1F                 RRA
0804 76                 HALT
0000                    END

0900                    ORG     0900H
0900 97                 SUB     A
0901 3EE7               LD      A,0E7H
0903 CB1F               RR      A
0905 76                 HALT
0000                    END
```

SOLUTION:

0800 and 0900 Accumulator is cleared

Flags register	C	Z	P/V	S	N	H
	0	1	0	0	1	0

0801 and 0901 Accumulator = E7 or 11100111.
No effect on flags.

		Cy	ACC	C	Z	P/V	S	N	H
0803	Before RRA	0	11100111	0	1	0	0	1	0
	After RRA	1	01110011	1	1	0	0	0	0

		Cy	ACC	C	Z	P/V	S	N	H
0903	Before RR A	0	11100111	0	1	0	0	1	0
	After RR A	1	01110011	1	0	0	0	0	0

The accumulator has the same result in either case. Only the zero flag differs. In the RRA instruction the zero flag is not affected, so it remains a 1.

In the RR A instruction, the zero flag is reset because the result in the accumulator is not equal to zero. As shown in Appendix C, the RRA requires one machine cycle and four states, whereas the RA A instruction requires two machine cycles and eight states.

6.2 CONDITIONAL JUMP INSTRUCTIONS

Thus far we have learned to load and exchange registers, operate on data with logical and arithmetic instructions, and input and output data. This set of instructions provides the microprocessor with decision-making capabilities. The processor can jump to a new location in the program to fetch the next instruction if certain conditions are met. Those conditions involve the state of the flags. A 3-bit code is assigned to the conditions that can exist, as shown in Figure 6–7.

These codes are used in the instruction JP cc,nn, where cc is one of the conditions listed in Figure 6–7, and nn is a 16-bit address that contains the next instruction to be performed if the conditions for the jump are met. For example, JP Z,09E0H means jump to address 09E0 to obtain the next instruction if the zero flag is set. If the zero flag is cleared, disregard the instruction and continue with the next instruction. The op code

CC	Condition
000	NZ nonzero
001	Z zero
010	NC noncarry
011	C carry
100	PO parity odd
101	PE parity even
110	P sign positive
111	M sign negative

FIGURE 6–7 Jump conditions

is 11CCC010, where CCC is the 3-bit condition code shown in Figure 6–7. Jump on zero would be 11001010 or CAnn.

EXAMPLE: What will be the contents of the accumulator after the following program has run?

```
0800                ORG   0800H
0800 97             SUB   A
0801 1E02           LD    E,02H
0803 0681           LD    B,81H
0805 80             ADD   A,B
0806 1D             DEC   E
0807 CA1008         JP    Z,0810H
080A 80             ADD   A,B
080B 1D             DEC   E
080C CA1008         JP    Z,0810H
080F 80             ADD   A,B
0810 D300           OUT   (00H),A
0812 76             HALT
0000                END
```

SOLUTION:

0800 Accumulator = 00H and Z=1
0801 E = 02H Z unchanged
0803 B = 81H Z unchanged
0805 A = 81H Add affects the Z flag, Z=0
0806 E = 01H 8-bit decrement affects the zero flag, Z = 0
0807 Zero flag not set, instruction disregarded.
Does not jump to 0810, but takes next instruction from 080A
080A A = 81H+81H = 1000 0001

```
                    1000 0001
                    1000 0001
                  1 0000 0010
```

080B E = 0. 8-bit decrement affects the zero flag, so Z=1
080C Since Z=1, 0810H is loaded into the program counter, and the next instruction is taken from address 0810. The instruction at 080F is skipped.
0810 02H output to port 00.

The parity flag acts as an odd-parity generator. After a logical operation is performed (AND, OR, XOR), if the number of 1's in the accumulator is even, the parity flag is set, and vice versa. The instruction JP PE means jump to the given address on even parity (parity flag = 1). JP PO means jump on odd parity (parity flag = 0). If the condition is not met, the instruction is ignored.

The sign flag is set or reset by bit 7 of the register operated upon. If the result is negative, bit 7 is set. JP M means jump or minus (sign flag = 1). If the result is positive, bit 7 is reset. JP P means jump on positive (sign flag = 0).

The flag register is not affected by the JUMP instructions. Figure 6–8 summarizes the conditional jump op codes. They all use the immediate extended addressing mode.

			CONDITION: UN-COND.	CARRY	NON CARRY	ZERO	NON ZERO	PARITY EVEN	PARITY ODD	M: SIGN NEG	P: SIGN POS	REG B≠0
JUMP 'JP'	IMMED. EXT.	nn	C3 n n	DA n n	D2 n n	CA n n	C2 n n	EA n n	E2 n n	FA n n	F2 n n	

FIGURE 6–8 Conditional jumps

			CONDITION: UN-COND.	CARRY	NON CARRY	ZERO	NON ZERO	PARITY EVEN	PARITY ODD	M: SIGN NEG	P: SIGN POS	REG B≠0
JUMP 'JP'	REG. INDIR.	(HL)	E9									
JUMP 'JP'		(IX)	DD E9									
JUMP 'JP'		(IY)	FD E9									

FIGURE 6–9 Unconditional jumps

6.3 UNCONDITIONAL JUMP INSTRUCTIONS

JP nn is a mandatory unconditional jump to address nn specified by bytes 3 and 2 of the instruction. Its op code is C3nn. It does not depend on any conditions being met. Figure 6–9 summarizes the unconditional JUMP instructions.

There are three other unconditional jumps, but they use register indirect addressing. Jump to the address pointed to by HL, JP (HL), jump to the address pointed to by IX index register, JP (IX), and jump to the address pointed to by IY index register, JP (IY) are the three instructions. The flags are not affected.

EXAMPLE: Predict what will be displayed at output ports 00, 01, and 02H

```
0800                    ORG     0800H
0800 DD212009           LD      IX,0920H
0804 FD214009           LD      IY,0940H
0808 216009             LD      HL,0960H
080B 97                 SUB     A
080C C38009             JP      0980H
080F D300               OUT     (00H),A
0811 DDE9               JP      (IX)
0813 D301               OUT     (01H),A
0815 FDE9               JP      (IY)
0817 D302               OUT     (02H),A
0819 76                 HALT
```

```
0920                     ORG     0920H
0920 B6                  OR      A,(HL)
0921 EA1308              JP      PE,0813H
0924 A6                  AND     A,(HL)
0925 E21308              JP      PO,0813H
0928 76                  HALT
0940                     ORG     0940H
0940 23                  INC     HL
0941 3EF0                LD      A,0F0H
0943 FEF0                CP      0F0H
0945 C21708              JP      NZ,0817H
0948 E60F                AND     0FH
094A CA1708              JP      Z,0817H
0960                     ORG     0960H
0960 80                  DB      80H          ;DATA
0961 01                  DB      01H          ;DATA
0962 FF                  DB      0FFH         ;DATA
0980                     ORG     0980H
0980 86                  ADD     A,(HL)
0981 CB17                RL      A
0983 C21308              JP      NZ,0813H
0986 C644                ADD     A,44H
0988 D20F08              JP      NC,080FH
098B 76                  HALT
0000                     END
```

SOLUTION:

0800	IX = 0920H
0804	IY = 0940H
0808	HL = 0960H
080B	A = 0 Carry Flag = 0 Z = 1
080C	Unconditional jump to 0980H
0980	The contents of HL, 80H, are added to A A = 80H Cy = 0 Z = 0
0981	Before RL A A = 1000 0000 Cy = 0 After RL A A = 0000 0000 Cy = 1 As a result of the rotate, Z = 1
0983	Jump on nonzero is ignored
0986	A = 00 + 44H = 44H Cy = 0
0988	Jump on no carry to 080F
080F	A = 44 is output to port 00H
0811	Jump to 0920
0920	A = 44, 0960 contains 80, 44 OR 84 = C4H C4 contains three 1's, so the P flag is reset
0921	Jump on parity even means jump if P = 1. The instruction is ignored.
0924	C4H, HL contains 80, C4 AND 80 = 80 80 contains one 1, so the P flag is reset.
0925	Jump on parity odd means jump if P = 0. The jump to 0813 is taken.
0813	A = 80 is output to port 01H.

0815	Jump to 0940.
0940	HL = HL + 1 = 0961H
0941	A = F0H
0943	A is compared to F0. Z = 1
0945	Jump on nonzero to 0817 is ignored
0948	F0 and 0F equals 00. Z = 1
094A	Jump on zero to 0817H is taken.
0817	A = 00H is output to port 02.
0819	HALT
	Port 00 contains 44H, port 01 contains 80H,and port 02 contains 00H.

6.4 RELATIVE JUMP INSTRUCTIONS

A different type of jump is the relative jump. Instead of specifying an absolute address to which to jump, the relative JUMP instruction supplies a displacement value, e: e is an 8-bit signed 2's complement number that specifies the number of bytes to jump to obtain the next instruction. The program counter (PC) contains the address of the next instruction to be performed. After the contents of the PC have been placed on the address bus so that the next instruction can be fetched, the PC is incremented to point to the next instruction. When a relative jump is encountered, e is added to PC to point to the new location of the next instruction.

EXAMPLE: Suppose that address 085E contains the 2-byte relative JUMP instruction JR e, where e is 24H. From which address will the next instruction be fetched?

SOLUTION: While the relative jump is being fetched and decoded, the PC is incremented to point to the next address as if a relative jump were not going to take place.

$$085E + 02 = 0860$$

The displacement 24H is added to that new value.

$$0860 + 24 = 0884H$$

The next instruction is contained at 0884H.

EXAMPLE: If the 2-byte relative JUMP instruction JR e is contained at address 083A, what value of e will cause the next instruction to be taken from address 0843?

SOLUTION: After fetching JR e, the program counter will contain 083C. 0843 − 083C equals 7. e = 07H.

Jump relative, JR, is an unconditional jump. Its op code is 18e. No flags are affected. There are also four relative conditional jumps. They are jump relative on carry (JR C), jump relative on noncarry (JR NC), jump relative on zero (JR Z), and jump relative on nonzero (JR NZ). The op codes for the relative jumps are shown in Figure 6–10.

Note that in using the assembler program to write the following program, the displacement byte, e, was calculated by the computer. The instruction at location 0806H

			CONDITION							M	P	
			UN-COND.	CARRY	NON CARRY	ZERO	NON ZERO	PARITY EVEN	PARITY ODD	SIGN NEG	SIGN POS	REG B≠0
JUMP 'JR'	RELATIVE		18 e-2	38 e-2	30 e-2	28 e-2	20 e-2					

FIGURE 6–10 Relative jumps

was entered as JR NZ, 0803H. Even though the jump is relative, the absolute address was supplied, and the computer supplied the op code with displacement byte, 20 FB.

An alternate approach is to label the address that will be jumped to and use the same label in the relative jump mnemonic code.

EXAMPLE: What data will be output to port 00H as a result of the following program?

```
0800                ORG    0800H
0800 97             SUB    A              ;CLEAR ACCUMULATOR
0801 0E03           LD     C,03H          ;INITIALIZE COUNTER
0803 C60F           ADD    A,0FH
0805 0D             DEC    C              ;DECREMENT COUNTER
0806 20FB           JR     NZ,0803H       ;JUMP TO ADD
0808 D300           OUT    (00H),A        ;OUT A TO 00H
080A 76             HALT
0000                END
```

SOLUTION:

0800 Accumulator is cleared.

0801 Register C is to be used as a counter. It is initialized with the value 3.

0803 A = 00+0F = 0FH

0805 C is decremented to 2. Dec C affects the zero flag. Since C is not zero, the zero flag is reset.

0806 After the relative JUMP instruction is fetched, the program counter is incremented to 0808, the address of the next instruction if the relative jump is not taken. Because the zero flag is reset, the jump is taken. FB is added to the contents of the program counter to determine the address of the next instruction.

$$\begin{array}{rcllll} PC = 0808H & = & 0000 & 1000 & 0000 & 1000 \\ FBH & = & \underline{1111} & \underline{1111} & \underline{1111} & \underline{1011} \\ & & 0000 & 1000 & 0000 & 0011 \end{array}$$

Address of next instruction = 0803H

Note that the most significant byte is added as FF.

0803 Accumulator = 0F+0FH

$$\begin{array}{ll} 0000 & 1111 \\ \underline{0000} & \underline{1111} \\ 0001 & 1110 = 1E\ H \end{array}$$

0805 C is decremented to 1. The zero flag is reset.

0806 The relative jump is taken to 0803.

0803 Accumulator = 1E+0FH = 0001 1110

0000 1111

0010 1101 = 2DH

0805 C is decremented to 00H. The zero flag is set.

0806 The relative jump is not taken since it is a jump on nonzero. The next instruction is taken from 0808.

0808 2DH is output to port 00H.

EXAMPLE: Rewrite the program in the previous example and use a label to specify the target address.

SOLUTION:

```
0800                         ORG     0800H
0800 97                      SUB     A
0801 0E03                    LD      C,03H
0803 C60F       LOOP:        ADD     A,0FH
0805 0D                      DEC     C
0806 20FB                    JR      NZ,LOOP
0808 D300                    OUT     (00H),A
080A 76                      HALT
0000                         END
```

In this example the C register was used as a counter. It was initialized to 3, and as a result of the program 0FH was added to the accumulator three times.

If the B register is used as a counter, the instruction DJNZ,e decrements the B register and performs a relative jump if B is not yet zero. This instruction combines a decrement with a relative jump on nonzero. Its op code is 10e.

EXAMPLE: Rewrite the program in the last example, using the DJNZ,e instruction.

SOLUTION:

```
0800                         ORG     0800H
0800 97                      SUB     A
0801 0603                    LD      B,03H
0803 C60F                    ADD     A,0FH
0805 10FC                    DJNZ    0803H
0807 D300                    OUT     (00H),A
0809 76                      HALT
0000                         END
```

The absolute jumps require the programmer to know the exact address of the instruction to be jumped to. The relative jumps allow the programmer to write the complete program without tying it down to absolute addresses. A program written with relative jumps can be relocated in memory and still be operable.

The displacement byte, e, works the same way that the displacement byte, d, works with indexed addressing.

EXAMPLE: If the 2-byte instruction DJNZ (decrement B, jump if nonzero) is contained at address 0908, what displacement byte should be used to cause a relative jump to address 08F5?

SOLUTION: After the instruction is fetched, the program counter will contain 090A. We will use the 2's complement method to find the difference.

08F5		0000	1000	1111	0101
− 090A	−	0000	1001	0000	1010
		0000	1000	1111	0101
2's comp.		1111	0110	1111	0110
		1111	1111	1110	1011

e = EBH.

Check: 090A	0000	1001	0000	1010
+ EB	1111	1111	1110	1011
	0000	1000	1111	0101

The next instruction would be at location 08F5, as required.

6.5 *BIT SET, RESET, AND TEST*

By using one of the bit manipulation instructions, any bit of a word in memory or in registers A,B,C,D,E,H, or L can be set to a 1, reset to a zero, or tested to determine whether the bit is a 1 or 0.

The mnemonic code for setting a bit in one of the registers is SET b,r. The first byte in this 2-byte instruction is always CB. The second byte follows the format 11bbbrrr, where bbb is the octal code for the bit to be used (000 through 111). This is called *bit addressing*. The register to be used is specified in bits rrr by using register addressing. The 3-bit register code shown in Figure 4–4 is used. No flags are affected by this operation. It requires two machine cycles and eight T states.

EXAMPLE: What does the instruction CBD4 do?

SOLUTION: D4H = 11010100
This is the proper format for a SET b,r instruction, where b = 010 and r = 100. Bit 2 in register H is set.

The SET instructions are summarized in Figure 6–11.

EXAMPLE: Use Figure 6–11 to find the op code for SET 7,A.

SOLUTION: Read down the A column and across the SET BIT 7 row to find CBFF.

Any bit in memory can be set by using the HL register pair or IX + d or IY + d to point to the operand.

		REGISTER ADDRESSING							REG. INDIR.	INDEXED	
	BIT	A	B	C	D	E	H	L	(HL)	(IX+d)	(IY+d)
TEST 'BIT'	0	CB 47	CB 40	CB 41	CB 42	CB 43	CB 44	CB 45	CB 46	DD CB d 46	FD CB d 46
	1	CB 4F	CB 48	CB 49	CB 4A	CB 4B	CB 4C	CB 4D	CB 4E	DD CB d 4E	FD CB d 4E
	2	CB 57	CB 50	CB 51	CB 52	CB 53	CB 54	CB 55	CB 56	DD CB d 56	FD CB d 56
	3	CB 5F	CB 58	CB 59	CB 5A	CB 5B	CB 5C	CB 5D	CB 5E	DD CB d 5E	FD CB d 5E
	4	CB 67	CB 60	CB 61	CB 62	CB 63	CB 64	CB 65	CB 66	DD CB d 66	FD CB d 66
	5	CB 6F	CB 68	CB 69	CB 6A	CB 6B	CB 6C	CB 6D	CB 6E	DD CB d 6E	FD CB d 6E
	6	CB 77	CB 70	CB 71	CB 72	CB 73	CB 74	GB 75	CB 76	DD CB d 76	FD CB d 76
	7	CB 7F	CB 78	CB 79	CB 7A	CB 7B	CB 7C	CB 7D	CB 7E	DD CB d 7E	FD CB d 7E
RESET BIT 'RES'	0	CB 87	CB 80	CB 81	CB 82	CB 83	CB 84	CB 85	CB 86	DD CB d 86	FD CB d 86
	1	CB 8F	CB 88	CB 89	CB 8A	CB 8B	CB 8C	CB 8D	CB 8E	DD CB d 8E	FD CB d 8E
	2	CB 97	CB 90	CB 91	CB 92	CB 93	CB 94	CB 95	CB 96	DD CB d 96	FD CB d 96
	3	CB 9F	CB 98	CB 99	CB 9A	CB 9B	CB 9C	CB 9D	CB 9E	DD CB d 9E	FD CB d 9E
	4	CB A7	CB A0	CB A1	CB A2	CB A3	CB A4	CB A5	CB A6	DD CB d A6	FD CB d A6
	5	CB AF	CB A8	CB A9	CB AA	CB AB	CB AC	CB AD	CB AE	DD CB d AE	FD CB d AE
	6	CB B7	CB B0	CB B1	CB B2	CB B3	CB B4	CB B5	CB B6	DD CB d B6	FD CB d B6
	7	CB BF	CB B8	CB B9	CB BA	CB BB	CB BC	CB BD	CB BE	DD CB d BE	FD CB d BE
SET BIT 'SET'	0	CB C7	CB C0	CB C1	CB C2	CB C3	CB C4	CB C5	CB C6	DD CB d C6	FD CB d C6
	1	CB CF	CB C8	CB C9	CB CA	CB CB	CB CC	CB CD	CB CE	DD CB d CE	FD CB d CE
	2	CB D7	CB D0	CB D1	CB D2	CB D3	CB D4	CB D5	CB D6	DD CB d D6	FD CB d D6
	3	CB DF	CB D8	CB D9	CB DA	CB DB	CB DC	CB DD	CB DE	DD CB d DE	FD CB d DE
	4	CB E7	CB E0	CB E1	CB E2	CB E3	CB E4	CB E5	CB E6	DD CB d E6	FD CB d E6
	5	CB EF	CB E8	CB E9	CB EA	CB EB	CB EC	CB ED	CB EE	DD CB d EE	FD CB d EE
	6	CB F7	CB F0	CB F1	CB F2	CB F3	CB F4	CB F5	CB F6	DD CB d F6	FD CB d F6
	7	CB FF	CB F8	CB F9	CB FA	CB FB	CB FC	CB FD	CB FE	DD CB d FE	FD CB d FE

FIGURE 6–11 Bit manipulation op codes

EXAMPLE: What does the op code DDCBE4F6 do? Suppose IX contains 0900H.

SOLUTION: DDCBE4F6 is of the format DDCBdF6 where d is the displacement byte. Figure 6–11 shows that this is the op code for SET 6, (IX+d), where d=E4.

IX contains 0900 =	0000	1001	0000	0000
d = FFE4 =	1111	1111	1110	0100
	0000	1000	1110	0100

Bit 6 of memory location 08E4 will be SET. Using HL to point to the operand requires four machine cycles and 15 T states. Using IX or IY requires six machine cycles and 23 T states.

The RES instruction can be used to reset any bit in memory or in registers A,B,C,D,E,H, or L. These instructions follow the same format as the SET instructions except that the second byte is of the form 10bbbrrr. The RES op codes are summarized in Figure 6–11. No flags are affected.

Any bit in registers A,B,C,D,E,H or L or any bit in memory can be tested by using the BIT instruction. The zero flag is set if the selected bit is 0, and reset if it is a 1. The remaining flags are affected as shown in Figure 6–12. The operand can be specified by using register addressing, register indirect addressing (HL register pair only), or indexed addressing. These are summarized in Figure 6–11.

S	Z	X	H	X	P/V	N	C
X	↕	–	1	–	X	0	•

FIGURE 6–12 Effect of BIT instruction on flags

EXAMPLE: Write a program that will input a byte from port 0 and test bits 6 and 7 of that byte. If bit 6 is a 0, output FFH to output port 0. If bit 7 is 0, output FF to port 1.

SOLUTION:

```
        ORG     0800H
        LD      A,0FFH      ;INITIALIZE A'
        EX      AF,AF'
        SUB     A           ;CLEAR A
        LD      C,00H       ;INITIALIZE C FOR OUT
        IN      A,(00H)     ;INPUT BYTE
TEST6:  BIT     6,A         ;TEST BIT 6
        JR      NZ,TEST7    ;IF 1,TEST BIT 7
        EX      AF,AF'
        OUT     (00H),A     ;IF 0,OUTPUT FF
        EX      AF,AF'
```

```
TEST7:     BIT     7,A          ;TEST BIT 7
           JR      NZ,FINISH    ;IF 1,FINISH
           EX      AF,AF'
           OUT     (01H),A      ;IF 0,OUTPUT FF
FINISH:    HALT
           END
```

The assembled program looks like this.

```
0800                   ORG    0800H
0800  3EFF             LD     A,0FFH      ;INITIALIZE A'
0802  08               EX     AF,AF'
0803  97               SUB    A           ;CLEAR A
0804  0E00             LD     C,00H       ;INITIALIZE C FOR OUT
0806  DB00             IN     A, (00H)    ;INPUT BYTE
0808  CB77   TEST6:    BIT    6,A         ;TEST BIT 6
080A  2004             JR     NZ,TEST7    ;IF 1,TEST BIT 7
080C  08               EX     AF,AF'
080D  D300             OUT    (00H),A     ;IF 0,OUTPUT FF
080F  08               EX     AF,AF'
0810  CB7F   TEST7:    BIT    7,A         ;TEST BIT 7
0812  2003             JR     NZ,FINISH   ;IF 1,FINISH
0814  08               EX     AF,AF'
0815  D301             OUT    (01H),A     ;IF 0,OUTPUT FF
0817  76     FINISH:   HALT
0000                   END
```

EXERCISE 6

1. Describe the difference between ROTATE and SHIFT instructions.
2. Draw a diagram that represents the effect of a ROTATE LEFT CIRCULAR instruction.
3. Draw a diagram that represents the effect of a ROTATE RIGHT CIRCULAR instruction.
4. Draw a diagram that represents the effect of a ROTATE LEFT instruction.
5. Draw a diagram that represents the effect of a ROTATE RIGHT instruction.
6. Draw a diagram that represents the effect of a SHIFT LEFT ARITHMETIC instruction.
7. Draw a diagram that represents the effect of a SHIFT RIGHT ARITHMETIC instruction.
8. Draw a diagram that represents the effect of a SHIFT RIGHT logical instruction.
9. Draw a diagram that represents the effect of a ROTATE DIGIT LEFT instruction.
10. Draw a diagram that represents the effect of a ROTATE DIGIT RIGHT instruction.
11. Describe the effect of the op code CB24.
12. Describe the effect of the op code FDCBFA2E.
13. What op code will cause the contents of the C register to be shifted left with bit 7 shifting into the carry flag and a 0 shifting into bit 0?
14. Discuss the difference between RRC A and RRCA.

15. Discuss the difference between RR A and RRA.
16. List the eight conditions that can be tested for a JUMP instruction.
17. What is the op code for a jump on zero to 0950H?
18. Discuss the parity flag and its relation to the conditional jump.
19. Discuss the sign flag and its relation to the conditional jump.
20. If a 2-byte relative JUMP instruction is contained at address 0890 and the displacement byte is F0, at what address is the next instruction contained?
21. If a 2-byte relative JUMP instruction is contained at address 0944 and the displacement byte is 4F, at what address is the next instruction contained?
22. Write a program that will use the DJNZ instruction to add 08H to the accumulator five times.
23. Write a program that will subtract 04H from the HL register pair eight times.
24. Write the op code (and displacement byte) of a relative jump that will cause the next instruction to be taken from 0877H if the zero flag is set. The op code is to be stored at location 0897H.
25. Write the op code and displacement byte of a relative jump that will cause the next instruction to be taken from 0950 if the parity flag is set. The op code is to be stored at location 0940.

Lab 6

OBJECTIVES

After completing this lab, you should be able to

- write and implement programs using ROTATE, SHIFT, and JUMP instructions.
- predict and verify the effect of a program.

Procedure

1. Enter the first example of Section 6.3. Predict the results. Run the program to verify.
2. Write a program using DJNZ that will add the contents of memory location 0900 to the accumulator as many times as specified in location of 0901. Output the result to port 00H. Run and debug the program.

Chapter 7

SUBROUTINES, STACK, AND INTERRUPT INSTRUCTIONS

OBJECTIVES

After completing this chapter, you should be able to

- use subroutines in programming.
- describe the eight conditions upon which conditional calls and returns are based.
- describe how PUSH and POP instructions affect the stack and stack pointer.
- discuss the difference between maskable and nonmaskable interrupts.
- describe the difference between modes 0, 1, and 2 interrupts.
- use RESTART instructions in conjunction with mode 0 interrupts.

7.1 CALL AND RETURN

In Chapter 6 several jump instructions were studied. A different type of jump is the CALL instruction. CALL allows the programmer to jump to a part of the program called a subroutine. A *subroutine* is a portion of the program that performs a particular function. The main program can call that subroutine any number of times as needed. The last instruction in the subroutine is RETURN. It causes the CPU to return to the main program to continue from where it left off. It fetches the instruction that follows the CALL instruction that caused the jump to subroutine. There are unconditional and conditional CALL to subroutine instructions just as there were conditional and unconditional JUMP instructions. The CALL op codes are listed in Figure 7–1. They use the immediate extended mode of addressing. The address of the first instruction of the subroutine is specified by bytes 2 and 3 of the instruction, in LOW byte, HIGH byte order.

Each subroutine terminates in a RETURN instruction. The RETURN signals the CPU to return to the main program for the next instruction. The mnemonic code for RETURN is RET. RETURNs can be unconditional or conditional, as shown in Figure 7–2. The RETURNs use register indirect addressing in that the address of the next instruction is pointed to by the stack pointer.

			CONDITION							M	P	
			UN- COND.	CARRY	NON CARRY	ZERO	NON ZERO	PARITY EVEN	PARITY ODD	SIGN NEG	SIGN POS	REG $B \neq 0$
'CALL'	IMMED. EXT.	nn	CD n n	DC n n	D4 n n	CC n n	C4 n n	EC n n	E4 n n	FC n n	F4 n n	

FIGURE 7–1 CALL op codes

			CONDITION							M	P	
			UN- COND.	CARRY	NON CARRY	ZERO	NON ZERO	PARITY EVEN	PARITY ODD	SIGN NEG	SIGN POS	REG $B \neq 0$
RETURN 'RET'	REG. INDIR.	(SP) (SP+1)	C9	D8	D0	C8	C0	E8	E0	F8	F0	

FIGURE 7–2 RETURN FROM SUBROUTINE op codes

EXAMPLE: Determine the contents of output ports 00, 01, 02 after the following program has run.

```
0800                         ORG      0800H
0800 97                      SUB      A
0801 0EFF                    LD       C,0FFH
0803 CD3008                  CALL     0830H
0806 ED79                    OUT      (C),A
0808 CD3008                  CALL     0830H
080B ED79                    OUT      (C),A
080D CD3008                  CALL     0830H
0810 ED79                    OUT      (C),A
0812 76                      HALT
0830                         ORG      0830H
0830 C604                    ADD      A,04H
0832 0C                      INC      C
0833 C9                      RET
0000                         END
```

SOLUTION: The main program begins at 0800. The subroutine begins at 0830 and is called three times.

0800 The accumulator is cleared.
0801 FFH is loaded into C.
0803 The subroutine at 0830 is called.
0830 04H is added to the accumulator: A = 04H.
0832 C is incremented: FF + 01 = 00H.
0833 RETURN sends the CPU back to 0806 for the next instruction.
0806 04H is output to port 00.
0808 The subroutine is called again.
0830 04H is added to the accumulator: A = 08H.

0832 C is incremented: C=01H.
0833 The RETURN sends the CPU to 080BH for the next instruction.
080B 08H is output to port pointed to by the C register: 01H.
080D The subroutine is called again.
0830 04H is addcd to thc accumulator: Λ=0C.
0832 C is incremented: C=02H.
0833 The RETURN sends the CPU to 0810H for the next instruction.
0810 0CH is output to port 02H.
0812 HALT

Port 00 should display 04H, port 01 should display 08H, and port 02 should display 0C.

There is a time delay subroutine stored in ROM beginning at location 00E4H. We will study that subroutine later in the chapter, but we will use it now in the following example.

EXAMPLE: Predict the effect of the following program on output port 00H. Run the program to verify your results.

```
0800                ORG     0800H
0800 97             SUB     A
0801 3C             INC     A
0802 D300           OUT     (00H),A
0804 CDE400         CALL    00E4H
0807 CB07           RLC     A
0809 C30208         JP      0802H
080C 76             HALT
0000                END
```

SOLUTION:

0800 The accumulator is cleared.
0801 A = 01H.
0802 01H to output port 00.
0804 The subroutine at address 00E4H is called. It provides a 10-ms delay to slow the program enough so that our eyes can observe the output. The RETURN instruction in the subroutine causes the CPU to select the next instruction from address 0807.
0807 Rotate left circular shifts the "1" left. Since this rotate shifts bit 7 into bit 0, the status of the carry flag was not important.
0809 A jump is made to the OUT statement in line 0802. This program will run in this loop until the trainer is reset.

To slow the action even more, we will use a "nested" subroutine. *Nested* implies that one subroutine is called from within another subroutine. A diagram of this is shown in Figure 7–3.

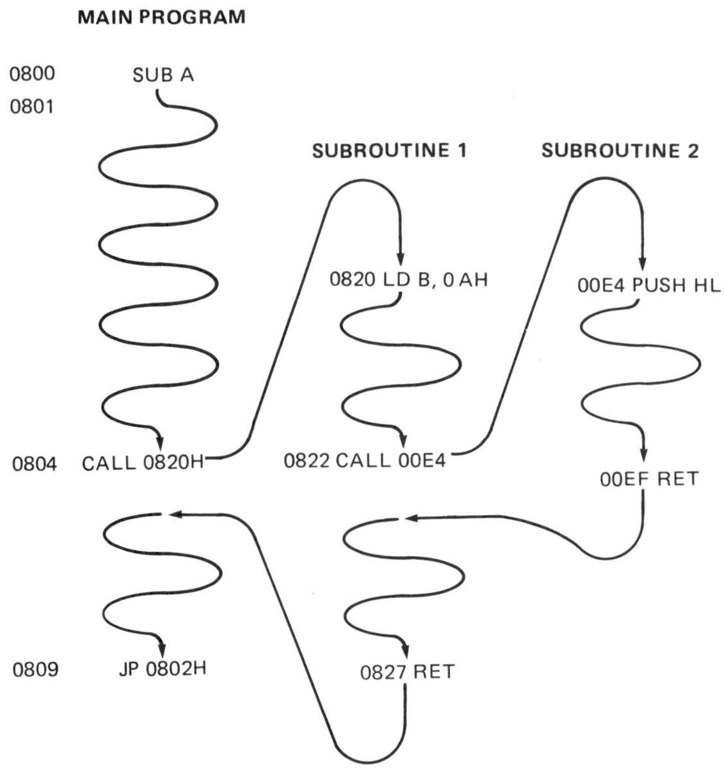

FIGURE 7–3 Nested subroutines

EXAMPLE: Determine how the following program produces a longer delay than that in the preceding example.

```
0800                                ORG     0800H
0800 97                             SUB     A
0801 3C                             INC     A
0802 D300                           OUT     (00H),A
0804 CD2008                         CALL    0820H
0807 CB07                           RLC     A
0809 C30208                         JP      0802H
0820                                ORG     0820H
0820 060A                           LD      B,0AH
0822 CDE400     LOOP:               CALL    00E4H
0825 10FB                           DJNZ    LOOP
0827 C9                             RET
0828 76                             HALT
0000                                END
```

SOLUTION: Instead of calling the delay subroutine that begins at 00E4H, the main program calls a subroutine at 0820H that acts as a counter.

0820H B is loaded with 0AH or 10 decimal.

0822 The 10-ms time-delay subroutine at 00E4H is called. After a 10-ms delay the program returns to 0825.

0825 B is decremented to 9. The zero flag is not set, so the relative jump is taken. FBH causes a jump to address 0822, which calls the 10-ms delay subroutine again. This is repeated until B=0. When B=0, the relative jump is ignored. The subroutine at 00E4 is called 10 times. This yields a delay of approximately 100 ms.

0827 RETURN causes the next instruction to be taken from the main program at 0807.

0807 Rotates the accumulator left circular.

0809 The program jumps to 0802 where the accumulator is output to port 00H.

The length of delay can be controlled by initializing B to one-tenth the desired time delay in milliseconds.

7.2 STACK AND STACK POINTER

If the subroutine at 0820H in the last example were to be called from many places in the program, care would have to be taken that loading the B register with the counter number does not interfere with work being done in the main program. The subroutine needs to be made "transparent" to the main program. Transparent implies that upon returning from the subroutine, all registers will contain their original values. This can be accomplished by storing the data contained in any register to be used in the subroutine in a special place in RAM called the *stack*. Just before returning from the subroutine, the original data is returned to the registers from the stack.

One of the tasks performed by ROM upon resetting the trainer is loading the stack pointer with the address in RAM where the stack is to be placed. If the stack pointers were loaded with 0950, the first byte of data would be loaded or pushed onto 094F, then 094E, 094D, and so on. Data would be removed or popped from the stack in the opposite order: "last in, first out."

Data is pushed onto or popped off the stack two bytes (16 bits) at a time. The HIGH byte of the register pair being pushed onto the stack is loaded first, followed by the LOW byte.

As a byte of data is pushed onto the stack, the stack pointer is decremented so that the next byte of data is always pushed onto the address contained in SP-1.

EXAMPLE: Suppose that the stack pointer contains 0A00 and the BC register pair contains C904H. What will be the contents of the stack pointer and the stack after BC is pushed onto the stack?

SOLUTION: The HIGH byte is pushed onto the address pointed to by SP-1 or 09FF. The LOW byte is pushed onto 09FE. The stack pointer will be decremented twice. At the conclusion, SP will contain 09FEH. Address 09FFH will contain C9H, and memory location 09FEH will contain 04H.

Address	Data	
09FE	04	data from C
09FF	C9	data from B

The final order in memory is LOW byte, HIGH byte as usual.

To pop data off of the stack into a register pair, the byte pointed to by the stack pointer is loaded into the LOW byte of the register pair. The stack pointer is then incremented to point to the data that is loaded into the HIGH byte of the register pair. Finally, the stack pointer is incremented again.

EXAMPLE: Suppose that the stack pointer contains 097FH, address 097FH contains D6H, and 0980H contains 05H. If the stack is popped into register pair HL, what will be the contents of H, L, and the stack pointer?

SOLUTION: The byte pointed to by the stack pointer will be loaded into the L register. L contains D6H. The stack pointer is incremented: SP = 0980. The contents of 0980 are loaded into the H register. H contains 05H. The stack pointer is incremented again: SP = 0981.

L contains D6H
H contains 05H
SP contains 0981H

Figure 7–4 contains the op codes of the PUSH and POP instructions. The contents of register pairs AF, BC, DE, HL, IX, or IY can be pushed onto or popped from the stack.

PUSH and POP instructions will be used to write a subroutine that is transparent to the main program. (The data in all registers will be the same upon returning from the subroutine, as they were when the subroutine was called.)

EXAMPLE: In the last example in Section 7.1, rewrite the subroutine beginning at address 0820 so that it is transparent to the main program.

SOLUTION: Register B is the only register used in this subroutine. First, push pair BC onto the stack. Pop BC just before returning.

```
0820                          ORG     0820H
0820 C5                       PUSH    BC
0821 060A                     LD      B,0AH
0823 CDE400     LOOP:         CALL    00E4H
0826 10FB                     DJNZ    LOOP
0828 C1                       POP     BC
0829 C9                       RET
082A 76                       HALT
0000                          END
```

The time-delay subroutine beginning at address 00E4H is transparent.

EXAMPLE: Use your trainer to read the contents of ROM beginning at 00E4H. Explain why the subroutine is considered transparent.

SOLUTION: By entering REBOOT, 00, H, E4, L and stepping through the program, we obtain the following op codes:

```
E5        PUSH HL
21DB05    LD HL,05DB
2D        DEC L
20FD      JR NZ,FD
25        DEC H
20FA      JR NZ,FA
E1        POP HL
00        NOP
C9        RET
```

The only registers used in the subroutine are H and L. The HL pair is pushed at the beginning and popped just before return. The original contents of HL are not disturbed.

			SOURCE						
			REGISTER						
			AF	BC	DE	HL	SP	IX	IY
PUSH INSTRUCTIONS →	REG. IND.	(SP)	F5	C5	D5	E5		DD E5	FD E5

NOTE: The Push and Pop Instructions adjust the SP after every execution.

			REG. INDIR.
			(SP)
DESTINATION	REGISTER	AF	F1
		BC	C1
		DE	D1
		HL	E1
		SP	
		IX	DD E1
		IY	FD E1

↑ POP INSTRUCTIONS

FIGURE 7–4 PUSH and POP op codes

7.3 INTERRUPTS AND RESTARTS

An external or peripheral device that needs servicing can signal the Z 80 for an interrupt. When the Z 80 responds, it issues an $\overline{\text{IORQ}}$, an $\overline{\text{RD}}$, and an $\overline{\text{MI}}$ signal. These signals are used to place an instruction on the data bus. That instruction usually leads the CPU to the location of the start of an interrupt subroutine. The subroutine is designed to service the needs of the peripheral device. The interrupt subroutine ends with a RETURN FROM INTERRUPT instruction that directs the CPU back to the main program, where it resumes operation from the point at which it was interrupted.

There are two general types of interrupts: maskable and nonmaskable. The nonmaskable interrupt (NMI) cannot be disabled by the programmer. Whenever an NMI is called for, the Z 80 finishes the instruction that it is executing and takes its next instruction from location 0066H. An NMI is signaled for on pin 17 of the Z 80. In our trainer, NMI is generated by the reboot circuit shown in Figure 7–5.

When the REBOOT button is pressed, the capacitor is discharged. While it is charging through the zero range, the output of the Schmitt trigger inverter, IC4, is HIGH and the output of the 7406 inverter is LOW. This provides the active low NMI signal.

The next instruction is taken from 0066H which is the start of the monitor routine stored in ROM. It causes the HIGH byte of the first location in RAM, 08, to be displayed in port 00, the LOW byte, 00, to be displayed in port 01, and the contents of that address to be displayed in port 02. It scans the keypad for input, either a hex digit or one of the commands H, L, S, or RUN.

An NMI might be used to signal the Z 80 that the level of liquid in a reservoir has fallen too low. The subroutine that is called might start a pump to correct the situation.

The maskable interrupt, INT, can be enabled or disabled by the programmer. The

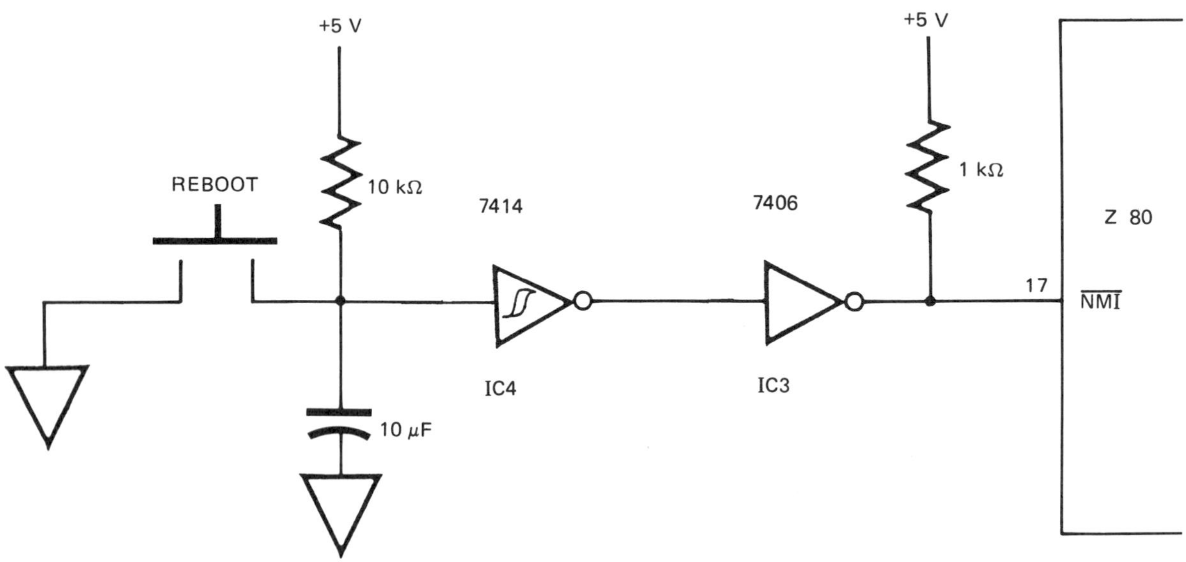

FIGURE 7–5 Reboot circuit

Op code	Op code Format	LOW Byte	Mnemonic Code
C7	11 000 111	00H	RST 00H
CF	11 001 111	08H	RST 08H
D7	11 010 111	10H	RST 10H
DF	11 011 111	18H	RST 18H
E7	11 100 111	20H	RST 20H
EF	11 101 111	28H	RST 28H
F7	11 110 111	30H	RST 30H
FF	11 111 111	38H	RST 38H

FIGURE 7–6 RESTART instructions

instruction DISABLE INTERRUPT (DI) resets the interrupt flip-flop (IFF). While reset, all maskable interrupts are ignored. The op code for DI is F3H.

IFF can be set with the instruction ENABLE INTERRUPT (EI). The op code for EI is FBH. While set, the CPU can respond to three different modes of maskable interrupts: modes 0, 1, and 2. Once the CPU responds to an interrupt request, the IFF is reset. The programmer must issue another EI instruction before the CPU will accept another interrupt. This is usually done just before returning from the interrupt subroutine. The Z 80 automatically enters mode 0 after a reset (reboot).

The system can be set to interrupt mode 0 with the instruction IM0, op code ED46H. In mode 0 the Z 80 responds to interrupts exactly the way that the 8080 does. The CPU issues $\overline{\text{IORQ}}$, $\overline{\text{RD}}$, and $\overline{\text{M1}}$ signals. These signals ORed together produce an interrupt acknowledge signal, $\overline{\text{INTACK}}$. $\overline{\text{INTACK}}$ can be used to enable tri-state gates that pass eight bits onto the data bus. That byte is the op code of the next instruction to be executed. Although it can be any 1-byte instruction, it often is a RESTART (RST) instruction. There are eight RESTART instructions. Each causes the CPU to jump to a specific memory location in the zero page of ROM to obtain the next instruction. Zero page implies that the HIGH byte is 00H. The LOW byte can vary, as shown in Figure 7–6. The op codes for the RESTART instructions are of the form lltttlll, where ttt is the 3-bit code shown in Figure 7–6.

When an RST instruction is implemented, the program counter contents are pushed onto the stack. The program counter is then loaded with 00P, where P is the LOW byte of the address called by the RST instruction. The address 00P often contains a JUMP instruction to a location in RAM where more room is available for an interrupt and where the program can be changed at will.

RETURN FROM INTERRUPT (RETI) causes the address that was pushed onto the stack to be popped back into the program counter so that the program can continue from where it left off. The op code for RETI is ED4DH.

EXAMPLE: The program beginning at 0800H is run. What will be the effect on the accumulator? What will happen when an interrupt is called for and op code D7H is placed on the data bus? What will happen when an interrupt is called for and the instruction RST 20H is placed on the data bus?

```
0010                    ORG     0010H
0010 C31008             JP      0810H
0020                    ORG     0020H
0020 C32008             JP      0820H
0800                    ORG     0800H
0800 97        START:   SUB     A          ;START OF MAIN PROGRAM
0801 37                 SCF                ;TO SHIFT LIGHTS LEFT
0802 FB                 EI                 ;ENABLE IFF
0803 CB17      RLEFT:   RL A               ;ROTATE LEFT
0805 D300               OUT     (00H),A    ;OUT A TO 00H
0807 CD2508             CALL    0825H      ;DELAY 100 MILLISECONDS
080A 18F7               JR      RLEFT      ;JUMP TO ROTATE LEFT
0810                    ORG     0810H      ;START OF INTERRUPT
0810 0604               LD      B,04H      ;SUBROUTINE TO SHIFT
0812 CB1F      RRIGHT:  RR      A          ;LIGHT RIGHT
0814 D300               OUT     (00H),A    ;FOUR SPACES
0816 CD2508             CALL    0825H      ;DELAY 100 MILLISECONDS
0819 10F7               DJNZ    RRIGHT     ;REPEAT UNTIL B=0
081B FB                 EI                 ;ENABLE INTERRUPT
081C ED4D               RETI
0820                    ORG     0820H      ;START OF INTERRUPT
0820 97                 SUB     A          ;SUBROUTINE TO MAKE
0821 37                 SCF                ;LIGHT START OVER
0822 FB                 EI                 ;ENABLE INTERRUPT
0823 ED4D               RETI
0825 C5                 PUSH BC            ;START OF TIME DELAY
0826 060A               LD      B,0AH      ;SUBROUTINE  100 MS
0828 CDE400    LOOP:    CALL    00E4H
082B 10FB               DJNZ    LOOP
082D C1                 POP     BC
082E C9                 RET
0000                    END
```

SOLUTION:

0800	The accumulator is cleared.
0801	Carry flag = 1.
0802	Interrupt FF is enabled.
0803	After rotate left, ACC = 01H.
0805	01H is output to port 00.
0807	Time-delay subroutine is called.
080A	Jump back to RL A.

One lit LED continuously shifts left through output port 00. Port 00 is blank as the "1" shifts through the carry flag.

Since the IFF is enabled, when an interrupt is called for and D7H is placed on the data bus, D7H will be taken as the op code of the next instruction. D7H is a RESTART instruction that directs the CPU to address 0010H for the next instruction. The instruction there is jump to 0810H.

0810	B is loaded with 04H to set up a counter.
0812	The accumulator is rotated right.
0814	Accumulator to port 00.

0816	Time-delay subroutine is called.
0819	B is decremented. If B $\neq$ 0, a jump is made back up to rotate right, 0812.
081B	The interrupt flag is enabled to allow further interrupts.
081C	Return to main program.

As a result of this interrupt, the lit LED was shifted to the right four times. Since the IFF was enabled at the end of the last interrupt subroutine, the CPU will allow another interrupt. If RST 20H, op code E7, is placed on the data bus, the CPU will jump to 0020H for the next instruction. In this program, that instruction is JP 0820H. The subroutine at 0820H clears the accumulator and sets the carry flag. The IFF is enabled and the return causes the next instruction to be taken from the main program. In summary, the main program causes the lit LED to shift left. D7H causes the lit LED to shift right four times. E7H causes the shift sequence to start from 00 again.

Figure 7–7 shows the hardware required to implement the interrupts of the last example. Switch 0 is pressed to call for interrupt 0. A clock pulse is generated that turns on 7476(A) (J = 1 and K = 0). When $\overline{Q}$ goes low, the output of NAND gate 1 on set/reset flip-flop 3 goes high. The flip-flop remains in that state until a different interrupt is signalled for. The 1 is inverted to a 0 and enables OR gate 3. $\overline{Q}$ also generates the $\overline{INT}$ signal at AND gate 1 that calls for an interrupt at pin 16 of the Z 80. Since IFF has been set by the program, the Z 80 responds to the $\overline{INT}$ by generating $\overline{IOREQ}$, $\overline{RD}$, and $\overline{M1}$. These are ORed together with OR gates 1 and 2 to make interrupt acknowledge ($\overline{INTACK}$). With flip-flop A on and $\overline{INTACK}$ present, the output of OR gate 3 goes LOW and enables 74LS245/1. With the direction input (pin 1) tied HIGH, data passes from pin 2 to pin 18, and so on. The op code D7H is passed through to the data bus. As discussed in the example, this causes the lit LED to shift right four times.

$\overline{INTACK}$ causes the output of AND gate 2 to be 0, which resets (clears) 7476A. Once the instruction has been read by the Z 80, $\overline{INTACK}$ goes high, and the 74LS245/1 returns to its HiZ state. The reset, pin 26 of the Z 80, is fed into AND gate 2 to insure that both 7476(A) and 7476(B) are reset upon power-up. To implement reset 20H, press switch 1. Only one of the switches can be pressed at one time.

The IM1 instruction, op code ED56H, causes the CPU to operate in interrupt mode 1. In this mode the CPU responds to an interrupt by executing a restart to location 0038H. That is, the next instruction is taken from 0038H. In our trainer the instruction at 0038H is a jump to address 0838H. The next instruction is taken from that address.

The IM2 instruction, op code ED5EH, causes the CPU to operate in interrupt mode 2. Mode 2 is the most versatile of the three interrupt modes. A table of starting addresses is formed in RAM. The HIGH byte of the address of the table is loaded into the I register using the LD I,A instruction. The LOW byte of the address in the table is supplied at the time of interrupt by the interrupting device. The LOW byte is placed on the data bus in response to an interrupt acknowledge signal. That address formed points to a location in the table that contains the LOW byte of the starting address of the interrupt subroutine to be used to service the interrupt device. The following byte is the HIGH byte of the starting address. The entries in the table of starting addresses always begin at an even address (least significant bit = 0) and alternate: LOW byte, HIGH byte, and so on.

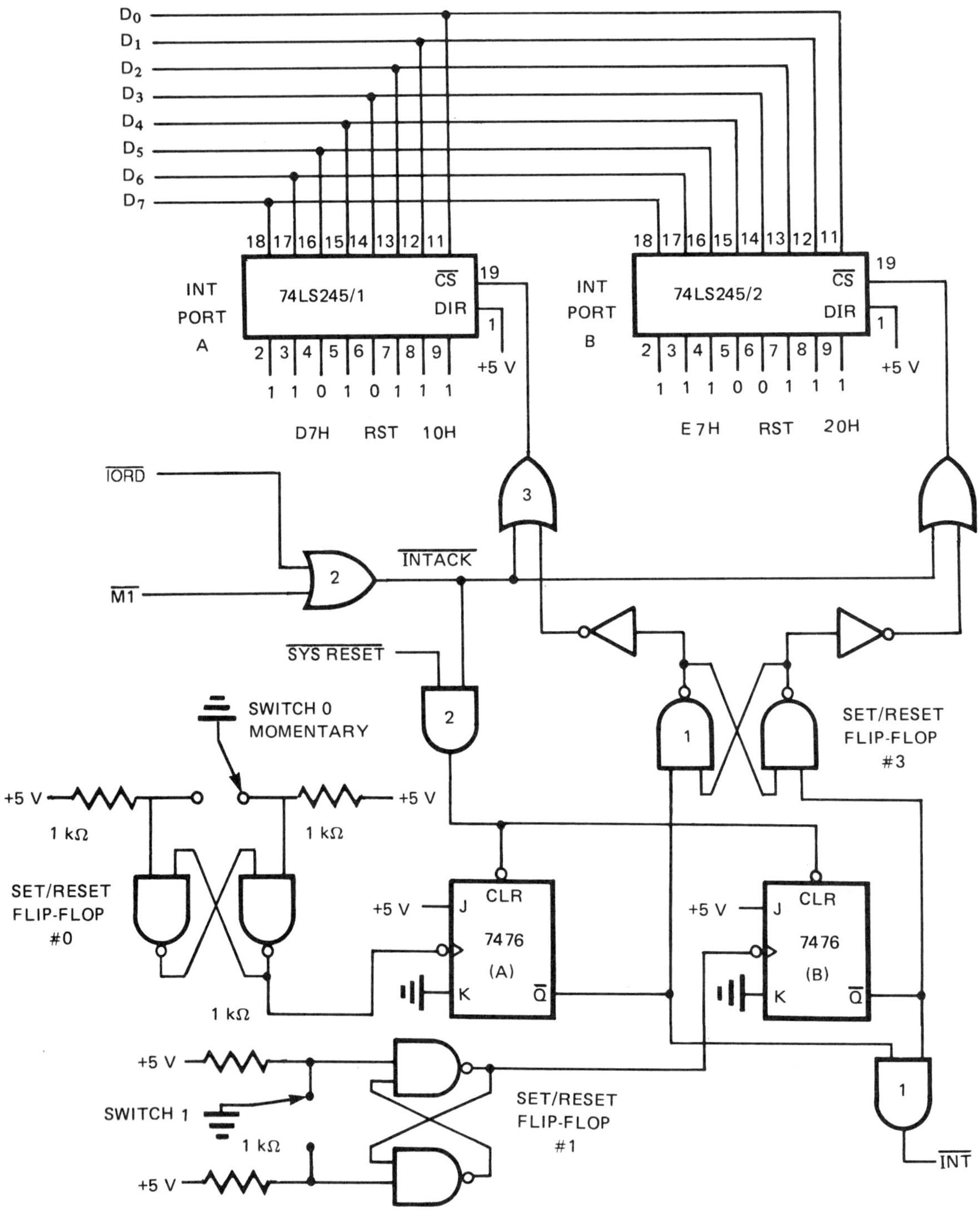

FIGURE 7–7 Mode 0 interrupt hardware

EXAMPLE: Set up a table of starting addresses for mode 2 interrupts that will place interrupt subroutines at 0900, 0920, 0940, and 0960H. Place the table at 0980H.

SOLUTION: Beginning at 0980H the starting address of each interrupt subroutine is listed in LOW byte, HIGH byte order.

Address	Data
0980	00
0981	09
0982	20
0983	09
0984	40
0985	09
0986	60
0987	09

EXAMPLE: What instructions must be included in the program to use the table in the previous example in a mode 2 interrupt scheme?

SOLUTION: The HIGH byte of the location of the table, 09, must be loaded into the I register via the accumulator (LD I,A). The system must be set to mode 2 interrupt (IM2). The interrupt flip-flop must be enabled (EI).

EXAMPLE: In the previous examples, if the I register contains 09H and the interrupting device places 82H on the data bus, what will be the starting address of the interrupt subroutine?

SOLUTION: 0982 becomes a pointer to the table. 0982 contains 20 and 0983 contains 09. The starting address is 0920H.

Once the LOW byte is supplied by the interrupting device, the program counter is pushed onto the stack. The starting address from the table is then loaded into the program counter. When a RETURN from interrupt is reached, the address in the stack is popped back into the program counter.

EXERCISE 7

1. What instruction terminates a subroutine?
2. Name eight conditions upon which a CALL or RET can be based.
3. What is a nested subroutine?
4. If the stack pointer contains 0950H and HL is pushed onto the stack, where will H be stored? Where will L be stored?
5. If the stack pointer contains 0C00H and the accumulator and flags register are pushed onto the stack, where will the accumulator be stored? Where will the flags be stored?
6. If the stack pointer contains 0A0AH and POP DE is implemented, what address will be the source of data for D? for E?

7. If the stack pointer contains 09FFH and POP AF is implemented, what address will be the source of data for A? for F?
8. Name two general categories of interrupts.
9. Name three types of maskable interrupts.
10. When the Z 80 is reset, into what interrupt mode does it enter?
11. What instruction allows the Z 80 to process a maskable interrupt?
12. What instruction prohibits maskable interrupts from being implemented?
13. When a mode 0 interrupt is called for, from where is the next instruction taken?
14. When a mode 1 interrupt is called for, from where is the next instruction taken?
15. When a mode 2 interrupt is called for, from where is the next instruction taken?
16. Which interrupt mode makes use of RESTART instructions?
17. List the RESTART instructions and the addresses they call out.
18. In Figure 7–7, is flip-flop B set or cleared when switch 1 is pushed?
19. In Figure 7–7, what is the output of AND gate 1 when switch 1 is pressed?
20. In Figure 7–7, flip-flops A and B must be off initially for this scheme to work. How do we know they will be off until an interrupt is called for?
21. In Figure 7–7, what conditions must exist for the 74LS245/2 to be enabled?
22. In Figure 7–7, how can the schematic be modified to implement an instruction at address 0030H when switch 1 is pressed?

Lab 7

OBJECTIVES

After completing this lab, you should be able to

- use subroutines in programming.
- use PUSH and POP instructions to produce a transparent subroutine.
- produce time delay that is a multiple of 10 ms.
- use interrupts.

Procedure

1. Enter the program in the last example of Section 7.1. Run the program and observe the time delay. Initialize B with different values and observe the effect when the program is run. Summarize your results.
2. The circuit in Figure 7-7 will be used in conjunction with the program in the first example in Section 7.3. Port A will be used to place the op code D7H (RST 10H) on the data bus for an interrupt, and port B will be used to place the op code E7H (RST 20H) on the data bus. Enter and run the program. Summarize your results.
3. Write a program that will have the following effect on the LEDs. Light the MSB of port 00H and the LSB of port 01H. After a 100-ms delay, shift port 00H right and port 01H left. Continue until the LEDs meet in the middle (LSB of port 00 lit and MSB of port 01 lit). After a delay, reverse the process so that the lights diverge. Run the program in a loop so that the LEDs continuously shift in and out.
4. Write a transparent subroutine that will output the contents of the accumulator to port 00H and the contents of the flags register to port 01H.

Chapter 8

PROGRAMMING METHODS AND THE OPERATING SYSTEM

OBJECTIVES

After completing this chapter, you should be able to

- describe the Biggy trainer operating system.
- develop the tools to write complex assembly or machine level programs.
- write timing loop programs for a precise delay.
- explain how to use a voltmeter scope and logic probe to test and troubleshoot computer equipment.
- explain the operation and use of CPU emulators.
- explain the operation and use of logic analyzers.
- describe and use typical software methods of debugging and troubleshoot computer hardware.

8.1 THE PROGRAM

The program is the fuel that gives the computer hardware its power. Good programs can do very powerful things very quickly, and bad programs can make a fast and potentially powerful computer act like a turtle. The following three things will enable you to program any computer:

1. Understand the instruction set of the CPU.
2. Be able to read and write to the computer's memory.
3. Start a program at any point in memory you desire.

If you can do these three things with a computer, you can control it.

There are five basic steps to writing a computer program that apply even if you are using a higher-level language such as BASIC or FORTRAN. They are:

1. Define the operations you wish the computer to do.
2. Derive a system or method that the computer can use to perform the operation you defined in number 1.
3. Sequence the system or method of number 2 into an orderly procedure and draw a flowchart to define the order in which the operations are to take place.

4. Write a computer program to accomplish each part of the flowchart and put each program together in an appropriate place in the computer's memory.
5. Test the program and debug it. Very few—and this means *very few*—programs work perfectly when first run.

We will use these five basic steps to build the Biggy trainer operating system and, by doing so, learn some basic methods of good computer programming.

8.2 DEFINING THE PROBLEM

When the hardware for the Biggy trainer was designed, provisions were made for the CPU to be able to display binary numbers to the operator by using the three output ports 00H, 01H, and 02H, which each have eight LEDs. The input was provided for with a single input port (00H) that was connected to a multiplexed keyboard. The selects of the multiplexer inputs were controlled by a 4-bit output port (03H).

This then is the basic computer hardware with which the program has to operate. The first step in writing the operating system is to define the basic goals of the program. They are as follows:

Goal 1: Be able to read and write to any memory location in the computer.
Goal 2: Be able to start the execution of a program at any place in memory.
Goal 3: Provide for interrupts to a RAM location.

These are very broad goals, so we will break each part into smaller parts which will better define them.

Goal 1

A. Port 0 will display the most significant byte of the current address.

B. Port 1 will display the least significant byte of the current address.

C. Port 2 will display the contents of the memory address that is displayed on ports 0 and 1 until a Hex key is pressed, at which time port 2 will display the Hex key as follows: When a Hex key is pressed, the byte displayed on port 2 will be shifted four places to the left and the value of the Hex key pressed will be placed on the least significant four bits of port 2.

D. When the H key is pressed, the byte displayed on port 2 will be transferred to port 0, and port 2 will then display the contents of the new address displayed on ports 0 and 1.

E. When the L key is pressed, the byte displayed on port 2 will be transferred to port 1, and the contents of the new address displayed on ports 0 and 1 will be displayed on port 2.

F. When the shift key is pressed, the byte displayed on port 2 will be stored or written to the memory location whose address is displayed on ports 0 and 1. Then the address displayed on ports 0 and 1 will be incremented by 1, and the content of the new address displayed on ports 0 and 1 will be displayed on port 2.

G. When the computer is rebooted or has power applied to it, the address displayed on ports 0 and 1 will be the first address of usable RAM (0800H) in the computer, and the byte displayed on port 2 will be the content of that memory location.

Goal 2

When the RUN button is pressed, the CPU will start execution of the instructions in memory, starting at the address displayed on ports 0 and 1.

Goal 3

Jumps will be made to locations in usable RAM for as many restart call to subroutine instructions as feasible.

8.3 DERIVING A METHOD FOR ACCOMPLISHING THE PROBLEM

To accomplish the goals set forth in Section 8.2, we must consider what we have in computer hardware and the innate CPU instruction set. A list of what is to be accomplished, and a simple method of accomplishing it will help.

1. The program must start at address 0000H and 0066H so that the power on reset and nonmaskable interrupts can start the program.
2. The program must reside in ROM so it will not be lost when power is turned off. This means that the contents of the program cannot be changed.
3. Room must be left for unconditional jumps to RAM locations for the restart call to subroutine instructions.
4. When the program starts, necessary tasks such as loading the stack pointer and displaying the proper address on ports 0 and 1 must be done first.
5. The keyboard must be scanned and the pressed key returned. The keyboard must also be debounced.
6. The value of the pressed key must be determined and acted upon.
7. If a Hex key is pressed, a routine to shift port 2 and display the key must be used.
8. If the key pressed is the H or L key, a routine to transfer the byte displayed on port 2 to ports 0 or 1 must be executed.
9. If the key pressed is the shift key, then a routine to implement this key must be executed.
10. If the run button is pressed, then the program counter must be loaded with the address displayed on ports 0 and 1.

8.4 THE FLOWCHART

A flowchart is a graphic method of showing the sequence of the operations that make up a program. There are three basic symbols used in a flowchart, as shown in Figure 8–1.

When you put your steps into a flowchart, remember that these steps will eventually

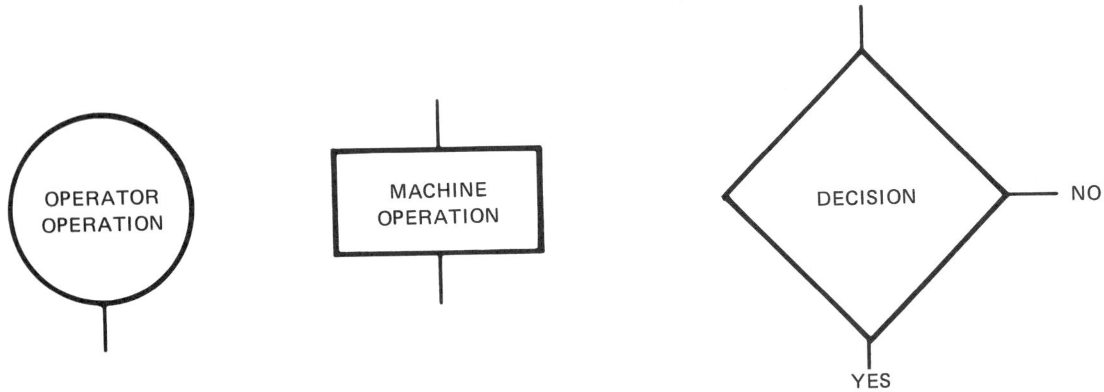

FIGURE 8–1

become small machine language programs, so don't make them too large or too hard to accomplish in machine language.

This part of the process of writing a program is often the hardest, and it may demand a great deal of trial and error as well as creativity. You may start down a road just to see that you have boxed yourself in at the end and have to start over again.

A routine, which is the same or very similar, that you find yourself doing over and over again should become a subroutine. Subroutines should also be used for parts of the program that you may see a need to use as a part of a later program. Figures 8–2 and 8–3 show the flowchart for the Biggy trainer operating system.

8.5 WRITING THE ASSEMBLY OR MACHINE LANGUAGE PROGRAMS FOR THE PARTS OF THE FLOWCHART

An assembler was used to write the final program shown in Figure 8–4. The use of an assembler is much preferred to hand assembly of op codes because the assembly program will check for common errors in coding, and you can easily edit the code if needed. It is also much faster.

360–430	Lines 360 to 430 equate labels used through the program to real Hex values.
460	Line 460 originates or starts the program at 0000 Hex.
470	Line 470 jumps to the start of the operating system, and lines 480–610 set up jump to RAM for the restart call to subroutine instructions. These jumps will allow us to use all but RST 0 for interrupts later on.
630	Line 630 sets the stack pointer to one byte past the last memory location in RAM (0C00H).

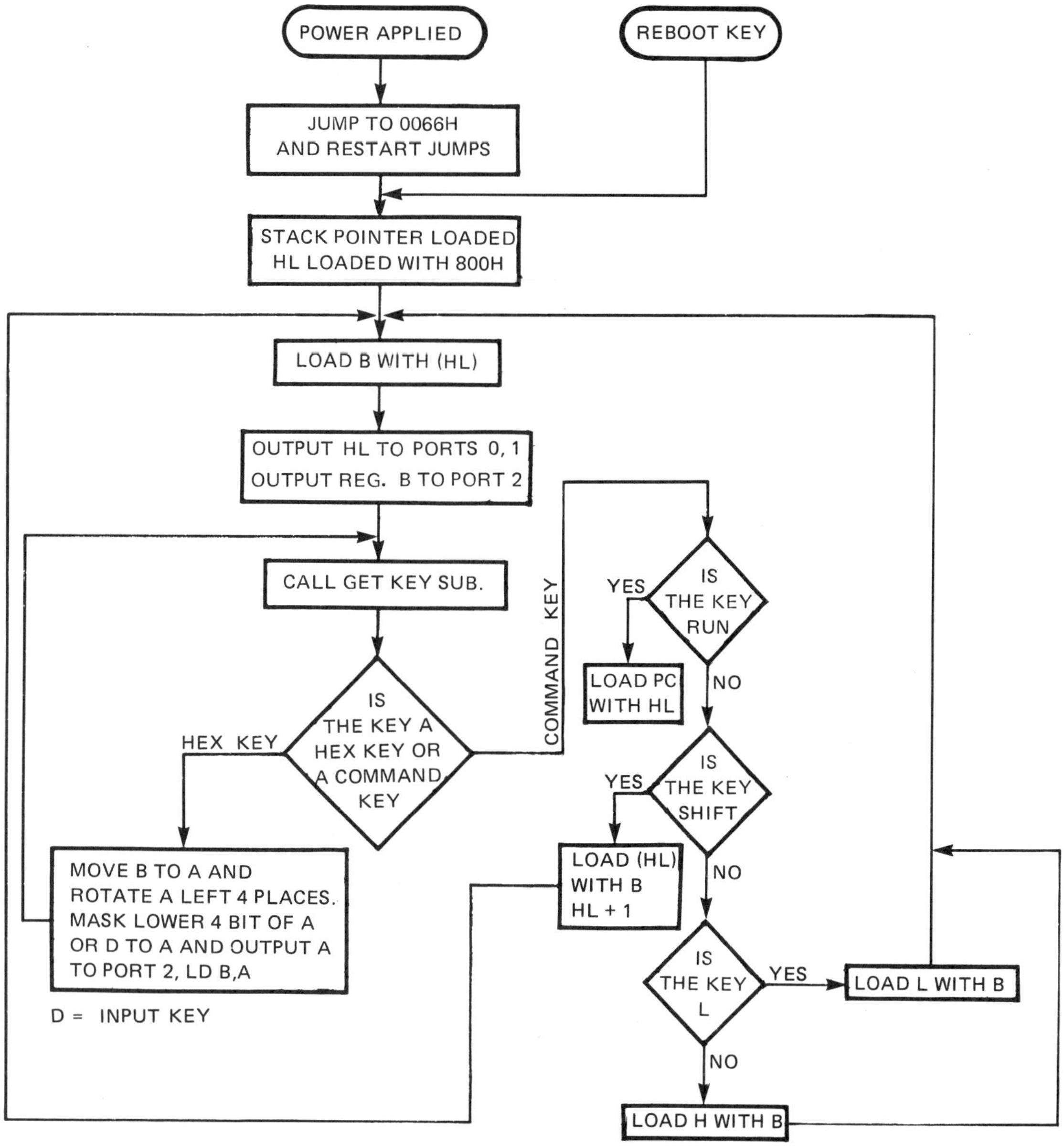

FIGURE 8–2 Biggy trainer operating system flowchart

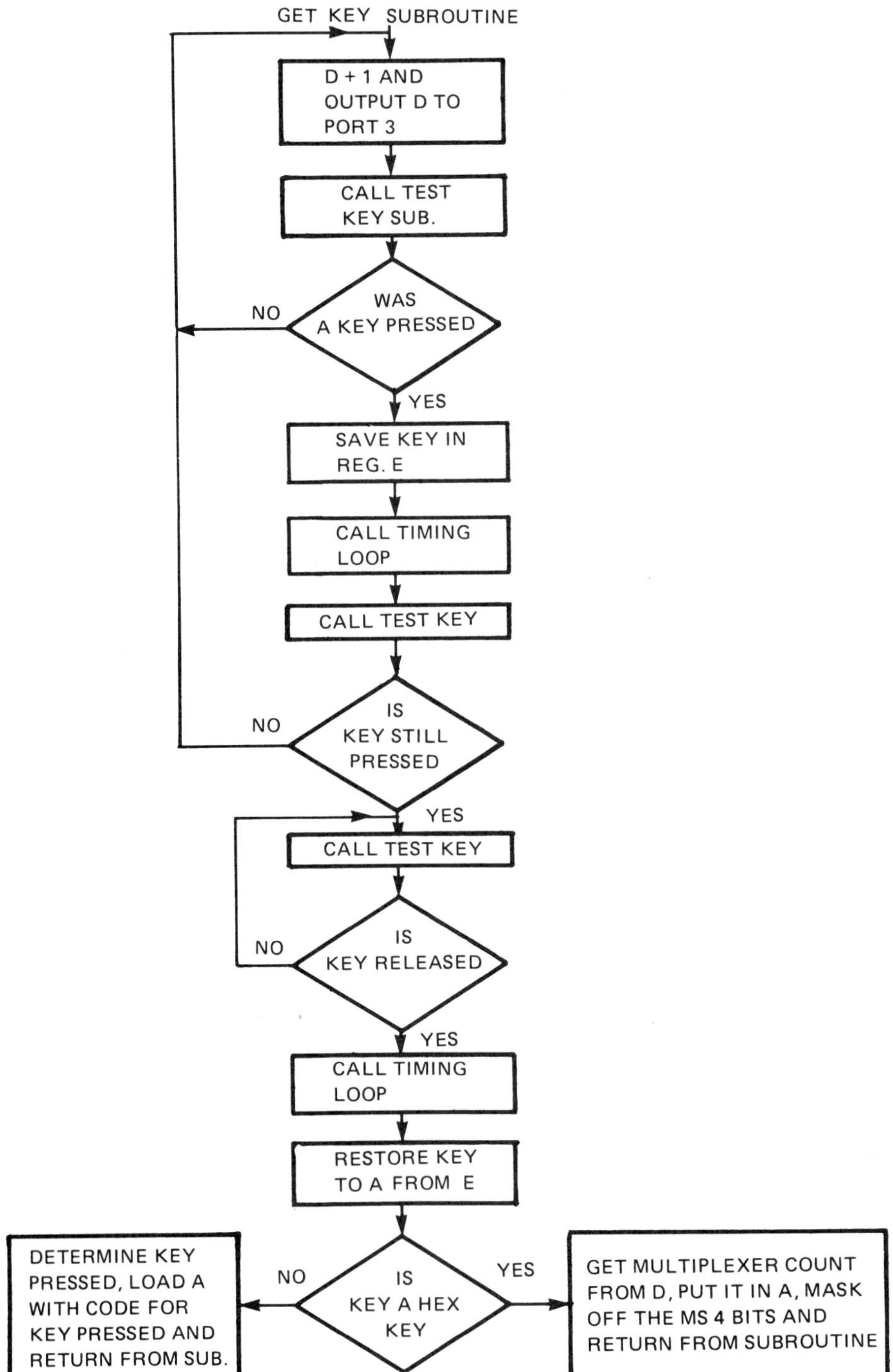
GET KEY SUBROUTINE
D + 1 AND OUTPUT D TO PORT 3
CALL TEST KEY SUB.
WAS A KEY PRESSED
NO
YES
SAVE KEY IN REG. E
CALL TIMING LOOP
CALL TEST KEY
IS KEY STILL PRESSED
NO
YES
CALL TEST KEY
IS KEY RELEASED
NO
YES
CALL TIMING LOOP
RESTORE KEY TO A FROM E
IS KEY A HEX KEY
NO
YES
DETERMINE KEY PRESSED, LOAD A WITH CODE FOR KEY PRESSED AND RETURN FROM SUB.
GET MULTIPLEXER COUNT FROM D, PUT IT IN A, MASK OFF THE MS 4 BITS AND RETURN FROM SUBROUTINE

FIGURE 8–3

```
             ;*****************************************************
             ;*      THE BIGGY TRAINER OPERATING SYSTEM           *
             ;*****************************************************
             ;
             ;
             ;
             ;            KEY DEFINITIONS
             ;
             ; 0 THROUGH F -  PRODUCES THE HEX VALUE FOR INPUT
             ; H   --  MOVES THE BYTE DISPLAYED ON PORT 2 TO PORT 0
             ;         WHICH IS THE HIGH BYTE OF THE ADDRESS
             ; L   --  MOVES THE BYTE DISPLAYED ON PORT 2 TO PORT 1
             ;         WHICH IS THE LOW BYTE OF THE ADDRESS
             ; S   --  STORES THE BYTE DISPLAYED ON PORT 2 IN THE
             ;         MEMORY LOCATION OF THE ADDRESS DISPLAYED ON
             ;         PORTS 0 AND 1 THEN INCREMENTS THE ADDRESS
             ;         DISPLAYED ON PORTS 0 AND 1 AND DISPLAYS THE
             ;         CONTENT OF THE NEW ADDRESS DISPLAYED ON
             ;         PORTS 0 AND 1
             ; RUN --  STARTS THE CPU EXECUTING INSTRUCTIONS AT THE
             ;         ADDRESS DISPLAYED ON PORTS 0 AND 1
             ;REBOOT-  REBOOTS THE COMPUTER VIA THE NONMASKABLE
             ;         INTERRUPT AND DISPLAYS 08 00 XX ON PORTS 0 1  2
             ;
             ;
             ;
0800         RAMSTA  EQU     800H             ;FIRST RAM BYTE
0BFF         RAMEND  EQU     0BFFH            ;LAST RAM BYTE
0000         OUT0    EQU     000H             ;ADD. OF OUTPUT PORT 0
0001         OUT1    EQU     001H             ;ADD. OF OUTPUT PORT 1
0002         OUT2    EQU     002H             ;ADD. OF OUTPUT PORT 2
0003         OUT3    EQU     003H             ;ADD. OF OUTPUT PORT 3
0000         IN0     EQU     000H             ;ADD. OF INPUT PORT 0
0066         REBOOT  EQU     66H              ;ADD. OF NMI RESTART
             ;
             ;
0000                 ORG     000H             ;START OF PROGRAM
0000 C36600  START   JP      REBOOT           ;JUMP TO BEGINNING
0008                 ORG     08H              ;ADD OR RST 08 INSTR.
0008 C30808          JP      808H             ;JUMP TO RAM LOCATION
0010                 ORG     010H             ;ADD OF RST 10 INSTR.
0010 C31008          JP      810H             ;JUMP TO RAM LOCATION
0018                 ORG     018H             ;ADD OF RST 18 INSTR.
0018 C31808          JP      818H             ;JUMP TO RAM LOCATION
0020                 ORG     020H             ;ADD. OF RST 20 INSTR.
0020 C32008          JP      820H             ;JUMP TO RAM LOCATION
0028                 ORG     028H             ;ADD. OF RST 28 INSTR.
0028 C32808          JP      828H             ;JUMP TO RAM LOCATION
0030                 ORG     30H              ;ADD. OF RST 30 INSTR.
0030 C33008          JP      830H             ;JUMP TO RAM LOCATION
0038                 ORG     038H             ;ADD. OF RST 38 INSTR.
0038 C33808          JP      0838H            ;JUMP TO RAM LOCATION
0066                 ORG     066H             ;BEGINNING OF OP. SYSTEM
0066 31000C          LD      SP,RAMEND+1      ;ADD OF STACK POINTER
0069 210008          LD      HL,RAMSTA        ;ADDRESS OF FIRST BYTE
006C 0E00    LOOP1   LD      C,OUT0           ;ADD. OF HIGH BYTE OF ADD
006E 46              LD      B,(HL)           ;GET CONTENT OF ADD IN HL
006F ED61            OUT     (C),H            ;OUTPUT H TO PORT 0
0071 0C              INC     C                ;INC. C TO PORT 1 ADDRESS
0072 ED69            OUT     (C),L            ;OUTPUT L TO PORT 1
0074 0C              INC     C                ;INC. C TO PORT 2 ADDRESS
0075 ED41            OUT     (C),B            ;OUTPUT CONTENT OF HL
0077 CDA300  LOOP    CALL    GETKEY           ;CALL GETKEY SUBROUTINE
```

FIGURE 8–4

```
007A CB67               BIT     4,A             ;BIT 4 TEST FOR COMMAND
007C 200E               JR      NZ,INTERP       ;JUMP TO INTERPRETER
007E 57                 LD      D,A             ;STORE HEX DIGIT
007F 78                 LD      A,B             ;GET STORED BYTE
0080 07                 RLCA                    ;ROTATE LEFT 4 BITS
0081 07                 RLCA
0082 07                 RLCA
0083 07                 RLCA
0084 E6F0               AND     0F0H            ;MASK OFF LS 4 BITS
                ;                               TO ADD NEW HEX DIGIT
0086 B2                 OR      D               ;OR HEX DIGIT TO BYTE
0087 47                 LD      B,A             ;STORE BYTE IN REG. B
0088 D302               OUT     (OUT2),A        ;DISPLAY NEW BYTE
008A 18EB               JR      LOOP            ;DO AGAIN
008C FE13       INTERP  CP      13H             ;TEST FOR GO KEY
008E 2812               JR      Z,GO            ;JUMP TO GO ROUTINE
0090 FE12               CP      12H             ;TEST FOR STEP KEY
0092 2807               JR      Z,STEP          ;JUMP TO STEP ROUTINE
0094 FE11               CP      11H             ;TEST FOR LOW KEY
0096 2807               JR      Z,LOW           ;JUMP TO LOW ROUTINE
0098 60                 LD      H,B             ;NEW BYTE TO H REGISTER
0099 18D1               JR      LOOP1           ;DO AGAIN
009B 70         STEP    LD      (HL),B          ;PUT BYTE IN MEMORY
009C 23                 INC     HL              ;BUMP BYTE POINTER BY 1
009D 18CD               JR      LOOP1           ;JUMP TO OUTPUT NEW ADD
009F 68         LOW     LD      L,B             ;MOVE BYTE TO REG. L
00A0 18CA               JR      LOOP1           ;JUMP TO OUTPUT NEW ADD
00A2 E9         GO      JP      (HL)            ;START PROGRAM AT ADD. HL
                ;
                ;       *****************************************
                ;       *    GETKEY SUBROUTINE                  *
                ;       *****************************************
                ;
                ;THIS SUBROUTINE WILL FETCH AND DEBOUNCE A PRESSED KEY
                ;FROM THE KEYBOARD
                ;
00A3 14         GETKEY  INC     D               ;ADD 1 TO REGISTER D
00A4 7A                 LD      A,D             ;MOVE D TO A TO OUTPUT IT
00A5 D303               OUT     (OUT3),A        ;D TO KEYBOARD MUX.
00A7 CDDD00             CALL    TESKEY          ;TEST FOR VALID KEY
00AA 28F7               JR      Z,GETKEY        ;DO OVER IF NO KEY PUSHED
00AC 5F                 LD      E,A             ;SAVE KEY PRESSED
00AD CDE400             CALL    TIME            ;PAUSE TO DEBOUNCE KEY
00B0 CDDD00             CALL    TESKEY          ;IS KEY STILL PRESSED
00B3 28EE               JR      Z,GETKEY        ;DO OVER IF NOT PRESSED
00B5 CDDD00     LOOP2   CALL    TESKEY          ;WAIT FOR KEY TO BE LET
00B8 20FB               JR      NZ,LOOP2        ;UP
00BA CDE400             CALL    TIME            ;PAUSE TO DEBOUNCE KEY
00BD 7B                 LD      A,E             ;RESTORE KEY TO A REG.
00BE 17                 RLA                     ;TEST FOR A HEX KEY
00BF 380C               JR      C,HEX           ;JUMP TO PRODUCE HEX KEY
00C1 17                 RLA                     ;TEST FOR HIGH KEY
00C2 300D               JR      NC,HIGH
00C4 17                 RLA                     ;TEST FOR LOW KEY
00C5 300D               JR      NC,LOW1
00C7 17                 RLA                     ;TEST FOR STEP KEY
00C8 300D               JR      NC,STEP1
00CA 17                 RLA                             ;TEST FOR GO KEY
00CB 300D               JR      NC,GO1
00CD 7A         HEX     LD      A,D             ;GET THE HEX COUNT
00CE E60F               AND     0FH             ;MASK OFF THE 4 MS BITS
00D0 C9                 RET
00D1 3E10       HIGH    LD      A,10H           ;16 BASE 10 OR HIGH CODE
```

FIGURE 8–4 (cont.)

```
00D3 C9                      RET
00D4 3E11         LOW1       LD       A,11H             ;17 BASE 10 OR LOW CODE
00D6 C9                      RET
00D7 3E12         STEP1      LD       A,12H             ;18 BASE 10 OR STEP CODE
00D9 C9                      RET
00DA 3E13         GO1        LD       A,13H             ;19 BASE 10 OR GO CODE
00DC C9                      RET
                  ;
                  ;
                  ;          ****************************************
                  ;          *     TEST KEY SUBROUTINE                *
                  ;          ****************************************
                  ;
                  ;THIS SUBROUTINE WILL TEST THE KEYBOARD AND RETURN WITH
                  ;THE ZERO FLAG SET IF NO KEY WAS PRESSED .  THE ZERO FLAG
                  ;WILL BE RESET TO 0 IF A KEY WAS PRESSED.
                  ;
                  ;
00DD DB00         TESKEY     IN       A,(IN0)           ;GET KEYBOARD BYTE
00DF E6F8                    AND      0F8H              ;MASK UNWANTED BITS
00E1 FE78                    CP       78H               ;SET Z IF NO KEY PRESSED
00E3 C9                      RET
                  ;
                  ;
                  ;          **************************************
                  ;          *  10 MILLISECOND TIMING LOOP        *
                  ;          **************************************
                  ;
                  ;THIS SUBROUTINE WILL WASTE 10 MILL SECONDS OF TIME TO
                  ;BE USED ANY PLACE TIME IS NEEDED SUCH AS KEY DEBOUNCE
                  ;
                  ;
00E4 E5           TIME       PUSH     HL                ;SAVE HL
00E5 21DB05                  LD       HL,05DBH          ;LOAD HL WITH TIME COUNT
00E8 2D           LOOP3      DEC      L                 ;FAST COUNTER -1
00E9 20FD                    JR       NZ,LOOP3          ;DO TILL L = 0
00EB 25                      DEC      H                 ;SLOW COUNTER -1
00EC 20FA                    JR       NZ,LOOP3          ;DO TILL H = 0
00EE E1                      POP      HL                ;RESTORE HL
00EF 00                      NOP                        ;ADD 4 CLOCK CYCLES
00F0 C9                      RET
0000                         END
00000 Total Errors

LOOP3   00E8     OUT3     0003
GO1     00DA     OUT2     0002
STEP1   00D7     OUT1     0001
LOW1    00D4     OUT0     0000
HIGH    00D1     RAMEND   0BFF
HEX     00CD     RAMSTA   0800
LOOP2   00B5
TIME    00E4
TESKEY  00DD
LOW     009F
STEP    009B
GO      00A2
INTERP  008C
GETKEY  00A3
LOOP    0077
LOOP1   006C
START   0000
REBOOT  0066
IN0     0000
```

FIGURE 8–4 (cont.)

640	Line 640 sets the HL register pair to the first address in RAM (0800H). HL will always contain the current memory address being displayed.
650–710	Lines 650–710 load B from the memory location pointed to by HL register pair and output B to port 2. This displays the current address and its memory content to the user.
720	Line 720 calls the GETKEY subroutine, which will only return if a key is pressed. The value of the key pressed will be in the A register. A Hex key will be from 0 to FH, H key is 10H, L key is 11H, shift key is 12H, and the RUN button is 13H.
730–740	Lines 730 and 740 test bit 4 of the key pressed to determine if a Hex key or command was pressed. If a command key was pressed, then the program jumps to label INTERP or line 870.
750–860	Lines 750–860 rotate the B register four places to the left and replace the least significant four bits with the Hex key that was just pressed. B is output to port 2. After doing this the program jumps to "loop," which is line 720, where the program looks for a new key.
870–1000	Lines 870–1000 interpret the command key pressed and perform the action that the key indicates. If the key pressed is H, L, or shift, then the program jumps to LOOP 1, where the new address and memory content is displayed. If the key pressed is the RUN button, then the content of the HL register pair is loaded into the program counter. This causes the CPU to jump to memory location contained in HL, which is also displayed on ports 0 and 1.
1090–1200	Lines 1090–1200 scan and debounce the keyboard to determine if a key has been pressed. Debouncing the key closure is done with a 10-ms timing loop. When a key is detected by the TESKEY subroutine, the program waits 10 ms and tests the key again for key closure. If the key is still closed, then the program waits for the key to open back up, then waits an additional 10 ms and continues. This ensures that the key is not bouncing when it is used by the rest of the program.
1210	Line 1210 restores the content of input port 0 that was saved in line 1140 and contains the key definition of the key that was just pressed.
1220–1230	Lines 1220–1230 test bit 7 to determine if the key pressed was a Hex key or a command key. If a Hex key was pressed, then the output of the multiplexer, which is bit 7, would be high. The Hex number of that key would be in the D register because the D register was output to port 3 to select the key on the multiplexer. A HIGH on bit 7 causes the program to jump to label HEX, which is line 1320. A LOW on bit 7 passes the shifted A register on to line 1240.
1240–1420	Lines 1240–1420 determine the type of command key, places the appropriate code for that key in the A register, and then return from subroutine.
1540–1570	Lines 1540–1570 test input port 0 for any key closure and set the Z flag if no key was pressed.
1680–1760	Lines 1680–1760 is the timing loop, which is 10 ms long. The method of setting the time to 10 ms is covered in Section 8.7.

8.6 DEBUGGING THE PROGRAM

Debugging a program that must exist in ROM is no easy job. The main problem with debugging a program such as the Biggy trainer system is that, if it doesn't work, you cannot run the computer to test or debug the program. If you have a good minicomputer or good debugger software for a microcomputer, you can debug the newly written software in that computer before you burn it into an EPROM.

Debugger software allows the user to define the hardware environment in which the program you are going to debug will run. It then simulates running your new program in that hardware environment. This type of software debugger is very powerful and can save a lot of time, but it usually requires a minicomputer such as a VAX 750 and can be quite costly.

The cheaper approach, is to observe the operation of the program after it has been burned into the EPROM and is running in the actual hardware it was designed for. By observing and using test instruments such as a scope and logic analyzer, you can make conclusions about the probable cause of the bug in the program and reprogram the EPROM with the change.

Debugging software requires a thorough knowledge of how the programs work and the hardware environment in which it runs.

8.7 TIMING LOOP

Timing loops are short programs or subroutines that do nothing but take up time. They can be made very precise and as long as needed or as short as four clock cycles of the clock.

The operating system uses a 10-ms timing loop to debounce the keypad. We will examine it and compute the exact time to execute the subroutine. The first step in computing the time it will take to execute a program is to write down each instruction and the number of clock cycles it takes to execute each instruction. This is shown in Figure 8–5.

			Clock Cycles
	CALLTIME		17
Time	Push	HL	11
	LD	HL,05DBH	10
LOOP 3	DEC	L	4
	JR	NZ, LOOP 3	12 for Jump, 7 no Jump
	DEC	H	4
	JR	NZ, LOOP 3	12 for Jump, 7 no Jump
	POP	HL	10
	NOP		4
	RET		10

FIGURE 8–5

The second step is to determine the number of times that each instruction is executed. This requires the programmer to analyze the subroutine's operation and compute the number of times each instruction is executed.

The subroutine of Figure 8–5 has a nested loop that decrements L until L is 0; then it falls past the conditional jump and decrements H. The program then jumps up to DEC L, and the L register is decremented again, but this time L is already 00H, so after L is decremented it will contain FF. This means that L will be decremented 256 times until it once again is equal to 00H, and then H will be decremented again. This will continue until the H register turns to 00H, at which time the program will fall through the conditional jump, POP HL, and then return from subroutine.

The HL register is pushed onto the stack at the very beginning of the program to save its content because it is used in the timing loop. The number that HL is loaded with will determine the length of the timing loop. The first time through the DEC L loop will be for the number of times contained in L. After that, L will be decremented 256 times for each count in the H register.

			CLOCK CYCLES	NUMBER OF TIMES EXECUTED	TOTAL CLOCK CYCLES
	CALL	TIME	17	1	17
TIME	PUSH	HL	11	1	11
	LD	HL,05DBH	10	1	10
LOOP 3	DEC	L	4	L+256(H−1) 219+256(5−1) 1243	4972
	JR	NZ,LOOP 3	12 or 7	[L+256(H−1)]−(5/12)H 1243−2.1 1240.9	14891
	DEC	H	4	H H=5	20
	JR	NZ,LOOP 3	12 or 7	$H-(5/12)=4.58\overline{3}$	55
	POP	HL	10	1	10
	NOP		4	1	4
	RET		10	1	10

TOTAL CLOCK CYCLES ⟶ 20000

TOTAL TIME = (TOTAL CLOCK CYCLES) (Per of clock)
TOTAL TIME = (20 000) (0.5×10^{-6} s)
TOTAL TIME = 10.0000 ms

FIGURE 8–6

Therefore, the instructions in the DEC L loop will be executed L + 256(H-1), because the first time through the DEC L loop will be only the value of the L register.

The JR NZ,LOOP3 instruction has two different clock cycle counts: one for a jump, and one for no jump. Therefore, each time L reaches 00H the cycle count for JR NZ,LOOP3 will be 7, not 12. The count for the instruction is $[L+256(H-1)]-(5/12)H$ because the no jump count is 5/12 less the jump count, and the 7-cycle count happens the number of times contained in the register H.

Examine the program shown in Figure 8–6 and confirm the instruction count. Notice that the call to subroutine is also included in the clock cycle count because it must be executed to make the timing loop run.

The third step is to obtain the total number of clock cycles and multiply it by the time for one clock cycle.

This process can be reversed by dividing the desired time for a timing loop by the timing for one clock cycle to obtain the total cycle count needed to make the desired timing loop. Then the proper values for H and L are computed to give the end total count desired.

8.8 INTRODUCTION TO TESTING DIGITAL COMPUTER HARDWARE

Testing or troubleshooting digital computer hardware is quite different in many ways from testing and troubleshooting analog circuits such as amplifiers or transmitters.

In most cases the actual value of a voltage is unimportant as long as it is in the valid 0 or 1 range. The timing and sequence of the data flow is much more critical in digital circuits than in most analog circuits.

To troubleshoot any circuit, be it analog or digital, you must first understand the theory of the operation of the circuit. This means that you must not only have adequate knowledge of electronics but also have all the information about the circuit, such as the schematics and operation manuals. To try and fix a computer that is down without a schematic is like trying to write in the dark; you are not sure just what you are doing.

Second, fix the inputs of the circuit to known values. For example, if the circuit to be troubleshot is a digital decoder, then place a known binary number on the inputs of the decoder.

Third, after placing a known value on the circuit inputs, test the outputs of the circuit. Based on the value of the inputs, the value of the outputs, and your knowledge of the circuit's operation, make a conclusion as to the possible problem and then proceed to test for that problem. These three steps may seem quite simple, but they are often overlooked when a student tries to fix a circuit.

There are a few things that test technicians will often see in the circuits they get for testing. Power supply shorts can be very hard to find in a newly made printed circuit board that was just run over the wave solder. If the power supply is loaded down, test the ICs for heat. A chip that was placed in backwards will quite often be reversed biased, and it will get hot. A touch will let you k ow if it is hot. Quite often a freshly soldered board will have a fine solder jump across the power supply that is not readily seen by the naked eye. These can be very hard to locate, but you can remove them by placing a very large capacitor (50 000 μF to 100 000 μF) charged to 5 V across the power supply. The capacitor will discharge through the short, producing a very large current at the short point causing it to burn out. Because the capacitor was only charged to 5 V, the ICs will not be affected by this burnout procedure.

Another source of intermittent circuit failure in digital circuits is power supply spikes. These are quite often caused by TTL ICs that do not have despiking capacitors across their power supply pin or an electromagnetic device, such as a relay, with no spike suppressor diode. Intermittent circuit failure can often be caused by input left unconnected, such as JK inputs on flip-flops. This is often a problem with CMOS type ICs.

When testing an IC on a circuit board, put the test probe on the IC's pin, not on the track soldered to the pin. This will detect a cold solder joint at the IC pin.

8.9 EQUIPMENT TO TEST LOGIC AND VOLTAGE LEVEL

The voltage level of digital inputs or outputs can be tested with a variety of test equipment. The voltmeter is probably the best instrument to test the static voltage level of digital inputs or outputs because it gives an indication of the input or output loads by the value of the 1 or 0 voltages. A simple logic probe can show you the logic state 1 or 0 with an LED, but it cannot tell you how close the 1 or 0 is to the limit of the 1 or 0 voltage values for a valid 0 or 1.

Neither the voltmeter nor logic probe can give the technician an accurate reading when the logic level is changing quickly. The voltmeter will read the average input voltage, and the logic probe will indicate both 0 and 1 values. The best tool for testing a dynamic digital circuit is an oscilloscope. There is nothing that can replace a good dual-trace scope for troubleshooting a running digital circuit.

The scope can measure voltage levels frequency and the duty cycle of a running circuit. With a dual-trace scope you can compare two signals with respect to time to determine if they are high or low at the same time. You can even measure current with a scope. Suppose you want to dynamically monitor the current flow of the power supply to a computer. Just place a 0.1-Ω resistor in series with the +5 V of the power supply. Then put your scope across the 0.1-Ω resistor. The voltage drop divided by 0.1Ω is the current flowing; therefore, the current flowing is 10 times the scale reading in the scope. The voltage drop produced by the 0.1 ohm resistor is usually not noticeable to the computer. With the oscilloscope you can observe power increase that occurs as the computer controls various parts of its system. There is nothing that can replace a good scope. You should know how your particular brand of scope works and you should use it often.

8.10 THE STATIC CPU EMULATOR

The fact that a computer is constantly changing the status of its various parts makes the testing of logic levels quite hard. You cannot test the address decoder, for example, if the CPU is constantly changing the input to the decoder.

One simple solution to this problem is to get rid of the CPU and replace it with a static emulator that you can statically control. There are various commercial models of CPU emulators that have dynamic test features as well as static testing, but they are quite costly. A simple static CPU emulator can be made with some switches and LEDs, as shown in Figure A–6 of Appendix A. This little device has a switch connected to each CPU output and an LED to indicate logic 0 or 1. All the CPU inputs have just a buffered LED to indicate the logic state of the CPU input.

To use this device, the technician first removes the CPU chip and puts the CPU emulator in its place. The technician can then act like the CPU and make any output low, high, or HiZ. The technician can place an address on the address bus, make $\overline{\text{MREQ}}$, and $\overline{\text{RD}}$ low, and then read the memory location at the data bus. The switches can make an output high, low, or HiZ. To read a memory location or input port, the data bus is made HiZ. This allows the external memory or input port to drive the LEDs of the static emulator. The value of the CPU output can be held in a fixed state that allows the technician to use a voltmeter to test the logic state of the rest of the computer in a systematic, straightforward manner. About the only part of the computer that cannot be tested with this device is dynamic memory, but the address decoders, chip select lines, and bidirectional bus drives to the memory can be checked. This little device has saved many hours of work and is one of the best troubleshooting tools.

One should remember that not all problems can be found by statically testing digital circuits. Memory ICs or CMOS ICs often break down at high speed, and the static emulator cannot find this type of problem.

8.11 USING A LOGIC ANALYZER TO DYNAMICALLY TEST A COMPUTER

When a computer has dynamic memory or has a problem that cannot be tested statically, the technician must resort to a device called a *logic analyzer*. This device is nothing more than a sophisticated and very fast latch or digital memory. The logic analyzer is designed to store the contents of its inputs each time a clock makes a transition of either HIGH to LOW or LOW to HIGH. If you place the inputs of the logic analyzer on the data bus of the computer and use the $\overline{\text{MRD}}$ signal from the CPU, the logic analyzer will latch its memory full of the thing that the CPU reads from the bus. Figures 8–7A and 8–7B show a very simple 8-channel logic analyzer that will latch 16 bytes of information.

The input data is fed to eight 74LS75 flip-flops that are clocked by the control clock. The control clock is used to determine the time in which the data present on the data input is to be latched. The word-select switches and the 74LS30 IC allow the operator to set a beginning word that when found starts the logic analyzer saving the next 16 bytes to be clocked in.

When an input word matches the switch setting, all the inputs of the 74LS30 will be HIGH, causing its output to go LOW. This causes the 74LS76 JK flip-flop to set Q to a logic 1 and $\overline{\text{Q}}$ to 0. The LOW on the $\overline{\text{Q}}$ enables the OR gate at pin 4 of IC5, allowing the clock pulse to pass on to a set of 74121 one-shots. The first one-shot (IC7) produces a 200-ns positive-going pulse that is used to toggle the 74LS93 counter when it falls LOW at the end of the 200 ns. The rising edge of this 200-ns pulse triggers the next one-shot (IC8) and produces a shorter 100 ns negative going pulse. This pulse is

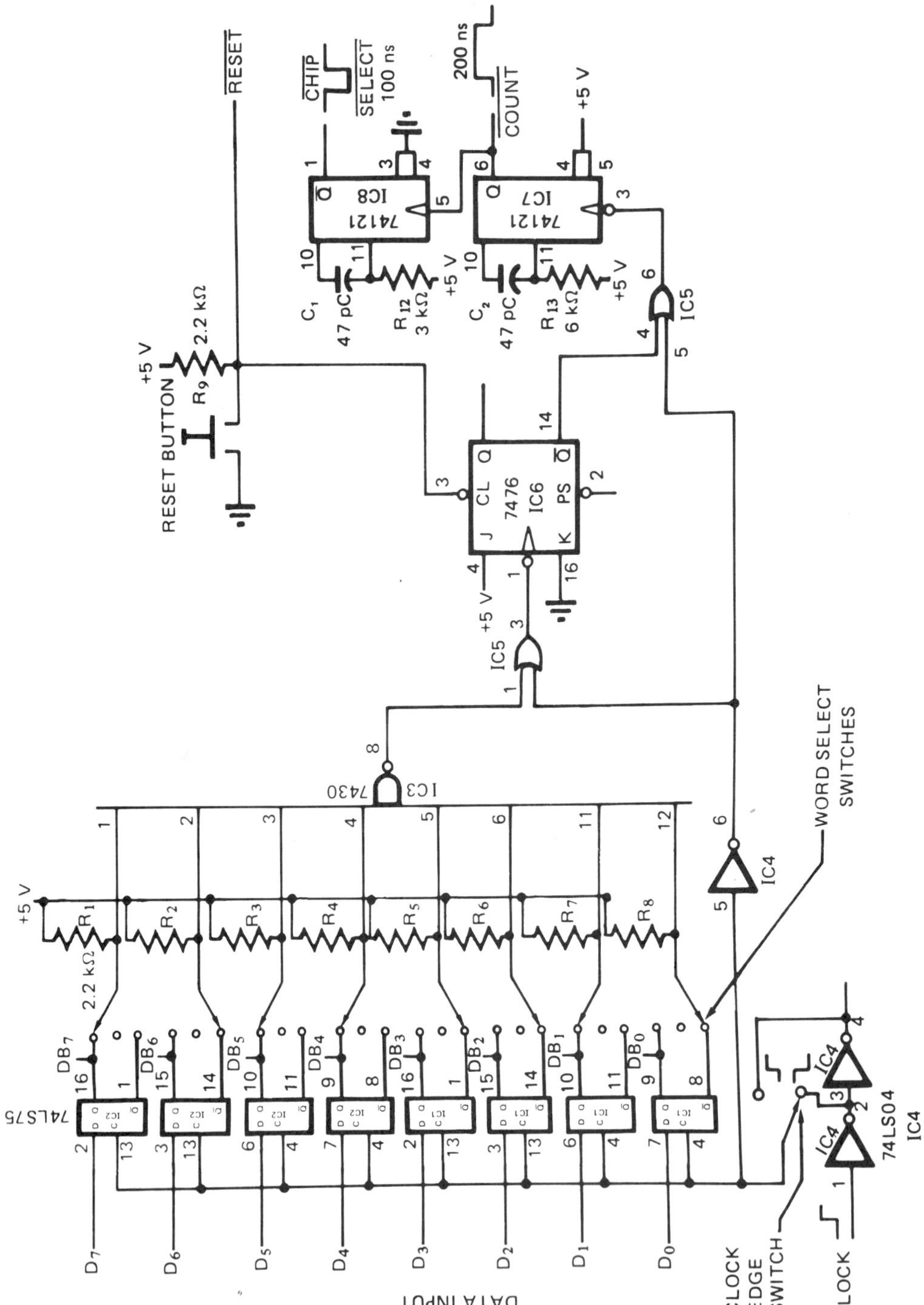

FIGURE 8–7A A simple logic analyzer

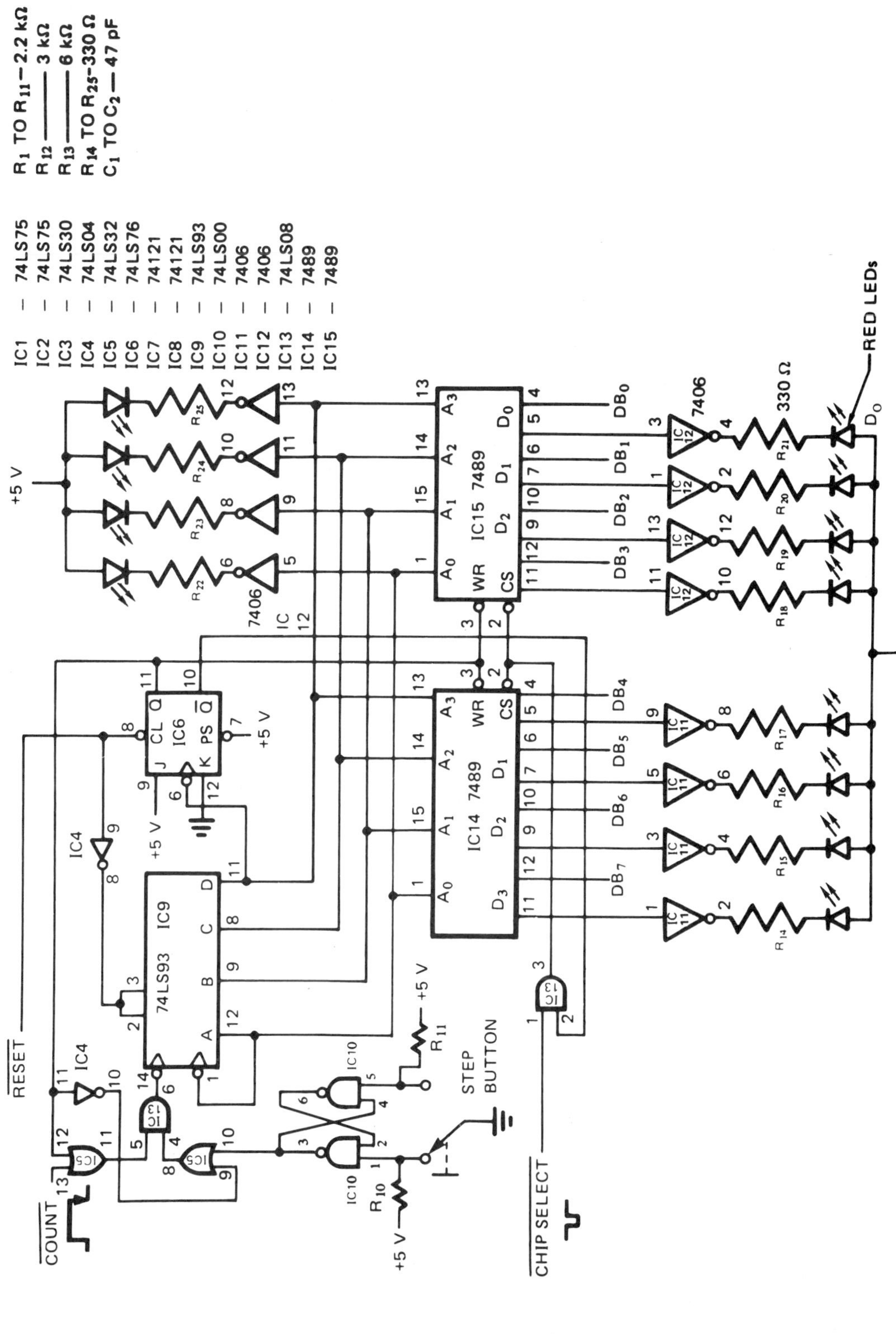

FIGURE 8–7B A simple logic analyzer

used to strobe the chip select of the 7489 memories. Each time a clock pulse is input after the trigger word was encountered, the data on the inputs will be stored in the 7489 memory, and the 74LS93 counter will be incremented. This will continue until the counter sets the end JK flip, which causes the count input of the 74LS93 to be switched to a manual push button, and the 7489 memories are switched from write to read. Now the operator can step through the last 16 bytes after the select word was encountered. The four LEDs on the counter outputs are buffered with a 7406 IC and tell the operator the order in which the bytes were latched. With this type of device a technician can accurately determine what was on the bus or control bus at a specific instant in time.

Good commercial logic analyzers are quite expensive and often have very advanced features such as a microcomputer to disassemble the instructions latched in off the data bus and display them in mnemonics for you. With a good logic analyzer you can pick apart any program or computer, but the really good logic analyzers are not cheap.

8.12 USING THE COMPUTER TO TEST ITSELF

If the computer to be repaired can still be programmed, then you can use the computer itself to test the parts that you want to troubleshoot.

Suppose output port 0 was not working correctly on the Biggy trainer. A short program such as the following will produce a continuous low-going device-select pulse at the clock of the 7475 latches that make up the output port.

```
LOOP    INC     A          ;add 1 to A
        OUT     (00),A     ;output A to port 0
        JP      LOOP       ;do it again
```

By using a scope you can look at the device select and the waveform of each of the output data lines on port 0. If there is no low-going pulse on the enable pins of the 7475 latches, then the problem is probably further up in the computer logic, perhaps the I/O decoder. If the device select is present at the enable pins of the 7475 latches but the display still gives incorrect outputs, check the waveform of D_0 or the least significant bit to the next bit, D_1. The scope should show the D_0 output of the port to be twice the frequency of D_1, and D_3 should be twice the frequency of D_2, and so on. This is because the port is being made to count by the program. If the frequencies of the port output bits are not in multiples of 2, then they are out of order and should be fixed.

This is, of course, a simple example of diagnostic software. Properly used by a knowledgeable technician, diagnostic software can be a powerful tool for troubleshooting the computer.

Diagnostic software is quite often placed in ROM chips, and then the computer is run using this software to test various parts of the system. ROM software of this type usually has a portion to test the RAM, and the program is written in such a manner as to avoid any CALL to subroutine or instruction that uses RAM. In this way the diagnostic software will run even though the RAM will not.

Most large minicomputers and mainframes have extensive diagnostic software written for debugging hardware problems.

EXERCISE 8

1. What are the three things needed to control any computer?
2. Describe the five steps for writing a complicated program.
3. What are the three basic symbols used in a flowchart?
4. What is the address of the 10-ms timing loop in the Biggy trainer operating system?
5. Change the timing loop in the Biggy trainer to 25 ms.
6. Give two methods for locating and repairing power supply shorts in a freshly soldered board.
7. What is a static CPU emulator?
8. Explain how a scope can be used to measure current.
9. Give a brief description of a logic analyzer and what it is used for.
10. Give one example of a short program that could be used to test a computer's hardware.
11. How much time does it take to run the TESTKEY subroutine in the Biggy trainer operating system?
12. Write a 1-s timing loop. Write a flowchart and make it a subroutine.
13. Write a short testing loop to test the Biggy trainer input port.
14. Where is the stack started when the Biggy trainer is rebooted?
15. What is the highest RAM address in the Biggy trainer?
16. Why does the operating system start the job of setting up the stack ect. at address 0066 Hex in the Biggy Trainer?
17. List all the codes that the GETKEY subroutine will return with for the H, L, SHIFT, and RUN keys.
18. How much ROM is unused in the Biggy trainer?
19. What type of binary information would be latched into the logic analyzer if it were connected to the data bus and the clock were obtained from ORing the $\overline{M1}$ and $\overline{MRD}$ control signals together?
20. What Biggy trainer control signal would be used to latch the interrupt input bytes with a logic analyzer?

Lab 8

OBJECTIVES

After completing this lab, you should be able to
- draw a flowchart to outline a complicated program.
- write a program in assembly language to implement the flowchart.
- debug the program so that it functions perfectly.

Procedure

Suppose that an external timing device supplies a pulse once each second. Using that pulse as an interrupt signal (mode 1 will require the least external hardware), write a program that will keep track of seconds, minutes, and hours. Outport the time to ports 0, 1, and 2 in BCD. Make provisions to initialize the time before starting the program.

1. Draw a flowchart and have it approved.
2. Write the program in assembly language. If no assembler is available, then hand assemble it.
3. Debug the program until it runs perfectly. To debug the program, write a short program that will call the 10-ms timing loop in the ROM at 00E4H 100 times. Then use this 1-s time delay to space calls to your clock subroutine. Save your clock program because you will use it in Lab 10 with an external interrupt signal.

Chapter 9

PARALLEL COMPUTER INTERFACING THE 8255 IC

OBJECTIVES

After completing this chapter, you should be able to

- explain the difference between memory mapped input/output and direct input/output ports.
- describe the operation of the 8255 programmable peripheral interface IC.
- describe the operation of the Centronic parallel printer port.

9.1 MEMORY MAPPED PARALLEL INTERFACE VERSUS DIRECT INPUT/OUTPUT PORTS

Figure 9–1 shows a typical memory mapped output interface to a seven-segment LED and an input from a set of switches. The switches might be used by the computer to configure other ICs when the computer starts up from a cold boot. The seven-segment LED might be used to give a test technician a read back on certain tests that might be run on the computer system.

Notice that all 16 address lines are used by the address decoder because the input/output appears to the computer as a place in its central or core memory. The address decoder decodes a unique block of eight possible addresses instead of a single unique address. This is done because many parallel interface chips, such as the 8255, 8251, and Z8420, decode the lower two or three bits of the address themselves.

Memory mapped input/output allows the programmer to use any instruction that will affect memory as an input/output instruction because the input/output is a contiguous part of the core memory of the computer. This can make for easy programming, but the drawback is that you must sacrifice some of the usable memory for this input/output.

In some CPUs memory mapping is the only way that input/output can be accomplished. The 8080A, 8085, and the Z 80 all have another way, which was discussed in Chapter 3—input/output ports.

Figure 9–2 shows a typical Z 80 input/output port configuration. By using an input/output port to do the I/O operations you do not have to sacrifice any of the central

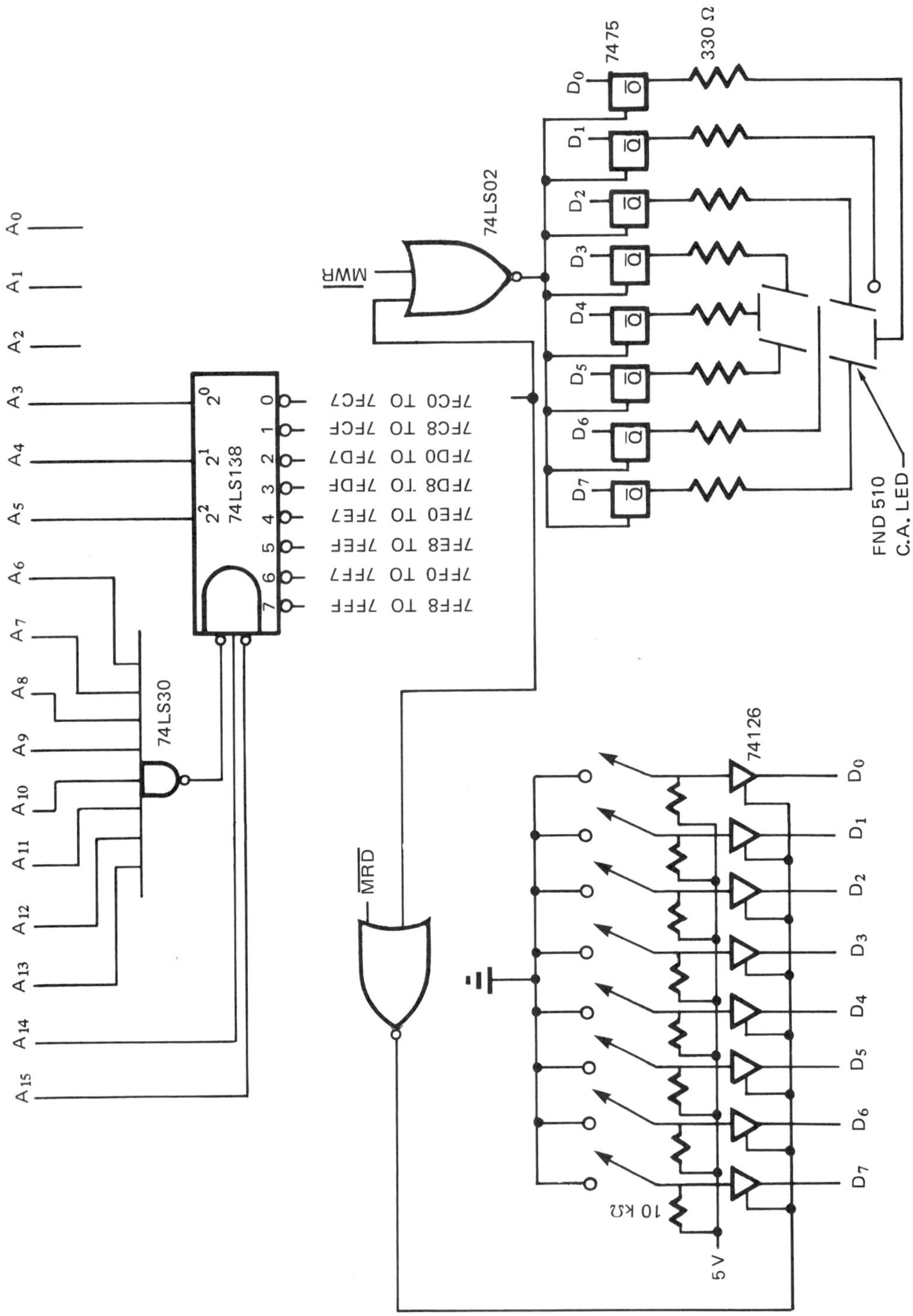

FIGURE 9–1 Memory mapped input/output

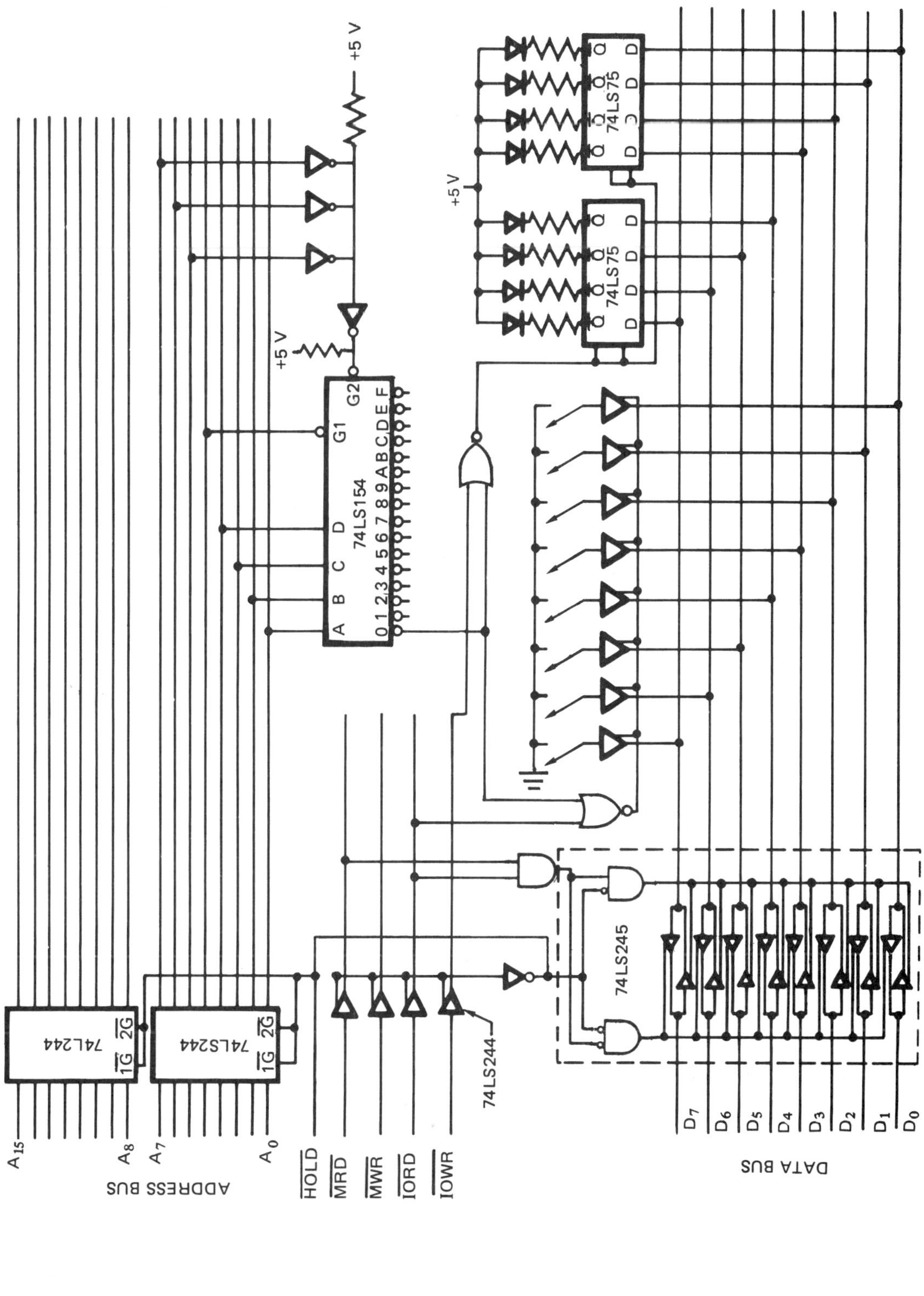
+5 V
74LS75
74LS75
74LS154
74LS245
74LS244
74LS244
74L244
ADDRESS BUS
DATA BUS
HOLD
MRD
MWR
IORD
IOWR

FIGURE 9–2

or core memory, but you are limited to the number of instructions that you can use to access the input/output ports.

In the 8080A and 8085 CPUs there are only two instructions that can access the input/output ports: IN A,(NN) and OUT (NN), A. All data that is input or output must flow through the A register. In the Z 80 you can use these two instructions, and you can also use the C register as the input/output port address and input or output from any of the general-purpose registers:

IN R,(C) and OUT (C),R

where R=A, B, C, D, E, H, or L. Also the two instructions OUTD and OUTI can be used for block output port operation.

9.2 THE 8255 PARALLEL PERIPHERAL INTERFACE IC

The 8255 is a programmable parallel interface IC made by Intel Corp. Other companies, such as ZILOG, which makes the Z 80, also make similar ICs. We will study the 8255 because it is widely used and it does more than most parallel interface ICs.

The 8255 is an NMOS 40-pin IC that uses +5 V as a power supply. It can handle two TTL loads on its outputs and has an input load of 10 μA. Figure 9–3 shows the pinout and block diagram of the 8255 IC.

The 8255 has three input/output ports, a bidirectional data bus to communicate with the computer on, and a set of address and control signal inputs to allow the CPU to control the IC.

The control of the 8255 is accomplished by using three control lines ($\overline{RD}$, $\overline{WR}$, and $\overline{CS}$) and two address lines (A_0 and A_1). As shown in Figure 9–4, the $\overline{RD}$ and $\overline{WR}$ inputs to the 8255 are usually connected to the $\overline{IORD}$ and $\overline{IOWR}$ outputs of the Z-80 or 8080A CPU, and the $\overline{CS}$ (chip select) is used by the input/output address decode to select or enable the IC. The two address inputs to the 8255 usually are connected to the A_0 and A_1 address lines of the CPU's address bus. The two address inputs (A_0 and A_1) select the particular port inside the 8255 that the CPU is going to access. 00 is port A, 01 is port B, 10 is port C, and 11 is the control register. The IC is programmed by writing a control byte to the control register, which is address 11. This will configure the 8255 into a particular pattern of input or output ports, and it will remain that way until it is reprogrammed with a new byte written to the control register.

The data bus is a true bidirectional data bus, but it does not have enough current-driving capability to drive the computer's data bus by itself, so a 74LS245 bidirectional data bus drive was used to buffer the 8255 data bus.

The RESET input pin is used to force the 8255 into a fixed configuration. When the RESET is brought HIGH, the 8255 configured all its input/output ports as input ports. The RESET is often connected to the computer system reset so that when the computer is reset the 8255 will be automatically configured as input ports so the CPU can read data from the three input ports to get information that will be used to program other LSI ICs used by the computer.

intel®

8255A/8255A-5
PROGRAMMABLE PERIPHERAL INTERFACE

- MCS-85™ Compatible 8255A-5
- 24 Programmable I/O Pins
- Completely TTL Compatible
- Fully Compatible with Intel® Microprocessor Families
- Improved Timing Characteristics
- Direct Bit Set/Reset Capability Easing Control Application Interface
- 40-Pin Dual In-Line Package
- Reduces System Package Count
- Improved DC Driving Capability

The Intel® 8255A is a general purpose programmable I/O device designed for use with Intel® microprocessors. It has 24 I/O pins which may be individually programmed in 2 groups of 12 and used in 3 major modes of operation. In the first mode (MODE 0), each group of 12 I/O pins may be programmed in sets of 4 to be input or output. In MODE 1, the second mode, each group may be programmed to have 8 lines of input or output. Of the remaining 4 pins, 3 are used for handshaking and interrupt control signals. The third mode of operation (MODE 2) is a bidirectional bus mode which uses 8 lines for a bidirectional bus, and 5 lines, borrowing one from the other group, for handshaking.

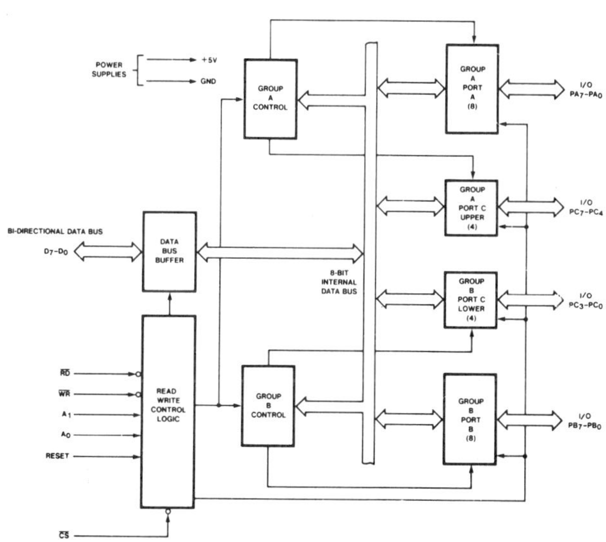

8255A Block Diagram

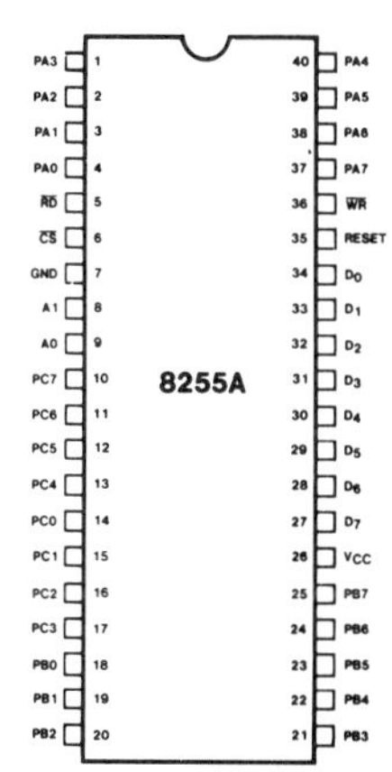

Pin Configuration

FIGURE 9–3

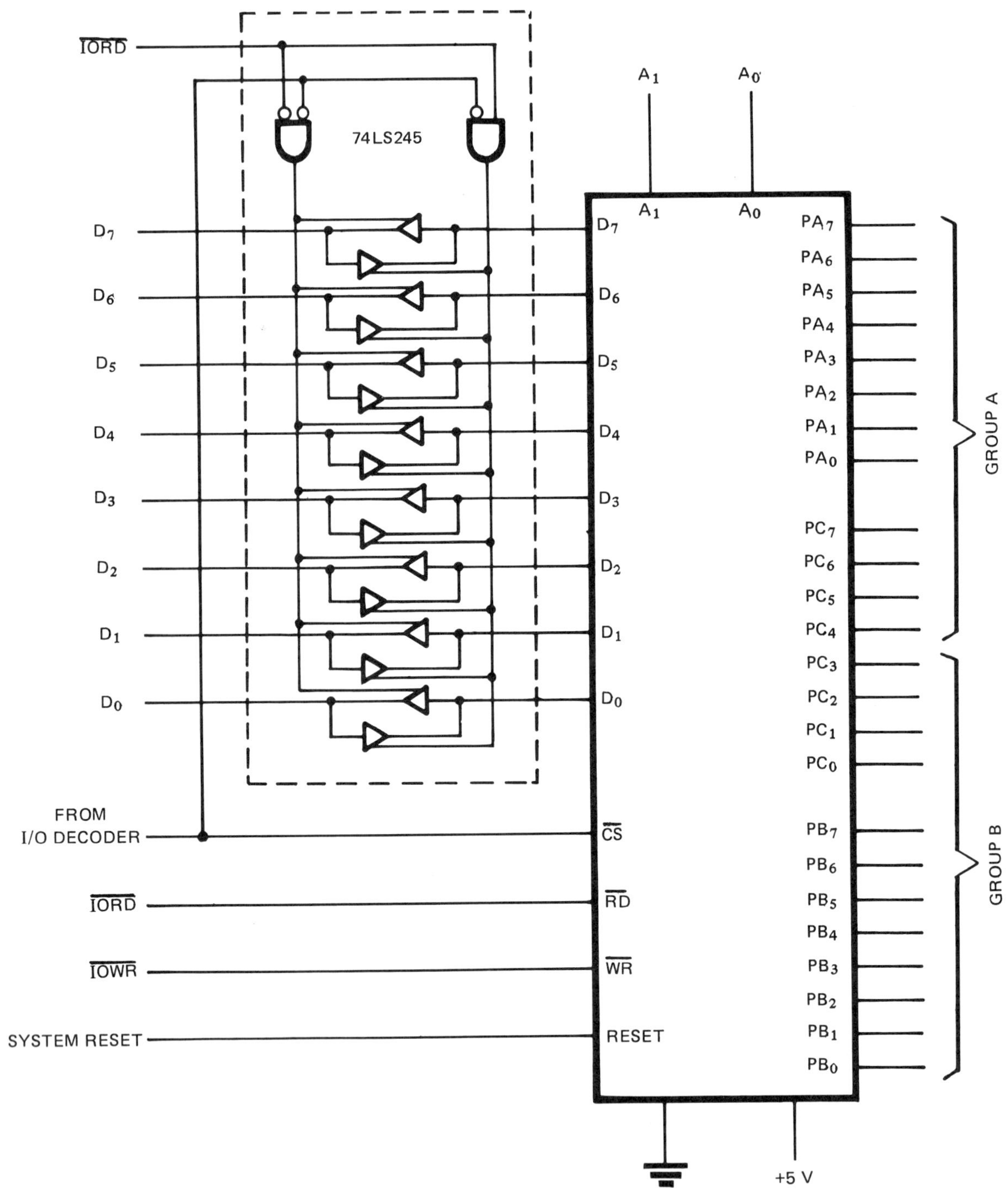

$\overline{IORD}$
74LS245
A_1
A_0
D_7
D_6
D_5
D_4
D_3
D_2
D_1
D_0
PA_7
PA_6
PA_5
PA_4
PA_3
PA_2
PA_1
PA_0
PC_7
PC_6
PC_5
PC_4
PC_3
PC_2
PC_1
PC_0
PB_7
PB_6
PB_5
PB_4
PB_3
PB_2
PB_1
PB_0
GROUP A
GROUP B
FROM I/O DECODER
$\overline{CS}$
$\overline{IORD}$
$\overline{RD}$
$\overline{IOWR}$
$\overline{WR}$
SYSTEM RESET
RESET
+5 V

FIGURE 9–4

intel **8255A/8255A-5**

8255A FUNCTIONAL DESCRIPTION

General

The 8255A is a programmable peripheral interface (PPI) device designed for use in Intel® microcomputer systems. Its function is that of a general purpose I/O component to interface peripheral equipment to the microcomputer system bus. The functional configuration of the 8255A is programmed by the system software so that normally no external logic is necessary to interface peripheral devices or structures.

Data Bus Buffer

This 3-state bidirectional 8-bit buffer is used to interface the 8255A to the system data bus. Data is transmitted or received by the buffer upon execution of input or output instructions by the CPU. Control words and status information are also transferred through the data bus buffer.

Read/Write and Control Logic

The function of this block is to manage all of the internal and external transfers of both Data and Control or Status words. It accepts inputs from the CPU Address and Control busses and in turn, issues commands to both of the Control Groups.

($\overline{CS}$)

Chip Select. A "low" on this input pin enables the communiction between the 8255A and the CPU.

($\overline{RD}$)

Read. A "low" on this input pin enables the 8255A to send the data or status information to the CPU on the data bus. In essence, it allows the CPU to "read from" the 8255A.

($\overline{WR}$)

Write. A "low" on this input pin enables the CPU to write data or control words into the 8255A.

(A_0 and A_1)

Port Select 0 and Port Select 1. These input signals, in conjunction with the RD and WR inputs, control the selection of one of the three ports or the control word registers. They are normally connected to the least significant bits of the address bus (A_0 and A_1).

8255A BASIC OPERATION

A_1	A_0	$\overline{RD}$	$\overline{WR}$	$\overline{CS}$	INPUT OPERATION (READ)
0	0	0	1	0	PORT A ⇒ DATA BUS
0	1	0	1	0	PORT B ⇒ DATA BUS
1	0	0	1	0	PORT C ⇒ DATA BUS
					OUTPUT OPERATION (WRITE)
0	0	1	0	0	DATA BUS ⇒ PORT A
0	1	1	0	0	DATA BUS ⇒ PORT B
1	0	1	0	0	DATA BUS ⇒ PORT C
1	1	1	0	0	DATA BUS ⇒ CONTROL
					DISABLE FUNCTION
X	X	X	X	1	DATA BUS ⇒ 3-STATE
1	1	0	1	0	ILLEGAL CONDITION
X	X	1	1	0	DATA BUS ⇒ 3-STATE

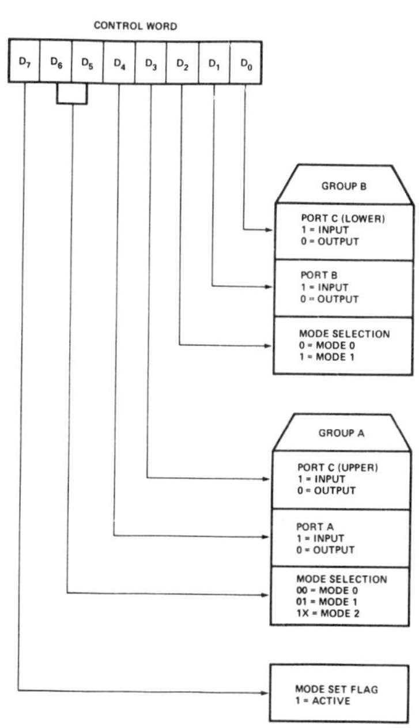

Mode Definition Format

FIGURE 9–5

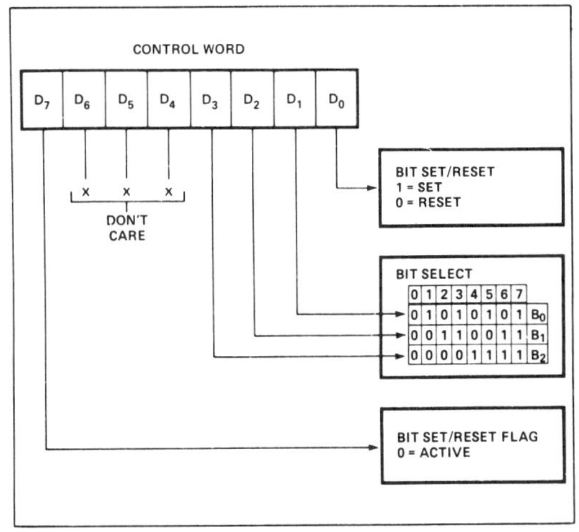

Bit Set/Reset Format

FIGURE 9–6

The three input/output ports are read from or written to by placing the correct port address on the address input, bringing the $\overline{CS}$ LOW and strobing either the $\overline{RD}$ or $\overline{WR}$ LOW when the data is read into or output from the CPU.

For programming and port configuration the three ports are grouped into two groups (Group A and Group B). Group A is made up of port A and the upper four bits of port C (PC_4 to PC_7). Group B is made up of port B and the lower four bits of port C (PC_0 to PC_3). Group A can be configured to run in three different modes (modes 0, 1, and 2), but Group B can only use modes 0 and 1.

The mode of operation for each group is programmed by the control byte written to the 8255 control register by the CPU. The format for this control byte is shown in Figure 9–5. This is the format for the mode control word. Bit 7 of this word or byte determines the mode format from the bit set/reset format shown in Figure 9–6.

The bit set/reset control word allows you to set or reset any one of the port C bits without affecting any of the other six bits in port C.

9.3 MODE 0 OPERATION OF THE 8255

Mode 0 is the basic input/output port mode of the 8255. When Group A or Group B is programmed in mode 0, ports A, B, or C can be made an input or an output port. Port C can be split into half input and half output, if desired. In mode 0, the two ports A and B are often used as either input or output ports, while port C is used as control signal to peripheral because the bits of port C can be set or reset by the bit set/reset control word. Mode 0 port configurations are shown in Figure 9–7.

MODE 0 Port Definition

A		B		GROUP A			GROUP B	
D_4	D_3	D_1	D_0	PORT A	PORT C (UPPER)	#	PORT B	PORT C (LOWER)
0	0	0	0	OUTPUT	OUTPUT	0	OUTPUT	OUTPUT
0	0	0	1	OUTPUT	OUTPUT	1	OUTPUT	INPUT
0	0	1	0	OUTPUT	OUTPUT	2	INPUT	OUTPUT
0	0	1	1	OUTPUT	OUTPUT	3	INPUT	INPUT
0	1	0	0	OUTPUT	INPUT	4	OUTPUT	OUTPUT
0	1	0	1	OUTPUT	INPUT	5	OUTPUT	INPUT
0	1	1	0	OUTPUT	INPUT	6	INPUT	OUTPUT
0	1	1	1	OUTPUT	INPUT	7	INPUT	INPUT
1	0	0	0	INPUT	OUTPUT	8	OUTPUT	OUTPUT
1	0	0	1	INPUT	OUTPUT	9	OUTPUT	INPUT
1	0	1	0	INPUT	OUTPUT	10	INPUT	OUTPUT
1	0	1	1	INPUT	OUTPUT	11	INPUT	INPUT
1	1	0	0	INPUT	INPUT	12	OUTPUT	OUTPUT
1	1	0	1	INPUT	INPUT	13	OUTPUT	INPUT
1	1	1	0	INPUT	INPUT	14	INPUT	OUTPUT
1	1	1	1	INPUT	INPUT	15	INPUT	INPUT

MODE 0 Configurations

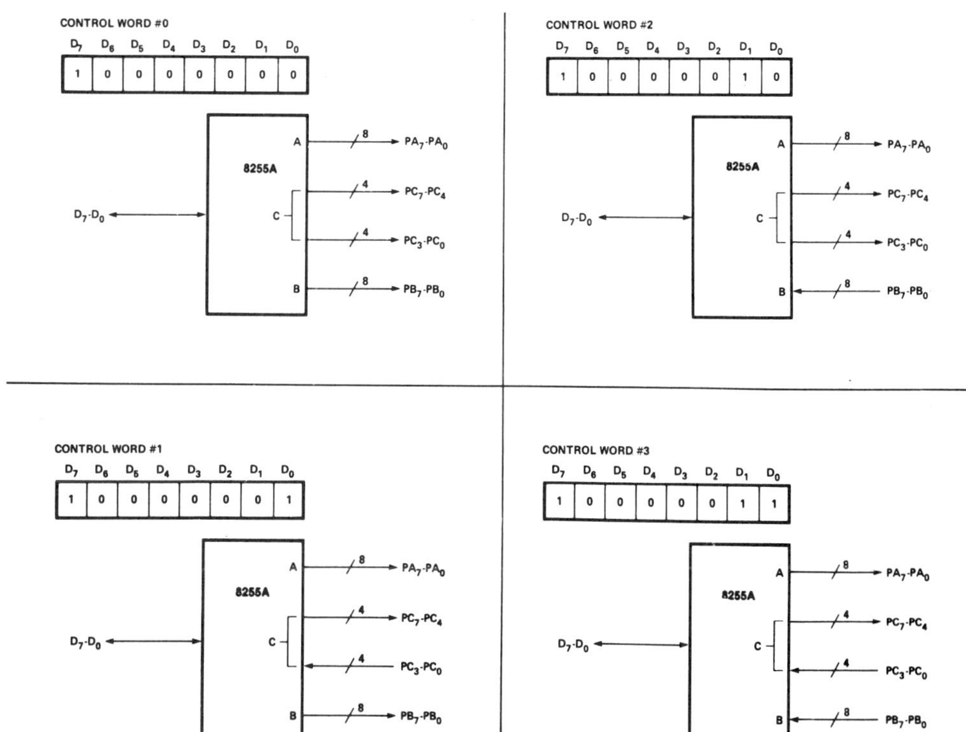

FIGURE 9–7

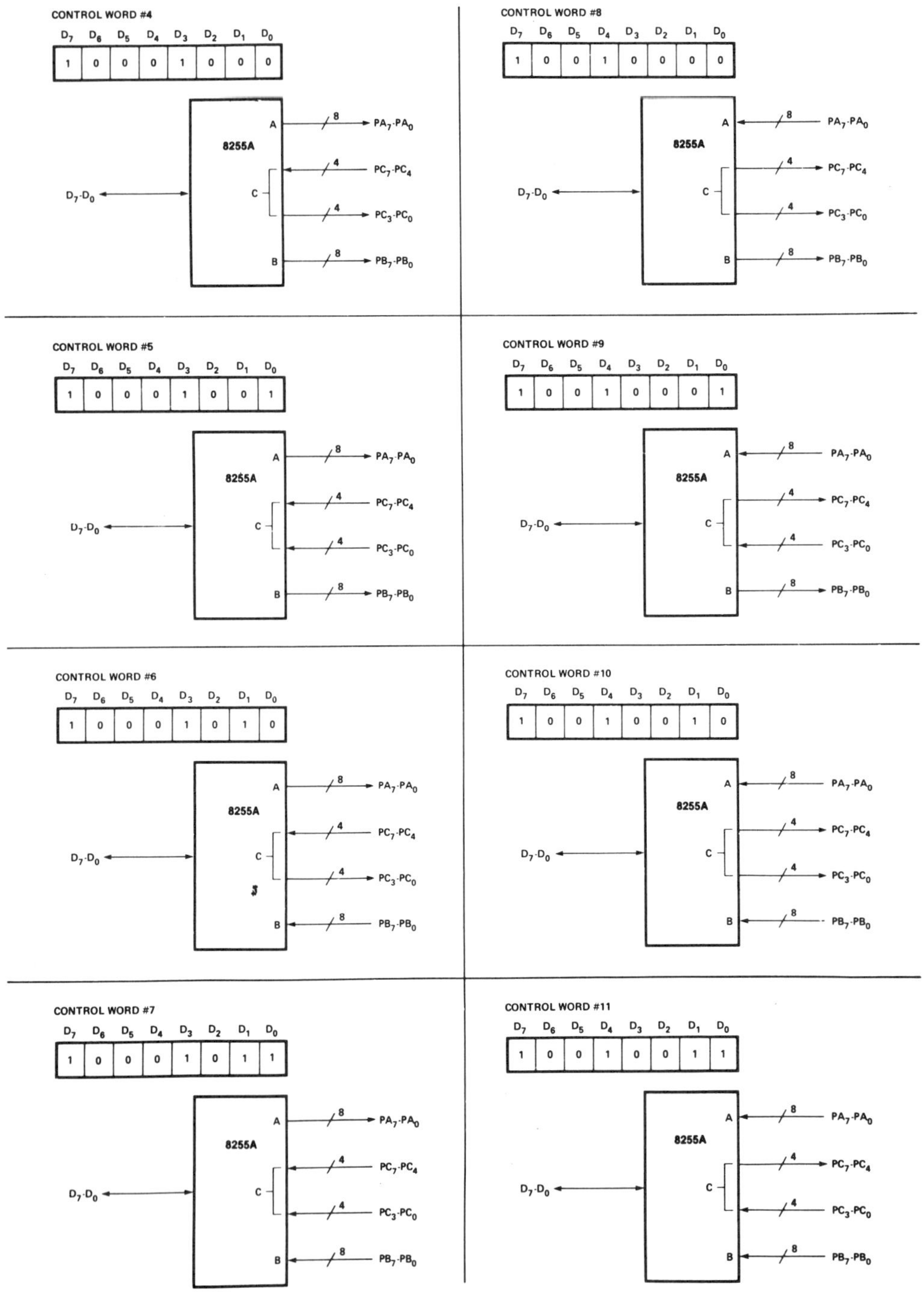

FIGURE 9–7 (cont.)

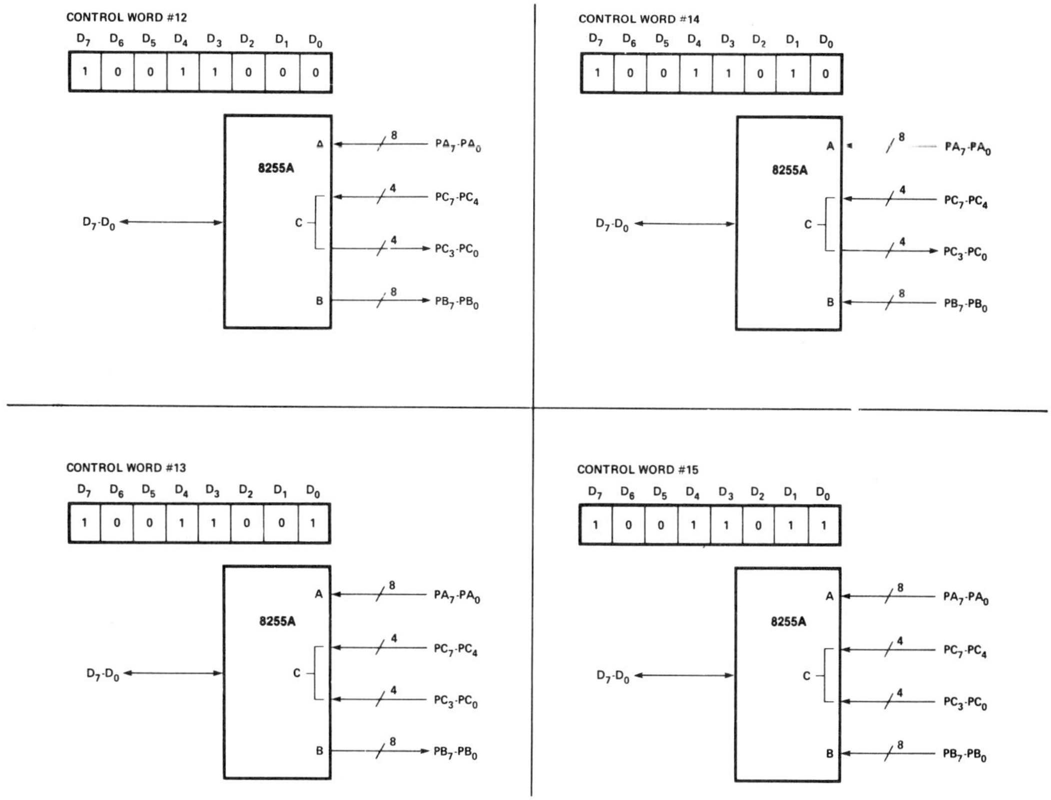

FIGURE 9–7 (cont.)

Operating Modes

MODE 1 (Strobed Input/Output). This functional configuration provides a means for transferring I/O data to or from a specified port in conjunction with strobes or "handshaking" signals. In mode 1, port A and Port B use the lines on port C to generate or accept these "handshaking" signals.

Mode 1 Basic Functional Definitions:

- Two Groups (Group A and Group B)
- Each group contains one 8-bit data port and one 4-bit control/data port.
- The 8-bit data port can be either input or output. Both inputs and outputs are latched.
- The 4-bit port is used for control and status of the 8-bit data port.

9.4 MODE 1 OPERATION OF THE 8255

Mode 1 is input or output using control signal or handshaking. Figure 9–8 shows the port configuration for mode 1 input and the control word for Group A and Group B. In mode 1, the four bits of port C are used as control or handshaking signals for the main eight bits of ports A or B.

When in mode 1 input, the $\overline{STB}_A$ or $\overline{STB}_B$ is used to latch data from an outside source into the 8255 A or B input register. When the $\overline{STB}_A$ or $\overline{STB}_B$ goes LOW to latch the data, the IBF_A (input buffer full) or IBF_B goes HIGH to indicate that data has been latched into ports A or B and that the external source should not latch anymore data until the CPU has read ports A or B. When the CPU reads ports A or B, the associated IBF will be reset to a 0, thus allowing the external source to latch in another byte to ports A or B.

This method of handshaking allows the external source to supply data to the CPU as fast as the CPU handles it without losing any data by too fast an input. As can be seen in Figure 9–8, the IBF_A signal is ANDed with the PC_4 bit to produce an interrupt

Input Control Signal Definition

STB (Strobe Input). A "low" on this input loads data into the input latch.

IBF (Input Buffer Full F/F)

A "high" on this output indicates that the data has been loaded into the input latch; in essence, an acknowledgement. IBF is set by STB input being low and is reset by the rising edge of the RD input.

INTR (Interrupt Request)

A "high" on this output can be used to interrupt the CPU when an input device is requesting service. INTR is set by the $\overline{STB}$ is a "one", IBF is a "one" and INTE is a "one". It is reset by the falling edge of $\overline{RD}$. This procedure allows an input device to request service from the CPU by simply strobing its data into the port.

INTE A

Controlled by bit set/reset of PC_4.

INTE B

Controlled by bit set/reset of PC_2.

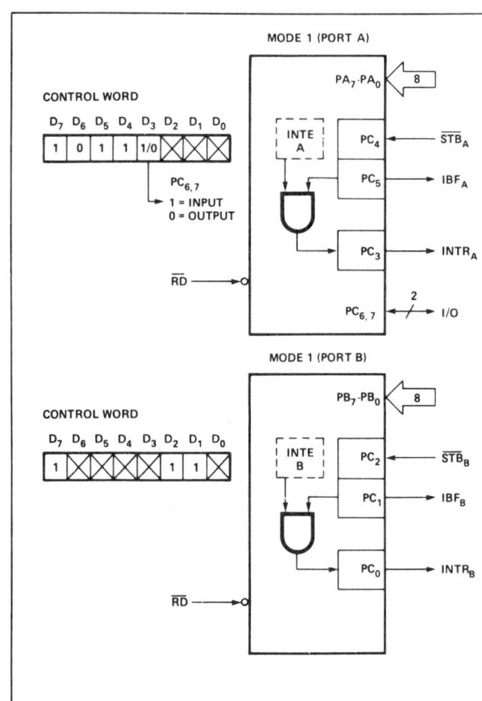

MODE 1 Input

FIGURE 9–8

Output Control Signal Definition

$\overline{OBF}$ (Output Buffer Full F/F). The OBF output will go "low" to indicate that the CPU has written data out to the specified port. The OBF F/F will be set by the rising edge of the WR input and reset by ACK Input being low.

$\overline{ACK}$ (Acknowledge Input). A "low" on this input informs the 8255A that the data from port A or port B has been accepted. In essence, a response from the peripheral device indicating that it has received the data output by the CPU.

INTR (Interrupt Request). A "high" on this output can be used to interrupt the CPU when an output device has accepted data transmitted by the CPU. INTR is set when ACK is a "one", OBF is a "one" and INTE is a "one". It is reset by the falling edge of WR.

INTE A

Controlled by bit set/reset of PC_6.

INTE B

Controlled by bit set/reset of PC_2.

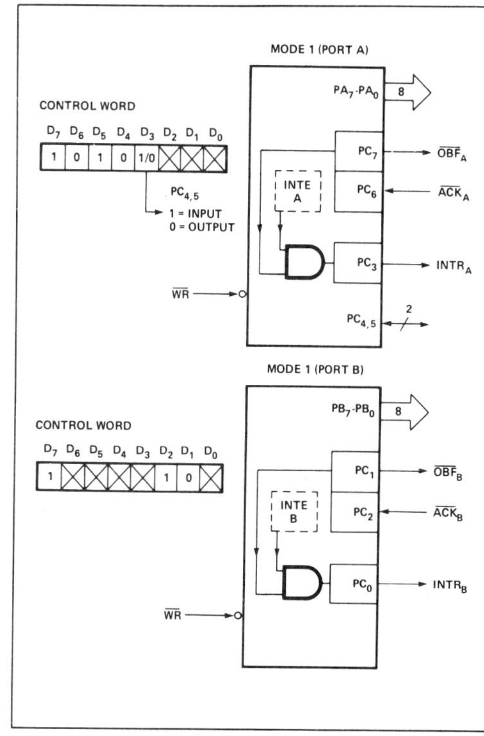

MODE 1 Output

FIGURE 9–9

signal that is fed to PC_3. This signal can be enabled or disabled by using a bit set/reset command to set or reset PC_4. If PC_3 is connected to the INT (interrupt input) of the CPU, then when the IBF_A goes high and PC_4 is set to 1, a 1 will be placed on PC_3, thus interrupting the CPU. The CPU will then jump to a subroutine that will input the byte latched into port A from the external source. This interrupt method can also be implemented with port B.

The mode 1 output operation is shown in Figure 9–9. When the CPU outputs to port A, the $\overline{OBF}_A$ (output buffer full) is brought LOW, which tells the external output device that data is present on port A to be used by that device. When the external output device has finished or latched the data present on port A, it will bring the $\overline{ACK}_A$ (acknowledge) LOW, which will signal the CPU that a new byte can be output to port A. The C register can be read and tested to determine the value of PC_6 or PC_2 for this purpose. When $\overline{ACK}_A$ goes LOW, $\overline{OBF}_A$ is set back to 1, indicating that no new data is present on port A.

When $\overline{OBF}_A$ is set back to 1 and PC_6 is set to 1, an interrupt signal is placed on PC_3 to indicate that a new byte could be output. The CPU would then be interrupted and a call to subroutine would be executed. This subroutine would then output a new byte to port A that would make $\overline{OBF}_A$ go LOW, thus removing the interrupt signal from PC_3. Notice that PC_3 is the interrupt output pin for mode 1 for both input and output. PC_3 is also the interrupt output for Group A mode 2. This allows us to hardwire PC_3 to the CPU's INT input and use any of the interrupt options offered by the 8255.

9.5 MODE 2 OPERATION OF THE 8255

Mode 2 can only be used on Group A. It is a combination of mode 1 input and output operations. As can be seen in Figure 9–10, both sets of control or handshaking signals for input and output are present in mode 2 operation. Port A is used as a bidirectional port that can input data and also output data. The $\overline{OBF}_A$ will go LOW when the CPU writes out data to port A and will be set by the $\overline{ACK}_A$ going LOW, just as in mode 1 output. The only thing different is that the output lines of port A will be in the HiZ state until the $\overline{ACK}_A$ goes LOW.

The $\overline{STB}_A$ and $\overline{IBF}_A$ work just as in mode 1 input. The two associated interrupt outputs for the mode 1 input and output are ORed together, and the output is fed to PC_3. This allows either input or output to interrupt the CPU.

There are many applications for the 8255 and LSI ICs such as the 8255. They are used wherever parallel input/output is needed. Figure 9–11 shows an 8255 used to scan a keyboard and return the ASCII code for the key pressed. Figure 9–12 is the program for the keyboard.

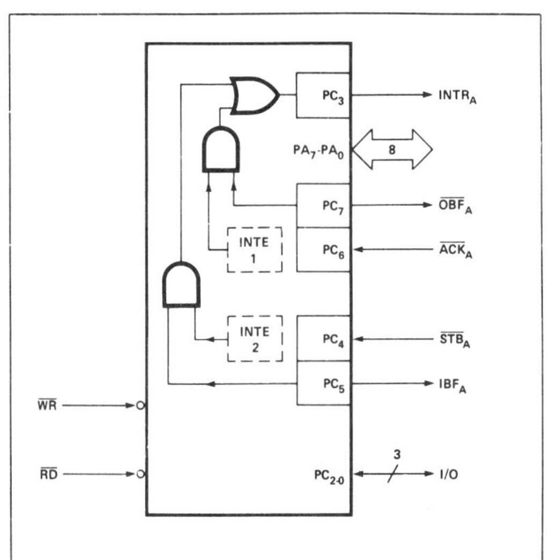

MODE 2

FIGURE 9–10

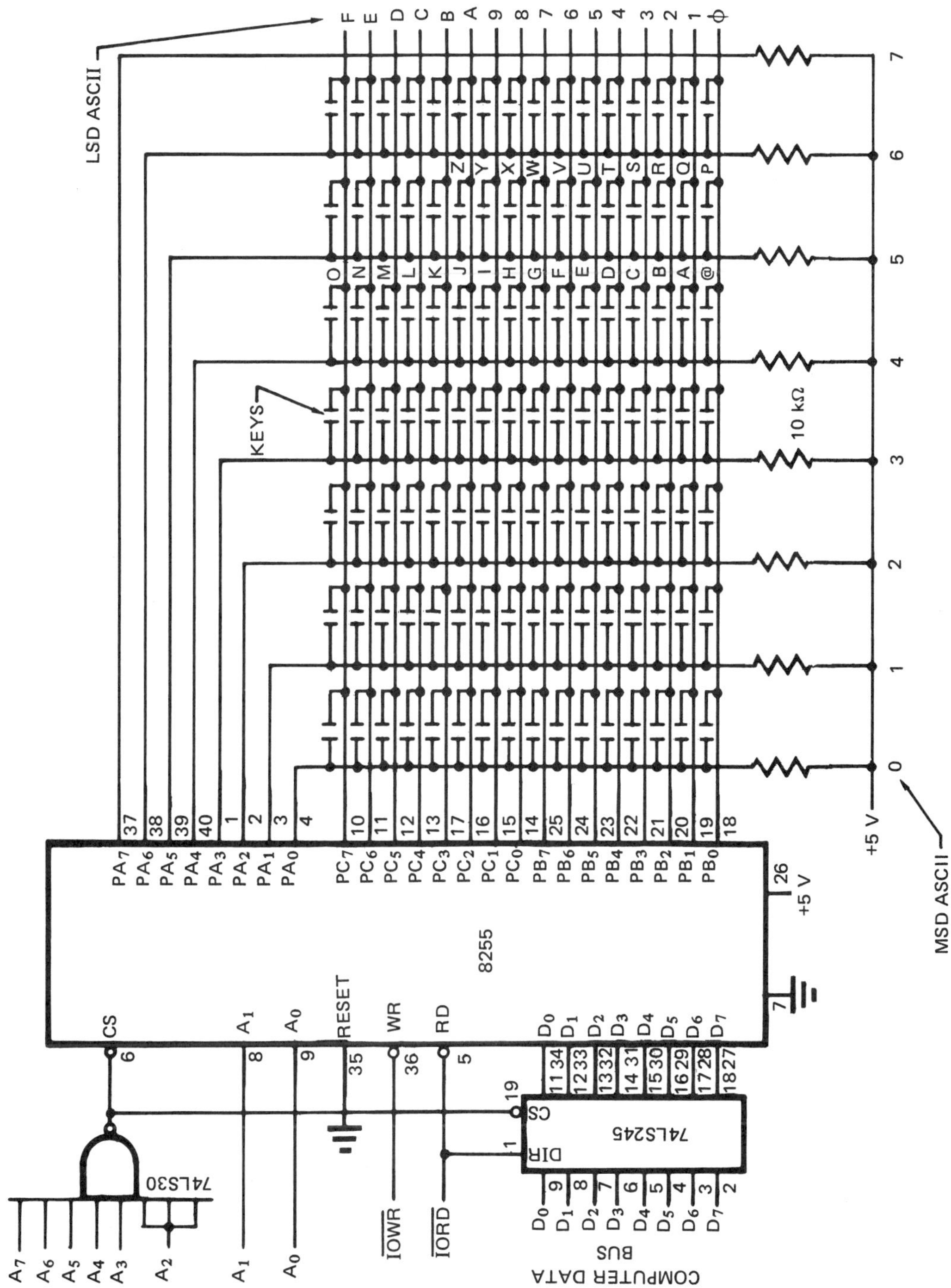

FIGURE 9–11 ASCII keyboard

```
               ;*****************************************************
               ;*  SUBROUTINE TO RETURN THE ASCII CODE OF THE PRESSED  *
               ;*             KEY IN THE A REGISTER                    *
               ;*****************************************************
               ;
               ;
00FF           CONTRO  EQU   0FFH       ;ADDRESS OF CONTROL REG.
00FC           PORTA   EQU   0FCH       ;ADDRESS OF PORT A, 8255
00FD           PORTB   EQU   0FDH       ;ADDRESS OF PORT B, 8255
00FE           PORTC   EQU   0FEH       ;ADDRESS OF PORT C, 8255
               ;
0900                   ORG   900H       ;START OF PROGRAM
0900 C5        START   PUSH  BC         ;SAVE BC
0901 E5                PUSH  HL         ;SAVE HL
0902 0EFF              LD    C,CONTRO   ;CONTROL ADD TO C REG.
0904 3E90              LD    A,90H      ;PORT A INPUT B ,C OUTPUT
0906 ED79              OUT   (C),A      ;PROGRAM 8255
0908 210100    BEGIN   LD    HL,01H     ;CLEAR ROW SELECT REG.
090B 0600              LD    B,00H      ;CLEAR ROW BINARY REG.
090D 7D        AGAIN   LD    A,L        ;MOVE LOW ROW BYTE TO A
090E 2F                CPL              ;COMPLEMENT A
090F D3FD              OUT   (PORTB),A  ;OUT LSB OF ROW TO KEYS
0911 7C                LD    A,H        ;HIGH BYTE OF ROW TO A
0912 2F                CPL              ;COMPLEMENT A
0913 D3FE              OUT   (PORTC),A  ;OUT MSB OF ROW TO KEYS
0915 DBFC              IN    A,(PORTA)  ;GET COLUMN OF KEYBOARD
0917 2F                CPL              ;COMPLEMENT A FOR TEST
0918 E6FF              AND   0FFH       ;SET Z FLAG IF NO KEY
091A 2009              JR    NZ,GETKEY  ;JUMP IF A KEY PRESSED
091C 04                INC   B          ;ADD 1 OF BINARY COUNTER
091D 29                ADD   HL,HL      ;SELECT NEXT ROW
091E 3E0F              LD    A,0FH      ;MASK OFF THE MSB 4 BITS
0920 A0                AND   B          ;OF THE BINARY COUNTER
0921 20EA              JR    NZ,AGAIN           ;TEST NEXT ROW
0923 18E3              JR    BEGIN      ;START ROW TEST AT BEGIN
0925 0E00      GETKEY  LD    C,00H      ;CLEAR REGISTER C
0927 CB0F      ROTA    RRC   A          ;ROTATE BIT TO C FLAG
0929 DA3009            JP    C,DONE     ;JUMP TO END
092C 0C                INC   C          ;CONVERT C TO BINARY MSD
092D C32709            JP    ROTA       ;DO AGAIN
0930 79        DONE    LD    A,C        ;ROTATE THE 4 LSB TO THE
0931 CB07              RLC   A          ;TO THE MS 4 BITS
0933 CB07              RLC   A
0935 CB07              RLC   A
0937 CB07              RLC   A
0939 B0                OR    B          ;OR IN THE LOWER 4 BITS
093A E1                POP   HL         ;RESTORE HL
093B C1                POP   BC         ;RESTORE BC
093C C9                RET              ;RETURN FROM SUB
0000                   END
00000 Total Errors
```

FIGURE 9–12

9.6 THE CENTRONIC PARALLEL PRINTER PORT

Centronic is a company that makes computer printers and other hardware. The parallel interface used to drive their printer has become widely used on todays microcomputers. This parallel interface is designed to transfer bytes of data, usually ASCII code, to a printer and return information about the printer's operation.

Figure 9–13 shows the pinout of the 36-pin connectors used for the Centronic printer parallel interface. Data, usually in the form of ASCII code, is placed on the data bits (pins 2 to 9), and the data strobe is brought LOW to latch the data out to the printer. Because the printers of old were very much a mechanical device, the data strobe is defined as being at least 1 μs in length. The output data and input data are all TTL levels and often use twisted pairs of wire to reduce noise. The busy signal is used to signal the computer that the printer is printing, paper is out, or any other things that would prevent the output of another byte of data. When the busy returns LOW, the $\overline{\text{ACKNOWLEDGE}}$

SIGNAL PIN NO.	SIGNAL NAME	REMARKS
1	$\overline{\text{STROBE}}$	DATA STROBE INPUT FROM COMPUTER
2	DATA 1	PARALLEL DATA FROM COMPUTER
3	DATA 2	
4	DATA 3	
5	DATA 4	
6	DATA 5	
7	DATA 6	
8	DATA 7	
9	DATA 8	
10	$\overline{\text{ACK}}$	DATA ACKNOWLEDGE OUTPUT FROM PRINTER
11	BUSY	BUSY OUTPUT FROM PRINTER
12	PE	PAPER EMPTY OUTPUT FROM PRINTER
13	SLCT	SELECTED OUTPUT FROM PRINTER
14	=0 V	NOT USED–NOT TERMINATED
15	OSCXT	NOT USED–NOT TERMINATED
16	GROUND	SIGNAL GROUND
17	GROUND	CHASSIS GROUND
18	+5 V	
19–30		
31	INPUT PRIME	
32	$\overline{\text{FAULT}}$	
33–36		

INPUT CONNECTOR: The input connector is a 36-pin D connector.
AMP champ series (AMP P/N 2-552275-1)

FIGURE 9–13A Centronic printer interface

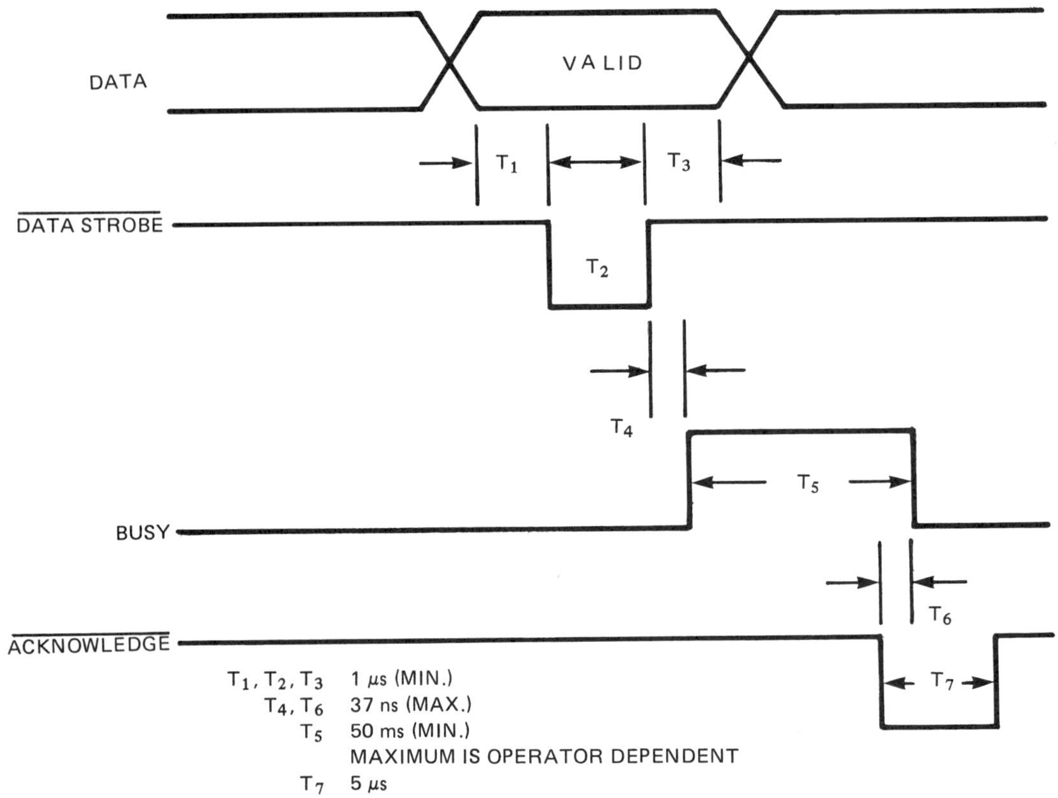

FIGURE 9–13B Timing for the Centronic printer interface

signal follows the busy and indicates the completion of a printer operation. Out of paper indicates an out of paper situation, and select indicates the online or offline status of the printer. The fault line is used to indicate to the computer the presence of any trouble that could hamper printing. The input prime is a signal from the computer that resets the printer logic and homes the print head.

Only five of these control signals are usually used (data strobe, busy, out of paper, select, and fault). Figure 9–14 shows a Centronic parallel printer output port that uses these five control signals. Notice the 74121 one-shot used to stretch the output strobe to a 1-µs pulse length.

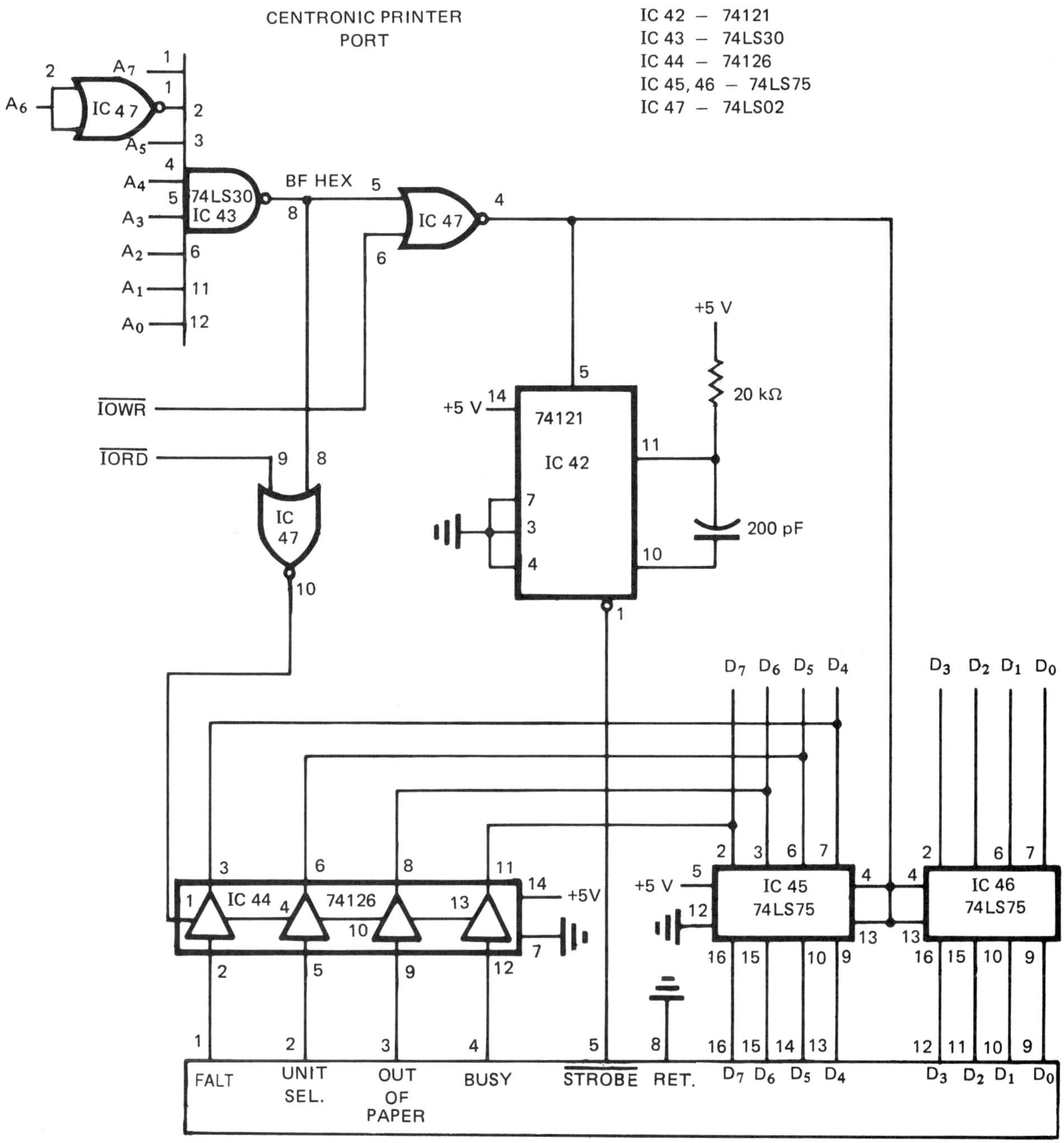
CENTRONIC PRINTER PORT
IC 42 – 74121
IC 43 – 74LS30
IC 44 – 74126
IC 45, 46 – 74LS75
IC 47 – 74LS02
A_7
A_6
A_5
A_4
A_3
A_2
A_1
A_0
IC 47
74LS30
IC 43
BF HEX
IC 47
$\overline{IOWR}$
$\overline{IORD}$
IC 47
+5 V
20 kΩ
200 pF
+5 V
74121
IC 42
D_7 D_6 D_5 D_4
D_3 D_2 D_1 D_0
IC 44
74126
+5V
+5 V
IC 45
74LS75
IC 46
74LS75
FALT
UNIT SEL.
OUT OF PAPER
BUSY
$\overline{STROBE}$
RET.
D_7 D_6 D_5 D_4
D_3 D_2 D_1 D_0

FIGURE 9–14

EXERCISE 9

1. Explain the difference between memory mapped and direct input/output ports.
2. List all the Z 80 input/output instructions.
3. Into how many modes can Group B of the 8255 be programmed?
4. Which mode of the 8255 is used for bidirectional data transfer?
5. What is the value of the first two bits of the address for the control register in the 8255?
6. Write a short program to set the 8255 to all output ports.
7. Write a short program to input data from port B of the 8255 and output it to port A (use circuit in Lab 9).
8. Why is PC_3 the pin used for all the interrupts in all the modes of the 8255?
9. How is the interrupt disabled in mode 1 Group A in the 8255?
10. What is the address of the A port in Figure 9–11?
11. When PB_1 row select line in Figure 9–11 is made LOW and the PA_4 input line goes LOW, what happens to the keys on the keyboard?
12. What is the port configuration of the 8255 in Figure 9–11 if the program in Figure 9–12 is run with the hardware?
13. What is the address of the Centronic printer port in Figure 9–14?
14. What is the bit location (D_0 to D_7) of the busy signal in the Centronic printer port in Figure 9–14?
15. Does the Centronic printer interface have seven or eight data lines?
16. What is the purpose of the select input signal from the Centronic printer port in Figure 9–14?
17. Which bit controls whether a control word will be a mode control word or a bit set/reset control word in the 8255?
18. Which port in the 8255 can have an individual bit set or reset with a bit set/reset control word?
19. Why can't both Group A and Group B be programmed in mode 2?
20. Draw the interface circuit to interface an 8255 to the Biggy trainer at the memory locations of 0FFF, 0FFE, 0FFD, and 0FFC Hex.

Lab 9

OBJECTIVES

After completing this lab, you should be able to

- use the 8255 and program it.
- construct an input port using the 8255.
- construct an output port using the 8255.

Procedure

1. Construct the circuit shown and debug it by using the following procedure:
   A. Use a small continual input/output loop to test the address decoder and the $\overline{IOWR}$ and $\overline{IORD}$ control signals.

```
again   OUT   (02H), A
        IN    A , (FF)
        JP    again
```

   B. After entering this short loop, use a scope and look for low-going strobes at $\overline{CS}$, $\overline{RD}$, and $\overline{WR}$. If they are not present, then check your wiring of the circuit.
   C. Remove the wires from the IC side of the 74LS245 bidirectional bus driver. Use the short input loop and the probe to test each bit of the input of the 74LS245 as shown.

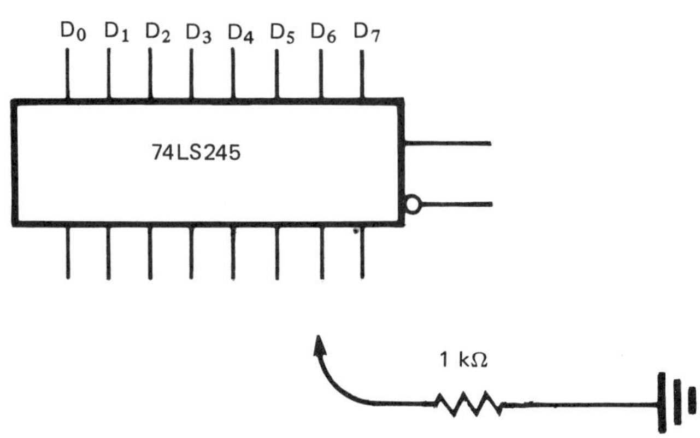

2. Write a program that will take the binary number on input port B of the 8255 and display it on port 2 of the Biggy trainer. Loop the program so that as the dip switch is changed, port 2 will reflect the change.
3. Write a program that will turn PC_4 on for 5 s and off for 10 s. Use the 10-ms timing loop in the Biggy trainer operating system.

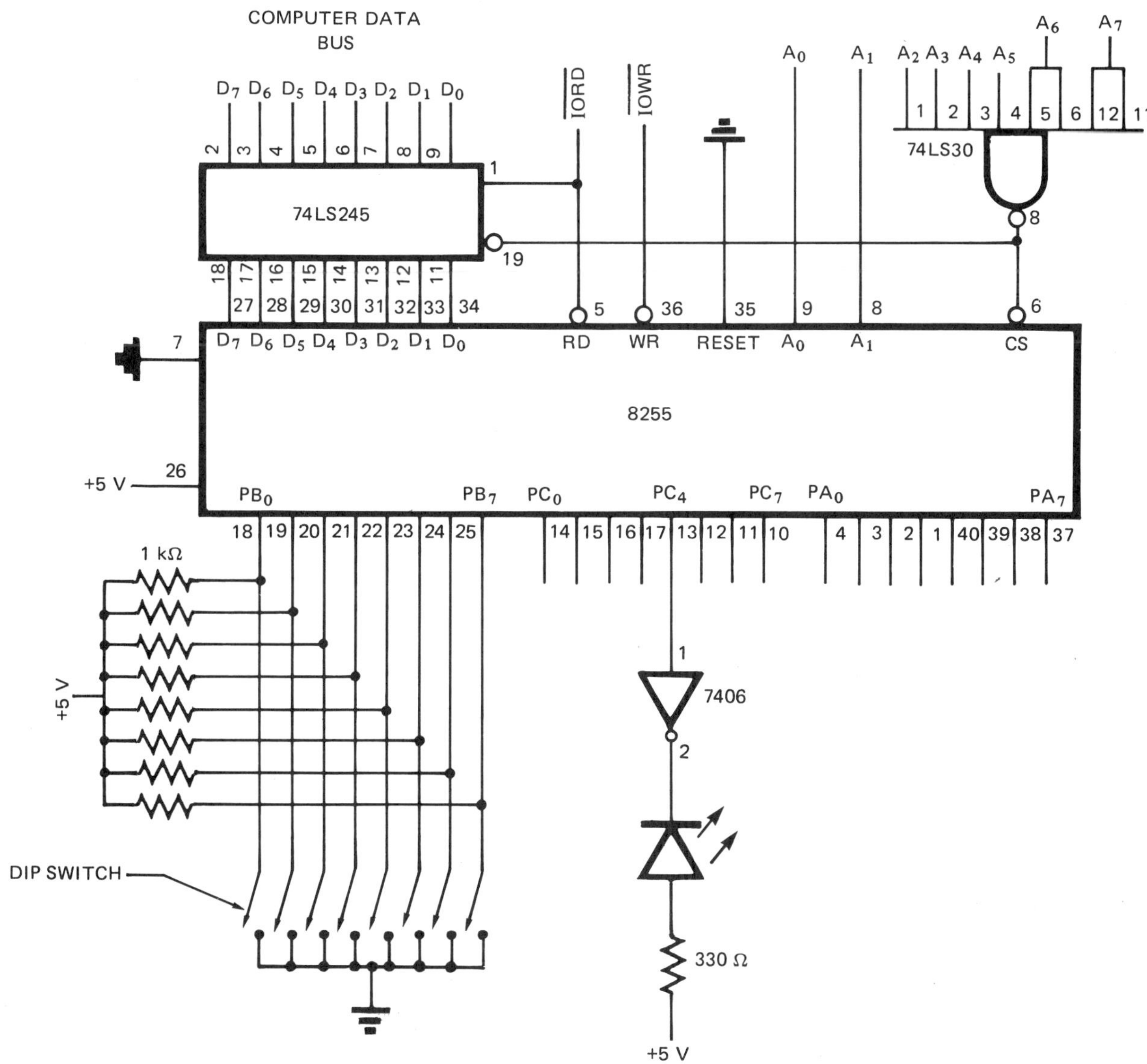
COMPUTER DATA BUS
D_7 D_6 D_5 D_4 D_3 D_2 D_1 D_0
$\overline{IORD}$
$\overline{IOWR}$
A_0
A_1
A_2 A_3 A_4 A_5
A_6
A_7
74LS30
74LS245
8255
RD
WR
RESET
CS
+5 V
PB_0
PB_7
PC_0
PC_4
PC_7
PA_0
PA_7
1 kΩ
DIP SWITCH
7406
330 Ω

Chapter 10

PROGRAMMABLE TIMERS, COUNTERS, AND 8253 ICs

OBJECTIVES

After completing this chapter, you should be able to
- explain the use of a programmable counter as a clock generator.
- explain the 8253 and its programming.

10.1 PROGRAMMABLE DOWN COUNTERS

Quite often a clock generator that the computer can control the frequency of is needed. It may be used to generate the clock for a UART, which is part of a serial port or some other peripheral.

A clock of this type could be produced by having the CPU turn on a bit of an output port and run a fixed timing loop, turning off the output port, and then repeating the whole operation. The only problem is that this will tie up the CPU and nothing else will get done. The answer is to use an external down counter to divide the CPU clock or any external clock by a binary number that the CPU could output to the down counter. The down counter would then divide the clock by the number supplied by the CPU and output a pulse each time the count reached 0, then start over again. This would allow the CPU to output the binary divisor and then forget about the clock generator down counter until the CPU wished to change its output frequency.

Figure 10–1 shows a typical programmable down counter that will produce an even-duty-cycle clock with an output frequency of one-half the external clock frequency divided by the binary number latched out to the output port of the circuit.

The 7430 and the 7402 make a simple 8-bit address decoder that selects the output port made up of D latches. This output port can hold an 8-bit binary number that the CPU can change if desired. Flip-flops A through H are JK flip-flops set to toggle and are used to make an 8-bit ripple down counter. The counter will down count because the $\overline{Q}$ output of each flip-flop provides the clock input to the next flip-flop. The $\overline{\text{PRESET}}$ and $\overline{\text{CLEAR}}$ inputs of each flip-flop are controlled by a set of NAND gates that will either set or clear the Q output of the JK flip-flops when the NAND gates are enabled by a HIGH on the load input. Whether the JK flip-flops are set or reset when the load

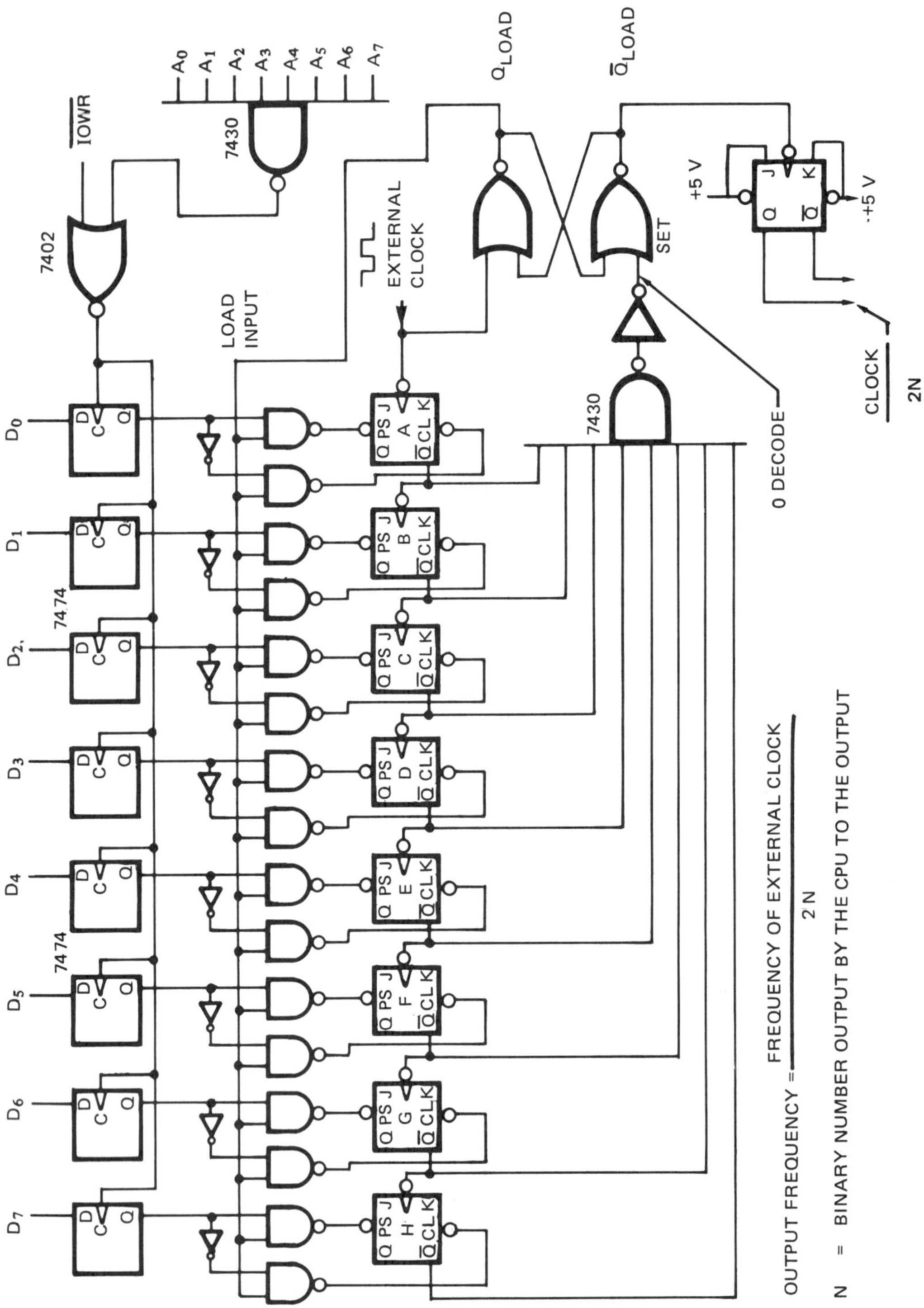

FIGURE 10–1 Programmable clock generator

input goes high is controlled by the logic state of the associated D flip-flops of the output port.

Therefore, when the load input goes high, the binary number stored in the D latches of the output port is impressed on the Q and $\overline{Q}$ outputs of the down counter. When the load input returns to a logic LOW state, the down counter then starts to count down from the binary number just impressed on it to 0 at which time it would then set all its Q outputs to 1's and start counting down to 0 again, except for the 7430 and the SET RESET crossed NOR flip-flop.

When the down counter's Q outputs reach 0, all the $\overline{Q}$ outputs are 1's. This causes the output of the 7430 to set the Q output of the SET RESET crossed NOR flip-flop to 1, thus loading the stored binary number in the D latch into the down counter. When this happens, the counter's output is no longer all 1's for the $\overline{Q}$ outputs, and the SET input to the SET RESET crossed NOR flip-flop goes to 0. This does not reset the Q output of the crossed NOR flip-flop though. To reset a SET RESET flip-flop, you must make the RESET input active while keeping the SET input inactive. This happens when the external clock again returns HIGH and resets the crossed NOR flip-flop Q output, thus releasing the down counter to start a down count from the stored number once again.

Every time the down counter reaches 0 the counter is reloaded with the stored binary number and allowed to start counting down again. If the stored binary number is 6, then every sixth clock cycle of the external clock will produce a negative-going clock pulse on the $\overline{Q}$ output of the SET RESET crossed NOR flip-flop. This is then fed to the clock of a JK flip-flop set to toggle. This toggling flip-flop will further divide the external clock by two and in the process produce an even-duty-cycle clock. Therefore, the final output frequency is

$$F = \frac{f}{2N}$$

where F = output frequency
f = frequency of external clock
N = number output by the CPU

Figure 10–2 shows the waveforms for the divide by 6 down count.

10.2 THE 8253 PROGRAMMABLE INTERVAL TIMER

The 8253 is an LSI NMOS IC made by Intel Co. It has three 16-bit programmable down counters that are very similar to the 8-bit down counter just discussed. The outputs are capable of handling one TTL load, and the inputs draw about 10 μA each. The clock inputs to each of the counters have a maximum frequency of 2 MHz. The 8254 is functionally the same IC as the 8253, except that its clock inputs are rated at 10 MHz.

Figure 10–3 shows the block drawing and pinout of the 8253 IC. The bidirectional data bus is used to interface to the computer's data bus. Because the outputs of the 8253 can only handle one TTL load, the data bus must be buffered as shown in Figure 10–4. The 74LS245 bidirectional bus driver was used for buffering the data bus in the example

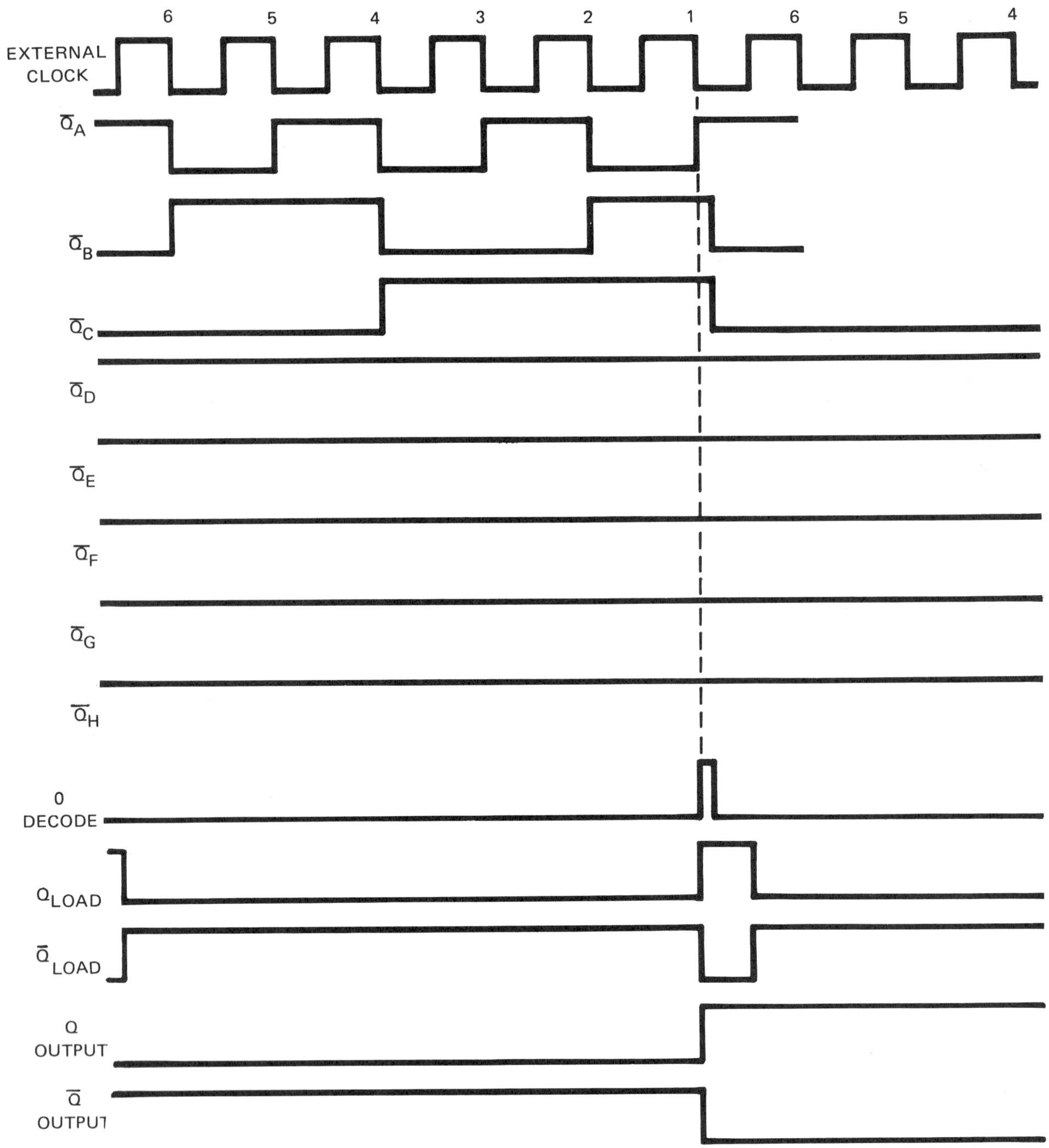

FIGURE 10–2 Waveforms for divide by 6 set into the programmable clock of Figure 10–1

intel®

8253/8253-5
PROGRAMMABLE INTERVAL TIMER

- **MCS-85™ Compatible 8253-5**
- **3 Independent 16-Bit Counters**
- **DC to 2 MHz**
- **Programmable Counter Modes**
- **Count Binary or BCD**
- **Single +5V Supply**
- **24-Pin Dual In-Line Package**

The Intel® 8253 is a programmable counter/timer chip designed for use as an Intel microcomputer peripheral. It uses nMOS technology with a single +5V supply and is packaged in a 24-pin plastic DIP.

It is organized as 3 independent 16-bit counters, each with a count rate of up to 2 MHz. All modes of operation are software programmable.

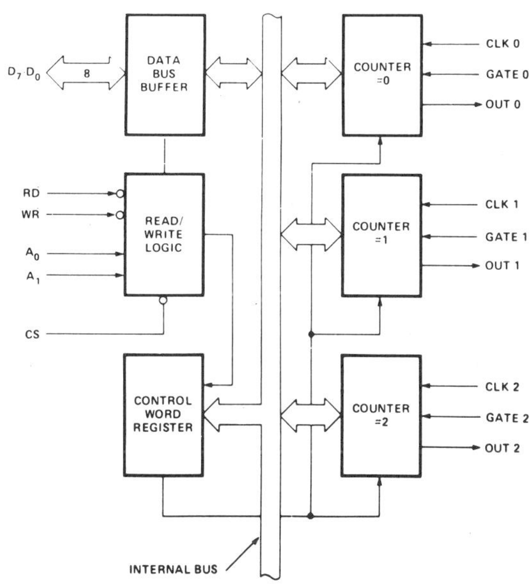

Block Diagram

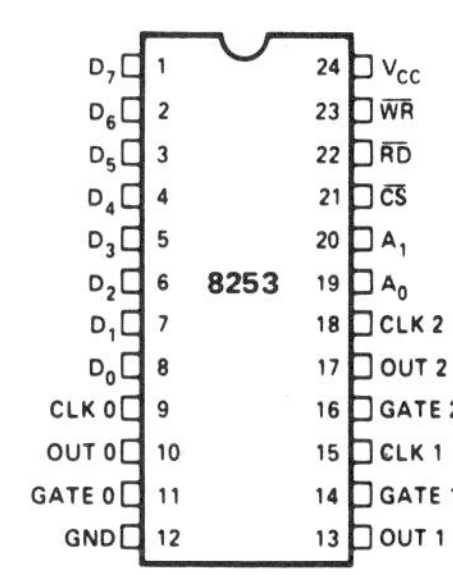

Pin Configuration

FIGURE 10–3

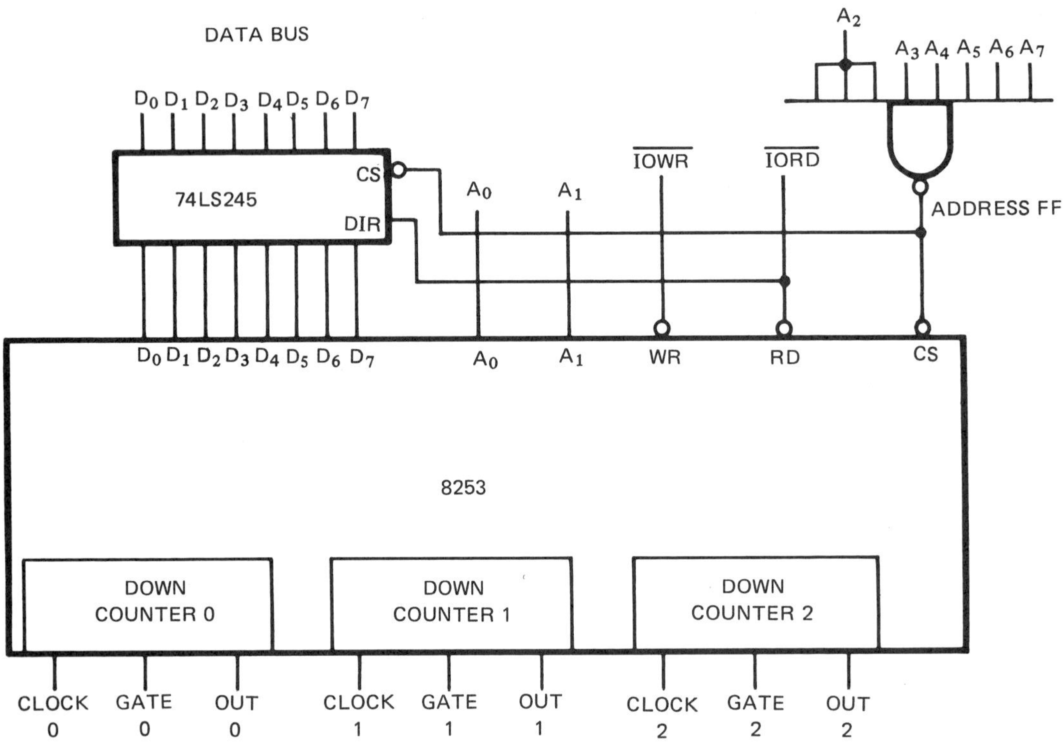

FIGURE 10–4 The 8253 interfaced to a computer

interface of Figure 10–4. The $\overline{RD}$, $\overline{WR}$, and $\overline{CS}$ control the read/write and select to the 8253 just as they did in the 8255 LSI IC, which we studied earlier.

The address inputs A_0 and A_1 address the internal registers that are to be written to or read from. The addresses for the registers are shown in the table of Figure 10–5.

Each of the three 16-bit counters has a gate input, clock input, and a single output. The gate input is used to gate the clock to the counter, and the output is used to produce a pulse at the termination or 0 count of the down counter.

10.3 PROGRAMMING THE 8253

There are six modes to which any of the three down counters can be set. The control word format is shown in Figure 10–6. When this 1-byte control word is written out to the control register of the 8253 (address $A_0 = 1$, $A_1 = 1$), the down counter addressed by the two most significant bits (D_7 and D_6) of the byte is configured in the mode indicated by the rest of the control byte. D_4 and D_5 determine how the down counter is to be loaded with the binary number to which it will preset itself. If D_4 and D_5 are 00, then

$\overline{CS}$	$\overline{RD}$	$\overline{WR}$	A_1	A_0	
0	1	0	0	0	Load Counter No. 0
0	1	0	0	1	Load Counter No. 1
0	1	0	1	0	Load Counter No. 2
0	1	0	1	1	Write Mode Word
0	0	1	0	0	Read Counter No. 0
0	0	1	0	1	Read Counter No. 1
0	0	1	1	0	Read Counter No. 2
0	0	1	1	1	No-Operation 3-State
1	X	X	X	X	Disable 3-State
0	1	1	X	X	No-Operation 3-State

FIGURE 10–5

the content of the selected counter is latched into a storage register, so the CPU can read that register to determine the value of the counter when the control word to latch was written out to the control register. A 01 on D_4 and D_5 will cause the next byte written out to the selected register to be loaded into the least significant byte of the 16-bit down counter register. A 10 will load the most significant byte in the same manner. When D_4 and D_5 are 11, both bytes of the down counter are loaded by first writing out the least significant byte and then the most significant byte.

Control Word Format

D_7	D_6	D_5	D_4	D_3	D_2	D_1	D_0
SC1	SC0	RL1	RL0	M2	M1	M0	BCD

Definition of Control

SC — Select Counter:

SC1	SC0	
0	0	Select Counter 0
0	1	Select Counter 1
1	0	Select Counter 2
1	1	Illegal

RL — Read/Load:

RL1	RL0	
0	0	Counter Latching operation (see READ/WRITE Procedure Section)
1	0	Read/Load most significant byte only.
0	1	Read/Load least significant byte only.
1	1	Read/Load least significant byte first, then most significant byte.

M — MODE:

M2	M1	M0	
0	0	0	Mode 0
0	0	1	Mode 1
X	1	0	Mode 2
X	1	1	Mode 3
1	0	0	Mode 4
1	0	1	Mode 5

BCD:

0	Binary Counter 16-bits
1	Binary Coded Decimal (BCD) Counter (4 Decades)

FIGURE 10–6 The 8253 control word format

D_1, D_2, and D_3 determine the mode of operation of the selected down counter, and D_0 is used to set the type of down counter to be used. If D_0 is a 1, the down count is a BCD counter, and you would load it with BCD numbers such as 9999 (1001,1001, 1001, 1001). A 0 on D_0 configures the down counter as a regular binary counter.

The following is a sample program for loading the 0 counter of the 8253.

```
             ;*****************************************************
             ;    LOADING THE 0 COUNTER OF THE 8253 TIMER           *
             ;*****************************************************
             ;
0800                    ORG     800H
0800 3E30               LD      A,30H           ;CONTROL WORD
0802 D3FF               OUT     (0FFH),A        ;LS BYTE TO COUNTER 0
0804 3E00               LD      A,00H           ;LS BYTE OF 0 COUNTER
0806 D3FC               OUT     (0FCH),A        ;OUT TO COUNTER 0
0808 3E01               LD      A,01H           ;MS BYTE OF COUNTER 0
080A D3FC               OUT     (0FCH),A        ;OUT TO COUNTER 0
080C 76                 HALT
0000                    END
00000 Total Errors
```

This program will set counter 0 to be a binary counter and operate in mode 0. The down count that will determine the divisor of the clock input to counter 0 is 0100H, and it is loaded in a 2-byte output operation: least significant byte then the most significant byte. After the most significant byte is loaded, the down counter will start to run.

10.4 MODE 0 OPERATION OF THE 8253

Mode 0 is a CPU-controlled one-shot. When the down counter is loaded, the output is LOW and the down counter begins to count down from the loaded count to 0. When the 0 count is reached, the output stays HIGH and will not go LOW again until the counter is reloaded with a new count. If the down counter is reloaded before the terminal or 0 count is reached, the output will stay LOW, and the counter will start again at the new count just loaded. Therefore, the down counter acts just like a retriggerable one-shot that is triggered by the CPU when the down count is loaded into the down counter of the 8253.

A typical use for this type of one-shot operation would be in process control of machinery. For example, a small CPU could control all the functions of an orange juice processing machine that would take the oranges off a conveyor belt one at a time and squeeze them. If no oranges came down the conveyor belt, then the CPU would turn off the juice squeezer part of the machine. A photosenser could detect the passage of an orange just before it fell off the conveyor belt into the squeezer and interrupt the CPU, which had been busy with other tasks. When the CPU was interrupted, it would call to a short subroutine that would output a count to an 8253 that controls the juice squeezer.

When the down count was loaded in the 8253, its output would go LOW, which would start the juice squeezer and keep it running for the time it would take to squeeze the orange, and the CPU could then go on its merry way. If one orange after another came down the conveyor belt, the juice squeezer would just keep going because the down counter in the 8253 would reload faster than the counter could count down to 0. Therefore, the squeezer would only run when it was needed, and the CPU would only have to start it when an orange came along. Also, the length of time to run the squeezer per orange could easily be controlled by the number output to the 8253 down counter.

10.5 MODE 1 OPERATION OF THE 8253

Mode 1 operation is very similar to mode 0 operation except that the counter is triggered or started to count by the rising edge of the gate input to the counter on the 8253 IC. The output will be HIGH until the rising edge of the gate input, at which time the output will go LOW until the down counter reaches the 0 count. The counter will then be preset to the original count and stay there until the rising edge of the next gate input. The one-shot is retriggerable if the gate is triggered before the 0 count is reached. If a new count is loaded into the down counter of the 8253 before the terminal or 0 count is reached, the new count will be reloaded and the down counter will start counting down to 0 again.

If the photosensor in the juice squeezer just described was connected to the gate of the 8253 down counter, and the 8253 was programmed in mode 1, then the CPU would not have to be interrupted to start the juice squeezer.

10.6 MODE 2 OPERATION OF THE 8253

Mode 2 operation is used to make a divide by N counter to produce different frequencies for any application that a computer may need. When the down counter is loaded, it begins to count down to 0. When the terminal count or 0 is reached, the output goes LOW for one clock period of the input clock to the down counter. The counter is then preset to the original count, and the process starts over again. Therefore, the input frequency is divided by the number loaded into the down counter. If the gate input is LOW, the output will stay HIGH until the gate returns HIGH, at which time the counter will start counting again from the beginning. This allows the counter to be externally synchronized to another clock if needed.

This mode of operation is often used to produce baud rate frequencies for UART ICs or for CRT control of monitors.

10.7 MODE 3 OPERATION OF THE 8253

This is the same as mode 2 except that the output is HIGH for half of the down count and LOW for the second half of the count. This is done by decrementing the down counter by 2 each time the input clock goes from HIGH to LOW. Odd number down counts decrement the counts by 1 on the first clock and by 2 thereafter. On the next cycle the first clock decrements the down counter by 3, and then by 2 until 0 is reached again, and the process repeats itself.

The output will be HIGH for N + 1 divided by 2, and LOW for N − 1 divided by 2. If these two terms are added together, the sum is N:

$$\frac{N+1}{2} + \frac{N-1}{2} = \frac{(N+1) \quad + \quad (N-1)}{2} = \frac{2N+1-1}{2} = \frac{2N}{2} = N$$

By this means an odd number can be used as a divider even though the output is not quite an even duty cycle.

10.8 MODE 4 OPERATION OF THE 8253

Mode 4 operation is exactly the same as mode 0, except that the output will be HIGH until the counter reaches the 0 count; it will then go LOW for one clock period of the input clock. The output is a one-shot that produces a short one clock, low-going strobe.

10.9 MODE 5 OPERATION OF THE 8253

Mode 5 operation is the same as mode 1, except that at the terminal or 0 count the output will produce a low-going strobe for one clock cycle of the input clock.

10.10 READING THE 8253 DOWN COUNTER REGISTERS

It is possible to read any of the three down counters in the 8253 while they are running by simply executing a READ operation by the CPU to the desired down counter. The only problem is that you may get invalid data if you just happen to read the counter at the moment it is changing count. If all this number is to be used for is a random number, then this is no problem; but if this number is to be used by the CPU to determine the progress of the counter, then a different method of reading the counter is used.

To read the counter accurately while it is down counting, the CPU must write out the read control word to the control register for the down counter it wishes to read. This causes the content of the down counter to be latched into a register, where it will remain until the CPU reads it. To read the count latched in this storage register, the CPU reads the down counter just as before. The first READ operation reads the LOW byte, and the second reads the HIGH byte of the latched counter value.

By reading the value of a selected down counter, the CPU can tell how much time is left for a certain process to complete or how much of a process has yet to be done.

EXERCISE 10

1. What is the address of the output port in Figure 10–1?
2. What would be the binary number to be output to the down counter in Figure 10–1 to produce a 300-Hz frequency if the input to the external clock was 2 MHz?
3. How many modes can the 8253 be programmed in?
4. What do bits 4 and 5 of the 8253 control word determine?
5. What is the control word to program counter 0 of the 8253 in mode 3 with a dual counter load, and as a binary counter?
6. Which mode of the 8253 will produce an even-duty-cycle waveform?
7. What are the addresses of the counters and control words for the 8253 in Lab 10?
8. What mode will produce a one-shot that is controlled by an external input and where the output will be a short, low-going pulse?
9. How are the 8253 counters read to determine the count of a counter?
10. Why was the 74LS245 used to buffer the data bus of the 8253?
11. Write a short program to produce an output frequency of 1000 Hz at pin 10 of the circuit in Lab 10.
12. Write a short program to produce a computer-controlled one-shot of 50 ms in length.
13. Write a short program to read the 0 counter of the Lab 10 circuit and place the count on port 2 of the trainer.
14. Draw the block drawing of the 8253.
15. Draw the circuit to memory map the 8253 into memory locations FDFF Hex, FDFE Hex, FDFD Hex, and FDFC Hex.
16. What would be the time-out period for an 8253 programmed in mode 0 if all three counters were cascaded together and loaded FFFF Hex? (Use an input frequency of 2 MHz.)
17. What is the control word to program counter 2 in mode 5 with a low byte counter load only?
18. What is the maximum clock speed for the standard 8253?
19. What will happen if the $\overline{CS}$ is LOW and $\overline{RD}$ and $\overline{WR}$ are HIGH in the 8253?
20. What are the V_{CC} and ground pins of the 8253?

Lab 10

OBJECTIVES

After completing this lab, you should be able to

- program the 8253.
- construct an interface circuit using the 8253.

Procedure

1. Construct the circuit shown and debug it by using the following procedure:
   A. Use a small continual input/output loop to test the address decoder and the $\overline{IOWR}$ and $\overline{IORD}$ control signals.

```
again   OUT   (02H), A
        IN    A , (FF)
        JP    again
```

   B. After entering this short loop, use a scope and look for low-going strobes at $\overline{CS}$, $\overline{RD}$, and $\overline{WR}$. If they are not present then check your wiring of the circuit.
   C. Remove the wires from the IC side of the 74LS245 bidirectional bus driver. Use the short input loop and the probe to test each bit of the input of the 74LS245 as shown.

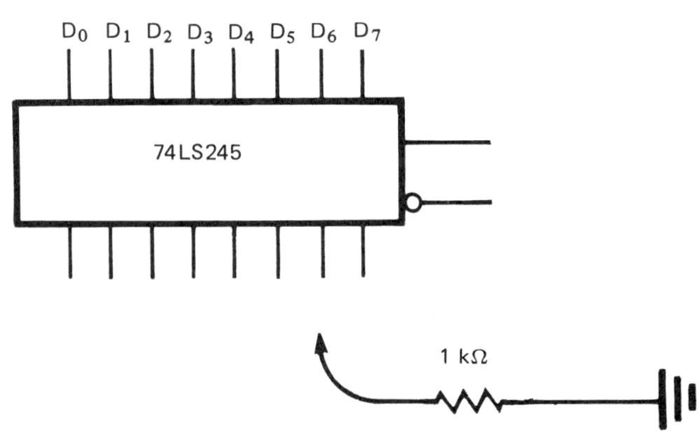

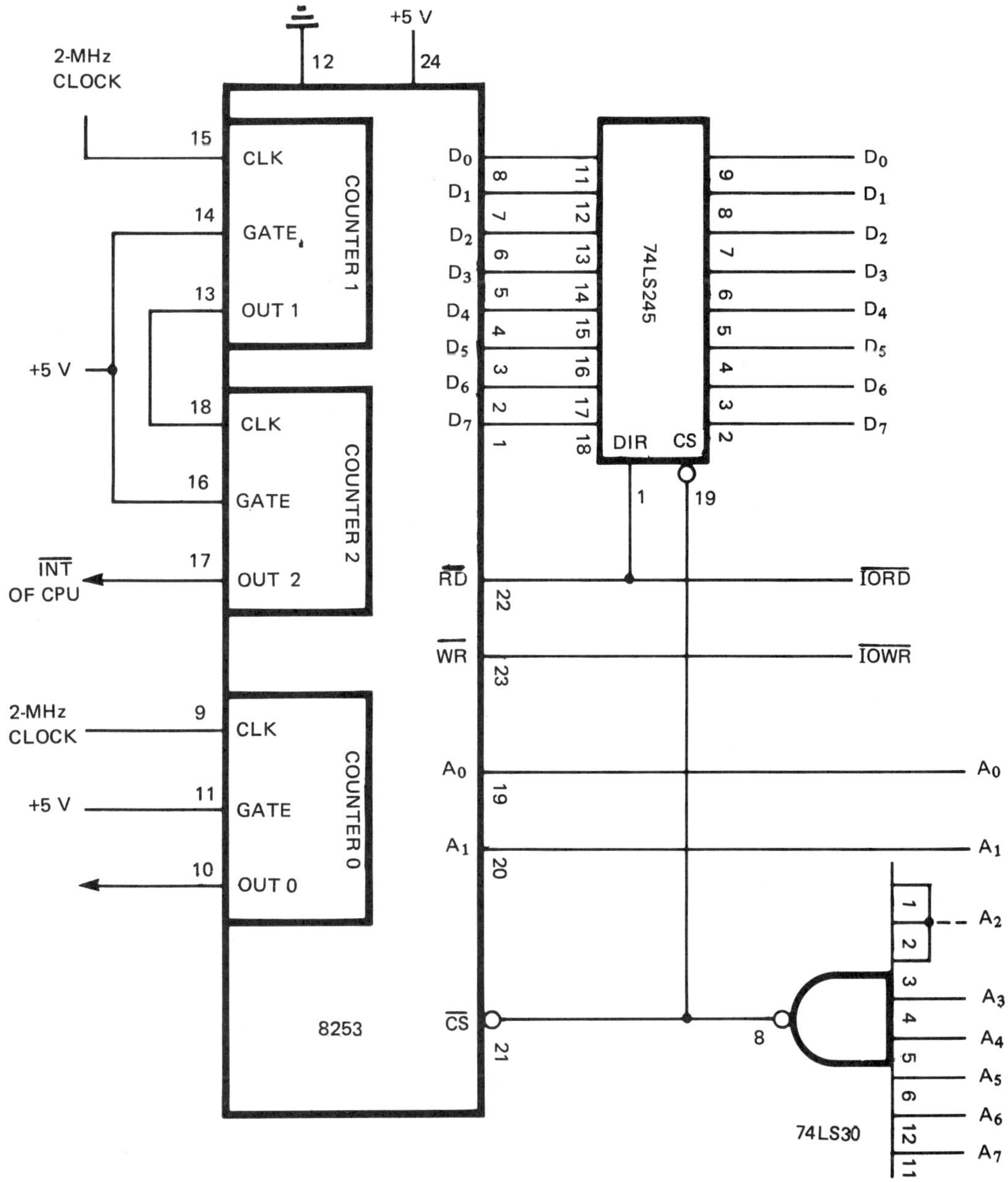
2-MHz CLOCK
+5 V
12
24
15
CLK
14
GATE
13
OUT 1
COUNTER 1
18
CLK
16
GATE
17
OUT 2
COUNTER 2
INT OF CPU
2-MHz CLOCK
9
CLK
11
GATE
10
OUT 0
COUNTER 0
8253
D0 D1 D2 D3 D4 D5 D6 D7
RD
22
WR
23
A0
19
A1
20
CS
21
74LS245
DIR
CS
1
19
IORD
IOWR
A0 A1 A2 A3 A4 A5 A6 A7
74LS30
8

D. If Steps A–C prove to function correctly, then enter the short program shown and test the output frequency of counter 0 with the scope. The output frequency should be one-half of the input clock frequency.

```
  LD   A, 36H
 OUT   (FF), A
  LD   A, 02H
 OUT   (FC), A
  LD   A,00H
 OUT   (FC), A
HALT
```

2. Write a short program to make the output of counter 2 have a 1-Hz rate exactly (use mode 2).
3. Use the $\overline{\text{INT}}$ input mode 1 interrupt of the Z 80 and the clock program you wrote in Lab 8 to produce an accurate clock from the 1-Hz signal of the output of counter 2.

Note: To make the interrupt work well, set the down counter of the 1 counter to divide by 32. This will give a short pulse of long-enough duration to be used as the interrupt strobe coming out of the output of counter 2 at a 1-Hz rate. There is a JP 838 Hex instruction at memory location 0038 Hex. Therefore place your clock subroutine at 838 Hex in RAM.

Chapter 11

SERIAL COMMUNICATION

OBJECTIVES

After completing this chapter, you should be able to

- describe asynchronous and synchronous serial communication formats.
- use the 8251-A universal synchronous asynchronous receiver transmitter and program it.
- describe the EIA RS-232C serial communication standard.
- use the ASCII code.

11.1 ASYNCHRONOUS SERIAL COMMUNICATION

Until now, all the data that the computer has moved around has been moved by using a bus. A bus has one line or wire for each bit of the binary number being moved. This is a very fast method of transferring information inside a computer, but it becomes impractical to have one line for each bit when the data communication is over a longer distance. The use of a bus to transfer digital data is called *parallel data communication*.

Serial data communication uses only two lines or wires to transfer data. This requires that the bits be sent one at a time down the wire at a precise rate and reassembled into a parallel form at the other end. This is done with a parallel in/serial out shift register as a transmitter and a serial in/parallel out shift register as a receiver. The rate at which the bits are shifted out of the shift register is usually called the *baud* rate. In most instances, the bit rate of a serial transmitter and the baud rate are the same. There are a few methods used mainly in telephone modems in which more than one bit of data is encoded on one transition of the baud rate clock. In these cases the baud rate and bit rate are not at the same frequency. For the rest of this discussion the baud rate and bit rate will mean the same thing.

Asynchronous serial communication uses a low-going start bit to signal the serial receiver to start clocking in the data to the shift register. The serial transmission line is held at a logic HIGH until a byte of data is to be transmitted down the line. To transmit a byte, the line is brought LOW for one bit; then the contents of the data byte are

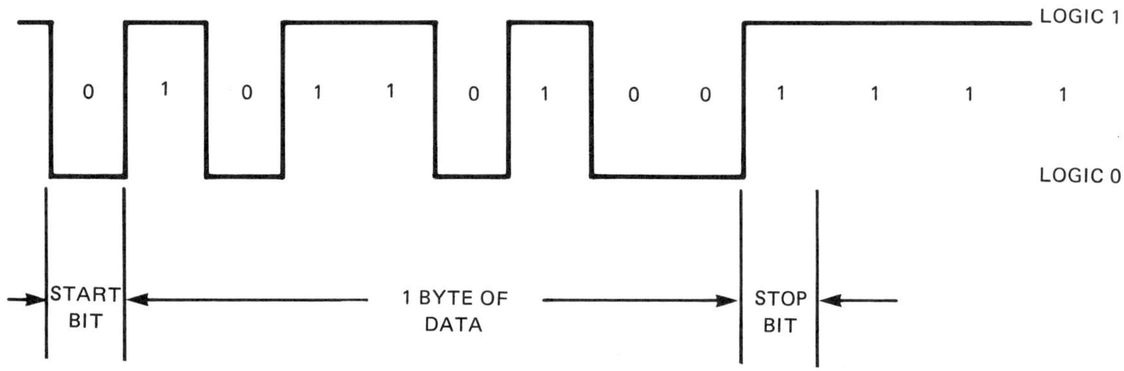

FIGURE 11–1 The asynchronous serial format

transmitted one bit at a time, followed by at least one bit of logic HIGH called the stop bit. This format is shown in Figure 11–1. The use of a low-going start bit is not something dreamed up for computer communication, but it is the leftover method used by old teletype communication. The old teletype used a current of 20–60 mA as a logic 1, which held a rotary distributor from turning. When the current was broken, the electric magnet holding the rotary distributor let go and the bits were transferred to relays as the wheel turned around one time. A stop bit was necessary to ensure that the magnet would stop the wheel after one turn. A 20–60-mA current (logic 1) was called a MARK, and the absence of current (logic 0) was called a SPACE. These terms are still sometimes used today.

To make sure that the same data transmitted is shifted into the receiver, the clocks of the transmitter and receiver must be extremely accurate. Crystal-controlled clocks are used to generate the clock frequency for the serial transmitter and receiver. The 8253 internal timer is often used to generate the correct baud rate frequency for serial communication in a computer system because its frequency or baud rate is programmable over a wide frequency range.

11.2 SYNCHRONOUS SERIAL COMMUNICATION

In the asynchronous serial format just discussed, it takes 10 bits to send one byte of data (one start bit, eight data bits, and one stop bit). This means that 20% of the transmitter time is spent sending the framing bits (start and stop bits). Synchronous serial communication does not use framing bits and uses eight bits to send eight bits or one byte. Therefore, more data can be sent in the same time period with synchronous than asynchronous serial communication. To keep the transmitter and receiver in sync with each other, a predefined sync word is continually transmitted while no data is being sent down the wire. The receiver shifts in the bits one at a time and compares the word in the shift register to the predefined sync word. When the word in the shift register is the same as the predefined sync word, the shift register will clock in a whole new word and compare it to the predefined sync word again. If it matches, the receiver will bring a control bit

HIGH to tell the CPU that it is in sync with the transmitter of the other device that is sending the sync word.

After the receiver is in sync, any change in the bit pattern shifted into the shift register is considered a data word. Usually data is transmitted in blocks of 256 or 1024 bytes, with the first byte being a predefined start code and the ending byte a cyclic redundancy byte to check for errors in transmission.

Synchronous methods of serial communication are used on disk and tape storage systems to squeeze as much storage as possible on the storage media.

11.3 THE ASYNCHRONOUS SERIAL TRANSMITTER

Figure 11–2 is the logic circuit for an asynchronous serial transmitter, which will follow the format shown in Figure 11–1. The transmitter is made of three basic parts: transmitter buffer, shift register, and control sequencer.

When the CPU outputs a byte to the transmitter buffer, the byte is stored in the D latches that make up the buffer, and the TRANS flip-flop is set. The TRANS READY flag will go LOW which is usually interfaced to the CPU through an input port so that the CPU can test it. This flag is used to tell the CPU that the transmitter buffer is full and that it should wait to output another byte to it.

Setting the TRANS flip-flop also places a 1 on the input of the NOR gate which controls the counters of the sequencer part of the serial transmitter. This allows the counters to start counting from the 0 count. A 74154, 74145, and three OR gates are used to decode the 1, 7, and 9F counts of this counter. When the 1 count comes along, it sets the RUN flip-flop and broadside loads the byte stored in the transmitter buffer into the JK flip-flops used for the shift register. Setting the RUN flip-flop also places a 1 on the input to the NOR gate which controls the counter CLEARs. This will ensure that the counter will keep running until the RUN flip-flop and the TRANS flip-flop are both reset. Once the shift register is loaded, the 7 count resets the TRANS flip-flop, which makes the TRANS READY flag HIGH. This tells the CPU that it can output a new byte to the transmitter buffer. When the 7 count resets the TRANS flip-flop, the counters are not reset to 0 because the RUN flip-flop is set, which keeps the counters running. This method of using a buffer to store the next byte to be shifted out is called *double buffering* and is used in almost all LSI asynchronous serial ICs.

After the 7 count resets the TRANS flip-flop, the XF count is used to produce the clock for the shift register, which now contains the byte to shift out. Notice that the first JK flip-flop is hard wired to be reset to 0 when the shift register is broadside loaded. This is the start bit, which is always 0.

The shift register is now clocked each time the XF count comes along. When the 9F count goes low, it resets the RUN flip-flop, which will reset the counters to 0 if a new byte has not been loaded into the transmitter buffer. If a new byte had been loaded in the transmitter buffer before the shift register was finished shifting out the last byte, then the TRANS flip-flop would be set and the counter would keep on counting and start a whole new cycle of loading and shifting out the next byte once again.

The clock that drives the counters is 16 times the bit rate or baud rate of the transmitter and will determine the speed of the asynchronous serial transmitter. Figure 11–3 shows the waveforms for the transmitter of Figure 11–2.

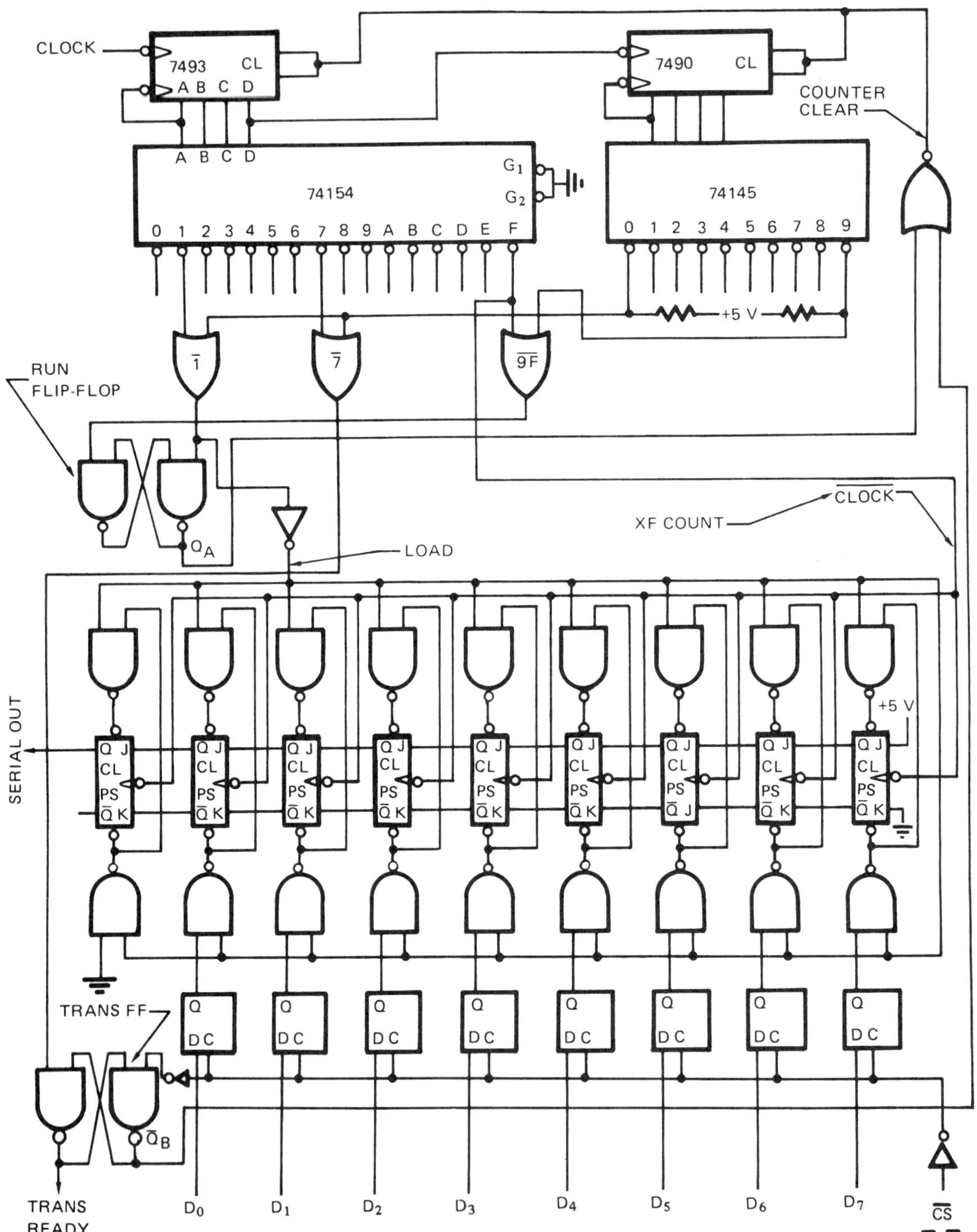

FIGURE 11–2 Serial transmitter

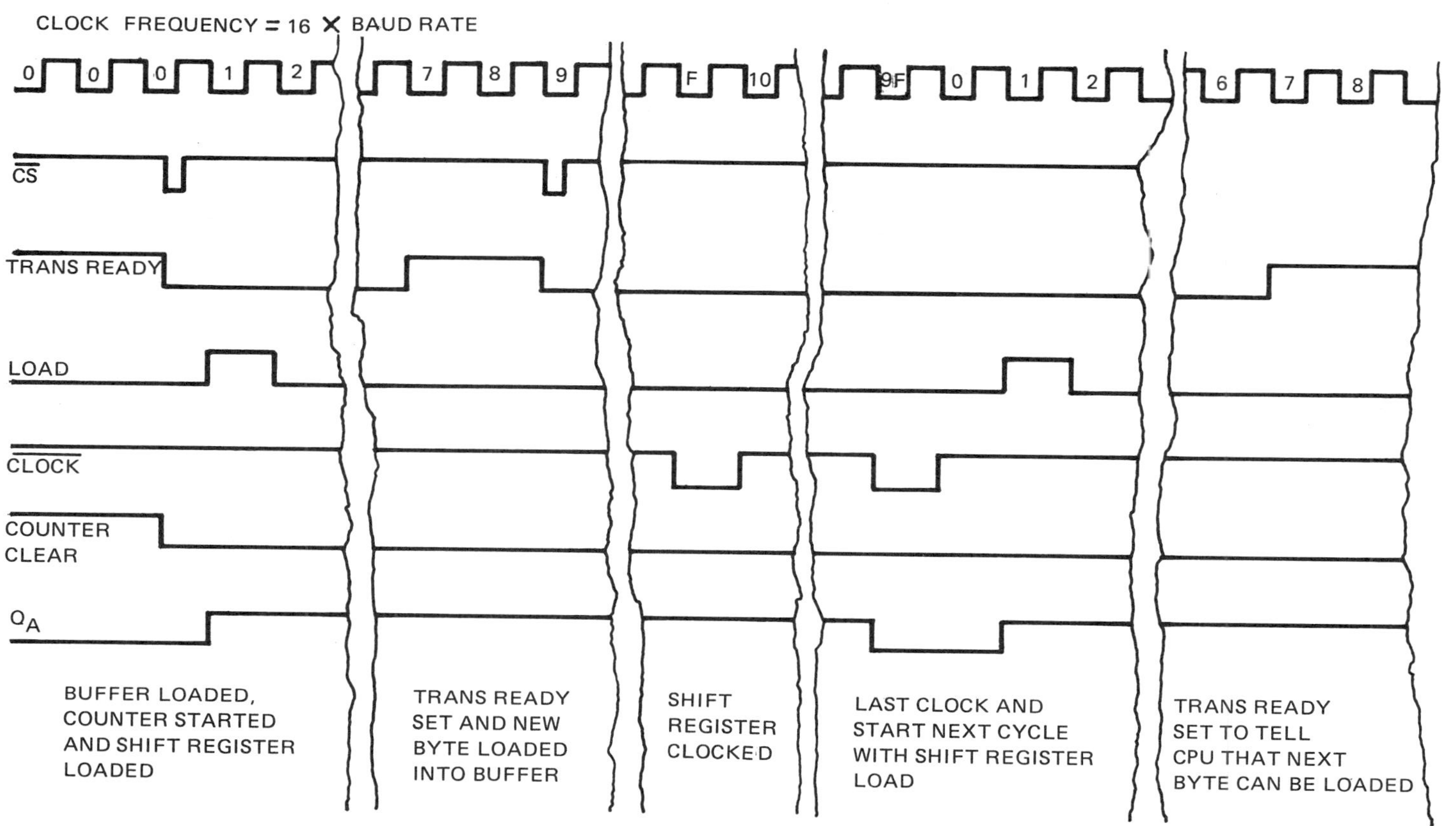

FIGURE 11–3 Waveforms for serial transmitter of Figure 11–2

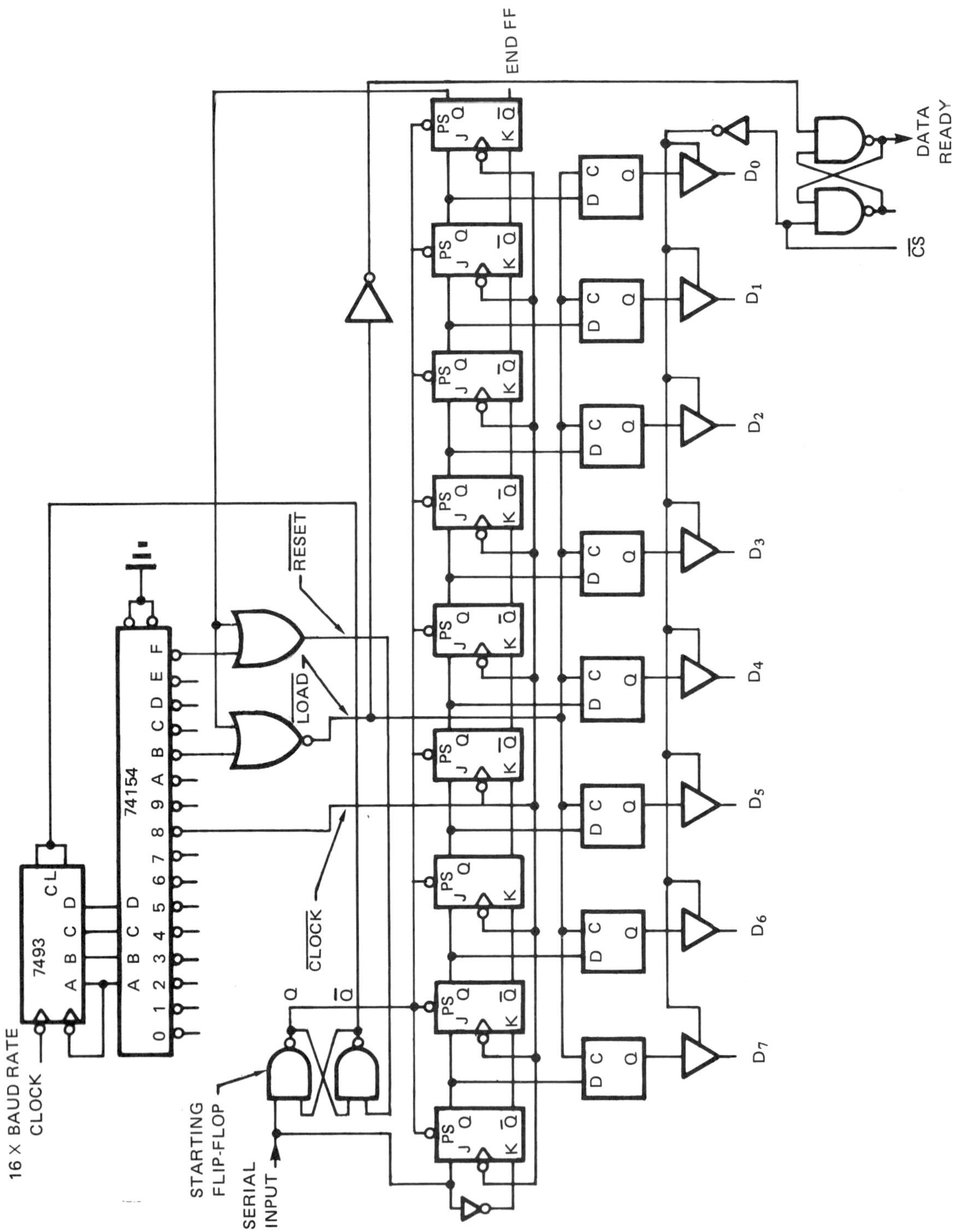

FIGURE 11–4A Serial receiver

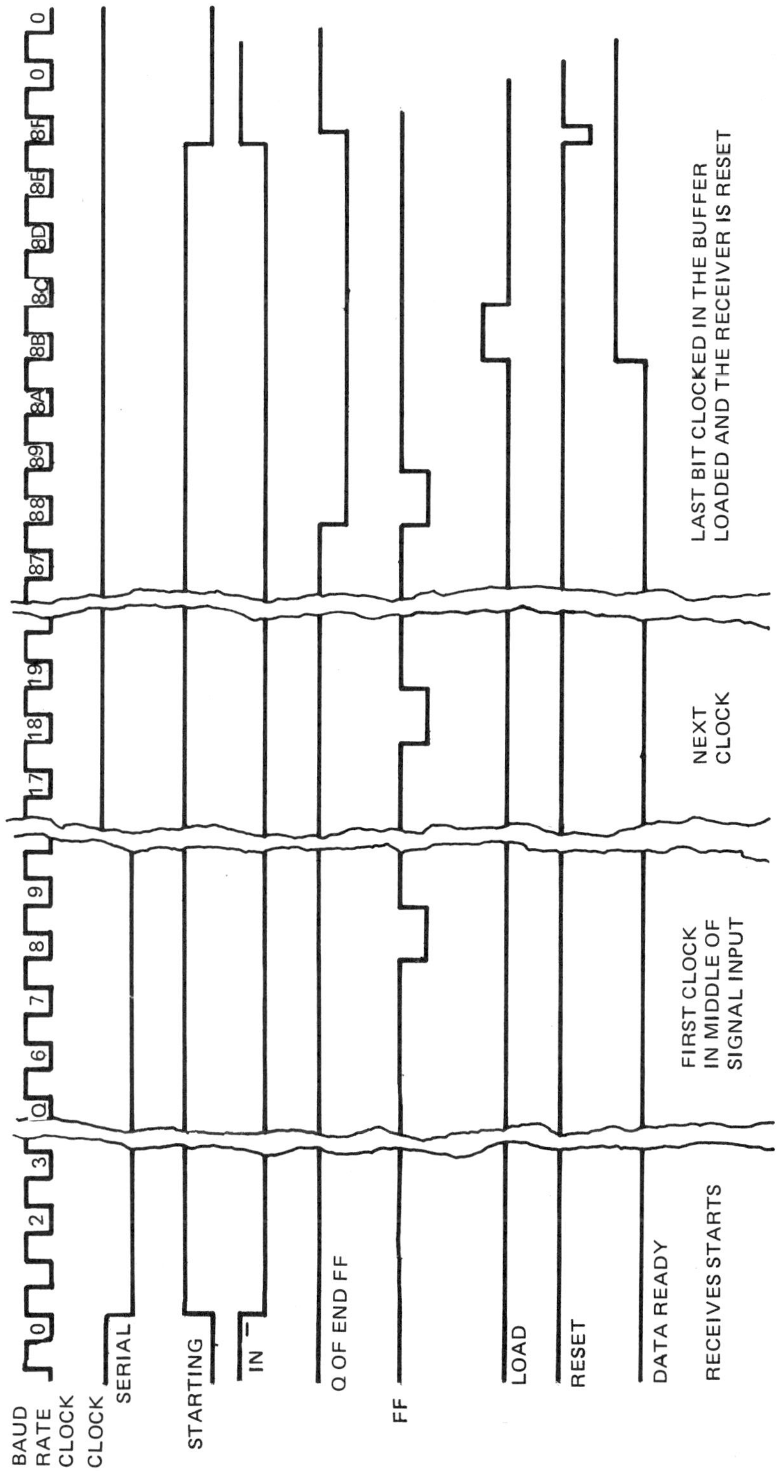

FIGURE 11–4B Waveforms for Figure 11–4A

11.4 THE ASYNCHRONOUS SERIAL RECEIVER

The logic circuit for an asynchronous serial receiver that will receive data transmitted in the format of Figure 11–1 is shown in Figure 11–4. The receiver has three basic parts: receiver buffer, shift register, and sequencer.

When the start bit sets the STARTING flip-flop, the 7493 16-bit counter is released and starts to count from 0 to F. The outputs of this counter are fed to a 74154, which decodes the X8 count for the shift register clock, the XB count, and the XF count.

Eight counts of the counter after the falling edge of the serial input, the shift register is clocked and the 0 starting bit is clocked into the first JK flip-flop. This means that the serial input signal will be sampled or shifted into the shift register in the middle of each bit sent down the wire. This prevents possible data loss due to noise at the transition of each bit. Also, if the two baud rate generators of the transmitter and receiver are slightly off, the error will not effect the data transmission.

The clocking or shifting of the data bits into the shift register will continue until the LOW start bit reaches the end flip-flop of the shift register. Because all the JK flip-flops of the shift register were preset to 1 when the receiver was reset after the last byte was received, the end flip-flop was 1 until the 0 start bit reached it. The 0 on the Q of the end flip-flop caused the load to go HIGH at the XB count. This loads the receiver buffer (which is made of D flip-flops) with the content of the byte just shifted into shift register. The load strobe also sets the DATA READY control signal that the CPU will monitor through an input port.

After the data is loaded into the receiver buffer, the reset strobe is generated by the XF count of the sequencer. This resets the starting flip-flop and presets all the JK flip-flops to 1 for the next byte to come down the wire.

The CPU must monitor the DATA READY line to detect a new byte and input that byte before the next byte is loaded over the top of the first byte, or data will be lost. This type of data error is often called *overrun*, and many LSI asynchronous serial ICs have error-control signals to indicate to the CPU that this has taken place.

11.5 THE 8251-A PROGRAMMABLE COMMUNICATION INTERFACE

The 8251-A is an LSI universal synchronous asynchronous receiver transmitter IC (USART) made by Intel Corp. Other IC manufacturers make similar serial communication ICs, such as Zilog's Z8031 asynchronous serial communication controller (ASCC). The 8251-A is widely used for all types of serial communications and is a good general-purpose IC to study. It is made from NMOS technology, and the outputs can handle 1 TTL load. The pinout and block drawing are shown in Figure 11–5.

There are five basic parts to the 8251-A: a bidirectional data bus buffer, read/write control logic, modem controls, a serial transmitter, and a serial receiver. There are two write-only registers (transmitter output buffer and control register) and two read only registers (receiver input buffer and status register). Which register is to be read from or written to is controlled by the value of the $C/\overline{D}$ (control/data) pin and the $\overline{CS}$, $\overline{RD}$, or

intel®

8251A/S2657
PROGRAMMABLE COMMUNICATION INTERFACE

- **Synchronous and Asynchronous Operation**
- **Synchronous 5-8 Bit Characters; Internal or External Character Synchronization; Automatic Sync Insertion**
- **Asynchronous 5-8 Bit Characters; Clock Rate—1, 16 or 64 Times Baud Rate; Break Character Generation; 1, 1½, or 2 Stop Bits; False Start Bit Detection; Automatic Break Detect and Handling**
- **Synchronous Baud Rate — DC to 64K Baud**
- **Asynchronous Baud Rate — DC to 19.2K Baud**
- **Full Duplex, Double Buffered, Transmitter and Receiver**
- **Error Detection — Parity, Overrun and Framing**
- **Fully Compatible with 8080/8085 CPU**
- **28-Pin DIP Package**
- **All Inputs and Outputs are TTL Compatible**
- **Single +5V Supply**
- **Single TTL Clock**

The Intel® 8251A is the enhanced version of the industry standard, Intel® 8251 Universal Synchronous/Asynchronous Receiver/Transmitter (USART), designed for data communications with Intel's new high performance family of microprocessors such as the 8085. The 8251A is used as a peripheral device and is programmed by the CPU to operate using virtually any serial data transmission technique presently in use (including IBM "bi-sync"). The USART accepts data characters from the CPU in parallel format and then converts them into a continuous serial data stream for transmission. Simultaneously, it can receive serial data streams and convert them into parallel data characters for the CPU. The USART will signal the CPU whenever it can accept a new character for transmission or whenever it has received a character for the CPU. The CPU can read the complete status of the USART at any time. These include data transmission errors and control signals such as SYNDET, TxEMPTY. The chip is constructed using N-channel silicon gate technology.

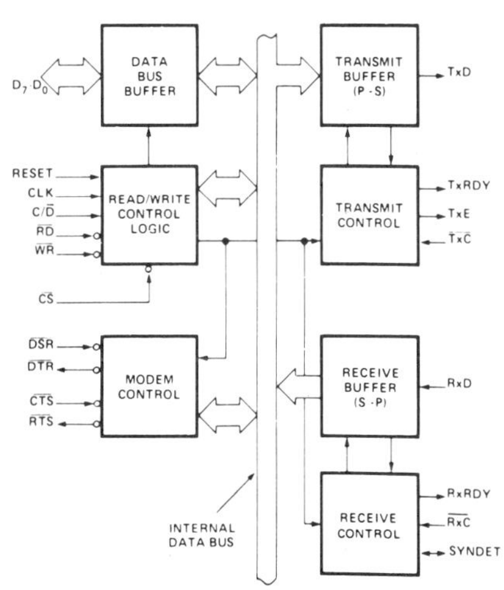

Block Diagram

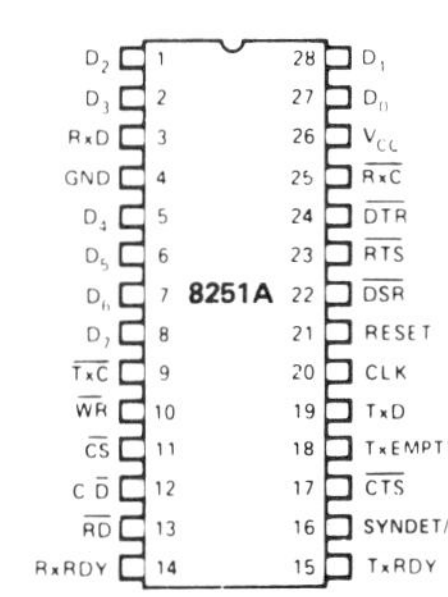

Pin Configuration

FIGURE 11–5

$\overline{WR}$ pins. If the C/$\overline{D}$ pin is LOW when a read is performed by the CPU, then the receiver input buffer is read. If a write operation is performed by the CPU when the C/$\overline{D}$ pin is LOW, then the transmitter output buffer is written to.

When the C/$\overline{D}$ pin is HIGH, the control register is written to and the status register is read from. Because the C/$\overline{D}$ pin controls which internal register is accessed, it is usually tied to the A_0 line of the computer's address bus. A typical 8251-A interface circuit is shown in Figure 11–6. Notice that it is very similar to the interface of the 8255 and 8253, which were studied earlier.

The 74LS245 is used to buffer the 8251-A data bus because the 8251-A can only drive a little more than a 1-TTL load. The computer data bus will require a device that can drive many times a 1-TTL load. The 74LS245 bidirectional data bus drive can sink up to 24 mA and is ideal for this job. The $\overline{CS}$ control input selects the chip and is usually connected to the address decoder, as shown in Figure 11–6. In Figure 11–6 the address decoder is only eight bits because the $\overline{IORD}$ and $\overline{IOWR}$ are used to strobe the $\overline{RD}$ and $\overline{WR}$ of the 8251-A. This means that the interface is an input/output port and only needs an 8-bit address. If the interface had been a memory mapped interface, then $\overline{MRD}$ and $\overline{MWR}$ would have been used, and the address decoder would have been 16 bits wide.

The RESET pin of the 8251-A is connected to the system reset of the computer, so that when the computer is powered up or physically reset by the operator, the 8251-A will be placed in the idle state so it can be reprogrammed for proper operation. A clock input is used to synchronize the internal operation of this IC to the system clock of the CPU. This clock must be at least 30 times the bit rate, or the IC will not function. If the system clock is 2 MHz, then the maximum baud rate would be 2 MHz/30 or 66.6 kHz, which is higher than the 64K maximum baud rate for this IC. As you will see later, it is possible to program the 8251-A to divide the $\overline{RXC}$ or $\overline{TXC}$ clocks by 1, 16, or 64 to produce a lower bit rate.

The transmitter and receiver are separate parts of the 8251-A and can be run at different baud rates if desired. The RXD and TXD are the TTL level serial input and serial output of the internal shift registers. The receiver and transmitter are very similar to the receiver and transmitter studied in Sections 11.3 and 11.4 and are both double buffered. The RXRDY output goes HIGH to indicate that a byte or word has been shifted in and is ready to be read from the receiver. When the byte is read, the RXRDY is reset to 0 until the next byte is shifted into the receiver buffer. This pin can be used to interrupt the CPU if desired. The TXRDY output is used to indicate that the transmitter buffer is empty and can have a new byte loaded to it by the CPU. This output pin can also be used to interrupt the CPU if desired. The TXE output pin goes HIGH to indicate that the transmitter shift register has finished shifting its last bit and no more transmission will be done. The primary use for this output is to indicate to external logic that the transmission line can now be used for receiving a word or byte. The use of one set of wires for both transmitting and receiving is called *half-duplex operation*. When there are three wires (one for receiving, one for transmitting, and a common ground), the operation is called *full duplex*.

SYNDET can be either an output or an input, depending upon how the 8251-A is programmed; it will be discussed later.

One nice feature of the 8251-A is its four modem controls. They are the four standard controls used by the EIA RS-232C standard, which is probably the most widely used

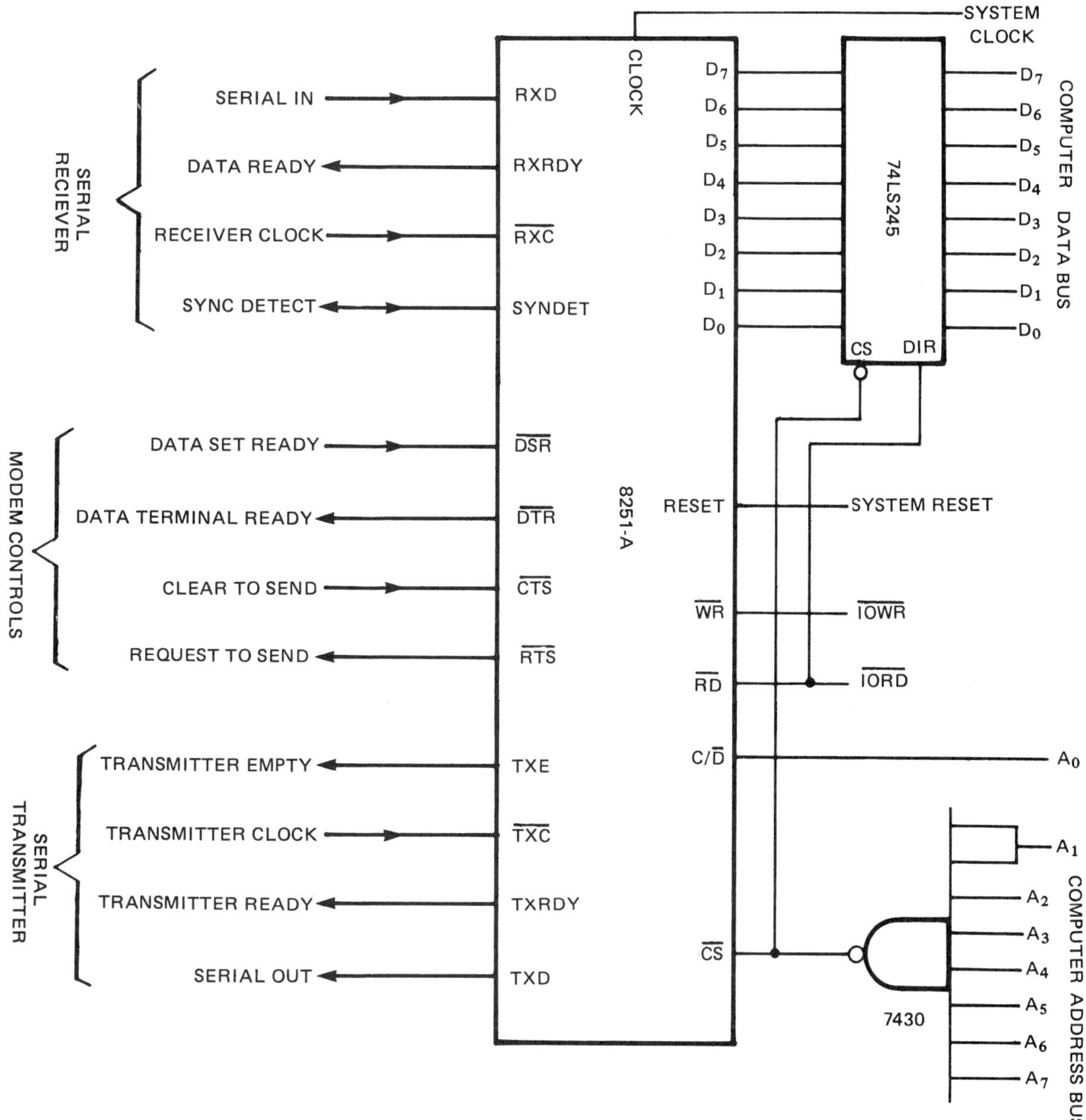

FIGURE 11–6 The 8251-A interface

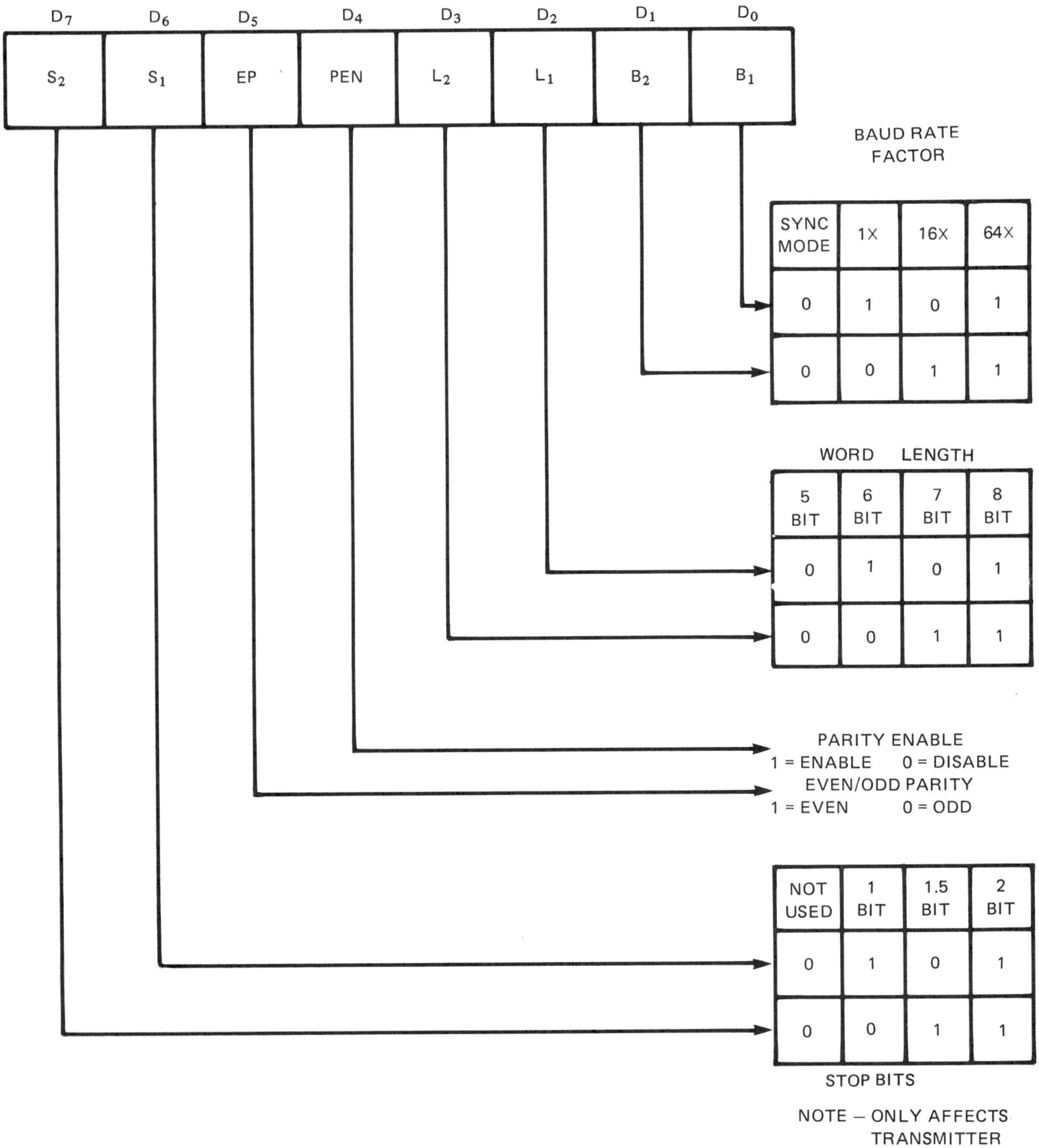

FIGURE 11–7 Asynchronous-mode control word format

serial communication standard used today. These four inputs and outputs are simple 1-bit ports that can be read or set by the CPU. The only one of these four that has any direct control over the 8251-A is the $\overline{\text{CTS}}$ (clear to send). If the $\overline{\text{CTS}}$ is made HIGH, the transmitter will be disabled after it is finished shifting out its last bit. This is used by modems or other peripherals to control the flow of bytes or word sent to it.

11.6 ASYNCHRONOUS OPERATION OF THE 8251-A

Before the 8251-A can shift any data in or out, it must be programmed to fit the type of serial communication the CPU needs. This is done by first resetting the 8251-A by the CPU. After the 8251-A is reset, a mode-control word is written out to the control register, which tells the IC the configuration to be used.

There are two types of mode control words: asynchronous and synchronous. As shown in Figure 11–7, if the least significant two bits (D_O and D_1) are both 0, then the mode control word is for synchronous operation; otherwise, the mode control word is for asynchronous operation. When the 8251-A is run in asynchronous mode, the bit width, baud rate factor, parity, and number of stop bits can be controlled by the asynchronous control word written to the 8251-A control register.

After the serial configuration is set by the mode control word, the 8251-A is ready to perform serial communication. The TXRDY line is brought HIGH to indicate that the transmitter output buffer is ready to accept data; if a serial word is shifted in, the RXRDY line is brought HIGH to indicate that a data word has been received and that the CPU should read the receiver buffer. These status lines also appear in the status register as bits D_O and D_1. This is shown in Figure 11–8. The TXRDY line and status bit are reset to 0 on the falling edge of the $\overline{\text{WR}}$ strobe, and the RXRDY line and status bit are reset to 0 on the falling edge of the $\overline{\text{RD}}$ strobe. It should be noted that these bits are only reset when the C/$\overline{\text{D}}$ pin is LOW, which indicates that a read from the receiver buffer or a write to the transmitter buffer is to be done.

The status register is read when the C/$\overline{\text{D}}$ pin is HIGH and the $\overline{\text{RD}}$ is strobed LOW. The status register format is shown in Figure 11–8. It can be read by the CPU and tested to determine the operating status of the 8251-A. All of these bits have the same definition in synchronous mode as they do in asynchronous, except for the SYNDET/BRKDET bit. In asynchronous mode this bit indicates that the serial input line has been broken or disconnected when it goes LOW and stays LOW for more than the time it takes to shift in two complete words.

The $\overline{\text{CTS}}$ input pin and the TXEN bit of the command word do not affect the operations of the TXRDY bit in the status register, but they do mask the operation of the TXRDY output pin. This means that the transmitter can be full and shifting out a word when the $\overline{\text{CTS}}$ pin disables the transmitter with a 0 on the $\overline{\text{CTS}}$ pin. This would cause the TXRDY output pin to go LOW, but the TXRDY bit in the status register would go HIGH again when the transmitter output buffer is ready to receive a new word. This is done because the TXRDY pin is often used as an external interrupt to the CPU and can be enabled or disabled by either the $\overline{\text{CTS}}$ or the TXEN of the command word.

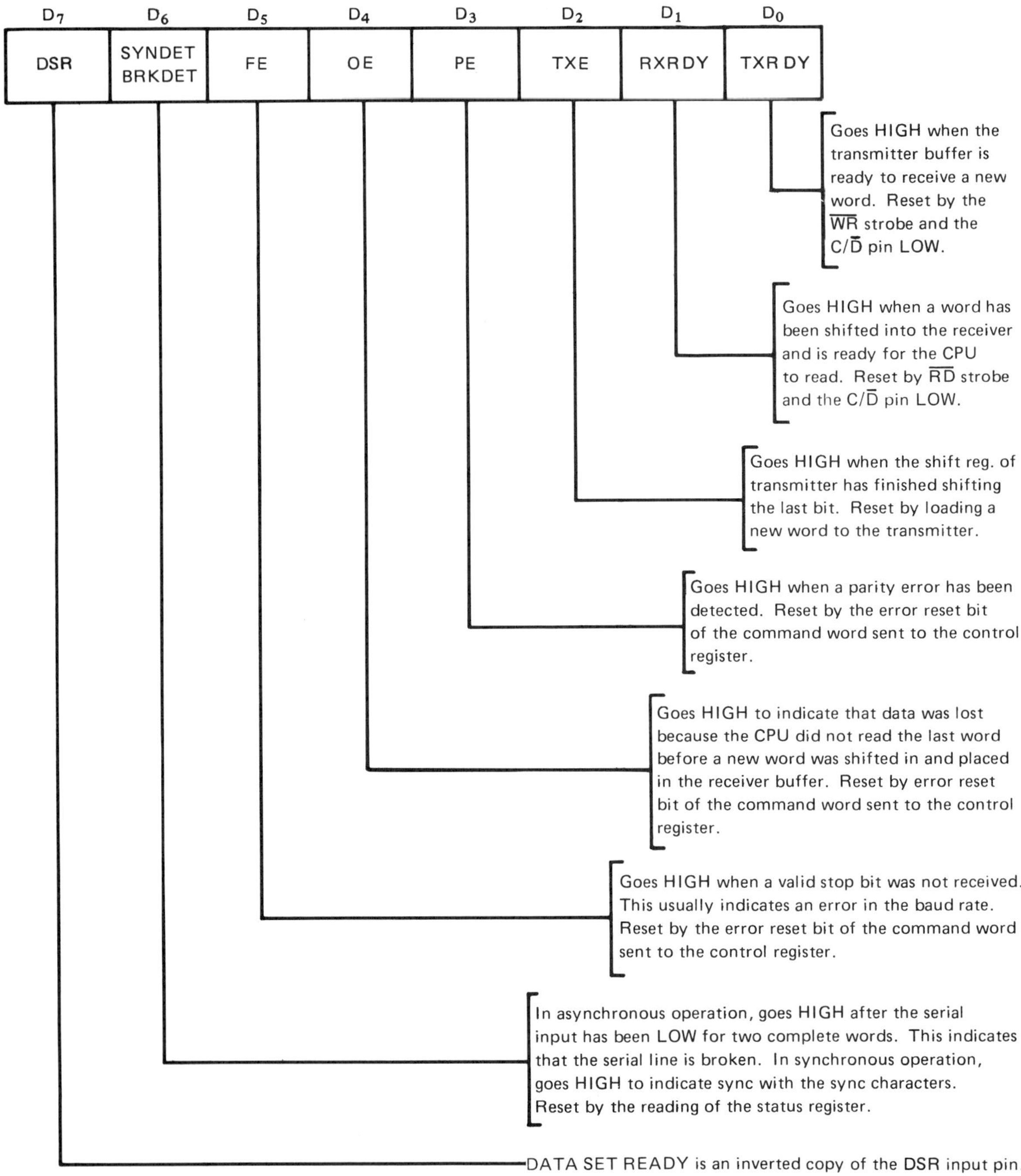

FIGURE 11–8 The status register format for the 8251-A

The command word is used to reset, or give the 8251-A operating instructions. The format for the command word is shown in Figure 11–9. Any word written to the 8251-A control register after the mode word (and sync character for synchronous operation) is considered a command word and will be interrupted according to definitions shown in Figure 11–9.

The short program that follows is an example of programming the 8251-A for asynchronous operation.

```
              ;*****************************************************
              ;*  PROGRAM TO CONFIGURE THE 8251 TO ASYNCHRONOUS    *
              ;*                    OPERATION                      *
              ;*****************************************************
              ;
0800                         ORG     800H
0800 3E40     START          LD      A,40H          ;INTERNAL RESET
0802 D3FF                    OUT     (0FFH),A       ;OUT A TO CONTROL REG.
0804 3E4E                    LD      A,4EH          ;MODE CONTROL WORD FOR
                                                    ;1 STOP BIT, NO PARITY
                                                    ;8 BIT DATA LENGTH AND
                                                    ;16X BAUD RATE FACTOR
0806 D3FF                    OUT     (0FFH),A       ;OUT MODE WORD TO CONTROL
                                                    ;REGISTER OF 8251
0808 3E37                    LD      A,37H          ;COMMAND WORD TO ENABLE
                                                    ;THE TRANS., RECEIVER
                                                    ;BREAK OF 1, RESET ERROR
                                                    ;FLAGS, MAKE RST AND DTR
080A D3FF                    OUT     (0FFH),A       ;LOW AND NO RESET
0000                         END
00000 Total Errors

START    0800
```

After programming the operation of the 8251-A, a short subroutine can be used to output a byte when needed. This subroutine can be called whenever needed, and the content of the A register will be serially outputted.

```
              ;*****************************************************
              ;* SUBROUTINE TO OUTPUT THE A REGISTER SERIALLY THROUGH *
              ;*                     THE 8251                         *
              ;*****************************************************
              ;
0900                         ORG     900H
0900 F5       SOUT           PUSH    AF             ;SAVE THE BYTE TO OUTPUT
0901 DBFF     LOOP           IN      A,(0FFH)       ;READ STATUS WORD
0903 1F                      RRA                    ;SHIFT TXRDY BIT TO C. F.
0904 30FB                    JR      NC,LOOP        ;TEST AGAIN IF NOT READY
0906 F1                      POP     AF             ;RESTORE BYTE TO OUTPUT
0907 D3FE                    OUT     (0FEH),A       ;OUTPUT BYTE TO TRANS.
0909 C9                      RET                    ;RETURN FROM SUBROUTINE
0000                         END
00000 Total Errors

LOOP     0901
SOUT     0900
```

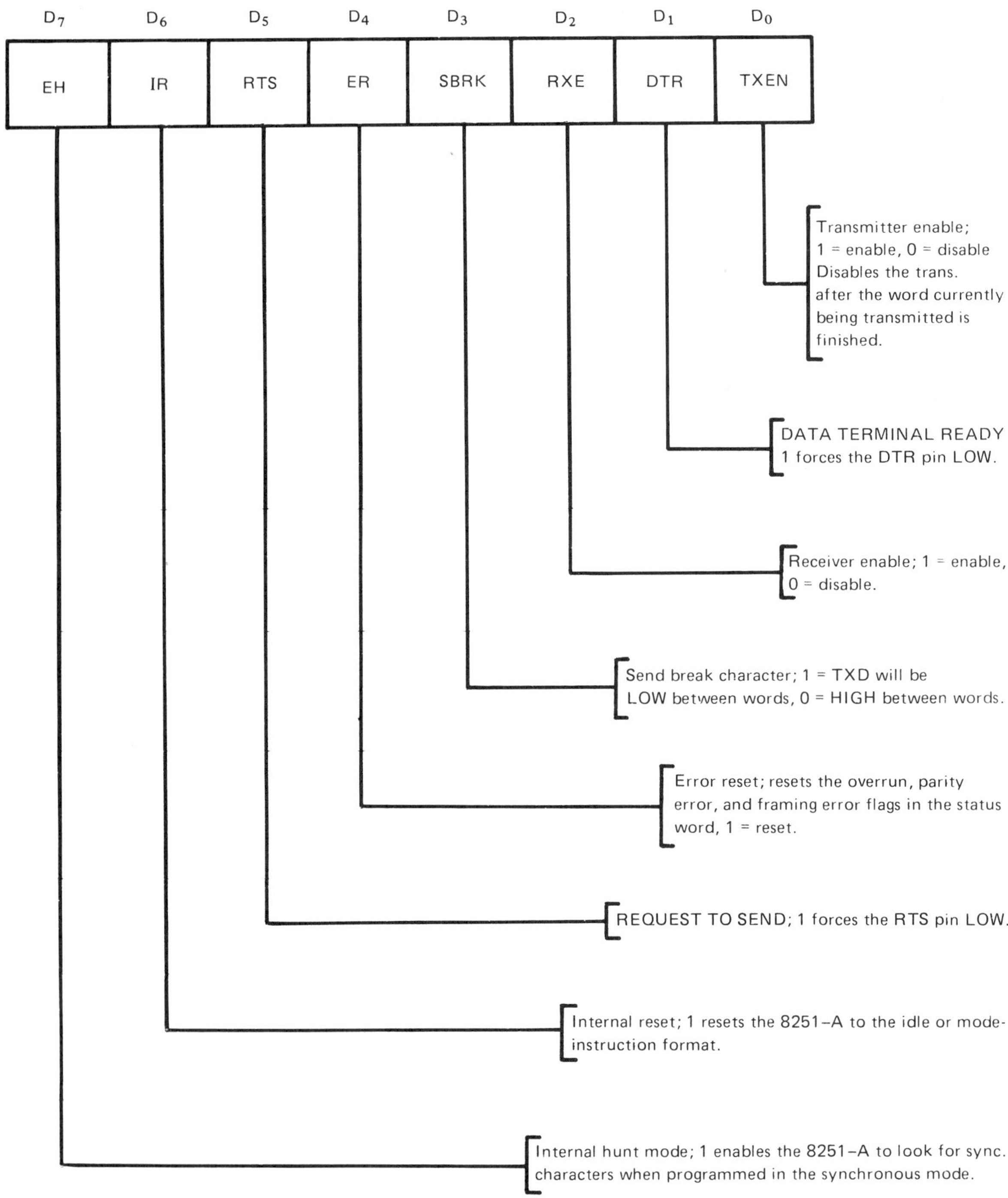

FIGURE 11–9 Command word format for the 8251-A

To receive a byte, the CPU would use this short subroutine. When the subroutine is called, it will continually test the RXRDY bit in the status register for a received byte; it will then return with the content of the received byte in the A register.

```
                ;*****************************************************
                ;* SUBROUTINE TO INPUT A SERIALLY RECEIVED BYTE THROUGH *
                ;*          THE 8251 AND INTO THE A REGISTER           *
                ;*****************************************************
                ;
0A00                         ORG     0A00H
0A00 DBFF       SIN          IN      A,(0FFH)       ;READ THE STATUS REG.
0A02 1F                      RRA                    ;ROTATE THE RXREDY BIT
0A03 1F                      RRA                    ; INTO THE C. F.
0A04 30FA                    JR      NC,SIN         ;LOOP UNTIL BYTE RECEIVED
0A06 DBFE                    IN      A,(0FEH)       ;INPUT THE RECEIVED BYTE
0A08 C9                      RET                    ;RETURN FROM SUBROUTINE
0000                         END
00000 Total Errors

SIN       0A00
```

11.7 SYNCHRONOUS OPERATION OF THE 8251-A

The synchronous-mode control word format is shown in Figure 11–10. As previously stated, when the synchronous mode is in operation there are no framing bits used; but a single or double sync word or character is used to synchronize the receiver. The operation of detecting the sync characters can be internal to the 8251-A or external, if desired. This is determined when the synchronous-mode control word is written out to the control register. If the external method is programmed, then the SYNDET pin will be an input pin. A HIGH placed on the SYNDET pin when the external sync detect has been programmed will cause the receiver to start shifting in data, and the SYNDET bit of the status word is set to 1.

When the 8251-A is looking for the sync characters, it is in the hunt mode. It can be placed in the hunt mode by setting D_7 of the command word. This can be done for both internal and external sync detects.

The internal sync-detect mode configures the sync-detect pin as an output pin, and it will go HIGH when the 8251-A has achieved sync.

After a command word is written to the control register, which forces the synchronously programmed 8251-A to enter the hunt operation, the shift register will shift one bit and test for the sync character. This 1-bit shift and test will continue until the sync characters are found. After sync is obtained, the SYNDET will go HIGH and will be reset on every read of the status word. If sync is still present, the bit will just be set back to 1 after the next sync character is shifted in. This way if the sync character is lost, the CPU can determine it.

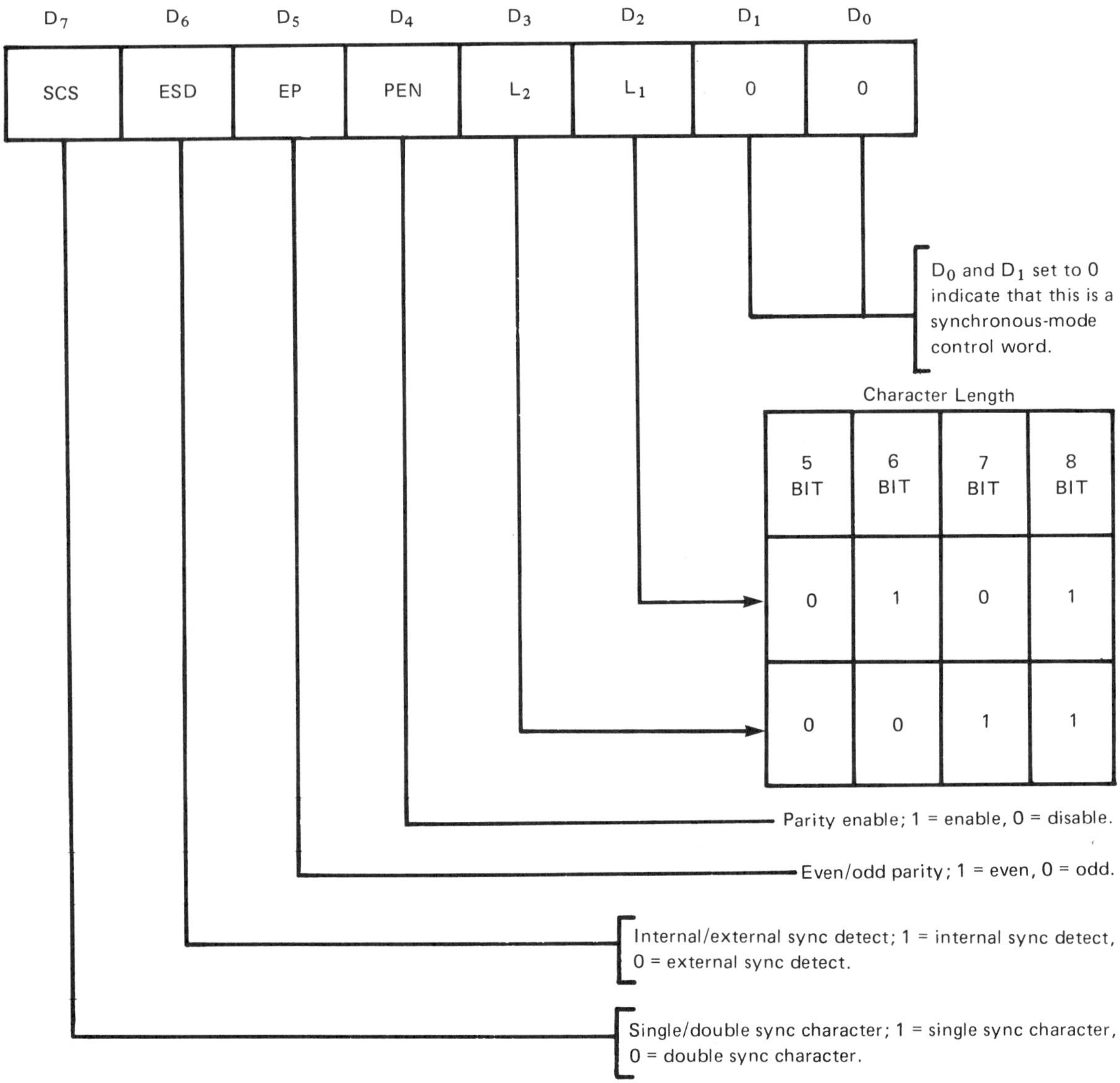

FIGURE 11–10 The synchronous-mode control word for the 8251-A

The short program that follows will program the 8251-A for synchronous operation.

```
          ;*****************************************************
          ;* PROGRAM TO PROGRAM THE 8251 FOR SYNCHRONOUS OPERATION
          ;*****************************************************
          ;
0800             ORG    800H
0800 3E40        LD     A,40H        ;RESET TO MODE FORMAT
0802 D3FF        OUT    (0FFH),A     ;OUTPUT TO CONTROL REG.
0804 3ECC        LD     A,0CCH       ;CONTROL WORD FOR
                                     ;SYNCHRONOUS MODE, 8 BIT
                                     ;DATA LENGTH, NO PARITY
                                     ;AND INTERNAL SYNC
0806 D3FF        OUT    (0FFH),A     ;OUTPUT TO CONTROL REG.
0808 3E80        LD     A,80H        ;SYNC CHARACTER
080A D3FF        OUT    (0FFH),A     ;OUTPUT SYNC CHAR. TO
                                     ;CONTROL REGISTER
080C 3EB7        LD     A,0B7H       ;COMMAND WORD TO ENTER
                                     ;HUNT MODE FOR SYNC CHR.
080E D3FF        OUT    (0FFH),A     ;OUTPUT COMMAND WORD
0810 76          HALT
0000             END
00000 Total Errors
```

The synchronous use of the 8251-A is one feature that many similar LSI ICs lack. Because it can sync on two characters, it can be used to communicate with the IBM "bisync" format.

It should be noted that if the external reset of the 8251-A is not reset by the system reset of the computer upon system power-up, it could come up in any mode or configuration. If this is the case, then the program should output three 00H bytes to the control register, followed by a 40H byte to reset the 8251-A to the mode or idle formats.

11.8 THE EIA RS-232C SERIAL COMMUNICATION STANDARD

EIA stands for Electronic Industries Association. This association produces standards for many types of computer serial communication, but the one most widely used today for microcomputers is the RS-232C standard. The RS-232C was published in 1969. The letters "RS" stand for "recommended standard"; the 232 is the identification number, and the letter "C" indicates the third revision of the standard.

There are three basic parts to the standard: electrical standards, handshaking lines, and type of equipment. First, we will look at the electrical part of the standard.

Figure 11–11 shows the minimum and maximum voltage levels for the RS-232C standard. Notice that it is a negative logic system because the 1 voltage is lower than the 0 voltage. There is a 2-V noise margin, and the signal will be a true AC voltage because the logic 1 is below ground. This makes for good signal transmission with less noise. The shunt capacitance between conductors and the terminator is limited to 2500 pF by the standard, but with slow baud rates and a good serial transmitter this can be increased. This capacitance limit is the reason the standard restricts the RS-232C cable length to 50 ft, but with good cable and good equipment the length can be greatly increased. This

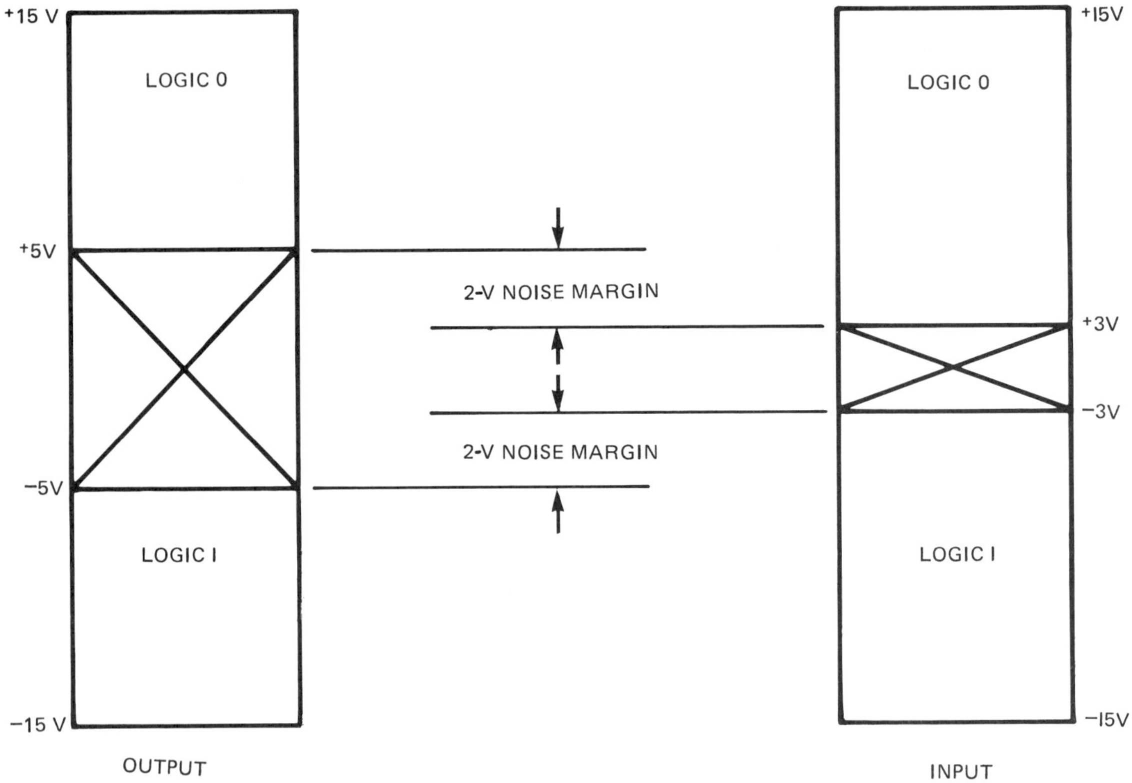

FIGURE 11–11 **RS-232C minimum and maximum logic voltages**

author has seen RS-232C cables as long as ¼ mile at 9600 baud rate with no problems. There has become several standard baud rates used on the RS-232C, which are

75	600	4800
110—old teletype	1200	9600—most computer terminals
300—Bell 103 modem	2400	19,200

There are several handshaking lines in the RS-232C standards, but only four are ever used very much. They are REQUEST TO SEND ($\overline{RTS}$), CLEAR TO SEND ($\overline{CTS}$), DATA SET READY ($\overline{DSR}$), and DATA TERMINAL READY ($\overline{DTR}$). The $\overline{RTS}$ is made logic LOW to indicate the desires of a device to serially transmit data; if the receiving device is ready, then it brings $\overline{CTS}$ to a logic LOW to indicate its readiness. The DATA TERMINAL READY ($\overline{DTR}$) is brought LOW to request the readiness of a receiver to receive, and the receiver will answer with a logic LOW on the $\overline{DSR}$ when it is ready. These four handshaking signals are not often used, except on such equipment as telephone modems. Most computer terminals and printers use only the transmitter data line, receiver data, and signal ground.

The RS-232C standard classifies the transmitting and receiving equipment into two categories called data communication equipment (DCE) and data terminating equipment (DTE). Originally, DTE equipment was meant to be a computer or terminal, and the DCE was a telephone modem often called a data set, but today the DCE could be a microcomputer, and the DTE could be a printer or another, larger, computer. The distinction between DCE and DTE has blurred with time.

One way to tell a DCE piece of equipment is to look at its DB-25 connector: If it is female, then it is a DCE piece of equipment. It should be noted that the EIA RS-232C standard does not specify a connector type, but the DB-25 connector is a de facto standard in use today. The pin definition for the DB-25 connector is shown in Figure 11–12. Pin

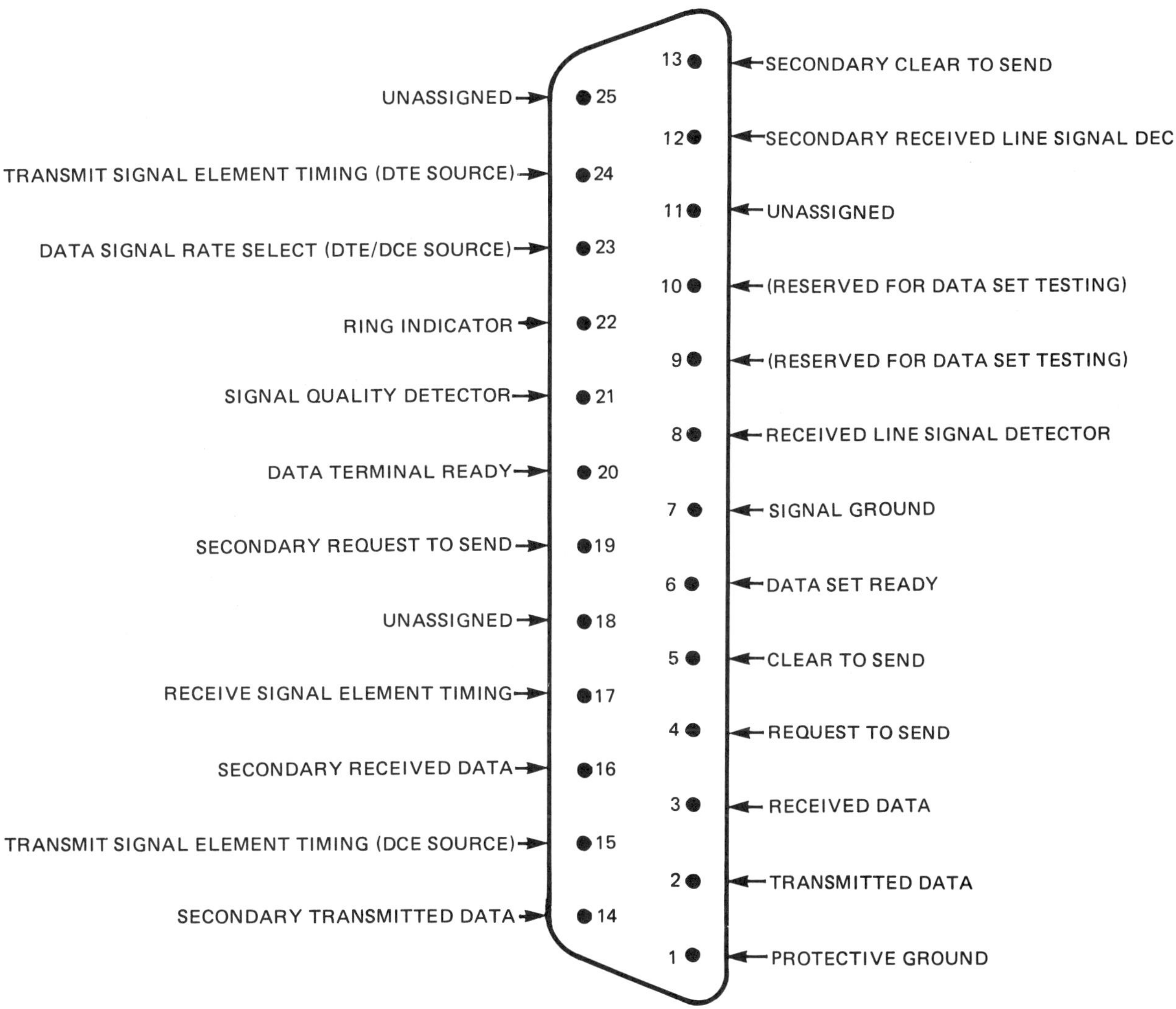

FIGURE 11–12 EIA RS-232C (DTE) male DB-25 connector

1489

QUAD RS232 RECEIVER

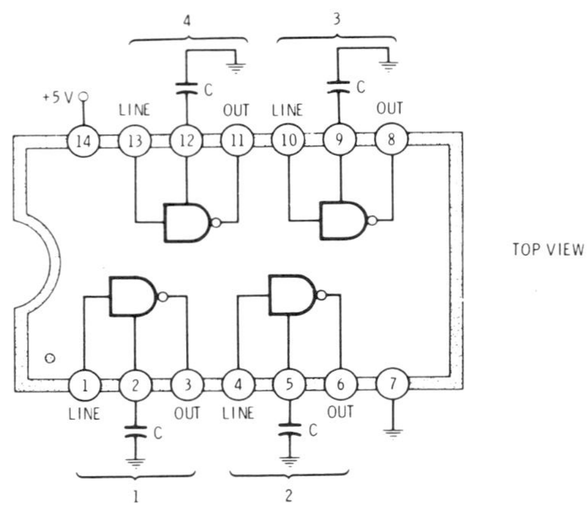

This package converts four separate bipolar RS232-C input logic swings into TTL logic levels. Each of the four separate receivers inverts its logic sense.

On any single receiver, a negative input voltage greater than −3 V will be read as a logic 1. A positive input voltage greater than +3 V will be read as a logic 0.

The capacitors may be used to minimize impulse noise. A value of at least 330 pF is normally used. Resistive connection of this terminal to an external power supply can also be used to shift the trip points and hysteresis of the receiver.

The output can drive up to 10 TTL loads and any number of CMOS loads.

Power-supply current is 25 mA.

1488

QUAD RS232 DRIVER

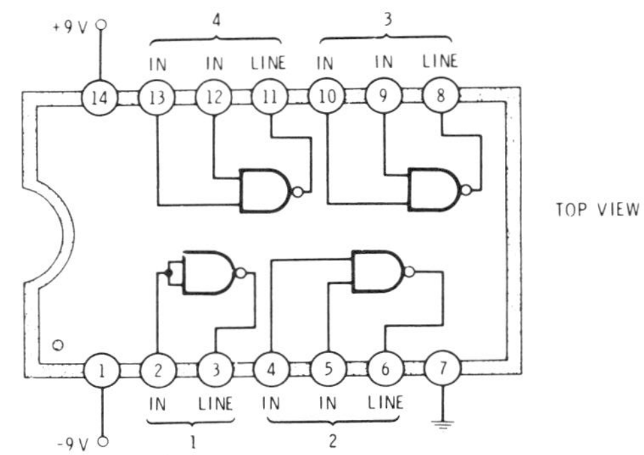

This package converts input TTL logic levels into bipolar voltages suitable for driving an RS232-C interface. There are four separate drivers. One has a single input. The others have dual NAND inputs.

A digital logic 0 at the input is inverted to a 1 and converted to a +9-V line voltage. A digital logic 1 at the input is inverted to a 0 and converted to a −9-V line voltage.

The inputs are TTL compatible and need 1.6 mA of input current in the low state. CMOS logic having this much output sinking current may also be used.

A capacitor of not less than 330 pF must be placed on each output to limit the slew rate to values within the RS232 spec.

Series power diodes on both supply lines are recommended for fail-safe operation.

Power-supply current from each supply is 20 mA.

FIGURE 11–13

ASCII CODE CONVERSION TABLE

BITS 4 thru 6	—	0	1	2	3	4	5	6	7
BITS 0 thru 3	0	NUL	DLE	SP	0	@	P	` `	p
	1	SOH	DC1	!	1	A	Q	a	q
	2	STX	DC2	”	2	B	R	b	r
	3	ETX	DC3	#	3	C	S	c	s
	4	EOT	DC4	$	4	D	T	d	t
	5	ENQ	NAK	%	5	E	U	e	u
	6	ACK	SYN	&	6	F	V	f	v
	7	BEL	ETB	’	7	G	W	g	w
	8	BS	CAN	(	8	H	X	h	x
	9	HT	EM	)	9	I	Y	i	y
	A	LF	SUB	*	:	J	Z	j	z
	B	VT	ESC	+	;	K	[	k	{
	C	FF	FS	,	<	L	\	l	¦
	D	CR	GS	-	=	M	]	m	}
	E	SO	RS	.	>	N	∧	n	~
	F	SI	US	/	?	O	—	o	DEL

NUL	NULL	DLE	DATA LINK ESCAPE
SOH	START OF HEADING	DC1	DIRECT CONTROL 1
STX	START TEXT	DC2	DIRECT CONTROL 2
ETX	END TEXT	DC3	DIRECT CONTROL 3
EOT	END OF TRANSMISSION	DC4	DIRECT CONTROL 4
ENQ	ENQUIRY	NAK	NEGATIVE ACKNOWLEDGE
ACK	ACKNOWLEDGE	SYN	SYNCHRONOUS IDLE
BEL	BELL	ETB	END TRANSMISSION BLOCK
BS	BACKSPACE	CAN	CANCEL
HT	HORIZONTAL TAB	EM	END OF MEDIUM
LF	LINE FEED	SUB	SUBSTITUTE
VT	VERTICAL TAB	ESC	ESCAPE
FF	FORM FEED	FS	FORM SEPARATOR
CR	CARRIAGE RETURN	GS	GROUP SEPARATOR
SO	SHIFT OUT	RS	RECORD SEPARATOR
SI	SHIFT IN	US	UNIT SEPARATOR

FIGURE 11–14 The ASCII code and machine control code definitions

2 is the transmit pin for DTE equipment and the receive pin for DCE equipment. A cable that has the lines between pins 2 and 3 crossed will allow serial communication between two DCE devices or two DTE devices. This type of cable is called a *null modem* cable and is often used today for various RS-232C installations.

The job of interfacing the TTL logic to a negative RS-232C logic can be done quite easily with the two ICs shown in Figure 11–13. The 1488 is an RS-232C line drive that will produce a negative voltage when a TTL logic 1 is input. The 1489 is an RS-232C receive and will convert the plus or minus voltage to a TTL logic. They both have standard TTL input loads and outputs.

11.9 THE ASCII CODE

ASCII stands for American Standard Code for Information Interchange (pronounce ASKEY). It is a standard 7-bit binary code used to represent letter, numbers, and machine operations such as line feed. The ASCII code is not the only such code in use today, but it is probably the most widely used. Some others are the old Baudot code and EPIDIC. A normal computer terminal will use this code to transmit the letters you type to the computer. Figure 11–14 shows the ASCII code.

EXERCISE 11

1. Draw the waveforms for an RS-232C asynchronous serial output for the binary number 41 Hex (no parity bit and two stop bits).
2. What is the difference between asynchronous and synchronous serial communication?
3. What is meant by an overrun error?
4. What is meant by the term "double buffering"?
5. What is the purpose of the $C/\overline{D}$ pin on the 8251-A USART?
6. How is the mode configuration changed on the 8251-A USART?
7. What is the purpose of the clock input of the 8251-A?
8. Draw the pinout of the 8251-A USART.
9. What is the use of the SYNDET pin on the 8251-A USART?
10. Which two bits of the mode control word determine the synchronous or asynchronous operation of the 8251-A USART?
11. What is the voltage for a logic 1 output of the RS-232C standard?
12. What must be the baud rate factor used in lab 11 to make the 8251-A USART run at 9600 baud?
13. What are the two types of equipment used in the EIA RS-232C standard?
14. What is the mode control word for asynchronous operation, with seven data bits, a baud rate factor of 16, no parity bit, and two stop bits in the 8251-A USART?
15. Which bit of the status register in the 8251-A USART is used to indicate that a byte has been received?

16. What is the difference between TXE and TXRDY pins in the 8251-A USART?
17. Which pin of the DB-25 connector used for an RS-232C connector is the DCE receiver?
18. Which pin of the DB-25 connector is used for signal ground?
19. What is the ASCII code for the letter "B"?
20. What is the ASCII code for line feed?

Lab 11

OBJECTIVES

After completing this lab, you should be able to

- interface the 8251 to the Biggy trainer.
- use the RS-232C serial standard.
- use the RS-232C interface ICs.
- program the 8251 USART.

Procedure

1. Construct the RS-232C serial port shown in the following order.
   A. Wire the 74LS93 counters and measure the final output frequency. It should be 153846 Hz. If it isn't, then debug the counters before going on.
   B. Wire the 74LS245 bidirectional bus driver and use a short software loop to input from the input port created and display it on port 2 of the Biggy trainer. Then use a 1kΩ resistor connected to ground as a probe to test the input port, as was done in previous labs.
   C. Wire the LM1489 and LM1488 ICs and test them for correct operation. Don't forget the positive and negative 12-V power supply and ground on the LM1488 IC.
   D. Wire the 8251 USART to the tested and debugged parts in A, B, and C and check the wiring for errors. Don't forget to connect the $\overline{CTS}$ pin to ground and to connect the reset pin to $P0_7$. $P0_7$ will be used to reset the 8251 USART for a new mode control word.
2. Connect the DB-25 connector to the DTE connector of a terminal and set the terminal to a baud rate of 9600 and 1 stop bit.
3. Write a program that will take the ASCII code shifted into the 8251 USART and place it on output port 1 of the Biggy trainer.
4. Write a program that will output your name through the 8251 USART to the CRT of the terminal.
5. Have your instructor OK the operation of parts 3 and 4.

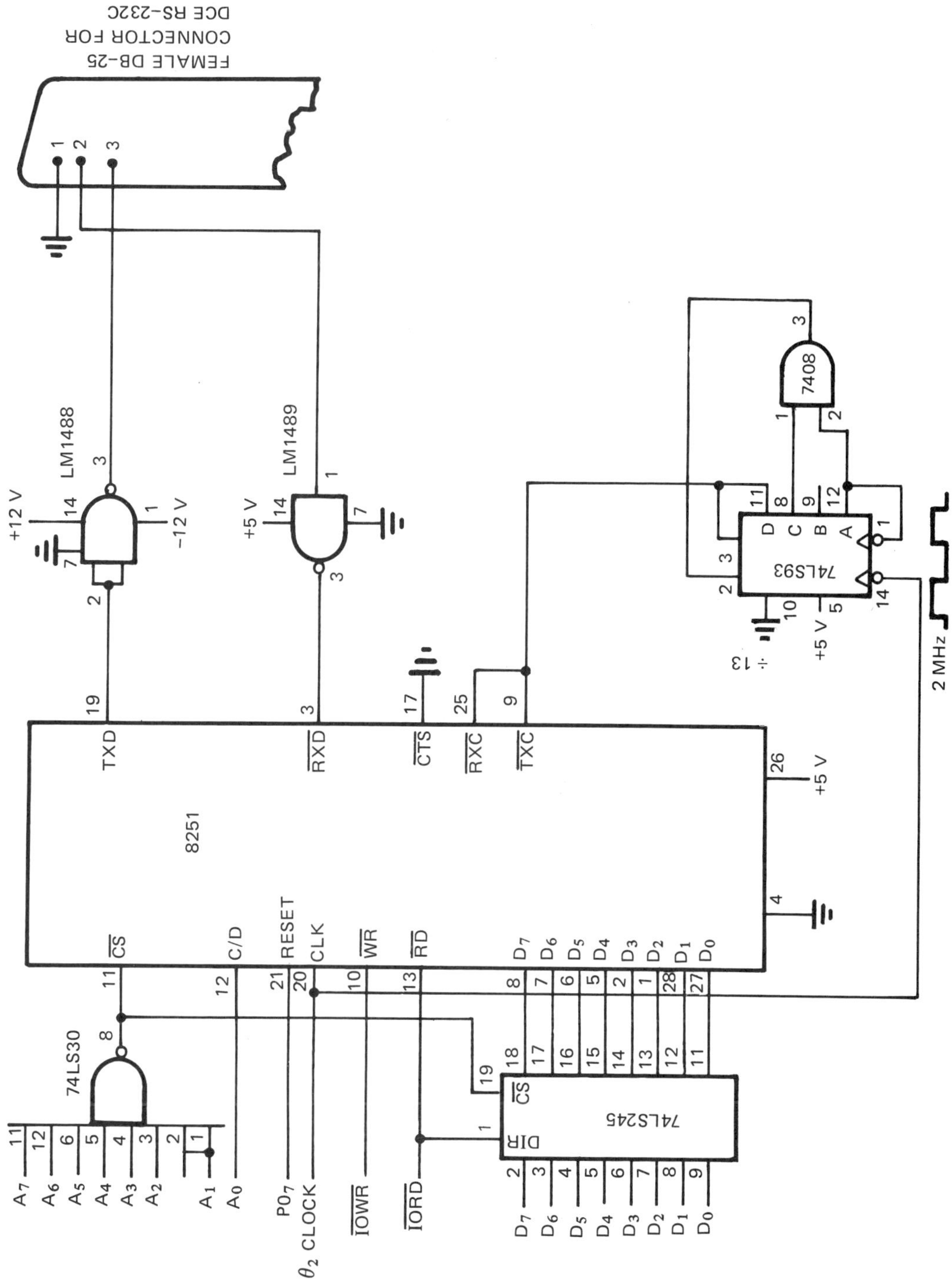
FEMALE DB-25
CONNECTOR FOR
DCE RS-232C
LM1488
LM1489
+12 V
−12 V
+5 V
7408
74LS93
÷ 13
2 MHz
8251
TXD
RXD
CTS
RXC
TXC
CS
C/D
RESET
CLK
WR
RD
74LS30
74LS245
DIR
P0₇
θ₂ CLOCK
IOWR
IORD

Chapter 12

DIGITAL TO ANALOG AND ANALOG TO DIGITAL

OBJECTIVES

After completing this chapter, you should be able to

- describe the binary and 2R ladder methods of digital-to-analog conversion.
- describe the count-up and successive approximation methods of analog-to-digital conversion.
- apply the methods of digital-to-analog and analog-to-digital conversions to the microcomputer.
- use typical analog-to-digital LSI ICs and interface them to a microcomputer.

12.1 REVIEW OF DIGITAL-TO-ANALOG METHODS

We will review the basic method of digital-to-analog (D/A) and analog-to-digital (A/D) conversion methods used by non-micro-oriented circuits and then apply these methods to the microcomputer.

First, we will look at two resistor networks to do the job of converting a binary number to a proportional analog voltage. The first is the binary ladder. Figure 12–1 shows the binary ladder made with switches for each binary bit instead of TTL outputs. This is so we can better understand its operation.

The binary number set by the switches is 1000 or decimal 8. The largest number that the four switches could express is 1111 or decimal 15. In this case, a 1 is +15 V, and a 0 is ground. Therefore, if the binary number 1111 or decimal 15 were put on the switches, the output of the binary ladder would be tied right to the +15-V supply through all the resistors in parallel, as shown in Figure 12–2. This would be 15 V in this case.

If all the switches were switched to the 0 position, the output would be 0 V or ground, as shown in Figure 12–3.

Now let us analyze the switch configuration in Figure 12–1, which is binary 1000 or decimal 8. The equivalent circuit is shown in Figure 12–4. If we reduce the circuit to two series equivalent resistors, then the voltage output would be the voltage drop across

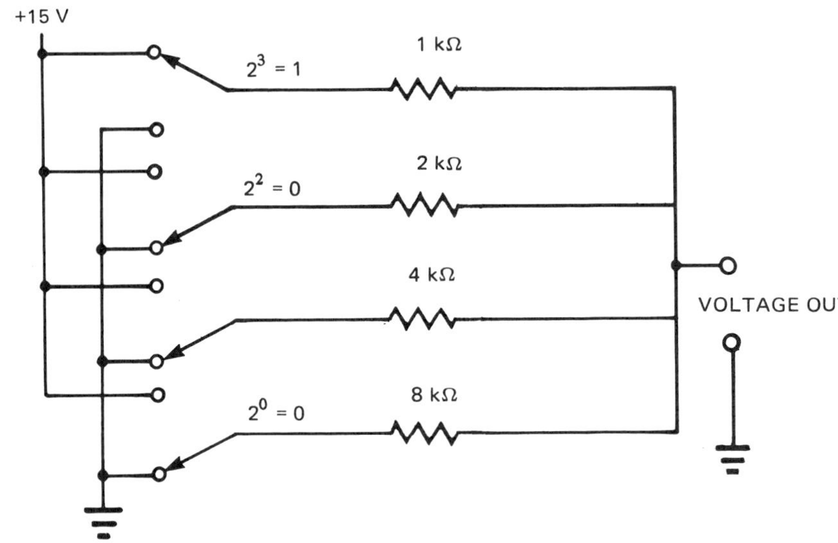

FIGURE 12–1

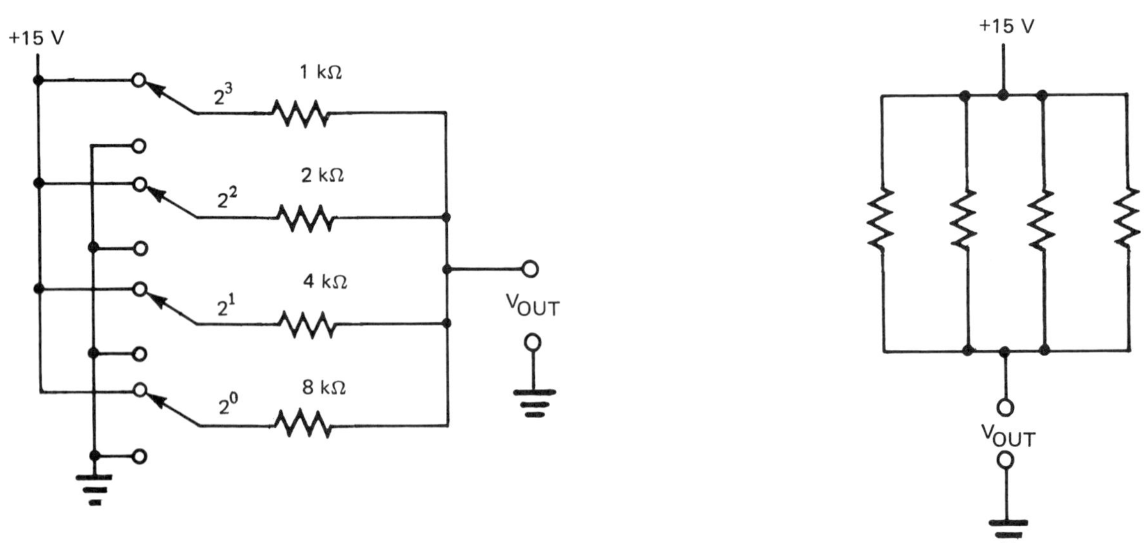

FIGURE 12–2

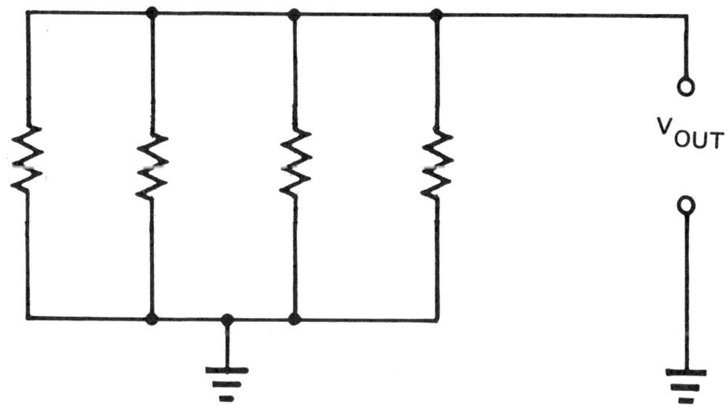

FIGURE 12–3

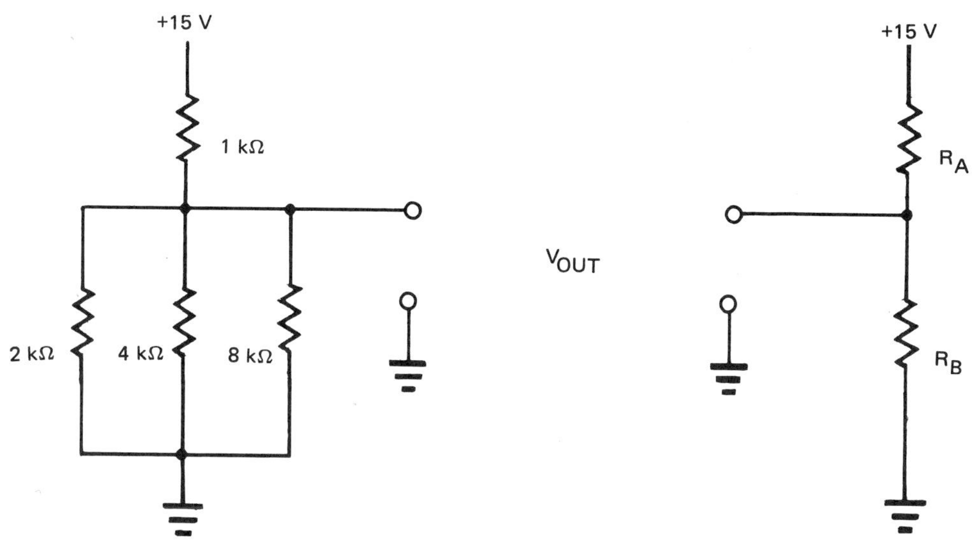

$$R_B = \frac{1}{\frac{1}{2K} + \frac{1}{4K} + \frac{1}{8K}} = 1.1429\ \text{k}\Omega$$

$$V_{OUT} = V_S\left(\frac{R_B}{R_A + R_B}\right) = 15\left(\frac{1.1429\ \text{k}\Omega}{1\ \text{k}\Omega + 1.1429\ \text{k}\Omega}\right)$$

$$V_{OUT} = 8\ \text{V}$$

FIGURE 12–4

the R_B resistor. Using the voltage divider formula, we find that the output voltage for the binary number 1000 is 8 V.

The output voltage for the other possible binary number inputs could be computed in a similar manner, and it would be found that the voltage increments would be 1 V in this case. Binary number 1010 would produce a voltage of 10 V, and binary number 0111 would produce a voltage of 7 V. In other words, the supply voltage is divided into increments equal to the supply voltage divided by the largest binary number that could be input to the resistor network. Therefore, the voltage increments that the output would increase by when the binary number increased by 1 would be equal to the following formula:

$$\text{binary ladder voltage increment} = \frac{V_S}{2^N - 1}$$

where N equals the number of bits in the binary number input to the binary ladder, and $2^N - 1$ is the largest number that can be expressed for a binary number of N bits. If this formula is the amount of each increment, then the final output voltage must be equal to the binary number input to the binary ladder multiplied by the voltage increment.

This is shown in the next formula, which is the voltage output of the circuit shown in Figure 12–1.

$$\text{binary ladder } V_{out} = (\text{binary number input}) \frac{V_S}{2^N - 1}$$

Note that the resistor values in the binary ladder are divided by 2 as the binary power increases; that is, 2^0 resistor is 8 kΩ, 2^1 resistor is 4 kΩ, 2^2 resistor is 2 kΩ, and 2^3 resistor is 1 kΩ. If a 5 bit were added to the binary ladder, the resistor value would be one-half of the 2^3 resistor or 500 Ω. You can see that the larger the binary number is, the smaller the resistor must be. Also, it is not easy to get exact values of resistors that fit this pattern.

These two problems can be eliminated by using another type of resistor network to produce the proportional output voltage. This is the 2R network shown in Figure 12–5.

Using the same method as in Figure 12–4, we can determine the output voltage for the binary number switched into the 2R network in Figure 12–5. This is shown in Figure 12–6.

The 2R network is similar to the binary ladder, except that the voltage increments are equal to the voltage supply divided by the total number of combinations in the binary number input. The total number of combinations in a binary number of N bits is 2^N; therefore, the formula for the voltage output of the 2R network is equal to the binary number input multiplied by the voltage supply divided by 2^N.

$$\text{2R network } V_{out} = \text{binary number} \left(\frac{V_S}{2^N}\right)$$

Both of these networks will give very accurate output voltages as long as the output load impedance is very high with respect to the network's impedance. If the load resistance is increased, the linearity of the output is reduced. To reduce this problem, a HiZ buffer is usually used, such as an operational amplifier to drive the analog load.

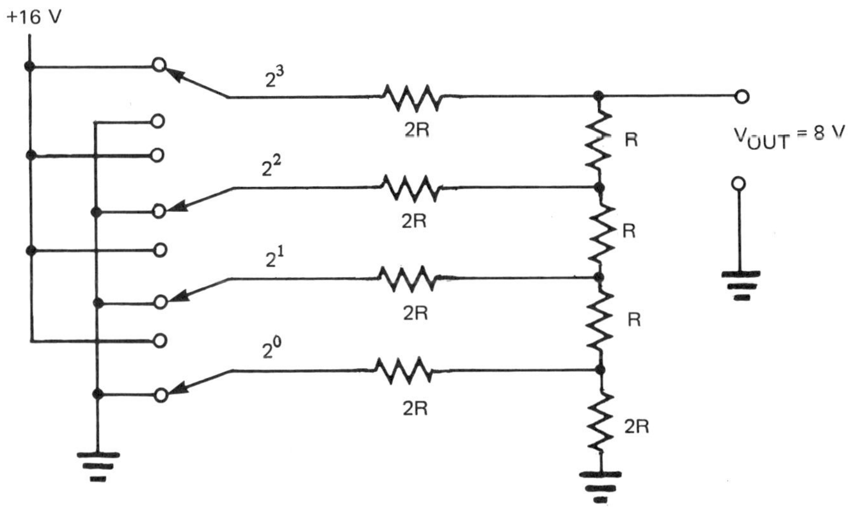

FIGURE 12–5

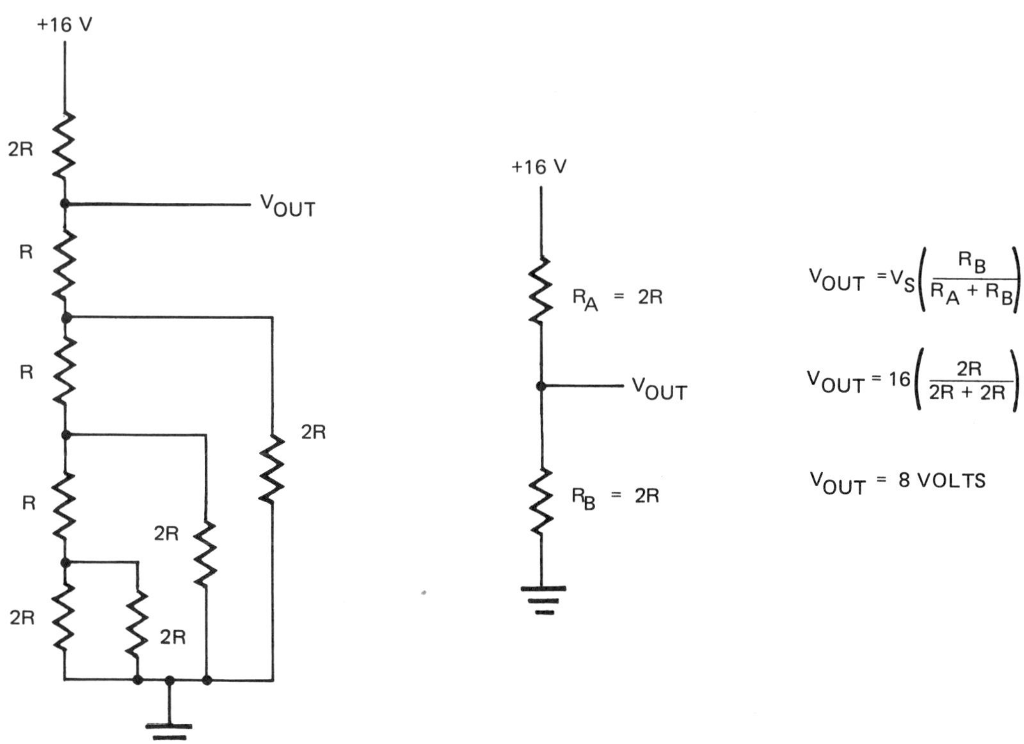

FIGURE 12–6

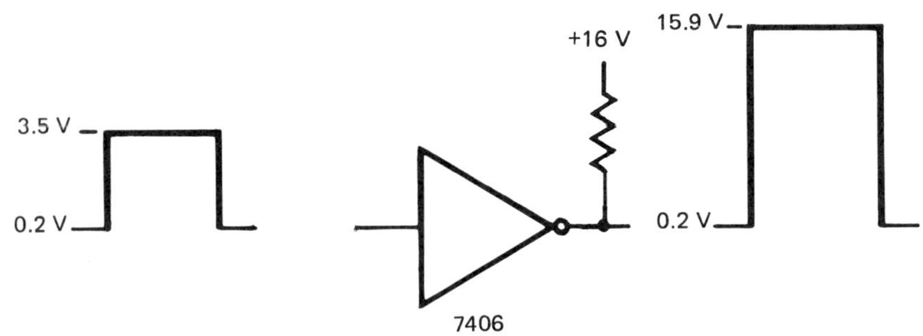

FIGURE 12–7

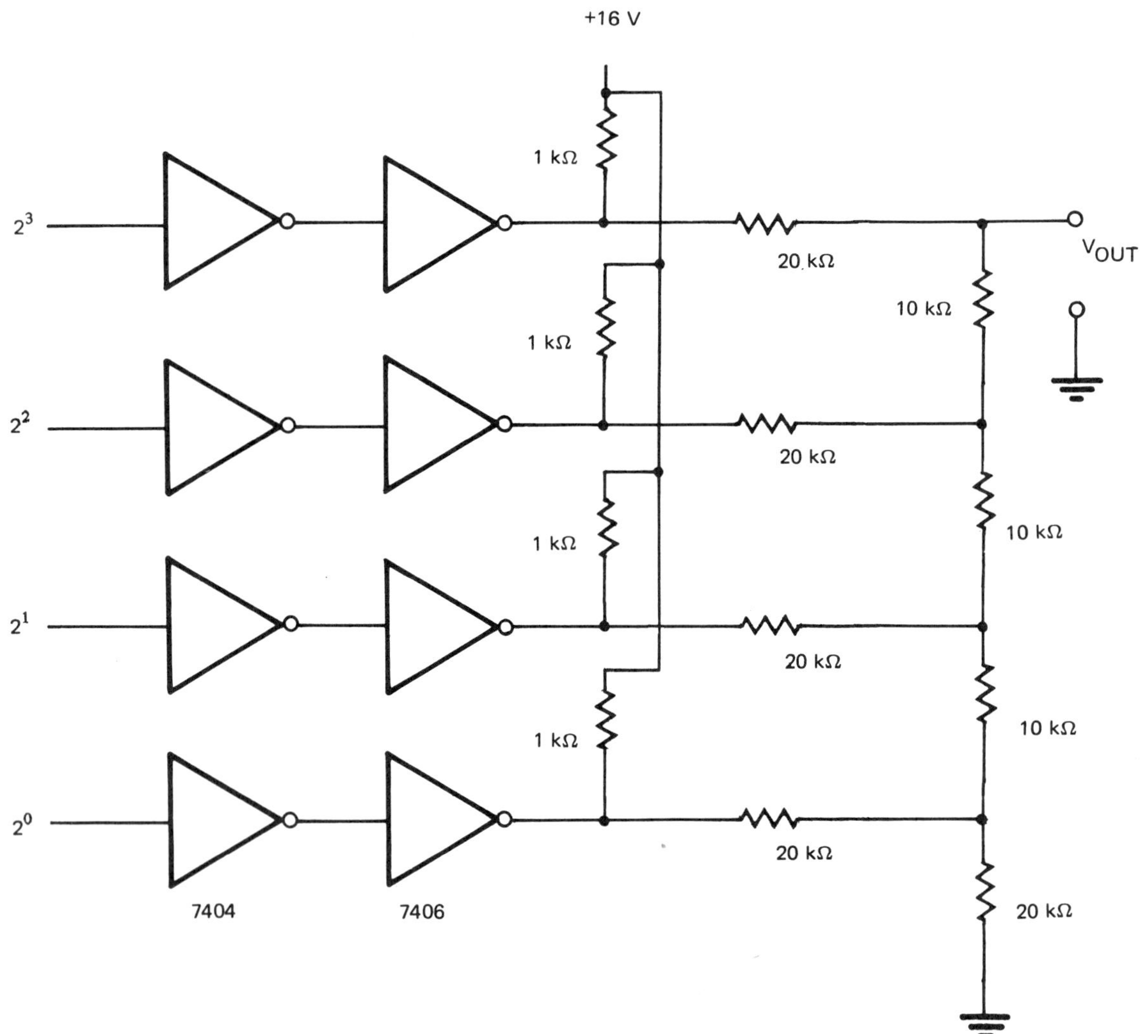

FIGURE 12–8

12.2 THE TTL DIGITAL-TO-ANALOG CONVERTER

The binary number in the networks just discussed was not a TTL level input. To make the network work, the 1 voltage must be voltage supply, and the 0 voltage must be ground or 0. The TTL output voltage will give a good 0 voltage or, in the worst case, 0.4 V, but the 1 voltage is typically about 3.5. By using an open-collector output, such as the 7406 inverter or 7407 noninverting buffer, and a pull-up resistor to V_S supply of the D/A network, we can convert the TTL level voltages to the voltage needed by the D/A network. The output voltage of the 7406 or 7407 is not absolute ground or absolute voltage supply, but it is very close. This is shown in Figure 12–7.

Figure 12–8 shows this type of buffer used to make a TTL D/A converter, where the top output voltage is 15 V.

When the output of the 7406 goes LOW, it will go to 0.1 or 0.2 V above ground at best, which introduces some error into the D/A converter, and when the 7406 output goes to HiZ the 1-kΩ resistor pulls the 20-kΩ resistor up to +16 V, but in doing so it adds its 1-kΩ to the 20-kΩ resistor. This means that the 2R resistor is a little larger (by 5% in this case) when it is at +16 V and does not quite reach ground when it is brought LOW.

These errors can be eliminated by other methods, but for many uses of D/A converters these errors are tolerable. Figure 12–9 shows a D/A converter used to control the speed of a small DC motor, such as might be used on a small robotic arm.

Notice the operational amplifier used to buffer the D/A converter.

12.3 ANALOG TO DIGITAL USING VOLTAGE COMPARATORS

An analog-to-digital converter produces a binary number that is in direct proportion to an analog voltage input.

Figure 12–10 shows a 3-bit A/D converter made from seven LM339 voltage comparators. The negative input of each comparator is tied to a resistor voltage divider that divides the 8-V supply into 1-V increments. Each voltage comparator has a reference voltage of 1 V greater than the comparator below it. All of the positive inputs to the comparators are tied together, so the input voltage will increase on all comparators at the same time.

If the input voltage increases to 2.5 V, then the output of the first two comparators will be +5 or logic 1, because the + input will be greater than the − input, but the rest of the comparators' outputs will be at ground or logic 0. The output of the LM339 is an open-collector output, so by using a pull-up resistor to +5 V the output will be standard TTL levels, even though the input may go as high as 8 V. As the voltage increases to 3.5 V, the third comparator's output will change to a logic 1. If the analog voltage increases to above 7 V, all the comparators will be at logic 1. The comparators will go to logic 0 when the input voltage goes below the reference voltage that is set by the voltage divider.

The output of all the comparators is decoded to form a 3-bit binary number by the

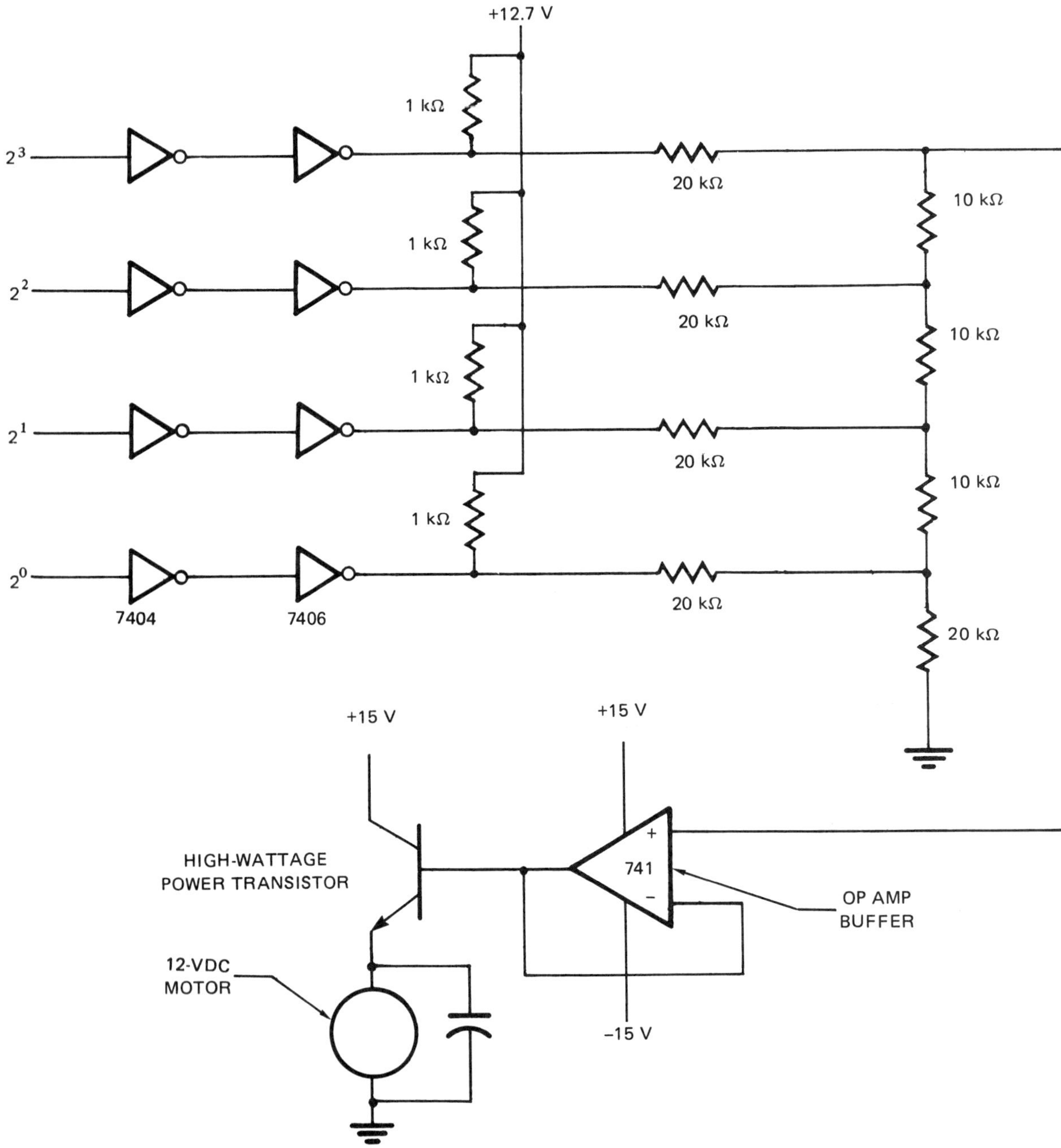
+12.7 V
1 kΩ
1 kΩ
1 kΩ
1 kΩ
2^3
2^2
2^1
2^0
7404
7406
20 kΩ
20 kΩ
20 kΩ
20 kΩ
10 kΩ
10 kΩ
10 kΩ
20 kΩ
+15 V
+15 V
HIGH-WATTAGE
POWER TRANSISTOR
741
OP AMP
BUFFER
12-VDC
MOTOR
–15 V

FIGURE 12–9

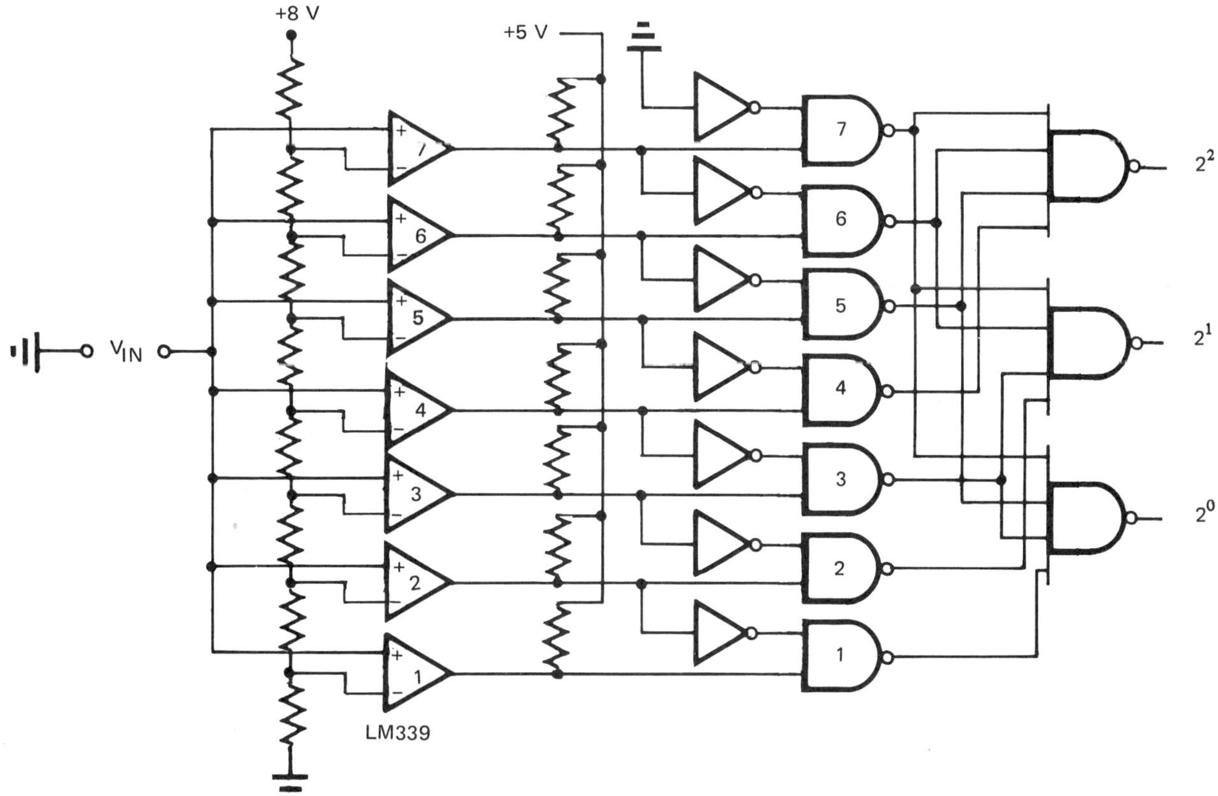

FIGURE 12–10

logic gates shown in Figure 12–10. When all the comparators' outputs are at logic 0, the outputs of their corresponding NAND gates are 1's, because any 0 into a NAND gate produces a 1 output. If the analog input voltage rises to 1.5 V, the first comparator's output goes to logic 1, which is fed to the two input NAND gate. The other input to this NAND gate is from the inverter, which comes off the output of the next higher comparator. The output of the second comparator is still 0, because the analog voltage is still 1.5 V and is not yet great enough to change the state of the second comparator. This 0 is inverted to a 1 and fed to the input of the NAND gate for the first comparator. At this point, the first NAND gate has 1 and 1 on its inputs and a 0 on its output, which is fed to the 2^0 NAND gate. This produces a logic 1 on the output of the 2^0 NAND gate, or binary number 1. A binary 1 on the output means that the analog input voltage lies between 1 and 2 V.

When the input voltage increases to 2.5 V, the second comparator's output will be logic 1 also. This produces a 0 on the inverter, which disables the first NAND gate, thus removing the 1 on the 2^0 NAND gate's output. The logic 1 on the second comparator's output enables the second NAND gate, producing a 0 on its output, which produces a logic 1 on the output of the 2^1 NAND gate, or binary number 10. This means that the analog input lies between 2 and 3 V.

It can be seen that as the voltage increases, the binary output of the A/D converter will change to reflect the value of the analog input.

In order to increase the accuracy of the comparator in Figure 12–10, you would need more comparators and NAND gates. This is a major drawback to this type of A/D converter, but it operates very fast. The only thing to slow it down is the propagation delay of the comparators and gates, which is in the order of 50 to 75 ns.

12.4 THE COUNT-UP AND COMPARE ANALOG-TO-DIGITAL CONVERTER

This type of A/D converter uses one voltage comparator and a D/A converter. Figure 12–11 shows a count-up and compare A/D comparator using an LM339 voltage comparator and a 2R resistor network.

The D/A converter is driven by a 7493 binary counter, which can count from 0000 to 1111 binary or 0 to 15 decimal. The output of the D/A converter is fed to the negative input of a voltage comparator and the + input comes from the analog voltage that we want to measure. The output of the LM339 voltage comparator is used to enable or disable a NAND gate that feeds the clock to the 7493 counter. If the NAND gate is disabled, then the counter will not receive a clock pulse and stop counting.

When the reset button is pushed, the counter is cleared, and all its outputs go to logic 0. This puts a 0 or ground voltage on the − input of the voltage comparator. Let us say that the analog input to the voltage comparator has 7.75 V on it. This means that the + input is greater than the − input of the voltage comparator, and its output will be at logic 1. A logic 1 on the input of the NAND gate that is fed from the comparator enables the NAND gate, and the clock is passed on to the 7493 counter. As the counter counts, the binary number on its outputs gets larger, and the analog voltage output of the 2R resistor network also gets larger.

When the voltage at the − input of the voltage comparator gets larger than the analog voltage input to the + input of the comparator, the output of the comparator goes LOW, which disables the NAND gate and stops the clock and the 7493 counter. The stopped counter will now contain the binary number that produces a voltage that is one increment of the D/A converter larger than the analog input voltage.

The A/D converter will stay at this point until the reset button is pushed or the analog input voltage increases, at which time the counter would simply count back up to the new voltage. If the analog input voltage dropped after the counter had stopped, the counter could not change and would have to be reset to count back up to the lower voltage. Figure 12–12 shows the waveform for the analog output of the D/A converter as the analog input voltage changes.

To increase the accuracy of the count-up and compare A/D converter, all you have to do is increase the size of the counter and the D/A converter. In the case of the A/D converter in Figure 12–11, if you added one more 7493 to the converter, the +16 V

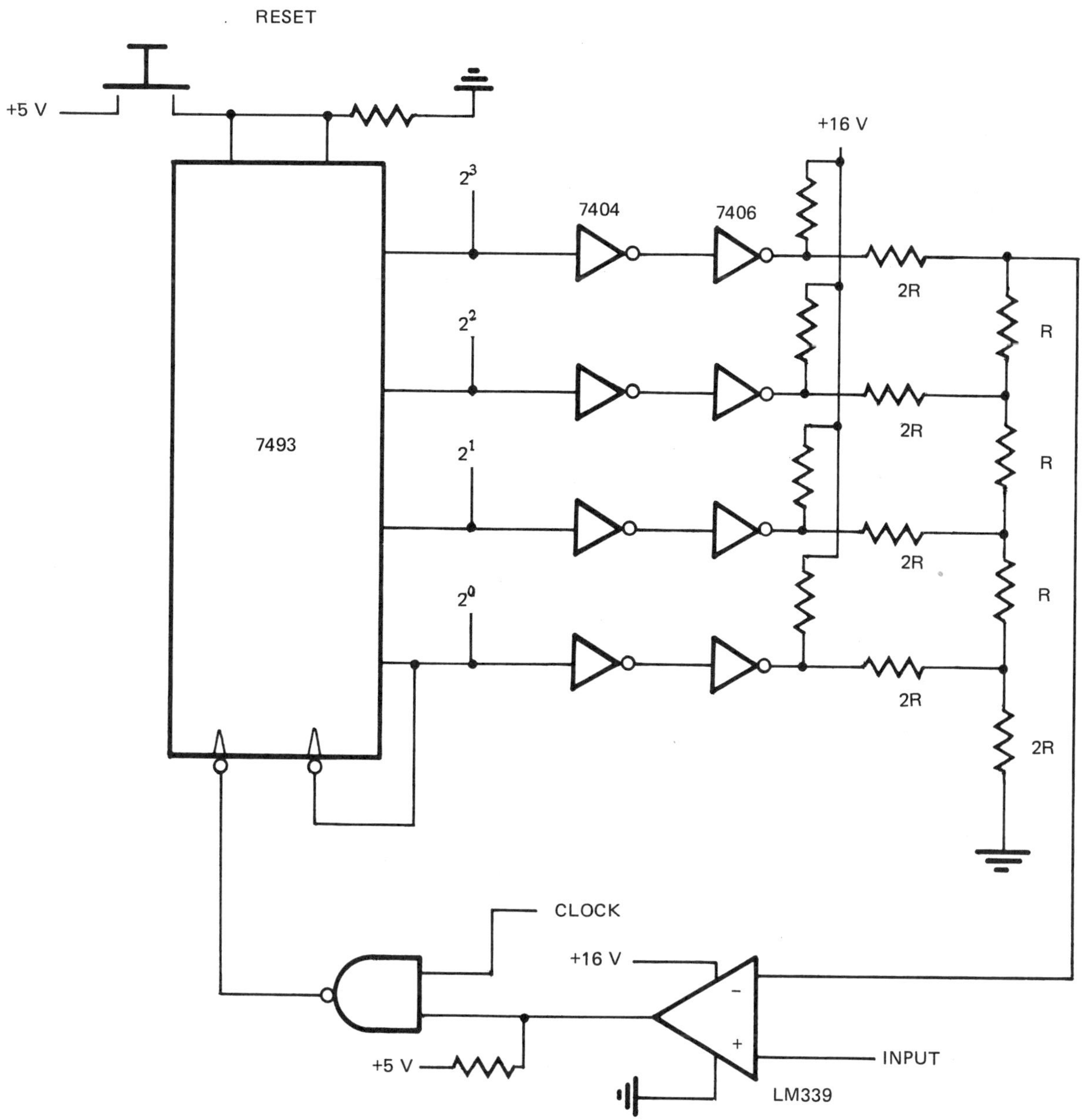
RESET
+5 V
+16 V
7493
2^3
2^2
2^1
2^0
7404
7406
2R
R
2R
R
2R
R
2R
2R
CLOCK
+16 V
+5 V
INPUT
LM339

FIGURE 12–11

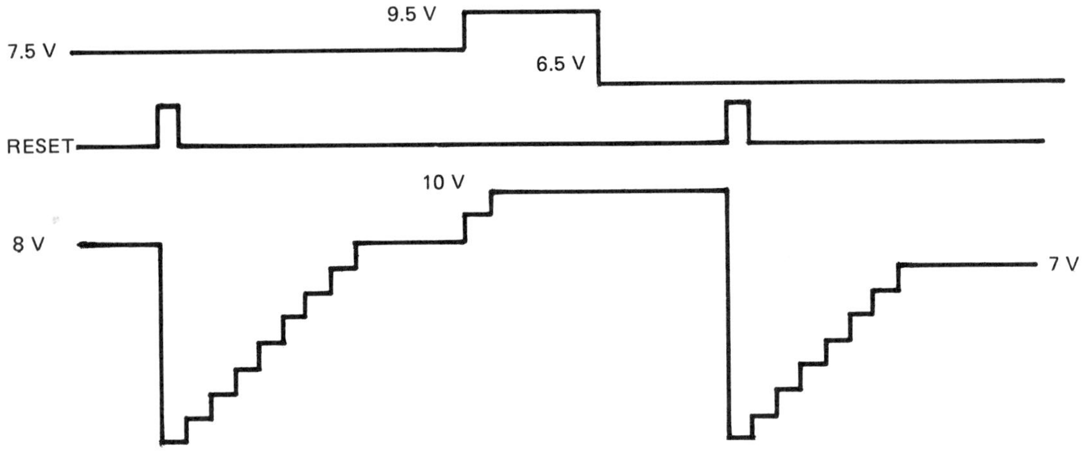

FIGURE 12–12

would be divided into 256 increments as compared to 16 increments with one 7493 counter. This is an increase of 16 times in the resolutions and, therefore, in the accuracy. The main drawback to this type of A/D converter is lack of speed, because of the time it takes to count up and compare.

12.5 THE SUCCESSIVE APPROXIMATION ANALOG-TO-DIGITAL CONVERTER

This type of A/D converter uses a D/A converter and a voltage comparator also, but it uses a different technique to determine the binary number to feed to the D/A converter.

To study this technique, let us use the D/A converter and voltage comparator in Figure 12–13.

To determine the correct binary number using the successive approximation method, you first set the most significant bit of the D/A converter to a logic 1, then test the output of the D/A converter against the input analog voltage to be measured and see if the D/A output is larger or smaller. If the voltage generated by the D/A converter is smaller, then you leave the most significant bit at a logic 1; but if it is larger, then you bring it LOW to a logic 0. In the example in Figure 12–13, the LED is off, indicating that the binary number 1000 is too small; therefore, we keep the 1 in the most significant place and bring the next place to a logic 1. Now, we have the binary number 1100, or decimal 12, input to the D/A converter. The LED is still off because the analog voltage being measured is greater than 12 V; therefore, we leave the second bit at logic 1 also. Next, we bring the third bit HIGH. Now we have binary number 1110 or 14 decimal on the input to the D/A converter. The voltage output of the D/A converter is now larger than the 12.5 V of the analog input voltage, and the LED is on. In this case, we remove the

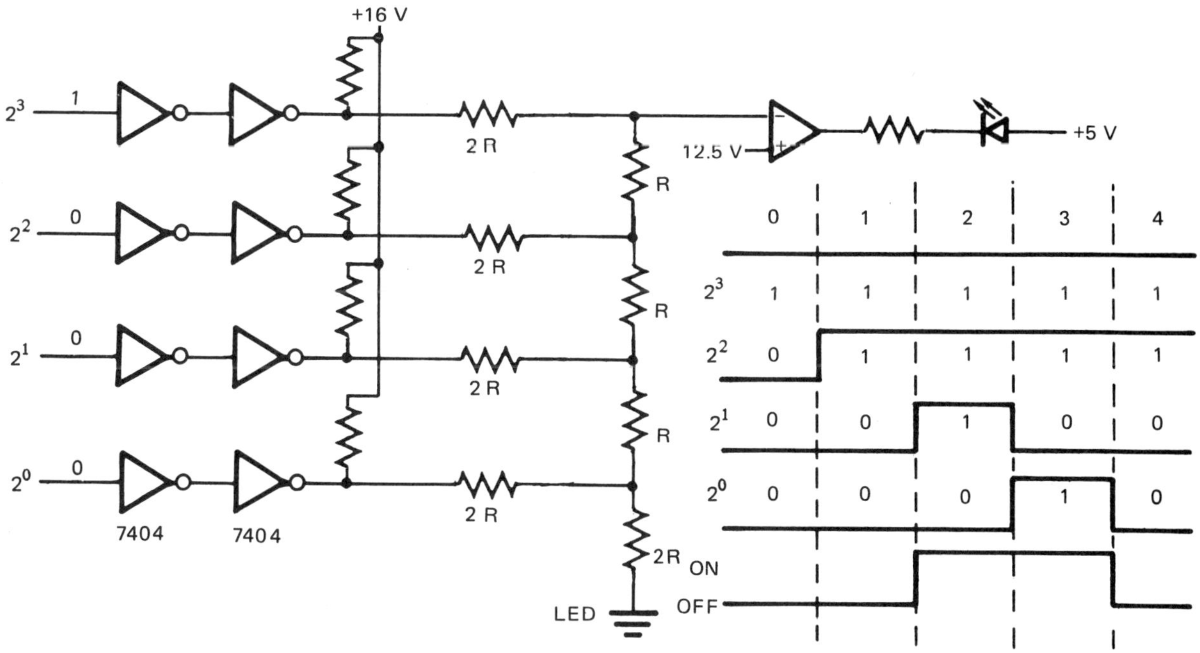

FIGURE 12–13

1 on the third bit and put a 1 on the last, and least significant, bit. This gives us the binary number 1101 input to the D/A converter. The output voltage is now 13 V, which is still greater than the analog input voltage, and the LED is still on; therefore, we remove the 1 and make it a 0. This gives us the final binary number 1100, or decimal 12, which is one increment of the D/A converter less than the actual analog input voltage being measured.

The successive approximation method just described takes only four cycles to determine the correct binary number for the given analog input voltage, and it takes the same time to determine a large number as a small one. Therefore, the successive approximation method is faster than the count-up method but not as fast as the voltage compare method.

Figure 12–14 shows a successive approximation A/D converter that uses a CP and CP′ nonoverlapping clock generator, shift register, and storage registers. When the reset button is pushed, the clock generator and A flip-flop are preset to 1, and all the rest of the flip-flops are reset to 0. The A/D converter will stay in this configuration until the reset button is released, allowing the clock generator flip-flop to run. After the clock is allowed to run, Q_A is preset to 1, which places a 1 on the 2^3 or most significant bit of the D/A converter. The content of the comparator is fed to an AND gate, which is controlled by the CP clock of the nonoverlapping clock generator. When it goes HIGH, the contents of the comparator are passed through the AND gate to the AS storage flip-flop NAND gate. If the comparator is 1, then the flip-flop will be set; if it is 0, then the flip-flop won't be set. Next comes the CP′ clock, which shifts the A, B, C, and D flip-flops shift register one place. This makes Q_B 1, and the cycle is repeated. After the 1 that was generated in Q_A by the reset pulse is shifted out of the A, B, C, and D flip-flop shift register, the correct binary number is present on the 2^0 to 2^3 outputs.

Notice that it took only four CP′ pulses to obtain the correct binary number. Figure 12-15 shows the waveforms for the operation of the A/D converter in Figure 12-14 for an anolog input voltage of 12.5 V.

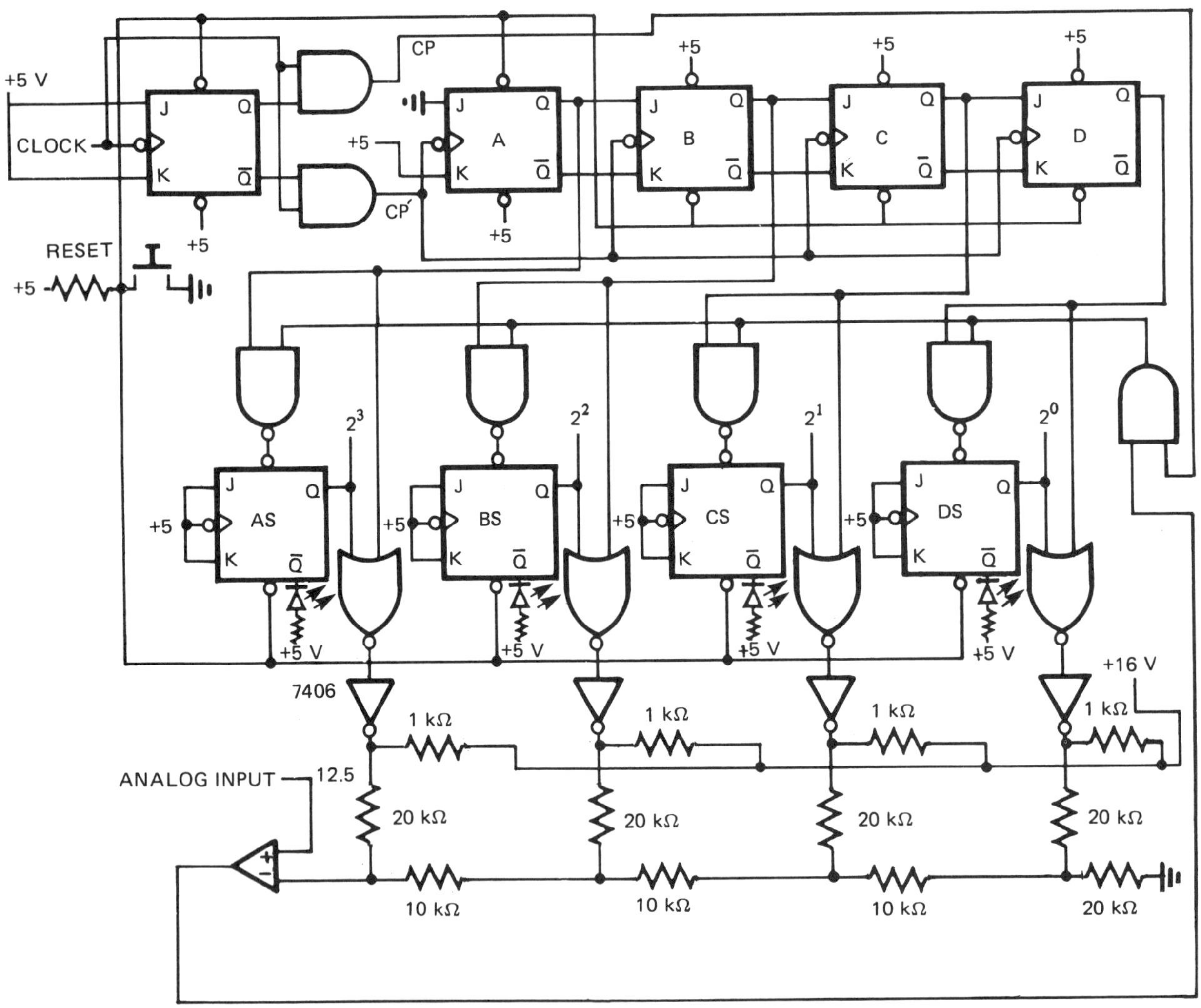

FIGURE 12-14 4 bit successive approximation analog-to-digital converter

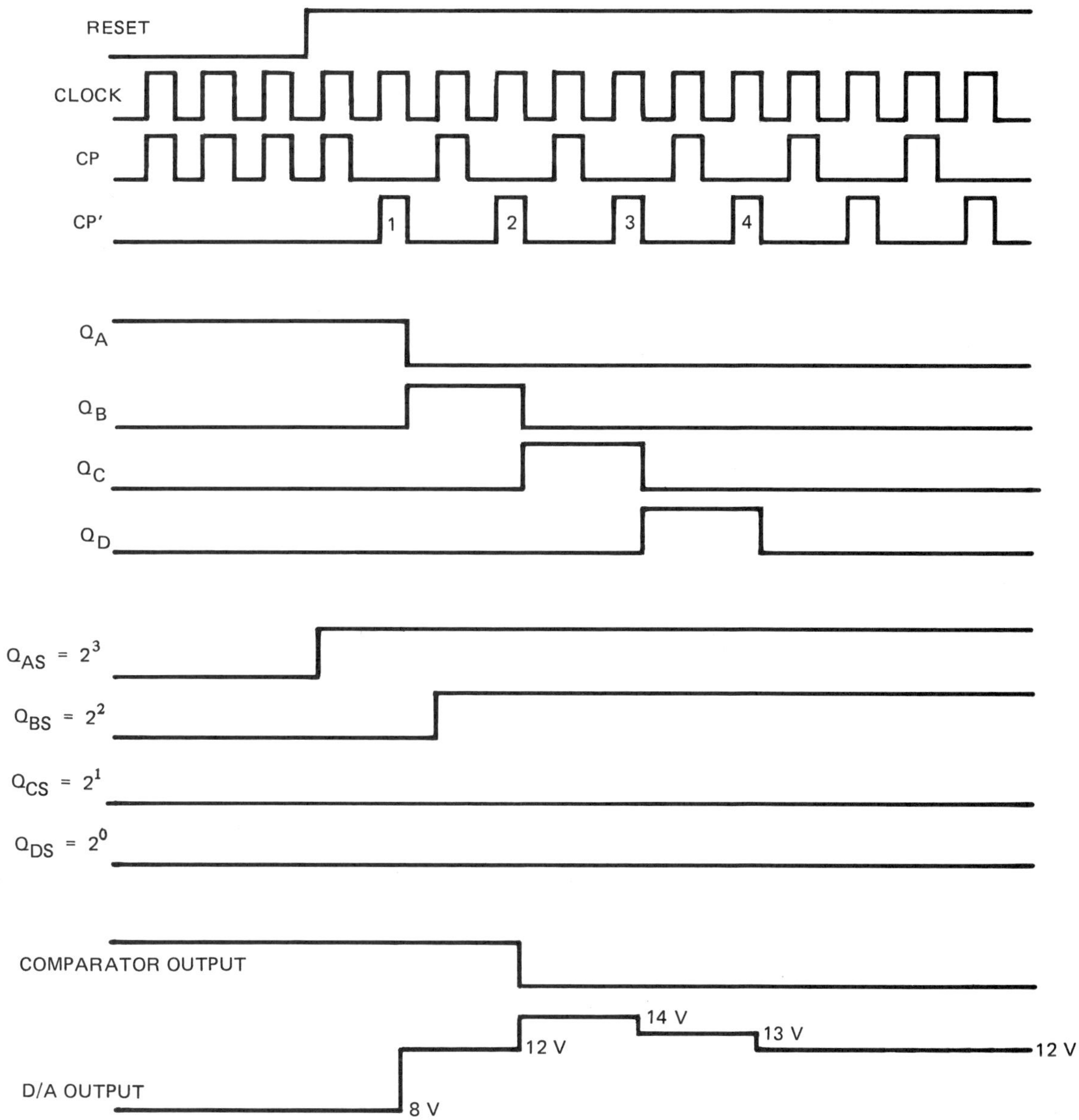

FIGURE 12–15 Wave forms for the A to D converter in Figure 12–14

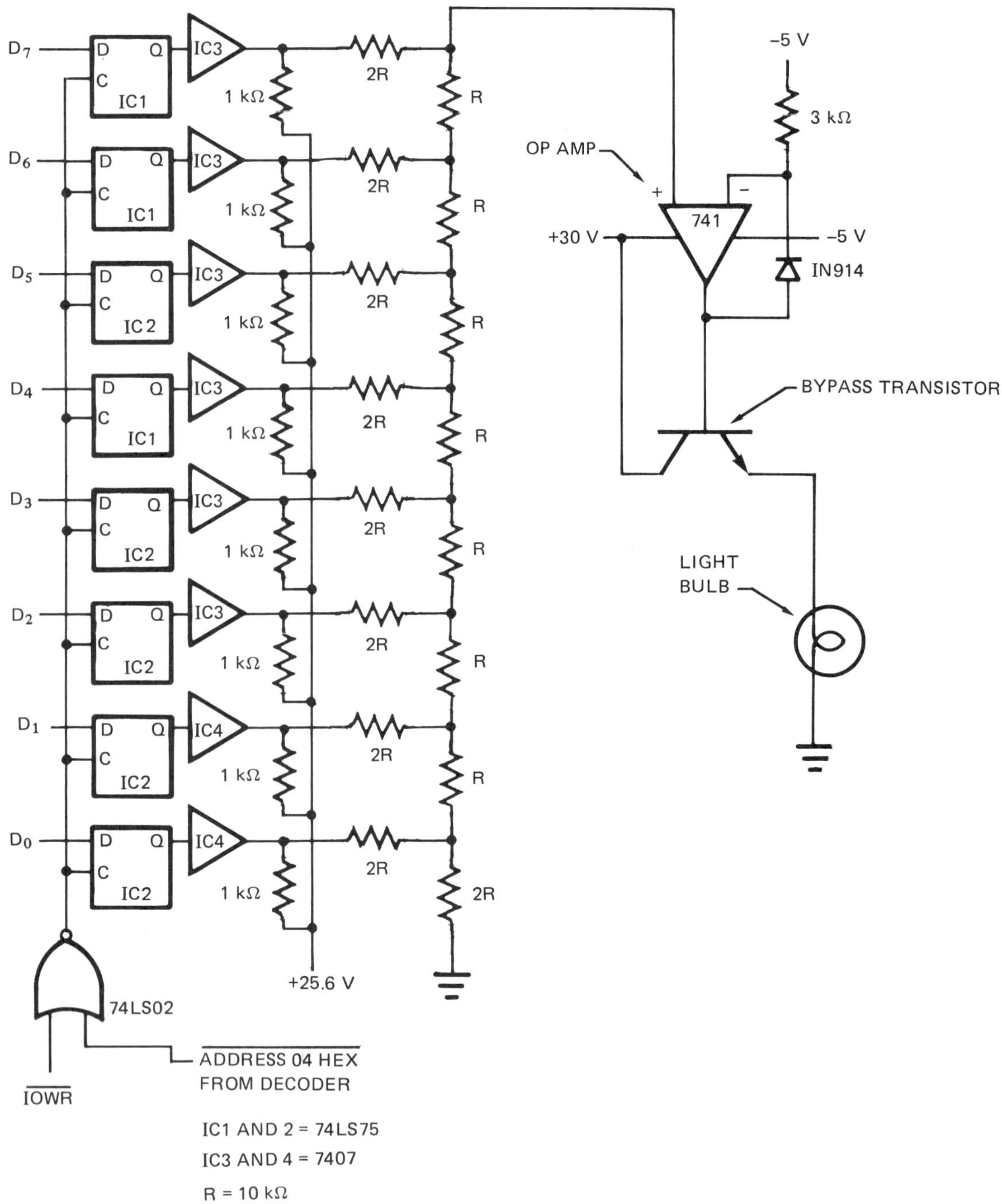

D7
D6
D5
D4
D3
D2
D1
D0
D
Q
C
IC1
IC2
IC3
IC4
1 kΩ
2R
R
+25.6 V
74LS02
IOWR
ADDRESS 04 HEX
FROM DECODER
IC1 AND 2 = 74LS75
IC3 AND 4 = 7407
R = 10 kΩ
OP AMP
741
+30 V
−5 V
3 kΩ
IN914
BYPASS TRANSISTOR
LIGHT
BULB

FIGURE 12–16

12.6 INTERFACING DIGITAL-TO-ANALOG CONVERTER TO THE MICROCOMPUTER

Figure 12–16 shows a digital-to-analog converter that is controlled by a computer through an output port. The output port is made of eight D latches and has a port address of 04 Hex. The Q outputs of the D latches drive a 2R D/A converter, as described earlier in this chapter.

The resolution or accuracy of this D/A converter is 0.1 V because the 25.6 V supply voltage to the 2R resistor network is divided by 2^8 or 256. This means that the computer can control the D/A converter's output in 0.1 V steps. The output voltage of the 2R network would be the binary number latched out to the output port multiplied by 0.1 V. Therefore, a binary number of 10001111 or decimal 143 would produce a voltage at the 2R resistor network of (143)(0.1 V) or 14.3 V. The same small problem of inaccuracy discussed earlier with this type of D/A converter still exists, but the voltage will still be quite accurate for the most part.

The output of a D/A converter driven by a computer is usually used to control some device such as a motor or electronics device. Therefore, the output of the 2R resistor network must be buffered to prevent loading and the distortion in linearity it causes.

The type of buffering used will depend on the use of the analog voltage. In Figure 12–16 the analog voltage produced by the output of the 2R resistor network is used to control the light intensity of a negative enlarger for an automated film processor. The light bulb will draw from 0 to 2 A of current when fully lit. This current is supplied by a bypass transistor capable of handling the current load. The base current of the power transistor is supplied by a 741 operational amplifier. The operational amplifier has very high input impedance, so it will not load the 2R resistor network, and the op amp's output can supply the larger base current of the bypass transistor. Because the voltage drop from emitter to base of the bypass transistor is about 0.7 V, a silicon diode with a 0.7 V drop was placed in the feedback loop of the op amp. This will cause the op amp's output voltage to always be 0.7 V more than the voltage of the 2R resistor network at the + input of the op amp. This will produce the same voltage at the emitter of the bypass transistor as the 2R resistor network puts out. The −5 V supply is used to ensure the current flow in the feedback loop of the op amp and to maintain at least 2–4 V difference between $-V_{sat}$ and the + input of the op amp.

12.7 THE ANALOG-TO-DIGITAL CONVERTER INTERFACED TO THE MICROCOMPUTER

When constructing an A/D converter for a microcomputer, it is possible to eliminate much of the hardware previously necessary and replace it with the software of the computer. This was done with the example in Figure 12–17. The output of the D/A part of the A/D converter is controlled by the computer through an output port. The computer can determine the state of the LM339 voltage comparator by inputting port 05 Hex and testing bit 7 for a 0 or a 1 value.

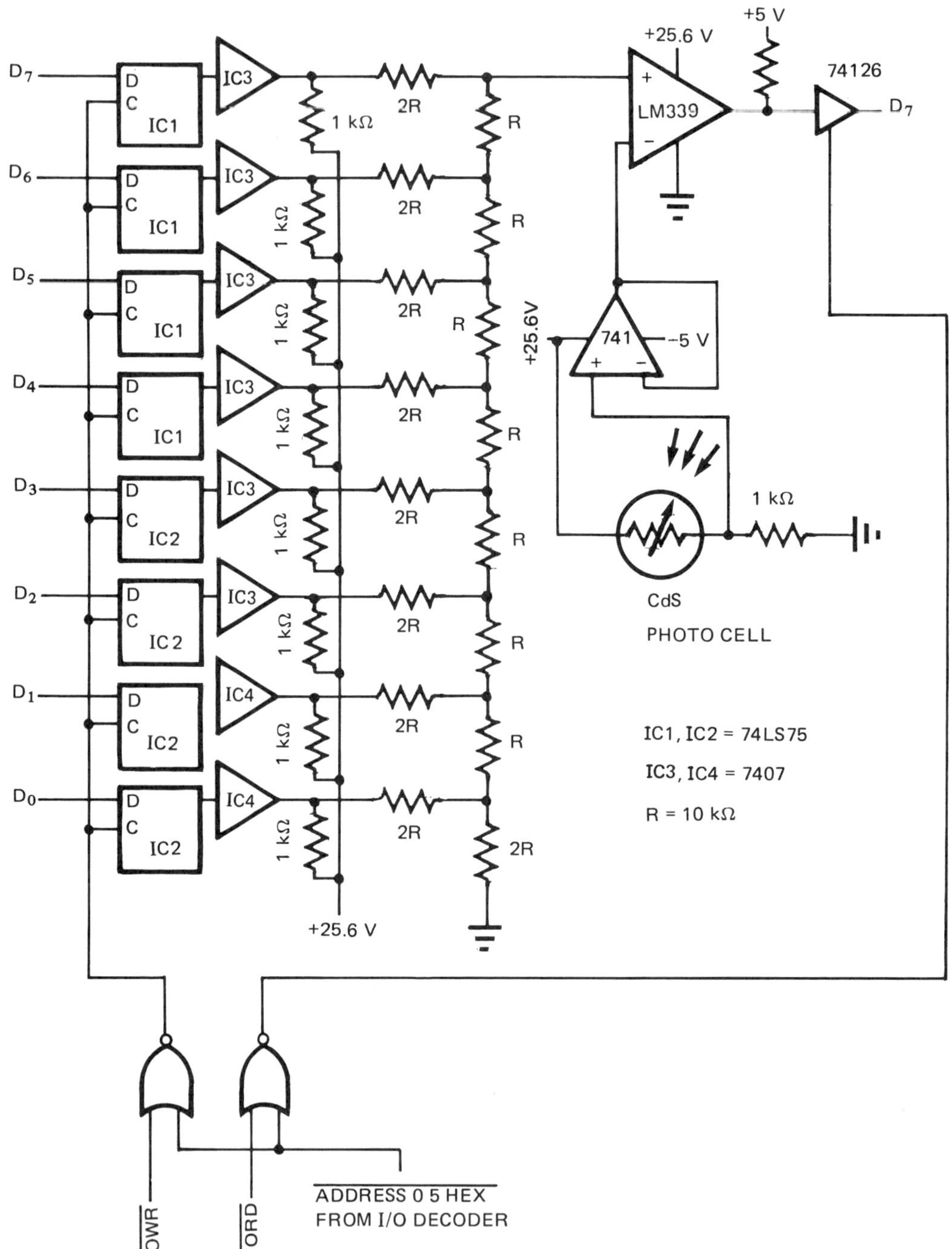
D7
D6
D5
D4
D3
D2
D1
D0
D
C
IC1
IC2
IC3
IC4
1 kΩ
2R
R
+25.6V
+25.6 V
+5 V
LM339
74126
741
−5 V
CdS
PHOTO CELL
IC1, IC2 = 74LS75
IC3, IC4 = 7407
R = 10 kΩ
IOWR
IORD
ADDRESS 0 5 HEX
FROM I/O DECODER

FIGURE 12–17

With this hardware, software can be written to determine the value of the voltage input to the − input of the LM339 comparator to the resolution of the D/A part of the analog converter. The analog voltage is supplied in Figure 12–17 by the output of an operational amplifier. The voltage controlling the op amp's output is the voltage drop across the 1-kΩ resistor in series with the cadium sulfide photocell. This input voltage will vary with the light falling on it. The voltage will get larger as the light intensity gets greater. This is the other half of the photoenlarger system that Figure 12–16 was used for.

The computer software or programming will determine the digital value of the light intensity incident on the printing paper by using the A/D converter in Figure 12–17 and will then adjust the light source with the D/A converter in Figure 12–16. This is a typical example of process control using a microcomputer. This control system has feedback, so the computer can evaluate the results of the control.

12.8 THE COUNT-UP SOFTWARE FOR THE ANALOG-TO-DIGITAL CONVERTER

The following program uses the count-up and compare method of obtaining voltage value input to the analog converter in Figure 12–17.

```
               ;*****************************************************
               ;*  SUBROUTINE TO OBTAIN THE VALUE OF THE VOLTAGE AT    *
               ;          THE A TO D CONVERTER WITH THE
               ;           COUNT UP AND COMPARE METHOD                 *
               ;*****************************************************
               ;
               ;THE SUBROUTINE WILL RETURN WITH THE VOLTAGE x 10^-1 IN
               ;THE A REGISTER.  NO OTHER REGISTERS ARE CHANGED
               ;
               ;
               ;
0005           INOUT   EQU     05H           ;PORT ADDRESS OF A TO D
               ;
0900                   ORG     900H          ;START OF PROGRAM
0900 C5        CONVER  PUSH    BC            ;SAVE BC
0901 0E05              LD      C,INOUT       ;PORT ADDRESS TO REG. C
0903 06FF              LD      B,0FFH        ;CLEAR COUNTER FOR D TO A
0905 04        LOOP    INC     B             ;BUMP COUNTER BY 1
0906 ED41              OUT     (C),B         ;OUTPUT COUNTER TO D TO A
0908 ED78              IN      A,(C)         ;INPUT COMPARATOR VALUE
090A 17                RLA                   ;PUT D7 IN THE CARRY FLAG
090B D20509            JP      NC,LOOP       ;JUMP IF COUNT IS TO LOW
090E 78                LD      A,B           ;PUT ANSWER IN A REGISTER
090F C1                POP     BC            ;RESTORE BC REGISTER
0910 C9                RET                   ;RETURN FROM SUBROUTINE
0000                   END
00000 Total Errors

LOOP     0905
CONVER   0900
INOUT    0005
```

12.9 THE SUCCESSIVE APPROXIMATION SOFTWARE FOR ANALOG-TO-DIGITAL CONVERTER

The following program will obtain the value of the voltage input to the A/D converter in Figure 12–17 using the successive approximation method.

```
                ;*******************************************************
                ;*  SUBROUTINE TO OBTAIN THE VOLTAGE FROM THE A TO D   *
                ;*          CONVERTER USING THE SUCCESSIVE             *
                ;*               APPROXIMATION METHOD                  *
                ;*******************************************************
                ;
0005            INOUT:  EQU     05H             ;ADDRESS OF THE A TO D
                ;
0900                    ORG     900H            ;START OF SUBROUTINE
0900 C5         CONVER: PUSH    BC              ;SAVE REGISTER
0901 D5                 PUSH    DE
0902 118000             LD      DE,0080H        ;SET D TO 0, E TO 80H
0905 0E05               LD      C,INOUT         ;PORT ADDRESS TO C REG.
0907 7B         LOOP:   LD      A,E             ;NEXT BIT TO A REGISTER
0908 B2                 OR      D               ;GEN. VALUE FOR D TO A
0909 ED79               OUT     (C),A           ;OUTPUT VALUE TO D TO A
090B F5                 PUSH    AF              ;SAVE VOLTAGE VALUE
090C ED78               IN      A,(C)           ;GET COMPARATOR VALUE
090E 17                 RLA                     ;PUT D7 IN CARRY FLAG
090F DA1F09             JP      C,REMOV         ;JUMP IF VOLTS TO LARGE
0912 F1                 POP     AF              ;RESTORE VOLTAGE VALUE
0913 B2                 OR      D               ;ADD TO THE VOLTAGE
0914 57                 LD      D,A             ;PUT VOLTAGE VALUE IN D
0915 7B         AGAIN:  LD      A,E             ;GET NEXT BIT TO TEST
0916 1F                 RRA                     ;SHIFT RIGHT, NEXT BIT
0917 5F                 LD      E,A             ;SAVE SHIFTED BIT IN E
0918 D20709             JP      NC,LOOP         ;JUMP IF NOT DONE
091B 7A                 LD      A,D             ;GET VOLTAGE IN A REG.
091C D1                 POP     DE              ;RESTORE REGISTERS
091D C1                 POP     BC
091E C9                 RET                     ;RETURN FROM SUBROUTINE
                ;
091F F1         REMOV:  POP     AF              ;RESTORE VOLTAGE VALUE
0920 C31509             JP      AGAIN           ;JUMP, VOLTAGE TO HIGH
0000                    END

***** NO ERRORS DETECTED *****
```

National Semiconductor

ADC0808, ADC0809 8-Bit μP Compatible A/D Converters With 8-Channel Multiplexer

General Description

The ADC0808, ADC0809 data acquisition component is a monolithic CMOS device with an 8-bit analog-to-digital converter, 8-channel multiplexer and microprocessor compatible control logic. The 8-bit A/D converter uses successive approximation as the conversion technique. The converter features a high impedance chopper stabilized comparator, a 256R voltage divider with analog switch tree and a successive approximation register. The 8-channel multiplexer can directly access any of 8-single-ended analog signals.

The device eliminates the need for external zero and full-scale adjustments. Easy interfacing to microprocessors is provided by the latched and decoded multiplexer address inputs and latched TTL TRI-STATE® outputs.

The design of the ADC0808, ADC0809 has been optimized by incorporating the most desirable aspects of several A/D conversion techniques. The ADC0808, ADC0809 offers high speed, high accuracy, minimal temperature dependence, excellent long-term accuracy and repeatability, and consumes minimal power. These features make this device ideally suited to applications from process and machine control to consumer and automotive applications. For 16-channel multiplexer with common output (sample/hold port) see ADC0816 data sheet. (See AN-247 for more information.)

Features

- Resolution—8-bits
- Total unadjusted error—$\pm \frac{1}{2}$ LSB and ± 1 LSB
- No missing codes
- Conversion time—100 μS
- Single supply—5 V_{DC}
- Operates ratiometrically or with 5 V_{DC} or analog span adjusted voltage reference
- 8-channel multiplexer with latched control logic
- Easy interface to all microprocessors, or operates "stand alone"
- Outputs meet T^2L voltage level specifications
- 0V to 5V analog input voltage range with single 5V supply
- No zero or full-scale adjust required
- Standard hermetic or molded 28-pin DIP package
- Temperature range −40°C to +85°C or −55°C to +125°C
- Low power consumption—15 mW
- Latched TRI-STATE output

Block Diagram

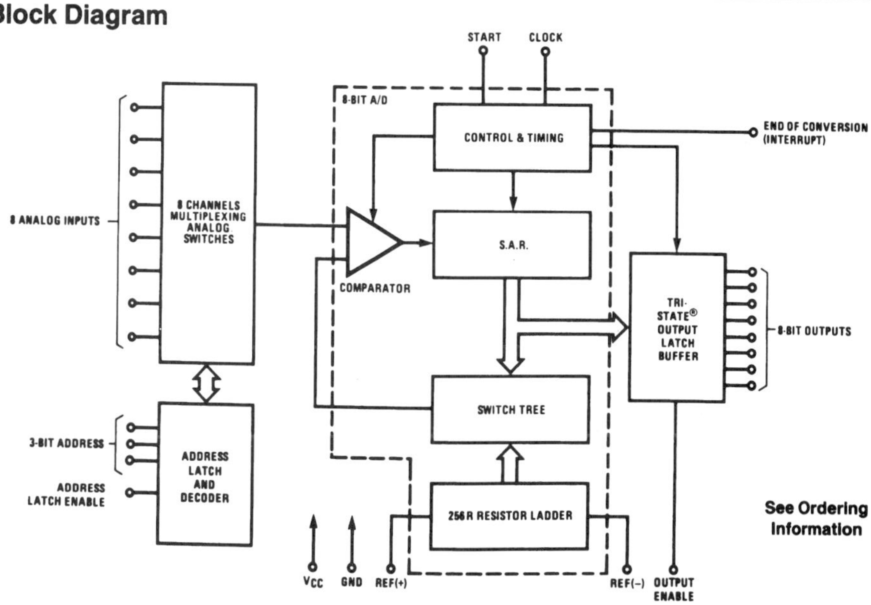

See Ordering Information

FIGURE 12–18

Functional Description

Multiplexer. The device contains an 8-channel single-ended analog signal multiplexer. A particular input channel is selected by using the address decoder. Table I shows the input states for the address lines to select any channel. The address is latched into the decoder on the low-to-high transition of the address latch enable signal.

TABLE I

SELECTED ANALOG CHANNEL	ADDRESS LINE		
	C	B	A
IN0	L	L	L
IN1	L	L	H
IN2	L	H	L
IN3	L	H	H
IN4	H	L	L
IN5	H	L	H
IN6	H	H	L
IN7	H	H	H

CONVERTER CHARACTERISTICS

The Converter

The heart of this single chip data acquisition system is its 8-bit analog-to-digital converter. The converter is designed to give fast, accurate, and repeatable conversions over a wide range of temperatures. The converter is partitioned into 3 major sections: the 256R ladder network, the successive approximation register, and the comparator. The converter's digital outputs are positive true.

The 256R ladder network approach *(Figure 1)* was chosen over the conventional R/2R ladder because of its inherent monotonicity, which guarantees no missing digital codes. Monotonicity is particularly important in closed loop feedback control systems. A non-monotonic relationship can cause oscillations that will be catastrophic for the system. Additionally, the 256R network does not cause load variations on the reference voltage.

The bottom resistor and the top resistor of the ladder network in *Figure 1* are not the same value as the remainder of the network. The difference in these resistors causes the output characteristic to be symmetrical with the zero and full-scale points of the transfer curve. The first output transition occurs when the analog signal has reached $+\frac{1}{2}$ LSB and succeeding output transitions occur every 1 LSB later up to full-scale.

The successive approximation register (SAR) performs 8 iterations to approximate the input voltage. For any SAR type converter, n-iterations are required for an n-bit converter. *Figure 2* shows a typical example of a 3-bit converter. In the ADC0808, ADC0809, the approximation technique is extended to 8 bits using the 256R network.

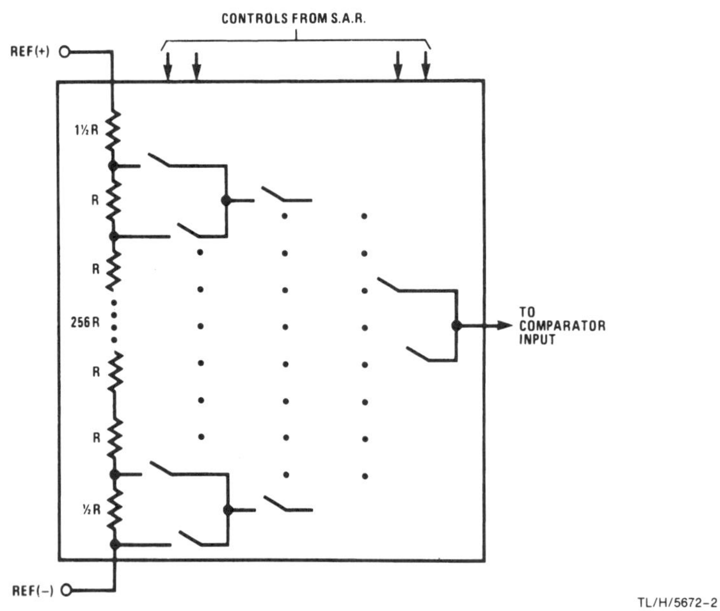

Resistor Ladder and Switch Tree

FIGURE 12–19

12.10 A TYPICAL LSI ANALOG-TO-DIGITAL CONVERTER

Today most computers that use an analog voltage to input information about some device use an LSI (large-scale intergration) IC to do the job. The same process and much of the same types of circuits are employed in these chips, but they are all on board the IC and can be directly accessed by the CPU or microcomputer.

The block diagram of a typical A/D converter on a single IC is shown in Figure 12–18. This IC is National Semiconductor's ADC0808, ADC0809 microprocessor compatible A/D converters. Notice that there are eight analog inputs. Any one of the eight can be selected by the 3-bit address and address latch enable to pass its voltage to the voltage comparators. The actual conversion from analog to digital is done with a successive approximation register and a D/A converter that they call a *switch tree*. The control of the successive approximation registers and the final output to micro output port latches is controlled by an external clock and a start input. The resistor ladder in this IC is actually a series string of 256 resistors of equal value. The switching tree takes the binary number output by the successive approximation register and taps the series resistor at the proper level to produce the desired voltage for the comparator. This is shown in Figure 12–19. The voltage across this string of 256 resistors is applied at the REF + and REF − input and cannot be more than + 5 V. The 8-bit latched output port is tri-state but can only drive about a 1-TTL load, so they must be buffered in most applications. This IC could be used very well to interface such devices as a joystick and a position indicator to a computer.

The full IC specifications for the ADC0808, ADC0809 are shown in Appendix D.

EXERCISE 12

1. Draw the circuit for an 8-bit 2R D/A converter that can be driven from an 8-bit output port of a microcomputer.
2. What would be the output voltage of the D/A converter in Figure 12–1 if the supply voltage was 20 V and the binary number A Hex was switched into the input?
3. Give two reasons why the TTL D/A converter in Figure 12–8 will not be absolutely accurate.
4. Why is the 741 op amp used in the circuit of Figure 12–9?
5. Draw the waveforms for the A/D converter of Figure 12–11 for the binary number of B Hex.
6. Draw the waveforms for the circuit in Figure 12–17 for an input voltage of 13.44 V, and use the successive approximation method.
7. Draw the circuit for a 5-bit binary ladder D/A converter with TTL inputs.
8. Why is the IN914 silicon diode in the feedback loop of the 741 op amp buffer in Figure 12–16?

9. Draw the pinout for the ADC0808 A/D converter.
10. How many analog inputs does the ADC0808 have?
11. What type of resistor network does the ADC0808 use to obtain the analog voltage for its comparator?
12. What would be the voltage increment for the A/D converter in lab 12 if the supply voltage to the resistor network was 6.4 V?
13. What would you expect to see on the scope if the scope probe was on the output of the D/A resistor network of Figure 12–11 and the output of the op amp became disconnected from the NAND gate input?
14. What would you expect to see on the scope if the scope probe was on the output of the op amp in Figure 12–11 and the op amp's output was disconnected from the NAND gate's input?
15. What would be the voltage increment of the A/D converter in Figure 12–10 if the supply voltage to the voltage comparators was 24 V?
16. Write a short program to determine the value of the input voltage to the LM339 comparator in Figure 12–17 and display it on port 2 of the Biggy trainer (use the count-up and compare method).
17. Repeat problem 16 but use the successive approximation method.
18. What is the input port address of the voltage comparator in lab 12?
19. What would be the output voltage of the D/A converter in Figure 12–8 if the binary number 9 were placed on its inputs?
20. Give two typical uses for an A/D converter used with a microcomputer.

Lab 12

OBJECTIVES

After completing this lab, you should be able to

- construct an analog-to-digital converter.
- write a program to operate the analog-to-digital converter by count-up and successive approximation methods.
- observe the stair-step and successive approximation waveforms on the scope.

Procedure

1. Construct the given circuit on the protoboard of the trainer.
2. Write a short program to make port 2 count from 0 to 256 and repeat itself.
3. Put a scope probe on pin 5 of the LM339 and observe the stair-step wave pattern on the scope. Have the instructor approve its operation, and then graph it.
4. Write a program similar to the one in the text to obtain the binary value of the analog input voltage put out by the 10-kΩ pot. Make the program output the value of the voltage on port 0. (Use the count-up method.) Make the program loop so you can observe the stair-step output as the input voltage changes. Have the instructor approve its operation.
5. Repeat part 4 but use the successive approximation method to obtain the analog voltage.
6. The voltage steps for this A/D converter are

$$\frac{V_s}{2^N} = \frac{12.8}{256} = 0.05 \text{ V}$$

With this information, make a graph of actual input voltage versus the measure input voltage of the A/D converter.

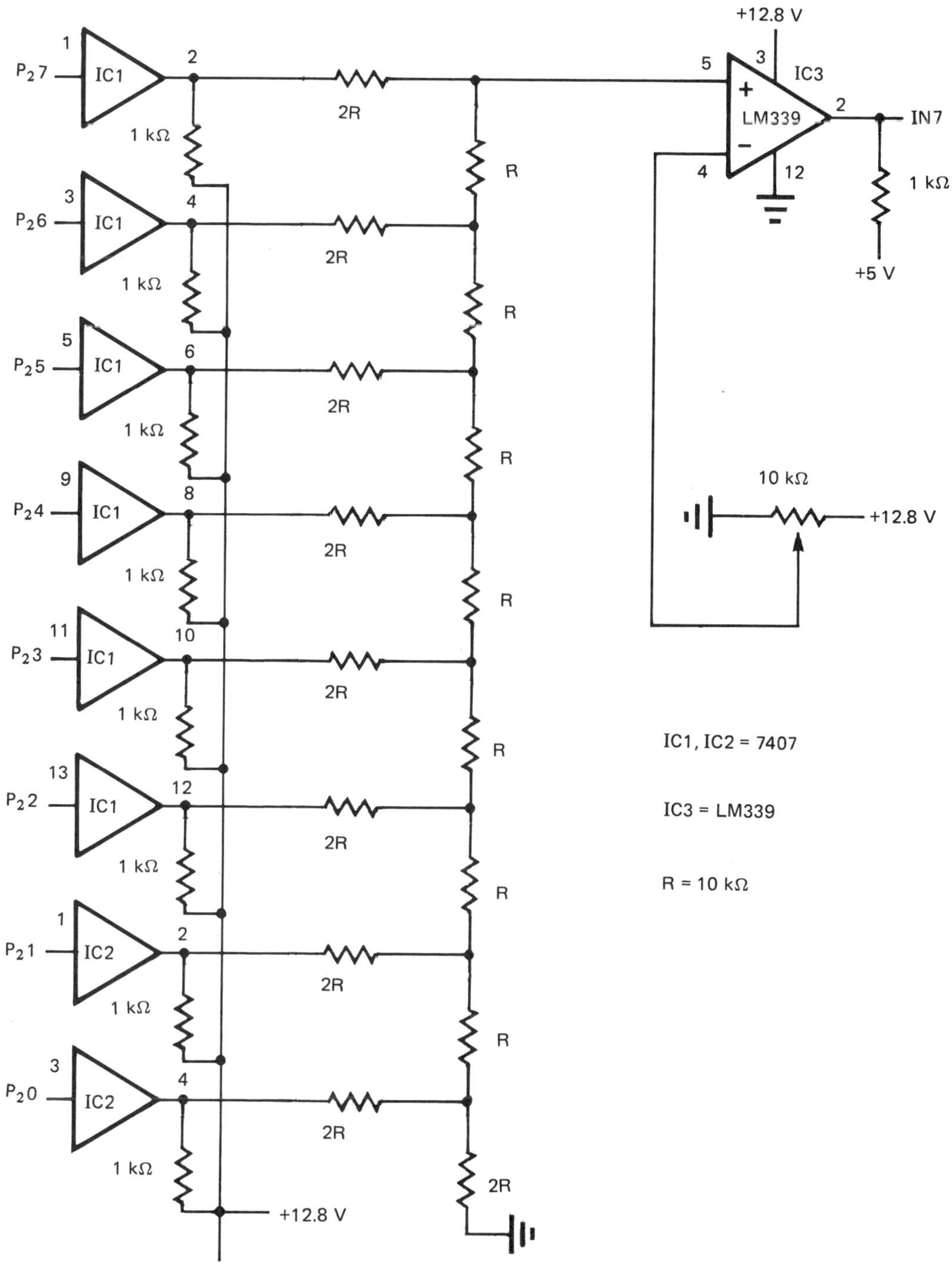
+12.8 V
IC3
LM339
IN7
1 kΩ
+5 V
P27
P26
P25
P24
P23
P22
P21
P20
IC1
IC2
2R
R
1 kΩ
10 kΩ
+12.8 V
IC1, IC2 = 7407
IC3 = LM339
R = 10 kΩ

Chapter **13**

COMPUTER PROCESS CONTROL

OBJECTIVES

After completing this chapter, you should be able to

- interface high current relays and small DC motors to a typical computer system.
- control a small stepper motor with computer hardware and software.
- use relays and optical couplers to isolate the computer from other electrical circuits.
- identify the difference between open-loop and closed-loop controls with a microcomputer.

13.1 INTRODUCTION TO COMPUTER PROCESS CONTROL

Obtaining input from the real world and controlling real-world devices with the computer is what we mean by the term *computer process control*. Process control in the past has been accomplished by using analog circuits and relays designed to fit the specific machinery or process to be controlled. These noncomputerized control systems were often slow and very hard to change once designed and operating. Such noncomputerized systems of control ranged from the mechanical governor of a small lawn mower engine to the frequency control system of a larger generator.

Today many of the process control systems of the past have an extra part, the computer, that can be programmed to make the decision necessary to control the process correctly based on input from the process being controlled. The control of a process is based on the input to the computer, and what the computer does is a direct function of its program. Therefore, the way in which the computer controls the process can be changed by simply using a different software program; no hardware need be changed. Also, the computer is capable of doing vast amounts of calculations to produce the proper control sequence or values to use in control of the process. For these and other reasons, the computer is an invaluable tool to control processes of all types.

The use of computer process control was rather limited until the advent of the microprocessor because of the cost and size of the computer. The micro, on the other hand, made it possible to think of using a computer to control such jobs as running a washing machine, running a fire alarm, and even running a simple toy train. This trend of using a microcomputer to control processes of all kind is going to grow very fast in the future. You only have to look at the auto industry and all the microcomputer process controls that are employed in new cars today to realize that the microcomputer will have a tremendous impact on the way machines work in the future.

To control any real-world process, the computer must be able to gain input from the real world and be able to control the real world. This input and output interface to the real world is the hardware part of process control. The other part is the program, which is just as important as the hardware. The design of the input/output hardware depends a great deal on what the computer is to control. Therefore, we will not be able to cover every aspect of this topic in this chapter, but we will look at some very typical methods of input/output hardware for process control.

For programming, the same constraints apply. Therefore, the programming presented will apply to the examples used in the chapter.

13.2 OUTPUT CONTROL OF THE REAL WORLD WITH RELAYS

When the computer is asked to control the real world, it is not dealing with + 5 VDC but anything from millivolts to megavolts and milliwatts to megawatts. The goal of the process control engineer is to run the whole world on a 5 V signal, and someday he may succeed.

Most of the time the computer must start and stop or control the direction of motors, valves, or solenoids, which run on 110-, 220- or 440-VAC at high currents. This means that the computer circuitry must be isolated from the motors or solenoids in some way. There are two basic methods of isolating the computer electrically from another circuit: relays and optocouplers.

A relay is a switch that is controlled by an electric magnet. The switch is open or closed by energizing or not energizing the magnet. Figure 13–1 shows a drawing of a small relay and the two schematic symbols used for relays. Figure 13–1B shows the symbol for a coil of wire wound on a magnetic core with switch contacts just above it. This is an old way of drawing a relay in a circuit. Figure 13–1C is the method of drawing a relay most often used today. The coil is drawn separately and labeled with a letter. The contacts that the coil controls are then drawn and shown any place that they are used in a schematic. When the contacts are drawn, they are drawn in their unenergized state (the open or closed state when the magnet has no current flow).

Because the only thing connecting the coil circuit and the switch contacts is the magnetic pull of an electric magnet, the relay offers very good electrical isolation, but because it is mechanical in nature, it is slow to switch. The amount of current or voltage that the relay can turn on or off is limited to the size of the contact, not the current necessary to close the contact with the coil of the electric magnet. Therefore, the relay is ideal for controlling large machines with high voltages and currents.

Most relays are measured for size by the electrical specifications needed to energize the coil and the electrical specifications for the switch contacts of the output. Relay coils

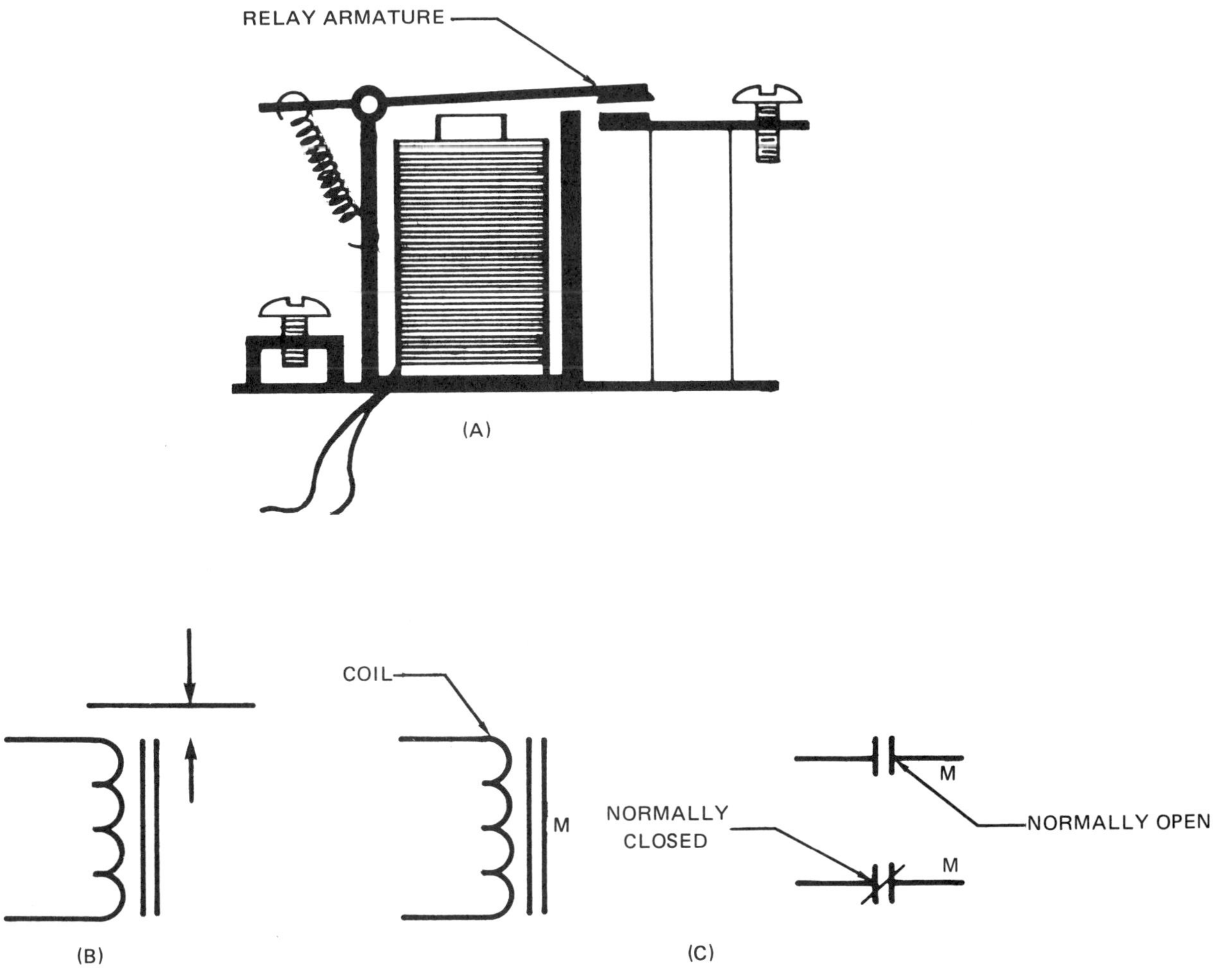

FIGURE 13–1

are usually specified by the voltage needed to energize the coil, by the resistance of the coil, or by the current needed to energize the coil. Often a relay will have a pickup current specified, which means that a specified amount of current is needed to energize the relay or pick up the armature of the relay. The type of switch contacts and the current and voltage capabilities of the contacts used in the relay is the other specification used. The contacts of the relays in Figure 13–1B and C are single-pole double-throw.

Because most relay coils need higher voltages and greater current than a typical TTL output can supply, it is necessary to design an interface circuit, such as in Figure 13–2, to drive the coil.

In Figure 13–2 the 1-bit output port supplies a TTL logic 1 or 0 to the 7406 open-collector inverter. The 7406 is a buffer IC capable of handling up to 40 mA of sink current and 30 V on its output. This is an ideal IC to use as a small transistor driver.

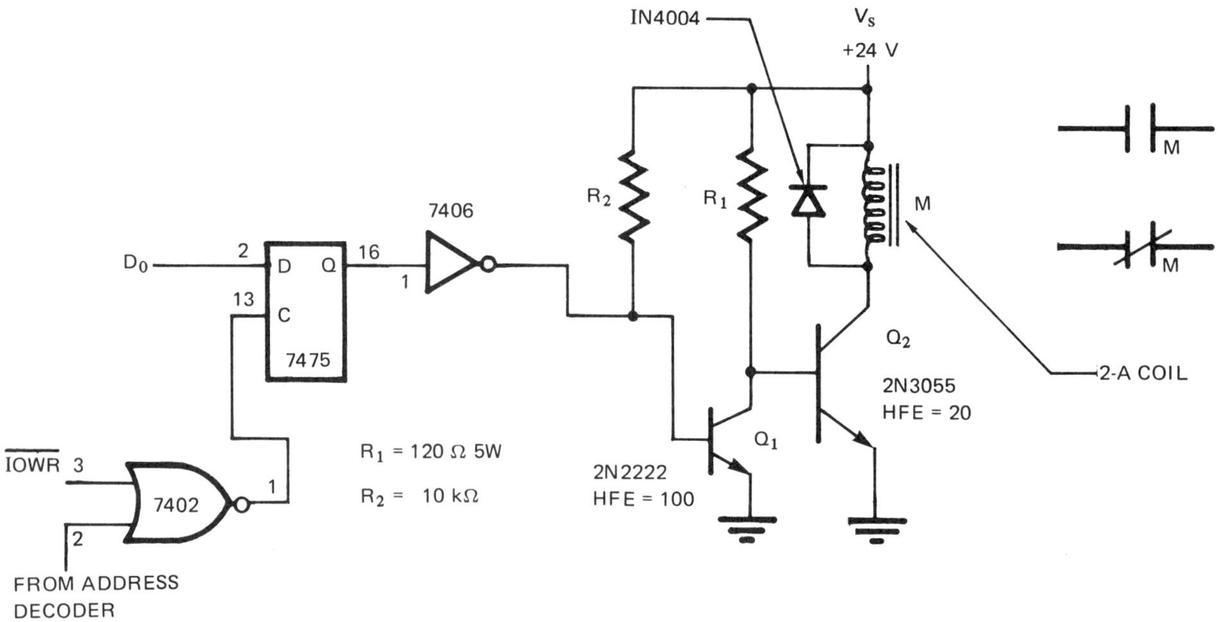

FIGURE 13–2

When the 7406 output goes to Hiz, the Q1 transistor will turn on and bring the base voltage of Q2 to about 0.2 V. This low base voltage on Q2 causes it to turn off, thus causing the relay to open. Where the output of the 7406 goes to a logic LOW, the Q1 transistor turns off and the base of Q2 is pulled high through the 120-Ω R1 resistor. This supplies Q2 with a substantial base current, and the Q2 collector current goes quite high, thus energizing the 2-A relay coil.

Because the 2-A relay coil has a large inductance, the current does not rise quickly, but when the current is cut off to the coil, the magnetic lines of force fall very quickly across the winding of the coil, causing a very large voltage and current in the same direction as the former current flow. This voltage kick can be quite damaging to the whole computer circuit if not suppressed. To suppress this voltage and current, a diode is placed across the relay coil in reverse bias to the power supply. Figure 13–3 shows the graph of current versus time for turning on the relay. When the current is cut off to the relay coil, the voltage induced looks like a battery in series with the power supply. The diode is forward biased to this induced voltage and shorts it out, thus protecting the rest of the computer from the large kick that would have been produced.

A 2-A relay coil is very large. A relay that large could have very high voltage and current capacities on the contacts. Such a relay could conceivably turn on or off very large motors at very high AC voltage if needed.

The Q2 transistor is the transistor that must directly supply the current to the relay coil and must have a collector current rating large enough to supply the 2 A needed.

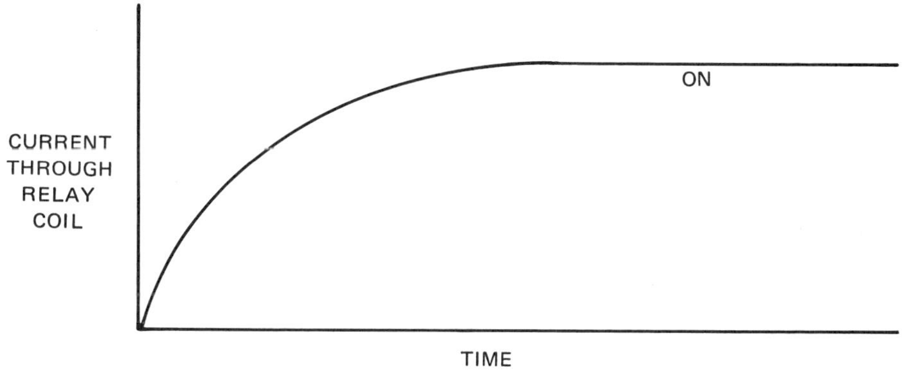

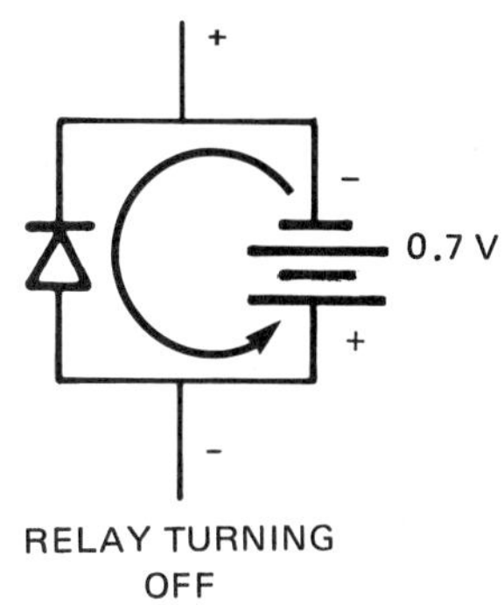

The 2N3055 is a typical silicon power transistor with a typical Ic rating of 15 A and maximum collector voltage of 60 V. The HFE (change in collector current ÷ change in base current: $\Delta Ic/\Delta Ib$) is 20 at an Ic of 4 A. As can be seen, this transistor will more than do the job.

The base current needed to supply the 2 A of collector current is equal to the collector current divided by the HFE.

$$Ib = \frac{Ic}{HFE}$$

$$Ib = \text{base current}$$

$$Ic = \text{collector current}$$

$$HFE = \frac{Ic}{Ib}$$

To compute the necessary base current for the relay in Figure 13–2, we will use a collector current of twice the actual Ic. This will insure that Q2 will be turned on hard with very little, if any, voltage drop across it.

$$Ib = \frac{Ic}{HFE}$$
$$Ib = \frac{4\ A}{20}$$
$$Ib = 200\ mA$$

When Q2 is turned on, the voltage at the base is 0.7 V, because a forward-biased PN junction has about 0.7 V drop across it. Therefore, the voltage drop across R1 is

$$V_{R1} = V_S - 0.7$$
$$V_{R1} = 24 - 0.7$$
$$V_{R1} = 23.3\ V$$

The current through R1 must be 200 mA because it supplies the base current for Q2. Therefore, the value of R1 and the wattage of R1 are computed as follows:

$$R1 = \frac{V_{R1}}{I_{R1}} \qquad W_{R1} = (I_{R1})\,(V_{R1})$$
$$R1 = \frac{23.3\ V}{200\ mA} \qquad W_{R1} = (200\ mA)\,(23.3\ V)$$
$$R1 = 116.5 \qquad W_{R1} = 4.66\ W$$

A 120-Ω, 5-W resistor will do the job quite nicely for R1.

The 200-mA base current is diverted through Q1 when we wish to turn off Q2. This could have been done by the 7406, but the 7406 IC is not capable of handling 200 mA of current. So a second transistor is used to handle the 200 mA. The 200-mA current is well within the collector current capability of the 2N2222 transistor selected.

The 2N2222 has an HFE of 100 at an Ic of 150 mA. Therefore, the Ib would be

$$Ib = \frac{Ic}{HFE}$$
$$Ib = \frac{200\ mA}{100}$$
$$Ib = 2\ mA$$

The 7406 can more than handle 2 mA of current, and a 10-kΩ resistor (R2) will supply about 2.33 mA of base current for Q1.

For many applications one transistor will do, but in this case Q1 was needed because of the high base current caused by the 2-A relay.

13.3 OUTPUT CONTROL OF THE REAL WORLD WITH OPTOCOUPLERS

An optocoupler is an enclosed package containing an LED and phototransistor or photodiode. Figure 13–4 shows the schematic symbols for optocouplers. The LED is interfaced to the computer, and the photodiode or phototransistor is used as the corresponding output. The only thing connecting the two circuits is the light of the LED. Therefore,

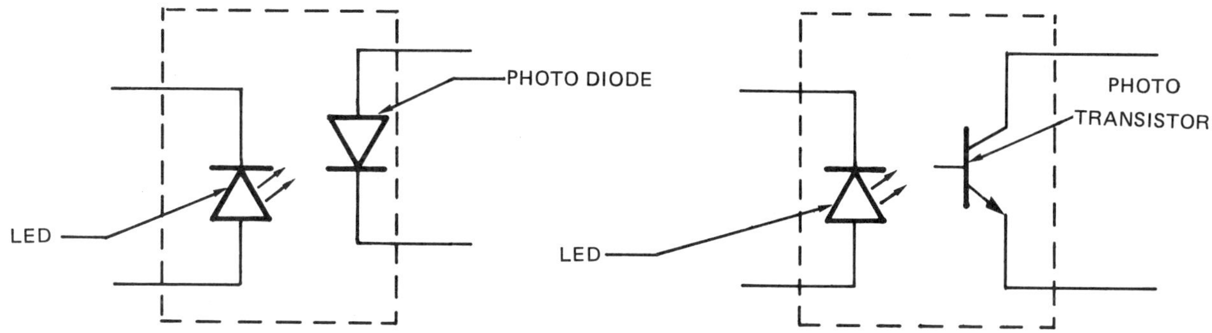

FIGURE 13–4

the optocoupler offers excellent circuit isolation, and it can operate very fast. The speed of the optocoupler is in the neighborhood of 5–10 ns, so it could easily be used to transfer serial data from a computer to a remote radio-frequency transmitter or other device.

Figure 13–5 shows a typical optocoupler interface to drive a digital transmission wire pair that might be used to carry the digital signal to a remote site.

Optocouplers can work fast, but, unlike the relay, they cannot handle great currents or voltages. This has changed somewhat with the introduction of optocouplers with triacs and large power capabilities, but they still cannot match the relay for switching high-

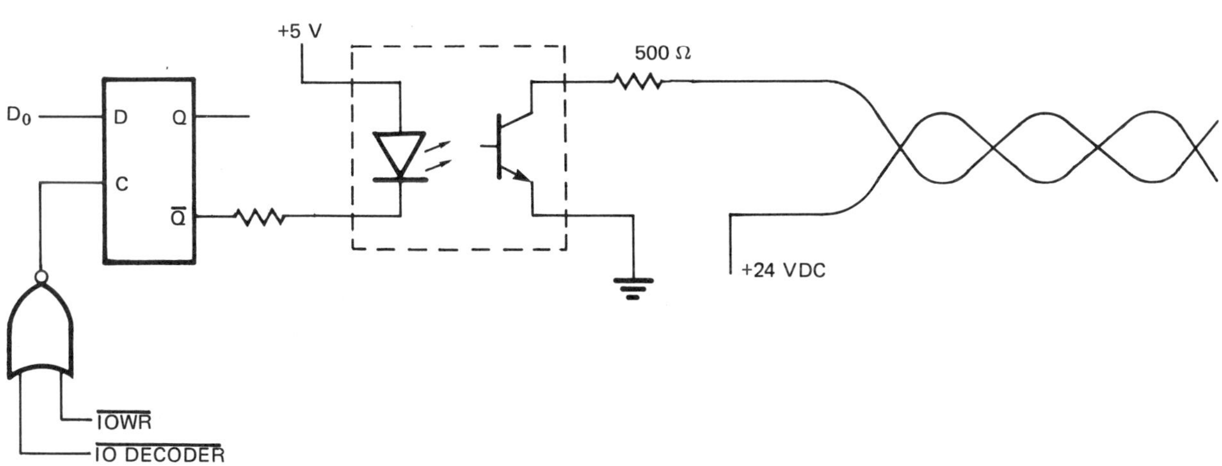

FIGURE 13–5 Optocoupler used to drive a long transmission wire pair

power devices. Unlike relays, the optocouplers can pass an analog voltage quite well. This is because the light intensity of an LED is directly proportional to the current flowing through it. This aspect of the optocoupler is quite useful when circuit isolation and analog voltages are involved.

13.4 CONTROL OF A TYPICAL STEPPER MOTOR

Stepper motors are electrical motors designed to be rotated in steps with electrical pulses. Because they move a certain amount of rotation with each step or electrical pulse, they are very easy to interface to a computer. The computer can put out three pulses, and the stepper motor will rotate three steps. If each step is 15°, then the motor shaft will have rotated 45° or one-eighth turn. Stepper motors are used wherever the computer needs to control the angular rotation of mechanical control devices, such as the injectors of a diesel engine or the bed feed of a milling machine. Almost all disk drives use stepper motors to move the head from track to track.

There are two basic types of stepper motors in use today with computers. They are the three-phase motor and the magnetic-rotor stepper motor. First, we will examine the operation of these two types of motors. Then we will see how to interface them to the computer.

Figure 13–6 shows the basic layout of a three-phase motor, sometimes called a least-reluctance motor. It consists of an iron rotor with poles on it. The field of the motor is also iron with poles on it, but the field has more poles than the rotor. The field has coils of wire wrapped around its poles to form three separate sets of electromagnets, as shown in Figure 13–6. Only the first three coils are shown in Figure 13–6, but the rest of the field is also wrapped with the same three coils. When coil 1 is energized by putting a current through it, two north/south magnets are produced, as shown in Figure 13–6. This magnetic field causes the iron rotor to align itself to produce the least reluctance or resistance to the magnetic circuit. That means that the two poles of the field and rotor will align themselves as shown in Figure 13–6. Notice that when the rotor is aligned to a set of poles, the pole next to it is right in the middle of the two poles on the field. That is because the rotor has eight poles and the field has 12. As long as coil 1 is energized, the motor will stay in a fixed position, and it will take considerable force to move it or cause it to slip as it is called. The holding force of a stepper motor is a typical specification given when specifying the properties of a stepper motor.

To rotate the motor from the position shown in Figure 13–7A, coil 1 is de-energized and current is applied to coil 2, causing coil 2 to become a set of north/south magnets that pull the iron rotor into alignment with it. As shown in Figure 13–7B, this rotates the rotor 15°. Then coil 2 is de-energized, and coil 3 is energized, causing coil 3 to produce a set of north/south magnets. This pulls the rotor 15° more to align it with the magnetic poles of coil 3, as shown in Figure 13–7C. To continue the rotation, coil 1 is energized next, and the whole process starts over. The direction of rotation is determined by the order in which the coils are turned on or off. If you use a sequence of 123123, then the motor will rotate counterclockwise as shown. If the on/off sequence is 321321, then the direction is opposite or clockwise.

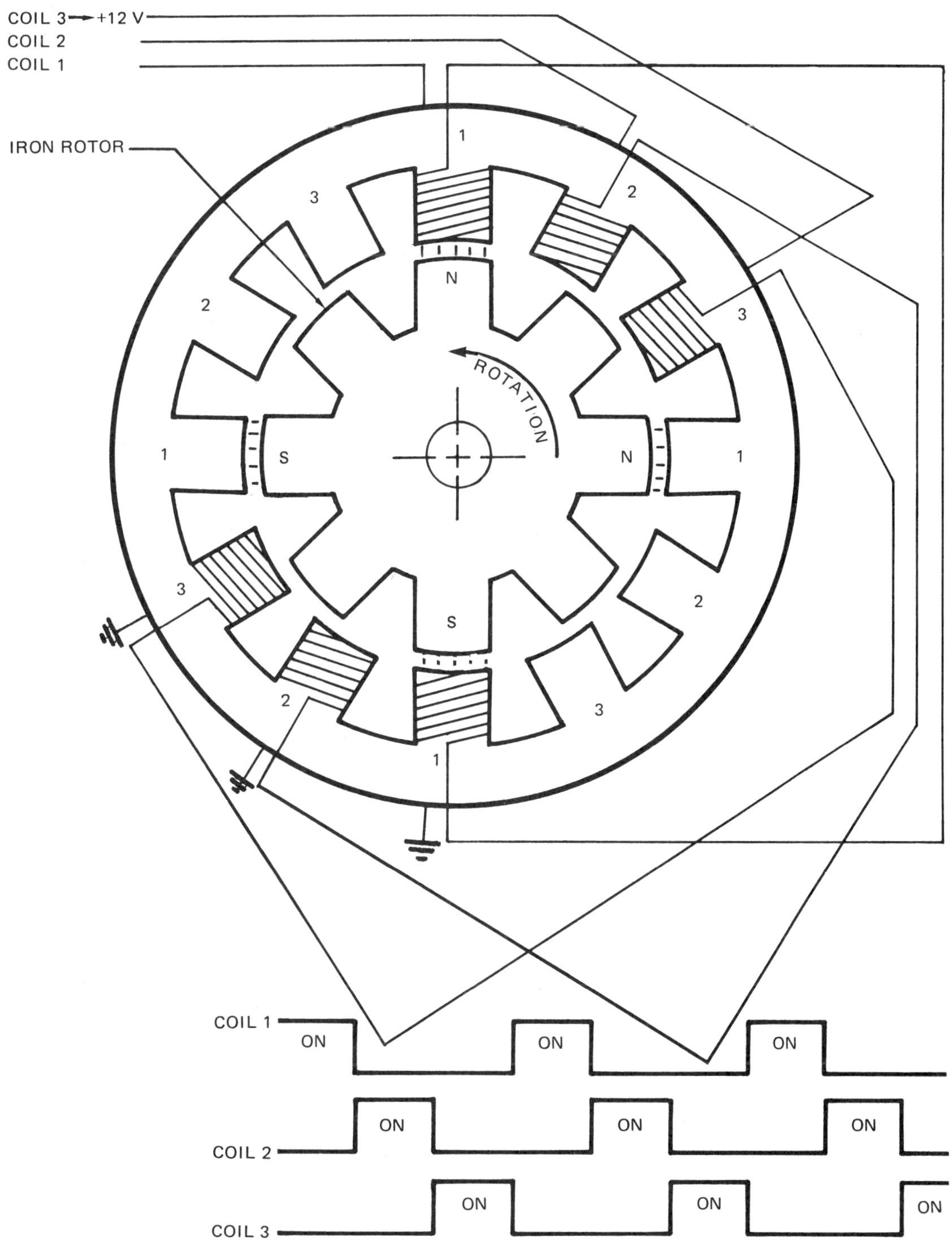
COIL 3 → +12 V
COIL 2
COIL 1
IRON ROTOR
1
2
3
N
S
ROTATION
COIL 1
ON
COIL 2
ON
COIL 3
ON

FIGURE 13–6

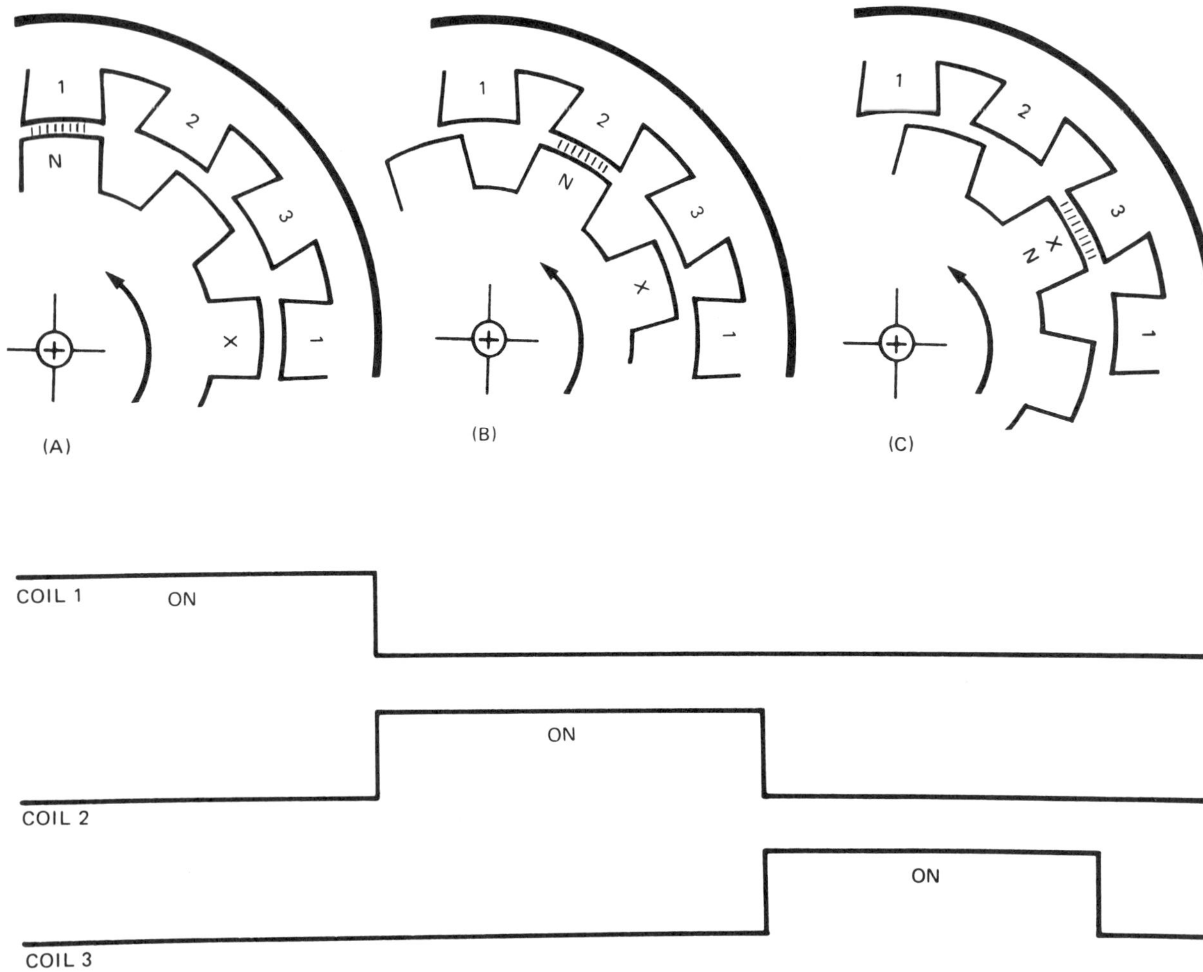

FIGURE 13–7

Notice the waveforms for the rotation of the three-phase motor in Figures 13–6 and 13–7. They are out of phase by 120° and could easily be generated by a shift register with output tied back to the input.

The permanent-magnet stepper motor is constructed a bit differently as shown in Figure 13–8. The field consists of two halves. On each half two coils are wound in opposite directions. The metal cores on which the coils are wound have small triangle tails that are bent down, one beside the other. This makes a north/south magnet when one of the coils is energized. If the other coil is energized, the north/south poles will change their polarities because it is wound in the opposite direction, and the current will flow in the opposite direction around the coil. The rotor is a set of permanent magnets that are set in the rotor, as shown in Figure 13–8.

To understand how these stepper motors work, we will look at one of the rotor magnets as it passes the changing magnetic poles of the field. This is shown in Figure 13–9. The rotation sequence starts in Figure 13–9A, where coil 1 (C1) and coil 2 (C2) are energized. This pulls the rotor magnet into a place of least reluctance for the magnetic circuit. This is shown in Figure 13–9A. To rotate the rotor 7.5°, the polarity of the top set of magnets in the field is changed by energizing coil 3 (C3). This pulls the rotor magnet to the right to a new place of least reluctance. Next, the bottom set of magnets on the field is changed by energizing coil (C4), which moves the rotor magnet 7.5° to the right again, as shown in Figure 13–9C. Then the top set of magnets is changed. Next, the pattern returns to the beginning, as shown in Figure 13–9A. Notice that this motor uses four coils and four steps to complete one cycle. Also, two coils are on at a time. The sequence for rotation is shown in the table in Figure 13–9. It could also be easily derived from a properly set up shift register.

Stepping motors of this type have good holding torque and good turning torque. This is because of the added strength of the permanent magnets. The type of stepper motor shown in Figures 13–8 and 13–9 is quite often used in 5¼-in floppy-disk drives and small robotic arms.

Figure 13–10 shows a typical drive circuit for a stepper motor like the one shown in Figure 13–8. Because the current of the stepper motor is quite high (2–3 A), a power transistor is used to supply the current, as discussed earlier in this chapter. Notice the induction-kick-suppressor diodes for each coil. The on/off state of the transistor or the coils is controlled by the computer through a standard 4-bit output port made from D latches. The computer can move the motor at will simply by outputting the proper sequence of 4-bit words to the output port. To do this, the computer must have a simple program to produce the proper sequence to rotate the motor left or right, fast or slow.

The program shown in Figure 13–11 will take a signed 2's complement number in the A register and step the motor counterclockwise if the number is positive or clockwise if it is negative for the number of times the A register contains. The rate of stepping is contained in the B register. The stepping rate is the value of B multiplied by 10 ms per step. This program is designed to work with the hardware of Figure 13–10. Notice that a 4-bit shift register is made from an 8-bit register by rotating the memory location two times. This way, the two on bits can be rotated around the shift register in order, as shown in Figure 13–11. Notice that the bit pattern is the same for the rotation of the stepper motor in Figure 13–9.

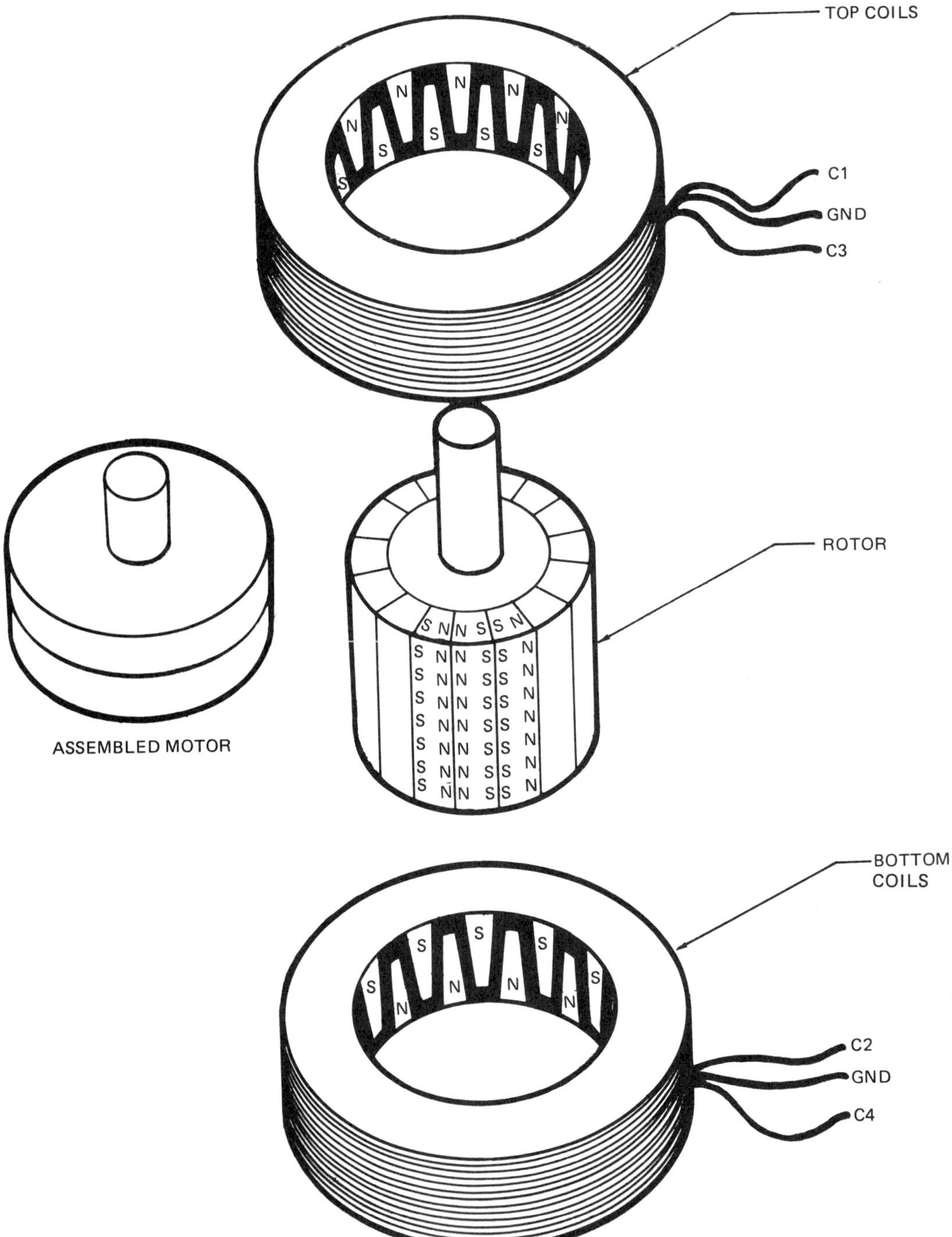
TOP COILS
C1
GND
C3
ROTOR
ASSEMBLED MOTOR
BOTTOM COILS
C2
GND
C4

FIGURE 13–8

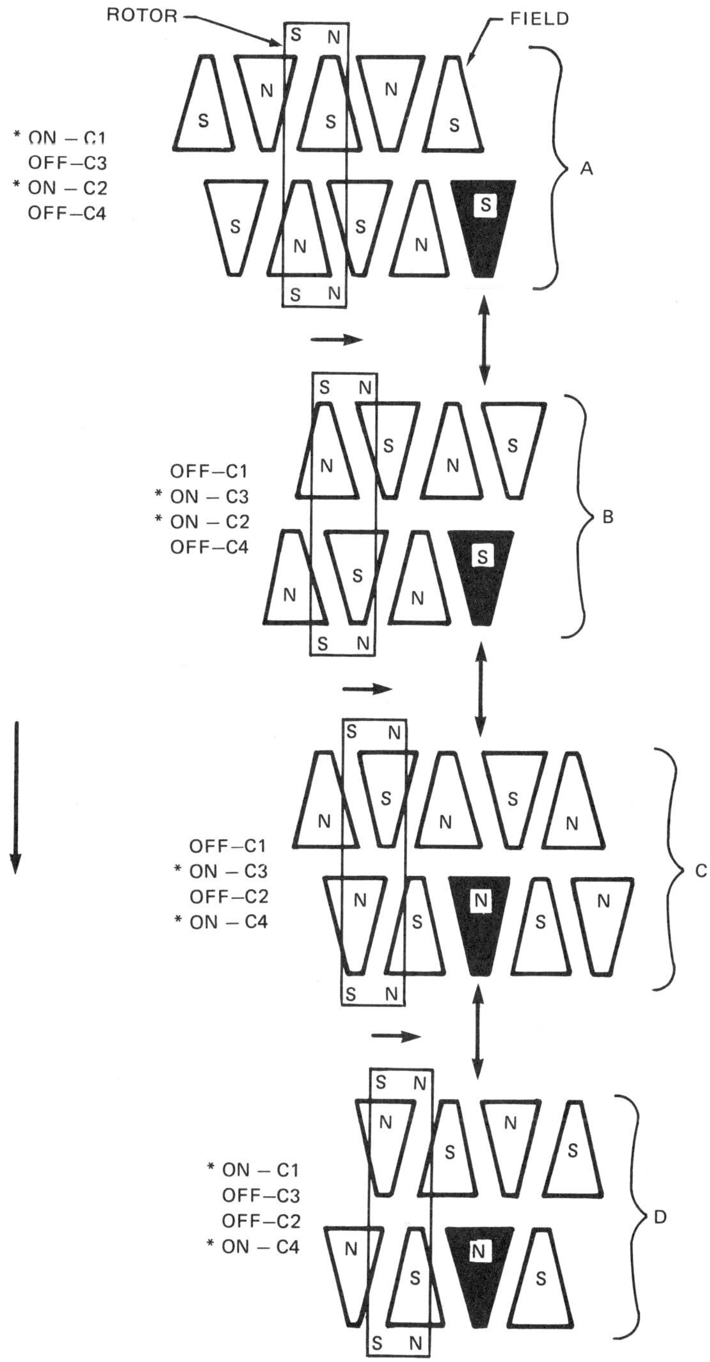

	C1	C2	C3	C4
A	1	1	0	0
B	0	1	1	0
C	0	0	1	1
D	1	0	0	1

FIGURE 13–9

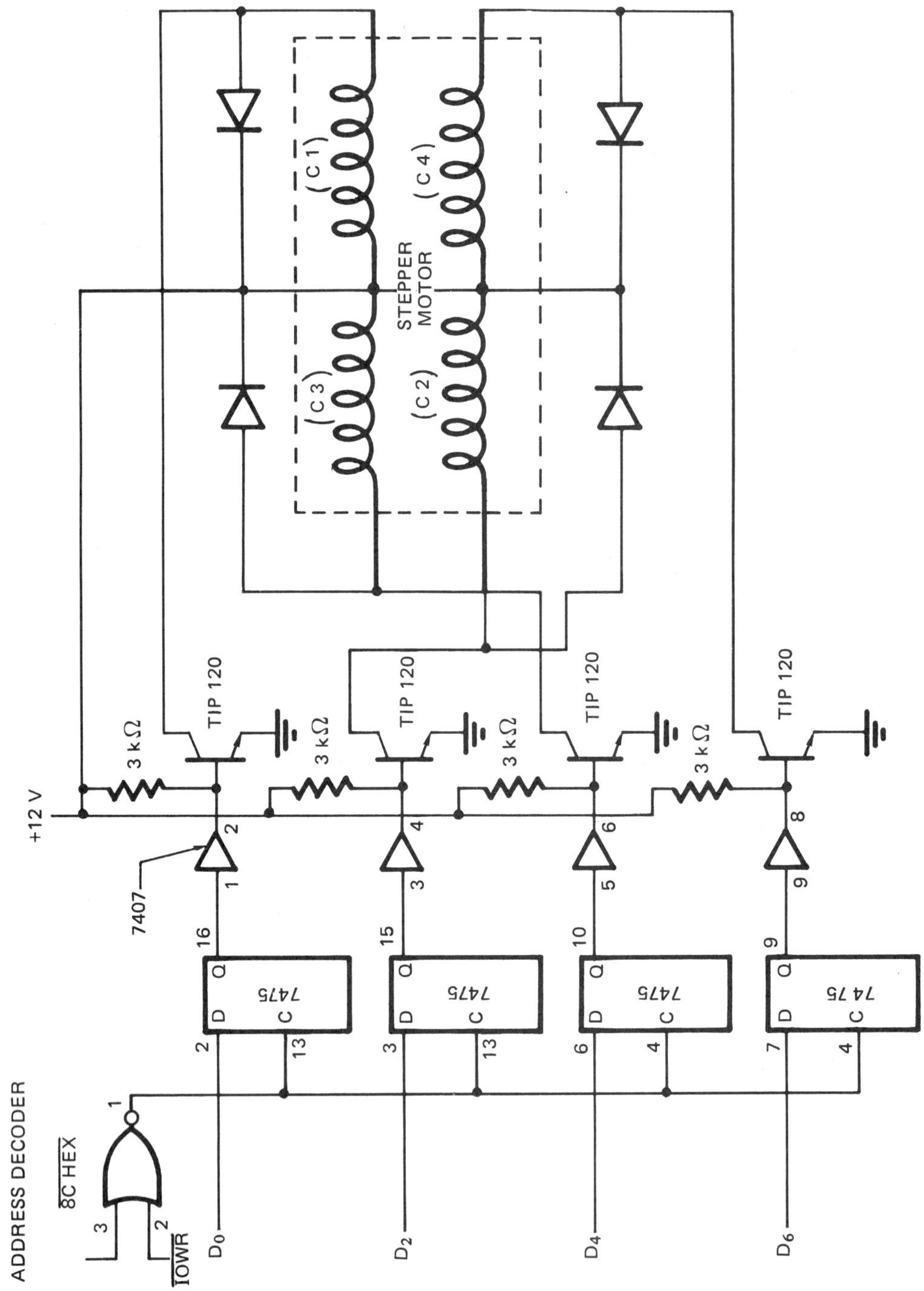
ADDRESS DECODER
8C HEX
IOWR
D0
D2
D4
D6
7475
7407
+12 V
3 kΩ
TIP 120
STEPPER MOTOR
(C 1)
(C 2)
(C 3)
(C 4)

FIGURE 13–10

```
                ;***  SUBROUTINE TO ROTATE STEPPING MOTOR   ***
                ;
                ;A REG. CONTAINS THE NO. OF STEPS IN SIGNED 2'S COMP FORM
                ;B REG. CONTAINS THE RATE IN INCREMENTS OF .01 SEC./ STEP
                ;
                ;
09FF            SAVE    EQU     09FFH           ;ADD. OF MOTOR COIL STATE
00E4            TIME    EQU     00E4H           ;ADD. OF 10 MILL SEC. LOOP
008C            PORT    EQU     8CH             ;ADD. OF MOTOR OUTPUT
                ;
0920                    ORG     0920H           ;MEM. LOC. OF SUBROUTINE
0920 C5         ROTATE  PUSH    BC              ;SAVE BC
0921 D5                 PUSH    DE              ;SAVE DE
0922 E5                 PUSH    HL              ;SAVE HL
0923 F5                 PUSH    AF              ;SAVE AF
0924 21FF09             LD      HL,SAVE         ;HL POINT TO MOTOR STATE
0927 0E8C               LD      C,PORT          ;PUT MOTOR PORT ADD IN C
0929 50                 LD      D,B             ;SAVE RATE IN D
092A E6FF               AND     0FFH            ;SET FLAGS FOR TEST
092C FA4309             JP      M,CW            ;TEST FOR NEG. 2'S COMP.
092F CB06       LOOP1   RLC     (HL)            ;ROTATE THE MOTOR COIL
0931 CB06               RLC     (HL)            ;MEM. LOC. TWO TO LEFT
0933 5E                 LD      E,(HL)          ;GET NEW MOTOR STATE TO E
0934 ED59               OUT     (C),E           ;OUTPUT NEW MOTOR STATE
0936 CDE400     LOOP    CALL    TIME            ;CALL 10 M SEC. LOOP
0939 10FB               DJNZ    LOOP            ;DO FOR B * 10 M SEC.
093B 42                 LD      B,D             ;RESTORE B FOR NEXT LOOP
093C 3D                 DEC     A               ;TEST FOR NO. OF STEPS
093D C22F09             JP      NZ,LOOP1        ;DO TILL A = 0
0940 C35409             JP      DONE            ;JUMP TO EXIT ROUTINE
0943 CB0E       CW      RRC     (HL)            ;ROTATE (HL) RIGHT TWO
0945 CB0E               RRC     (HL)            ;BITS , MOTOR COIL STATE
0947 5E                 LD      E,(HL)          ;GET MOTOR COIL STATE
0948 ED59               OUT     (C),E           ;OUTPUT MOTOR COIL STATE
094A CDE400     LOOP2   CALL    TIME            ;CALL 10 M SEC. LOOP
094D 10FB               DJNZ    LOOP2           ;DO FOR B * 10 MILL SEC.
094F 42                 LD      B,D             ;RESTORE B FOR NEXT LOOP
0950 3C                 INC     A               ;COUNT UP TO 0 , 2'S COMP
0951 C24309             JP      NZ,CW           ;DO TILL A = 0
0954 F1         DONE    POP     AF              ;RESTORE AF
0955 E1                 POP     HL              ;RESTORE HL
0956 D1                 POP     DE              ;RESTORE DE
0957 C1                 POP     BC              ;RESTORE BC
0958 C9                 RET                     ;RETURN FROM SUBROUTINE
0000                    END
00000 Total Errors

LOOP2    094A
DONE     0954
LOOP     0936
LOOP1    092F
CW       0943
ROTATE   0920
PORT     008C
TIME     00E4
SAVE     09FF
```

Memory location of HL used to store the motor coil state and how they are shifted to rotate the motor

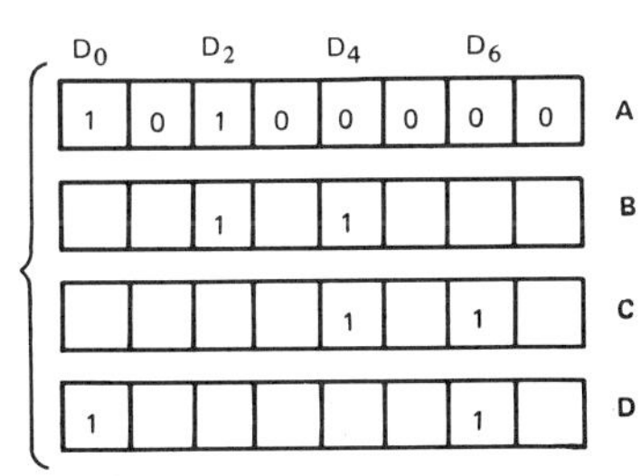

FIGURE 13–11

13.5 OBTAINING INPUT FROM THE REAL WORLD

Monitoring real-world phenomena and converting it to electrical pulses or voltages is a large subject, much too large to completely cover in this textbook. So we will only look at some typical input methods used to gain information about mechanical devices and how they are moving. A simple switch closer can tell the computer a great deal about the machine it is monitoring. A switch closer could indicate that a robot arm is fully extended or that a shaft has made a complete rotation. Switches are mechanical devices, and bounce when opened or closed. This bounce can cause the computer to think that the switch has opened and closed several times, when in fact the switch just opened once. Therefore, the first thing to do when interfacing a switch to the computer is to debounce the switch. This can be done with software, as was done with the keys of the Biggy trainer, or with hardware, as shown in Figure 13–12.

Figure 13–12A shows a double-throw single-pole switch with a follower arm that is riding on a cam. The switch is debounced with a crossed NAND $\overline{\text{SET}}$ $\overline{\text{RESET}}$ flip-flop. The computer can determine the state of the switch and thereby the position of the cam by inputing the associated input bit D_7 with an $\overline{\text{IORD}}$ to the associated input port. Figure 13–12B shows a mercury switch much like that used on typical household thermostats that is interfaced to the nonmaskable interrupt of the computer. An edge-triggered JK flip-flop was used to latch the switch closer and allow the computer to clear the interrupt if needed. This would be typical of an input control that was of critical interest to the controlling computer, such as a temperature rise in a freezer.

Because the computer can control the way in which a device samples or records the physical phenomena it is designed to measure, the measuring circuit can be made much simpler. An example of this is the circuit shown in Figure 13–13. This circuit is designed to tell the computer the frequency of the AC current flowing from a diesel generator. The way in which the circuit operates is a function of the computer program that runs the input circuit.

The generator is a typical emergency AC generator designed to produce 110 VAC at 60 Hz. An increased electrical load placed on the generator will cause the mechanical torque needed to keep the generator turning at 60 Hz to increase. Therefore, the diesel engine will have to respond with more power, or the rpms of the engine will decrease, causing the frequency of the generator to fall below 60 Hz. On the other side of the coin, when the electrical load decreases, the diesel engine must decrease in its power output, or the generator frequency will climb too high. The frequency sampling circuit in Figure 13–13 could be used to sample the frequency of the generator and feed it to the computer. The computer could then raise or lower the diesel engine's power by controlling the engine injector's setting with a small stepper motor.

The AC voltage is isolated and converted to a TTL level by an optocoupler. Because the LED inside the optocoupler is a diode, it will produce light only when it is forward biased and not when the AC current reverse biases it. This will produce a nice on/off transition for each cycle of the AC current, isolating the AC from the computer. The on/off output of the optocoupler is fed to the input of a NAND gate whose output is fed to an 8-bit counter made of two 74LS93 ICs. The NAND gate is used to gate the

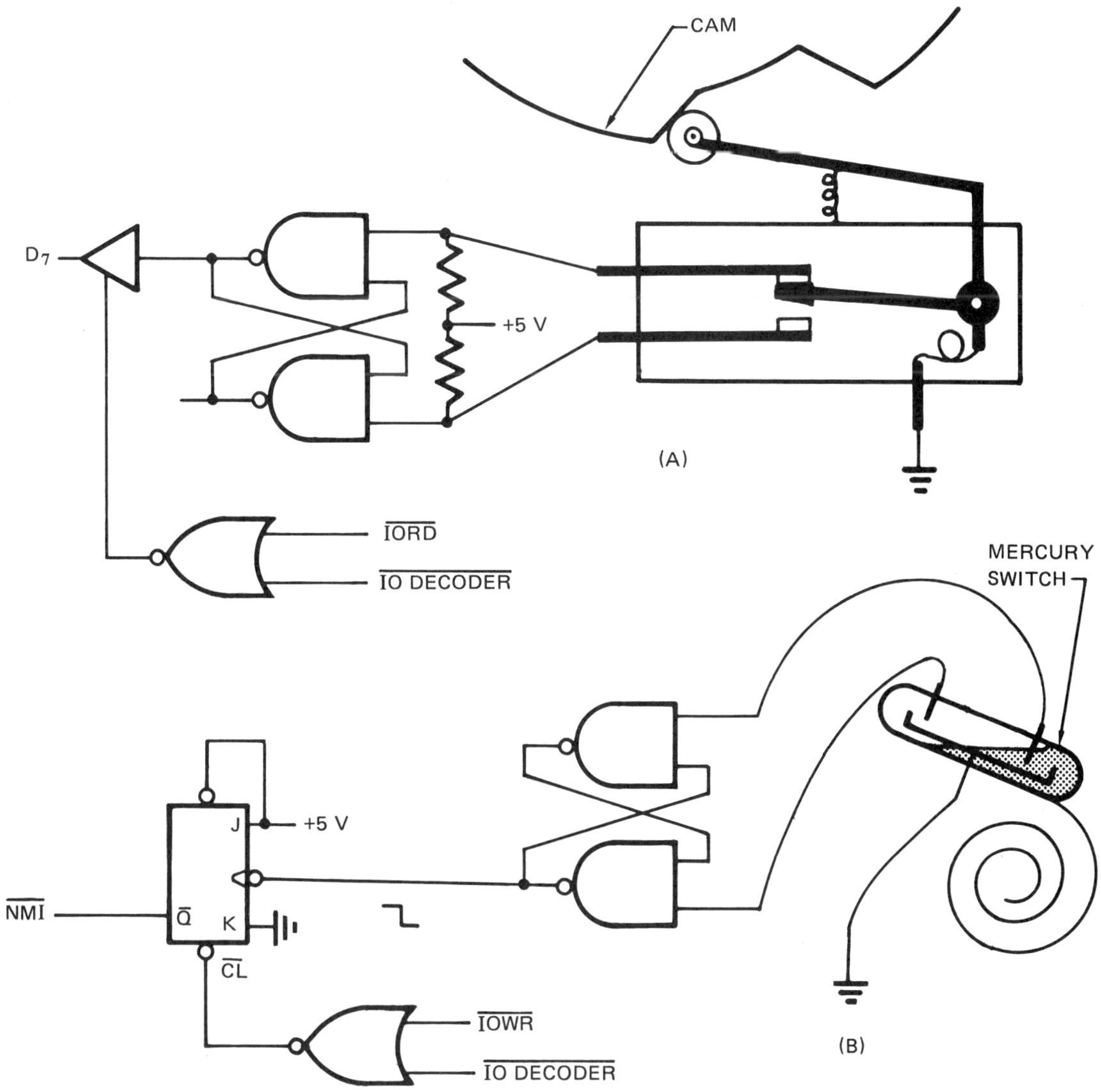

FIGURE 13–12

optocoupler's output to the 8-bit counter. Whether or not the optocoupler's output is passed on to the counter depends on the logic state of the other input to the NAND gate. This is controlled by a $\overline{\text{SET/RESET}}$ flip-flop made from two crossed NAND gates. The logic state of the Q output is controlled by the computer through an output port made up of the 74LS138 address decoder and some NOR gates. The counter can also be cleared by the computer, and the count value of the counter can also be input using the 74LS138 address decoder and the associated NOR gate.

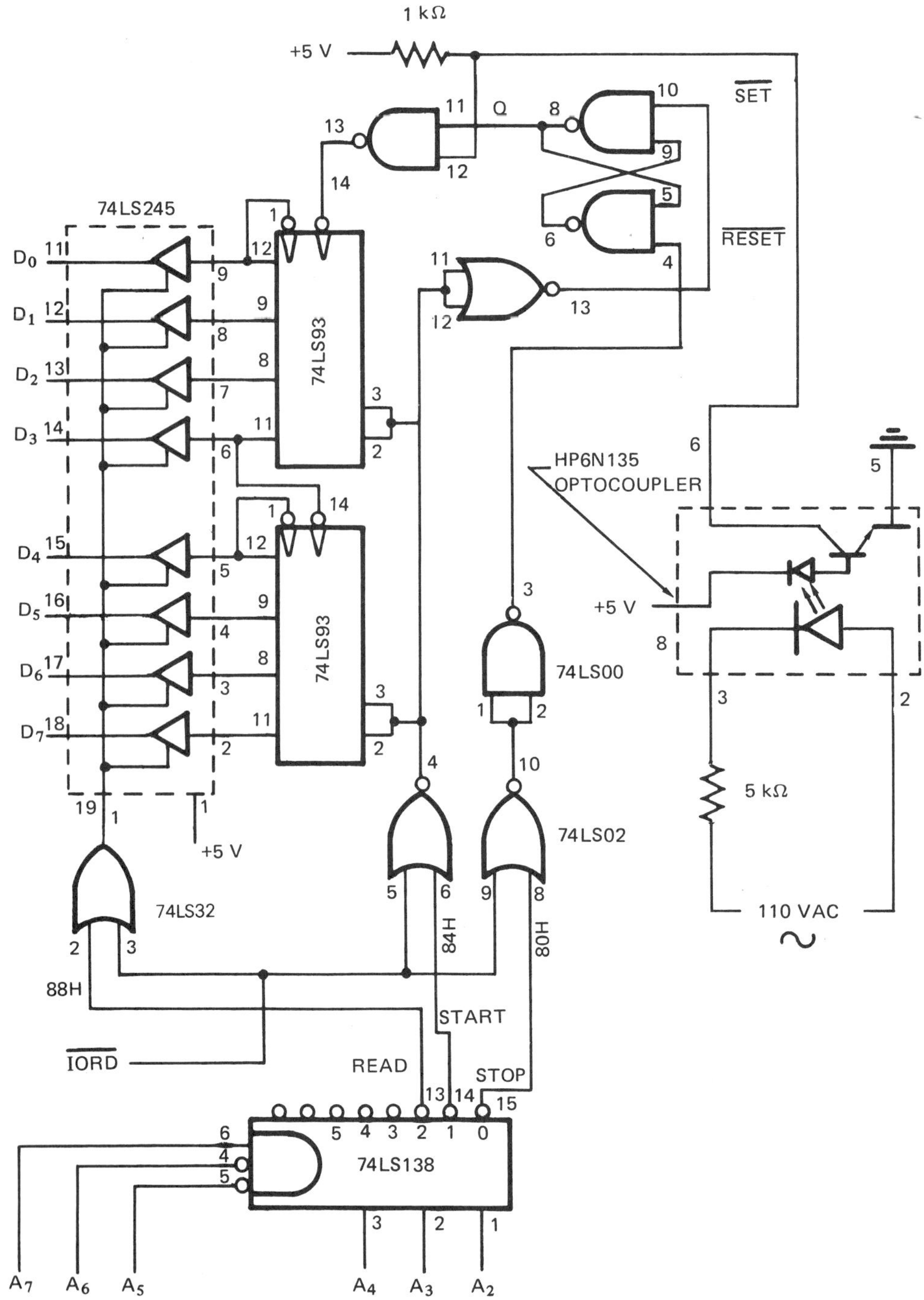

FIGURE 13–13 Generator frequency input

```
                ;***   SAMPLE PROGRAM   ***
                ;
                ;THE CYCLES PER SEC. WILL BE RETURNED IN A
                ;
                ;
00E4            TIME    EQU     00E4H       ;ADD. OF 10 M SEC LOOP
0084            START   EQU     84H         ;PORT ADD. OF START COUNT
0080            STOP    EQU     80H         ;PORT ADD. OF STOP COUNT
0088            READ    EQU     88H         ;PORT ADD. OF INPUT COUNT
                ;
0900                    ORG     900H        ;MEMORY LOCATION OF SUB.
0900 C5         SAMPLE  PUSH    BC          ;SAVE REGISTER PAIR BC
0901 0664               LD      B,100       ;LOAD B FOR 1 SEC LOOP
0903 DB84               IN      A,(START)   ;START COUNT OF FREQ.
0905 CDE400     LOOP    CALL    TIME        ;CALL 10 M SEC LOOP
0908 10FB               DJNZ    LOOP        ;DO FOR 1 SEC. , B TIMES
090A DB80               IN      A,(STOP)    ;STOP COUNT AFTER 1 SEC.
090C DB88               IN      A,(READ)    ;READ COUNT AFTER 1 SEC.
090E C1                 POP     BC          ;RESTORE BC
090F C9                 RET                 ;RETURN FROM SUBROUTINE
0000                    END
00000 Total Errors

LOOP     0905
SAMPLE   0900
READ     0088
STOP     0080
START    0084
TIME     00E4
```

FIGURE 13–14 Program to find the cycles for 1 s

When the computer wishes to sample the frequency of the generator, it first does an $\overline{\text{IORD}}$ to port 84 Hex. This produces a short positive-going spike at pins 2 and 3 of the 74LS93 ICs, which clears them. Also the crossed NAND flip-flop is set, which allows the output of the optocoupler to pass to the counter input. This starts the counter counting the AC cycles. The computer then calls a 1 second timing loop. When the computer returns after 1 second, it stops the counter by doing an $\overline{\text{IORD}}$ to port 80 Hex. This resets the crossed NAND flip-flop and disables the output of the optocoupler to the counter. The number of cycles that accrued in the last second is now stored in the counter, which can now be read by the computer by executing an $\overline{\text{IORD}}$ to port 88 Hex.

The rate at which the computer samples the generator frequency, the time of the sample, and use of the sample data are all determined by the computer's program.

Figure 13–14 shows a typical subroutine to obtain the binary number of cycles per second in the A register by using the Biggy trainer as the controlling computer.

13.6 OPEN-LOOP AND CLOSED-LOOP PROCESS CONTROLS

When a computer is controlling a process but does not receive any feedback or input as to what results the control is having, it is called *open-loop control*. Examples of this type

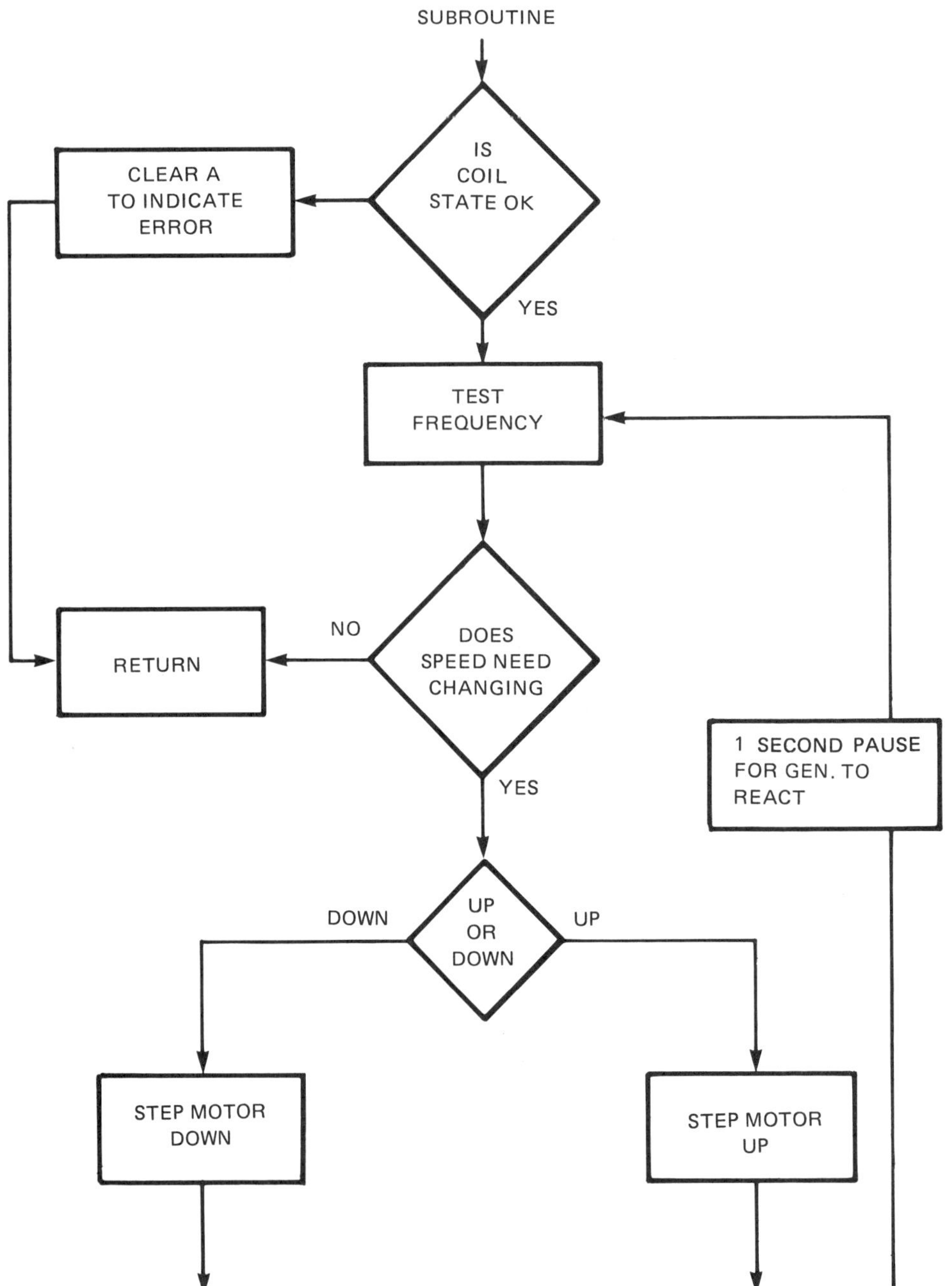

FIGURE 13–15A

```
                ;*****************************************************
                ;*   SUBROUTINE TO CONTROL THE FREQUENCY OF A GENERATOR *
                ;*****************************************************
                ;
                ;
00E4            TIME     EQU     0E4H          ;ADD OF 10 MIL SEC LOOP
09FF            SAVE     EQU     9FFH          ;ADD OF COIL STATE
0920            ROTATE   EQU     920H          ;ADD OF ROTATE SUBROUTINE
0900            SAMPLE   EQU     900H          ;ADD OF FREQUENCY SAMPLER
                ;
0838                     ORG     838H          ;MODE 1 INTERRUPT ADD
0838 E5         CONTRL   PUSH    HL            ;SAVE HL
0839 C5                  PUSH    BC            ;SAVE BC
083A 7E                  LD      A,(HL)        ;GET COIL STATE TO TEST
083B FE05                CP      05H           ;AND TEST IT FOR THE  4
083D 280F                JR      Z,OK          ;POSSIBLE VALUES THE COIL
083F FE14                CP      14H           ;STATE COULD HAVE
0841 280B                JR      Z,OK
0843 FE50                CP      50H
0845 2807                JR      Z,OK
0847 FE41                CP      41H
0849 2803                JR      Z,OK
084B 97                  SUB     A             ;CLEAR REG. A TO 0
084C 1807                JR      EXIT          ;TO INDICATE ERROR
084E CD0009     OK       CALL    SAMPLE        ;TEST GEN. FREQUENCY
0851 D63C                SUB     60            ;SUB 60 TO TEST FOR 60 HZ
0853 2003                JR      NZ,CHANGE     ;JUMP IF HZ NEEDS CHANGE
0855 C1         EXIT     POP     BC            ;RESTORE BC
0856 E1                  POP     HL            ;RESTORE HL
0857 C9                  RET                   ;RETURN FROM SUBROUTINE
0858 0603       CHANGE   LD      B,03H         ;SET ROTATE AT 30 MILL S.
085A CD2009              CALL    ROTATE        ;STEP INJECTOR STEPPER M.
085D 0664                LD      B,100         ;SET B FOR 1 SEC LOOP
085F CDE400     LOOP     CALL    TIME          ;CALL 10 MILL SEC LOOP
0862 10FB                DJNZ    LOOP          ;PAUSE FOR 1 SEC
0864 18E8                JR      OK            ;SAMPLE TEST AGAIN
0000                     END
00000 Total Errors

LOOP     085F
CHANGE   0858
EXIT     0855
OK       084E
CONTRL   0838
SAMPLE   0900
ROTATE   0920
SAVE     09FF
TIME     00E4
```

FIGURE 13–15B

of control are turning lights or motors on and off. In such cases the computer has no way of knowing if the light or motor is actually off or not. Many small robots are open-loop controlled and must first be brought to a known position so the computer will know where to expect the arm to be as it controls its movements.

Closed-loop control allows the computer to input the value of the results of its control. This means that the computer can take action based on the result of its previous actions and therefore correct for such things as overshooting the mark, not enough movement, etc. To have a closed-loop control system, you must have input from the physical phenomenon you wish to control and a means of controlling the same physical phenomenon.

A good example of closed-loop control is shown in the program in Figure 13–15. This program works with the frequency input device of Figure 13–13 and the stepper motor output device of Figure 13–10 to control the frequency output of a diesel generator. The frequency of the generator is controlled by using the stepper motor to adjust the injector control of the diesel engine. Controlling the injector of the engine will raise or lower the power output and rpm of the engine. The feedback as the result of controlling the injectors to the engine will come from the frequency input device of Figure 13–13.

This program is run as a subroutine that could be called at various intervals while the process is busy controlling other aspects of the generator control, such as output voltage control or phase sink to the grid. It is assumed that the generator in question has an approximate one-step-to-one-cycle ratio of stepper motor to generator output frequency, and that the generator is incapable of more than 255 Hz of generator frequency. If these parameters were to change, all that would have to change is the program, not the hardware. This is the great thing about computer process control.

EXERCISE 13

1. What is open-loop control of a machine?
2. Give two methods of isolating the computer circuits from an outside AC voltage.
3. What current would be needed to energize a relay with a 500-Ω coil that was designed to work at 24 V?
4. Draw the schematic for a double-throw double-pole relay.
5. What would be the value of the R1 resistor in Figure 13–2 if the relay coil required 700 mA to energize?
6. Why is the diode in the circuit of Figure 13–2?
7. Draw the symbol for an optocoupler with a phototransistor in it.
8. What would be the value of the resistor in the LED circuit of the optocoupler in Figure 13–13 if the AC voltage were 500 V?
9. List all the possible addresses for the STOP signal of the circuit in Figure 13–13.
10. Design a simple shift register to run the three-phase motor in Figure 13–6. (Use 7476 JK flip-flops and a 555 timer.)
11. Draw the circuit for a switch input to a 1-bit input port for a single-pole double-throw switch.
12. What is the wattage of the resistor in question 5?
13. If R1 of Figure 13–2 were 1000 Ω, what would be the maximum current that the transistor would supply before it would start to run in the analog region?
14. Design the receiver circuit for the transmitter circuit in Figure 13–5.
15. What is closed-loop control of a machine?

16. In which state, energized or unenergized, is the contact of a relay drawn in a schematic?
17. What is meant by the term "pickup current" in reference to a relay?
18. Draw a table like that in Figure 13–9 that will drive the motor in the opposite direction.
19. Write a program to make the stepper motor in Figure 13–10 rotate at a rate of 100 ms per step.
20. Why are there two transistors in Figure 13–2?

Lab 13

OBJECTIVE

After completing this lab, you should be able to

- control an AC current with the Biggy trainer and a relay.

Procedure

1. Construct the circuit shown and debug it.
2. Write a program to change the state of the relay every 5 s.
3. What is the collector voltage when the relay is energized?

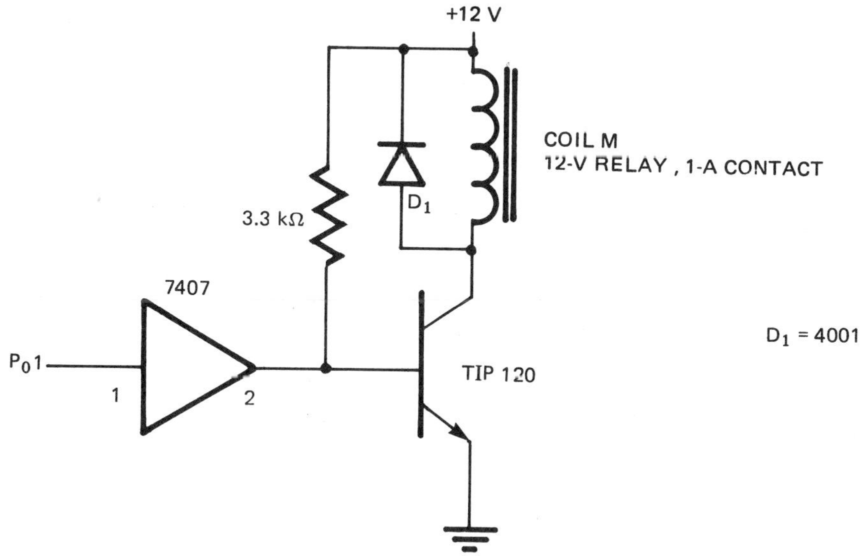
+12 V
COIL M
12-V RELAY , 1-A CONTACT
3.3 kΩ
D1
7407
D1 = 4001
P01
1
2
TIP 120

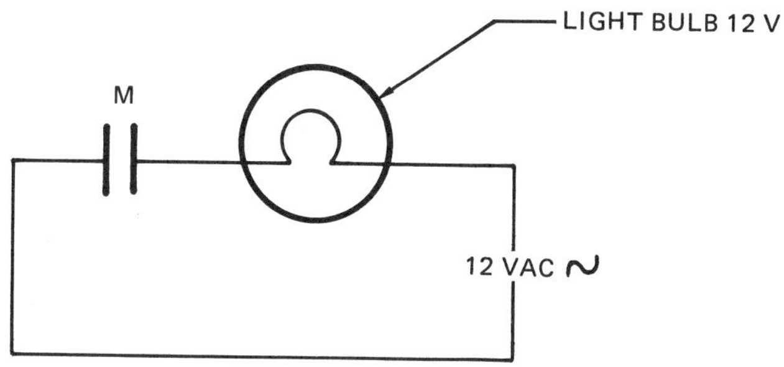
LIGHT BULB 12 V
M
12 VAC ~

Chapter 14

SURVEY OF PROCESSORS AND CONTROLLERS

OBJECTIVES

After completing this chapter, you should be able to

- describe the difference between a microprocessor and a microcomputer or microcontroller.
- describe in general the processors and controllers available from Motorola, Zilog, and Intel.
- describe in general the features available on microcontroller ICs.

14.1 MOTOROLA'S 6800 GROUP

The 6800 microprocessor was introduced by Motorola in 1974. The 6800 family has evolved in many directions since that time. The first six sections of this chapter offer an overview of the Motorola family of microprocessors and single-chip microcomputer data.

The 6800 microprocessor has two 8-bit accumulators, ACCA and ACCB. Both are active. That is, the programmer designates which is to be used for arithmetic, logic, or load operations. It has a 16-bit index register, program counter, and stack pointer. An 8-bit condition codes register contains six flags similar to those in the Z 80.

The 6800 is a 40-pin IC that operates from a single 5-V supply. Eight pins are used for a bidirectional tri-state data bus that can directly drive one TTL load. For direct memory access (DMA) operations, the data bus can be placed into the high-impedance state by holding the data bus enable (DBE) control input low. Sixteen pins are dedicated to the 16-bit address bus, which enables the 6800 to directly access 64 kilobytes (Kbytes) of memory. Two pins are used to input nonoverlapping clocks, $\phi 1$ and $\phi 2$. The remaining pins are used for processor and bus control.

The 6800 instruction set contains no IN or OUT instructions. Input/output operations are accomplished by treating the input/output ports as if they were locations in memory. This approach is called memory mapped I/O. An advantage to memory mapping is that the instructions involved with loading data to or from memory become input/output instructions. More options become available to the programmer.

Motorola also introduced support ICs to interface with the 6800. The 6821 peripheral interface adapter (PIA) is a programmable parallel port IC used to interface the 6800 to external peripherals. It contains two 8-bit ports, whose bits can be programmed as input or output as needed, and four interrupt control lines, two of which are bidirectional.

The 6850 asynchronous communications interface adapter (ACIA) is a serial interface port. The ACIA formats the data to be sent serially and checks for parity errors as programmed during initialization.

The 6871 1-MHz, two-phase clock generator develops $\phi 1$ and $\phi 2$ for the 6800 and $\phi 2$ TTL for timing with TTL and memory chips in the system. The 6810 128-by-8-bit RAM and the 6830 1024-by-8-bit ROM were developed to interface directly to the 6800.

These ICs together produced a 6800 based microcomputer that has evolved in several directions. The following groups will be summarized: 6801, 6802, 6804, 6805.

14.2 MOTOROLA'S 6801 GROUP

The 6801 is an 8-bit single-chip microcomputer unit (MCU). It contains an upgraded 6800 microprocessor unit (MPU) in which some execution times have been improved and some instructions added. The two 8-bit accumulators ACCA and ACCB can act separately or as one 16-bit accumulator, D. The MUL multiply instruction multiplies ACCA by ACCB and stores the result in D. Other new instructions include loading and adding with the double accumulator D.

Included on the same chip are 2048 bytes of ROM, 128 bytes of RAM, a serial communications interface (SCI), three 8-bit parallel ports, one 5-bit parallel port, and a three-function programmable timer.

The 6801 can be operated in one of three general modes. In the single-chip mode it functions as is. In the expanded nonmultiplexed mode, parallel port 3 functions as a bidirectional data bus, and port 4 as the low byte of the address bus. In this mode the 6801 can address 256 bytes of external memory. In the expanded multiplexed mode, parallel port 3 is a multiplexed address/data bus, and port 4 is address bus. With the full 16-bit address bus available, the 6801 can address a total of 64 kbytes of memory. Variations on how this memory space is used and variations in the other modes lead to a total of eight modes of operation.

The 6801 is upward compatible with the 6800. That is, source and object code written for the 6800 will run as is on the 6801. The 6801 is constructed of high-density N-channel MOS (HMOS) and operates from a 5-V supply. A V_{CC} standby input is provided to supply power to the standby portion of RAM (64 bytes). The 6801 supports maskable and nonmaskable interrupts.

The 6803 MPU is the same as the 6801 except that it has no internal ROM. It must be operated in the expanded multiplexed mode. The 68701 is an EPROM version of the 6801. It is used to develop systems that will be driven by the 6801 or 6803. The 6801 clock can range from 0.5 MHz to 1 MHz; the 6801-1 clock can range from 0.5 MHz to 1.5 MHz; and the 68B01 clock can range from 0.5 MHz to 2 MHz.

The 6801U4 MCU is an enhancement of the 6801. It contains 4096 bytes of ROM, 192 bytes of RAM, and a six-function programmable timer. The 6803U4 MPU is an enhancement of the 6803. It contains 192 bytes of RAM, but no ROM. The 68701U4 has 4096 bytes of EPROM in place of ROM.

The 68HC11A4 is a CMOS version of the 6801. CMOS dissipates less power (10 to 20 times less) and can operate over a wider range of supply voltages, 3–6 V in this case. CMOS MCUs are static in nature and can operate down to 0 Hz. The 68HC11A4 operates on a 2-MHz clock. It contains 4 kbytes of ROM, 512 bytes of EEPROM, and 256 bytes of static RAM. It contains an 8-channel A/D converter, a serial communications interface (SCI), and a serial peripheral interface (SPI). The timer functions are expanded over that of the 6801 and a computer operating properly (COP) watchdog system that helps protect against software failure has been added.

14.3 MOTOROLA'S 6802 GROUP

The 6802 MPU has the same internal registers as the 6800. In addition, the 6802 contains 128 bytes of RAM located at 0000H through 007FH. Pin 35, VCC standby, is used to provide auxiliary DC power to the MCU during low-power or power-down conditions. This retains any data that is stored in the first 32 bytes of RAM (through 001FH). The 6802 can address 64 kbytes of memory. The 6802 also has an on-board clock oscillator that can be controlled by an external crystal. The circuit divides the crystal frequency by four so that a 4-MHz crystal can be used (this is cheaper). The instruction set for the 6802 is identical to that of the 6800: 72 instructions with seven modes of addressing.

The 6802NS is identical to the 6802, except that it has no standby RAM feature. The 6808 is identical to the 6802, except that it has no on-board RAM. The 68A02 and 68A08 can operate at 1.5 MHz, and the 68B02 and 68B08 can operate at 2.0 MHz.

The 6846 is a ROM–I/O–timer IC that provides 2048 bytes of mask programmable ROM, an 8-bit bidirectional input/output port with control lines, and a 16-bit programmable timer/counter. This IC interfaces directly with the 6802 to produce a basic two-chip microcomputer system.

14.4 MOTOROLA'S 6805 GROUP

The 6805 group is composed of a series of single-chip 8-bit microcomputers and microprocessors. In addition to varying amounts of on-board RAM and ROM, members of this group contain bidirectional I/O lines and on-chip clock generators and timers. They have a self-test function that is implemented by placing 9 V on the timer input. These MCUs function in the single-chip mode and are not expandable to 64K memory.

The 6805P2 was the original MCU of this group. It has one 8-bit accumulator, not two as in the 6800, an 8-bit index register, an 11-bit program counter, an 11-bit stack pointer, and a 5-bit condition code register (flags). It is HMOS with 64 bytes of RAM and 1100 bytes of ROM on board. It has 20 software-controlled bidirectional I/O lines. The 6805P2 can be driven from an external 4-MHz crystal, which is divided by 4 internally, from an external signal, or internally to minimize total parts. The user must specify the internal clock upon purchase.

The 6805P4 differs from the P2 in that it has 112 bytes of RAM that is backed up from a standby power source. The user can order open-collector (open-drain)-style ports on ports B and C if desired. The 6805P6 has 64 bytes of RAM (not backed up) and 1796 bytes of user ROM.

The 68705 series has 3776 bytes of on-board user EPROM and 112 bytes of RAM. The 68705R3 and R5 have an A/D converter built in.

The 6805S2 has an A/D converter, a serial peripherial interface (SPI) and three on-board timers. The 6805T2 is an MCU with an on-board phase-locked loop (PLL) for radio-frequency synthesis applications.

The 68HC05C4 is a CMOS version of the 6805. It has 176 bytes of RAM, 4160 bytes of ROM, and 24 bidirectional I/O lines. It can operate at a clock frequency of 2.1 MHz at 5 V and 1.0 MHz at 3 V.

The 6804J2 is similar to the 6805. In place of a stack pointer it has a last-in, first-out (LIFO) stack that is four levels deep. It has 32 bytes of RAM, 1008 bytes of program ROM, 64 bytes of data ROM, and 12 bidirectional I/O lines.

The 6804P2 also has a 4-level stack. Its program ROM has been increased to 1024 bytes, and its I/O lines to 20.

14.5 MOTOROLA'S 6809 GROUP

The 6809 MPU has two 8-bit accumulators, A and B, as the 6800 does. In some operations A and B function as one 16-bit accumulator, D. In addition to the registers contained in the 6800, the 6809 contains a direct page register, a user stack pointer, and a second index register.

The 8-bit direct page register, DP, is used with the direct addressing mode. During direct addressing execution, the contents of DP are placed on the HIGH byte of the address bus. The instruction specifies the LOW byte of the address to be used. DP is cleared during reset and provides zero-page addressing until loaded with another page number.

The 6809 contains both a user stack pointer, U, and a hardware stack pointer, S. The hardware stack pointer is used by the processor during subroutines and interrupts. The user stack pointer is controlled completely by the programmer. Both stack pointers point to the top of the stack as the Z 80 did, whereas the 6808 stack pointer points to the next available location on the stack.

The 6809 has two 16-bit index registers, X and Y, for use in the indexed mode of addressing. X, Y, U, and S can all be used as index registers. These registers allow for 10 addressing modes, which are used with 59 basic instructions, giving the 6809 1464 different instructions. This flexibility makes it the most powerful processor in the 6800 family.

The 6809 operates at 4 MHz, the 68A09 at 6 MHz, and the 68B09 at 8 MHz. The 6809E is similar to the 6809, except that H does not contain an on-board clock oscillator. The 6809E has clock input pins E and Q to allow for synchronization with peripherals or other systems or MPUs. The 68HC09E is a high-density CMOS (HCMOS) version of the 6809E.

14.6 MOTOROLA'S 68000

The 68000 is a HMOS 16-bit microprocessor unit. The 68000 has eight 32-bit data registers called D_0–D_7. They can be used for data operations for bytes (8 bits), words (16 bits), or long words (32 bits). They can also be used as index registers. There are seven 32-bit address registers (A_0–A_6) that can be used as stack pointers for 16-bit or 32-bit address operations. A_7 is a 32-bit system stack pointer.

The 68000 has a 24-bit address bus with which it can directly address 16 megabytes (Mbytes) of memory. The 16-bit status register contains a user byte that monitors five condition codes (flags) and a system byte that monitors whether the processor is in the trace mode, supervisor state, or interrupt mode.

The 68000 has 14 addressing modes. The instruction set includes 56 basic instructions, including signed and unsigned multiply, with 21 variations to these basic instructions. Coupled with the 14 addressing modes and the fact that instructions can operate on bytes, words, or long words, more than 1000 instructions are available.

The 6800 peripherals discussed earlier interface directly with the 68000. In addition, a more powerful set of peripheral interface ICs has been developed. The 68451 memory management unit (MMU) provides address translation in multiprocess systems. The 68341 is a floating-point ROM programmed for the 68000 instruction set. The 68450 is a direct memory access controller (DMAC). The 68122 is a cluster terminal controller (CTC) that coordinates the communications between terminals attached to the 68000. The 68230 is a parallel interface/timer (PI/T) that is used to connect peripheral devices to the 68000. The 68230 connects directly to the 68000 and to the DMAC.

The 68560 is a serial direct memory access (SDMA) IC. A primary SDMA is connected to one or more secondary SDMAs. The 68560 uses IBM's synchronous data link control protocol.

The 68561 multiprotocol communications controller (MPCC) is an asynchronous serial data communications interface IC. It contains an on-board crystal oscillator and baud rate generator. The 68120 is a programmable intelligent peripheral controller (IPC). It contains its own 8-bit CPU. It has 21 parallel I/O lines, 2 Kbytes of ROM, 128 bytes of RAM, a timer, and a serial communications interface.

14.7 ZILOG'S Z 80 FAMILY

The Z 80 CPU is the base of Zilog's 8400 family of related ICs. The Z 80 CPU itself is called the Z8400. The following chips were developed to work directly with the Z8400.

The Z8410 DMA IC was designed to manage transfer of data between memory and I/O peripherals independent of the CPU.

The Z8420 is a parallel input/output (PIO) controller. It provides two 8-bit parallel ports. All data is transferred via interrupt control.

The Z8430 CTC contains four independent programmable counter/timer channels. Each has a divide by 16 or divide by 256 prescaler. The Z8430 can be used with the Z8440 as a baud rate generator.

The Z8440 serial input/output (SIO) controller has two independent channels with separate control and status lines for modems. The SIO can function in the asynchronous or synchronous modes.

The Z8470 dual asynchronous receiver/transmitter (DART) is a dual-channel asynchronous interface IC that does not provide for synchronous operation as the SIO did.

The Z8400 operates a 2.4 MHz, the Z8400A at 4 MHz, and the Z8400B at 6 MHz.

The Z8300 family is a low-power version of the 8400 group. The Z8300-1 is a Z 80 that operates at 1-MHz clock frequency and draws a maximum of 20 mA from the power supply at 25° C. The Z8300-3 operates at 2.5 MHz and draws a maximum of 30 mA, whereas the 8400 operating at 2.5 MHz draws a maximum of 150 mA. The following low-power interface ICs were developed to work with the Z 8300. They are equivalent to their 8400 family counterparts.

- Z8320 PIO
- Z8330 CTC
- Z8340 SIO

14.8 ZILOG'S Z8000 FAMILY

At the base of the Z8000 family are the Z8001 and Z8002 HMOS 16-bit CPUs. The Z8002 has a 16-bit bus that is time multiplexed between address and data lines. In addition, the Z8001 has a 7-bit segment address that points to any one of 128 beginning addresses in memory. The 16-bit address on the address bus provides the offset from the beginning segment address. This segmented approach provides for 128 segments of 64 kbytes each for a total of 8 Mbytes of addressing space.

The Z8010 -ZMMU is designed to work with the Z8001 CPU. The addresses used by the programmer and the Z8001 are called logical addresses. Through a process called relocation, the MMU converts logical addresses into the physical addresses used to access memory. The process uses a translation table located in the MMU that is updated as needed by the MMU to make efficient use of memory. The process is transparent to the user. Each MMU can manage 64 segments that can vary in size from 256 to 65,536 bytes. These segments are mapped into a physical address space of 16 Mbytes. The Z8001-2 can operate at 4, 6, or 10 MHz.

The Z8003, Z8004 virtual memory processing unit CPUs are the same as the Z8001, Z8002, except for the addition of an abort request function and a test and set status. An external memory management system issues the abort signal when the CPU requests an address that is not in main memory. Upon receipt of the abort signal, the instruction being executed is stopped immediately. The page or segment containing the address needed is brought into memory, and the execution of the instruction continues. The Z8015 paged memory management unit (PMMU) was designed to work directly with the Z8003 processor. The PMMU divides 16 Mbytes of physical memory into 2048 byte pages. PMMUs translate the 8 Mbytes of logical addresses output by the CPU into 16 Mbytes of physical memory. Each PMMU can manage sixty-four 2048-byte pages. The Z8003 and Z8004 CPUs can operate at 4, 8, or 10 MHz. The support ICs developed for use with the Z8000 CPUs are summarized as follows.

The Z8016 Z-DTC direct memory access transfer controller works with the Z8000

CPUs. In a system operating at 4 MHz, the DTC can transfer data from memory to peripheral at the rate of 2.66 Mbytes per second and from memory to memory at 1.33 Mbytes per second.

The Z8030 Z-SCC serial communications controller has two independent channels that operate from 0 to 1 Mbit per second. Each channel has its own crystal oscillator and baud rate generators and can be operated synchronously or asynchronously.

The Z8031 Z-ASCC asynchronous serial communicators controller is similar to the Z8030 without the synchronous mode capability.

The Z8036 Z-CIO counter/timer and parallel I/O unit provides two 8-bit and one 4-bit bidirectional I/O ports with four handshaking modes. Also contained on the IC are three independent 16-bit counters/timers with four external access lines to each counter.

The Z8038 Z-FIO input/output interface unit is an asynchronous buffer. It provides 128 bytes of first in–first out (FIFO) buffering between two CPUs or between a CPU and an external device.

The Z8060 Z-FIFO buffer unit is a 128-by-8-bit FIFO memory that can be used to expand the Z8038.

The Z8065 Z-BEP burst error processor provides error detection and correction for high-speed, serial data transfers such as high-density disk systems. It provides four polynomials that detect errors.

The Z8068 Z-DCP data ciphering processor uses the National Bureau of Standards encryption algorithm to encrypt and decrypt data at 1 Mbyte per second rates and higher.

14.9 ZILOG'S Z8 FAMILY

The Z8601 is a single-chip microcomputer that contains 2 Kbytes of ROM, 128 bytes of RAM, and 32 I/O lines. The Z8601 can address 64 kbytes of program memory. The first 2 kbytes are on-board mask programmed ROM and the remaining 62 kbytes are external. In addition, the 8601 can address 62 kbytes of external data memory. The 8601 also contains two 8-bit programmable timers, a full-duplex UART, and an on-board oscillator. The on-board oscillator can be replaced with a power-down standby option that retains the contents of the 144 internal registers (124 general-purpose registers, 4 I/O port registers, and 16 control and status registers). With this option an external oscillator must be used.

The Z8603 microcomputer protopack emulator is a ROMless version of the Z8601. The 8603 has a 24-pin socket piggybacked on it for interfacing to a 2716 EPROM. The 2716 provides the first 2 kbytes of program memory. The 2716 can be reprogrammed as needed to prototype the system. When the final program has been developed, the 8601 can be mask programmed for high-volume production.

The Z8611 is a single-chip microcomputer that can be configured as a stand-alone microcomputer with 4 kbytes of internal ROM, a processor that addresses 120 kbytes of external memory, or a parallel processor operating in a system with other processors. The Z8612 is identical to the Z8611 except that it has no internal ROM. The Z8613 is pin compatible with the Z8611 and piggybacks a 2732 EPROM. Either the 8612 or 8613 can be used for prototype development. Once the operating system has been finalized, it can be mask programmed into the Z8611 for high-volume production.

The Z8671 single-chip microcomputer contains a 2 kbyte BASIC/debug program.

The MCU is programmed through the on-board UART. The BASIC interpreter can call machine language subroutines for increased speed of operation. The Z8671 operates at 8 MHz, and the Z8671-12 operates at 12 MHz.

The Z8681 and Z8682 differ only slightly. They are both microcomputers that lack ROM. They each contain 24 I/O lines, 124 general-purpose registers, 3 I/O registers, and 16 status and control registers. They contain an on-board UART, clock oscillator, and low-power standby option. They operate at 8 or 12 MHz.

Universal peripheral controllers (UPC) are intelligent peripheral controllers that perform such functions as formatting data, controlling I/O devices, and performing arithmetic functions. This frees the master processor of these duties. The Z8590, Z8594, Z8090, and Z8094 are such devices. They contain 2 kbytes of internal program ROM, 256-byte register files, three 8-bit I/O ports, and two counter/timers. The Z8590 and Z8594 interface to CPUs that do not use a multiplexed address/data bus, such as the Z 80. The Z8090 and Z8094 interface to multiplexed address data buses such as used on the Z8000. The Z8594 and Z8094 are prototype development processors that are pin compatable with the Z8590 and Z8090, respectively.

14.10 ZILOG'S Z800 FAMILY

The Z800 family contains both 8-bit and 16-bit processors. The 8-bit processors have a bus structure identical to the Z 80, and the 16-bit processors have an address/data bus structure called the Z-bus. Each comes in either a 40-pin or 64-pin package. Each processor has an on-board memory management unit (MMU) that enables the 40-pin CPUs to address 512 kbytes of memory and the 64-pin CPUs to address 16 Mbytes of memory.

These CPUs are upward compatible to the Z 80, meaning that Z 80 code can run as is on the Z800 processors. In addition to all the instructions in the Z 80 instruction set, the Z800 processors support an indexed mode of addressing with 16-bit displacement, program counter relative with 16-bit displacement, stack pointer relative with 16-bit displacement, and base index mode. In base index mode the contents of HL, IX, or IY are added to HL, IX, or IY. The result points to the operand.

Each Z800 CPU contains four on-board 16-bit counter/timers, four on-chip direct memory access (DMA) channels, and a full-duplex UART.

The Z8108 and Z8208 are 8-bit processors. Their 8-bit data bus is multiplexed with the low byte of the address bus. The 8108 is packaged in a 40-pin IC and can address 512 kbytes of memory. The Z8208 is packaged in a 64-pin IC and can address 16 Mbytes of memory.

The Z8116 and Z8216 are 16-bit processors. Their 16-bit data bus is multiplexed with the lower 16 bits of the address bus. The Z8116 is packaged as a 40-pin IC and can address 512 kbytes of memory. The Z8216 is packaged as a 64-pin IC and can address 16 Mbytes of memory.

Each of these processors supports eight traps. *Traps* are synchronous events that occur internally when particular conditions arise during the execution of an instruction. Examples are the stack warning trap and the single-step trap.

14.11 ZILOG'S Z80000 CPU

The Z80000 is a 32-bit CPU that can directly address 4 gigabytes (4 billion bytes) of memory. It has sixteen 32-bit general-purpose registers, a 32-bit program counter, and a 16-bit flag and control word (FCW) register. The 32-bit address and data bus are time multiplexed.

The Z80000 uses the Zilog extended processing architecture (EPA) facility to extend operations by software or hardware. Up to four extended processing units (EPUs) can be used in a single system. One example of an EPU is the Z8070 arithmetic processing unit (APU) or a software package that emulates an APU. When the CPU reaches an EPA instruction, the instruction is sent via the external bus to the appropriate EPU. The CPU can continue processing while the EPU performs the operation.

The Z80000 supports four types of exceptions: reset, bus error, interrupts, and traps. Whereas an interrupt is an asychronous event that happens when an external device signals for attention, a trap is a synchronous event that occurs when a particular condition arises during the execution of an instruction.

14.12 INTEL'S 8080A AND 8085A MICROPROCESSORS

The 8080 is an 8-bit processor that contains six general-purpose registers arranged in pairs: BC, DE, HL. It has separate 16-bit address and 8-bit data buses. The 8080 works in conjunction with an 8224 clock generator and an 8228 system controller and bus driver. It requires a +5- and +12-V power supply. The 8080A can directly address 64 kbytes of memory and 512 I/O ports.

The 8085A is an enhancement of the 8080. It incorporates on board the clock generator and system controller and requires only a +5-V supply. The 8085A is completely software compatible with the 8080A. The on-board oscillator divides by 2. The 8085A is operated with a 6-MHz crystal (max) for an internal clock of 3 MHz. The 8085A-2 can be operated with a 10-MHz crystal for an internal clock of 5 MHz. The 8085 has three maskable vector interrupt pins and one nonmaskable trap interrupt. It also has a serial input data (SID) and serial output data (SOD) for serial interface.

The 8085AH and 8085AH-2 are HMOS versions of the 8085A. They use 30% less supply current than N-channel counterparts. The HMOS versions draw a maximum of 120 mA, whereas the N-channel versions draw 170 mA.

The 8155 and 8156 are static RAM, I/O port, timer ICs designed for use with the 8085A or 8088 (to be discussed later). The only difference between the two is that pin 8 (chip enable) is active LOW on the 8155 ($\overline{CE}$) and active HIGH on the 8156 (CE). They provide 256 bytes of RAM, two programmable 8-bit I/O ports, one programmable 6-bit I/O port, and a 14-bit binary counter/timer. The 8155-2 and 8156-2 have maximum access times of 330 ns for use with the 8085A-2 or the 8088 operating at 5 MHz.

14.13 INTEL'S 8086 AND 8088 PROCESSORS

Intel's 8086 or IAPX86/10 is a 16-bit processor. Its 16-bit data bus is time multiplexed with the lower 16 bits of the address bus. The upper four bits of the address bus are multiplexed with status information. The 20-bit address bus enables the 8086 to directly address 1 Mbyte of memory. Internally the 8086 is divided into two units: the bus interface unit (BIU) and the execution unit (EU). The BIU has a 6-byte FIFO buffer from which the EU extracts instruction bytes as required. Whenever there is a 2-byte vacancy in the buffer, the BIU does a word fetch memory cycle. This prefetching of instructions increases processor performances. The EU receives prefetched instructions from the BIU buffer and provides unrelocated operand addresses to the BIU. The BIU performs the required address relocations. Operands are passed through the BIU for processing by the EU, and the results are passed back through the BIU for storage.

The 8086 can operate in either a single-processor minimum mode or a more complex multiple-processor configuration (maximum mode). To limit the package to 40 pins and still support a wide range of configurations, the 8086 has an input pin 33 called MN/$\overline{\text{MX}}$. The definitions and functions of pins 24–31 change, depending on the status of pin 33. When strapped to ground for the maximum mode, pins 26, 27, and 28 feed status information into an 8288 bus controller, which generates bus timing and control signals.

Address lines A_0–A_{15} are used in I/O operation. This enables the 8086 to address up to 64K I/O byte ports or 32K I/O word ports (16-bit ports).

The 8088 (IAPX88/10) is an 8-bit processor with the same internal architecture as the 8086. The 8088 handles the external busses the same way that the 8086 does, except that the 8088 brings in data eight bits at a time. Two other differences are that 8088's BIU has a 4-byte buffer instead of a 6-byte, and the 8088's BIU fetches a new instruction into the buffer when there is a 1-byte vacancy. The 8086 and 8088 are completely software compatable.

The 8087 is a numeric processor extension (NPX). It is a 40-pin IC that executes instructions as a coprocessor to an 8086 or 8088 functioning in the maximum mode. Trigonometric, logarithimic, and exponential functions are built into the hardware of the 8087. The 8087 in conjunction with the 8086 (IAPX86/10) constitutes the IAPX86/20 numeric data processor (NDP). The 8087 in conjunction with the 8088 (IAPX88/10) constitutes the IAPX88/20 NDP.

14.14 INTEL'S MICROCONTROLLERS

At the center of Intel's MCS-48 "microcontroller" family is the 8048. The 8048 is an 8-bit controller with 1 kbyte of program memory, 64 bytes of RAM data memory, a control-oriented instruction set, 27 I/O lines, and a clock oscillator.

The 8748H is an EPROM version of the 8048 with 1 kbyte of EPROM replacing the 1 kbyte of ROM.

In the 8049AH the ROM has increased to 2 kbytes, and the RAM to 128 bytes. The

8749H has 2 kbytes of EPROM in place of the ROM. In the 8050AH the ROM has been increased to 4 kbytes, and the RAM to 256 bytes.

The 8021 is a low-cost version of the 8048. It operates from a single +5-V supply and contains 1 kbyte of ROM, 64 bytes of RAM, and 21 I/O lines. It contains an on-board interval timer/counter and clock oscillator. Its instruction set is a subset of the 8048. The 8021 has zero cross-detection circuitry built in that can detect when an AC signal crosses its average DC level. This allows the use of the 60-Hz power signal as the basis for system timing, including time of day.

The 8022 is similar to the 8021, except that on-board ROM has been increased to 2 kbytes. On-board RAM remains the same with 64 bytes, and the number of I/O lines has been increased to 28. In addition, the 8022 has an 8-bit A/D converter with two multiplexed input channels. The converter uses successive approximation techniques to update the conversion every four instruction cycles. The 8035AHL, 8039AHL, and 8040AHL are equivalent, respectively, to the 8048AH, 8049AH, and 8050H, except that they have no internal ROM or EPROM.

The 80C48, 80C35, 80C49, 80C39, 80C50, and 80C40 are HCMOS versions of their counterparts and are pin-to-pin compatible with them. These microcomputers can be battery operated and can maintain operation during AC power interruptions.

At the center of Intel's MSL-51 family is the 8051. The 8031/8051/8751 group of single-component 8-bit microcomputers contains four 8-bit ports, two 16-bit timers/counters, full-duplex serial channels (UART), and an on-board clock oscillator.

The 8031 has no on-chip program memory. It can address 64 kbytes of external program memory and 64 kbytes of external data memory. The 8051 is an 8031 with the lower 4 kbytes of program memory implemented as on-board mask programmable ROM and 128 bytes of RAM. The 8751 has 4 kbytes of EEPROM.

These microcomputers are enhancements of the 8048 processors. Additions to the instruction set include multiply, divide, subtract, and compare. With a 12-MHz crystal, 58% of the instructions execute in 1 μs, and another 40% in 2 μs. Multiply and divide require 4 μs.

The 8052 is an 8-bit microcomputer with 8 kbytes of ROM, 256 bytes of RAM, four 8-bit I/O parts, three 16-bit timers/counters, programmable UART, and an on-board oscillator. The 8032 is identical, except that it lacks on-board ROM.

The controllers in the 8044/8344/8744 group are remote universal peripheral interface ICs (RUPI). These RUPIs contain the same architecture and instruction set as the 8051. The serial interface on the 8051 has been replaced with a more powerful serial interface unit (SIU). The SIU works concurrently with the processor for increased speed. Also 64 more bytes of RAM have been added. The 8044 has 4 kbytes of mask programmable ROM. EPROM replaces the ROM in the 8744, and the 8344 has no internal program memory.

EXERCISE 14

1. Name an advantage of memory mapped I/O.
2. Do Motorola's processors have IN and OUT instructions?
3. Is the 6801 a microprocessor unit or a microcomputer unit?
4. Describe the three general modes of operation of a 6801.
5. Describe the use of the 6809's direct page register.
6. How wide is the 68000 address bus, and how much memory can it address?
7. Describe the internal registers in the 68000.
8. Describe the segment address system used with the Z8001.
9. List the following processors in order of relative performance from the highest to the lowest: 6800, 6801, 6802, 6805, 6809.
10. What is the difference between logical addresses and physical addresses?
11. What is a DART?
12. What is direct memory access?
13. How does the Z8603 protopack emulator support the 8601?
14. Describe the difference between the Z8116 and the Z8216.
15. What is the difference between a trap and an interrupt?
16. Will a program written for the 8080 run on an 8085?
17. Which processor has a 16-bit data bus, the 8086 or the 8088?
18. Describe the interaction between the EU and the BIU in an 8086.
19. How many input ports can an 8086 address?
20. Describe the function of an 8087 numeric processor extension.
21. What is an IAPX86/20?
22. What is contained on an 8048?

Appendix A

Construction of the Biggy Trainer

A.1 INTRODUCTION

The Biggy trainer is a bare-bones Z 80 computer designed to be simple to build and understand but versatile enough to allow students to use it for interfacing to other LSI ICs. It has a simple operating system in ROM that uses three output ports (constructed of D latches and LEDs) to display memory address and contents of memory to its user. The input is a single Hex key pad that can be constructed from bolts and a probe if money is a concern.

The ROM is a 2716 EPROM, of which only about one-fourth is used. Therefore, there is plenty of room for future expansion of ROM-based programs if desired. The RAM is made of two 2114 1K by 4 static RAMs. This gives the user 1K of memory storage. The RAM storage could be expanded easily to 6 kbytes of RAM without adding another address decoder if the user wished to add the extra RAM at construction time.

The clock is derived from a 4-MHz crystal oscillator, which is divided by 2 to produce a 2-MHz even-duty-cycle clock for the Z 80 CPU.

All control signals, data bus lines, address lines, and output port lines are brought out to a protoboard or wireless breadboard so that students can use them for interfacing work.

An on-board 5-V power supply was not included in the design of the Biggy trainer because most educational electronics labs have a good 1-A or greater, 5-V power source on the lab bench. If this is not the case for your operation, then we have supplied a simple 5-V power supply that can be built in A.5 of Appendix A.

A complete list of component parts needed to build the Biggy trainer is listed in A.6 of Appendix A. The cost of these parts will range from $100 to $200 depending on the supplier and the method of construction. It is suggested by both authors that the trainer be built by the class and used by that class throughout the rest of the course. The first three labs can be used for the trainer construction. Nothing reinforces the material being taught better than the hands-on construction of the actual electronic circuit being discussed in class.

One problem with building a computer of this type is that in order to make it run you must have a properly programmed EPROM to hold the operating system. If you had the computer up and running, you could use it to program the 2716 EPROM with the operating system program, but you can't get a running computer without the EPROM already being programmed. It is kind of like the old chicken or the egg problem. If you have the equipment to program an EPROM, then you will have no problem with getting your first EPROM programmed for the Biggy trainer; but if you don't, you have a problem.

A.7 of Appendix A shows you a simple but painstaking circuit and method of programming your first EPROM. A.8 of Appendix A shows how to use the Biggy trainer to program as many 2716 EPROMS as you wish quickly and easily. By using the circuits and procedure in A.7 and A.8 of Appendix A, you can solve the computer chicken and egg problem quite inexpensively.

The construction of the Biggy trainer is divided into three parts: hardware and CPU; RAM, ROM, and address decoder; input/output ports. We suggest that the construction be accomplished in the first three lab sessions of Chapters 1–3 so that the student can have a complete and operational computer to learn the Z 80 instruction set in Chapters 4–7.

If the construction of the computers is not accomplished in the first three lab sessions, the instructor can use the lab sessions of Chapters 4–7 to complete the construction by the students. One completed trainer could be used in class for demonstrations if this were the case. The student will need a completed trainer for the labs after Chapter 7.

A.2 HARDWARE AND CPU CONSTRUCTION OF THE BIGGY TRAINER

A. Hardware considerations: The use of a printed circuit board is easy for students to mount parts on, and there are no problems of incorrect wiring. But the time and expense of developing a printed circuit board makes this option only feasible for those with the resources capable of doing the job. A much cheaper and easier method is to use 30-gauge wire-wrap sockets and a suitable board to mount the sockets and other components on. Wire-wrapping the computer will take each student longer, but it means that the time and development cost of a printed circuit board can be avoided. A commercial wire-wrap board, such as a standard S100 board, can be used, or the student can design the chip layout on a sheet of 0.1-inch graph paper. One-tenth-inch graph paper is nice to design IC layouts on because a standard IC dual inline package's pins are 0.1 inch apart, and the chip is either 0.3 inch or 0.6 inch wide. A suggested chip layout is shown in Figure A-1. Once the chip layout is completed, the graph paper can be glued to a sheet of formica or thin ⅛-inch plywood and the holes drilled with a number 60 or number 80 drill. The paper can be left on the board or removed if desired. The computer in Figure A-2A was made by gluing the layout sheet to a ⅛-inch piece of plywood.

B. Mounting the hardware to the wire-wrap board: After the board is drilled, place the wire-wrap sockets on the board and glue them in place with a drop of superglue in the middle of the socket. Be careful not to let the glue wick up into the socket and coat the contacts. This is shown in Figure A-3. All hardware such as the keyboard, protoboards, and binding posts should be mounted on the board at this time also. Parts such as capacitors and resistors can be mounted on dip headers that can then be plugged into wire-wrap sockets or simply mounted directly on the board.

C. Soldering the despike capacitors and miscellaneous components: After all the hardware, such as wire-wrap sockets, protoboards, keyboards, and binding posts are mounted, the major part of soldering components should take place. This will avoid having to

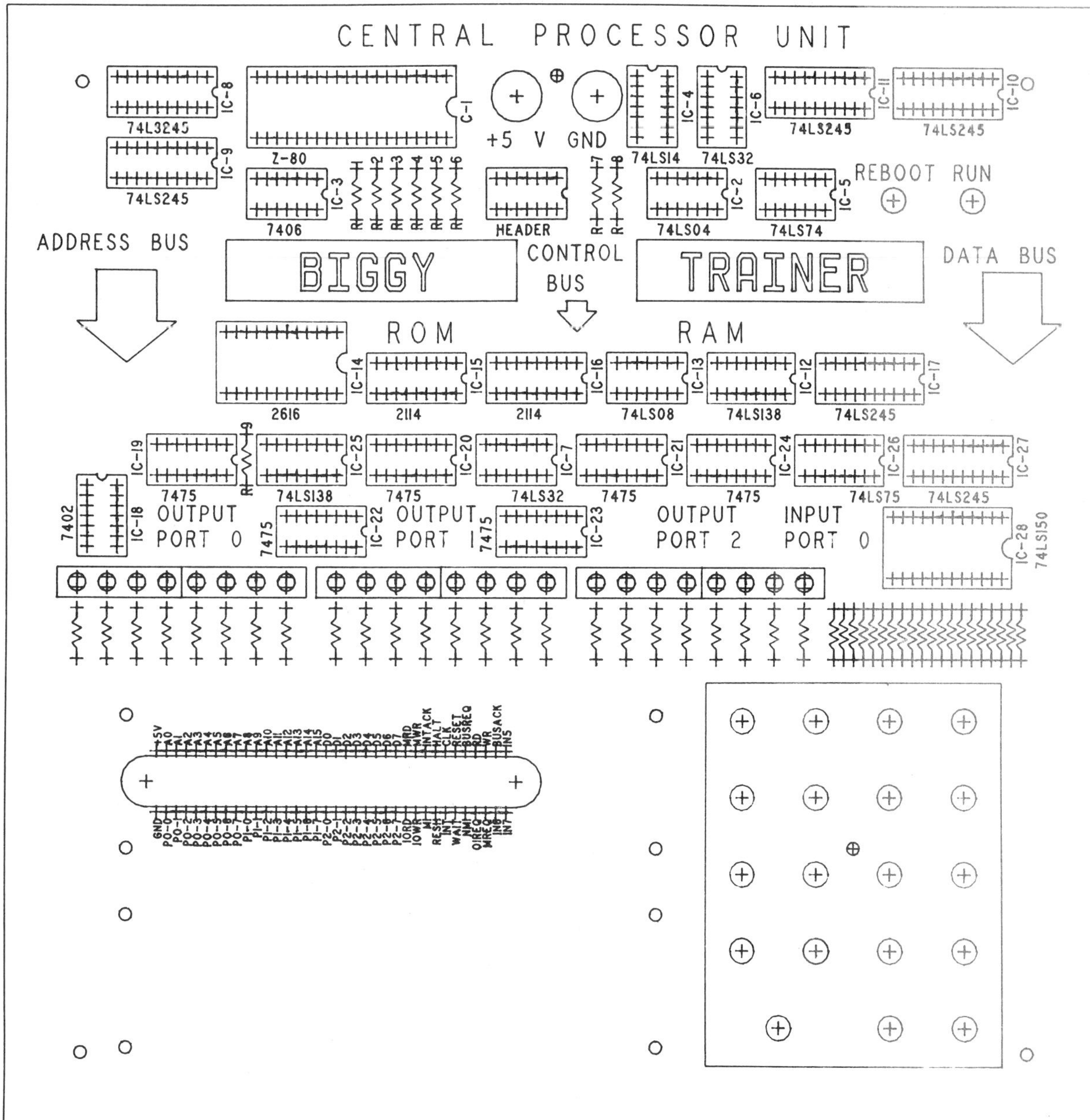

FIGURE A-1 Front panel and chip layout of the Biggy trainer

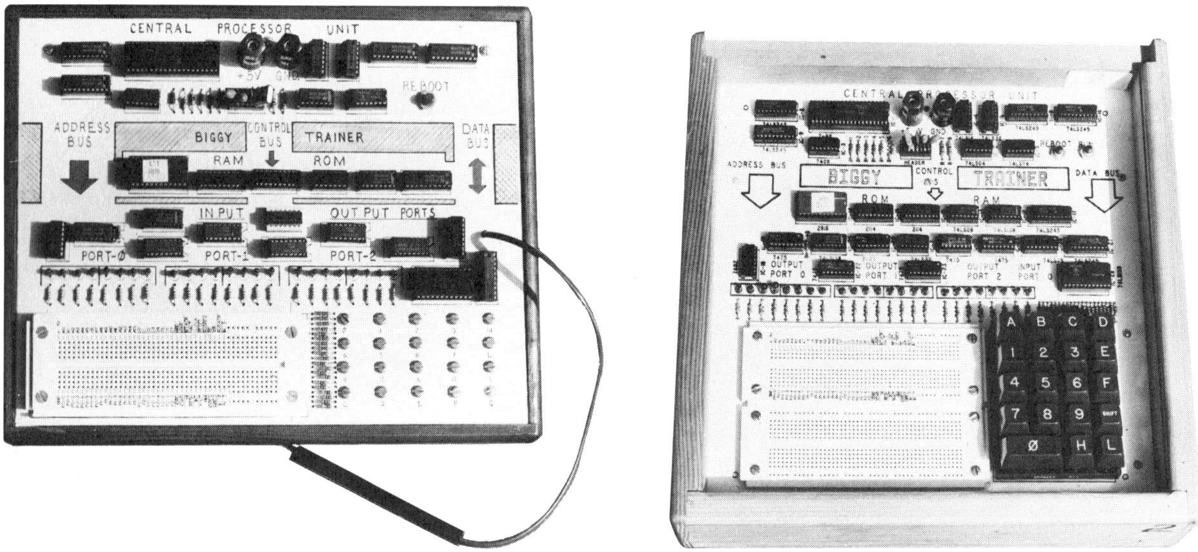

FIGURE A-2 The Biggy trainer

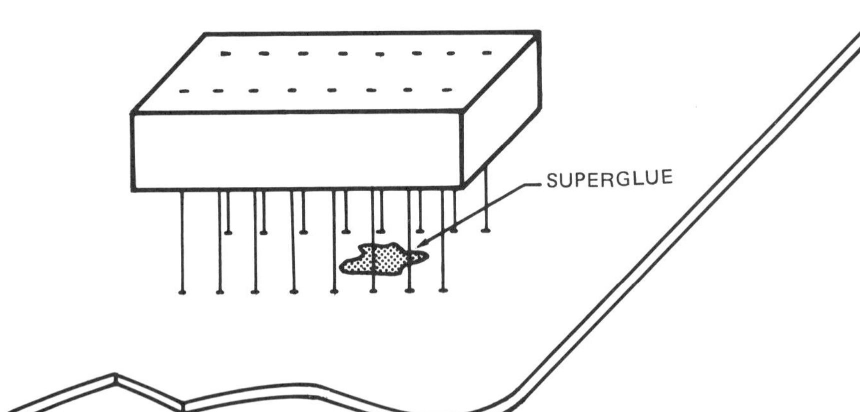

FIGURE A-3 Gluing a wire-wrap socket

solder components after the wire from the wire wrapping is in place. The first components to solder in place are the despiking capacitors used to supress the TTL power spike produced when a typical TTL totem-pole output changes states. Figure A-4 shows how these components should be soldered in place across the power supply pins of each IC in the Biggy trainer. Soldering the despike capacitor in place will prevent the wire-wrap socket from ever coming out of the board.

D. Wire all the power to the ICs using the wire-wrap tool and 30-gauge insulated wire. Figure A-5 shows an enlarged view of the wire-wrap tool end and how it is used to wrap the stripped end of the 30-ga. wire around the square 0.025-inch pin of the wire-wrap socket. Be sure to wire all the ICs with power and check the completed wiring with an ohmmeter for continuity from the top or IC side of the board. After you have wired the power to the ICs, place ground and +5 V on the power connectors of the trainer and use a voltmeter to check each IC socket for ground and +5 V at their proper power pins.

E. Using the schematic in A.9 wire the CPU clock, data, address and control lines, buffers, reset, nonmaskable interrupt, and the lines running to the protoboard from the buffers. Wire everything on the CPU schematic sheet.

F. After the wiring of the CPU portion of the trainer, place all the ICs used in the CPU sheet of the schematic in their proper socket on the trainer, except the Z 80 CPU. Put +5 V power on the trainer and use a scope to test the operation of the clock and other parts of the CPU portion of the trainer. The Z 80 static emulator shown in Figure A-6 is a very handy device to debug Z 80 computers of all types because it allows you to control the address bus, data bus, and control lines at will and keep them in a static state so you can trace their signal throughout the computer. The same thing can be accomplished by jumping wires from the Z 80 IC socket to blank spots on the protoboard and then making them HIGH, LOW, or HiZ.

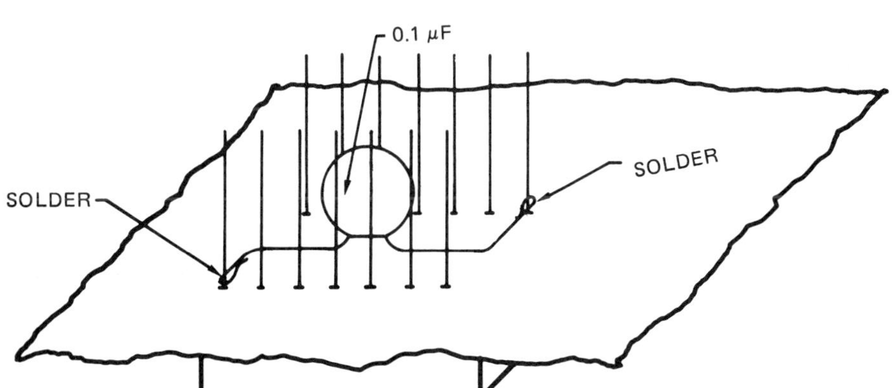

FIGURE A-4 Bottom view of IC wire-wrap socket and despike capacitor

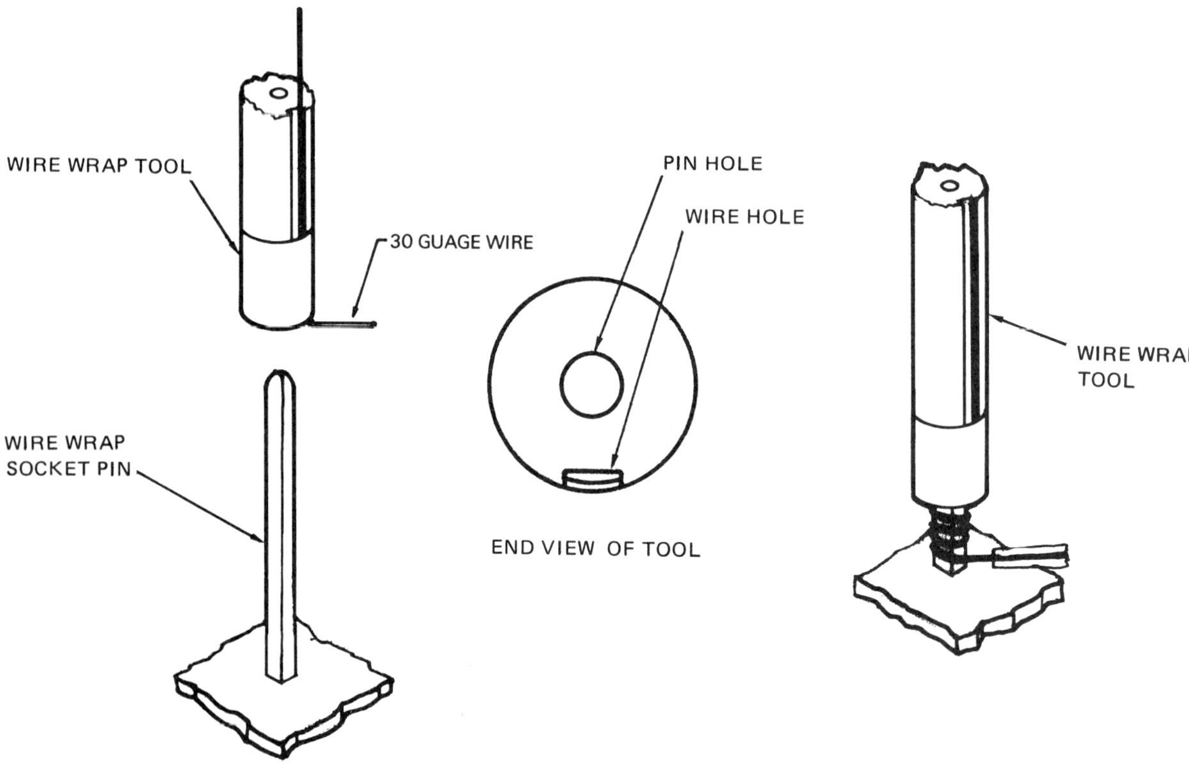

FIGURE A-5 Wire-wrap tool

A.3 WIRING OF THE RAM AND ROM

A. After the CPU portion of the trainer has been wired and debugged, wire-wrap the memory decoder and memories. After wiring the memories and decoder on the ROM schematic sheet, check your wiring for continuity with an ohmmeter.

B. After wiring and checking, insert the ICs for the decoder, buffer, RAM, and a programmed 2716 EPROM. Check to be sure the memories are functioning properly. If they are not, then use the static Z 80 emulator or a protoboard with wires to replace the Z 80. Then follow the debugging procedure listed in C.

C.
1. Move the data bus switches of the Z 80 emulator to the middle position or HiZ.
2. Put a logic 1 on all control signal outputs.
3. Place logic 0 on all address lines.
4. Now plug the emulator socket into the Z 80 wire-wrap socket.

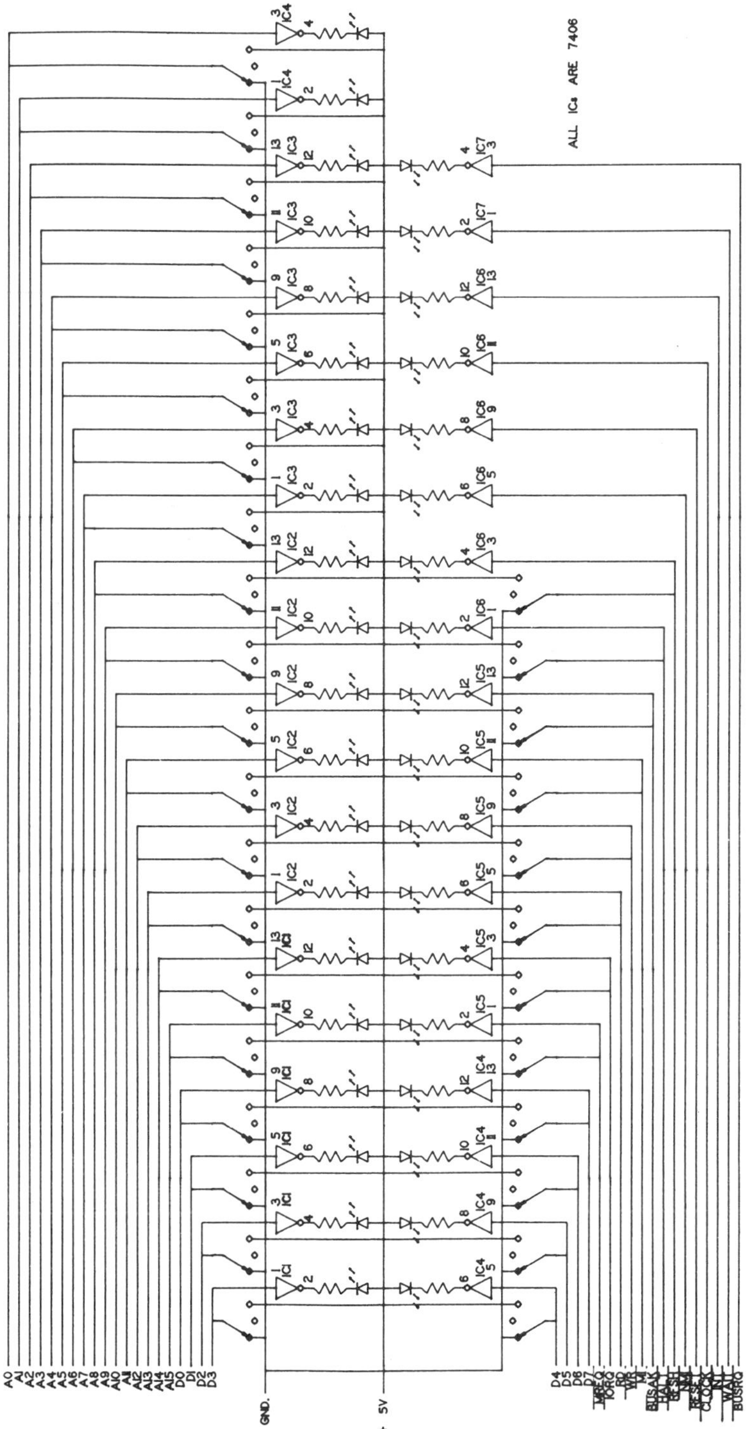

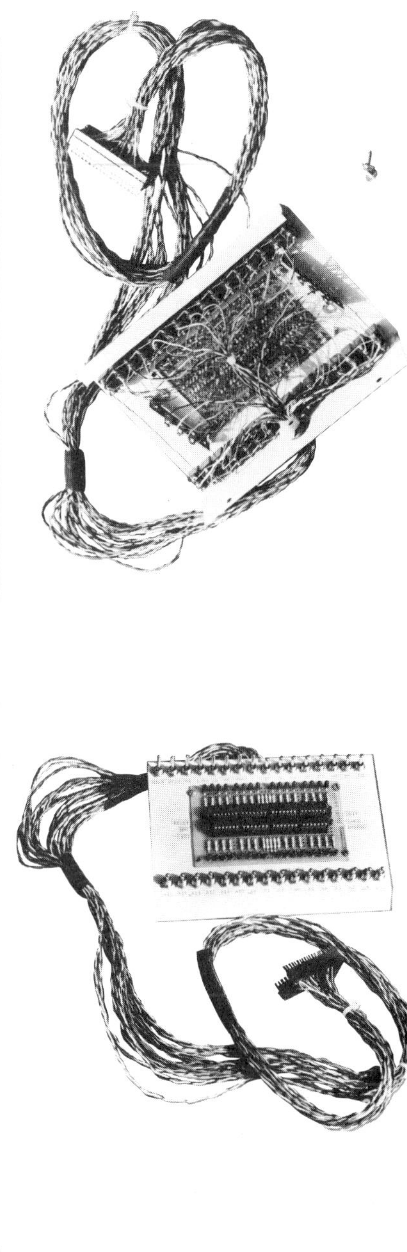

FIGURE A-6 Z 80 Static emulator

5. Move the $\overline{\text{MREQ}}$ and $\overline{\text{RD}}$ switches to the zero position. *This should read the address 0000 Hex, which should be C3 Hex.* If the D_0 to D_7 data lines do not read C3, then use a voltmeter to check the $\overline{\text{MRD}}$ control signal through the CPU buffer to the memory decoder and on to the 2716 EPROM's $\overline{\text{CS}}$ pin.
6. If the $\overline{\text{CS}}$ of the 2716 EPROM is LOW, then switch the $\overline{\text{RD}}$ or $\overline{\text{MREQ}}$ to HIGH and then to LOW to ensure that they control the EPROM's $\overline{\text{CS}}$.
7. If the $\overline{\text{CS}}$ responds to the changing of the $\overline{\text{RD}}$ or $\overline{\text{MREQ}}$ control signal, then use the voltmeter to check the data outputs of the EPROM for C3 Hex. If it is there, then follow the signal back through the memory buffer to the Z 80.
8. After the C3 Hex is obtained on the data LEDs of the emulator, check the memory content of several ROM locations against the ROM listing in Appendix B.
9. After the ROM is functioning, check the RAM by using the $\overline{\text{MREQ}}$ and $\overline{\text{WR}}$ control lines to write a byte to memory location 0800 Hex. This is the first RAM location in the Biggy trainer. Now turn around and read the byte by using the $\overline{\text{MREQ}}$ and $\overline{\text{RD}}$ control signals. Remember to place the data bus switches of the Z 80 emulator in the HiZ position when reading memory.
10. Remember that in order to select the RAM or ROM, the address bus and address decoder must work properly. If you can't get the correct data out of the RAM or ROM, then check the address bus and decoder.

A.4 THE CONSTRUCTION OF THE INPUT/OUTPUT SYSTEM OF THE BIGGY TRAINER

A. First, wire the keyboard and LEDs of the input/output ports of the Biggy trainer, because you may have to solder some resistors and keyboard connections, and it will be easier to do it before the final wire wrapping. Complete the Biggy trainer construction by wiring all the chips and components on the third and final schematic sheet, which is the input/output schematic sheet in Section A.9.
B. Use the ohmmeter and the Z 80 static CPU emulator to debug the input/output ports of the Biggy trainer. By making $\overline{\text{IORQ}}$ and $\overline{\text{RD}}$ or $\overline{\text{WR}}$ active, you should be able to read or write to the input/output ports and trace the control signal with a voltmeter.
C. After you are sure the input/output system is functioning, replace the Z 80 CPU IC and apply power to the computer. The LEDs should display the value 08 00 xx Hex. This is the address of the first memory location in RAM, and your Biggy trainer is waiting for you to program it.
D. Complete lab 3 to ensure that the Biggy trainer is operating.

A.5 THE POWER SUPPLY

The power supply shown in Figure A-7 is a 2-A, 5-V supply and a 1-A variable-voltage power supply. This power supply can be constructed from easily obtained parts and will power the Biggy trainer very nicely. The variable power supply can be used to supply the 25 V needed for the programming of the 2716 EPROM. Figure A-7 also shows photos of a completed power supply housed in a metal cabinet.

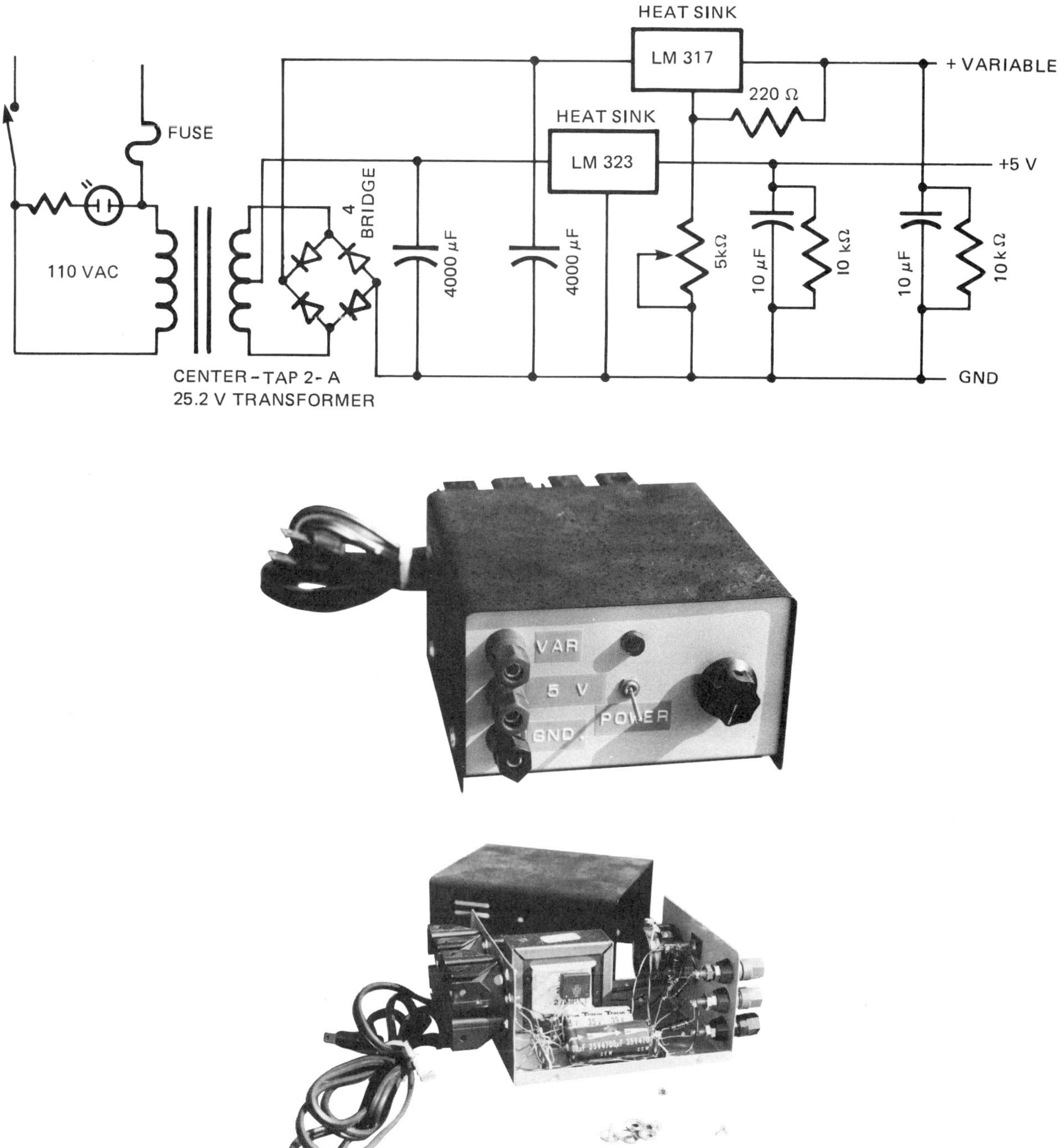

FIGURE A-7 Biggy trainer power supply

Biggy Trainer Power Supply

QUANTITY	PART DESCRIPTION
1	0.5-A slow blow fuse and holder
1	neon pilot light and resistor
1	spst switch for power switch
1	25.2-V center-tapped 2-A transformer
1	4-A diode bridge
2	4000-μF, 40-V capacitors
2	10-μF 40-V capacitors
1	LM323 5-V, 3-A voltage regulator
1	LM317 variable voltage regulator
1	220-Ω, ½-W resistor
1	5-kΩ pot
2	10-kΩ, ¼-W resistors
1	metal cabinet
3	4-pole terminal strips to mount parts on
2	T03 heat sinks with insulation
3	binding posts for power outputs
1	18-ga. power cord
1	¼-in knob for the voltage adjust pot

A.6 PARTS LIST FOR THE BIGGY TRAINER

The Biggy Trainer Electronic Parts List

QUANTITY	IC NO.	PART DESCRIPTION
1	IC 1	Z-80 CPU
1	IC 2	74LS04
1	IC 3	7406
1	IC 4	74LS14
1	IC 5	74LS74
2	IC 6,7	74LS32
6	IC 8,9,10,11,17,27	74LS245
1	IC 18	74LS02
6	IC 19,20,21,22,23,24	7475
2	IC 25,12	74LS138
1	IC 26	74LS75
1	IC 28	74LS150
1	IC 13	74LS08
1	IC 14	2716 EPROM
2	IC 15,16	2114 RAMs
28	RESISTORS	1 kΩ, ¼ W
2	RESISTORS	10 kΩ, ¼ W
25	RESISTORS	330 Ω, ¼ W
24		RED LEDs
1	CRYSTAL	4 MHz
29	CAPACITORS	0.1 μF
2	TANTALUM CAPACITOR	10 μF
1	TRANSISTOR	2N3906 PNP
1	RESISTOR	470 Ω, ¼ W

The Biggy Trainer Hardware Parts List

QUANTITY	PART DESCRIPTION
1	40-PIN WIRE-WRAP SOCKET
2	24-PIN WIRE-WRAP SOCKET
6	20-PIN WIRE-WRAP SOCKET
2	18-PIN WIRE-WRAP SOCKET
9	16-PIN WIRE-WRAP SOCKET
9	14-PIN WIRE-WRAP SOCKET
2	½-IN BINDING POST
2	6-IN PROTOBOARDS
1	20-KEY KEYBOARD OR 20 PUSH BUTTONS
1	WIRE-WRAP BOARD TO MOUNT SOCKETS ON
200 FT	30-GA. WIRE-WRAP WIRE
1	SMALL ROLL OF 60/40 SOLDER
9	⅛-IN-BY-¾-IN BOLTS AND NUTS
1	16-PIN DIP HEADER
2	NORMALLY-OPEN PUSH-BUTTON SWITCHES

A.7 THE EPROM PROGRAMMER

Figure A-8 shows a 50-ms one-shot that can be triggered by a debounce switch. This 50-ms pulse is fed to the $\overline{CS}$ of the 2716 EPROM to be programmed. We suggest that the 2716 be placed in a protoboard along with the 74121 and 7400. Hard-wire the address to be programmed and the data into the 2716 EPROM. Place the $\overline{OE}$ input at +5 V,

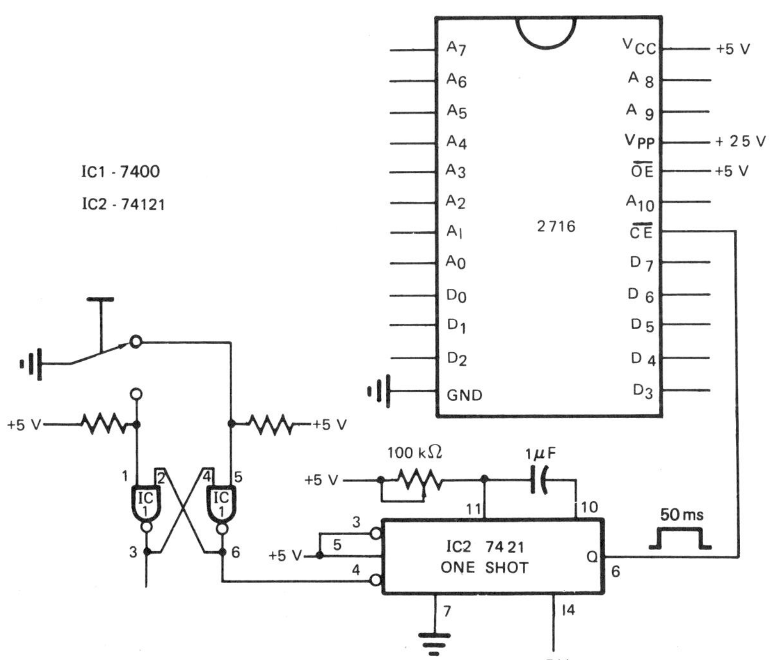

FIGURE A-8 EPROM programmer using a one-shot

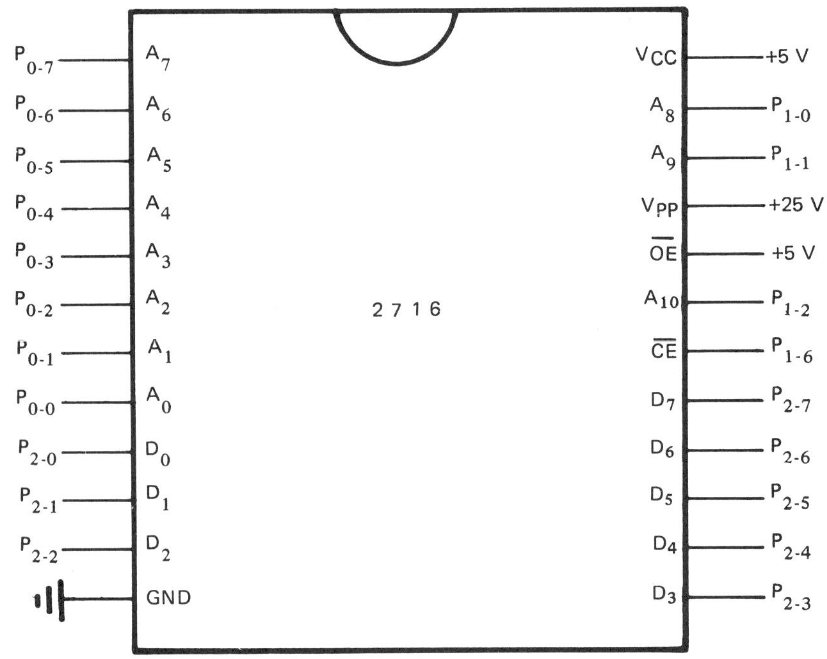

FIGURE A-9 Pin connection for using the Biggy trainer to program a 2716 EPROM

the $\overline{CS}$ to the 50-ms one-shot, and the VPP pin to +25 V. Use a good voltmeter to set the +25 V for the VPP pin because too much voltage can damage the 2716, and too little voltage will not program the bits.

Once everything is set up, trigger the one-shot with the button of the debounce flip-flop. This will pulse the 2716 EPROM $\overline{CS}$ HIGH for 50 ms. It should be noted that the one-shot should be tested and calibrated on a good scope for a perfect 50-ms pulse before programming begins.

Only trigger the one-shot once for each new address and data byte. Use the op codes in the program listing for the Biggy trainer operating system in Appendix B to program the EPROM.

This is a very slow and painstaking process, but it will properly program the 2716 EPROM and give you the one chip needed to run the Biggy trainer, which cannot be bought preprogrammed.

A.8 A FASTER PROGRAMMING METHOD

After the first EPROM is programmed and you have a running Biggy trainer, you can wire up a cleared 2716 EPROM to the trainer, as shown in Figure A-9, and use the following program to program the EPROM faster. This program will simply copy the block of memory from the memory location pointed to by HL through the memory location pointed to by DE to the EPROM. The starting address for the EPROM is the content of BC. These points are the first thing loaded in this program and can be changed if you wish to add to the Biggy trainer operating system.

```
            ;*****************************************************
            ;* PROGRAM TO PROGRAM A 2716 WITH THE BIGGY TRAINER    *
            ;*****************************************************
            ;
            ;OUTPUT PORT 0 AND 1 ARE THE ADDRESS OF THE EPROM
            ;OUTPUT PORT 2 WILL BE THE DATA TO BE PROGRAMMED
            ;BIT P1 7 WILL BE THE CE OF THE 2716 AND BE PULSED FOR
            ;50 MILLISEC. TO PROGRAM THE EPROM
            ;
            ;HL = BEGINNING ADDRESS OF MEMORY TO BE PROGRAMMED
            ;DE = ENDING ADDRESS OF MEMORY TO BE PROGRAMMED
            ;BC = BEGINNING ADDRESS OF THE EPROM TO BE PROGRAMMED
            ;
            ;TO USE THIS PROGRAM REBOOT THE BIGGY TRAINER AND
            ;PUT + 5 VOLTS ON VPP (PIN 21) OF THE 2716 SOCKET
            ;IN THE PROTOBOARD ON THE BIGGY TRAINER THEN PLACE
            ;THE 2716 TO BE PROGRAMMED IN THE PROTOBOARD AND
            ;AFTER IT IS IN PLACE PUT +25 VOLTS FROM THE POWER
            ;SUPPLY ON VPP (PIN 21).  NEXT START THE PROGRAM BY
            ;PRESSING THE RUN BUTTON.  THE EPROM WILL BE PROGRAMMED
            ;AND ALL THE OUTPUT PORTS WILL GO TO 00 HEX AT THE
            ;COMPLETION.  THEN PUT +5 VOLTS BACK ON VPP (PIN 21)
            ;AND REMOVE THE PROGRAMMED 2716 EPROM.
            ;
0000        BEGIN   EQU     00H             ;BEGINNING ADD OF ROM
00F0        ENDIN   EQU     0F0H            ;ENDING ADDRESS OF ROM
0000        START   EQU     00H             ;EPROM BEGINNING ADDRESS
00E4        TIME    EQU     0E4H            ;ADD OF 10 MILLISEC LOOP
            ;
0800                ORG     800H            ;START OF PROGRAM
0800 210000 PROG    LD      HL,BEGIN
0803 11F000         LD      DE,ENDIN
0806 010000         LD      BC,START
0809 79     AGAIN   LD      A,C             ;OUTPUT ADDRESS TO EPROM
080A D300           OUT     (00H),A
080C 7E             LD      A,(HL)          ;BYTE TO PROGRAM TO ROM
080D D302           OUT     (02H),A
080F 78             LD      A,B             ;GET MSB OF EPROM ADD
0810 F640           OR      40H             ;SET BIT 6 TO 1
0812 D301           OUT     (01H),A         ;START 50 MILL SEC TIME
0814 3E05           LD      A,05H           ;SET UP FOR 50 MILLISEC.
0816 CDE400 LOOP    CALL    TIME            ;CALL 10 MILL LOOP IN ROM
0819 3D             DEC     A
081A 20FA           JR      NZ,LOOP
081C 78             LD      A,B             ;STOP PROGRAMMING
081D E6BF           AND     0BFH            ;RESET BIT 6 TO 0
081F D301           OUT     (01H),A
0821 23             INC     HL              ;BUMP POINTER
0822 03             INC     BC              ;BUMP EPROM POINTER
0823 7D             LD      A,L             ;TEST FOR END OF
0824 BB             CP      E               ;PROGRAMMING THE EPROM
0825 20E2           JR      NZ,AGAIN
0827 7C             LD      A,H
0828 BA             CP      D
0829 20DE           JR      NZ,AGAIN
082B 3E00           LD      A,00H           ;SET A TO CLEAR ALL PORTS
082D D300           OUT     (00),A          ;TO INDICATE THE END OF
082F D301           OUT     (01H),A         ;THE PROGRAMMING
0831 D302           OUT     (02H),A
0833 76             HALT
0000                END
00000 Total Errors
```

A.9 BIGGY TRAINER SCHEMATICS

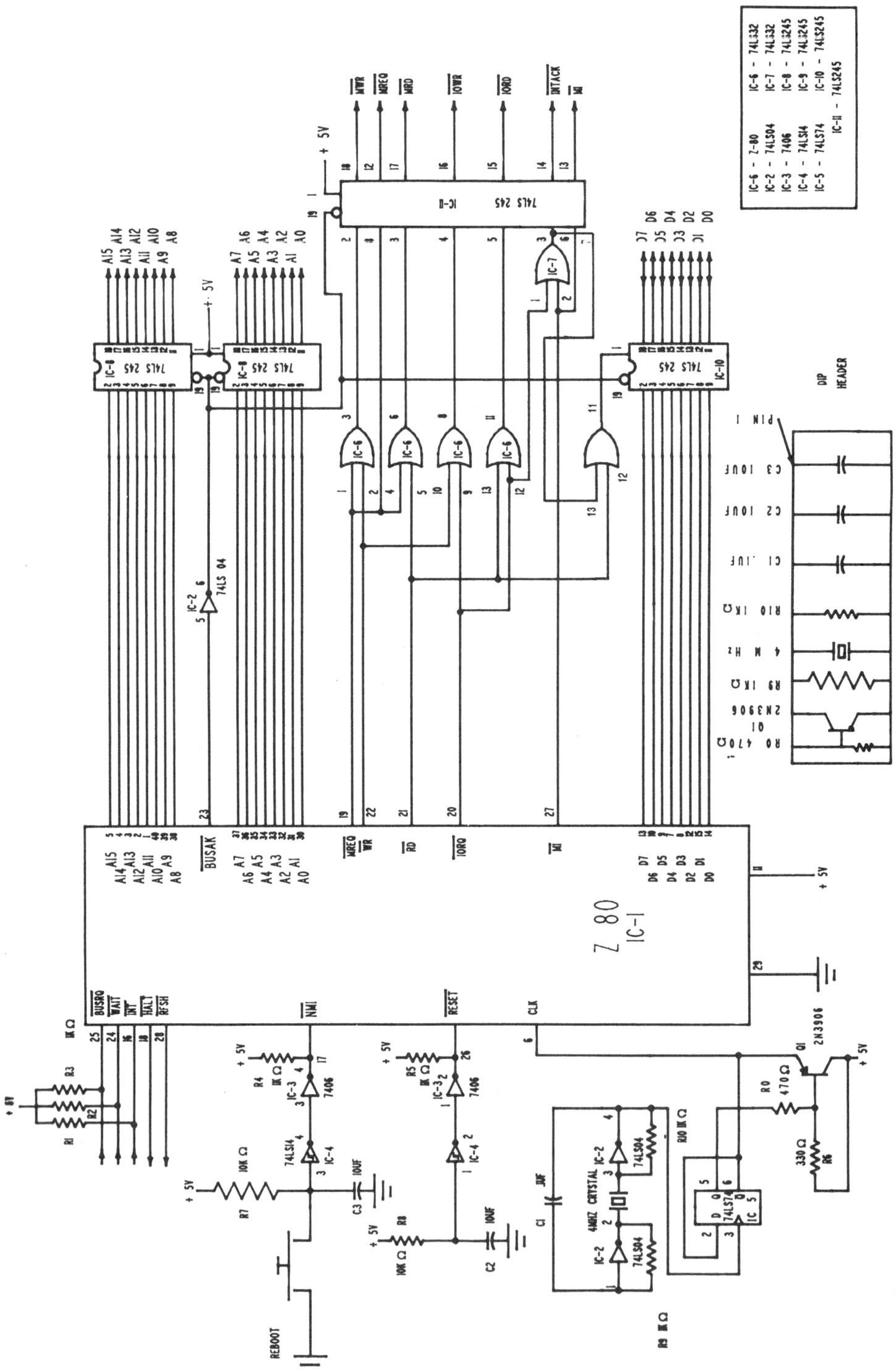

FIGURE A-10 Biggy trainer CPU

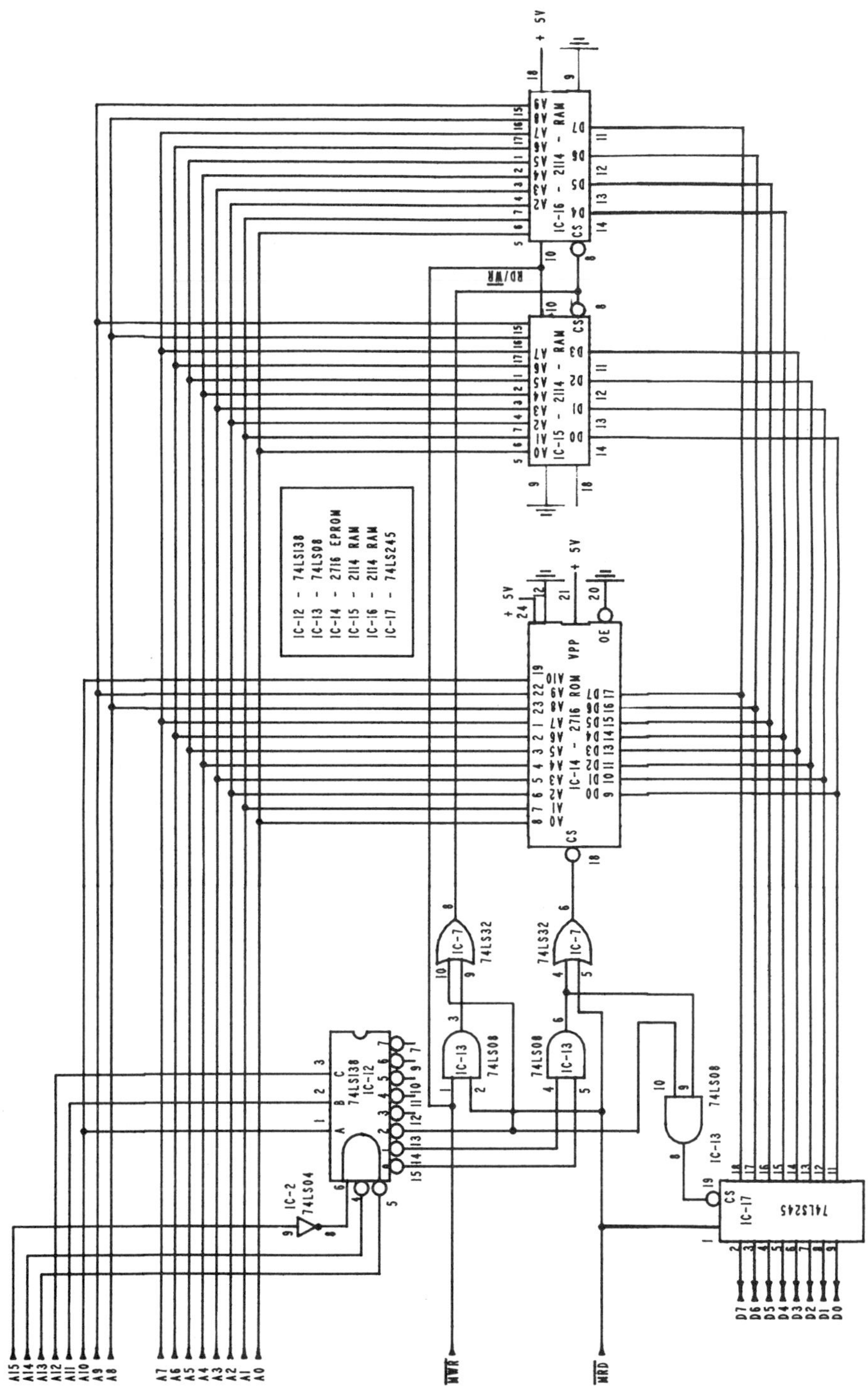

FIGURE A-11 Biggy trainer RAM and ROM

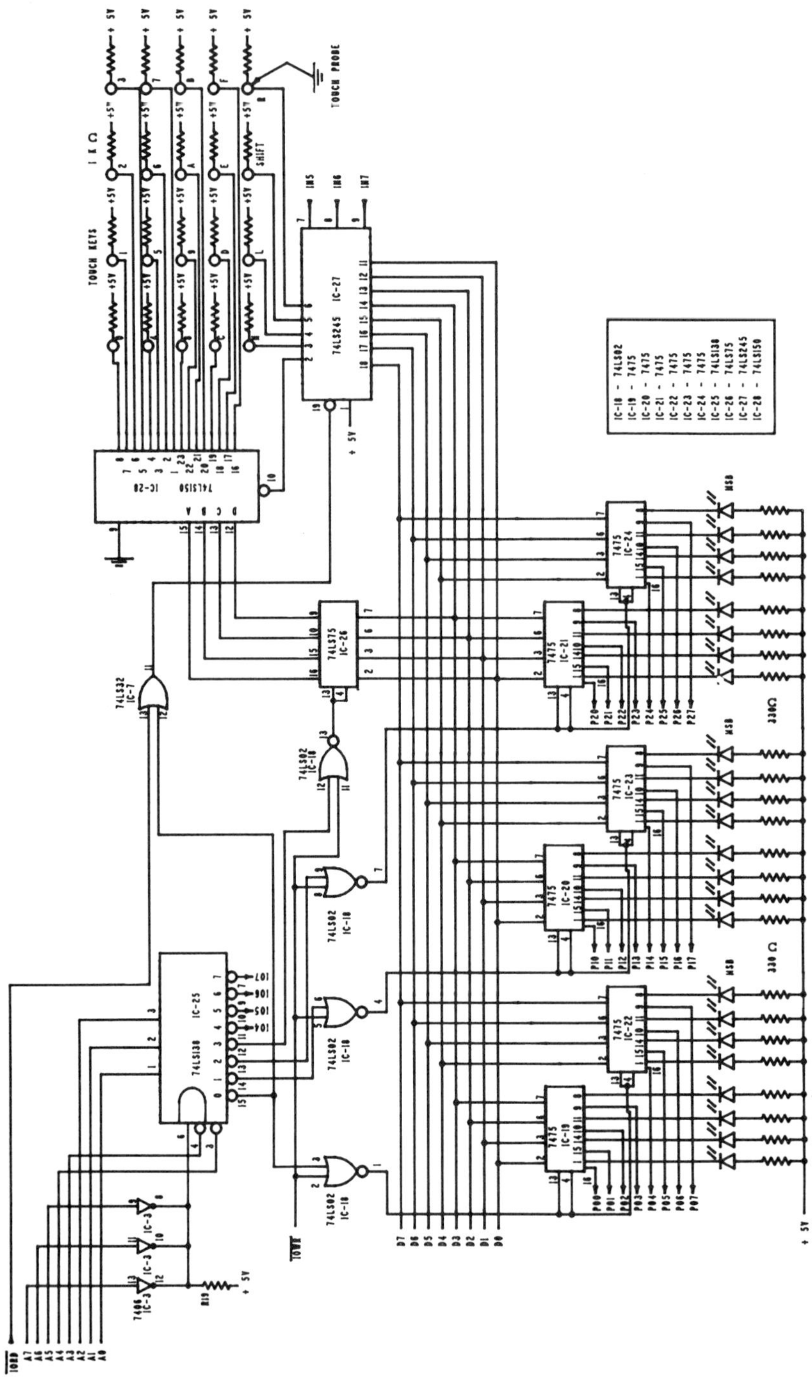

FIGURE A-12 Biggy trainer I/O

Appendix B

The Biggy Trainer Operating System

B.1 USING THE BIGGY TRAINER

1. The three output ports are made of eight LEDs each and are used by the computer to display the following:
   A. Port 0: HIGH byte of the current address being used by the operator.
   B. Port 1: LOW byte of the current address being used by the operator.
   C. Port 2: Displays content of the currently addressed memory and the value of the last-pressed hex keys.
2. When the computer is turned on, ports 0 and 1 will display the first RAM memory address (0800 Hex). Port 2 will display the content of that address.
3. Pressing the shift key will cause the current address displayed on ports 0 and 1 to be incremented by 1, and the content of the new address to be displayed on port 2. In this way you can look at the contents of memory.
4. Pressing a hex key will cause port 2 to be shifted left four bits, and the binary value of the pressed key to be placed on the least significant four bits of port 2. In this way you can change the value displayed on port 2.
5. Pressing the shift key after changing the value of port 2 will cause the new value of port 2 to be loaded into the current memory address displayed on ports 0 and 1.
6. Pressing the H key will move the byte displayed on port 2 to port 0. In this way you can change the HIGH byte of the current address.
7. Pressing the L key will move the byte displayed on port 2 to port 1. In this way you can change the LOW byte of the current address.
8. Pressing the reboot key will activate the nonmaskable interrupt and cause the Biggy trainer to warm boot (start over again) and display the 0800 Hex address on ports 0 and 1. A warm boot or reboot does not erase any of the RAM memory. This is a quick way to get back to the first RAM memory location.
9. Pressing the run key will cause the computer to fetch the next instruction from the current address shown on ports 0 and 1. This is how you execute a program.

B.2 THE BIGGY TRAINER OPERATING SYSTEM

```
                 ;*****************************************************
                 ;*      THE BIGGY TRAINER OPERATING SYSTEM           *
                 ;*****************************************************
                 ;
                 ;
                 ;
                 ;              KEY DEFINITIONS
                 ;
                 ; 0 THROUGH F -  PRODUCES THE HEX VALUE FOR INPUT
                 ; H  --  MOVES THE BYTE DISPLAYED ON PORT 2 TO PORT 0
                 ;        WHICH IS THE HIGH BYTE OF THE ADDRESS
                 ; L  --  MOVES THE BYTE DISPLAYED ON PORT 2 TO PORT 1
                 ;        WHICH IS THE LOW BYTE OF THE ADDRESS
                 ; S  --  STORES THE BYTE DISPLAYED ON PORT 2 IN THE
                 ;        MEMORY LOCATION OF THE ADDRESS DISPLAYED ON
                 ;        PORTS 0 AND 1 THEN INCREMENTS THE ADDRESS
                 ;        DISPLAYED ON PORTS 0 AND 1 AND DISPLAYS THE
                 ;        CONTENT OF THE NEW ADDRESS DISPLAYED ON
                 ;        PORTS 0 AND 1
                 ; RUN -- STARTS THE CPU EXECUTING INSTRUCTIONS AT THE
                 ;        ADDRESS DISPLAYED ON PORTS 0 AND 1
                 ;REBOOT- REBOOTS THE COMPUTER VIA THE NONMASKABLE
                 ;        INTERRUPT AND DISPLAYS 08 00 XX ON PORTS 0 1  2
                 ;
                 ;
                 ;
0800             RAMSTA  EQU     800H            ;FIRST RAM BYTE
0BFF             RAMEND  EQU     0BFFH           ;LAST RAM BYTE
0000             OUT0    EQU     000H            ;ADD. OF OUTPUT PORT 0
0001             OUT1    EQU     001H            ;ADD. OF OUTPUT PORT 1
0002             OUT2    EQU     002H            ;ADD. OF OUTPUT PORT 2
0003             OUT3    EQU     003H            ;ADD. OF OUTPUT PORT 3
0000             IN0     EQU     000H            ;ADD. OF INPUT PORT 0
0066             REBOOT  EQU     66H             ;ADD. OF NMI RESTART
                 ;
                 ;
0000                     ORG     000H            ;START OF PROGRAM
0000 C36600      START   JP      REBOOT          ;JUMP TO BEGINNING
0008                     ORG     08H             ;ADD OR RST 08 INSTR.
0008 C30808              JP      808H            ;JUMP TO RAM LOCATION
0010                     ORG     010H            ;ADD OF RST 10 INSTR.
0010 C31008              JP      810H            ;JUMP TO RAM LOCATION
0018                     ORG     018H            ;ADD OF RST 18 INSTR.
0018 C31808              JP      818H            ;JUMP TO RAM LOCATION
0020                     ORG     020H            ;ADD. OF RST 20 INSTR.
0020 C32008              JP      820H            ;JUMP TO RAM LOCATION
0028                     ORG     028H            ;ADD. OF RST 28 INSTR.
0028 C32808              JP      828H            ;JUMP TO RAM LOCATION
0030                     ORG     30H             ;ADD. OF RST 30 INSTR.
0030 C33008              JP      830H            ;JUMP TO RAM LOCATION
0038                     ORG     038H            ;ADD. OF RST 38 INSTR.
0038 C33808              JP      0838H           ;JUMP TO RAM LOCATION
0066                     ORG     066H            ;BEGINNING OF OP. SYSTEM
0066 31000C              LD      SP,RAMEND+1     ;ADD OF STACK POINTER
0069 210008              LD      HL,RAMSTA       ;ADDRESS OF FIRST BYTE
006C 0E00        LOOP1   LD      C,OUT0          ;ADD. OF HIGH BYTE OF ADD
006E 46                  LD      B,(HL)          ;GET CONTENT OF ADD IN HL
006F ED61                OUT     (C),H           ;OUTPUT H TO PORT 0
0071 0C                  INC     C               ;INC. C TO PORT 1 ADDRESS
0072 ED69                OUT     (C),L           ;OUTPUT L TO PORT 1
0074 0C                  INC     C               ;INC. C TO PORT 2 ADDRESS
0075 ED41                OUT     (C),B           ;OUTPUT CONTENT OF HL
0077 CDA300      LOOP    CALL    GETKEY          ;CALL GETKEY SUBROUTINE
```

```
007A CB67              BIT     4,A             ;BIT 4 TEST FOR COMMAND
007C 200E              JR      NZ,INTERP       ;JUMP TO INTERPRETER
007E 57                LD      D,A             ;STORE HEX DIGIT
007F 78                LD      A,B             ;GET STORED BYTE
0080 07                RLCA                    ;ROTATE LEFT 4 BITS
0081 07                RLCA
0082 07                RLCA
0083 07                RLCA
0084 E6F0              AND     0F0H            ;MASK OFF LS 4 BITS
            ;                                  TO ADD NEW HEX DIGIT
0086 B2                OR      D               ;OR HEX DIGIT TO BYTE
0087 47                LD      B,A             ;STORE BYTE IN REG. B
0088 D302              OUT     (OUT2),A        ;DISPLAY NEW BYTE
008A 18EB              JR      LOOP            ;DO AGAIN
008C FE13   INTERP     CP      13H             ;TEST FOR GO KEY
008E 2812              JR      Z,GO            ;JUMP TO GO ROUTINE
0090 FE12              CP      12H             ;TEST FOR STEP KEY
0092 2807              JR      Z,STEP          ;JUMP TO STEP ROUTINE
0094 FE11              CP      11H             ;TEST FOR LOW KEY
0096 2807              JR      Z,LOW           ;JUMP TO LOW ROUTINE
0098 60                LD      H,B             ;NEW BYTE TO H REGISTER
0099 18D1              JR      LOOP1           ;DO AGAIN
009B 70     STEP       LD      (HL),B          ;PUT BYTE IN MEMORY
009C 23                INC     HL              ;BUMP BYTE POINTER BY 1
009D 18CD              JR      LOOP1           ;JUMP TO OUTPUT NEW ADD
009F 68     LOW        LD      L,B             ;MOVE BYTE TO REG. L
00A0 18CA              JR      LOOP1           ;JUMP TO OUTPUT NEW ADD
00A2 E9     GO         JP      (HL)            ;START PROGRAM AT ADD. HL
            ;
            ;          ****************************************
            ;          *    GETKEY SUBROUTINE                 *
            ;          ****************************************
            ;
            ;THIS SUBROUTINE WILL FETCH AND DEBOUNCE A PRESSED KEY
            ;FROM THE KEYBOARD
            ;
00A3 14     GETKEY     INC     D               ;ADD 1 TO REGISTER D
00A4 7A                LD      A,D             ;MOVE D TO A TO OUTPUT IT
00A5 D303              OUT     (OUT3),A        ;D TO KEYBOARD MUX.
00A7 CDDD00            CALL    TESKEY          ;TEST FOR VALID KEY
00AA 28F7              JR      Z,GETKEY        ;DO OVER IF NO KEY PUSHED
00AC 5F                LD      E,A             ;SAVE KEY PRESSED
00AD CDE400            CALL    TIME            ;PAUSE TO DEBOUNCE KEY
00B0 CDDD00            CALL    TESKEY          ;IS KEY STILL PRESSED
00B3 28EE              JR      Z,GETKEY        ;DO OVER IF NOT PRESSED
00B5 CDDD00 LOOP2      CALL    TESKEY          ;WAIT FOR KEY TO BE LET
00B8 20FB              JR      NZ,LOOP2        ;UP
00BA CDE400            CALL    TIME            ;PAUSE TO DEBOUNCE KEY
00BD 7B                LD      A,E             ;RESTORE KEY TO A REG.
00BE 17                RLA                     ;TEST FOR A HEX KEY
00BF 380C              JR      C,HEX           ;JUMP TO PRODUCE HEX KEY
00C1 17                RLA                     ;TEST FOR HIGH KEY
00C2 300D              JR      NC,HIGH
00C4 17                RLA                     ;TEST FOR LOW KEY
00C5 300D              JR      NC,LOW1
00C7 17                RLA                     ;TEST FOR STEP KEY
00C8 300D              JR      NC,STEP1
00CA 17                RLA                             ;TEST FOR GO KEY
00CB 300D              JR      NC,GO1
00CD 7A     HEX        LD      A,D             ;GET THE HEX COUNT
00CE E60F              AND     0FH             ;MASK OFF THE 4 MS BITS
00D0 C9                RET
00D1 3E10   HIGH       LD      A,10H           ;16 BASE 10 OR HIGH CODE
```

```
00D3 C9                    RET
00D4 3E11        LOW1      LD      A,11H         ;17 BASE 10 OR LOW CODE
00D6 C9                    RET
00D7 3E12        STEP1     LD      A,12H         ;18 BASE 10 OR STEP CODE
00D9 C9                    RET
00DA 3E13        GO1       LD      A,13H         ;19 BASE 10 OR GO CODE
00DC C9                    RET
                 ;
                 ;
                 ;         ****************************************
                 ;         *     TEST KEY SUBROUTINE              *
                 ;         ****************************************
                 ;
                 ;THIS SUBROUTINE WILL TEST THE KEYBOARD AND RETURN WITH
                 ;THE ZERO FLAG SET IF NO KEY WAS PRESSED .  THE ZERO FLAG
                 ;WILL BE RESET TO 0 IF A KEY WAS PRESSED.
                 ;
                 ;
00DD DB00        TESKEY    IN      A,(IN0)       ;GET KEYBOARD BYTE
00DF E6F8                  AND     0F8H          ;MASK UNWANTED BITS
00E1 FE78                  CP      78H           ;SET Z IF NO KEY PRESSED
00E3 C9                    RET
                 ;
                 ;
                 ;         **************************************
                 ;         *  10 MILLISECOND TIMING LOOP        *
                 ;         **************************************
                 ;
                 ;THIS SUBROUTINE WILL WASTE 10 MILL SECONDS OF TIME TO
                 ;BE USED ANY PLACE TIME IS NEEDED SUCH AS KEY DEBOUNCE
                 ;
                 ;
00E4 E5          TIME      PUSH    HL            ;SAVE HL
00E5 21DB05                LD      HL,05DBH      ;LOAD HL WITH TIME COUNT
00E8 2D          LOOP3     DEC     L             ;FAST COUNTER -1
00E9 20FD                  JR      NZ,LOOP3      ;DO TILL L = 0
00EB 25                    DEC     H             ;SLOW COUNTER -1
00EC 20FA                  JR      NZ,LOOP3      ;DO TILL H = 0
00EE E1                    POP     HL            ;RESTORE HL
00EF 00                    NOP                   ;ADD 4 CLOCK CYCLES
00F0 C9                    RET
0000                       END
00000 Total Errors

LOOP3    00E8    OUT3     0003
GO1      00DA    OUT2     0002
STEP1    00D7    OUT1     0001
LOW1     00D4    OUT0     0000
HIGH     00D1    RAMEND   0BFF
HEX      00CD    RAMSTA   0800
LOOP2    00B5
TIME     00E4
TESKEY   00DD
LOW      009F
STEP     009B
GO       00A2
INTERP   008C
GETKEY   00A3
LOOP     0077
LOOP1    006C
START    0000
REBOOT   0066
IN0      0000
```

Appendix C

Z 80 Instruction Set

C.1 INTRODUCTION

This appendix contains two tables. The first lists all Z 80 mnemonic codes in alphabetical order. For each mnemonic code the corresponding op code is given along with the effect on the flags and the number of machine cycles and T states required. The flags appear in the same order that they are arranged in the flags register, with the two unused bits omitted.

The second table is identical except that it is arranged in numerical order according to op codes.

The symbols used in the tables are summarized.

.	Flag not changed by the operation.
0	Flag is reset.
1	Flag is set.
X	Resulting state of flag could be 1 or 0.
↕	Flag is affected according to the result of the operation.
P	The P/V flag is affected according to the number of 1's in the result.
V	Flag is affected according to the result of a signed 2's complement arithmetic operation. (V = 1 indicates result is incorrect)
e	8-bit offset for relative jumps
n	8-bit value
nn	16-bit value
d	8-bit offset indexed addressing
S	Sign flag
Z	Zero flag
H	Half-carry flag
P/V	Parity/overflow flag
N	Add/subtract flag
C	Carry flag

C.2 Z 80 MNEMONIC CODES IN ALPHABETICAL ORDER

MNEMONIC	OP CODE	COMMENT	S	Z	H	P/V	N	C	M CYCLES	T STATES
ADC A,(HL)	8E	Add contents of memory pointed to by HL and carry flag to the accumulator	↕	↕	↕	V	0	↕	2	7
ADC A,(IX+d)	DD8Ed	Add contents of memory pointed to by IX+d and carry flag to the accumulator	↕	↕	↕	V	0	↕	5	19
ADC A,(IY+d)	FD8Ed	Add contents of memory pointed to by IY+d and carry flag to the accumulator	↕	↕	↕	V	0	↕	5	19
ADC A,A	8F	Add contents of accumulator and carry flag to the accumulator	↕	↕	↕	V	0	↕	1	4
ADC A,B	88	Add contents of register B and carry flag to the accumulator	↕	↕	↕	V	0	↕	1	4
ADC A,C	89	Add contents of register C and carry flag to the accumulator	↕	↕	↕	V	0	↕	1	4
ADC A,D	8A	Add contents of register D and carry flag to the accumulator	↕	↕	↕	V	0	↕	1	4
ADC A,E	8B	Add contents of register E and carry flag to the accumulator	↕	↕	↕	V	0	↕	1	4
ADC A,H	8C	Add contents of register H and carry flag to the accumulator	↕	↕	↕	V	0	↕	1	4
ADC A,L	8D	Add contents of register L and carry flag to the accumulator	↕	↕	↕	V	0	↕	1	4
ADC A,n	CEn	Add byte 2 and carry flag to the accumulator	↕	↕	↕	V	0	↕	2	7
ADC HL,BC	ED4A	Add contents of register pair BC and carry flag to HL	↕	↕	X	V	0	↕	4	15
ADC HL,DE	ED5A	Add contents of DE and carry flag to HL	↕	↕	X	V	0	↕	4	15
ADC HL,HL	ED6A	Add contents of register pair HL and carry flag to HL	↕	↕	X	V	0	↕	4	15
ADC HL,SP	ED7A	Add contents of SP and the carry flag to HL	↕	↕	X	V	0	↕	4	15
ADD A,(HL)	86	Add contents of memory pointed to by HL to the accumulator	↕	↕	↕	V	0	↕	2	7
ADD A,(IX+d)	DD86d	Add contents of memory pointed to by IX+d to the accumulator	↕	↕	↕	V	0	↕	5	19
ADD A,(IY+d)	FD86d	Add contents of memory pointed to by IY+d to the accumulator	↕	↕	↕	V	0	↕	5	19
ADD A,A	87	Add contents of accumulator to itself	↕	↕	↕	V	0	↕	1	4
ADD A,B	80	Add contents of register B to the accumulator	↕	↕	↕	V	0	↕	1	4
ADD A,C	81	Add contents of register C to the accumulator	↕	↕	↕	V	0	↕	1	4
ADD A,D	82	Add contents of register D to the accumulator	↕	↕	↕	V	0	↕	1	4
ADD A,E	83	Add contents of register E to the accumulator	↕	↕	↕	V	0	↕	1	4
ADD A,H	84	Add contents of register H to the accumulator	↕	↕	↕	V	0	↕	1	4

MNEMONIC	OP CODE	COMMENT	FLAGS S	Z	H	P/V	N	C	M CYCLES	T STATES
ADD A,L	85	Add contents of register L to the accumulator	↕	↕	↕	V	0	↕	1	4
ADD A,n	C6n	Add byte 2 to the accumulator	↕	↕	↕	V	0	↕	2	7
ADD HL,BC	09	Add contents of register pair BC to HL	.	.	X	.	0	↕	3	11
ADD HL,DE	19	Add contents of register pair DE to HL	.	.	X	.	0	↕	3	11
ADD HL,HL	29	Add contents of register pair HL to HL	.	.	X	.	0	↕	3	11
ADD HL,SP	39	Add contents of the stack pointer to HL	.	.	X	.	0	↕	3	11
ADD IX,BC	DD09	Add contents of register pair BC to IX	.	.	X	.	0	↕	4	15
ADD IX,DE	DD19	Add contents of register pair DE to IX	.	.	X	.	0	↕	4	15
ADD IX,IX	DD29	Add contents of index register IX to IX	.	.	X	.	0	↕	4	15
ADD IX,SP	DD39	Add contents of the stack pointer to IX	.	.	X	.	0	↕	4	15
ADD IY,BC	FD09	Add contents of register pair BC to IY	.	.	X	.	0	↕	4	15
ADD IY,DE	FD19	Add contents of register pair to DE to IY	.	.	X	.	0	↕	4	15
ADD IY,IY	FD29	Add contents of index register IY to IY	.	.	X	.	0	↕	4	15
ADD IY,SP	FD39	Add contents of the stack pointer to IY	.	.	X	.	0	↕	4	15
AND (HL)	A6	AND contents of memory pointed to by HL with the accumulator	↕	↕	1	P	0	0	2	7
AND (IX+d)	DDA6d	AND contents of memory pointed to by IX+d with the accumulator	↕	↕	1	P	0	0	5	19
AND (IY+d)	FDA6d	AND contents of memory pointed to by IY+d with the accumulator	↕	↕	1	P	0	0	5	19
AND A	A7	AND contents of accumulator with accumulator	↕	↕	1	P	0	0	1	4
AND B	A0	AND contents of register B with the accumulator	↕	↕	1	P	0	0	1	4
AND C	A1	AND contents of register C with the accumulator	↕	↕	1	P	0	0	1	4
AND D	A2	AND contents of register D with the accumulator	↕	↕	1	P	0	0	1	4
AND E	A3	AND contents of register E with accumulator	↕	↕	1	P	0	0	1	4
AND H	A4	AND contents of register H with the accumulator	↕	↕	1	P	0	0	1	4
AND L	A5	AND contents of register L with the accumulator	↕	↕	1	P	0	0	1	4
AND n	E6n	AND byte 2 with the accumulator	↕	↕	1	P	0	0	2	7
BIT 0,(HL)	CB46	If bit 0 of memory pointed to by HL is 0, set the zero flag (Z=1). Otherwise Z=0	X	↕	1	X	0	.	3	12
BIT 0,(IX+d)	DDCBd46	If bit 0 of memory pointed to by IX+d is 0, set the zero flag (Z=1). Otherwise Z=0	X	↕	1	X	0	.	5	20
BIT 0,(IY+d)	FDCBd46	If bit 0 of memory pointed to by IY+d is 0, set the zero flag (Z=1). Otherwise Z=0	X	↕	1	X	0	.	5	20
BIT 0,A	CB47	If bit 0 of the accumulator is 0, set the zero flag (Z=1). Otherwise Z=0	X	↕	1	X	0	.	2	8
BIT 0,B	CB40	If bit 0 of register B is 0, set the zero flag (Z=1). Otherwise Z=0	X	↕	1	X	0	.	2	8
BIT 0,C	CB41	If bit 0 of register C is 0, set the zero flag (Z=1). Otherwise Z=0	X	↕	1	X	0	.	2	8

MNEMONIC	OP CODE	COMMENT	FLAGS S	Z	H	P/V	N	C	M CYCLES	T STATES
BIT 0,D	CB42	If bit 0 of register D is 0, set the zero flag (Z=1). Otherwise Z=0	X	↕	1	X	0	.	2	8
BIT 0,E	CB43	If bit 0 of register E is 0, set the zero flag (Z=1). Otherwise Z=0	X	↕	1	X	0	.	2	8
BIT 0,H	CB44	If bit 0 of register H is 0, set the zero flag (Z=1). Otherwise Z=0	X	↕	1	X	0	.	2	8
BIT 0,L	CB45	If bit 0 of register L is 0, set the zero flag (Z=1). Otherwise Z=0	X	↕	1	X	0	.	2	8
BIT 1,(HL)	CB4E	If bit 1 of memory pointed to by HL is 0, set the zero flag (Z=1). Otherwise Z=0	X	↕	1	X	0	.	3	12
BIT 1,(IX+d)	DDCBd4E	If bit 1 of memory pointed to by IX+d is 0, set the zero flag (Z=1). Otherwise Z=0	X	↕	1	X	0	.	5	20
BIT 1,(IY+d)	FDCBd4E	If bit 1 of memory poined to by IY+d is 0, set the zero flag (Z=1). Otherwise Z=0	X	↕	1	X	0	.	5	20
BIT 1,A	CB4F	If bit 1 of the accumulator is 0, set the zero flag (Z=1). Otherwise Z=0	X	↕	1	X	0	.	2	8
BIT 1,B	CB48	If bit 1 of register B is 0, set the zero flag (Z=1). Otherwise Z=0	X	↕	1	X	0	.	2	8
BIT 1,C	CB49	If bit 1 of register C is 0, set the zero flag (Z=1). Otherwise Z=0	X	↕	1	X	0	.	2	8
BIT 1,D	CB4A	If bit 1 of register D is 0, set the zero flag (Z=1). Otherwise Z=0	X	↕	1	X	0	.	2	8
BIT 1,E	CB4B	If bit 1 of register E is 0, set the zero flag (Z=1). Otherwise Z=0	X	↕	1	X	0	.	2	8
BIT 1,H	CB4C	If bit 1 of register H is 0, set the zero flag (Z=1). Otherwise Z=0	X	↕	1	X	0	.	2	8
BIT 1,L	CB4D	If bit 1 of register L is 0, set the zero flag (Z=1). Otherwise Z=0	X	↕	1	X	0	.	2	8
BIT 2,(HL)	CB56	If bit 2 of memory pointed to by HL is 0, set the zero flag (Z=1). Otherwise Z=0	X	↕	1	X	0	.	3	12
BIT 2,(IX+d)	DDCBd56	If bit 2 of memory pointed to by IX+d is 0, set the zero flag (Z=1). Otherwise Z=0	X	↕	1	X	0	.	5	20
BIT 2,(IY+d)	FDCBd56	If bit 2 of memory pointed to by IY+d is 0, set the zero flag (Z=1). Otherwise Z=0	X	↕	1	X	0	.	5	20
BIT 2,A	CB57	If bit 2 of the accumulator is 0, set the zero flag (Z=1). Otherwise Z=0	X	↕	1	X	0	.	2	8
BIT 2,B	CB50	If bit 2 of register B is 0, set the zero flag (Z=1). Otherwise Z=0	X	↕	1	X	0	.	2	8
BIT 2,C	CB51	If bit 2 of register C is 0, set the zero flag (Z=1). Otherwise Z=0	X	↕	1	X	0	.	2	8
BIT 2,D	CB52	If bit 2 of register D is 0, set the zero flag (Z=1). Otherwise Z=0	X	↕	1	X	0	.	2	8
BIT 2,E	CB53	If bit 2 of register E is 0, set the zero flag (Z=1). Otherwise Z=0	X	↕	1	X	0	.	2	8
BIT 2,H	CB54	If bit 2 of register H is 0, set the zero flag (Z=1). Otherwise Z=0	X	↕	1	X	0	.	2	8

MNEMONIC	OP CODE	COMMENT	S	Z	H	P/V	N	C	M CYCLES	T STATES
			FLAGS							
BIT 2,L	CB55	If bit 2 of register L is 0, set the zero flag (Z=1). Otherwise Z=0	X	↕	1	X	0	.	2	8
BIT 3,(HL)	CB5E	If bit 3 of memory pointed to by HL is 0, set the zero flag (Z=1). Otherwise Z=0	X	↕	1	X	0	.	3	12
BIT 3,(IX+d)	DDCBd5E	If bit 3 of memory pointed to by IX+d is 0, set the zero flag (Z=1). Otherwise Z=0	X	↕	1	X	0	.	5	20
BIT 3,(IY+d)	FDCBd5E	If bit 3 of memory pointed to by IY+d is 0, set the zero flag (Z=1). Otherwise Z=0	X	↕	1	X	0	.	5	20
BIT 3,A	CB5F	If bit 3 of the accumulator is 0, set the zero flag (Z=1). Otherwise Z=0	X	↕	1	X	0	.	2	8
BIT 3,B	CB58	If bit 3 of register B is 0, set the zero flag (Z=1). Otherwise Z=0	X	↕	1	X	0	.	2	8
BIT 3,C	CB59	If bit 3 of register C is 0, set the zero flag (Z=1). Otherwise Z=0	X	↕	1	X	0	.	2	8
BIT 3,D	CB5A	If bit 3 of register D is 0, set the zero flag (Z=1). Otherwise Z=0	X	↕	1	X	0	.	2	8
BIT 3,E	CB5B	If bit 3 of register E is 0, set the zero flag (Z=1). Otherwise Z=0	X	↕	1	X	0	.	2	8
BIT 3,H	CB5C	If bit 3 of register H is 0, set the zero flag (Z=1). Otherwise Z=0	X	↕	1	X	0	.	2	8
BIT 3,L	CB5D	If bit 3 of register L is 0, set the zero flag (Z=1). Otherwise Z=0	X	↕	1	X	0	.	2	8
BIT 4,(HL)	CB66	If bit 4 of memory pointed to by HL is 0, set the zero flag (Z=1). Otherwise Z=0	X	↕	1	X	0	.	3	12
BIT 4,(IX+d)	DDCBd66	If bit 4 of memory pointed to by IX+d is 0, set the zero flag (Z=1). Otherwise Z=0	X	↕	1	X	0	.	5	20
BIT 4,(IY+d)	FDCBd66	If bit 4 of memory pointed to by IY+d is 0, set the zero flag (Z=1). Otherwise Z=0	X	↕	1	X	0	.	5	20
BIT 4,A	CB67	If bit 4 of the accumulator is 0, set the zero flag (Z=1). Otherwise Z=0	X	↕	1	X	0	.	2	8
BIT 4,B	CB60	If bit 4 of register B is 0, set the zero flag (Z=1). Otherwise Z=0	X	↕	1	X	0	.	2	8
BIT 4,C	CB61	If bit 4 of register C is 0, set the zero flag (Z=1). Otherwise Z=0	X	↕	1	X	0	.	2	8
BIT 4,D	CB62	If bit 4 of register D is 0, set the zero flag (Z=1). Otherwise Z=0	X	↕	1	X	0	.	2	8
BIT 4,E	CB63	If bit 4 of register E is 0, set the zero flag (Z=1). Otherwise Z=0	X	↕	1	X	0	.	2	8
BIT 4,H	CB64	If bit 4 of register H is 0, set the zero flag (Z=1). Otherwise Z=0	X	↕	1	X	0	.	2	8
BIT 4,L	CB65	If bit 4 of register L is 0, set the zero flag (Z=1). Otherwise Z=0	X	↕	1	X	0	.	2	8
BIT 5,(HL)	CB6E	If bit 5 of memory pointed to by HL is 0, set the zero flag (Z=1). Otherwise Z=0	X	↕	1	X	0	.	3	12
BIT 5,(IX+d)	DDCBd6E	If bit 5 of memory pointed to by IX+d is 0, set the zero flag (Z=1). Otherwise Z=0	X	↕	1	X	0	.	5	20
BIT 5,(IY+d)	FDCBd6E	If bit 5 of memory pointed to by IY+d is 0, set the zero flag (Z=1). Otherwise Z=0	X	↕	1	X	0	.	5	20

MNEMONIC	OP CODE	COMMENT	S	Z	H	P/V	N	C	M CYCLES	T STATES
			FLAGS							
BIT 5,A	CB6F	If bit 5 of the accumulator is 0, set the zero flag (Z=1). Otherwise Z=0	X	↕	1	X	0	.	2	8
BIT 5,B	CB68	If bit 5 of register B is 0, set the zero flag (Z=1). Otherwise Z=0	X	↕	1	X	0	.	2	8
BIT 5,C	CB69	If bit 5 of register C is 0, set the zero flag (Z=1). Otherwise Z=0	X	↕	1	X	0	.	2	8
BIT 5,D	CB6A	If bit 5 of register D is 0, set the zero flag (Z=1). Otherwise Z=0	X	↕	1	X	0	.	2	8
BIT 5,E	CB6B	If bit 5 of register E is 0, set the zero flag (Z=1). Otherwise Z=0	X	↕	1	X	0	.	2	8
BIT 5,H	CB6C	If bit 5 of register H is 0, set the zero flag (Z=1). Otherwise Z=0	X	↕	1	X	0	.	2	8
BIT 5,L	CB6D	If bit 5 of register L is 0, set the zero flag (Z=1). Otherwise Z=0	X	↕	1	X	0	.	2	8
BIT 6,(HL)	CB76	If bit 6 of memory pointed to by HL is 0, set the zero flag (Z=1). Otherwise Z=0	X	↕	1	X	0	.	3	12
BIT 6,(IX+d)	DDCBd76	If bit 6 of memory pointed to by IX+d is 0, set the zero flag (Z=1). Otherwise Z=0	X	↕	1	X	0	.	5	20
BIT 6,(IY+d)	FDCBd76	If bit 6 of memory pointed to by IY+d is 0, set the zero flag (Z=1). Otherwise Z=0	X	↕	1	X	0	.	5	20
BIT 6,A	CB77	If bit 6 of the accumulator is 0, set the zero flag (Z=1). Otherwise Z=0	X	↕	1	X	0	.	2	8
BIT 6,B	CB70	If bit 6 of register B is 0, set the zero flag (Z=1). Otherwise Z=0	X	↕	1	X	0	.	2	8
BIT 6,C	CB71	If bit 6 of register C is 0, set the zero flag (Z=1). Otherwise Z=0	X	↕	1	X	0	.	2	8
BIT 6,D	CB72	If bit 6 of register D is 0, set the zero flag (Z=1). Otherwise Z=0	X	↕	1	X	0	.	2	8
BIT 6,E	CB73	If bit 6 of register E is 0, set the zero flag (Z=1). Otherwise Z=0	X	↕	1	X	0	.	2	8
BIT 6,H	CB74	If bit 6 of register H is 0, set the zero flag (Z=1). Otherwise Z=0	X	↕	1	X	0	.	2	8
BIT 6,L	CB75	If bit 6 of register L is 0, set the zero flag (Z=1). Otherwise Z=0	X	↕	1	X	0	.	2	8
BIT 7,(HL)	CB7E	If bit 7 of memory pointed to by HL is 0, set the zero flag (Z=1). Otherwise Z=0	X	↕	1	X	0	.	3	12
BIT 7,(IX+d)	DDCBd7E	If bit 7 of memory pointed to by IX+d is 0, set the zero flag (Z=1). Otherwise Z=0	X	↕	1	X	0	.	5	20
BIT 7,(IY+d)	FDCBd7E	If bit 7 of memory pointed to by IY+d is 0, set the zero flag (Z=1). Otherwise Z=0	X	↕	1	X	0	.	5	20
BIT 7,A	CB7F	If bit 7 of the accumulator is 0, set the zero flag (Z=1). Otherwise Z=0	X	↕	1	X	0	.	2	8
BIT 7,B	CB78	If bit 7 of register B is 0, set the zero flag (Z=1). Otherwise Z=0	X	↕	1	X	0	.	2	8
BIT 7,C	CB79	If bit 7 of register C is 0, set the zero flag (Z=1). Otherwise Z=0	X	↕	1	X	0	.	2	8
BIT 7,D	CB7A	If bit 7 of register D is 0, set the zero flag (Z=1). Otherwise Z=0	X	↕	1	X	0	.	2	8

MNEMONIC	OP CODE	COMMENT	S	Z	H	P/V	N	C	M CYCLES	T STATES
					FLAGS					
BIT 7,E	CB7B	If bit 7 of register E is 0, set the zero flag (Z=1). Otherwise Z−0	X	↕	1	X	0	.	2	8
BIT 7,H	CB7C	If bit 7 of register H is 0, set the zero flag (Z=1). Otherwise Z=0	X	↕	1	X	0	.	2	8
BIT 7,L	CB7D	If bit 7 of register L is 0, set the zero flag (Z=1). Otherwise Z=0	X	↕	1	X	0	.	2	8
CALL C,nn	DCnn	If carry flag=0, disregard instruction. If carry flag=1, call subroutine at address pointed to by bytes 3 and 2	.	.	.	.	.	.	3 (if C=0) 5 (if C=1)	10 17
CALL M,nn	FCnn	If sign flag=0, disregard instruction. If sign flag=1, call subroutine at address pointed to by bytes 3 and 2	.	.	.	.	.	.	3 (if S=0) 5 (if S=1)	10 17
CALL NC,nn	D4nn	If carry flag=1, disregard instruction. If carry flag=0 call subroutine at address pointed to by bytes 3 and 2	.	.	.	.	.	.	3 (if C=1) 5 (if C=0)	10 17
CALL nn	CDnn	Call subroutine at address pointed to by bytes 3 and 2	.	.	.	.	.	.	5	17
CALL NZ,nn	C4nn	If zero flag=1, disregard instruction. If zero flag=0, call subroutine at address pointed to by bytes 3 and 2	.	.	.	.	.	.	3 (if Z=1) 5 (if Z=0)	10 17
CALL P,nn	F4nn	If sign flag=1, disregard instruction. If sign flag=0, call subroutine at address pointed to by bytes 3 and 2	.	.	.	.	.	.	3 (if S=1) 5 (if S=0)	10 17
CALL PE,nn	ECnn	If parity flag=0, disregard instruction. If parity flag=1, call subroutine at address pointed to by bytes 3 and 2	.	.	.	.	.	.	3 (if P=0) 5 (if P=1)	10 17
CALL PO,nn	E4nn	If parity flag=1, disregard instruction. If parity flag=0, call subroutine at address pointed to by bytes 3 and 2	.	.	.	.	.	.	3 (if P=1) 5 (if P=0)	10 17
CALL Z,nn	CCnn	If zero flag=0, disregard instruction. If zero flag=1, call subroutine at address pointed to by bytes 3 and 2	.	.	.	.	.	.	3 (if Z=0) 5 (if Z=1)	10 17
CCF	3F	Complement the carry flag.	.	.	X	.	0	↕	1	4
CP (HL)	BE	Compare the contents of memory pointed to by HL with the accumulator	↕	↕	↕	V	1	↕	2	7
CP (IX+d)	DDBEd	Compare the memory pointed to by IX+d with the accumulator	↕	↕	↕	V	1	↕	5	19
CP (IY+d)	FDBEd	Compare the contents of memory pointed to by IY+d with the accumulator	↕	↕	↕	V	1	↕	5	19

MNEMONIC	OP CODE	COMMENT	FLAGS S	Z	H	P/V	N	C	M CYCLES	T STATES
CP A	BF	Compare the contents of accumulator with the accumulator	↕	↕	↕	V	1	↕	1	4
CP B	B8	Compare the contents of register B with the accumulator	↕	↕	↕	V	1	↕	1	4
CP C	B9	Compare the contents of register C with the accumulator	↕	↕	↕	V	1	↕	1	4
CP D	BA	Compare the contents of register D with the accumulator	↕	↕	↕	V	1	↕	1	4
CP E	BB	Compare the contents of register E with the accumulator	↕	↕	↕	V	1	↕	1	4
CP H	BC	Compare the contents of register H with the accumulator	↕	↕	↕	V	1	↕	1	4
CP L	BD	Compare the contents of register L with the accumulator	↕	↕	↕	V	1	↕	1	4
CP n	FEn	Compare byte 2 with contents of accumulator	↕	↕	↕	V	1	↕	2	7
CPD	EDA9	Compare the contents of memory pointed to by HL with the accumulator. Decrement HL and BC. When BC = 0, P/V = 0; otherwise P/V = 1. When A = (HL), Z = 1; otherwise Z = 0	↕	↕	↕	↕	1	.	4	16
CPDR	EDB9	Compare the contents of memory pointed to by HL with the accumulator. Decrement HL and BC. Repeat until the memory pointed by HL equals A or until BC = 0. When BC = 0, P/V = 0; otherwise P/V = 1. When A = (HL), Z = 1; otherwise Z = 0	↕	↕	↕	↕	1	.	5 [if BC ≠ 0 and A ≠ (HL)] 4 [if BC = 0 or A = (HL)]	21 16
CPI	EDA1	Compare the contents of memory pointed to by HL with the accumulator. Increment HL. Decrement BC. When BC = 0, P/V = 0; otherwise P/V = 1. When A = (HL), Z = 1; otherwise Z = 0	↕	↕	↕	↕	1	.	4	16
CPIR	EDB1	Compare the contents of memory pointed to by HL with the accumulator. Increment HL. Decrement BC. Repeat until memory pointed to by HL = A or until BC = 0. When BC = 0, P/V = 0; otherwise P/V = 1. When A = (HL), Z = 1; otherwise Z = 0	↕	↕	↕	↕	1	.	5 [if BC ≠ 0 and A ≠ (HL)] 4 [if BC = 0 or A = (HL)]	21 16
CPL	2F	Complement accumulator (1's complement)	.	.	1	.	1	.	1	4
DAA	27	Decimal adjust the accumulator	↕	↕	↕	P	.	↕	1	4
DEC (HL)	35	Decrement the contents of memory pointed to by HL	↕	↕	↕	V	1	.	3	11
DEC (IX + d)	DD35d	Decrement the contents of memory pointed to by IX + d	↕	↕	↕	V	1	.	6	23

MNEMONIC	OP CODE	COMMENT	S	Z	H	P/V	N	C	M CYCLES	T STATES
DEC (IY+d)	FD35d	Decrement the contents of memory pointed to by IY+d	↕	↕	↕	V	1	.	6	23
DEC A	3D	Decrement contents of accumulator	↕	↕	↕	V	1	.	1	4
DEC B	05	Decrement B	↕	↕	↕	V	1	.	1	4
DEC BC	0B	Decrement BC	.	.	.	.	.	.	1	6
DEC C	0D	Decrement C	↕	↕	↕	V	1	.	1	4
DEC D	15	Decrement D	↕	↕	↕	V	1	.	1	4
DEC DE	1B	Decrement DE	.	.	.	.	.	.	1	6
DEC E	1D	Decrement E	↕	↕	↕	V	1	.	1	4
DEC H	25	Decrement H	↕	↕	↕	V	1	.	1	4
DEC HL	2B	Decrement HL	.	.	.	.	.	.	1	6
DEC IX	DD2B	Decrement contents of IX	.	.	.	.	.	.	2	10
DEC IY	FD2B	Decrement contents of IY	.	.	.	.	.	.	2	10
DEC L	2D	Decrement L	↕	↕	↕	V	1	.	1	4
DEC SP	3B	Decrement contents of the stack pointer	.	.	.	.	.	.	1	6
DI	F3	Disable interrupt (reset interrupt flip-flop to 0)	.	.	.	.	.	.	1	4
DJNZ,e	10e	Decrement B. If B=0, continue to next instruction. If B≠0, jump to PC+e	.	.	.	.	.	.	2 (if B=0) 3 (if B≠0)	8 13
EI	FB	Enable interrupt (set interrupt flip-flop to 1)	.	.	.	.	.	.	1	4
EX (SP),HL	E3	Exchange contents of L with contents of memory pointed to by SP. Exchange contents of H with contents of memory pointed to by SP+1	.	.	.	.	.	.	5	19
EX (SP),IX	DDE3	Exchange contents of the stack pointer with the LOW byte of IX. Exchange the contents of SP+1 with the HIGH byte of IX	.	.	.	.	.	.	6	23
EX (SP),IY	FDE3	Exchange contents of the stack pointer with the LOW byte of IY. Exchange the contents of SP+1 with the HIGH byte of IY	.	.	.	.	.	.	6	23
EX AF,AF′	08	Exchange contents of A and A′ and F and F′	.	.	.	.	.	.	1	4
EX DE,HL	EB	Exchange contents of L with contents of E and contents of H with contents of D	.	.	.	.	.	.	1	4
EXX	D9	Exchange contents of BC, DE, HL with BC′, DE′, HL′, respectively	.	.	.	.	.	.	1	4
HALT	76	HALT	.	.	.	.	.	.	1	4
IM 0	ED46	Set interrupt mode to 0	.	.	.	.	.	.	2	8
IM 1	ED56	Set interrupt mode to 1	.	.	.	.	.	.	2	8
IM 2	ED5E	Set interrupt mode to 2	.	.	.	.	.	.	2	8
IN A,(C)	ED78	Input the data from the port pointed to by C into the accumulator	↕	↕	↕	P	0	.	3	12

MNEMONIC	OP CODE	COMMENT	S	Z	H	P/V	N	C	M CYCLES	T STATES
			FLAGS							
IN A,(n)	DBn	Input contents of input port pointed to by byte 2 into the accumulator	↕	↕	↕	P	0	.	3	11
IN B,(C)	ED40	Input data from port pointed to by C into register B	↕	↕	↕	P	0	.	3	12
IN C,(C)	ED48	Input data from port pointed to by C into register C	↕	↕	↕	P	0	.	3	12
IN D,(C)	ED50	Input data from port pointed to by C into register D	↕	↕	↕	P	0	.	3	12
IN E,(C)	ED58	Input data from port pointed to by C into register E	↕	↕	↕	P	0	.	3	12
IN H,(C)	ED60	Input data from port pointed to by C into register H	↕	↕	↕	P	0	.	3	12
IN L,(C)	ED68	Input data from port pointed to by C into register L	↕	↕	↕	P	0	.	3	12
INC (HL)	34	Increment contents of memory pointed to by HL	↕	↕	↕	V	0	.	3	11
INC (IX+d)	DD34d	Increment contents of memory pointed to by IX+d	↕	↕	↕	V	0	.	6	23
INC (IY+d)	FD34d	Increment contents of memory pointed to by IY+d	↕	↕	↕	V	0	.	6	23
INC A	3C	Increment contents of accumulator	↕	↕	↕	V	0	.	1	4
INC B	04	Increment B	↕	↕	↕	V	0	.	1	4
INC BC	03	Increment BC	.	.	.	.	.	.	1	6
INC C	0C	Increment C	↕	↕	↕	V	0	.	1	4
INC D	14	Increment D	↕	↕	↕	V	0	.	1	4
INC DE	13	Increment DE	.	.	.	.	.	.	1	6
INC E	1C	Increment E	↕	↕	↕	V	0	.	1	4
INC H	24	Increment H	↕	↕	↕	V	0	.	1	4
INC HL	23	Increment HL	.	.	.	.	.	.	1	6
INC IX	DD23	Increment contents of IX	.	.	.	.	.	.	2	10
INC IY	FD23	Increment contents of IY	.	.	.	.	.	.	2	10
INC L	2C	Increment L	↕	↕	↕	V	0	.	1	4
INC SP	33	Increment stack pointer	.	.	.	.	.	.	1	6
IND	EDAA	Input data from input port pointed to by C into memory pointed to by HL. Decrement B and set the zero flag if B=0; otherwise Z=0. Decrement HL	X	↕	X	X	1	X	4	16
INDR	EDBA	Input data from input port pointed to by C into memory pointed to by HL. Decrement B. Decrement HL. Repeat until B=0	X	1	X	X	1	X	5 (if B≠0) 4 (if B=0)	21 16
INI	EDA2	Input data from input port pointed to by C into memory pointed to by HL. Decrement B and set the zero flag if B=0; otherwise Z=0. Increment HL	X	↕	X	X	1	X	4	16

MNEMONIC	OP CODE	COMMENT	S	Z	H	P/V	N	C	M CYCLES	T STATES
INIR	EDB2	Input data from input port pointed to by C into memory pointed to by HL. Decrement B. Increment HL. Repeat B=0	X	1	X	X	1	X	5 (if B≠0) 4 (if B=0)	12 16
JP (HL)	E9	Jump to the address pointed to by HL	.	.	.	.	.	.	1	4
JP (IX)	DDE9	Jump to the address pointed to by IX	.	.	.	.	.	.	2	8
JP (IY)	FDE9	Jump to the address pointed to by IY	.	.	.	.	.	.	2	8
JP C,nn	DAnn	If C=0, disregard instruction. If C=1, jump to address pointed to by bytes 3 and 2	.	.	.	.	.	.	3	10
JP M,nn	FAnn	If sign flag=0, disregard instruction. If sign flag=1, jump to address pointed to by bytes 3 and 2	.	.	.	.	.	.	3	10
JP NC,nn	D2nn	If carry flag=1, disregard instruction. If carry flag=0, jump to address pointed to by bytes 3 and 2	.	.	.	.	.	.	3	10
JP nn	C3nn	Unconditional jump to address pointed to by bytes 3 and 2	.	.	.	.	.	.	3	10
JP NZ,nn	C2nn	If zero flag=1 disregard instruction. If zero flag=0, jump to address pointed to bytes 3 and 2	.	.	.	.	.	.	3	10
JP P,nn	F2nn	If sign flag=1, disregard instruction. If sign flag=0, jump to address pointed to by bytes 3 and 2	.	.	.	.	.	.	3	10
JP PE,nn	EAnn	If parity flag=0, disregard instruction. If parity flag=1, jump to address pointed to by bytes 3 and 2	.	.	.	.	.	.	3	10
JP PO,nn	E2nn	If parity flag=1, disregard instruction. If parity flag=0, jump to address pointed to by bytes 3 and 2	.	.	.	.	.	.	3	10
JP Z,nn	CAnn	If zero flag=0, then disregard instruction. If zero flag=1, then jump to address pointed to by bytes 3 and 2	.	.	.	.	.	.	3	10
JR C,e	38e	If carry flag=0, disregard instruction. If carry flag=1, jump to PC+e	.	.	.	.	.	.	2 (if C=0) 3 (if C=1)	7 12
JR e	18e	Unconditional relative jump to PC + e	.	.	.	.	.	.	3	12
JR NC,e	30e	If carry flag=1, disregard jump. If C=0, jump to PC+e	.	.	.	.	.	.	2 (if C=1) 3 (if C=0)	7 12
JR NZ,e	20e	If Z=1, disregard instructions. If Z=0, jump to PC+e	.	.	.	.	.	.	2 (if Z=1) 3 (if Z=0)	7 12

MNEMONIC	OP CODE	COMMENT	FLAGS S	Z	H	P/V	N	C	M CYCLES	T STATES
JR Z,e	28e	If Z=0, continue. If Z=1, jump to PC+e	.	.	.	.	.	.	2 (if Z=0) 3 (if Z=1)	7 12
LD (BC),A	02	Load accumulator into memory pointed to by BC	.	.	.	.	.	.	2	7
LD (DE),A	12	Load contents of accumulator into memory pointed to by DE	.	.	.	.	.	.	2	7
LD (HL),A	77	Load contents of accumulator into memory pointed to by HL	.	.	.	.	.	.	2	7
LD (HL),B	70	Load contents of B into memory pointed to by HL	.	.	.	.	.	.	2	7
LD (HL),C	71	Load contents of C into memory pointed to by HL	.	.	.	.	.	.	2	7
LD (HL),D	72	Load contents of D into memory pointed to by HL	.	.	.	.	.	.	2	7
LD (HL),E	73	Load contents of E into memory pointed to by HL	.	.	.	.	.	.	2	7
LD (HL),H	74	Load contents of H into memory pointed to by HL	.	.	.	.	.	.	2	7
LD (HL),L	75	Load contents of L into memory pointed by HL	.	.	.	.	.	.	2	7
LD (HL),n	36n	Load byte 2 into the address pointed to by HL	.	.	.	.	.	.	3	10
LD (IX+d),A	DD77d	Load contents of accumulator into memory pointed to by IX+d	.	.	.	.	.	.	5	19
LD (IX+d),B	DD70d	Load contents of register B into memory pointed to by IX+d	.	.	.	.	.	.	5	19
LD (IX+d),C	DD71d	Load contents of register C into memory pointed to by IX+d	.	.	.	.	.	.	5	19
LD (IX+d),D	DD72d	Load contents of register D into memory pointed to by IX+d	.	.	.	.	.	.	5	19
LD (IX+d),E	DD73d	Load contents of register E into memory pointed to by IX+d	.	.	.	.	.	.	5	19
LD (IX+d),H	DD74d	Load contents of register H into memory pointed to by IX+d	.	.	.	.	.	.	5	19
LD (IX+d),L	DD75d	Load contents of register L into memory pointed to by IX+d	.	.	.	.	.	.	5	19
LD (IX+d),n	DD36dn	Load data in byte 4 into memory pointed to by IX+d	.	.	.	.	.	.	5	19
LD (IY+d),A	FD77d	Load contents of the accumulator into memory pointed to by IY+d	.	.	.	.	.	.	5	19
LD (IY+d),B	FD70d	Load contents of register B into memory pointed to by IY+d	.	.	.	.	.	.	5	19
LD (IY+d),C	FD71d	Load contents of register C into memory pointed to by IY+d	.	.	.	.	.	.	5	19

MNEMONIC	OP CODE	COMMENT	S	Z	H	P/V	N	C	M CYCLES	T STATES
LD (IY+d),D	FD72d	Load contents of register D into memory pointed to by IY+d	.	.	.	.	.	.	5	19
LD (IY+d),E	FD73d	Load contents of register E into memory pointed to by IY+d	.	.	.	.	.	.	5	19
LD (IY+d),H	FD74d	Load contents of register H into memory pointed to by IY+d	.	.	.	.	.	.	5	19
LD (IY+d),L	FD75d	Load contents of register L into memory pointed to by IY+d	.	.	.	.	.	.	5	19
LD (IY+d),n	FD36dn	Load data in byte 4 into memory pointed to by IY+d	.	.	.	.	.	.	5	19
LD (nn),A	32nn	Load contents of A into memory pointed to by bytes 3 and 2	.	.	.	.	.	.	4	13
LD (nn),BC	ED43nn	Load contents of C into memory pointed to by bytes 4 and 3. Load B into the following address	.	.	.	.	.	.	6	20
LD (nn),DE	ED53nn	Load contents of E into memory pointed to by bytes 4 and 3. Load D into following address	.	.	.	.	.	.	6	20
LD (nn),HL	22nn	Load L into memory pointed to by bytes 3 and 2. Load H into the next higher address	.	.	.	.	.	.	5	16
LD (nn),IX	DD22nn	Load the LOW byte of the IX register into memory pointed to by bytes 4 and 3. Load the HIGH byte of IX into the next higher address	.	.	.	.	.	.	6	20
LD (nn),IY	FD22nn	Load the LOW byte of the IY register into memory pointed to by bytes 4 and 3. Load the HIGH byte of IY into the next higher address	.	.	.	.	.	.	6	20
LD (nn),SP	ED73nn	Load the LOW byte of the stack pointer into the address pointed to by bytes 4 and 3. Load the HIGH byte of SP into the next higher address	.	.	.	.	.	.	6	20
LD A,(BC)	0A	Load contents of memory pointed to by BC into the accumulator	.	.	.	.	.	.	2	7
LD A,(DE)	1A	Load contents of memory pointed to by DE into the accumulator	.	.	.	.	.	.	2	7
LD A,(HL)	7E	Load contents of memory pointed to by HL into the accumulator	.	.	.	.	.	.	2	7
LD A,(IX+d)	DD7Ed	Load contents of memory pointed to by IX+d into the accumulator	.	.	.	.	.	.	5	19
LD A,(IY+d)	FD7Ed	Load contents of memory pointed to by IY+d into the accumulator	.	.	.	.	.	.	5	19
LD A,(nn)	3Ann	Load contents of memory pointed to by bytes 3 and 2 into the accumulator	.	.	.	.	.	.	4	13
LD A,A	7F	Load contents of accumulator into the accumulator	.	.	.	.	.	.	1	4

MNEMONIC	OP CODE	COMMENT	FLAGS S	Z	H	P/V	N	C	M CYCLES	T STATES
LD A,B	78	Load contents of register B into A	.	.	.	.	.	.	1	4
LD A,C	79	Load contents of register C into A	.	.	.	.	.	.	1	4
LD A,D	7A	Load contents of register D into A	.	.	.	.	.	.	1	4
LD A,E	7B	Load contents of register E into A	.	.	.	.	.	.	1	4
LD A,H	7C	Load contents of register H into A	.	.	.	.	.	.	1	4
LD A,I	ED57	Load contents of register I into A. Contents of IFF (interrupt enable flip-flop) determines P/V.	↕	↕	0	↕	0	.	2	9
LD A,L	7D	Load contents of register L into A	.	.	.	.	.	.	1	4
LD A,n	3En	Load data in byte 2 into the accumulator	.	.	.	.	.	.	2	7
LD A,R	ED5F	Load contents of register R into accumulator. Contents of IFF (interrupt enable flip-flop) determines P/V	↕	↕	0	↕	.	.	2	9
LD B,(HL)	46	Load contents of memory pointed to by HL into B	.	.	.	.	.	.	2	7
LD B,(IX+d)	DD46d	Load contents of memory pointed to by IX+d into B	.	.	.	.	.	.	5	19
LD B,(IY+d)	FD46d	Load contents of memory pointed to by IY+d into B	.	.	.	.	.	.	5	19
LD B,A	47	Load contents of accumulator into B	.	.	.	.	.	.	1	4
LD B,B	40	Load contents of register B into B	.	.	.	.	.	.	1	4
LD B,C	41	Load contents of register C into B	.	.	.	.	.	.	1	4
LD B,D	42	Load contents of register D into B	.	.	.	.	.	.	1	4
LD B,E	43	Load contents of register E into B	.	.	.	.	.	.	1	4
LD B,H	44	Load contents of register H into B	.	.	.	.	.	.	1	4
LD B,L	45	Load contents of register L into B	.	.	.	.	.	.	1	4
LD B,n	06n	Load data in byte 2 into B	.	.	.	.	.	.	2	7
LD BC,(nn)	ED4Bnn	Load contents of memory pointed to by bytes 4 and 3 into C. Load the next byte in memory into B	.	.	.	.	.	.	6	20
LD BC,nn	01nn	Load the data in byte 2 into register C. Load the data in byte 3 into B	.	.	.	.	.	.	3	10
LD C,(HL)	4E	Load contents of memory pointed to by HL into C	.	.	.	.	.	.	2	7
LD C,(IX+d)	DD4Ed	Load contents of memory pointed to by IX+d into C	.	.	.	.	.	.	5	19
LD C,(IY+d)	FD4Ed	Load contents of memory pointed to by IY+d into C	.	.	.	.	.	.	5	19
LD C,A	4F	Load contents of accumulator into C	.	.	.	.	.	.	1	4
LD C,B	48	Load contents of register B into C	.	.	.	.	.	.	1	4
LD C,C	49	Load contents of register C into C	.	.	.	.	.	.	1	4
LD C,D	4A	Load contents of register D into C	.	.	.	.	.	.	1	4
LD C,E	4B	Load contents of register E into C	.	.	.	.	.	.	1	4
LD C,H	4C	Load contents of register H into C	.	.	.	.	.	.	1	4
LD C,L	4D	Load contents of register L into C	.	.	.	.	.	.	1	4
LD C,n	0En	Load data in byte 2 into C	.	.	.	.	.	.	1	4
LD D,(HL)	56	Load contents of memory pointed to by HL into D	.	.	.	.	.	.	2	7

MNEMONIC	OP CODE	COMMENT	S	Z	H	P/V	N	C	M CYCLES	T STATES
LD D,(IX+d)	DD56d	Load contents of memory pointed to by IX+d into D	.	.	.	.	.	.	5	19
LD D,(IY+d)	FD56d	Load contents of memory pointed to by IY+d into D	.	.	.	.	.	.	5	19
LD D,A	57	Load contents of accumulator into D	.	.	.	.	.	.	1	4
LD D,B	50	Load contents of register B into D	.	.	.	.	.	.	1	4
LD D,C	51	Load contents of register C into D	.	.	.	.	.	.	1	4
LD D,D	52	Load contents of register D into D	.	.	.	.	.	.	1	4
LD D,E	53	Load contents of register E into D	.	.	.	.	.	.	1	4
LD D,H	54	Load contents of register H into D	.	.	.	.	.	.	1	4
LD D,L	55	Load contents of register L into D	.	.	.	.	.	.	1	4
LD D,n	16n	Load data in byte 2 into D	.	.	.	.	.	.	2	7
LD DE,(nn)	ED5Bnn	Load contents of memory pointed to by bytes 4 and 3 into E. Load the next byte in memory into D	.	.	.	.	.	.	6	20
LD DE,nn	11nn	Load data in byte 2 into register E. Load data in byte 3 into D	.	.	.	.	.	.	3	10
LD E,(HL)	5E	Load contents of memory pointed to by HL into E	.	.	.	.	.	.	2	7
LD E,(IX+d)	DD5Ed	Load contents of memory pointed to by IX+d into E	.	.	.	.	.	.	5	19
LD E,(IY+d)	FD5Ed	Load contents of memory pointed to by IY+d into E	.	.	.	.	.	.	5	19
LD E,A	5F	Load contents of accumulator into E	.	.	.	.	.	.	1	4
LD E,B	58	Load contents of register B into E	.	.	.	.	.	.	1	4
LD E,C	59	Load contents of register C into E	.	.	.	.	.	.	1	4
LD E,D	5A	Load contents of register D into E	.	.	.	.	.	.	1	4
LD E,E	5B	Load contents of register E into E	.	.	.	.	.	.	1	4
LD E,H	5C	Load contents of register H into E	.	.	.	.	.	.	1	4
LD E,L	5D	Load contents of register L into E	.	.	.	.	.	.	1	4
LD E,n	1En	Load data in byte 2 into E	.	.	.	.	.	.	2	7
LD H,(HL)	66	Load contents of memory pointed to by HL into H	.	.	.	.	.	.	2	7
LD H,(IX+d)	DD66d	Load contents of memory pointed to IX+d into H	.	.	.	.	.	.	5	19
LD H,(IY+d)	FD66d	Load contents of memory pointed to IY+d into H	.	.	.	.	.	.	5	19
LD H,A	67	Load contents of accumulator into H	.	.	.	.	.	.	1	4
LD H,B	60	Load contents of register B into H	.	.	.	.	.	.	1	4
LD H,C	61	Load contents of register C into H	.	.	.	.	.	.	1	4
LD H,D	62	Load contents of register D into H	.	.	.	.	.	.	1	4
LD H,E	63	Load contents of register E into H	.	.	.	.	.	.	1	4
LD H,H	64	Load contents of register H into H	.	.	.	.	.	.	1	4
LD H,L	65	Load contents of register L into H	.	.	.	.	.	.	1	4
LD H,n	26n	Load data in byte 2 into H	.	.	.	.	.	.	2	7
LD HL,(nn)	2Ann	Load contents of memory pointed to by bytes 3 and 2 into L. Load the following byte into H	.	.	.	.	.	.	5	16

MNEMONIC	OP CODE	COMMENT	S	Z	H	P/V	N	C	M CYCLES	T STATES
LD HL,nn	21nn	Load byte 2 into L and load byte 3 into H	.	.	.	.	.	.	3	10
LD I,A	ED47	Load accumulator into interrupt register	.	.	.	.	.	.	2	9
LD IX,(nn)	DD2Ann	Load contents of memory pointed to by bytes 4 and 3 into the LOW byte of IX. Load the following byte into the HIGH byte of IX	.	.	.	.	.	.	6	20
LD IX,nn	DD21nn	Load byte 3 into LOW byte of IX and byte 4 into the HIGH byte of IX	.	.	.	.	.	.	4	14
LD IY,(nn)	FD2Ann	Load contents of memory pointed to by bytes 4 and 3 into the LOW byte of IY. Load the following byte into the HIGH byte of IY	.	.	.	.	.	.	6	20
LD IY,nn	FD21nn	Load byte 3 into LOW byte of IY and byte 4 into the HIGH byte of IY	.	.	.	.	.	.	4	14
LD L,(HL)	6E	Load contents of memory pointed to by HL into L	.	.	.	.	.	.	2	7
LD L,(IX+d)	DD6Ed	Load contents of memory pointed to by IX+d into L	.	.	.	.	.	.	5	19
LD L,(IY+d)	FD6Ed	Load contents of memory pointed to by IY+d into L	.	.	.	.	.	.	5	19
LD L,A	6F	Load contents of accumulator into L	.	.	.	.	.	.	1	4
LD L,B	68	Load contents of register B into L	.	.	.	.	.	.	1	4
LD L,C	69	Load contents of register C into L	.	.	.	.	.	.	1	4
LD L,D	6A	Load contents of register D into L	.	.	.	.	.	.	1	4
LD L,E	6B	Load contents of register E into L	.	.	.	.	.	.	1	4
LD L,H	6C	Load contents of register H into L	.	.	.	.	.	.	1	4
LD L,L	6D	Load contents of register L into L	.	.	.	.	.	.	1	4
LD L,n	2En	Load data in byte 2 into L	.	.	.	.	.	.	1	4
LD R,A	ED4F	Load contents of accumulator into R	.	.	.	.	.	.	1	4
LD SP,(nn)	ED7Bnn	Load contents of memory pointed to by bytes 3 and 2 into the LOW byte of SP and the contents of the next location in memory into the HIGH byte of SP	.	.	.	.	.	.	6	20
LD SP,HL	F9	Load contents of HL into stack pointer	.	.	.	.	.	.	1	6
LD SP,IX	DDF9	Load contents of IX into stack pointer	.	.	.	.	.	.	2	10
LD SP,IY	FDF9	Load contents of IY into stack pointer	.	.	.	.	.	.	2	10
LD SP,nn	31nn	Load byte 2 into the LOW byte of the stack pointer and byte 3 into the HIGH byte	.	.	.	.	.	.	3	10
LDD	EDA8	Load contents of memory pointed to by HL into memory pointed to by DE. Decrement HL. Decrement BC. Decrement DE. P/V Flag=0 if BC becomes 0 as a result of the decrement. Otherwise P/V=1	.	.	0	↕	0	.	4	16

MNEMONIC	OP CODE	COMMENT	S	Z	H	P/V	N	C	M CYCLES	T STATES
LDDR	EDB8	Load contents of memory pointed to by HL into memory pointed to by DE. Decrement DE. Decrement HL. Decrement BC. Repeat until BC = 0	.	.	0	0	0	.	5 (if BC ≠ 0) 4 (if BC = 0)	21 16
LDI	EDA0	Load contents of memory pointed to by HL into memory pointed to by DE. Increment DE. Increment HL. Decrement BC. P/V Flag = 0 if BC becomes 0 as a result of the decrement; otherwise P/V = 1	.	.	0	↕	0	.	4	16
LDIR	EDB0	Load contents of memory pointed to by HL into memory pointed to by DE. Increment DE. Increment HL. Decrement BC. Repeat until BC = 0	.	.	0	0	0	.	5 (if BC ≠ 0) 4 (if BC = 0)	21 16
NEG	ED44	Take the 2's complement of the accumulator (negate the accumulator)	↕	↕	↕	V	1	↕	2	8
OR (HL)	B6	OR contents of memory pointed to by HL with the accumulator	↕	↕	0	P	0	0	2	7
OR (IX + d)	DDB6d	OR contents of accumulator with contents of memory pointed to by IX + d	↕	↕	0	P	0	0	5	19
OR (IY + d)	FDB6d	OR contents of accumulator with contents of memory pointed to by IY + d	↕	↕	0	P	0	0	5	19
OR A	B7	OR contents of accumulator with contents of accumulator	↕	↕	0	P	0	0	1	4
OR B	B0	OR contents of B with contents of accumulator	↕	↕	0	P	0	0	1	4
OR C	B1	OR contents of C with contents of accumulator	↕	↕	0	P	0	0	1	4
OR D	B2	OR contents of D with contents of accumulator	↕	↕	0	P	0	0	1	4
OR E	B3	OR contents of E with contents of accumulator	↕	↕	0	P	0	0	1	4
OR H	B4	OR contents of H with contents of accumulator	↕	↕	0	P	0	0	1	4
OR L	B5	OR contents of L with contents of accumulator	↕	↕	0	P	0	0	1	4
OR n	F6n	OR byte 2 with contents of accumulator	↕	↕	0	P	0	0	2	7
OTDR	EDBB	Output contents of memory pointed to by HL to output port pointed to by C. Decrement B. Decrement HL. Repeat until B = 0	X	1	X	X	1	X	5 (if B ≠ 0) 4 (if B = 0)	21 16
OTIR	EDB3	Output contents of memory pointed to by HL to output port pointed to by C. Decrement B. Increment H. Repeat until B = 0	X	1	X	X	1	X	5 (if B ≠ 0) 4 (if B = 0)	21 16
OUT (C),A	ED79	Output accumulator to output port pointed to by C	.	.	.	.	.	.	3	12

MNEMONIC	OP CODE	COMMENT	S	Z	H	P/V	N	C	M CYCLES	T STATES
OUT (C),B	ED41	Output contents of register B to output port pointed to by C	.	.	.	.	.	.	3	12
OUT (C),C	ED49	Output contents of register C to output port pointed to by C	.	.	.	.	.	.	3	12
OUT (C),D	ED51	Output contents of register D to output port pointed to by C	.	.	.	.	.	.	3	12
OUT (C),E	ED59	Output contents of register E to output port pointed to by C	.	.	.	.	.	.	3	12
OUT (C),H	ED61	Output contents of register H to output port pointed to by C	.	.	.	.	.	.	3	12
OUT (C),L	ED69	Output contents of register L to output port pointed to by C	.	.	.	.	.	.	3	12
OUT (n),A	D3n	Output contents of accumulator to output port pointed to by byte 2	.	.	.	.	.	.	3	11
OUTD	EDAB	Output contents of memory pointed to by HL to the output port pointed to by register C. Decrement B. Decrement HL. If the result of B-1 is zero, then Z=1. Otherwise Z=0	X	↕	X	X	1	X	4	16
OUTI	EDA3	Output contents of memory pointed to by HL to the output port pointed to by register C. Decrement B. Increment HL. If the result of B-1 is zero, then Z=1. Otherwise Z=0	X	↕	X	X	1	X	4	16
POP AF	F1	Load contents of memory pointed to by SP into F and contents of memory pointed to by SP+1 into accumulator	.	.	.	.	.	.	3	10
POP BC	C1	Load contents of memory pointed to by stack pointer into C and contents of memory pointed to by SP+1 into B	.	.	.	.	.	.	3	10
POP DE	D1	Load contents of memory pointed to by SP into E and contents of memory pointed to by SP+1 into D	.	.	.	.	.	.	3	10
POP HL	E1	Load contents of memory pointed to by SP into L and contents of memory pointed to by SP+1 into H	.	.	.	.	.	.	3	10
POP IX	DDE1	Load contents of memory pointed to by stack pointer into LOW byte of IX and contents of memory pointed to by SP+1 into HIGH byte of IX	.	.	.	.	.	.	4	14
POP IY	FDE1	Load contents of memory pointed to by stack pointer into LOW byte of IY and contents of memory pointed to by SP+1 into HIGH byte of IY	.	.	.	.	.	.	4	14
PUSH AF	F5	Load contents of accumulator into memory pointed to by SP−1 and flags register into memory pointed to by SP−2	.	.	.	.	.	.	3	11

MNEMONIC	OP CODE	COMMENT	S	Z	H	P/V	N	C	M CYCLES	T STATES
PUSH BC	C5	Load B into memory pointed to by SP−1 and C into memory pointed to by SP−2	.	.	.	.	.	.	3	11
PUSH DE	D5	Load contents of D into memory pointed to by SP−1 and contents of E into memory pointed to by SP−2	.	.	.	.	.	.	3	11
PUSH HL	E5	Load contents of H into address pointed to by SP−1 and load L into address pointed to by SP−2	.	.	.	.	.	.	3	11
PUSH IX	DDE5	Load contents of HIGH byte of IX into memory pointed to by SP−1 and contents of LOW byte into memory pointed to by SP−2	.	.	.	.	.	.	4	15
PUSH IY	FDE5	Load contents of HIGH byte of IY into memory pointed to by SP−1 and contents of LOW byte into memory pointed to by SP−2	.	.	.	.	.	.	4	15
RES 0,(HL)	CB86	Reset bit zero in memory pointed to by HL to 0	.	.	.	.	.	.	4	15
RES 0,(IX+d)	DDCBd86	Reset bit zero in memory pointed to by IX+d to 0	.	.	.	.	.	.	6	23
RES 0,(IY+d)	FDCBd86	Reset first bit in memory pointed to by IY+d to 0	.	.	.	.	.	.	6	23
RES 0,A	CB87	Reset bit zero of accumulator to 0	.	.	.	.	.	.	2	8
RES 0,B	CB80	Reset bit zero of B register to 0	.	.	.	.	.	.	2	8
RES 0,C	CB81	Reset bit zero of C register to 0	.	.	.	.	.	.	2	8
RES 0,D	CB82	Reset bit zero of D register to 0	.	.	.	.	.	.	2	8
RES 0,E	CB83	Reset bit zero of E register to 0	.	.	.	.	.	.	2	8
RES 0,H	CB84	Reset bit zero of H register to 0	.	.	.	.	.	.	2	8
RES 0,L	CB85	Reset bit zero of L register to 0	.	.	.	.	.	.	2	8
RES 1,(HL)	CB8E	Reset bit 1 in memory pointed to by HL to 0	.	.	.	.	.	.	4	15
RES 1,(IX+d)	DDCBd8E	Reset bit 1 in memory pointed to by IX+d to 0	.	.	.	.	.	.	6	23
RES 1,(IY+d)	FDCBd8E	Reset bit 1 in memory pointed to by IY+d to 0	.	.	.	.	.	.	6	23
RES 1,A	CB8F	Reset bit 1 in accumulator to 0	.	.	.	.	.	.	2	8
RES 1,B	CB88	Reset bit 1 in B register to 0	.	.	.	.	.	.	2	8
RES 1,C	CB89	Reset bit 1 in C register to 0	.	.	.	.	.	.	2	8
RES 1,D	CB8A	Reset bit 1 in D register to 0	.	.	.	.	.	.	2	8
RES 1,E	CB8B	Reset bit 1 in E register to 0	.	.	.	.	.	.	2	8
RES 1,H	CB8C	Reset bit 1 in H register to 0	.	.	.	.	.	.	2	8
RES 1,L	CB8D	Reset bit 1 in L register to 0	.	.	.	.	.	.	2	8
RES 2,(HL)	CB96	Reset bit 2 in memory pointed to by HL to 0	.	.	.	.	.	.	4	15
RES 2,(IX+d)	DDCBd96	Reset bit 2 in memory pointed to by IX+d to 0	.	.	.	.	.	.	6	23
RES 2,(IY+d)	FDCBd96	Reset bit 2 in memory pointed to by IY+d to 0	.	.	.	.	.	.	6	23

MNEMONIC	OP CODE	COMMENT	S	Z	H	P/V	N	C	M CYCLES	T STATES
RES 2,A	CB97	Reset bit 2 in accumulator to 0	.	.	.	.	.	.	2	8
RES 2,B	CB90	Reset bit 2 in register B to 0	.	.	.	.	.	.	2	8
RES 2,C	CB91	Reset bit 2 in register C to 0	.	.	.	.	.	.	2	8
RES 2,D	CB92	Reset bit 2 in register D to 0	.	.	.	.	.	.	2	8
RES 2,E	CB93	Reset bit 2 in register E to 0	.	.	.	.	.	.	2	8
RES 2,H	CB94	Reset bit 2 in register H to 0	.	.	.	.	.	.	2	8
RES 2,L	CB95	Reset bit 2 in register L to 0	.	.	.	.	.	.	2	8
RES 3,(HL)	CB9E	Reset bit 3 in memory pointed to by HL to 0	.	.	.	.	.	.	4	15
RES 3,(IX+d)	DDCBd9E	Reset bit 3 in memory pointed to by IX+d to 0	.	.	.	.	.	.	6	23
RES 3,(IY+d)	FDCBd9E	Reset bit 3 in memory pointed to by IY+d to 0	.	.	.	.	.	.	6	23
RES 3,A	CB9F	Reset bit 3 in accumulator to 0	.	.	.	.	.	.	2	8
RES 3,B	CB98	Reset bit 3 in register B to 0	.	.	.	.	.	.	2	8
RES 3,C	CB99	Reset bit 3 in register C to 0	.	.	.	.	.	.	2	8
RES 3,D	CB9A	Reset bit 3 in register D to 0	.	.	.	.	.	.	2	8
RES 3,E	CB9B	Reset bit 3 in register E to 0	.	.	.	.	.	.	2	8
RES 3,H	CB9C	Reset bit 3 in register H to 0	.	.	.	.	.	.	2	8
RES 3,L	CB9D	Reset bit 3 in register L to 0	.	.	.	.	.	.	2	8
RES 4,(HL)	CBA6	Reset bit 4 in memory pointed to by HL to 0	.	.	.	.	.	.	4	15
RES 4,(IX+d)	DDCBdA6	Reset bit 4 in memory pointed to by IX+d to 0	.	.	.	.	.	.	6	23
RES 4,(IY+d)	FDCBdA6	Reset bit 4 in memory pointed to by IY+d to 0	.	.	.	.	.	.	6	23
RES 4,A	CBA7	Reset bit 4 in accumulator to 0	.	.	.	.	.	.	2	8
RES 4,B	CBA0	Reset bit 4 in register B to 0	.	.	.	.	.	.	2	8
RES 4,C	CBA1	Reset bit 4 in register C to 0	.	.	.	.	.	.	2	8
RES 4,D	CBA2	Reset bit 4 in register D to 0	.	.	.	.	.	.	2	8
RES 4,E	CBA3	Reset bit 4 in register E to 0	.	.	.	.	.	.	2	8
RES 4,H	CBA4	Reset bit 4 in register H to 0	.	.	.	.	.	.	2	8
RES 4,L	CBA5	Reset bit 4 in register L to 0	.	.	.	.	.	.	2	8
RES 5,(HL)	CBAE	Reset bit 5 in memory pointed to by HL to 0	.	.	.	.	.	.	4	15
RES 5,(IX+d)	DDCBdAE	Reset bit 5 in memory pointed to by IX+d to 0	.	.	.	.	.	.	6	23
RES 5,(IY+d)	FDCBdAE	Reset bit 5 in memory pointed to by IY+d to 0	.	.	.	.	.	.	6	23
RES 5,A	CBAF	Reset bit 5 in accumulator to 0	.	.	.	.	.	.	2	8
RES 5,B	CBA8	Reset bit 5 in register B to 0	.	.	.	.	.	.	2	8
RES 5,C	CBA9	Reset bit 5 in register C to 0	.	.	.	.	.	.	2	8
RES 5,D	CBAA	Reset bit 5 in register D to 0	.	.	.	.	.	.	2	8
RES 5,E	CBAB	Reset bit 5 in register E to 0	.	.	.	.	.	.	2	8
RES 5,H	CBAC	Reset bit 5 in register H to 0	.	.	.	.	.	.	2	8
RES 5,L	CBAD	Reset bit 5 in register L to 0	.	.	.	.	.	.	2	8
RES 6,(HL)	CBB6	Reset bit 6 in memory pointed to by HL to 0	.	.	.	.	.	.	4	15

MNEMONIC	OP CODE	COMMENT	S	Z	H	P/V	N	C	M CYCLES	T STATES
RES 6,(IX+d)	DDCBdB6	Reset bit 6 in memory pointed to by IX+d to 0	.	.	.	.	.	.	6	23
RES 6,(IY+d)	FDCBdB6	Reset bit 6 in memory pointed to by IY+d to 0	.	.	.	.	.	.	6	23
RES 6,A	CBB7	Reset bit 6 in accumulator to 0	.	.	.	.	.	.	2	8
RES 6,B	CBB0	Reset bit 6 in register B to 0	.	.	.	.	.	.	2	8
RES 6,C	CBB1	Reset bit 6 in register C to 0	.	.	.	.	.	.	2	8
RES 6,D	CBB2	Reset bit 6 in register D to 0	.	.	.	.	.	.	2	8
RES 6,E	CBB3	Reset bit 6 in register E to 0	.	.	.	.	.	.	2	8
RES 6,H	CBB4	Reset bit 6 in register H to 0	.	.	.	.	.	.	2	8
RES 6,L	CBB5	Reset bit 6 in register L to 0	.	.	.	.	.	.	2	8
RES 7,(HL)	CBBE	Reset bit 7 in memory pointed to by HL to 0	.	.	.	.	.	.	4	15
RES 7,(IX+d)	DDCBdBE	Reset bit 7 in memory pointed to by IX+d to 0	.	.	.	.	.	.	6	23
RES 7,(IY+d)	FDCBdBE	Reset bit 7 in memory pointed to by IY+d to 0	.	.	.	.	.	.	6	23
RES 7,A	CBBF	Reset bit 7 in accumulator to 0	.	.	.	.	.	.	2	8
RES 7,B	CBB8	Reset bit 7 in register B to 0	.	.	.	.	.	.	2	8
RES 7,C	CBB9	Reset bit 7 in register C to 0	.	.	.	.	.	.	2	8
RES 7,D	CBBA	Reset bit 7 in register D to 0	.	.	.	.	.	.	2	8
RES 7,E	CBBB	Reset bit 7 in register E to 0	.	.	.	.	.	.	2	8
RES 7,H	CBBC	Reset bit 7 in register H to 0	.	.	.	.	.	.	2	8
RES 7,L	CBBD	Reset bit 7 in register L to 0	.	.	.	.	.	.	2	8
RET	C9	Unconditional return from subroutine	.	.	.	.	.	.	3	10
RET C	D8	If carry flag=0, disregard instruction. If carry flag=1, return from subroutine	.	.	.	.	.	.	1 (if C=0) 3 (if C=1)	5 11
RET M	F8	If sign flag=0, disregard instruction. If sign flag=1, return from subroutine	.	.	.	.	.	.	1 (if S=0) 3 (if S=1)	5 11
RET NC	D0	If carry flag=1, disregard instruction. If carry flag=0, return from subroutine	.	.	.	.	.	.	1 (if C=1) 3 (if C=0)	5 11
RET NZ	C0	If zero flag= 1, disregard instruction. If zero flag=0, return from subroutine	.	.	.	.	.	.	1 (if Z=1) 3 (if Z=0)	5 11
RET P	F0	If sign flag=1, disregard instruction. If sign flag=0, return from subroutine	.	.	.	.	.	.	1 (if S=1) 3 (if S=0)	5 11
RET PE	E8	If parity flag=0, disregard instruction. If parity flag=1, return from subroutine	.	.	.	.	.	.	1 (if P=0) 3 (if P=1)	5 11

MNEMONIC	OP CODE	COMMENT	S	Z	H	P/V	N	C	M CYCLES	T STATES
			FLAGS							
RET PO	E0	If parity flag = 1, disregard instruction. If parity flag = 0, return from subroutine	.	.	.	.	.	.	1 (if P = 1)	5
									3 (if P = 0)	11
RET Z	C8	If zero flag = 0, disregard instruction. If zero flag = 1, return from subroutine	.	.	.	.	.	.	1 (if Z = 0)	5
									3 (if Z = 1)	11
RETI	ED4D	Return from interrupt	.	.	.	.	.	.	4	14
RETN	ED45	Return from nonmaskable interrupt	.	.	.	.	.	.	4	14
RL (HL)	CB16	Rotate left the contents of memory pointed to by HL	↕	↕	0	P	0	↕	4	15
RL (IX + d)	DDCBd16	Rotate left the contents of memory pointed to by IX + d	↕	↕	0	P	0	↕	6	23
RL (IY + d)	FDCBd16	Rotate left the contents of memory pointed to by IY + d	↕	↕	0	P	0	↕	6	23
RL A	CB17	Rotate left the contents of accumulator	↕	↕	0	P	0	↕	6	23
RL B	CB10	Rotate left the contents of register B	↕	↕	0	P	0	↕	2	8
RL C	CB11	Rotate left the contents of register C	↕	↕	0	P	0	↕	2	8
RL D	CB12	Rotate left the contents of register D	↕	↕	0	P	0	↕	2	8
RL E	CB13	Rotate left the contents of register E	↕	↕	0	P	0	↕	2	8
RL H	CB14	Rotate left the contents of register H	↕	↕	0	P	0	↕	2	8
RL L	CB15	Rotate left the contents of register L	↕	↕	0	P	0	↕	2	8
RLA	17	Rotate left the contents of the accumulator	.	.	0	.	0	↕	1	4
RLC (HL)	CB06	Rotate left circular the contents of memory pointed to by HL	↕	↕	0	P	0	↕	4	15
RLC (IX + d)	DDCBd06	Rotate left circular the contents of memory pointed to by IX + d	↕	↕	0	P	0	↕	6	23
RLC (IY + d)	FDCBd06	Rotate left circular the contents of memory pointed to by IY + d	↕	↕	0	P	0	↕	6	23
RLC A	CB07	Rotate left circular the accumulator	↕	↕	0	P	0	↕	2	8
RLC B	CB00	Rotate left circular the contents of register B	↕	↕	0	P	0	↕	2	8
RLC C	CB01	Rotate left circular the contents of register C	↕	↕	0	P	0	↕	2	8
RLC D	CB02	Rotate left circular the contents of register D	↕	↕	0	P	0	↕	2	8
RLC E	CB03	Rotate left circular the contents of register E	↕	↕	0	P	0	↕	2	8
RLC H	CB04	Rotate left circular the contents of register H	↕	↕	0	P	0	↕	2	8
RLC L	CB05	Rotate left circular the contents of register L	↕	↕	0	P	0	↕	2	8
RLCA	07	Rotate left circular the contents of the accumulator (1 byte instruction)	.	.	0	.	0	↕	1	4
RLD	ED6F	Rotate left digit	↕	↕	0	P	0	.	2	8

MNEMONIC	OP CODE	COMMENT	S	Z	H	P/V	N	C	M CYCLES	T STATES
RR (HL)	CB1E	Rotate right the contents of memory pointed to by HL	↕	↕	0	P	0	↕	4	15
RR (IX+d)	DDCBd1E	Rotate right the contents of memory pointed to by IX+d	↕	↕	0	P	0	↕	6	23
RR (IY+d)	FDCBd1E	Rotate right the contents of memory pointed to by IY+d	↕	↕	0	P	0	↕	6	23
RR A	CB1F	Rotate right the contents of register A	↕	↕	0	P	0	↕	2	8
RR B	CB18	Rotate right the contents of register B	↕	↕	0	P	0	↕	2	8
RR C	CB19	Rotate right the contents of register C	↕	↕	0	P	0	↕	2	8
RR D	CB1A	Rotate right the contents of register D	↕	↕	0	P	0	↕	2	8
RR E	CB1B	Rotate right the contents of register E	↕	↕	0	P	0	↕	2	8
RR H	CB1C	Rotate right the contents of register H	↕	↕	0	P	0	↕	2	8
RR L	CB1D	Rotate right the contents of register L	↕	↕	0	P	0	↕	2	8
RRA	1F	Rotate right accumulator	.	.	0	.	0	↕	1	4
RRC (HL)	CB0E	Rotate right circular the contents of memory pointed to by HL	↕	↕	0	P	0	↕	5	15
RRC (IX+d)	DDCBd0E	Rotate right circular the contents of memory pointed to by IX+d	↕	↕	0	P	0	↕	6	23
RRC (IY+d)	FDCBd0E	Rotate right circular the contents of memory pointed to by IY+d	↕	↕	0	P	0	↕	6	23
RRC A	CB0F	Rotate right circular the contents of the accumulator	↕	↕	0	P	0	↕	2	8
RRC B	CB08	Rotate right circular the contents of register B	↕	↕	0	P	0	↕	2	8
RRC C	CB09	Rotate right circular the contents of register C	↕	↕	0	P	0	↕	2	8
RRC D	CB0A	Rotate right circular the contents of register D	↕	↕	0	P	0	↕	2	8
RRC E	CB0B	Rotate right circular the contents of register E	↕	↕	0	P	0	↕	2	8
RRC H	CB0C	Rotate right circular the contents of register H	↕	↕	0	P	0	↕	2	8
RRC L	CB0D	Rotate right circular the contents of register L	↕	↕	0	P	0	↕	2	8
RRCA	0F	Rotate right circular accumulator	.	.	0	.	0	↕	1	4
RRD	ED67	Rotate right digit	↕	↕	0	P	0	.	5	18
RST 00H	C7	Restart at 0000H. Push contents of the program counter onto the stack. Load the program counter with 0000H	.	.	.	.	.	.	3	11
RST 08H	CF	Restart at 0008H. Push contents of the program counter onto the stack. Load program counter with 0008H	.	.	.	.	.	.	3	11
RST 10H	D7	Restart at 0010H. Push contents of the program counter onto the stack. Load the program counter with 0010H	.	.	.	.	.	.	3	11
RST 18H	DF	Restart at 0018H. Push contents of the program counter onto the stack. Load the program counter with 0018H	.	.	.	.	.	.	3	11

MNEMONIC	OP CODE	COMMENT	FLAGS S	Z	H	P/V	N	C	M CYCLES	T STATES
RST 20H	E7	Restart at 0020H. Push contents of the program counter onto the stack. Load the program counter with 0020H	.	.	.	.	.	.	3	11
RST 28H	EF	Restart at 0028H. Push contents of the program onto the stack. Load the program counter with 0028H	.	.	.	.	.	.	3	11
RST 30H	F7	Restart at 0030H. Push contents of the program counter onto the stack. Load the program counter with 0030H	.	.	.	.	.	.	3	11
RST 38H	FF	Restart at 0038H. Push contents of the program counter onto the stack. Load the program counter with 0038H	.	.	.	.	.	.	3	11
RST 0	C7	Same as RST 00H	.	.	.	.	.	.	3	11
RST 8	CF	Same as RST 08H	.	.	.	.	.	.	3	11
RST 16	D7	Same as RST 10H	.	.	.	.	.	.	3	11
RST 24	DF	Same as RST 18H	.	.	.	.	.	.	3	11
RST 32	E7	Same as RST 20H	.	.	.	.	.	.	3	11
RST 40	EF	Same as RST 28H	.	.	.	.	.	.	3	11
RST 48	F7	Same as RST 30H	.	.	.	.	.	.	3	11
RST 56	FF	Same as RST 38H	.	.	.	.	.	.	3	11
SBC A,(HL)	9E	Subtract contents of memory pointed to by HL and carry flag from accumulator	↕	↕	↕	V	1	↕	2	7
SBC A,(IX+d)	DD9Ed	Subtract contents of memory pointed to by IX+d and carry flag from accumulator	↕	↕	↕	V	1	↕	5	19
SBC A,(IY+d)	FD9Ed	Subtract contents of memory pointed to by IY+d and carry flag from accumulator	↕	↕	↕	V	1	↕	5	19
SBC A,A	9F	Subtract contents of accumulator and carry flag from accumulator	↕	↕	↕	V	1	↕	1	4
SBC A,B	98	Subtract contents of register B and carry flag from accumulator	↕	↕	↕	V	1	↕	1	4
SBC A,C	99	Subtract contents of register C and carry flag from contents of accumulator	↕	↕	↕	V	1	↕	1	4
SBC A,D	9A	Subtract contents of register D and carry flag from contents of accumulator	↕	↕	↕	V	1	↕	1	4
SBC A,E	9B	Subtract contents of register E and carry flag from contents of accumulator	↕	↕	↕	V	1	↕	1	4
SBC A,H	9C	Subtract contents of register H and carry flag from contents of accumulator	↕	↕	↕	V	1	↕	1	4
SBC A,L	9D	Subtract contents of register L and carry flag from contents of accumulator	↕	↕	↕	V	1	↕	1	4
SBC A,n	DEn	Subtract byte 2 and the carry flag from the accumulator	↕	↕	↕	V	1	↕	2	7
SBC HL,BC	ED42	Subtract contents of register pair BC and the carry flag from HL	↕	↕	X	V	1	↕	4	15
SBC HL,DE	ED52	Subtract contents of register pair DE and the carry flag from HL	↕	↕	X	V	1	↕	4	15
SBC HL,HL	ED62	Subtract contents of register HL and the carry flag from HL	↕	↕	X	V	1	↕	4	15

MNEMONIC	OP CODE	COMMENT	S	Z	FLAGS H	P/V	N	C	M CYCLES	T STATES
SBC HL,SP	ED72	Subtract contents of the stack pointer and the carry flag from HL	↕	↕	X	V	1	↕	4	15
SCF	37	Set carry flag	.	.	0	.	0	1	1	4
SET 0,(HL)	CBC6	Set bit 0 of memory pointed to by HL to 1	.	.	.	.	.	.	4	15
SET 0,(IX+d)	DDCBdC6	Set bit 0 of memory pointed to by IX+d to 1	.	.	.	.	.	.	6	23
SET 0,(IY+d)	FDCBdC6	Set bit 0 of memory pointed to by IY+d to 1	.	.	.	.	.	.	6	23
SET 0,A	CBC7	Set bit 0 of accumulator to 1	.	.	.	.	.	.	2	8
SET 0,B	CBC0	Set bit 0 of register B to 1	.	.	.	.	.	.	2	8
SET 0,C	CBC1	Set bit 0 of register C to 1	.	.	.	.	.	.	2	8
SET 0,D	CBC2	Set bit 0 of register D to 1	.	.	.	.	.	.	2	8
SET 0,E	CBC3	Set bit 0 of register E to 1	.	.	.	.	.	.	2	8
SET 0,H	CBC4	Set bit 0 of register H to 1	.	.	.	.	.	.	2	8
SET 0,L	CBC5	Set bit 0 of register L to 1	.	.	.	.	.	.	2	8
SET 1,(HL)	CBCE	Set bit 1 of memory pointed to by HL to 1	.	.	.	.	.	.	4	15
SET 1,(IX+d)	DDCBdCE	Set bit 1 of memory pointed to by IX+d to 1	.	.	.	.	.	.	6	23
SET 1,(IY+d)	FDCBdCE	Set bit 1 of memory pointed to by IY+d to 1	.	.	.	.	.	.	6	23
SET 1,A	CBCF	Set bit 1 of accumulator to 1	.	.	.	.	.	.	2	8
SET 1,B	CBC8	Set bit 1 of register B to 1	.	.	.	.	.	.	2	8
SET 1,C	CBC9	Set bit 1 of register C to 1	.	.	.	.	.	.	2	8
SET 1,D	CBCA	Set bit 1 of register D to 1	.	.	.	.	.	.	2	8
SET 1,E	CBCB	Set bit 1 of register E to 1	.	.	.	.	.	.	2	8
SET 1,H	CBCC	Set bit 1 of register H to 1	.	.	.	.	.	.	2	8
SET 1,L	CBCD	Set bit 1 of register L to 1	.	.	.	.	.	.	2	8
SET 2,(HL)	CBD6	Set bit 2 of memory pointed to by HL to 1	.	.	.	.	.	.	4	15
SET 2,(IX+d)	DDCBdD6	Set bit 2 of memory pointed to by IX+d to 1	.	.	.	.	.	.	6	23
SET 2,(IY+d)	FDCBdD6	Set bit 2 of memory pointed to by IY+d to 1	.	.	.	.	.	.	6	23
SET 2,A	CBD7	Set bit 2 of accumulator to 1	.	.	.	.	.	.	2	8
SET 2,B	CBD0	Set bit 2 of register B to 1	.	.	.	.	.	.	2	8
SET 2,C	CBD1	Set bit 2 of register C to 1	.	.	.	.	.	.	2	8
SET 2,D	CBD2	Set bit 2 of register D to 1	.	.	.	.	.	.	2	8
SET 2,E	CBD3	Set bit 2 of register E to 1	.	.	.	.	.	.	2	8
SET 2,H	CBD4	Set bit 2 of register H to 1	.	.	.	.	.	.	2	8
SET 2,L	CBD5	Set bit 2 of register L to 1	.	.	.	.	.	.	2	8
SET 3,(HL)	CBDE	Set bit 3 of memory pointed to by HL to 1	.	.	.	.	.	.	4	15
SET 3,(IX+d)	DDCBdDE	Set bit 3 of memory pointed to by IX+d to 1	.	.	.	.	.	.	6	23
SET 3,(IY+d)	FDCBdDE	Set bit 3 of memory pointed to by IY+d to 1	.	.	.	.	.	.	6	23

MNEMONIC	OP CODE	COMMENT	S	Z	FLAGS H	P/V	N	C	M CYCLES	T STATES
SET 3,A	CBDF	Set bit 3 of accumulator to 1	.	.	.	.	.	.	2	8
SET 3,B	CBD8	Set bit 3 of register B to 1	.	.	.	.	.	.	2	8
SET 3,C	CBD9	Set bit 3 of register C to 1	.	.	.	.	.	.	2	8
SET 3,D	CBDA	Set bit 3 of register D to 1	.	.	.	.	.	.	2	8
SET 3,E	CBDB	Set bit 3 of register E to 1	.	.	.	.	.	.	2	8
SET 3,H	CBDC	Set bit 3 of register H to 1	.	.	.	.	.	.	2	8
SET 3,L	CBDD	Set bit 3 of register L to 1	.	.	.	.	.	.	2	8
SET 4,(HL)	CBE6	Set bit 4 of memory pointed to by HL to 1	.	.	.	.	.	.	4	15
SET 4,(IX+d)	DDCBdE6	Set bit 4 of memory pointed to by IX+d to 1	.	.	.	.	.	.	6	23
SET 4,(IY+d)	FDCBdE6	Set bit 4 of memory pointed to by IY+d to 1	.	.	.	.	.	.	6	23
SET 4,A	CBE7	Set bit 4 of accumulator to 1	.	.	.	.	.	.	2	8
SET 4,B	CBE0	Set bit 4 of register B to 1	.	.	.	.	.	.	2	8
SET 4,C	CBE1	Set bit 4 of register C to 1	.	.	.	.	.	.	2	8
SET 4,D	CBE2	Set bit 4 of register D to 1	.	.	.	.	.	.	2	8
SET 4,E	CBE3	Set bit 4 of register E to 1	.	.	.	.	.	.	2	8
SET 4,H	CBE4	Set bit 4 of register H to 1	.	.	.	.	.	.	2	8
SET 4,L	CBE5	Set bit 4 of register L to 1	.	.	.	.	.	.	2	8
SET 5,(HL)	CBEE	Set bit 5 of memory pointed to by HL to 1	.	.	.	.	.	.	4	15
SET 5,(IX+d)	DDCBdEE	Set bit 5 of memory pointed to by IX+d to 1	.	.	.	.	.	.	6	23
SET 5,(IY+d)	FDCBdEE	Set bit 5 of memory pointed to by IY+d to 1	.	.	.	.	.	.	6	23
SET 5,A	CBEF	Set bit 5 of the accumulator to 1	.	.	.	.	.	.	2	8
SET 5,B	CBE8	Set bit 5 of register B to 1	.	.	.	.	.	.	2	8
SET 5,C	CBE9	Set bit 5 of register C to 1	.	.	.	.	.	.	2	8
SET 5,D	CBEA	Set bit 5 of register D to 1	.	.	.	.	.	.	2	8
SET 5,E	CBEB	Set bit 5 of register E to 1	.	.	.	.	.	.	2	8
SET 5,H	CBEC	Set bit 5 of register H to 1	.	.	.	.	.	.	2	8
SET 5,L	CBED	Set bit 5 of register L to 1	.	.	.	.	.	.	2	8
SET 6,(HL)	CBF6	Set bit 6 of memory pointed to by HL to 1	.	.	.	.	.	.	4	15
SET 6,(IX+d)	DDCBdF6	Set bit 6 of memory pointed to by IX+d to 1	.	.	.	.	.	.	6	23
SET 6,(IY+d)	FDCBdF6	Set bit 6 of memory pointed to by IY+d to 1	.	.	.	.	.	.	6	23
SET 6,A	CBF7	Set bit 6 of accumulator to 1	.	.	.	.	.	.	2	8
SET 6,B	CBF0	Set bit 6 of register B to 1	.	.	.	.	.	.	2	8
SET 6,C	CBF1	Set bit 6 of register C to 1	.	.	.	.	.	.	2	8
SET 6,D	CBF2	Set bit 6 of register D to 1	.	.	.	.	.	.	2	8
SET 6,E	CBF3	Set bit 6 of register E to 1	.	.	.	.	.	.	2	8
SET 6,H	CBF4	Set bit 6 of register H to 1	.	.	.	.	.	.	2	8
SET 6,L	CBF5	Set bit 6 of register L to 1	.	.	.	.	.	.	2	8
SET 7,(HL)	CBFE	Set bit 7 of memory pointed to by HL to 1	.	.	.	.	.	.	4	15

MNEMONIC	OP CODE	COMMENT	S	Z	FLAGS H	P/V	N	C	M CYCLES	T STATES
SET 7,(IX+d)	DDCBdFE	Set bit 7 of memory pointed to by IX+d to 1	.	.	.	.	.	.	6	23
SET 7,(IY+d)	FDCBdFE	Set bit 7 of memory pointed to by IY+d to 1	.	.	.	.	.	.	6	23
SET 7,A	CBFF	Set bit 7 of accumulator to 1	.	.	.	.	.	.	2	8
SET 7,B	CBF8	Set bit 7 of register B to 1	.	.	.	.	.	.	2	8
SET 7,C	CBF9	Set bit 7 of register C to 1	.	.	.	.	.	.	2	8
SET 7,D	CBFA	Set bit 7 of register D to 1	.	.	.	.	.	.	2	8
SET 7,E	CBFB	Set bit 7 of register E to 1	.	.	.	.	.	.	2	8
SET 7,H	CBFC	Set bit 7 of register H to 1	.	.	.	.	.	.	2	8
SET 7,L	CBFD	Set bit 7 of register L to 1	.	.	.	.	.	.	2	8
SLA (HL)	CB26	Shift left arithmetic the contents of memory pointed to by HL	↕	↕	0	P	0	↕	4	15
SLA (IX+d)	DDCBd26	Shift left arithmetic the contents of memory pointed to by IX+d	↕	↕	0	P	0	↕	6	23
SLA (IY+d)	FDCBd26	Shift left arithmetic the contents of memory pointed to by IY+d	↕	↕	0	P	0	↕	6	23
SLA A	CB27	Shift left arithmetic the contents of the accumulator	↕	↕	0	P	0	↕	2	8
SLA B	CB20	Shift left arithmetic the contents of register B	↕	↕	0	P	0	↕	2	8
SLA C	CB21	Shift left arithmetic the contents of register C	↕	↕	0	P	0	↕	2	8
SLA D	CB22	Shift left arithmetic the contents of register D	↕	↕	0	P	0	↕	2	8
SLA E	CB23	Shift left arithmetic the contents of register E	↕	↕	0	P	0	↕	2	8
SLA H	CB24	Shift left arithmetic the contents of register H	↕	↕	0	P	0	↕	2	8
SLA L	CB25	Shift left arithmetic the contents of register L	↕	↕	0	P	0	↕	2	8
SRA (HL)	CB2E	Shift right arithmetic the contents of memory pointed to by HL	↕	↕	0	P	0	↕	4	15
SRA (IX+d)	DDCBd2E	Shift right arithmetic the contents of memory pointed to by IX+d	↕	↕	0	P	0	↕	6	23
SRA (IY+d)	FDCBd2E	Shift right arithmetic the contents of memory pointed to by IY+d	↕	↕	0	P	0	↕	6	23
SRA A	CB2F	Shift right arithmetic the contents of accumulator	↕	↕	0	P	0	↕	2	8
SRA B	CB28	Shift right arithmetic the contents of register B	↕	↕	0	P	0	↕	2	8
SRA C	CB29	Shift right arithmetic the contents of register C	↕	↕	0	P	0	↕	2	8
SRA D	CB2A	Shift right arithmetic the contents of register D	↕	↕	0	P	0	↕	2	8
SRA E	CB2B	Shift right arithmetic the contents of register E	↕	↕	0	P	0	↕	2	8

MNEMONIC	OP CODE	COMMENT	S	Z	H	P/V	N	C	M CYCLES	T STATES
SRA H	CB2C	Shift right arithmetic the contents of register H	↕	↕	0	P	0	↕	2	8
SRA L	CB2D	Shift right arithmetic the contents of register L	↕	↕	0	P	0	↕	2	8
SRL (HL)	CB3E	Shift right logical the contents of memory pointed to by HL	↕	↕	0	P	0	↕	4	15
SRL (IX+d)	DDCBd3E	Shift right logical the contents of memory pointed to by IX+d	↕	↕	0	P	0	↕	6	23
SRL (IY+d)	FDCBd3E	Shift right logical the contents of memory pointed to by IY+d	↕	↕	0	P	0	↕	6	23
SRL A	CB3F	Shift right logical the contents of accumulator	↕	↕	0	P	0	↕	2	8
SRL B	CB38	Shift right logical the contents of register B	↕	↕	0	P	0	↕	2	8
SRL C	CB39	Shift right logical the contents of register C	↕	↕	0	P	0	↕	2	8
SRL D	CB3A	Shift right logical the contents of register D	↕	↕	0	P	0	↕	2	8
SRL E	CB3B	Shift right logical the contents of register E	↕	↕	0	P	0	↕	2	8
SRL H	CB3C	Shift right logical the contents of register H	↕	↕	0	P	0	↕	2	8
SRL L	CB3D	Shift right logical the contents of register L	↕	↕	0	P	0	↕	2	8
SUB (HL)	96	Subtract contents of memory pointed to by HL from accumulator	↕	↕	↕	V	1	↕	2	7
SUB (IX+d)	DD96d	Subtract contents of memory pointed to by IX+d from accumulator	↕	↕	↕	V	1	↕	5	19
SUB (IY+d)	FD96d	Subtract contents of memory pointed to by IY+d from accumulator	↕	↕	↕	V	1	↕	5	19
SUB A	97	Subtract contents of accumulator from the accumulator	↕	↕	↕	V	1	↕	1	4
SUB B	90	Subtract contents of register B from the accumulator	↕	↕	↕	V	1	↕	1	4
SUB C	91	Subtract contents of register C from the accumulator	↕	↕	↕	V	1	↕	1	4
SUB D	92	Subtract contents of register D from the accumulator	↕	↕	↕	V	1	↕	1	4
SUB E	93	Subtract contents of register E from the accumulator	↕	↕	↕	V	1	↕	1	4
SUB H	94	Subtract contents of register H from the accumulator	↕	↕	↕	V	1	↕	1	4
SUB L	95	Subtract contents of register L from the accumulator	↕	↕	↕	V	1	↕	1	4
SUB n	D6n	Subtract contents of second byte from contents of accumulator	↕	↕	↕	V	1	↕	2	7

MNEMONIC	OP CODE	COMMENT	S	Z	FLAGS H	P/V	N	C	M CYCLES	T STATES
XOR (HL)	AE	Exclusive-OR the contents of memory pointed to by HL with the accumulator	↕	↕	0	P	0	0	2	7
XOR (IX+d)	DDAEd	Exclusive-OR the contents of memory pointed to by IX+d with contents of accumulator	↕	↕	0	P	0	0	5	19
XOR (IY+d)	FDAEd	Exclusive-OR the contents of address pointed to by IY+d with contents of accumulator	↕	↕	0	P	0	0	5	19
XOR A	AF	Exclusive OR the contents of accumulator with the accumulator	↕	↕	0	P	0	0	1	4
XOR B	A8	Exclusive-OR the contents of register B with the accumulator	↕	↕	0	P	0	0	1	4
XOR C	A9	Exclusive-OR the contents of register C with the accumulator	↕	↕	0	P	0	0	1	4
XOR D	AA	Exclusive-OR the contents of register D with the accumulator	↕	↕	0	P	0	0	1	4
XOR E	AB	Exclusive-OR the contents of register E with the accumulator	↕	↕	0	P	0	0	1	4
XOR H	AC	Exclusive-OR the contents of register H with the accumulator	↕	↕	0	P	0	0	1	4
XOR L	AD	Exclusive-OR the contents of register L with the accumulator	↕	↕	0	P	0	0	1	4
XOR n	EEn	Exclusive-OR byte 2 with the accumulator	↕	↕	0	P	0	0	2	7

C.3 *Z 80 OP CODES IN NUMERICAL ORDER*

OP CODE	MNEMONIC	COMMENT	S	Z	FLAGS H	P/V	N	C	M CYCLES	T STATES
00	NOP	No operation	.	.	.	.	.	.	1	4
01nn	LD BC,nn	Load data in byte 2 into register C. Load data in byte 3 into B	.	.	.	.	.	.	3	10
02	LD (BC),A	Load accumulator into memory pointed to by BC	.	.	.	.	.	.	2	7
03	INC BC	Increment BC	.	.	.	.	.	.	1	6
04	INC B	Increment B	↕	↕	↕	V	0	.	1	4
05	DEC B	Decrement B	↕	↕	↕	V	1	.	1	4
06n	LD B,n	Load data in byte 2 into B	.	.	.	.	.	.	2	7
07	RLCA	Rotate left circular the contents of the accumulator (1 byte instruction)	.	.	0	.	0	↕	1	4
08	EX AF,AF'	Exchange contents of A and A' and F and F'	.	.	.	.	.	.	1	4
09	ADD HL,BC	Add contents of register pair BC to HL	.	.	X	.	0	↕	3	11

OP CODE	MNEMONIC	COMMENT	S	Z	H	P/V	N	C	M CYCLES	T STATES
			FLAGS							
0A	LD A,(BC)	Load contents of memory pointed to by BC into accumulator	.	.	.	.	.	.	2	7
0B	DEC BC	Decrement BC	.	.	.	.	.	.	1	6
0C	INC C	Increment C	↕	↕	↕	V	0	.	1	4
0D	DEC C	Decrement C	↕	↕	↕	V	1	.	1	4
0En	LD C,n	Load data in byte 2 into C	.	.	.	.	.	.	1	4
0F	RRCA	Rotate right circular accumulator	.	.	0	.	0	↕	1	4
10e	DJNZ,e	Decrement B. If B = 0, continue to next instruction. If B ≠ 0, jump to PC + e	.	.	.	.	.	.	2 (if B = 0)	8
									3 (if B ≠ 0)	13
11nn	LD DE,nn	Load data in byte 2 into register E. Load data in byte 3 into D	.	.	.	.	.	.	3	10
12	LD (DE),A	Load contents of accumulator into memory pointed to by DE	.	.	.	.	.	.	2	7
13	INC DE	Increment DE	.	.	.	.	.	.	1	6
14	INC D	Increment D	↕	↕	↕	V	0	.	1	4
15	DEC D	Decrement D	↕	↕	↕	V	1	.	1	4
16n	LD D,n	Load data in byte 2 into D	.	.	.	.	.	.	2	7
17	RLA	Rotate left the contents of the accumulator	.	.	0	.	0	↕	1	4
18e	JR e	Unconditional relative jump to PC + e	.	.	.	.	.	.	3	12
19	ADD HL,DE	Add contents of register pair DE to HL	.	.	X	.	0	↕	3	11
1A	LD A,(DE)	Load the contents of memory pointed to by DE into the accumulator	.	.	.	.	.	.	2	7
1B	DEC DE	Decrement DE	.	.	.	.	.	.	1	6
1C	INC E	Increment E	↕	↕	↕	V	0	.	1	4
1D	DEC E	Decrement E	↕	↕	↕	V	1	.	1	4
1En	LD E,n	Load data in byte 2 into E	.	.	.	.	.	.	2	7
1F	RRA	Rotate right accumulator	.	.	0	.	0	↕	1	4
20e	JR NZ,e	If Z = 1, disregard instructions. If Z = 0, jump to PC + e	.	.	.	.	.	.	2 (if Z = 1)	7
									3 (if Z = 0)	12
21nn	LD HL,nn	Load byte 2 into L and load byte 3 into H	.	.	.	.	.	.	3	10
22nn	LD (nn),HL	Load L into memory pointed to by bytes 3 and 2. Load H into the next higher address	.	.	.	.	.	.	5	16
23	INC HL	Increment HL	.	.	.	.	.	.	1	6
24	INC H	Increment H	↕	↕	↕	V	0	.	1	4
25	DEC H	Decrement H	↕	↕	↕	V	1	.	1	4
26n	LD H,n	Load data in byte 2 into H	.	.	.	.	.	.	2	7
27	DAA	Decimal adjust the accumulator	↕	↕	↕	P	.	↕	1	4
28e	JR Z,e	If Z = 0, continue. If Z = 1, jump to PC + e	.	.	.	.	.	.	2 (if Z = 0)	7
									3 (if Z = 1)	12
29	ADD HL,HL	Add contents of register pair HL to HL	.	.	X	.	0	↕	3	11

OP CODE	MNEMONIC	COMMENT	S	Z	H	P/V	N	C	M CYCLES	T STATES
					FLAGS					
2Ann	LD HL,(nn)	Load contents of memory pointed to by bytes 3 and 2 into L. Load the following byte into H	.	.	.	.	.	.	5	16
2B	DEC HL	Decrement HL	.	.	.	.	.	.	1	6
2C	INC L	Increment L	↕	↕	↕	V	0	.	1	4
2D	DEC L	Decrement L	↕	↕	↕	V	1	.	1	4
2En	LD L,n	Load data in byte 2 into L	.	.	.	.	.	.	1	4
2F	CPL	Complement accumulator (1's complement)	.	.	1	.	1	.	1	4
30e	JR NC,e	If carry flag=1, disregard jump. If C=0, jump to PC+e	.	.	.	.	.	.	2 (if C=1)	7
									3 (if C=0)	12
31nn	LD SP,nn	Load byte 2 into the LOW byte of the stack pointer and byte 3 into the HIGH byte	.	.	.	.	.	.	3	10
32nn	LD (nn),A	Load contents of A into memory pointed to by bytes 3 and 2	.	.	.	.	.	.	4	13
33	INC SP	Increment stack pointer	.	.	.	.	.	.	1	6
34	INC (HL)	Increment contents of memory location pointed to by HL	↕	↕	↕	V	0	.	3	11
35	DEC (HL)	Decrement contents of memory pointed to by HL	↕	↕	↕	V	1	.	3	11
36	LD (HL),n	Load byte 2 into address pointed to by HL	.	.	.	.	.	.	3	10
37	SCF	Set carry flag	.	.	0	.	0	1	1	4
38e	JR C,e	If carry flag=0, disregard instruction. If carry flag=1, jump to PC+e	.	.	.	.	.	.	2 (if C=0)	7
									3 (if C=1)	12
39	ADD HL,SP	Add contents of stack pointer to HL	.	.	X	.	0	↕	3	11
3Ann	LD A,(nn)	Load contents of memory pointed to by bytes 3 and 2 into accumulator	.	.	.	.	.	.	4	13
3B	DEC SP	Decrement contents of stack pointer	.	.	.	.	.	.	1	6
3C	INC A	Increment contents of accumulator	↕	↕	↕	V	0	.	1	4
3D	DEC A	Decrement contents of accumulator	↕	↕	↕	V	1	.	1	4
3En	LD A,n	Load data in byte 2 into accumulator	.	.	.	.	.	.	2	7
3F	CCF	Complement the carry flag	.	.	X	.	0	↕	1	4
40	LD B,B	Load contents of register B into B	.	.	.	.	.	.	1	4
41	LD B,C	Load contents of register C into B	.	.	.	.	.	.	1	4
42	LD B,D	Load contents of register D into B	.	.	.	.	.	.	1	4
43	LD B,E	Load contents of register E into B	.	.	.	.	.	.	1	4
44	LD B,H	Load contents of register H into B	.	.	.	.	.	.	1	4
45	LD B,L	Load contents of register L into B	.	.	.	.	.	.	1	4
46	LD B,(HL)	Load contents of memory pointed to by HL into B	.	.	.	.	.	.	2	7
47	LD B,A	Load contents of accumulator into B	.	.	.	.	.	.	1	4
48	LD C,B	Load contents of register B into C	.	.	.	.	.	.	1	4
49	LD C,C	Load contents of register C into C	.	.	.	.	.	.	1	4
4A	LD C,D	Load contents of register D into C	.	.	.	.	.	.	1	4

OP CODE	MNEMONIC	COMMENT	S	Z	H	P/V	N	C	M CYCLES	T STATES
4B	LD C,E	Load contents of register E into C	.	.	.	.	.	.	1	4
4C	LD C,H	Load contents of register H into C	.	.	.	.	.	.	1	4
4D	LD C,L	Load contents of register L into C	.	.	.	.	.	.	1	4
4E	LD C,(HL)	Load contents of memory pointed to by HL into C	.	.	.	.	.	.	2	7
4F	LD C,A	Load contents of accumulator into C	.	.	.	.	.	.	1	4
50	LD D,B	Load contents of register B into D	.	.	.	.	.	.	1	4
51	LD D, C	Load contents of register C into D	.	.	.	.	.	.	1	4
52	LD D,D	Load contents of register D into D	.	.	.	.	.	.	1	4
53	LD D,E	Load contents of register E into D	.	.	.	.	.	.	1	4
54	LD D,H	Load contents of register H into D	.	.	.	.	.	.	1	4
55	LD D,L	Load contents of register L into D	.	.	.	.	.	.	1	4
56	LD D,(HL)	Load contents of memory pointed to by HL into D	.	.	.	.	.	.	2	7
57	LD D,A	Load contents of accumulator into D	.	.	.	.	.	.	1	4
58	LD E,B	Load contents of register B into E	.	.	.	.	.	.	1	4
59	LD E,C	Load contents of register C into E	.	.	.	.	.	.	1	4
5A	LD E,D	Load contents of register D into E	.	.	.	.	.	.	1	4
5B	LD E,E	Load contents of register E into E	.	.	.	.	.	.	1	4
5C	LD E,H	Load contents of register H into E	.	.	.	.	.	.	1	4
5D	LD E,L	Load contents of register L into E	.	.	.	.	.	.	1	4
5E	LD E,(HL)	Load contents of memory pointed to by HL into E	.	.	.	.	.	.	2	7
5F	LD E,A	Load contents of accumulator into E	.	.	.	.	.	.	1	4
60	LD H,B	Load contents of register B into H	.	.	.	.	.	.	1	4
61	LD H,C	Load contents of register C into H	.	.	.	.	.	.	1	4
62	LD H,D	Load contents of register D into H	.	.	.	.	.	.	1	4
63	LD H,E	Load contents of register E into H	.	.	.	.	.	.	1	4
64	LD H,H	Load contents of register H into H	.	.	.	.	.	.	1	4
65	LD H,L	Load contents of register L into H	.	.	.	.	.	.	1	4
66	LD H,(HL)	Load contents of memory pointed to by HL into H	.	.	.	.	.	.	2	7
67	LD H,A	Load contents of accumulator into H	.	.	.	.	.	.	1	4
68	LD L,B	Load contents of register B into L	.	.	.	.	.	.	1	4
69	LD L,C	Load contents of register C into L	.	.	.	.	.	.	1	4
6A	LD L,D	Load contents of register D into L	.	.	.	.	.	.	1	4
6B	LD L,E	Load contents of register E into L	.	.	.	.	.	.	1	4
6C	LD L,H	Load contents of register H into L	.	.	.	.	.	.	1	4
6D	LD L,L	Load contents of register L into L	.	.	.	.	.	.	1	4
6E	LD L,(HL)	Load contents of memory pointed to by HL into L	.	.	.	.	.	.	2	7
6F	LD L,A	Load contents of accumulator into L	.	.	.	.	.	.	1	4
70	LD (HL),B	Load contents of B into memory pointed to by HL	.	.	.	.	.	.	2	7
71	LD (HL),C	Load contents of C into memory pointed to by HL	.	.	.	.	.	.	2	7
72	LD (HL),D	Load contents of D into memory pointed to by HL	.	.	.	.	.	.	2	7

OP CODE	MNEMONIC	COMMENT	S	Z	H	P/V	N	C	M CYCLES	T STATES
			FLAGS							
73	LD (HL),E	Load contents of E into memory pointed to by HL	.	.	.	.	.	.	2	7
74	LD (HL),H	Load contents of H into memory pointed to by HL	.	.	.	.	.	.	2	7
75	LD (HL), L	Load contents of L into memory pointed to by HL	.	.	.	.	.	.	2	7
76	HALT	HALT	.	.	.	.	.	.	1	4
77	LD (HL),A	Load contents of accumulator into memory pointed to by HL	.	.	.	.	.	.	2	7
78	LD A,B	Load contents of register B into A	.	.	.	.	.	.	1	4
79	LD A,C	Load contents of register C into A	.	.	.	.	.	.	1	4
7A	LD A,D	Load contents of register D into A	.	.	.	.	.	.	1	4
7B	LD A,E	Load contents of register E into A	.	.	.	.	.	.	1	4
7C	LD A,H	Load contents of register H into A	.	.	.	.	.	.	1	4
7D	LD A,L	Load contents of register L into A	.	.	.	.	.	.	1	4
7E	LD A,(HL)	Load contents of memory pointed to by HL into the accumulator	.	.	.	.	.	.	2	7
7F	LD A,A	Load contents of accumulator into the accumulator	.	.	.	.	.	.	1	4
80	ADD A,B	Add contents of register B to the accumulator	↕	↕	↕	V	0	↕	1	4
81	ADD A,C	Add contents of register C to the accumulator	↕	↕	↕	V	0	↕	1	4
82	ADD A,D	Add contents of register D to the accumulator	↕	↕	↕	V	0	↕	1	4
83	ADD A,E	Add contents of register E to the accumulator	↕	↕	↕	V	0	↕	1	4
84	ADD A,H	Add contents of register H to the accumulator	↕	↕	↕	V	0	↕	1	4
85	ADD A,L	Add contents of register L to the accumulator	↕	↕	↕	V	0	↕	1	4
86	ADD A,(HL)	Add contents of memory pointed to by HL to the accumulator	↕	↕	↕	V	0	↕	2	7
87	ADD A,A	Add contents of accumulator to itself	↕	↕	↕	V	0	↕	1	4
88	ADC A,B	Add contents of register B and carry flag to the accumulator	↕	↕	↕	V	0	↕	1	4
89	ADC A,C	Add contents of register C and carry flag to the accumulator	↕	↕	↕	V	0	↕	1	4
8A	ADC A,D	Add contents of register D and carry flag to the accumulator	↕	↕	↕	V	0	↕	1	4
8B	ADC A,E	Add contents of register E and carry flag to the accumulator	↕	↕	↕	V	0	↕	1	4
8C	ADC A,H	Add contents of register H and carry flag to the accumulator	↕	↕	↕	V	0	↕	1	4
8D	ADC A,L	Add contents of register L and carry flag to the accumulator	↕	↕	↕	V	0	↕	1	4
8E	ADC A,(HL)	Add contents of memory pointed to by HL and carry flag to the accumulator	↕	↕	↕	V	0	↕	2	7
8F	ADC A,A	Add contents of accumulator and carry flag to the accumulator	↕	↕	↕	V	0	↕	1	4
90	SUB B	Subtract contents of register B from the accumulator	↕	↕	↕	V	1	↕	1	4

OP CODE	MNEMONIC	COMMENT	FLAGS S	Z	H	P/V	N	C	M CYCLES	T STATES
91	SUB C	Subtract contents of register C from the accumulator	↕	↕	↕	V	1	↕	1	4
92	SUB D	Subtract contents of register D from the accumulator	↕	↕	↕	V	1	↕	1	4
93	SUB E	Subtract contents of register E from the accumulator	↕	↕	↕	V	1	↕	1	4
94	SUB H	Subtract contents of register H from the accumulator	↕	↕	↕	V	1	↕	1	4
95	SUB L	Subtract contents of register L from the accumulator	↕	↕	↕	V	1	↕	1	4
96	SUB (HL)	Subtract contents of memory pointed to by HL from accumulator	↕	↕	↕	V	1	↕	2	7
97	SUB A	Subtract contents of accumulator from the accumulator	↕	↕	↕	V	1	↕	1	4
98	SBC A,B	Subtract contents of register B and carry flag from the accumulator	↕	↕	↕	V	1	↕	1	4
99	SBC A,C	Subtract contents of register C and carry flag from contents of accumulator	↕	↕	↕	V	1	↕	1	4
9A	SBC A,D	Subtract contents of register D and carry flag from contents of accumulator	↕	↕	↕	V	1	↕	1	4
9B	SBC A,E	Subtract contents of register E and carry flag from contents of accumulator	↕	↕	↕	V	1	↕	1	4
9C	SBC A,H	Subtract contents of register H and carry flag from contents of accumulator	↕	↕	↕	V	1	↕	1	4
9D	SBC A,L	Subtract contents of L and carry flag from contents of accumulator	↕	↕	↕	V	1	↕	1	4
9E	SBC A,(HL)	Subtract contents of memory pointed to by HL and carry flag from accumulator	↕	↕	↕	V	1	↕	2	7
9F	SBC A,A	Subtract contents of accumulator and carry flag from the accumulator	↕	↕	↕	V	1	↕	1	4
A0	AND B	AND contents of register B with the accumulator	↕	↕	1	P	0	0	1	4
A1	AND C	AND contents of register C with the accumulator	↕	↕	1	P	0	0	1	4
A2	AND D	AND contents of register D with the accumulator	↕	↕	1	P	0	0	1	4
A3	AND E	AND contents of register E with accumulator	↕	↕	1	P	0	0	1	4
A4	AND H	AND contents of register H with the accumulator	↕	↕	1	P	0	0	1	4
A5	AND L	AND contents of register L with the accumulator	↕	↕	1	P	0	0	1	4
A6	AND (HL)	AND contents of memory pointed to by HL with the accumulator	↕	↕	1	P	0	0	2	7
A7	AND A	AND contents of accumulator with the accumulator	↕	↕	1	P	0	0	1	4
A8	XOR B	Exclusive-OR the contents of register B with the accumulator	↕	↕	0	P	0	0	1	4

OP CODE	MNEMONIC	COMMENT	S	Z	H	P/V	N	C	M CYCLES	T STATES
			FLAGS							
A9	XOR C	Exclusive-OR the contents of register C with the accumulator	↕	↕	0	P	0	0	1	4
AA	XOR D	Exclusive-OR the contents of register D with the accumulator	↕	↕	0	P	0	0	1	4
AB	XOR E	Exclusive-OR the contents of register E with the accumulator	↕	↕	0	P	0	0	1	4
AC	XOR H	Exclusive-OR the contents of register H with the accumulator	↕	↕	0	P	0	0	1	4
AD	XOR L	Exclusive-OR the contents of register L with the accumulator	↕	↕	0	P	0	0	1	4
AE	XOR (HL)	Exclusive-OR the contents of memory pointed to by HL with the accumulator	↕	↕	0	P	0	0	2	7
AF	XOR A	Exclusive-OR the contents of accumulator with the accumulator	↕	↕	0	P	0	0	1	4
B0	OR B	OR contents of B with contents of accumulator	↕	↕	0	P	0	0	1	4
B1	OR C	OR contents of C with contents of accumulator	↕	↕	0	P	0	0	1	4
B2	OR D	OR contents of D with contents of accumulator	↕	↕	0	P	0	0	1	4
B3	OR E	OR contents of E with contents of accumulator	↕	↕	0	P	0	0	1	4
B4	OR H	OR contents of H with contents of accumulator	↕	↕	0	P	0	0	1	4
B5	OR L	OR contents of L with contents of accumulator	↕	↕	0	P	0	0	1	4
B6	OR (HL)	OR contents of memory pointed to by HL with the accumulator	↕	↕	0	P	0	0	2	7
B7	OR A	OR contents of accumulator with contents of accumlator	↕	↕	0	P	0	0	1	4
B8	CP B	Compare contents of register B with the accumulator	↕	↕	↕	V	1	↕	1	4
B9	CP C	Compare contents of register C with the accumulator	↕	↕	↕	V	1	↕	1	4
BA	CP D	Compare contents of register D with the accumulator	↕	↕	↕	V	1	↕	1	4
BB	CP E	Compare contents of register E with the accumulator	↕	↕	↕	V	1	↕	1	4
BC	CP H	Compare contents of register H with the accumulator	↕	↕	↕	V	1	↕	1	4
BD	CP L	Compare contents of register L with contents of accumulator	↕	↕	↕	V	1	↕	1	4
BE	CP (HL)	Compare contents of memory pointed to by HL with the accumulator	↕	↕	↕	V	1	↕	2	7
BF	CP A	Compare contents of accumulator with the accumulator	↕	↕	↕	V	1	↕	1	4
C0	RET NZ	If zero flag=1, disregard instruction. If zero flag=0, return from subroutine	.	.	.	.	.	.	1 (if Z=1) 3 (if Z=0)	5 11
C1	POP BC	Load contents of memory pointed to by stack pointer into C and contents of memory pointed to by SP+1 into B	.	.	.	.	.	.	3	10

OP CODE	MNEMONIC	COMMENT	S	Z	H	P/V	N	C	M CYCLES	T STATES
C2nn	JP NZ,nn	If zero flag=1, disregard instruction. If zero flag=0, jump to address pointed to bytes 3 and 2	.	.	.	.	.	.	3	10
C3nn	JP nn	Unconditional jump to address pointed to by bytes 3 and 2	.	.	.	.	.	.	3	10
C4nn	CALL NZ,nn	If zero flag=1, disregard instruction. If zero flag=0, call subroutine at address pointed to by bytes 3 and 2	.	.	.	.	.	.	3 (if Z=1) 5 (if Z=0)	10 17
C5	PUSH BC	Load B into memory pointed to by SP-1 and C into memory pointed to by SP-2	.	.	.	.	.	.	3	11
C6n	ADD A,n	Add byte 2 to the accumulator	↕	↕	↕	V	0	↕	2	7
C7	RST 00H	Restart at 0000H. Push the contents of the program counter onto the stack. Load the program counter with 0000H	.	.	.	.	.	.	3	11
C8	RET Z	If zero flag=0, disregard instruction. If zero flag=1, return from subroutine	.	.	.	.	.	.	1 (if Z=0) 3 (if Z=1)	5 11
C9	RET	Unconditional return from subroutine	.	.	.	.	.	.	3	10
CAnn	JP Z,nn	If zero flag=0, disregard instruction. If zero flag=1, jump to address pointed to by bytes 3 and 2	.	.	.	.	.	.	3	10
CB00	RLC B	Rotate left circular the contents of register B	↕	↕	0	P	0	↕	2	8
CB01	RLC C	Rotate left circular the contents of register C	↕	↕	0	P	0	↕	2	8
CB02	RLC D	Rotate left circular the contents of register D	↕	↕	0	P	0	↕	2	8
CB03	RLC E	Rotate left circular the contents of register E	↕	↕	0	P	0	↕	2	8
CB04	RLC H	Rotate left circular the contents of register H	↕	↕	0	P	0	↕	2	8
CB05	RLC L	Rotate left circular the contents of register L	↕	↕	0	P	0	↕	2	8
CB06	RLC (HL)	Rotate left circular the contents of memory pointed to by HL	↕	↕	0	P	0	↕	4	15
CB07	RLC A	Rotate left circular the accumulator	↕	↕	0	P	0	↕	2	8
CB08	RRC B	Rotate right circular the contents of register B	↕	↕	0	P	0	↕	2	8
CB09	RRC C	Rotate right circular the contents of register C	↕	↕	0	P	0	↕	2	8
CB0A	RRC D	Rotate right circular the contents of register D	↕	↕	0	P	0	↕	2	8
CB0B	RRC E	Rotate right circular the contents of register E	↕	↕	0	P	0	↕	2	8
CB0C	RRC H	Rotate right circular the contents of register H	↕	↕	0	P	0	↕	2	8
CB0D	RRC L	Rotate right circular the contents of register L	↕	↕	0	P	0	↕	2	8
CB0E	RRC (HL)	Rotate right circular the contents of memory pointed to by HL	↕	↕	0	P	0	↕	5	15
CB0F	RRC A	Rotate right circular the contents of the accumulator	↕	↕	0	P	0	↕	2	8
CB10	RL B	Rotate left the contents of register B	↕	↕	0	P	0	↕	2	8
CB11	RL C	Rotate left the contents of register C	↕	↕	0	P	0	↕	2	8
CB12	RL D	Rotate left the contents of register D	↕	↕	0	P	0	↕	2	8
CB13	RL E	Rotate left the contents of register E	↕	↕	0	P	0	↕	2	8
CB14	RL H	Rotate left the contents of register H	↕	↕	0	P	0	↕	2	8

OP CODE	MNEMONIC	COMMENT	S	Z	H	P/V	N	C	M CYCLES	T STATES
			FLAGS							
CB15	RL L	Rotate left the contents of register L	↕	↕	0	P	0	↕	2	8
CB16	RL (HL)	Rotate left the contents of memory pointed to by HL	↕	↕	0	P	0	↕	4	15
CB17	RL A	Rotate left the contents of accumulator	↕	↕	0	P	0	↕	6	23
CB18	RR B	Rotate right the contents of register B	↕	↕	0	P	0	↕	2	8
CB19	RR C	Rotate right the contents of register C	↕	↕	0	P	0	↕	2	8
CB1A	RR D	Rotate right the contents of register D	↕	↕	0	P	0	↕	2	8
CB1B	RR E	Rotate right the contents of register E	↕	↕	0	P	0	↕	2	8
CB1C	RR H	Rotate right the contents of register H	↕	↕	0	P	0	↕	2	8
CB1D	RR L	Rotate right the contents of register L	↕	↕	0	P	0	↕	2	8
CB1E	RR (HL)	Rotate right the contents of memory pointed to by HL	↕	↕	0	P	0	↕	4	15
CB1F	RR A	Rotate right the contents of register A	↕	↕	0	P	0	↕	2	8
CB20	SLA B	Shift left arithmetic the contents of register B	↕	↕	0	P	0	↕	2	8
CB21	SLA C	Shift left arithmetic the contents of register C	↕	↕	0	P	0	↕	2	8
CB22	SLA D	Shift left arithmetic the contents of register D	↕	↕	0	P	0	↕	2	8
CB23	SLA E	Shift left arithmetic the contents of register E	↕	↕	0	P	0	↕	2	8
CB24	SLA H	Shift left arithmetic the contents of register H	↕	↕	0	P	0	↕	2	8
CB25	SLA L	Shift left arithmetic the contents of register L	↕	↕	0	P	0	↕	2	8
CB26	SLA (HL)	Shift left arithmetic the contents of memory pointed to by HL	↕	↕	0	P	0	↕	4	15
CB27	SLA A	Shift left arithmetic the contents of the accumulator	↕	↕	0	P	0	↕	2	8
CB28	SRA B	Shift right arithmetic the contents of register B	↕	↕	0	P	0	↕	2	8
CB29	SRA C	Shift right arithmetic the contents of register C	↕	↕	0	P	0	↕	2	8
CB2A	SRA D	Shift right arithmetic the contents of register D	↕	↕	0	P	0	↕	2	8
CB2B	SRA E	Shift right arithmetic the contents of register E	↕	↕	0	P	0	↕	2	8
CB2C	SRA H	Shift right arithmetic the contents of register H	↕	↕	0	P	0	↕	2	8
CB2D	SRA L	Shift right arithmetic the contents of register L	↕	↕	0	P	0	↕	2	8
CB2E	SRA (HL)	Shift right arithmetic the contents of memory pointed to by HL	↕	↕	0	P	0	↕	4	15
CB2F	SRA A	Shift right arithmetic the contents of the accumulator	↕	↕	0	P	0	↕	2	8
CB38	SRL B	Shift right logical contents of register B	↕	↕	0	P	0	↕	2	8
CB39	SRL C	Shift right logical contents of register C	↕	↕	0	P	0	↕	2	8
CB3A	SRL D	Shift right logical contents of register D	↕	↕	0	P	0	↕	2	8
CB3B	SRL E	Shift right logical contents of register E	↕	↕	0	P	0	↕	2	8
CB3C	SRL H	Shift right logical contents of register H	↕	↕	0	P	0	↕	2	8
CB3D	SRL L	Shift right logical contents of register L	↕	↕	0	P	0	↕	2	8
CB3E	SRL (HL)	Shift right logical the contents of memory pointed to by HL	↕	↕	0	P	0	↕	4	15
CB3F	SRL A	Shift right logical contents of accumulator	↕	↕	0	P	0	↕	2	8
CB40	BIT 0,B	If bit 0 of register B is 0, set the zero flag (Z=1). Otherwise Z=0	X	↕	1	X	0	.	2	8
CB41	BIT 0,C	If bit 0 of register C is 0, set the zero flag (Z=1). Otherwise Z=0	X	↕	1	X	0	.	2	8

OP CODE	MNEMONIC	COMMENT	FLAGS S	Z	H	P/V	N	C	M CYCLES	T STATES
CB42	BIT 0,D	If bit 0 of register D is 0, set the zero flag (Z=1). Otherwise Z=0	X	↕	1	X	0	.	2	8
CB43	BIT 0,E	If bit 0 of register E is 0, set the zero flag (Z=1). Otherwise Z=0	X	↕	1	X	0	.	2	8
CB44	BIT 0,H	If bit 0 of register H is 0, set the zero flag (Z=1). Otherwise Z=0	X	↕	1	X	0	.	2	8
CB45	BIT 0,L	If bit 0 of register L is 0, set the zero flag (Z=1). Otherwise Z=0	X	↕	1	X	0	.	2	8
CB46	BIT 0,(HL)	If bit 0 of memory pointed to by HL is 0, set the zero flag (Z=1). Otherwise Z=0	X	↕	1	X	0	.	3	12
CB47	BIT 0,A	If bit 0 of the accumulator is 0, set the zero flag (Z=1). Otherwise Z=0	X	↕	1	X	0	.	2	8
CB48	BIT 1,B	If bit 1 of register B is 0, set the zero flag (Z=1). Otherwise Z=0	X	↕	1	X	0	.	2	8
CB49	BIT 1,C	If bit 1 of register C is 0, set the zero flag (Z=1). Otherwise Z=0	X	↕	1	X	0	.	2	8
CB4A	BIT 1,D	If bit 1 of register D is 0, set the zero flag (Z=1). Otherwise Z=0	X	↕	1	X	0	.	2	8
CB4B	BIT 1,E	If bit 1 of register E is 0, set the zero flag (Z=1). Otherwise Z=0	X	↕	1	X	0	.	2	8
CB4C	BIT 1,H	If bit 1 of register H is 0, set the zero flag (Z=1). Otherwise Z=0	X	↕	1	X	0	.	2	8
CB4D	BIT I,L	If bit 1 of register L is 0, set the zero flag (Z=1). Otherwise Z=0	X	↕	1	X	0	.	2	8
CB4E	BIT 1,(HL)	If bit 1 of memory pointed to by HL is 0, set the zero flag (Z=1). Otherwise Z=0	X	↕	1	X	0	.	3	12
CB4F	BIT 1,A	If bit 1 of the accumulator is 0, set the zero flag (Z=1). Otherwise Z=0	X	↕	1	X	0	.	2	8
CB50	BIT 2,B	If bit 2 of register B is 0, set the zero flag (Z=1). Otherwise Z=0	X	↕	1	X	0	.	2	8
CB51	BIT 2,C	If bit 2 of register C is 0, set the zero flag (Z=1). Otherwise Z=0	X	↕	1	X	0	.	2	8
CB52	BIT 2,D	If bit 2 of register D is 0, set the zero flag (Z=1). Otherwise Z=0	X	↕	1	X	0	.	2	8
CB53	BIT 2,E	If bit 2 of register E is 0, set the zero flag (Z=1). Otherwise Z=0	X	↕	1	X	0	.	2	8
CB54	BIT 2,H	If bit 2 of register H is 0, set the zero flag (Z=1). Otherwise Z=0	X	↕	1	X	0	.	2	8
CB55	BIT 2,L	If bit 2 of register L is 0, set the zero flag (Z=1). Otherwise Z=0	X	↕	1	X	0	.	2	8
CB56	BIT 2,(HL)	If bit 2 of memory pointed to by HL is 0, set the zero flag (Z=1). Otherwise Z=0	X	↕	1	X	0	.	3	12
CB57	BIT 2,A	If bit 2 of the accumulator is 0, set the zero flag (Z=1). Otherwise Z=0	X	↕	1	X	0	.	2	8
CB58	BIT 3,B	If bit 3 of register B is 0, set the zero flag (Z=1). Otherwise Z=0	X	↕	1	X	0	.	2	8
CB59	BIT 3,C	If bit 3 of register C is 0, set the zero flag (Z=1). Otherwise Z=0	X	↕	1	X	0	.	2	8

OP CODE	MNEMONIC	COMMENT	S	Z	H	P/V	N	C	M CYCLES	T STATES
CB5A	BIT 3,D	If bit 3 of register D is 0, set the zero flag (Z=1). Otherwise Z=0	X	↕	1	X	0	.	2	8
CB5B	BIT 3,E	If bit 3 of register E is 0, set the zero flag (Z=1). Otherwise Z=0	X	↕	1	X	0	.	2	8
CB5C	BIT 3,H	If bit 3 of register H is 0, set the zero flag (Z=1). Otherwise Z=0	X	↕	1	X	0	.	2	8
CB5D	BIT 3,L	If bit 3 of register L is 0, set the zero flag (Z=1). Otherwise Z=0	X	↕	1	X	0	.	2	8
CB5E	BIT 3,(HL)	If bit 3 of memory pointed to by HL is 0, set the zero flag (Z=1). Otherwise Z=0	X	↕	1	X	0	.	3	12
CB5F	BIT 3,A	If bit 3 of the accumulator is 0, set the zero flag (Z=1). Otherwise Z=0	X	↕	1	X	0	.	2	8
CB60	BIT 4,B	If bit 4 of register B is 0, set the zero flag (Z=1). Otherwise Z=0	X	↕	1	X	0	.	2	8
CB61	BIT 4, C	If bit 4 of register C is 0, set the zero flag (Z=1). Otherwise Z=0	X	↕	1	X	0	.	2	8
CB62	BIT 4,D	If bit 4 of register D is 0, set the zero flag (Z=1). Otherwise Z=0	X	↕	1	X	0	.	2	8
CB63	BIT 4,E	If bit 4 of register E is 0, set the zero flag (Z=1). Otherwise Z=0	X	↕	1	X	0	.	2	8
CB64	BIT 4,H	If bit 4 of register H is 0, set the zero flag (Z=1). Otherwise Z=0	X	↕	1	X	0	.	2	8
CB65	BIT 4,L	If bit 4 of register L is 0, set the zero flag (Z=1). Otherwise Z=0	X	↕	1	X	0	.	2	8
CB66	BIT 4,(HL)	If bit 4 of memory pointed to by HL is 0, set the zero flag (Z=1). Otherwise Z=0	X	↕	1	X	0	.	3	12
CB67	BIT 4,A	If bit 4 of the accumulator is 0, set the zero flag (Z=1). Otherwise Z=0	X	↕	1	X	0	.	2	8
CB68	BIT 5,B	If bit 5 of register B is 0, set the zero flag (Z=1). Otherwise Z=0	X	↕	1	X	0	.	2	8
CB69	BIT 5,C	If bit 5 of register C is 0, set the zero flag (Z=1). Otherwise Z=0	X	↕	1	X	0	.	2	8
CB6A	BIT 5,D	If bit 5 of register D is 0, set the zero flag (Z=1). Otherwise Z=0	X	↕	1	X	0	.	2	8
CB6B	BIT 5,E	If bit 5 of register E is 0, set the zero flag (Z=1). Otherwise Z=0	X	↕	1	X	0	.	2	8
CB6C	BIT 5,H	If bit 5 of register H is 0, set the zero flag (Z=1). Otherwise Z=0	X	↕	1	X	0	.	2	8
CB6D	BIT 5,L	If bit 5 of register L is 0, set the zero flag (Z=1). Otherwise Z=0	X	↕	1	X	0	.	2	8
CB6E	BIT 5,(HL)	If bit 5 of memory pointed to by HL is 0, set the zero flag (Z=1). Otherwise Z=0	X	↕	1	X	0	.	3	12
CB6F	BIT 5,A	If bit 5 of the accumulator is 0, set the zero flag (Z=1). Otherwise Z=0	X	↕	1	X	0	.	2	8
CB70	BIT 6,B	If bit 6 of register B is 0, set the zero flag (Z=1). Otherwise Z=0	X	↕	1	X	0	.	2	8
CB71	BIT 6,C	If bit 6 of register C is 0, set the zero flag (Z=1). Otherwise Z=0	X	↕	1	X	0	.	2	8

OP CODE	MNEMONIC	COMMENT	FLAGS S	Z	H	P/V	N	C	M CYCLES	T STATES
CB72	BIT 6,D	If bit 6 of register D is 0, set the zero flag (Z=1). Otherwise Z=0	X	↕	1	X	0	.	2	8
CB73	BIT 6,E	If bit 6 of register E is 0, set the zero flag (Z=1). Otherwise Z=0	X	↕	1	X	0	.	2	8
CB74	BIT 6,H	If bit 6 of register H is 0, set the zero flag (Z=1). Otherwise Z=0	X	↕	1	X	0	.	2	8
CB75	BIT 6,L	If bit 6 of register L is 0, set the zero flag (Z=1). Otherwise Z=0	X	↕	1	X	0	.	2	8
CB76	BIT 6,(HL)	If bit 6 of memory pointed to by HL is 0, set the zero flag (Z=1). Otherwise Z=0	X	↕	1	X	0	.	3	12
CB77	BIT 6,A	If bit 6 of the accumulator is 0, set the zero flag (Z=1). Otherwise Z=0	X	↕	1	X	0	.	2	8
CB78	BIT 7,B	If bit 7 of register B is 0, set the zero flag (Z=1). Otherwise Z=0	X	↕	1	X	0	.	2	8
CB79	BIT 7,C	If bit 7 of register C is 0, set the zero flag (Z=1). Otherwise Z=0	X	↕	1	X	0	.	2	8
CB7A	BIT 7,D	If bit 7 of register D is 0, set the zero flag (Z=1). Otherwise Z=0	X	↕	1	X	0	.	2	8
CB7B	BIT 7,E	If bit 7 of register E is 0, set the zero flag (Z=1). Otherwise Z=0	X	↕	1	X	0	.	2	8
CB7C	BIT 7,H	If bit 7 of register H is 0, set the zero flag (Z=1). Otherwise Z=0	X	↕	1	X	0	.	2	8
CB7D	BIT 7,L	If but 7 of register L is 0, set the zero flag (Z=1). Otherwise Z=0	X	↕	1	X	0	.	2	8
CB7E	BIT 7,(HL)	If bit 7 memory pointed to by HL is 0, set the zero flag (Z=1). Otherwise Z=0	X	↕	1	X	0	.	3	12
CB7F	BIT 7,A	If bit 7 of the accumulator is 0, set the zero flag (Z=1). Otherwise Z=0	X	↕	1	X	0	.	2	8
CB80	RES 0,B	Reset bit 0 of B register to 0	.	.	.	.	.	.	2	8
CB81	RES 0,C	Reset bit 0 of C register to 0	.	.	.	.	.	.	2	8
CB82	RES 0,D	Reset bit 0 of D register to 0	.	.	.	.	.	.	2	8
CB83	RES 0,E	Reset bit 0 of E register to 0	.	.	.	.	.	.	2	8
CB84	RES 0,H	Reset bit 0 of H register to 0	.	.	.	.	.	.	2	8
CB85	RES 0,L	Reset bit 0 of L register to 0	.	.	.	.	.	.	2	8
CB86	RES 0,(HL)	Reset bit 0 in memory pointed to by HL to 0	.	.	.	.	.	.	4	15
CB87	RES 0,A	Reset bit 0 of accumulator to 0	.	.	.	.	.	.	2	8
CB88	RES 1,B	Reset bit 1 in B register to 0	.	.	.	.	.	.	2	8
CB89	RES 1,C	Reset bit 1 in C register to 0	.	.	.	.	.	.	2	8
CB8A	RES 1,D	Reset bit 1 in D register to 0	.	.	.	.	.	.	2	8
CB8B	RES 1,E	Reset bit 1 in E register to 0	.	.	.	.	.	.	2	8
CB8C	RES 1,H	Reset bit 1 in H register to 0	.	.	.	.	.	.	2	8
CB8D	RES 1,L	Reset bit 1 in L register to 0	.	.	.	.	.	.	2	8
CB8E	RES 1,(HL)	Reset bit 1 in memory pointed to by HL to 0	.	.	.	.	.	.	4	15
CB8F	RES 1,A	Reset bit 1 in accumulator to 0	.	.	.	.	.	.	2	8
CB90	RES 2,B	Reset bit 2 in B register to 0	.	.	.	.	.	.	2	8
CB91	RES 2,C	Reset bit 2 in C register to 0	.	.	.	.	.	.	2	8

OP CODE	MNEMONIC	COMMENT	FLAGS S	Z	H	P/V	N	C	M CYCLES	T STATES
CB92	RES 2,D	Reset bit 2 in D register to 0	.	.	.	.	.	.	2	8
CB93	RES 2,E	Reset bit 2 in E register to 0	.	.	.	.	.	.	2	8
CB94	RES 2,H	Reset bit 2 in H register to 0	.	.	.	.	.	.	2	8
CB95	RES 2,L	Reset bit 2 in L register to 0	.	.	.	.	.	.	2	8
CB96	RES 2,(HL)	Reset bit 2 in memory pointed to by HL to 0	.	.	.	.	.	.	4	15
CB97	RES 2,A	Reset bit 2 in accumulator to 0	.	.	.	.	.	.	2	8
CB98	RES 3,B	Reset bit 3 in B register to 0	.	.	.	.	.	.	2	8
CB99	RES 3,C	Reset bit 3 in C register to 0	.	.	.	.	.	.	2	8
CB9A	RES 3,D	Reset bit 3 in D register to 0	.	.	.	.	.	.	2	8
CB9B	RES 3,E	Reset bit 3 in E register to 0	.	.	.	.	.	.	2	8
CB9C	RES 3,H	Reset bit 3 in H register to 0	.	.	.	.	.	.	2	8
CB9D	RES 3,L	Reset bit 3 in L register to 0	.	.	.	.	.	.	2	8
CB9E	RES 3,(HL)	Reset bit 3 in memory pointed to by HL to 0	.	.	.	.	.	.	4	15
CB9F	RES 3,A	Reset bit 3 in accumulator to 0	.	.	.	.	.	.	2	8
CBA0	RES 4,B	Reset bit 4 in B register to 0	.	.	.	.	.	.	2	8
CBA1	RES 4,C	Reset bit 4 in C register to 0	.	.	.	.	.	.	2	8
CBA2	RES 4,D	Reset bit 4 in D register to 0	.	.	.	.	.	.	2	8
CBA3	RES 4,E	Reset bit 4 in E register to 0	.	.	.	.	.	.	2	8
CBA4	RES 4,H	Reset bit 4 in H register to 0	.	.	.	.	.	.	2	8
CBA5	RES 4,L	Reset bit 4 in L register to 0	.	.	.	.	.	.	2	8
CBA6	RES 4,(HL)	Reset bit 4 in memory pointed to by HL to 0	.	.	.	.	.	.	4	15
CBA7	RES 4,A	Reset bit 4 in accumulator to 0	.	.	.	.	.	.	2	8
CBA8	RES 5,B	Reset bit 5 in B register to 0	.	.	.	.	.	.	2	8
CBA9	RES 5,C	Reset bit 5 in C register to 0	.	.	.	.	.	.	2	8
CBAA	RES 5,D	Reset bit 5 in D register to 0	.	.	.	.	.	.	2	8
CBAB	RES 5,E	Reset bit 5 in E register to 0	.	.	.	.	.	.	2	8
CBAC	RES 5,H	Reset bit 5 in H register to 0	.	.	.	.	.	.	2	8
CBAD	RES 5,L	Reset bit 5 in L register to 0	.	.	.	.	.	.	2	8
CBAE	RES 5,(HL)	Reset bit 5 in memory pointed to by HL to 0	.	.	.	.	.	.	4	15
CBAF	RES 5,A	Reset bit 5 in accumulator to 0	.	.	.	.	.	.	2	8
CBB0	RES 6,B	Reset bit 6 in B register to 0	.	.	.	.	.	.	2	8
CBB1	RES 6,C	Reset bit 6 in C register to 0	.	.	.	.	.	.	2	8
CBB2	RES 6,D	Reset bit 6 in D register to 0	.	.	.	.	.	.	2	8
CBB3	RES 6,E	Reset bit 6 in E register to 0	.	.	.	.	.	.	2	8
CBB4	RES 6,H	Reset bit 6 in H register to 0	.	.	.	.	.	.	2	8
CBB5	RES 6,L	Reset bit 6 in L register to 0	.	.	.	.	.	.	2	8
CBB6	RES 6,(HL)	Reset bit 6 in memory pointed to by HL to 0	.	.	.	.	.	.	4	15
CBB7	RES 6,A	Reset bit 6 in accumulator to 0	.	.	.	.	.	.	2	8
CBB8	RES 7,B	Reset bit 7 in B register to 0	.	.	.	.	.	.	2	8
CBB9	RES 7,C	Reset bit 7 in C register to 0	.	.	.	.	.	.	2	8
CBBA	RES 7,D	Reset bit 7 in D register to 0	.	.	.	.	.	.	2	8
CBBB	RES 7,E	Reset bit 7 in E register to 0	.	.	.	.	.	.	2	8
CBBC	RES 7,H	Reset bit 7 in H register to 0	.	.	.	.	.	.	2	8
CBBD	RES 7,L	Reset bit 7 in L register to 0	.	.	.	.	.	.	2	8
CBBE	RES 7,(HL)	Reset bit 7 in memory pointed to by HL to 0	.	.	.	.	.	.	4	15
CBBF	RES 7,A	Reset bit 7 in accumulator to 0	.	.	.	.	.	.	2	8

OP CODE	MNEMONIC	COMMENT	S	Z	H	P/V	N	C	M CYCLES	T STATES
CBC0	SET 0,B	Set bit 0 of B register to 1	.	.	.	.	.	.	2	8
CBC1	SET 0,C	Set bit 0 of C register to 1	.	.	.	.	.	.	2	8
CBC2	SET 0,D	Set bit 0 of D register to 1	.	.	.	.	.	.	2	8
CBC3	SET 0,E	Set bit 0 of E register to 1	.	.	.	.	.	.	2	8
CBC4	SET 0,H	Set bit 0 of H register to 1	.	.	.	.	.	.	2	8
CBC5	SET 0,L	Set bit 0 of L register to 1	.	.	.	.	.	.	2	8
CBC6	SET 0,(HL)	Set bit 0 of memory pointed to by HL to 1	.	.	.	.	.	.	4	15
CBC7	SET 0,A	Set bit 0 of accumulator to 1	.	.	.	.	.	.	2	8
CBC8	SET 1,B	Set bit 1 of B register to 1	.	.	.	.	.	.	2	8
CBC9	SET 1,C	Set bit 1 of C register to 1	.	.	.	.	.	.	2	8
CBCA	SET 1,D	Set bit 1 of D register to 1	.	.	.	.	.	.	2	8
CBCB	SET 1,E	Set bit 1 of E register to 1	.	.	.	.	.	.	2	8
CBCC	SET 1,H	Set bit 1 of H register to 1	.	.	.	.	.	.	2	8
CBCD	SET 1,L	Set bit 1 of L register to 1	.	.	.	.	.	.	2	8
CBCE	SET 1,(HL)	Set bit 1 of memory pointed to by HL to 1	.	.	.	.	.	.	4	15
CBCF	SET 1,A	Set bit 1 of accumulator to 1	.	.	.	.	.	.	2	8
CBD0	SET 2,B	Set bit 2 of B register to 1	.	.	.	.	.	.	2	8
CBD1	SET 2,C	Set bit 2 of C register to 1	.	.	.	.	.	.	2	8
CBD2	SET 2,D	Set bit 2 of D register to 1	.	.	.	.	.	.	2	8
CBD3	SET 2,E	Set bit 2 of E register to 1	.	.	.	.	.	.	2	8
CBD4	SET 2,H	Set bit 2 of H register to 1	.	.	.	.	.	.	2	8
CBD5	SET 2,L	Set bit 2 of L register to 1	.	.	.	.	.	.	2	8
CBD6	SET 2,(HL)	Set bit 2 of memory pointed to by HL to 1	.	.	.	.	.	.	4	15
CBD7	SET 2,A	Set bit 2 of accumulator to 1	.	.	.	.	.	.	2	8
CBD8	SET 3,B	Set bit 3 of B register to 1	.	.	.	.	.	.	2	8
CBD9	SET 3,C	Set bit 3 of C register to 1	.	.	.	.	.	.	2	8
CBDA	SET 3,D	Set bit 3 of D register to 1	.	.	.	.	.	.	2	8
CBDB	SET 3,E	Set bit 3 of E register to 1	.	.	.	.	.	.	2	8
CBDC	SET 3,H	Set bit 3 of H register to 1	.	.	.	.	.	.	2	8
CBDD	SET 3,L	Set bit 3 of L register to 1	.	.	.	.	.	.	2	8
CBDE	SET 3,(HL)	Set bit 3 of memory pointed to by HL to 1	.	.	.	.	.	.	4	15
CBDF	SET 3,A	Set bit 3 of accumulator to 1	.	.	.	.	.	.	2	8
CBE0	SET 4,B	Set bit 4 of B register to 1	.	.	.	.	.	.	2	8
CBE1	SET 4,C	Set bit 4 of C register to 1	.	.	.	.	.	.	2	8
CBE2	SET 4,D	Set bit 4 of D register to 1	.	.	.	.	.	.	2	8
CBE3	SET 4,E	Set bit 4 of E register to 1	.	.	.	.	.	.	2	8
CBE4	SET 4,H	Set bit 4 of H register to 1	.	.	.	.	.	.	2	8
CBE5	SET 4,L	Set bit 4 of L register to 1	.	.	.	.	.	.	2	8
CBE6	SET 4,(HL)	Set bit 4 of memory pointed to by HL to 1	.	.	.	.	.	.	4	15
CBE7	SET 4,A	Set bit 4 of accumulator to 1	.	.	.	.	.	.	2	8
CBE8	SET 5,B	Set bit 5 of B register to 1	.	.	.	.	.	.	2	8
CBE9	SET 5,C	Set bit 5 of C register to 1	.	.	.	.	.	.	2	8
CBEA	SET 5,D	Set bit 5 of D register to 1	.	.	.	.	.	.	2	8
CBEB	SET 5,E	Set bit 5 of E register to 1	.	.	.	.	.	.	2	8
CBEC	SET 5,H	Set bit 5 of H register to 1	.	.	.	.	.	.	2	8
CBED	SET 5,L	Set bit 5 of L register to 1	.	.	.	.	.	.	2	8

OP CODE	MNEMONIC	COMMENT	S	Z	H	P/V	N	C	M CYCLES	T STATES
CBEE	SET 5,(HL)	Set bit 5 of memory pointed to by HL to 1	.	.	.	.	.	.	4	15
CBEF	SET 5,A	Set bit 5 of accumulator to 1	.	.	.	.	.	.	2	8
CBF0	SET 6,B	Set bit 6 of B register to 1	.	.	.	.	.	.	2	8
CBF1	SET 6,C	Set bit 6 of C register to 1	.	.	.	.	.	.	2	8
CBF2	SET 6,D	Set bit 6 of D register to 1	.	.	.	.	.	.	2	8
CBF3	SET 6,E	Set bit 6 of E register to 1	.	.	.	.	.	.	2	8
CBF4	SET 6,H	Set bit 6 of H register to 1	.	.	.	.	.	.	2	8
CBF5	SET 6,L	Set bit 6 of L register to 1	.	.	.	.	.	.	2	8
CBF6	SET 6,(HL)	Set bit 6 of memory pointed to by HL to 1	.	.	.	.	.	.	4	15
CBF7	SET 6,A	Set bit 6 of accumulator to 1	.	.	.	.	.	.	2	8
CBF8	SET 7,B	Set bit 7 of B register to 1	.	.	.	.	.	.	2	8
CBF9	SET 7,C	Set bit 7 of C register to 1	.	.	.	.	.	.	2	8
CBFA	SET 7,D	Set bit 7 of D register to 1	.	.	.	.	.	.	2	8
CBFB	SET 7,E	Set bit 7 of E register to 1	.	.	.	.	.	.	2	8
CBFC	SET 7,H	Set bit 7 of H register to 1	.	.	.	.	.	.	2	8
CBFD	SET 7,L	Set bit 7 of L register to 1	.	.	.	.	.	.	2	8
CBFE	SET 7,(HL)	Set bit 7 of memory pointed to by HL to 1	.	.	.	.	.	.	4	15
CBFF	SET 7,A	Set bit 7 of accumulator to 1	.	.	.	.	.	.	2	8
CCnn	CALL Z,nn	If zero flag=0, disregard instruction. If zero flag=1, call subroutine at address pointed to by bytes 3 and 2	.	.	.	.	.	.	3 (if Z=0) 5 (if Z=1)	10 17
CDnn	CALL nn	Call subroutine at address pointed to by bytes 3 and 2	.	.	.	.	.	.	5	17
CEn	ADC A,n	Add byte 2 and the carry flag to the accumulator	↕	↕	↕	V	0	↕	2	7
CF	RST 08H	Restart at 0008H. Push the contents of the program counter onto the stack. Load program counter with 0008H	.	.	.	.	.	.	3	11
D0	RET NC	If carry flag=1, disregard instruction. If carry flag=0, return from subroutine	.	.	.	.	.	.	1 (if C=1) 3 (if C=0)	5 11
D1	POP DE	Load contents of memory pointed to by SP into E and contents of memory pointed to by SP+1 into D	.	.	.	.	.	.	3	10
D2nn	JP NC,nn	If carry flag=1, disregard instruction. If carry flag=0, jump to address pointed to by bytes 3 and 2	.	.	.	.	.	.	3	10
D3n	OUT (n),A	Output contents of accumulator to output port pointed to by byte 2	.	.	.	.	.	.	3	11
D4nn	CALL NC,nn	If carry flag=1, disregard instruction. If carry flag=0, call subroutine at address pointed to by bytes 3 and 2	.	.	.	.	.	.	3 (if C=1) 5 (if C=0)	10 17
D5	PUSH DE	Load contents of D into memory pointed to by SP-1 and contents of E into memory pointed to by SP-2	.	.	.	.	.	.	3	11

OP CODE	MNEMONIC	COMMENT	S	Z	H	P/V	N	C	M CYCLES	T STATES
D6n	SUB n	Subtract contents of second byte from contents of accumulator	↕	↕	↕	V	1	↕	2	7
D7	RST 10H	Restart at 0010H. Push the contents of the program counter onto the stack. Load the program counter with 0010H	.	.	.	.	.	.	3	11
D8	RET C	If carry flag = 0, disregard instruction. If carry flag = 1, return from subroutine	.	.	.	.	.	.	1 (if C = 0) 3 (if C = 1)	5 11
D9	EXX	Exchange contents of BC, DE, HL with BC′, DE′, HL′, respectively	.	.	.	.	.	.	1	4
DAnn	JP C,nn	If C = 0, disregard instruction. If C = 1, jump to address pointed to by bytes 3 and 2	.	.	.	.	.	.	3	10
DBn	IN A,(n)	Input contents of input port pointed to by byte 2 into the accumulator	↕	↕	↕	P	0	.	3	11
DCnn	CALL C,nn	If carry flag = 0, disregard instruction. If carry flag = 1, call subroutine at address pointed to by bytes 3 and 2	.	.	.	.	.	.	3 (if C = 0) 5 (if C = 1)	10 17
DD09	ADD IX,BC	Add contents of register pair BC to IX	.	.	X	.	0	↕	4	15
DD19	ADD IX,DE	Add contents of register pair DE to IX	.	.	X	.	0	↕	4	15
DD21nn	LD IX,nn	Load byte 3 into LOW byte of IX and byte 4 into HIGH byte of IX	.	.	.	.	.	.	4	14
DD22nn	LD (nn),IX	Load LOW byte of the IX register into memory pointed to by bytes 4 and 3. Load HIGH byte of IX into the next higher address	.	.	.	.	.	.	6	20
DD23	INC IX	Increment contents of IX	.	.	.	.	.	.	2	10
DD29	ADD IX,IX	Add contents of index register IX to IX	.	.	X	.	0	↕	4	15
DD2Ann	LD IX,(nn)	Load contents of memory pointed to by bytes 4 and 3 into the LOW byte of IX. Load the following byte into the HIGH byte of IX	.	.	.	.	.	.	6	20
DD2B	DEC IX	Decrement contents of IX	.	.	.	.	.	.	2	10
DD34d	INC (IX+d)	Increment contents of memory pointed to by IX+d	↕	↕	↕	V	0	.	6	23
DD35d	DEC (IX+d)	Decrement contents of memory pointed to by IX+d	↕	↕	↕	V	1	.	6	23
DD36dn	LD (IX+d),n	Load data in byte 4 into memory pointed to by IX+d	.	.	.	.	.	.	5	19
DD39	ADD IX,SP	Add contents of stack pointer to IX	.	.	X	.	0	↕	4	15
DD46d	LD B,(IX+d)	Load contents of memory pointed to by IX+d into B	.	.	.	.	.	.	5	19
DD4Ed	LD C,(IX+d)	Load contents of memory pointed to by IX+d into C	.	.	.	.	.	.	5	19
DD56d	LD D,(IX+d)	Load contents of memory pointed to by IX+d into D	.	.	.	.	.	.	5	19
DD5Ed	LD E,(IX+d)	Load contents of memory pointed to by IX+d into E	.	.	.	.	.	.	5	19

OP CODE	MNEMONIC	COMMENT	S	Z	H	P/V	N	C	M CYCLES	T STATES
					FLAGS					
DD66d	LD H,(IX+d)	Load contents of memory pointed to by IX+d into H	.	.	.	.	.	.	5	19
DD6Ed	LD L,(IX+d)	Load contents of memory pointed to by IX+d into L	.	.	.	.	.	.	5	19
DD70d	LD (IX+d),B	Load contents of register B into memory pointed to by IX+d	.	.	.	.	.	.	5	19
DD71d	LD (IX+d),C	Load contents of C register into memory pointed to by IX+d	.	.	.	.	.	.	5	19
DD72d	LD (IX+d),D	Load contents of D register into memory pointed to by IX+d	.	.	.	.	.	.	5	19
DD73d	LD (IX+d),E	Load contents of E register into memory pointed to by IX+d	.	.	.	.	.	.	5	19
DD74d	LD (IX+d),H	Load contents of H register into memory pointed to by IX+d	.	.	.	.	.	.	5	19
DD75d	LD (IX+d),L	Load contents of L register into memory pointed to by IX+d	.	.	.	.	.	.	5	19
DD77d	LD (IX+d),A	Load contents of accumulator into memory pointed to by IX+d	.	.	.	.	.	.	5	19
DD7Ed	LD A,(IX+d)	Load contents of memory pointed to by IX+d into the accumulator	.	.	.	.	.	.	5	19
DD86d	ADD A,(IX+d)	Add contents of memory pointed to by IX+d to the accumulator	↕	↕	↕	V	0	↕	5	19
DD8Ed	ADC A,(IX+d)	Add contents of memory pointed to by IX+d and the carry flag to the accumulator	↕	↕	↕	V	0	↕	5	19
DD96d	SUB (IX+d)	Subtract contents of memory pointed to by IX+d from accumulator	↕	↕	↕	V	1	↕	5	19
DD9Ed	SBC A,(IX+d)	Subtract contents of memory pointed to by IX+d and the carry flag from the accumulator	↕	↕	↕	V	1	↕	5	19
DDA6d	AND (IX+d)	AND contents of memory pointed to by IX+d with the accumulator	↕	↕	1	P	0	0	5	19
DDAEd	XOR (IX+d)	Exclusive-OR contents of memory pointed to by IX+d with contents of accumulator	↕	↕	0	P	0	0	5	19
DDB6d	OR (IX+d)	OR contents of accumulator with contents of memory pointed to by IX+d	↕	↕	0	P	0	0	5	19
DDBEd	CP (IX+d)	Compare contents of memory pointed to by IX+d with the accumulator	↕	↕	↕	V	1	↕	5	19
DDCBd06	RLC (IX+d)	Rotate left circular the contents of memory pointed to by IX+d	↕	↕	0	P	0	↕	6	23
DDCBd0E	RRC (IX+d)	Rotate right circular the contents of memory pointed to by IX+d	↕	↕	0	P	0	↕	6	23
DDCBd16	RL (IX+d)	Rotate left the contents of memory pointed to by IX+d	↕	↕	0	P	0	↕	6	23
DDCBd1E	RR (IX+d)	Rotate right the contents of memory pointed to by IX+d	↕	↕	0	P	0	↕	6	23
DDCBd26	SLA (IX+d)	Shift left arithmetic the contents of memory pointed to by IX+d	↕	↕	0	P	0	↕	6	23

OP CODE	MNEMONIC	COMMENT	S	Z	H	P/V	N	C	M CYCLES	T STATES
DDCBd2E	SRA (IX+d)	Shift right arithmetic the contents of memory pointed to by IX+d	↕	↕	0	P	0	↕	6	23
DDCBd3E	SRL (IX+d)	Shift right logical contents of memory pointed to by IX+d	↕	↕	0	P	0	↕	6	23
DDCBd46	BIT 0,(IX+d)	If bit 0 of memory pointed to by IX+d is 0, set the zero flag (Z=1). Otherwise Z=0	X	↕	1	X	0	.	5	20
DDCBd4E	BIT 1,(IX+d)	If bit 1 of memory pointed to by IX+d is 0, set the zero flag (Z=1). Otherwise Z=0	X	↕	1	X	0	.	5	20
DDCBd56	BIT 2,(IX+d)	If bit 2 of memory pointed to by IX+d is 0, set the zero flag (Z=1). Otherwise Z=0	X	↕	1	X	0	.	5	20
DDCBd5E	BIT 3,(IX+d)	If bit 3 of memory pointed to by IX+d is 0, set the zero flag (Z=1). Otherwise Z=0	X	↕	1	X	0	.	5	20
DDCBd66	BIT 4,(IX+d)	If bit 4 of memory pointed to by IX+d is 0, set the zero flag (Z=1). Otherwise Z=0	X	↕	1	X	0	.	5	20
DDCBd6E	BIT 5,(IX+d)	If bit 5 of memory pointed to by IX+d is 0, set the zero flag (Z=1). Otherwise Z=0	X	↕	1	X	0	.	5	20
DDCBd76	BIT 6,(IX+d)	If bit 6 of memory poined to by IX+d is 0, set the zero flag (Z=1). Otherwise Z=0	X	↕	1	X	0	.	5	20
DDCBd7E	BIT 7,(IX+d)	If bit 7 of memory pointed to by IX+d is 0, set the zero flag (Z=1). Otherwise Z=0	X	↕	1	X	0	.	5	20
DDCBd86	RES 0,(IX+d)	Reset bit 0 in memory pointed to by IX+d to 0	.	.	.	.	.	.	6	23
DDCBd8E	RES 1,(IX+d)	Reset bit 1 in memory pointed to by IX+d to 0	.	.	.	.	.	.	6	23
DDCBd96	RES 2,(IX+d)	Reset bit 2 in memory pointed to by IX+d to 0	.	.	.	.	.	.	6	23
DDCBd9E	RES 3,(IX+d)	Reset bit 3 in memory pointed to by IX+d to 0	.	.	.	.	.	.	6	23
DDCBdA6	RES 4,(IX+d)	Reset bit 4 in memory pointed to by IX+d to 0	.	.	.	.	.	.	6	23
DDCBdAE	RES 5,(IX+d)	Reset bit 5 in memory pointed to by IX+d to 0	.	.	.	.	.	.	6	23
DDCBdB6	RES 6,(IX+d)	Reset bit 6 in memory pointed to by IX+d to 0	.	.	.	.	.	.	6	23
DDCBdBE	RES 7,(IX+d)	Reset bit 7 in memory pointed to by IX+d to 0	.	.	.	.	.	.	6	23
DDCBdC6	SET 0,(IX+d)	Set bit 0 of memory pointed to by IX+d to 1	.	.	.	.	.	.	6	23
DDCBdCE	SET 1,(IX+d)	Set bit 1 of memory pointed to by IX+d to 1	.	.	.	.	.	.	6	23
DDCBdD6	SET 2,(IX+d)	Set bit 2 of memory pointed to by IX+d to 1	.	.	.	.	.	.	6	23
DDCBdDE	SET 3,(IX+d)	Set bit 3 of memory pointed to by IX+d to 1	.	.	.	.	.	.	6	23
DDCBdE6	SET 4,(IX+d)	Set bit 4 of memory pointed to by IX+d to 1	.	.	.	.	.	.	6	23
DDCBdEE	SET 5,(IX+d)	Set bit 5 of memory pointed to by IX+d to 1	.	.	.	.	.	.	6	23
DDCBdF6	SET 6,(IX+d)	Set bit 6 of memory pointed to by IX+d to 1	.	.	.	.	.	.	6	23
DDCBdFE	SET 7,(IX+d)	Set bit 7 of memory pointed to by IX+d to 1	.	.	.	.	.	.	6	23
DDE1	POP IX	Load contents of memory pointed to by stack pointer into LOW byte of IX and contents of memory pointed to by SP+1 into HIGH byte of IX	.	.	.	.	.	.	4	14

OP CODE	MNEMONIC	COMMENT	S	Z	H	P/V	N	C	M CYCLES	T STATES
DDE3	EX (SP),IX	Exchange contents of stack pointer with LOW byte of IX. Exchange contents of SP+1 with HIGH byte of IX	.	.	.	.	.	.	6	23
DDE5	PUSH IX	Load contents of HIGH byte of IX into memory pointed to by SP−1 and contents of LOW byte into memory pointed to by SP−2	.	.	.	.	.	.	4	15
DDE9	JP (IX)	Jump to address pointed to by IX	.	.	.	.	.	.	2	8
DDF9	LD SP,IX	Load contents of IX into stack pointer	.	.	.	.	.	.	2	10
DEn	SBC A,n	Subtract byte 2 and the carry flag from the accumulator	$\updownarrow$	$\updownarrow$	$\updownarrow$	V	1	$\updownarrow$	2	7
DF	RST 18H	Restart at 0018H. Push the contents of the program counter onto the stack. Load the program counter with 0018H	.	.	.	.	.	.	3	11
E0	RET PO	If parity flag=1, disregard instruction. If parity flag=0, return from subroutine	.	.	.	.	.	.	1 (if P=1) 3 (if P=0)	5 11
E1	POP HL	Load contents of memory pointed to by SP into L and contents of memory pointed to by SP+1 into H	.	.	.	.	.	.	3	10
E2nn	JP PO,nn	If parity flag=1, disregard instruction. If parity flag=0, jump to address pointed to by bytes 3 and 2	.	.	.	.	.	.	3	10
E3	EX (SP),HL	Exchange contents of L with contents of memory pointed to by SP. Exchange contents of H with contents of memory pointed to by SP+1	.	.	.	.	.	.	5	19
E4nn	CALL PO,nn	If parity flag =1, disregard instruction. If parity flag=0, call subroutine at address pointed to by bytes 3 and 2	.	.	.	.	.	.	3 (if P=1) 5 (if P=0)	10 17
E5	PUSH HL	Load contents of H into address pointed to by SP−1 and load L into address pointed to by SP−2	.	.	.	.	.	.	3	11
E6n	AND n	AND byte 2 with accumulator	$\updownarrow$	$\updownarrow$	1	P	0	0	2	7
E7	RST 20H	Restart at 0020H. Push contents of the program counter onto the stack. Load program counter with 0020H	.	.	.	.	.	.	3	11
E8	RET PE	If parity flag=0, disregard instruction. If parity flag=1, return from subroutine	.	.	.	.	.	.	1 (if P=0) 3 (if P=1)	5 11
E9	JP (HL)	Jump to address pointed to by HL	.	.	.	.	.	.	1	4
EAnn	JP PE,nn	If parity flag=0, disregard instruction. If parity flag=1, jump to address pointed to by bytes 3 and 2	.	.	.	.	.	.	3	10
EB	EX DE,HL	Exchange contents of L with contents of E and contents of H with contents of D	.	.	.	.	.	.	1	4

OP CODE	MNEMONIC	COMMENT	FLAGS S	Z	H	P/V	N	C	M CYCLES	T STATES
ECnn	CALL PE,nn	If parity flag = 0, disregard insruction. If parity flag = 1, call subroutine at address pointed to by bytes 3 and 2	.	.	.	.	.	.	3 (if P = 0) 5 (if P = 1)	10 17
ED40	IN B,(C)	Input data from port pointed to by C into register B	↕	↕	↕	P	0	.	3	12
ED41	OUT (C),B	Output contents of register B to output port pointed to by C	.	.	.	.	.	.	3	12
ED42	SBC HL,BC	Subtract contents of register pair BC and the carry flag from HL	↕	↕	X	V	1	↕	4	15
ED43nn	LD (nn),BC	Load contents of C into memory pointed to by bytes 4 and 3. Load B into the following address	.	.	.	.	.	.	6	20
ED44	NEG	Take the 2's complement of the accumulator (negate the accumulator)	↕	↕	↕	V	1	↕	2	8
ED45	RETN	Return from nonmaskable interrupt	.	.	.	.	.	.	4	14
ED46	IM 0	Set interrupt mode to 0	.	.	.	.	.	.	2	8
ED47	LD I,A	Load accumulator into interrupt register	.	.	.	.	.	.	2	9
ED48	IN C,(C)	Input data from port pointed to by C into register C	↕	↕	↕	P	0	.	3	12
ED49	OUT (C),C	Output contents of register C to output port pointed to by C	.	.	.	.	.	.	3	12
ED4A	ADC HL,BC	Add contents of register pair BC and the carry flag to HL	↕	↕	X	V	0	↕	4	15
ED4Bnn	LD BC,(nn)	Load contents of memory pointed to by bytes 4 and 3 into C. Load next byte in memory into B	.	.	.	.	.	.	6	20
ED4D	RETI	Return from interrupt	.	.	.	.	.	.	4	14
ED4F	LD R,A	Load contents of accumulator into R	.	.	.	.	.	.	1	4
ED50	IN D,(C)	Input data from the port pointed to by C into register D	↕	↕	↕	P	0	.	3	12
ED51	OUT (C),D	Output contents of register D to output port pointed to by C	.	.	.	.	.	.	3	12
ED52	SBC HL,DE	Subtract contents of register pair DE and the carry flag from contents of HL	↕	↕	X	V	1	↕	4	15
ED53nn	LD (nn),DE	Load contents of E into memory pointed to by bytes 4 and 3. Load D into following address	.	.	.	.	.	.	6	20
ED56	IM 1	Set interrupt mode to 1	.	.	.	.	.	.	2	8
ED57	LD A,I	Load contents of register I into A. Contents of IFF (interrupt enable flip-flop) determine P/V.	↕	↕	0	↕	0	.	2	9
ED58	IN E,(C)	Input data from port pointed to by C into register E	↕	↕	↕	P	0	.	3	12
ED59	OUT (C),E	Output contents of register E to output port pointed to by C	.	.	.	.	.	.	3	12
ED5A	ADC HL,DE	Add contents of DE and the carry flag to HL	↕	↕	X	V	0	↕	4	15
ED5Bnn	LD DE,(nn)	Load contents of memory pointed to by bytes 4 and 3 into E. Load the next byte in memory into D	.	.	.	.	.	.	6	20

OP CODE	MNEMONIC	COMMENT	FLAGS S	Z	H	P/V	N	C	M CYCLES	T STATES
ED5E	IM 2	Set interrupt mode to 2	.	.	.	.	.	.	2	8
ED5F	LD A,R	Load contents of R register into accumulator. Contents of IFF (interrupt enable flip-flop) determine P/V	↕	↕	0	↕	.	.	2	9
ED60	IN H,(C)	Input data from port pointed to by C into register H	↕	↕	↕	P	0	.	3	12
ED61	OUT (C),H	Output contents of register H to output port pointed to by C	.	.	.	.	.	.	3	12
ED62	SBC HL,HL	Subtract contents of register HL and the carry flag from HL	↕	↕	X	V	1	↕	4	15
ED67	RRD	Rotate right digit	↕	↕	0	P	0	.	5	18
ED68	IN L,(C)	Input data from port pointed to by C into register L	↕	↕	↕	P	0	.	3	12
ED69	OUT (C),L	Output contents of register L to output port pointed to by C	.	.	.	.	.	.	3	12
ED6A	ADC HL,HL	Add contents of register pair HL and the carry flag to HL	↕	↕	X	V	0	↕	4	15
ED6F	RLD	Rotate left digit	↕	↕	0	P	0	.	2	8
ED72	BC HL,SP	Subtract contents of stack pointer and the carry flag from HL	↕	↕	X	V	1	↕	4	15
ED73nn	LD (nn),SP	Load LOW byte of stack pointer into address pointed to by bytes 4 and 3. Load HIGH byte of SP into next higher byte	.	.	.	.	.	.	6	20
ED78	IN A,(C)	Input data from port pointed to by C into the accumulator	↕	↕	↕	P	0	.	3	12
ED79	OUT (C),A	Output the accumulator to output port pointed to by C	.	.	.	.	.	.	3	12
ED7A	ADC HL,SP	Add contents of SP and the carry flag to HL	↕	↕	X	V	0	↕	4	15
ED7Bnn	LD SP,(nn)	Load contents of memory pointed to by bytes 3 and 2 into LOW byte of SP and the contents of the next location in memory into HIGH byte of SP	.	.	.	.	.	.	6	20
EDA0	LDI	Load contents of memory pointed to by HL into memory pointed to by DE. Increment DE. Increment HL. Decrement BC. P/V Flag = 0 if BC becomes 0 as a result of the decrement. Otherwise P/V = 1	.	.	0	↕	0	.	4	16
EDA1	CPI	Compare contents of memory pointed to by HL with accumulator. Increment HL. Decrement BC. When BC = 0, P/V = 0, otherwise P/V = 1. When A = (HL), Z = 1. Otherwise Z = 0	↕	↕	↕	↕	1	.	4	16
EDA2	INI	Input data from input port pointed to by C into memory pointed to by HL. Decrement B and set the zero flag if B = 0. Otherwise Z = 0. Increment HL	X	↕	X	X	1	X	4	16

OP CODE	MNEMONIC	COMMENT	S	Z	H	P/V	N	C	M CYCLES	T STATES
EDA3	OUTI	Output contents of memory pointed to by HL to output port pointed to by register C. Decrement B. Increment HL. If result of B − 1 is zero, then Z = 1. Otherwise Z = 0	X	↕	X	X	1	X	4	16
EDA8	LDD	Load contents of memory pointed to by HL into memory pointed to by DE. Decrement HL. Decrement BC. Decrement DE. P/V Flag = 0 if BC becomes 0 as a result of the decrement. Otherwise P/V = 1	.	.	0	↕	0	.	4	16
EDA9	CPD	Compare contents of memory pointed to by HL with the accumulator. Decrement HL and BC. When BC = 0, P/V = 0. Otherwise P/V = 1. When A = (HL), Z = 1. Otherwise Z = 0	↕	↕	↕	↕	1	.	4	16
EDAA	IND	Input data from input port pointed to by C into memory pointed to by HL. Decrement B and set the zero flag if B = 0. Otherwise Z = 0. Decrement HL	X	↕	X	X	1	X	4	16
EDAB	OUTD	Output contents of memory pointed to by HL to output port pointed to by register C. Decrement B. Decrement HL. If the result of B − 1 is zero, then Z = 1. Otherwise Z = 0	X	↕	X	X	1	X	4	16
EDB0	LDIR	Load contents of memory pointed to by HL into memory pointed to by DE. Increment DE. Increment HL. Decrement BC. Repeat until BC = 0	.	.	0	0	0	.	5 (if BC ≠ 0) 4 (if BC = 0)	21 16
EDB1	CPIR	Compare contents of memory pointed to by HL with the accumulator. Increment HL. Decrement BC. Repeat until memory pointed to by HL = A or until BC = 0. When BC = 0, P/V = 0. Otherwise P/V = 1. when A = (HL), Z = 1. Otherwise Z = 0	↕	↕	↕	↕	1	.	5 [if BC ≠ 0 and A ≠ (HL)] 4 [if BC = 0 or A = (HL)]	21 16
EDB2	INIR	Input data from input port pointed to by C into memory pointed to by HL. Decrement B. Increment HL. Repeat B = 0	X	1	X	X	1	X	5 (if B ≠ 0) 4 (if B = 0)	12 16
EDB3	OTIR	Output contents of memory pointed to by HL to output port pointed to by C. Decrement B. Increment H. Repeat until B = 0	X	1	X	X	1	X	5 (if B ≠ 0) 4 (if B = 0)	12 16
EDB8	LDDR	Load contents of memory pointed to by HL into memory pointed to by DE. Decrement DE. Decrement HL. Decrement BC. Repeat until BC = 0	.	.	0	0	0	.	5 (if BC ≠ 0) 4 (if BC = 0)	21 16

OP CODE	MNEMONIC	COMMENT	S	Z	H	P/V	N	C	M CYCLES	T STATES
EDB1	CPIR	Compare contents of memory pointed to by HL with the accumulator. Increment HL. Decrement BC. Repeat until memory pointed to by HL=A or until BC=0. When BC=0, P/V=0. Otherwise P/V=1. when A = (HL), Z=1. Otherwise Z=0	↕	↕	↕	↕	1	.	5 [if BC≠0 and A≠(HL)] 4 [if BC=0 or A=(HL)]	21 16
EDBA	INDR	Input data from input port pointed to by C into memory pointed to by HL. Decrement B. Decrement HL. Repeat until B=0	X	1	X	X	1	X	5 (if B≠0) 4 (if B=0)	21 16
EDBB	OTDR	Output contents of memory pointed to by HL to output port pointed to by C. Decrement B. Decrement HL. Repeat until B=0	X	1	X	X	1	X	5 (if B≠0) 4 (if B=0)	21 16
EEn	XOR n	Exclusive-OR byte 2 with the accumulator	↕	↕	0	P	0	0	2	7
EF	RST 28H	Restart at 0028H. Push contents of the program onto the stack. Load program counter with 0028H	.	.	.	.	.	.	3	11
F0	RET P	If sign flag=1, disregard instruction. If sign flag=0, return from subroutine	.	.	.	.	.	.	1 (if S=1) 3 (if S=0)	5 11
F1	POP AF	Load contents of memory pointed to by SP into F and contents of memory pointed to by SP+1 into accumulator	.	.	.	.	.	.	3	10
F2nn	JP P,nn	If sign flag=1, disregard instruction. If sign flag=0, jump to address pointed to by bytes 3 and 2	.	.	.	.	.	.	3	10
F3	DI	Disable interrupt (reset interrupt flip-flop to 0)	.	.	.	.	.	.	1	4
F4nn	CALL P,nn	If sign flag=1, disregard instruction. If sign flag=0, call subroutine at address pointed to by bytes 3 and 2	.	.	.	.	.	.	3 (if S=1) 5 (if S=0)	10 17
F5	PUSH AF	Load contents of accumulator into memory pointed to by SP−1 and flags register into memory pointed to by SP−2	.	.	.	.	.	.	3	11
F6n	OR n	OR byte 2 with contents of accumulator	↕	↕	0	P	0	0	2	7
F7	RST 30H	Restart at 0030H. Push contents of the program counter onto stack. Load program counter with 0030H	.	.	.	.	.	.	3	11
F8	RET M	If sign flag=0, disregard instruction. If sign flag=1, return from subroutine	.	.	.	.	.	.	1 (if S=0) 3 (if S=1)	5 11

OP CODE	MNEMONIC	COMMENT	S	Z	H	P/V	N	C	M CYCLES	T STATES
					FLAGS					
F9	LD SP,HL	Load contents of HL into stack pointer	.	.	.	.	.	.	1	6
FAnn	JP M,nn	If sign flag=0, disregard instruction. If sign flag=1, jump to address pointed to by bytes 3 and 2	.	.	.	.	.	.	3	10
FB	EI	Enable interrupt (set interrupt flip-flop to 1)	.	.	.	.	.	.	1	4
FCnn	CALL M,nn	If sign flag=0, disregard instruction. If sign flag=1, call subroutine at address pointed to by bytes 3 and 2	.	.	.	.	.	.	3 (if S=0) 5 (if S=1)	10 17
FD09	ADD IY,BC	Add contents of register pair BC to IY	.	.	X	.	0	↕	4	15
FD19	ADD IY,DE	Add contents of register pair DE to IY	.	.	X	.	0	↕	4	15
FD21nn	LD IY,nn	Load byte 3 into LOW byte of IY and byte 4 into HIGH byte of IY	.	.	.	.	.	.	4	14
FD22nn	LD (nn),IY	Load LOW byte of the IY register into memory pointed to by bytes 4 and 3. Load HIGH byte of IY into the next higher address	.	.	.	.	.	.	6	20
FD23	INC IY	Increment contents of IY	.	.	.	.	.	.	2	10
FD29	ADD IY,IY	Add contents of index register IY to IY	.	.	X	.	0	↕	4	15
FD2Ann	LD IY,(nn)	Load contents of memory pointed to by bytes 4 and 3 into LOW byte of IY. Load the following byte into HIGH byte of IY	.	.	.	.	.	.	6	20
FD2B	DEC IY	Decrement contents of IY	.	.	.	.	.	.	2	10
FD34d	INC (IY+d)	Increment contents of memory pointed to by IY+d	↕	↕	↕	V	0	.	6	23
FD35d	DEC (IY+d)	Decrement contents of memory pointed to by IY+d	↕	↕	↕	V	1	.	6	23
FD36dn	LD (IY+d),n	Load data in byte 4 into memory pointed to by IY+d	.	.	.	.	.	.	5	19
FD39	ADD IY,SP	Add contents of stack pointer to IY	.	.	X	.	0	↕	4	15
FD46d	LD B,(IY+d)	Load contents of memory pointed to by IY+d into B	.	.	.	.	.	.	5	19
FD4Ed	LD C,(IY+d)	Load contents of memory pointed to IY+d into C	.	.	.	.	.	.	5	19
FD56d	LD D,(IY+d)	Load contents of memory pointed to by IY+d into D	.	.	.	.	.	.	5	19
FD5Ed	LD E,(IY+d)	Load contents of memory pointed to by IY+d into E	.	.	.	.	.	.	5	19
FD66d	LD H,(IY+d)	Load contents of memory pointed to by IY+d into H	.	.	.	.	.	.	5	19
FD6Ed	LD L,(IY+d)	Load contents of memory pointed to by IY+d into L	.	.	.	.	.	.	5	19
FD70d	LD (IY+d),B	Load contents of register B into memory pointed to by IY+d	.	.	.	.	.	.	5	19
FD71d	LD (IY+d),C	Load contents of register C into memory pointed to by IY+d	.	.	.	.	.	.	5	19
FD72d	LD (IY+d),D	Load contents of register D into memory pointed to by IY+d	.	.	.	.	.	.	5	19

OP CODE	MNEMONIC	COMMENT	S	Z	H	P/V	N	C	M CYCLES	T STATES
FD73d	LD (IY+d),E	Load contents of register E into memory pointed to by IY+d	.	.	.	.	.	.	5	19
FD74d	LD (IY+d),H	Load contents of register H into memory pointed to by IY+d	.	.	.	.	.	.	5	19
FD75d	LD (IY+d),L	Load contents of register L into memory pointed to by IY+d	.	.	.	.	.	.	5	19
FD77d	LD (IY+d),A	Load contents of accumulator into memory pointed to by IY+d	.	.	.	.	.	.	5	19
FD7Ed	LD A,(IY+d)	Load contents of memory pointed to by IY+d into the accumulator	.	.	.	.	.	.	5	19
FD86d	ADD A,(IY+d)	Add contents of memory pointed to by IY+d to the accumulator	↕	↕	↕	V	0	↕	5	19
FD8Ed	ADC A,(IY+d)	Add contents of memory pointed to by IY+d and the carry flag to the accumulator	↕	↕	↕	V	0	↕	5	19
FD96d	SUB (IY+d)	Subtract contents of memory pointed to by IY+d from accumulator	↕	↕	↕	V	1	↕	5	19
FD9Ed	SBC A,(IY+d)	Subtract contents of memory pointed to by IY+d and the carry flag from the accumulator	↕	↕	↕	V	1	↕	5	19
FDA6d	AND (IY+d)	AND contents of memory pointed to by IY+d with the accumulator	↕	↕	1	P	0	0	5	19
FDAEd	XOR (IY+d)	Exclusive-OR the contents of address pointed to by IY+d with contents of accumulator	↕	↕	0	P	0	0	5	19
FDB6d	OR (IY+d)	OR contents of accumulator with contents of memory pointed to by IY+d	↕	↕	0	P	0	0	5	19
FDBEd	CP (IY+d)	Compare contents of memory pointed to by IY+d with the accumulator	↕	↕	↕	V	1	↕	5	19
FDCBd06	RLC (IY+d)	Rotate left circular the contents of memory pointed to by IY+d	↕	↕	0	P	0	↕	6	23
FDCBd0E	RRC (IY+d)	Rotate right circular the contents of memory pointed to by IY+d	↕	↕	0	P	0	↕	6	23
FDCBd16	RL (IY+d)	Rotate left the contents of memory pointed to by IY+d	↕	↕	0	P	0	↕	6	23
FDCBd1E	RR (IY+d)	Rotate right the contents of memory pointed to by IY+d	↕	↕	0	P	0	↕	6	23
FDCBd26	SLA (IY+d)	Shift left arithmetic the contents of memory pointed to by IY+d	↕	↕	0	P	0	↕	6	23
FDCBd2E	SRA (IY+d)	Shift right arithmetic the contents of memory pointed to by IY+d	↕	↕	0	P	0	↕	6	23
FDCBd3E	SRL (IY+d)	Shift right logical contents of memory pointed to by IY+d	↕	↕	0	P	0	↕	6	23
FDCBd46	BIT 0,(IY+d)	If bit 0 of memory pointed to by IY+d is 0, set the zero flag (Z=1). Otherwise Z=0	X	↕	1	X	0	.	5	20
FDCBd4E	BIT 1,(IY+d)	If bit 1 of memory pointed to by IY+d is 0, set the zero flag (Z=1). Otherwise Z=0	X	↕	1	X	0	.	5	20
FDCBd56	BIT 2,(IY+d)	If bit 2 of memory pointed to by IY+d is 0, set the zero flag (Z=1). Otherwise Z=0	X	↕	1	X	0	.	5	20
FDCBd5E	BIT 3,(IY+d)	If bit 3 of memory pointed to by IY+d is 0, set the zero flag (Z=1). Otherwise Z=0	X	↕	1	X	0	.	5	20

OP CODE	MNEMONIC	COMMENT	S	Z	H	P/V	N	C	M CYCLES	T STATES
FDCBd66	BIT 4,(IY+d)	If bit 4 of memory pointed to by IY+d is 0, set the zero flag (Z=1). Otherwise Z=0	X	↕	1	X	0	.	5	20
FDCBd6E	BIT 5,(IY+d)	If bit 5 of memory pointed to by IY+d is 0, set the zero flag (Z=1). Otherwise Z=0	X	↕	1	X	0	.	5	20
FDCBd76	BIT 6,(IY+d)	If bit 6 of memory pointed to by IY+d is 0, set the zero flag (Z=1). Otherwise Z=0	X	↕	1	X	0	.	5	20
FDCBd7E	BIT 7,(IY+d)	If bit 7 of memory pointed to by IY+d is 0, set the zero flag (Z=1). Otherwise Z=0	X	↕	1	X	0	.	5	20
FDCBd86	RES 0,(IY+d)	Reset first bit in memory pointed to by IY+d to 0	.	.	.	.	.	.	6	23
FDCBd8E	RES 1,(IY+d)	Reset bit 1 in memory pointed to by IY+d to 0	.	.	.	.	.	.	6	23
FDCBd96	RES 2,(IY+d)	Reset bit 2 in memory pointed to by IY+d to 0	.	.	.	.	.	.	6	23
FDCBd9E	RES 3,(IY+d)	Reset bit 3 in memory pointed to by IY+d to 0	.	.	.	.	.	.	6	23
FDCBdA6	RES 4,(IY+d)	Reset bit 4 in memory pointed to by IY+d to 0	.	.	.	.	.	.	6	23
FDCBdAE	RES 5,(IY+d)	Reset bit 5 in memory pointed to by IY+d to 0	.	.	.	.	.	.	6	23
FDCBdB6	RES 6,(IY+d)	Reset bit 6 in memory pointed to by IY+d to 0	.	.	.	.	.	.	6	23
FDCBdBE	RES 7,(IY+d)	Reset bit 7 in memory pointed to by IY+d to 0	.	.	.	.	.	.	6	23
FDCBdC6	SET 0,(IY+d)	Set bit 0 of memory pointed to by IY+d to 1	.	.	.	.	.	.	6	23
FDCBdCE	SET 1,(IY+d)	Set bit 1 of memory pointed to by IY+d to 1	.	.	.	.	.	.	6	23
FDCBdD6	SET 2,(IY+d)	Set bit 2 of memory pointed to by IY+d to 1	.	.	.	.	.	.	6	23
FDCBdDE	SET 3,(IY+d)	Set bit 3 of memory pointed to by IY+d to 1	.	.	.	.	.	.	6	23
FDCBdE6	SET 4,(IY+d)	Set bit 4 of memory pointed to by IY+d to 1	.	.	.	.	.	.	6	23
FDCBdEE	SET 5,(IY+d)	Set bit 5 of memory pointed to by IY+d to 1	.	.	.	.	.	.	6	23
FDCBdF6	SET 6,(IY+d)	Set bit 6 of memory pointed to by IY+d to 1	.	.	.	.	.	.	6	23
FDCBdFE	SET 7,(IY+d)	Set bit 7 of memory pointed to by IY+d to 1	.	.	.	.	.	.	6	23
FDE1	POP IY	Load contents of memory pointed to by stack pointer into LOW byte of IY and contents of memory pointed to by SP+1 into HIGH byte of IY	.	.	.	.	.	.	4	14
FDE3	EX (SP),IY	Exchange contents of stack pointer with LOW byte of IY. Exchange contents of SP+1 with HIGH byte of IY	.	.	.	.	.	.	6	23
FDE5	PUSH IY	Load contents of HIGH byte of IY into memory pointed to by SP−1 and contents of LOW byte into memory pointed to by SP−2	.	.	.	.	.	.	4	15
FDE9	JP (IY)	Jump to address pointed to by IY	.	.	.	.	.	.	2	8
FDF9	LD SP,IY	Load contents of IY into stack pointer	.	.	.	.	.	.	2	10
FEn	CP n	Compare byte 2 with contents of accumulator	↕	↕	↕	V	1	↕	2	7
FF	RST 38H	Restart at 0038H. Push contents of program counter onto stack. Load program counter with 0038H	.	.	.	.	.	.	3	11

C.4 SUMMARY OF ADDRESSING MODES

The method used to specify the operands that are to be used in an operation is called the mode of addressing. The 10 modes used in the Z-80 are summarized here for reference.

- Register Addressing
  The 3-bit register code is used within the op code to specify which internal register is to be used.

EXAMPLE: LD C,B

- Implied addressing
  The op code implies which register is to be involved.

EXAMPLE: EXX implies that the contents of BC,DE,HL will be swapped with BC′, DE′, HL′.

EXAMPLE: Sub C implies that C is to be subtracted from the accumulator.

- Register indirect addressing
  A register or register pair is used to point to the operand to be used.

EXAMPLE: LD (BC),A—The destination is specified by register indirect. BC contains the address in memory to be used as the destination.

EXAMPLE: OUT (C),B—The output port is pointed to by the C register.

- Immediate addressing
  The operand is included in the instruction as the last byte.

EXAMPLE: The op code for ADD A, 43H is C643.

- Immediate extended addressing
  The operand is included in the instruction as the last two bytes.

EXAMPLE: The op code to load BC with FF00H is 0100FF.

- Relative addressing
  Relative addressing is used with relative jump instructions. The last byte of the instruction is the displacement byte in 2's complement form.

EXAMPLE: 18FBH is the op code for an unconditional relative jump. FB, the displacement byte, is the 2's complement representation of −5. The next instruction will be taken from address PC − 5. The instruction uses only two bytes of program space to define the location of the next instruction.

- Extended addressing
  In extended addressing, two bytes of address are included in the instruction. (In immediate extended addressing, two bytes of data were included.)

EXAMPLE: ED43FF09 is the op code for LD (nn),BC, where (nn) is (09FFH). It means load C into memory pointed to by 09FFH, and load B into the following byte 0A00H.

- Indexed addressing
  A displacement byte in 2's complement form is included in the instruction. The displacement byte is added to the contents of one of the index registers IX or IY to point to the operand. The value in the index register does not change.

EXAMPLE: The op code for XOR (IX+08H) is DDAE08, where 08 is the displacement byte.

- Bit addressing
  In the instructions that set, reset, or test a bit in one of the registers or in a location in memory, a 3-bit code in the op code specifies which bit (0–7) is to be affected.

EXAMPLE: SET 3,A—The accumulator is specified by register addressing. Bit 3 is specified by bit addressing.

- Modified page zero addressing
  This mode of addressing is used with the restart instructions. The restart instruction specifies the LOW byte of the address of the next instruction. The HIGH byte is taken as 00H.

EXAMPLE: RST 18H causes the next instruction to be taken from 0018H.

Many instructions use more than one type of addressing; for example, LD C,(IX+d) uses indexed addressing to specify the source (memory pointed to by IX+d) and register addressing to specify the destination, register C.

Appendix D

LSI IC Specifications

National Semiconductor

ADC0808, ADC0809 8-Bit μP Compatible A/D Converters With 8-Channel Multiplexer

General Description

The ADC0808, ADC0809 data acquisition component is a monolithic CMOS device with an 8-bit analog-to-digital converter, 8-channel multiplexer and microprocessor compatible control logic. The 8-bit A/D converter uses successive approximation as the conversion technique. The converter features a high impedance chopper stabilized comparator, a 256R voltage divider with analog switch tree and a successive approximation register. The 8-channel multiplexer can directly access any of 8-single-ended analog signals.

The device eliminates the need for external zero and full-scale adjustments. Easy interfacing to microprocessors is provided by the latched and decoded multiplexer address inputs and latched TTL TRI-STATE® outputs.

The design of the ADC0808, ADC0809 has been optimized by incorporating the most desirable aspects of several A/D conversion techniques. The ADC0808, ADC0809 offers high speed, high accuracy, minimal temperature dependence, excellent long-term accuracy and repeatability, and consumes minimal power. These features make this device ideally suited to applications from process and machine control to consumer and automotive applications. For 16-channel multiplexer with common output (sample/hold port) see ADC0816 data sheet. (See AN-247 for more information.)

Features

- Resolution—8-bits
- Total unadjusted error—±½ LSB and ±1 LSB
- No missing codes
- Conversion time—100 μS
- Single supply—5 V_{DC}
- Operates ratiometrically or with 5 V_{DC} or analog span adjusted voltage reference
- 8-channel multiplexer with latched control logic
- Easy interface to all microprocessors, or operates "stand alone"
- Outputs meet T^2L voltage level specifications
- 0V to 5V analog input voltage range with single 5V supply
- No zero or full-scale adjust required
- Standard hermetic or molded 28-pin DIP package
- Temperature range −40°C to +85°C or −55°C to +125°C
- Low power consumption—15 mW
- Latched TRI-STATE output

Block Diagram

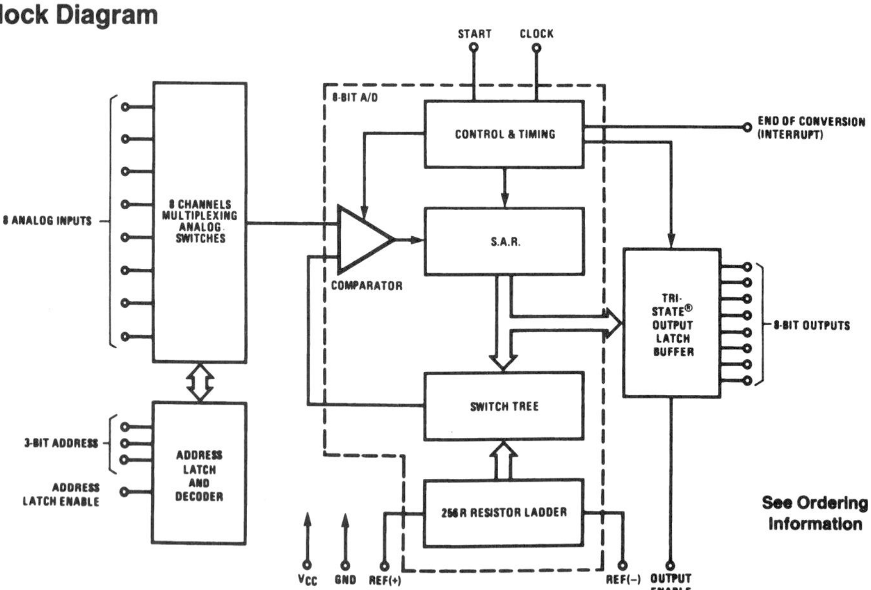

See Ordering Information

FIGURE A-13

Absolute Maximum Ratings (Notes 1 & 2)

Supply Voltage (V_{CC}) (Note 3)	6.5V
Voltage at Any Pin Except Control Inputs	−0.3V to (V_{CC}+0.3V)
Voltage at Control Inputs (START, OE, CLOCK, ALE, ADD A, ADD B, ADD C)	−0.3V to +15V
Storage Temperature Range	−65°C to +150°C
Package Dissipation at T_A=25°C	875 mW
Lead Temperature (Soldering, 10 seconds)	300°C

Operating Conditions (Notes 1 & 2)

Temperature Range (Note 1)	$T_{MIN} \le T_A \le T_{MAX}$
ADC0808CJ	$-55°C \le T_A \le +125°C$
ADC0808CCJ, ADC0808CCN, ADC0809CCN	$-40°C \le T_A \le +85°C$
Range of V_{CC} (Note 1)	4.5 V_{DC} to 6.0 V_{DC}

Electrical Characteristics

Converter Specifications: V_{CC}=5 V_{DC}=V_{REF+}, $V_{REF(-)}$=GND, $T_{MIN} \le T_A \le T_{MAX}$ and f_{CLK}=640 kHz unless otherwise stated.

Symbol	Parameter	Conditions	Min	Typ	Max	Units
	ADC0808 Total Unadjusted Error (Note 5)	25°C			±½	LSB
		T_{MIN} to T_{MAX}			±¾	LSB
	ADC0809 Total Unadjusted Error (Note 5)	0°C to 70°C			±1	LSB
		T_{MIN} to T_{MAX}			±1¼	LSB
	Input Resistance	From Ref(+) to Ref(−)	1.0	2.5		kΩ
	Analog Input Voltage Range	(Note 4) V(+) or V(−)	GND−0.10		V_{CC}+0.10	V_{DC}
$V_{REF(+)}$	Voltage, Top of Ladder	Measured at Ref(+)		V_{CC}	V_{CC}+0.1	V
$\frac{V_{REF(+)}+V_{REF(-)}}{2}$	Voltage, Center of Ladder		V_{CC}/2-0.1	V_{CC}/2	V_{CC}/2+0.1	V
$V_{REF(-)}$	Voltage, Bottom of Ladder	Measured at Ref(−)	−0.1	0		V
I_{IN}	Comparator Input Current	f_c=640 kHz, (Note 6)	−2	±0.5	2	μA

Electrical Characteristics

Digital Levels and DC Specifications: ADC0808CJ $4.5V \le V_{CC} \le 5.5V$, $-55°C \le T_A \le +125°C$ unless otherwise noted ADC0808CCJ, ADC0808CCN, and ADC0809CCN $4.75 \le V_{CC} \le 5.25V$, $-40°C \le T_A \le +85°C$ unless otherwise noted

Symbol	Parameter	Conditions	Min	Typ	Max	Units
ANALOG MULTIPLEXER						
$I_{OFF(+)}$	OFF Channel Leakage Current	V_{CC}=5V, V_{IN}=5V, T_A=25°C		10	200	nA
		T_{MIN} to T_{MAX}			1.0	μA
$I_{OFF(-)}$	OFF Channel Leakage Current	V_{CC}=5V, V_{IN}=0, T_A=25°C	−200	−10		nA
		T_{MIN} to T_{MAX}	−1.0			μA
CONTROL INPUTS						
$V_{IN(1)}$	Logical "1" Input Voltage		V_{CC}−1.5			V
$V_{IN(0)}$	Logical "0" Input Voltage				1.5	V
$I_{IN(1)}$	Logical "1" Input Current (The Control Inputs)	V_{IN}=15V			1.0	μA
$I_{IN(0)}$	Logical "0" Input Current (The Control Inputs)	V_{IN}=0	−1.0			μA
I_{CC}	Supply Current	f_{CLK}=640 kHz		0.3	3.0	mA

FIGURE A-14

Electrical Characteristics (Continued)

Digital Levels and DC Specifications: ADC0808CJ $4.5V \leq V_{CC} \leq 5.5V$, $-55°C \leq T_A \leq +125°C$ unless otherwise noted ADC0808CCJ, ADC0808CCN, and ADC0809CCN $4.75 \leq V_{CC} \leq 5.25V$, $-40°C \leq T_A \leq +85°C$ unless otherwise noted

Symbol	Parameter	Conditions	Min	Typ	Max	Units
DATA OUTPUTS AND EOC (INTERRUPT)						
$V_{OUT(1)}$	Logical "1" Output Voltage	$I_O = -360\ \mu A$	$V_{CC} - 0.4$			V
$V_{OUT(0)}$	Logical "0" Output Voltage	$I_O = 1.6\ mA$			0.45	V
$V_{OUT(0)}$	Logical "0" Output Voltage EOC	$I_O = 1.2\ mA$			0.45	V
I_{OUT}	TRI-STATE Output Current	$V_O = 5V$ $V_O = 0$	 −3		3	μA μA

Electrical Characteristics

Timing Specifications $V_{CC} = V_{REF(+)} = 5V$, $V_{REF(-)} = GND$, $t_r = t_f = 20$ ns and $T_A = 25°C$ unless otherwise noted.

Symbol	Parameter	Conditions	Min	Typ	Max	Units
t_{WS}	Minimum Start Pulse Width	*(Figure 5)*		100	200	ns
t_{WALE}	Minimum ALE Pulse Width	*(Figure 5)*		100	200	ns
t_s	Minimum Address Set-Up Time	*(Figure 5)*		25	50	ns
t_H	Minimum Address Hold Time	*(Figure 5)*		25	50	ns
t_D	Analog MUX Delay Time From ALE	$R_S = 0\Omega$ *(Figure 5)*		1	2.5	μS
t_{H1}, t_{H0}	OE Control to Q Logic State	$C_L = 50$ pF, $R_L = 10k$ *(Figure 8)*		125	250	ns
t_{1H}, t_{0H}	OE Control to Hi-Z	$C_L = 10$ pF, $R_L = 10k$ *(Figure 8)*		125	250	ns
t_c	Conversion Time	$f_c = 640$ kHz, *(Figure 5)* (Note 7)	90	100	116	μS
f_c	Clock Frequency		10	640	1280	kHz
t_{EOC}	EOC Delay Time	*(Figure 5)*	0		8+2 μS	Clock Periods
C_{IN}	Input Capacitance	At Control Inputs		10	15	pF
C_{OUT}	TRI-STATE Output Capacitance	At TRI-STATE Outputs, (Note 12)		10	15	pF

Note 1: Absolute maximum ratings are those values beyond which the life of the device may be impaired.

Note 2: All voltages are measured with respect to GND, unless othewise specified.

Note 3: A zener diode exists, internally, from V_{CC} to GND and has a typical breakdown voltage of 7 V_{DC}.

Note 4: Two on-chip diodes are tied to each analog input which will forward conduct for analog input voltages one diode drop below ground or one diode drop greater than the V_{CC}n supply. The spec allows 100 mV forward bias of either diode. This means that as long as the analog V_{IN} does not exceed the supply voltage by more than 100 mV, the output code will be correct. To achieve an absolute $0V_{DC}$ to $5V_{DC}$ input voltage range will therefore require a minimum supply voltage of 4.900 V_{DC} over temperature variations, initial tolerance and loading.

Note 5: Total unadjusted error includes offset, full-scale, linearity, and multiplexer errors. See *Figure 3*. None of these A/Ds requires a zero or full-scale adjust. However, if an all zero code is desired for an analog input other than 0.0V, or if a narrow full-scale span exists (for example: 0.5V to 4.5V full-scale) the reference voltages can be adjusted to achieve this. See *Figure 13*.

Note 6: Comparator input current is a bias current into or out of the chopper stabilized comparator. The bias current varies directly with clock frequency and has little temperature dependence *(Figure 6)*. See paragraph 4.0.

Note 7: The outputs of the data register are updated one clock cycle before the rising edge of EOC.

FIGURE A-15

Functional Description

Multiplexer. The device contains an 8-channel single-ended analog signal multiplexer. A particular input channel is selected by using the address decoder. Table I shows the input states for the address lines to select any channel. The address is latched into the decoder on the low-to-high transition of the address latch enable signal.

TABLE I

SELECTED ANALOG CHANNEL	ADDRESS LINE C	B	A
IN0	L	L	L
IN1	L	L	H
IN2	L	H	L
IN3	L	H	H
IN4	H	L	L
IN5	H	L	H
IN6	H	H	L
IN7	H	H	H

CONVERTER CHARACTERISTICS

The Converter

The heart of this single chip data acquisition system is its 8-bit analog-to-digital converter. The converter is designed to give fast, accurate, and repeatable conversions over a wide range of temperatures. The converter is partitioned into 3 major sections: the 256R ladder network, the successive approximation register, and the comparator. The converter's digital outputs are positive true.

The 256R ladder network approach *(Figure 1)* was chosen over the conventional R/2R ladder because of its inherent monotonicity, which guarantees no missing digital codes. Monotonicity is particularly important in closed loop feedback control systems. A non-monotonic relationship can cause oscillations that will be catastrophic for the system. Additionally, the 256R network does not cause load variations on the reference voltage.

The bottom resistor and the top resistor of the ladder network in *Figure 1* are not the same value as the remainder of the network. The difference in these resistors causes the output characteristic to be symmetrical with the zero and full-scale points of the transfer curve. The first output transition occurs when the analog signal has reached $+\frac{1}{2}$ LSB and succeeding output transitions occur every 1 LSB later up to full-scale.

The successive approximation register (SAR) performs 8 iterations to approximate the input voltage. For any SAR type converter, n-iterations are required for an n-bit converter. *Figure 2* shows a typical example of a 3-bit converter. In the ADC0808, ADC0809, the approximation technique is extended to 8 bits using the 256R network.

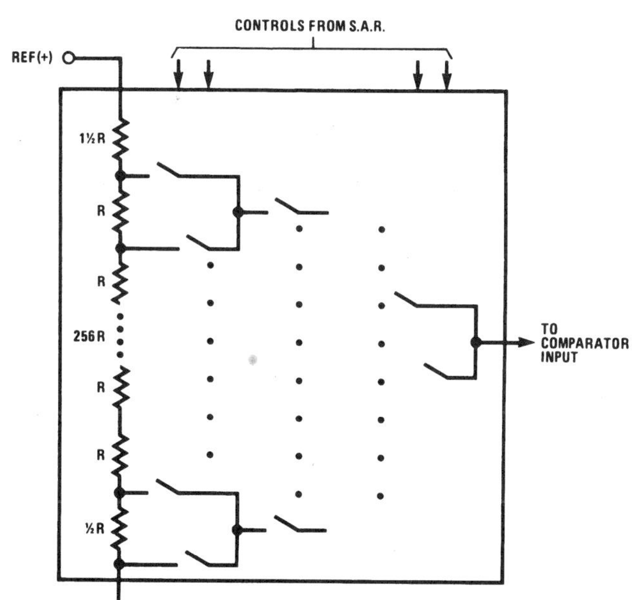

TL/H/5672–2

Resistor Ladder and Switch Tree

FIGURE A-16

Functional Description (Continued)

The A/D converter's successive approximation register (SAR) is reset on the positive edge of the start conversion (SC) pulse. The conversion is begun on the falling edge of the start conversion pulse. A conversion in process will be interrupted by receipt of a new start conversion pulse. Continuous conversion may be accomplished by tying the end-of-conversion (EOC) output to the SC input. If used in this mode, an external start conversion pulse should be applied after power up. End-of-conversion will go low between 0 and 8 clock pulses after the rising edge of start conversion.

The most important section of the A/D converter is the comparator. It is this section which is responsible for the ultimate accuracy of the entire converter. It is also the comparator drift which has the greatest influence on the repeatability of the device. A chopper-stabilized comparator provides the most effective method of satisfying all the converter requirements.

The chopper-stabilized comparator converts the DC input signal into an AC signal. This signal is then fed throught a high gain AC amplifier and has the DC level restored. This technique limits the drift component of the amplifier since the drift is a DC component which is not passed by the AC amplifier. This makes the entire A/D converter extremely insensitive to temperature, long term drift and input offset errors.

Figure 4 shows a typical error curve for the ADC0808 as measured using the procedures outlined in AN-179.

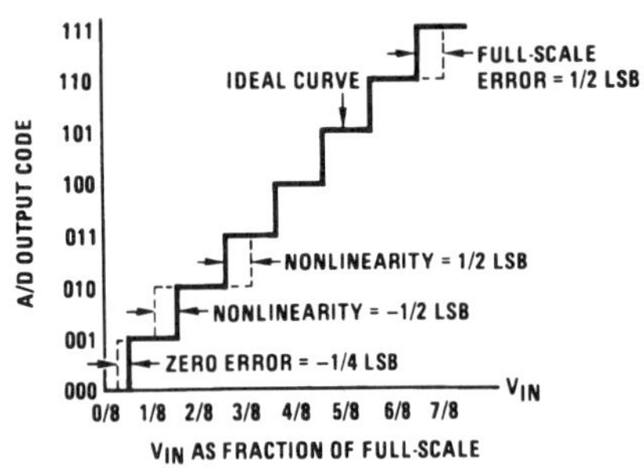

FIGURE 2. 3-Bit A/D Transfer Curve

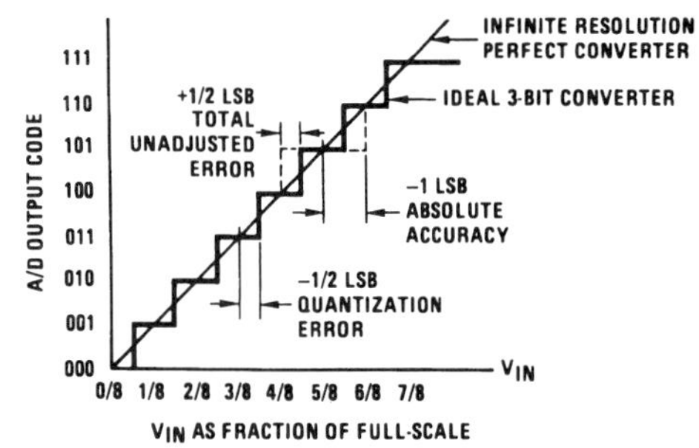

FIGURE 3. 3-Bit A/D Absolute Accuracy Curve

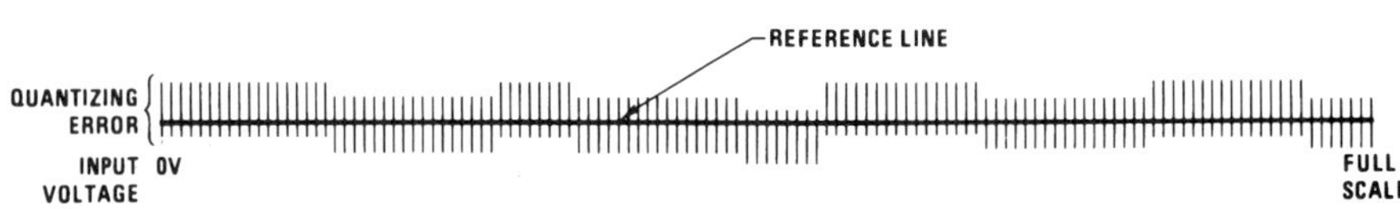

TL/H/5672–3

FIGURE 4. Typical Error Curve

FIGURE A-17

Connection Diagram

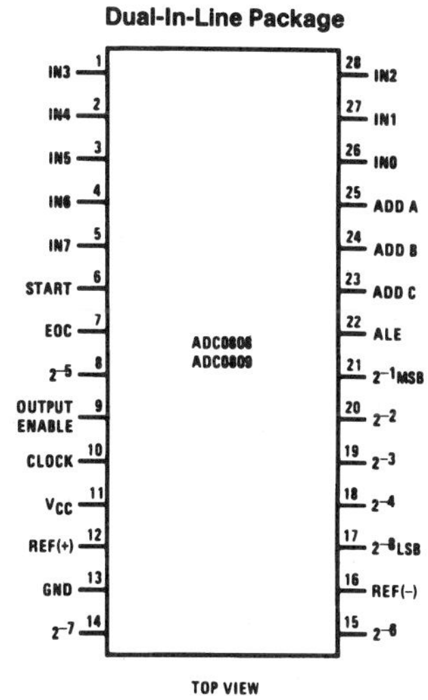

Timing Diagram

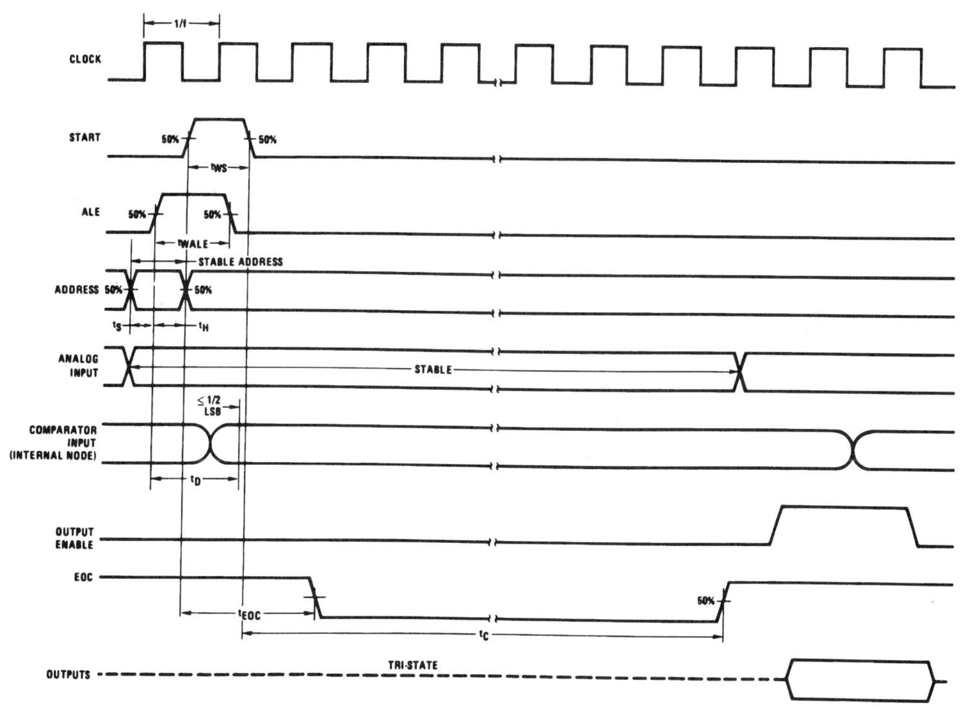

FIGURE A-18

Typical Performance Characteristics

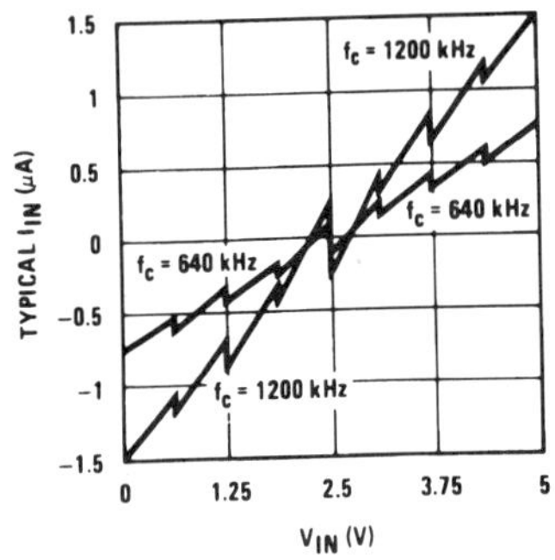

FIGURE 6. Comparator I_{IN} vs V_{IN} ($V_{CC} = V_{REF} = 5V$)

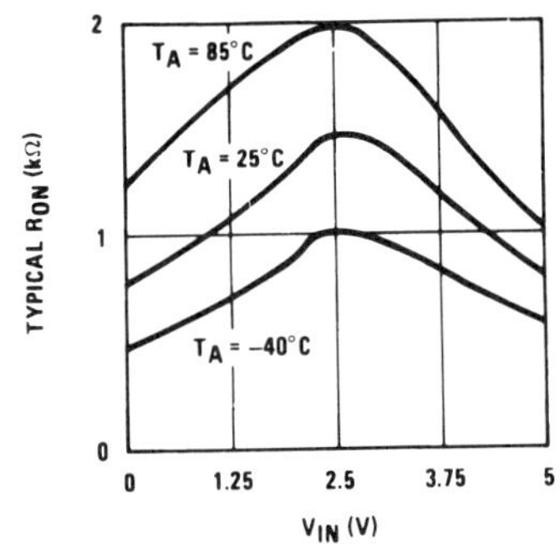

TL/H/5672-5

FIGURE 7. Multiplexer R_{ON} vs V_{IN} ($V_{CC} = V_{REF} = 5V$)

TRI-STATE Test Circuits and Timing Diagrams

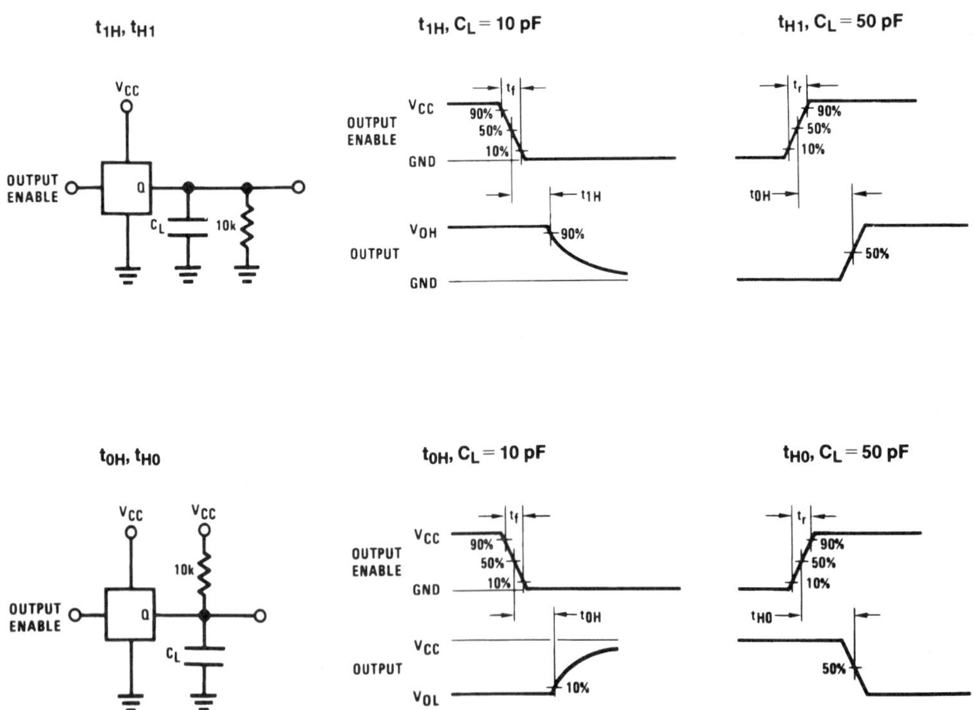

TL/H/5672-6

FIGURE A-19

Applications Information

OPERATION

1.0 RATIOMETRIC CONVERSION

The ADC0808, ADC0809 is designed as a complete Data Acquisition System (DAS) for ratiometric conversion systems. In ratiometric systems, the physical variable being measured is expressed as a percentage of full-scale which is not necessarily related to an absolute standard. The voltage input to the ADC0808 is expressed by the equation

$$\frac{V_{IN}}{V_{fs}-V_Z}=\frac{D_X}{D_{MAX}-D_{MIN}} \quad (1)$$

V_{IN} = Input voltage into the ADC0808

V_{fs} = Full-scale voltage

V_Z = Zero voltage

D_X = Data point being measured

D_{MAX} = Maximum data limit

D_{MIN} = Minimum data limit

A good example of a ratiometric transducer is a potentiometer used as a position sensor. The position of the wiper is directly proportional to the output voltage which is a ratio of the full-scale voltage across it. Since the data is represented as a proportion of full-scale, reference requirements are greatly reduced, eliminating a large source of error and cost for many applications. A major advantage of the ADC0808, ADC0809 is that the input voltage range is equal to the supply range so the transducers can be connected directly across the supply and their outputs connected directly into the multiplexer inputs, *(Figure 9)*.

Ratiometric transducers such as potentiometers, strain gauges, thermistor bridges, pressure transducers, etc., are suitable for measuring proportional relationships; however, many types of measurements must be referred to an absolute standard such as voltage or current. This means a system reference must be used which relates the full-scale voltage to the standard volt. For example, if $V_{CC}=V_{REF}=5.12V$, then the full-scale range is divided into 256 standard steps. The smallest standard step is 1 LSB which is then 20 mV.

2.0 RESISTOR LADDER LIMITATIONS

The voltages from the resistor ladder are compared to the selected into 8 times in a conversion. These voltages are coupled to the comparator via an analog switch tree which is referenced to the supply. The voltages at the top, center and bottom of the ladder must be controlled to maintain proper operation.

The top of the ladder, Ref(+), should not be more positive than the supply, and the bottom of the ladder, Ref(−), should not be more negative than ground. The center of the ladder voltage must also be near the center of the supply because the analog switch tree changes from N-channel switches to P-channel switches. These limitations are automatically satisfied in ratiometric systems and can be easily met in ground referenced systems.

Figure 10 shows a ground referenced system with a separate supply and reference. In this system, the supply must be trimmed to match the reference voltage. For instance, if a 5.12V is used, the supply should be adjusted to the same voltage within 0.1V.

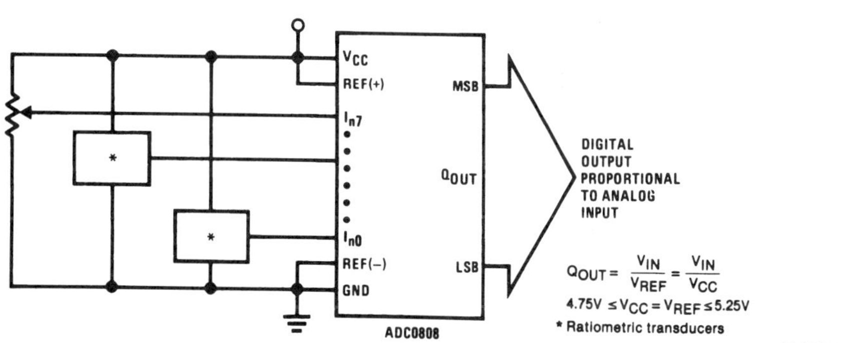

FIGURE 9. Ratiometric Conversion System

FIGURE A-20

Applications Information (Continued)

The ADC0808 needs less than a milliamp of supply current so developing the supply from the reference is readily accomplished. In *Figure 11* a ground referenced system is shown which generates the supply from the reference. The buffer shown can be an op amp of sufficient drive to supply the milliamp of supply current and the desired bus drive, or if a capacitive bus is driven by the outputs a large capacitor will supply the transient supply current as seen in *Figure 12*. The LM301 is overcompensated to insure stability when loaded by the 10 μF output capacitor.

The top and bottom ladder voltages cannot exceed V_{CC} and ground, respectively, but they can be symmetrically less than V_{CC} and greater than ground. The center of the ladder voltage should always be near the center of the supply. The sensitivity of the converter can be increased, (i.e., size of the LSB steps decreased) by using a symmetrical reference system. In *Figure 13*, a 2.5V reference is symmetrically centered about $V_{CC}/2$ since the same current flows in identical resistors. This system with a 2.5V reference allows the LSB bit to be half the size of a 5V reference system.

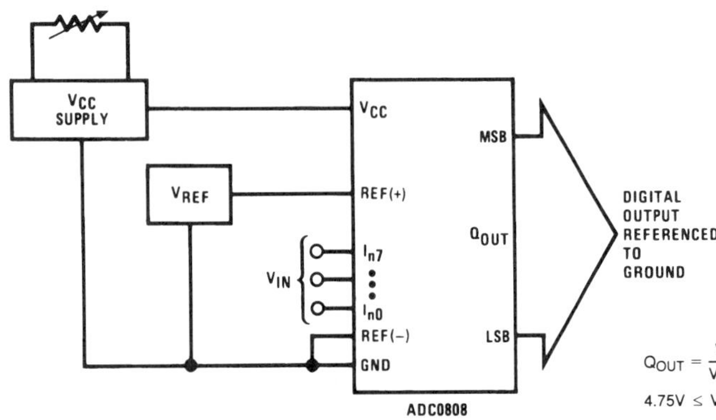

$$Q_{OUT} = \frac{V_{IN}}{V_{REF}}$$

$4.75V \leq V_{CC} = V_{REF} \leq 5.25V$

FIGURE 10. Ground Referenced Conversion System Using Trimmed Supply

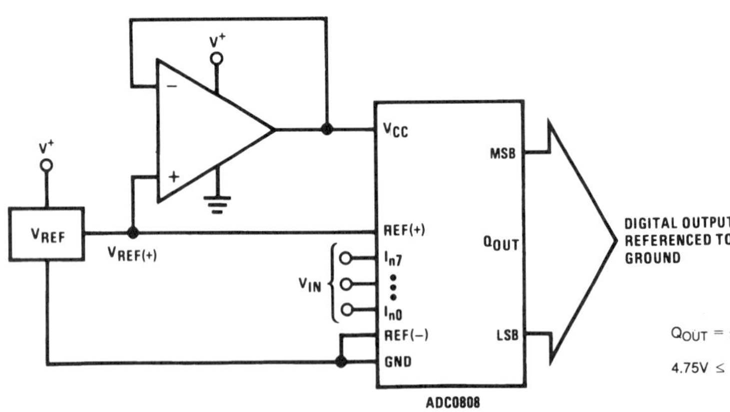

$$Q_{OUT} = \frac{V_{IN}}{V_{REF}}$$

$4.75V \leq V_{CC} = V_{REF} \leq 5.25V$

TL/H/5672–8

FIGURE 11: Ground Referenced Conversion System with Reference Generating V_{CC} Supply

FIGURE A-21

Applications Information (Continued)

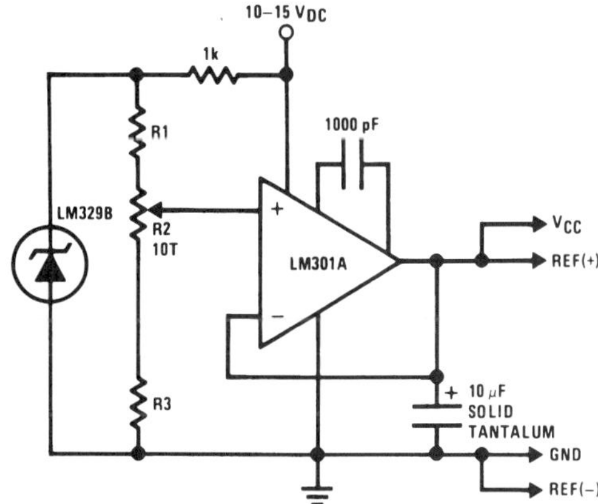

FIGURE 12. Typical Reference and Supply Circuit

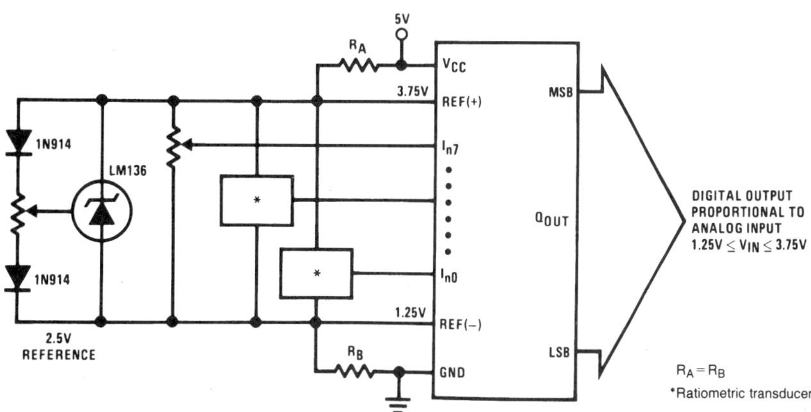

TL/H/5672–9

FIGURE 13. Symmetrically Centered Reference

3.0 CONVERTER EQUATIONS

The transition between adjacent codes N and N + 1 is given by:

$$V_{IN} = \left\{ (V_{REF(+)} - V_{REF(-)}) \left[\frac{N}{256} + \frac{1}{512} \right] \pm V_{TUE} \right\} + V_{REF(-)} \quad (2)$$

The center of an output code N is given by:

$$V_{IN} \left\{ (V_{REF(+)} - V_{REF(-)}) \left[\frac{N}{256} \right] \pm V_{TUE} \right\} + V_{REF(-)} \quad (3)$$

The output code N for an arbitrary input are the integers within the range:

$$N = \frac{V_{IN} - V_{REF(-)}}{V_{REF(+)} - V_{REF(-)}} \times 256 \pm \text{Absolute Accuracy} \quad (4)$$

where: V_{IN} = Voltage at comparator input

$V_{REF(+)}$ = Voltage at Ref(+)

$V_{REF(-)}$ = Voltage at Ref(−)

V_{TUE} = Total unadjusted error voltage (typically $V_{REF(+)} \div 512$)

4.0 ANALOG COMPARATOR INPUTS

The dynamic comparator input current is caused by the periodic switching of on-chip stray capacitances. These are connected alternately to the output of the resistor ladder/switch tree network and to the comparator input as part of the operation of the chopper stabilized comparator.

The average value of the comparator input current varies directly with clock frequency and with V_{IN} as shown in *Figure 6*.

If no filter capacitors are used at the analog inputs and the signal source impedances are low, the comparator input current should not introduce converter errors, as the transient created by the capacitance discharge will die out before the comparator output is strobed.

If input filter capacitors are desired for noise reduction and signal conditioning they will tend to average out the dynamic comparator input current. It will then take on the characteristics of a DC bias current whose effect can be predicted conventionally.

FIGURE A-22

Typical Application

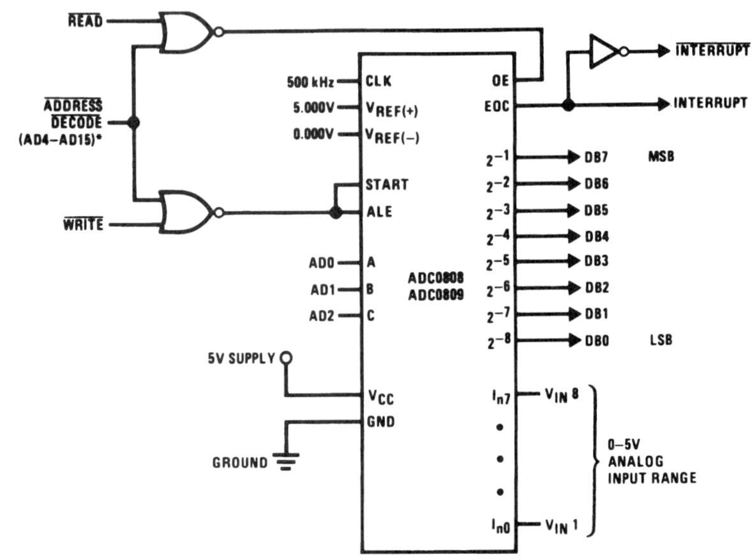

TL/H/5672–10

*Address latches needed for 8085 and SC/MP interfacing the ADC0808 to a microprocessor

MICROPROCESSOR INTERFACE TABLE

PROCESSOR	$\overline{\text{READ}}$	$\overline{\text{WRITE}}$	INTERRUPT (COMMENT)
8080	$\overline{\text{MEMR}}$	$\overline{\text{MEMW}}$	INTR (Thru RST Circuit)
8085	$\overline{\text{RD}}$	$\overline{\text{WR}}$	INTR (Thru RST Circuit)
Z-80	$\overline{\text{RD}}$	$\overline{\text{WR}}$	$\overline{\text{INT}}$ (Thru RST Circuit, Mode 0)
SC/MP	NRDS	NWDS	SA (Thru Sense A)
6800	VMA•ϕ2•R/W	VMA•ϕ•$\overline{\text{R/W}}$	$\overline{\text{IRQA}}$ or $\overline{\text{IRQB}}$ (Thru PIA)

Ordering Information

TEMPERATURE RANGE		−40°C to +85°C		−55°C to +125°C
Error	±½ Bit Unadjusted	ADC0808CCN	ADC0808CCJ	ADC0808CJ
	±1 Bit Unadjusted	ADC0809CCN		
Package Outline		N28A Molded DIP	J28A Hermetic DIP	J28A Hermetic DIP

FIGURE A-23

NPN PNP

TIP120 TIP125
TIP121 TIP126
TIP122 TIP127

PLASTIC MEDIUM-POWER COMPLEMENTARY SILICON TRANSISTORS

. . . designed for general-purpose amplifier and low-speed switching applications.

- High DC Current Gain —
  h_{FE} = 2500 (Typ) @ I_C = 4.0 Adc
- Collector-Emitter Sustaining Voltage — @ 100 mAdc
  $V_{CEO(sus)}$ = 60 Vdc (Min) — TIP120, TIP125
  = 80 Vdc (Min) — TIP121, TIP126
  = 100 Vdc (Min) — TIP122, TIP127
- Low Collector-Emitter Saturation Voltage —
  $V_{CE(sat)}$ = 2.0 Vdc (Max) @ I_C = 3.0 Adc
  = 4.0 Vdc (Max) @ I_C = 5.0 Adc
- Monolithic Construction with Built-In Base-Emitter Shunt Resistors
- TO-220AB Compact Package
- TO-66 Leadform Also Available

DARLINGTON
8 AMPERE
COMPLEMENTARY SILICON POWER TRANSISTORS
60-80-100 VOLTS
65 WATTS

***MAXIMUM RATINGS**

Rating	Symbol	TIP120, TIP125	TIP121, TIP126	TIP122, TIP127	Unit
Collector-Emitter Voltage	V_{CEO}	60	80	100	Vdc
Collector-Base Voltage	V_{CB}	60	80	100	Vdc
Emitter-Base Voltage	V_{EB}	← 5.0 →			Vdc
Collector Current — Continuous Peak	I_C	← 5.0 → ← 8.0 →			Adc
Base Current	I_B	← 120 →			mAdc
Total Power Dissipation @ T_C = 25°C Derate above 25°C	P_D	← 65 → ← 0.52 →			Watts W/°C
Total Power Dissipation @ T_A = 25°C Derate above 25°C	P_D	← 2.0 → ← 0.016 →			Watts W/°C
Unclamped Inductive Load Energy (1)	E	← 50 →			mJ
Operating and Storage Junction, Temperature Range	T_J, T_{stg}	← −65 to +150 →			°C

THERMAL CHARACTERISTICS

Characteristics	Symbol	Max	Unit
Thermal Resistance, Junction to Case	$R_{\theta JC}$	1.92	°C/W
Thermal Resistance, Junction to Ambient	$R_{\theta JA}$	62.5	°C/W

(1) I_C = 1 A, L = 100 mH, P.R.F. = 10 Hz, V_{CC} = 20 V, R_{BE} = 100 Ω.

FIGURE 1 — POWER DERATING

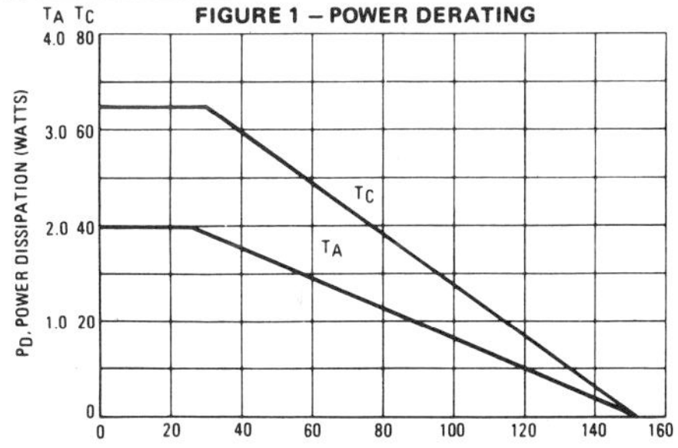

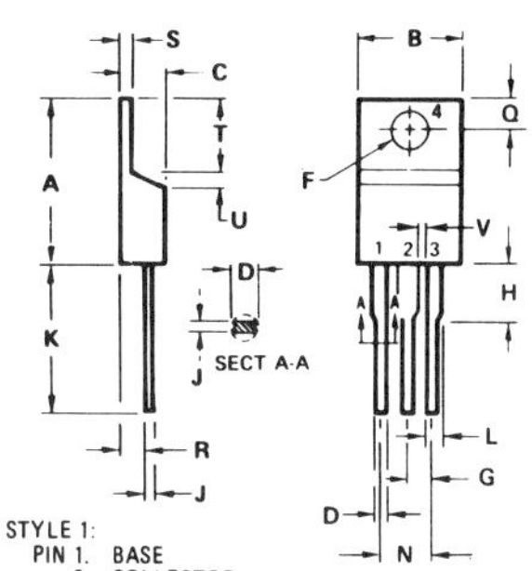

STYLE 1:
PIN 1. BASE
2. COLLECTOR
3. EMITTER
4. COLLECTOR

DIM	MILLIMETERS MIN	MILLIMETERS MAX	INCHES MIN	INCHES MAX
A	15.11	15.75	0.595	0.620
B	9.65	10.29	0.380	0.405
C	4.06	4.82	0.160	0.190
D	0.64	0.89	0.025	0.035
F	3.61	3.73	0.142	0.147
G	2.41	2.67	0.095	0.105
H	2.79	3.30	0.110	0.130
J	0.36	0.56	0.014	0.022
K	12.70	14.27	0.500	0.562
L	1.14	1.27	0.045	0.050
N	4.83	5.33	0.190	0.210
Q	2.54	3.04	0.100	0.120
R	2.04	2.79	0.080	0.110
S	1.14	1.39	0.045	0.055
T	5.97	6.48	0.235	0.255
U	0.76	1.27	0.030	0.050
V	1.14	-	0.045	-

CASE 221A-02
TO-220AB

FIGURE A-24

TIP120, TIP121, TIP122, NPN, TIP125, TIP126, TIP127, PNP

ELECTRICAL CHARACTERISTICS ($T_C = 25°C$ unless otherwise noted)

Characteristic		Symbol	Min	Max	Unit
OFF CHARACTERISTICS					
Collector-Emitter Sustaining Voltage (1)		$V_{CEO(sus)}$			Vdc
(I_C = 100 mAdc, I_B = 0)	TIP120, TIP125		60	–	
	TIP121, TIP126		80	–	
	TIP122, TIP127		100	–	
Collector Cutoff Current		I_{CEO}			mAdc
(V_{CE} = 30 Vdc, I_B = 0)	TIP120, TIP125		–	0.5	
(V_{CE} = 40 Vdc, I_B = 0)	TIP121, TIP126		–	0.5	
(V_{CE} = 50 Vdc, I_B = 0)	TIP122, TIP127		–	0.5	
Collector Cutoff Current		I_{CBO}			mAdc
(V_{CB} = 60 Vdc, I_E = 0)	TIP120, TIP125		–	0.2	
(V_{CB} = 80 Vdc, I_E = 0)	TIP121, TIP126		–	0.2	
(V_{CB} = 100 Vdc, I_E = 0)	TIP122, TIP127		–	0.2	
Emitter Cutoff Current (V_{BE} = 5.0 Vdc, I_C = 0)		I_{EBO}	–	2.0	mAdc
ON CHARACTERISTICS (1)					
DC Current Gain		h_{FE}			–
(I_C = 0.5 Adc, V_{CE} = 3.0 Vdc)			1000	–	
(I_C = 3.0 Adc, V_{CE} = 3.0 Vdc)			1000	–	
Collector-Emitter Saturation Voltage		$V_{CE(sat)}$			Vdc
(I_C = 3.0 Adc, I_B = 12 mAdc)			–	2.0	
(I_C = 5.0 Adc, I_B = 20 mAdc)			–	4.0	
Base-Emitter On Voltage (I_C = 3.0 Adc, V_{CE} = 3.0 Vdc)		$V_{BE(on)}$	–	2.5	Vdc
DYNAMIC CHARACTERISTICS					
Small-Signal Current Gain (I_C = 3.0 Adc, V_{CE} = 4.0 Vdc, f = 1.0 MHz)		$\|h_{fe}\|$	4.0	–	–
Output Capacitance		C_{ob}			pF
(V_{CB} = 10 Vdc, I_E = 0, f = 0.1 MHz)	TIP125, TIP126, TIP127		–	300	
	TIP120, TIP121, TIP122		–	200	

(1) Pulse Test: Pulse Width ⩽ 300 μs, Duty Cycle ⩽ 2%.

FIGURE 2 – SWITCHING TIMES TEST CIRCUIT

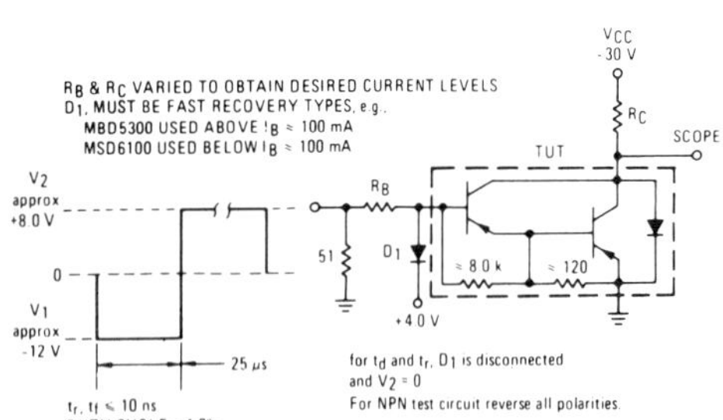

FIGURE 3 – SWITCHING TIMES

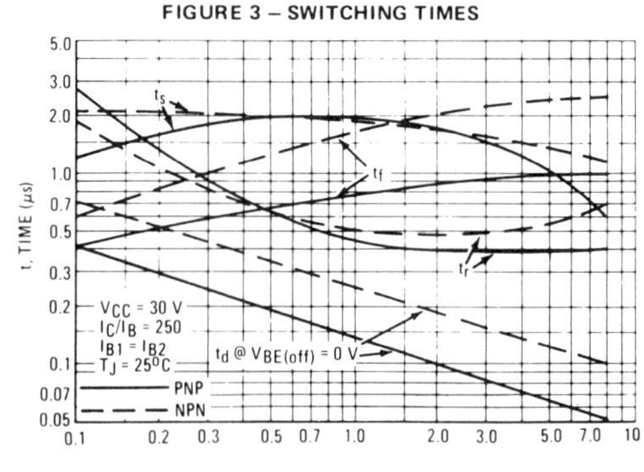

FIGURE A-25

NPN 2N3055 PNP MJ2955

COMPLEMENTARY SILICON POWER TRANSISTORS

. . . designed for general-purpose switching and amplifier applications.

- DC Current Gain – h_{FE} = 20–70 @ I_C = 4 Adc
- Collector-Emitter Saturation Voltage – $V_{CE(sat)}$ = 1.1 Vdc (Max) @ I_C = 4 Adc
- Excellent Safe Operating Area

15 AMPERE
POWER TRANSISTORS
COMPLEMENTARY SILICON

60 VOLTS
115 WATTS

MAXIMUM RATINGS

Rating	Symbol	Value	Unit
Collector-Emitter Voltage	V_{CEO}	60	Vdc
Collector-Emitter Voltage	V_{CER}	70	Vdc
Collector-Base Voltage	V_{CB}	100	Vdc
Emitter-Base Voltage	V_{EB}	7	Vdc
Collector Current – Continuous	I_C	15	Adc
Base Current	I_B	7	Adc
Total Power Dissipation @ T_C = 25°C Derate above 25°C	P_D	115 0.657	Watts W/°C
Operating and Storage Junction Temperature Range	T_J, T_{stg}	-65 to +200	°C

THERMAL CHARACTERISTICS

Characteristic	Symbol	Max	Unit
Thermal Resistance, Junction to Case	$R_{\theta JC}$	1.52	°C/W

FIGURE 1 – POWER DERATING

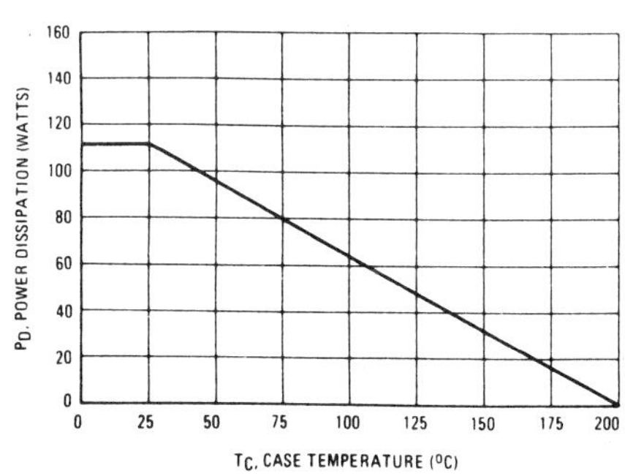

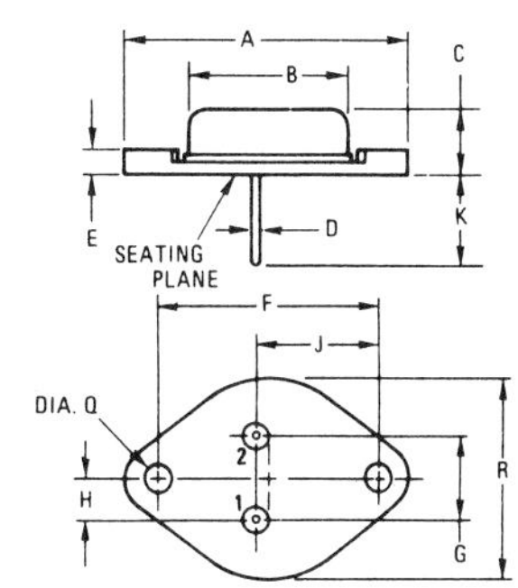

NOTE:
1. DIM "Q" IS DIA.

STYLE 1:
PIN 1. BASE
2. EMITTER
CASE: COLLECTOR

DIM	MILLIMETERS MIN	MILLIMETERS MAX	INCHES MIN	INCHES MAX
A	–	39.37	–	1.550
B	–	21.08	–	0.830
C	6.35	7.62	0.250	0.300
D	0.99	1.09	0.039	0.043
E	–	3.43	–	0.135
F	29.90	30.40	1.177	1.197
G	10.67	11.18	0.420	0.440
H	5.33	5.59	0.210	0.220
J	16.64	17.15	0.655	0.675
K	11.18	12.19	0.440	0.480
Q	3.84	4.09	0.151	0.161
R	–	26.67	–	1.050

Collector connected to case.
CASE 11-01
(TO-3)

FIGURE A-26

2N3055 NPN/MJ2955 PNP

ELECTRICAL CHARACTERISTICS (T_C = 25°C unless otherwise noted)

Characteristic	Symbol	Min	Max	Unit
***OFF CHARACTERISTICS**				
Collector-Emitter Sustaining Voltage (1) (I_C = 200 mAdc, I_B = 0)	$V_{CEO(sus)}$	60	–	Vdc
Collector-Emitter Sustaining Voltage (1) (I_C = 200 mAdc, R_{BE} = 100 Ohms)	$V_{CER(sus)}$	70	–	Vdc
Collector Cutoff Current (V_{CE} = 30 Vdc, I_B = 0)	I_{CEO}	–	0.7	mAdc
Collector Cutoff Current (V_{CE} = 100 Vdc, $V_{BE(off)}$ = 1.5 Vdc) (V_{CE} = 100 Vdc, $V_{BE(off)}$ = 1.5 Vdc, T_C = 150°C)	I_{CEX}	 – –	 1.0 5.0	mAdc
Emitter Cutoff Current (V_{BE} = 7.0 Vdc, I_C = 0)	I_{EBO}	–	5.0	mAdc
***ON CHARACTERISTICS (1)**				
DC Current Gain (I_C = 4.0 Adc, V_{CE} = 4.0 Vdc) (I_C = 10 Adc, V_{CE} = 4.0 Vdc)	h_{FE}	 20 5.0	 70 –	–
Collector-Emitter Saturation Voltage (I_C = 4.0 Adc, I_B = 400 mAdc) (I_C = 10 Adc, I_B = 3.3 Adc)	$V_{CE(sat)}$	–	 1.1 3.0	Vdc
Base-Emitter On Voltage (I_C = 4.0 Adc, V_{CE} = 4.0 Vdc)	$V_{BE(on)}$	–	1.5	Vdc
SECOND BREAKDOWN				
Second Breakdown Collector Current with Base Forward Biased (V_{CE} = 40 Vdc, t = 1.0 s; Nonrepetitive)	$I_{s/b}$	2.87	–	Adc
DYNAMIC CHARACTERISTICS				
Current Gain — Bandwidth Product (I_C = 0.5 Adc, V_{CE} = 10 Vdc, f = 1.0 MHz)	f_T	2.5	–	MHz
*Small-Signal Current Gain (I_C = 1.0 Adc, V_{CE} = 4.0 Vdc, f = 1.0 kHz)	h_{fe}	15	120	–
*Small-Signal Current Gain Cutoff Frequency (V_{CE} = 4.0 Vdc, I_C = 1.0 Adc, f = 1.0 kHz)	f_{hfe}	10	–	kHz

* Indicates Within JEDEC Registration. (2N3055)
(1) Pulse Test: Pulse Width ≤ 300 μs, Duty Cycle ≤ 2.0%.

FIGURE 2 – ACTIVE REGION SAFE OPERATING AREA

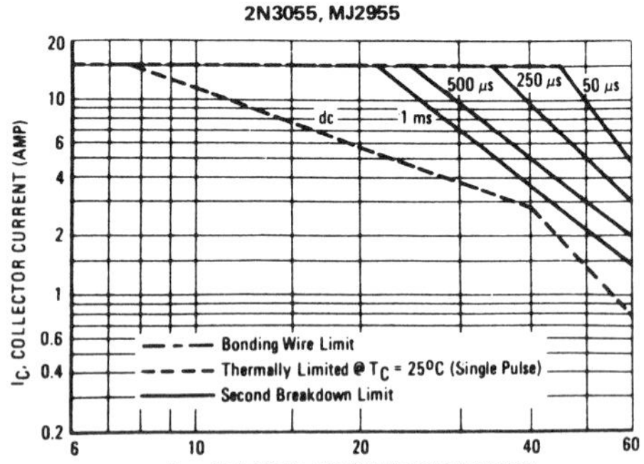

There are two limitations on the power handling ability of a transistor: average junction temperature and second breakdown. Safe operating area curves indicate I_C-V_{CE} limits of the transistor that must be observed for reliable operation; i.e., the transistor must not be subjected to greater dissipation than the curves indicate.

The data of Figure 2 is based on T_C = 25°C; $T_{J(pk)}$ is variable depending on power level. Second breakdown pulse limits are valid for duty cycles to 10% but must be derated for temperature according to Figure 1.

FIGURE A-27

2N2218,A/2N2219,A
2N2221,A/2N2222,A
2N5581/82

JAN, JTX, JTXV AVAILABLE

2N2218,A
2N2219,A
CASE 79-02
TO-39 (TO-205AD)

2N2221,A
2N2222,A
CASE 22-03
TO-18 (TO-206AA)

2N5581
2N5582
CASE 26-03
TO-46 (TO-206AB)

GENERAL PURPOSE TRANSISTOR

NPN SILICON

MAXIMUM RATINGS

Rating	Symbol	2N2218 2N2219 2N2221 2N2222	2N2218A 2N2219A 2N2221A 2N2222A	2N5581 2N5582	Unit
Collector-Emitter Voltage	V_{CEO}	30	40	40	Vdc
Collector-Base Voltage	V_{CBO}	60	75	75	Vdc
Emitter-Base Voltage	V_{EBO}	5.0	6.0	6.0	Vdc
Collector Current — Continuous	I_C	800	800	800	mAdc
		2N2218,A 2N2219,A	**2N2221,A 2N2222,A**	**2N5581 2N5582**	
Total Device Dissipation @ T_A = 25°C Derate above 25°C	P_D	0.8 4.57	0.4 2.28	0.6 3.33	Watt mW/°C
Total Device Dissipation @ T_C = 25°C Derate above 25°C	P_D	3.0 17.1	1.2 6.85	2.0 11.43	Watts mW/°C
Operating and Storage Junction Temperature Range	T_J, T_{stg}	−65 to +200			°C

ELECTRICAL CHARACTERISTICS (T_A = 25°C unless otherwise noted.)

Characteristic		Symbol	Min	Max	Unit
OFF CHARACTERISTICS					
Collector-Emitter Breakdown Voltage (I_C = 10 mAdc, I_B = 0)	Non-A Suffix A-Suffix, 2N5581, 2N5582	$V_{(BR)CEO}$	30 40	— —	Vdc
Collector-Base Breakdown Voltage (I_C = 10 μAdc, I_E = 0)	Non-A Suffix A-Suffix, 2N5581, 2N5582	$V_{(BR)CBO}$	60 75	— —	Vdc
Emitter-Base Breakdown Voltage (I_E = 10 μAdc, I_C = 0)	Non-A Suffix A-Suffix, 2N5581, 2N5582	$V_{(BR)EBO}$	5.0 6.0	— —	Vdc
Collector Cutoff Current (V_{CE} = 60 Vdc, $V_{EB(off)}$ = 3.0 Vdc)	A-Suffix, 2N5581, 2N5582	I_{CEX}	—	10	nAdc
Collector Cutoff Current (V_{CB} = 50 Vdc, I_E = 0) (V_{CB} = 60 Vdc, I_E = 0) (V_{CB} = 50 Vdc, I_E = 0, T_A = 150°C) (V_{CB} = 60 Vdc, I_E = 0, T_A = 150°C)	Non-A Suffix A-Suffix, 2N5581, 2N5582 Non-A Suffix A-Suffix, 2N5581, 2N5582	I_{CBO}	— — — —	0.01 0.01 10 10	μAdc
Emitter Cutoff Current (V_{EB} = 3.0 Vdc, I_C = 0)	A-Suffix, 2N5581, 2N5582	I_{EBO}	—	10	nAdc
Base Cutoff Current (V_{CE} = 60 Vdc, $V_{EB(off)}$ = 3.0 Vdc)	A-Suffix	I_{BL}	—	20	nAdc
ON CHARACTERISTICS					
DC Current Gain (I_C = 0.1 mAdc, V_{CE} = 10 Vdc)	2N2218,A, 2N2221,A, 2N5581(1) 2N2219,A, 2N2222,A, 2N5582(1)	h_{FE}	20 35	— —	—
(I_C = 1.0 mAdc, V_{CE} = 10 Vdc)	2N2218,A, 2N2221,A, 2N5581 2N2219,A, 2N2222,A, 2N5582		25 50	— —	
(I_C = 10 mAdc, V_{CE} = 10 Vdc)	2N2218,A, 2N2221,A, 2N5581(1) 2N2219,A, 2N2222,A, 2N5582(1)		35 75	— —	
(I_C = 10 mAdc, V_{CE} = 10 Vdc, T_A = −55°C)	2N2218A, 2N2221A, 2N5581 2N2219A, 2N2222A, 2N5582		15 35	— —	
(I_C = 150 mAdc, V_{CE} = 10 Vdc)(1)	2N2218,A, 2N2221,A, 2N5581 2N2219,A, 2N2222,A, 2N5582		40 100	120 300	

FIGURE A-28

2N2218/19/21/22, A SERIES, 2N5581/82

ELECTRICAL CHARACTERISTICS (continued) (T_A = 25°C unless otherwise noted.)

Characteristic		Symbol	Min	Max	Unit
(I_C = 150 mAdc, V_{CE} = 1.0 Vdc)(1)	2N2218,A, 2N2221,A, 2N5581		20	—	
	2N2219,A, 2N2222,A, 2N5582		50	—	
(I_C = 500 mAdc, V_{CE} = 10 Vdc)(1)	2N2218, 2N2221		20	—	
	2N2219, 2N2222		30	—	
	2N2218A, 2N2221A, 2N5581		25	—	
	2N2219A, 2N2222A, 2N5582		40	—	
Collector-Emitter Saturation Voltage(1)		$V_{CE(sat)}$			Vdc
(I_C = 150 mAdc, I_B = 15 mAdc)	Non-A Suffix		—	0.4	
	A-Suffix, 2N5581, 2N5582		—	0.3	
(I_C = 500 mAdc, I_B = 50 mAdc)	Non-A Suffix		—	1.6	
	A-Suffix, 2N5581, 2N5582		—	1.0	
Base-Emitter Saturation Voltage(1)		$V_{BE(sat)}$			Vdc
(I_C = 150 mAdc, I_B = 15 mAdc)	Non-A Suffix		0.6	1.3	
	A-Suffix, 2N5581, 2N5582		0.6	1.2	
(I_C = 500 mAdc, I_B = 50 mAdc)	Non-A Suffix		—	2.6	
	A-Suffix, 2N5581, 2N5582		—	2.0	
SMALL-SIGNAL CHARACTERISTICS					
Current-Gain — Bandwidth Product(2)		f_T			MHz
(I_C = 20 mAdc, V_{CE} = 20 Vdc, f = 100 MHz)	All Types, Except		250	—	
	2N2219A, 2N2222A, 2N5582		300	—	
Output Capacitance(3) (V_{CB} = 10 Vdc, I_E = 0, f = 100 kHz)		C_{obo}	—	8.0	pF
Input Capacitance(3)		C_{ibo}			pF
(V_{EB} = 0.5 Vdc, I_C = 0, f = 100 kHz)	Non-A Suffix		—	30	
	A-Suffix, 2N5581, 2N5582		—	25	
Input Impedance		h_{ie}			kohms
(I_C = 1.0 mAdc, V_{CE} = 10 Vdc, f = 1.0 kHz)	2N2218A, 2N2221A		1.0	3.5	
	2N2219A, 2N2222A		2.0	8.0	
(I_C = 10 mAdc, V_{CE} = 10 Vdc, f = 1.0 kHz)	2N2218A, 2N2221A		0.2	1.0	
	2N2219A, 2N2222A		0.25	1.25	
Voltage Feedback Ratio		h_{re}			$X 10^{-4}$
(I_C = 1.0 mAdc, V_{CE} = 10 Vdc, f = 1.0 kHz)	2N2218A, 2N2221A		—	5.0	
	2N2219A, 2N2222A		—	8.0	
(I_C = 10 mAdc, V_{CE} = 10 Vdc, f = 1.0 kHz)	2N2218A, 2N2221A		—	2.5	
	2N2219A, 2N2222A		—	4.0	
Small-Signal Current Gain		h_{fe}			—
(I_C = 1.0 mAdc, V_{CE} = 10 Vdc, f = 1.0 kHz)	2N2218A, 2N2221A		30	150	
	2N2219A, 2N2222A		50	300	
(I_C = 10 mAdc, V_{CE} = 10 Vdc, f = 1.0 kHz)	2N2218A, 2N2221A		50	300	
	2N2219A, 2N2222A		75	375	
Output Admittance		h_{oe}			μmhos
(I_C = 1.0 mAdc, V_{CE} = 10 Vdc, f = 1.0 kHz)	2N2218A, 2N2221A		3.0	15	
	2N2219A, 2N2222A		5.0	35	
(I_C = 10 mAdc, V_{CE} = 10 Vdc, f = 1.0 kHz)	2N2218A, 2N2221A		10	100	
	2N2219A, 2N2222A		25	200	
Collector Base Time Constant (I_E = 20 mAdc, V_{CB} = 20 Vdc, f = 31.8 MHz)	A-Suffix	$rb'C_c$	—	150	ps
Noise Figure (I_C = 100 μAdc, V_{CE} = 10 Vdc, R_S = 1.0 kohm, f = 1.0 kHz)	2N2219A, 2N2222A	NF	—	4.0	dB
Real Part of Common-Emitter High Frequency Input Impedance (I_C = 20 mAdc, V_{CE} = 20 Vdc, f = 300 MHz)	2N2218A, 2N2219A, 2N2221A, 2N2222A	$Re(h_{ie})$	—	60	Ohms

(1) Pulse Test: Pulse Width ≤ 300 μs, Duty Cycle ≤ 2.0%.
(2) f_T is defined as the frequency at which $|h_{fe}|$ extrapolates to unity.
(3) 2N5581 and 2N5582 are Listed C_{cb} and C_{eb} for these conditions and values.

FIGURE A-29

Absolute Maximum Ratings

Temperature Under Bias	Specified operating range
Storage Temperature	-65°C to +150°C
Voltage On Any Pin with Respect to Ground	-0.3V to +7V
Power Dissipation	1.5W

*Comment

Stresses above those listed under "Absolute Maximum Rating" may cause permanent damage to the device. This is a stress rating only and functional operation of the device at these or any other condition above those indicated in the operational sections of this specification is not implied. Exposure to absolute maximum rating conditions for extended periods may affect device reliability.

Note: For Z80-CPU all AC and DC characteristics remain the same for the military grade parts except I_{cc}.

I_{cc} = 200 mA

Z80-CPU D.C. Characteristics

T_A = 0°C to 70°C, V_{cc} = 5V ± 5% unless otherwise specified

Symbol	Parameter	Min.	Typ.	Max.	Unit	Test Condition
V_{ILC}	Clock Input Low Voltage	-0.3		0.45	V	
V_{IHC}	Clock Input High Voltage	V_{cc} -.6		V_{cc}+.3	V	
V_{IL}	Input Low Voltage	-0.3		0.8	V	
V_{IH}	Input High Voltage	2.0		V_{cc}	V	
V_{OL}	Output Low Voltage			0.4	V	I_{OL}=1.8mA
V_{OH}	Output High Voltage	2.4			V	I_{OH} = -250μA
I_{CC}	Power Supply Current			150	mA	
I_{LI}	Input Leakage Current			10	μA	V_{IN}=0 to V_{cc}
I_{LOH}	Tri-State Output Leakage Current in Float			10	μA	V_{OUT}=2.4 to V_{cc}
I_{LOL}	Tri-State Output Leakage Current in Float			-10	μA	V_{OUT}=0.4V
I_{LD}	Data Bus Leakage Current in Input Mode			±10	μA	$0 \leq V_{IN} \leq V_{cc}$

Capacitance

T_A = 25°C, f = 1 MHz,
unmeasured pins returned to ground

Symbol	Parameter	Max.	Unit
C_Φ	Clock Capacitance	35	pF
C_{IN}	Input Capacitance	5	pF
C_{OUT}	Output Capacitance	10	pF

Z80-CPU Ordering Information

C – Ceramic
P – Plastic
S – Standard 5V ±5% 0° to 70°C
E – Extended 5V ±5% -40° to 85°C
M – Military 5V ±10% -55° to 125°C

Z80A-CPU D.C. Characteristics

T_A = 0°C to 70°C, V_{cc} = 5V ± 5% unless otherwise specified

Symbol	Parameter	Min.	Typ.	Max.	Unit	Test Condition
V_{ILC}	Clock Input Low Voltage	-0.3		0.45	V	
V_{IHC}	Clock Input High Voltage	V_{cc} -.6		V_{cc}+.3	V	
V_{IL}	Input Low Voltage	-0.3		0.8	V	
V_{IH}	Input High Voltage	2.0		V_{cc}	V	
V_{OL}	Output Low Voltage			0.4	V	I_{OL}=1.8mA
V_{OH}	Output High Voltage	2.4			V	I_{OH} = -250μA
I_{CC}	Power Supply Current		90	200	mA	
I_{LI}	Input Leakage Current			10	μA	V_{IN}=0 to V_{cc}
I_{LOH}	Tri-State Output Leakage Current in Float			10	μA	V_{OUT}=2.4 to V_{cc}
I_{LOL}	Tri-State Output Leakage Current in Float			-10	μA	V_{OUT}=0.4V
I_{LD}	Data Bus Leakage Current in Input Mode			±10	μA	$0 \leq V_{IN} \leq V_{cc}$

Capacitance

T_A = 25°C, f = 1 MHz,
unmeasured pins returned to ground

Symbol	Parameter	Max.	Unit
C_Φ	Clock Capacitance	35	pF
C_{IN}	Input Capacitance	5	pF
C_{OUT}	Output Capacitance	10	pF

Z80A-CPU Ordering Information

C – Ceramic
P – Plastic
S – Standard 5V ±5% 0° to 70°C

FIGURE A-30

A.C. Characteristics — Z80A-CPU

$T_A = 0°C$ to $70°C$, $V_{cc} = +5V \pm 5\%$, Unless Otherwise Noted.

Signal	Symbol	Parameter	Min	Max	Unit	Test Condition
Φ	t_c	Clock Period	.25	[12]	μsec	
	$t_w(\Phi H)$	Clock Pulse Width, Clock High	110	[E]	nsec	
	$t_w(\Phi L)$	Clock Pulse Width, Clock Low	110	2000	nsec	
	$t_{r,f}$	Clock Rise and Fall Time		30	nsec	
A_{0-15}	$t_{D(AD)}$	Address Output Delay		110	nsec	$C_L = 50pF$
	$t_{F(AD)}$	Delay to Float		90	nsec	
	t_{acm}	Address Stable Prior to $\overline{MREQ}$ (Memory Cycle)	[1]		nsec	
	t_{aci}	Address Stable Prior to $\overline{IORQ}$, $\overline{RD}$ or $\overline{WR}$ (I/O Cycle)	[2]		nsec	
	t_{ca}	Address Stable from $\overline{RD}$, $\overline{WR}$, $\overline{IORQ}$ or $\overline{MREQ}$	[3]		nsec	
	t_{caf}	Address Stable From $\overline{RD}$ or $\overline{WR}$ During Float	[4]		nsec	
D_{0-7}	$t_{D(D)}$	Data Output Delay		150	nsec	$C_L = 50pF$
	$t_{F(D)}$	Delay to Float During Write Cycle		90	nsec	
	$t_{S\Phi(D)}$	Data Setup Time to Rising Edge of Clock During M1 Cycle	35		nsec	
	$t_{S\overline{\Phi}(D)}$	Data Setup Time to Falling Edge of Clock During M2 to M5	50		nsec	
	t_{dcm}	Data Stable Prior to $\overline{WR}$ (Memory Cycle)	[5]		nsec	
	t_{dci}	Data Stable Prior to $\overline{WR}$ (I/O Cycle)	[6]		nsec	
	t_{cdf}	Data Stable From $\overline{WR}$	[7]			
	t_H	Any Hold Time for Setup Time		0	nsec	
$\overline{MREQ}$	$t_{DL\overline{\Phi}(MR)}$	$\overline{MREQ}$ Delay From Falling Edge of Clock, $\overline{MREQ}$ Low		85	nsec	$C_L = 50pF$
	$t_{DH\Phi(MR)}$	$\overline{MREQ}$ Delay From Rising Edge of Clock, $\overline{MREQ}$ High		85	nsec	
	$t_{DH\overline{\Phi}(MR)}$	$\overline{MREQ}$ Delay From Falling Edge of Clock, $\overline{MREQ}$ High		85	nsec	
	$t_{w(\overline{MRL})}$	Pulse Width, $\overline{MREQ}$ Low	[8]		nsec	
	$t_{w(\overline{MRH})}$	Pulse Width, $\overline{MREQ}$ High	[9]		nsec	
$\overline{IORQ}$	$t_{DL\Phi(IR)}$	$\overline{IORQ}$ Delay From Rising Edge of Clock, $\overline{IORQ}$ Low		75	nsec	$C_L = 50pF$
	$t_{DL\overline{\Phi}(IR)}$	$\overline{IORQ}$ Delay From Falling Edge of Clock, $\overline{IORQ}$ Low		85	nsec	
	$t_{DH\Phi(IR)}$	$\overline{IORQ}$ Delay From Rising Edge of Clock, $\overline{IORQ}$ High		85	nsec	
	$t_{DH\overline{\Phi}(IR)}$	$\overline{IORQ}$ Delay From Falling Edge of Clock, $\overline{IORQ}$ High		85	nsec	
$\overline{RD}$	$t_{DL\Phi(RD)}$	$\overline{RD}$ Delay From Rising Edge of Clock, $\overline{RD}$ Low		85	nsec	$C_L = 50pF$
	$t_{DL\overline{\Phi}(RD)}$	$\overline{RD}$ Delay From Falling Edge of Clock, $\overline{RD}$ Low		95	nsec	
	$t_{DH\Phi(RD)}$	$\overline{RD}$ Delay From Rising Edge of Clock, $\overline{RD}$ High		85	nsec	
	$t_{DH\overline{\Phi}(RD)}$	$\overline{RD}$ Delay From Falling Edge of Clock, $\overline{RD}$ High		85	nsec	
$\overline{WR}$	$t_{DL\Phi(WR)}$	$\overline{WR}$ Delay From Rising Edge of Clock, $\overline{WR}$ Low		65	nsec	$C_L = 50pF$
	$t_{DL\overline{\Phi}(WR)}$	$\overline{WR}$ Delay From Falling Edge of Clock, $\overline{WR}$ Low		80	nsec	
	$t_{DH\Phi(WR)}$	$\overline{WR}$ Delay From Falling Edge of Clock, $\overline{WR}$ High		80	nsec	
	$t_{w(\overline{WRL})}$	Pulse Width, $\overline{WR}$ Low	[10]		nsec	
$\overline{M1}$	$t_{DL(M1)}$	$\overline{M1}$ Delay From Rising Edge of Clock, $\overline{M1}$ Low		100	nsec	$C_L = 50pF$
	$t_{DH(M1)}$	$\overline{M1}$ Delay From Rising Edge of Clock, $\overline{M1}$ High		100	nsec	
$\overline{RFSH}$	$t_{DL(RF)}$	$\overline{RFSH}$ Delay From Rising Edge of Clock, $\overline{RFSH}$ Low		130	nsec	$C_L = 50pF$
	$t_{DH(RF)}$	$\overline{RFSH}$ Delay From Rising Edge of Clock, $\overline{RFSH}$ High		120	nsec	
$\overline{WAIT}$	$t_{s(WT)}$	$\overline{WAIT}$ Setup Time to Falling Edge of Clock	70		nsec	
$\overline{HALT}$	$t_{D(HT)}$	$\overline{HALT}$ Delay Time From Falling Edge of Clock		300	nsec	$C_L = 50pF$
$\overline{INT}$	$t_{s(IT)}$	$\overline{INT}$ Setup Time to Rising Edge of Clock	80		nsec	
$\overline{NMI}$	$t_{w(\overline{NML})}$	Pulse Width, $\overline{NMI}$ Low	80		nsec	
$\overline{BUSRQ}$	$t_{s(BQ)}$	$\overline{BUSRQ}$ Setup Time to Rising Edge of Clock	50		nsec	
$\overline{BUSAK}$	$t_{DL(BA)}$	$\overline{BUSAK}$ Delay From Rising Edge of Clock, $\overline{BUSAK}$ Low		100	nsec	$C_L = 50pF$
	$t_{DH(BA)}$	$\overline{BUSAK}$ Delay From Falling Edge of Clock, $\overline{BUSAK}$ High		100	nsec	
$\overline{RESET}$	$t_{s(RS)}$	$\overline{RESET}$ Setup Time to Rising Edge of Clock	60		nsec	
	$t_{F(C)}$	Delay to Float ($\overline{MREQ}$, $\overline{IORQ}$, $\overline{RD}$ and $\overline{WR}$)		80	nsec	
	t_{mr}	M1 Stable Prior to IORQ (Interrupt Ack.)	[11]		nsec	

[12] $t_c = t_{w(\Phi H)} + t_{w(\Phi L)} + t_r + t_f$

[1] $t_{acm} = t_{w(\Phi H)} + t_f - 65$

[2] $t_{aci} = t_c - 70$

[3] $t_{ca} = t_{w(\Phi L)} + t_r - 50$

[4] $t_{caf} = t_{w(\Phi L)} + t_r - 45$

[5] $t_{dcm} = t_c - 170$

[6] $t_{dci} = t_{w(\Phi L)} + t_r - 170$

[7] $t_{cdf} = t_{w(\Phi L)} + t_r - 70$

[8] $t_{w(\overline{MR}L)} = t_c - 30$

[9] $t_{w(\overline{MR}H)} = t_{w(\Phi H)} + t_f - 20$

[10] $t_{w(\overline{WRL})} = t_c - 30$

[11] $t_{mr} = 2t_c + t_{w(\Phi H)} + t_f - 65$

NOTES:

A. Data should be enabled onto the CPU data bus when $\overline{RD}$ is active. During interrupt acknowledge data should be enabled when $\overline{M1}$ and $\overline{IORQ}$ are both active.

B. All control signals are internally synchronized, so they may be totally asynchronous with respect to the clock.

C. The $\overline{RESET}$ signal must be active for a minimum of 3 clock cycles.

D. Output Delay vs. Loaded Capacitance
TA = 70°C Vcc = +5V ±5%
Add 10nsec delay for each 50pf increase in load up to maximum of 200pf for data bus and 100pf for address & control lines.

E. Although static by design, testing guarantees $t_{w(\Phi H)}$ of 200 μsec maximum

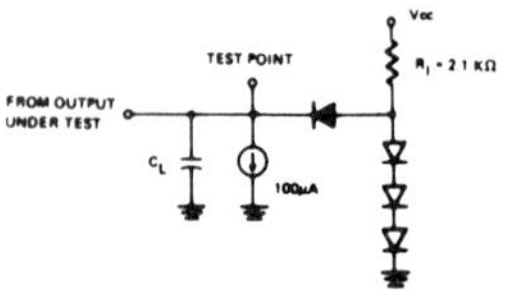

Load circuit for Output

FIGURE A-31

A.C. Timing Diagram

Timing measurements are made at the following voltages, unless otherwise specified:

	"1"	"0"
CLOCK	V_{cc} -.6V	.45V
OUTPUT	2.0 V	.8 V
INPUT	2.0 V	.8 V
FLOAT	Δ V	± 0.5 V

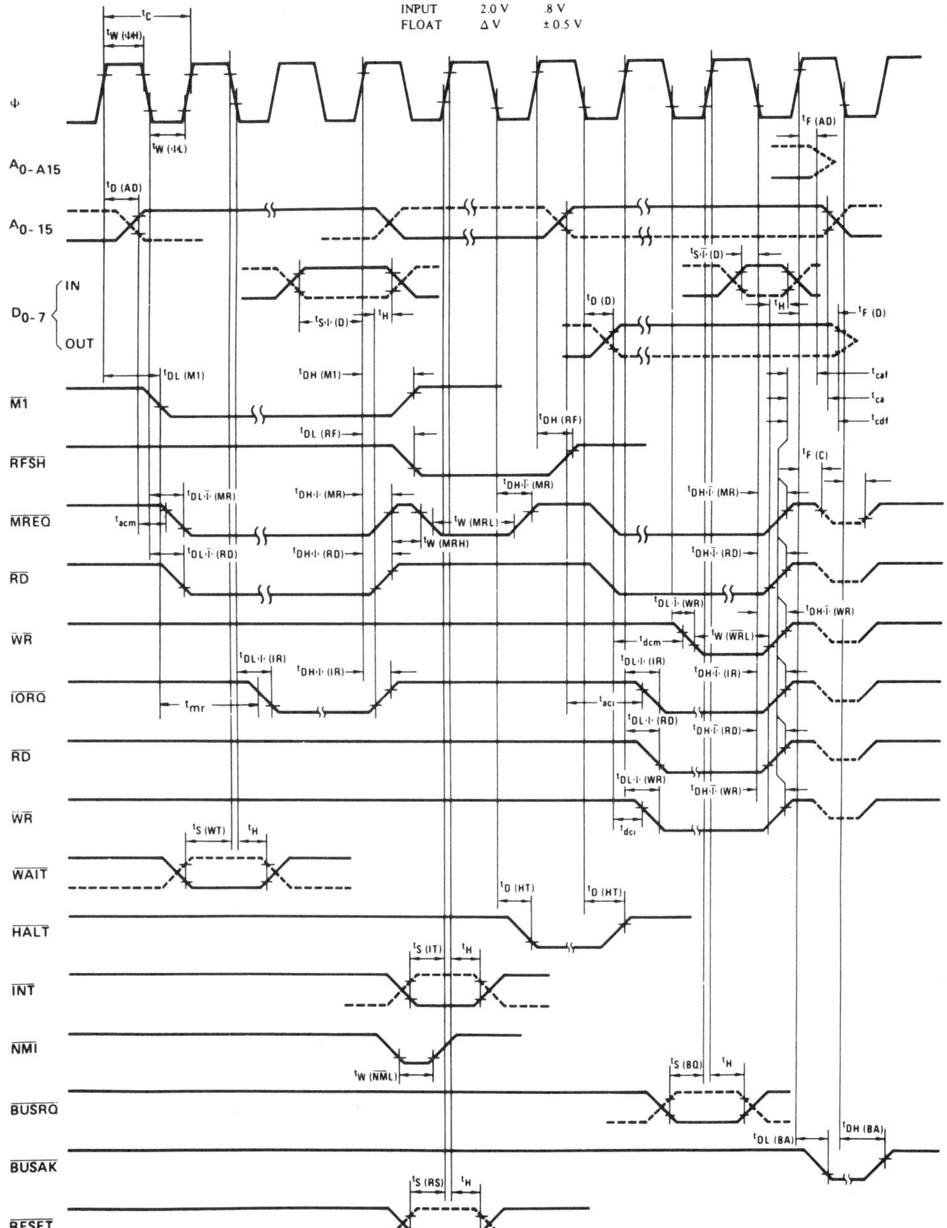

FIGURE A-32

A.C. Characteristics — Z80-CPU

$T_A = 0°C$ to $70°C$, $V_{CC} = +5V \pm 5\%$, Unless Otherwise Noted.

Signal	Symbol	Parameter	Min	Max	Unit	Test Condition
Φ	t_c	Clock Period	.4	[12]	μsec	
	$t_w(\Phi H)$	Clock Pulse Width, Clock High	180	[E]	nsec	
	$t_w(\Phi L)$	Clock Pulse Width, Clock Low	180	2000	nsec	
	$t_{r,f}$	Clock Rise and Fall Time		30	nsec	
A_{0-15}	$t_{D(AD)}$	Address Output Delay		145	nsec	$C_L = 50pF$
	$t_{F(AD)}$	Delay to Float		110	nsec	
	t_{acm}	Address Stable Prior to $\overline{MREQ}$ (Memory Cycle)	[1]		nsec	
	t_{aci}	Address Stable Prior to $\overline{IORQ}$, $\overline{RD}$ or $\overline{WR}$ (I/O Cycle)	[2]		nsec	
	t_{ca}	Address Stable from $\overline{RD}$, $\overline{WR}$, $\overline{IORQ}$ or $\overline{MREQ}$	[3]		nsec	
	t_{caf}	Address Stable From $\overline{RD}$ or $\overline{WR}$ During Float	[4]		nsec	
D_{0-7}	$t_{D(D)}$	Data Output Delay		230	nsec	$C_L = 50pF$
	$t_{F(D)}$	Delay to Float During Write Cycle		90	nsec	
	$t_{S\Phi(D)}$	Data Setup Time to Rising Edge of Clock During M1 Cycle	50		nsec	
	$t_{S\overline{\Phi}(D)}$	Data Setup Time to Falling Edge of Clock During M2 to M5	60		nsec	
	t_{dcm}	Data Stable Prior to $\overline{WR}$ (Memory Cycle)	[5]		nsec	
	t_{dci}	Data Stable Prior to $\overline{WR}$ (I/O Cycle)	[6]		nsec	
	t_{cdf}	Data Stable From $\overline{WR}$	[7]			
	t_H	Any Hold Time for Setup Time	0		nsec	
$\overline{MREQ}$	$t_{DL\overline{\Phi}(MR)}$	$\overline{MREQ}$ Delay From Falling Edge of Clock, $\overline{MREQ}$ Low		100	nsec	$C_L = 50pF$
	$t_{DH\Phi(MR)}$	$\overline{MREQ}$ Delay From Rising Edge of Clock, $\overline{MREQ}$ High		100	nsec	
	$t_{DH\overline{\Phi}(MR)}$	$\overline{MREQ}$ Delay From Falling Edge of Clock, $\overline{MREQ}$ High		100	nsec	
	$t_{w(\overline{MRL})}$	Pulse Width, $\overline{MREQ}$ Low	[8]		nsec	
	$t_{w(\overline{MRH})}$	Pulse Width, $\overline{MREQ}$ High	[9]		nsec	
$\overline{IORQ}$	$t_{DL\Phi(IR)}$	$\overline{IORQ}$ Delay From Rising Edge of Clock, $\overline{IORQ}$ Low		90	nsec	$C_L = 50pF$
	$t_{DL\overline{\Phi}(IR)}$	$\overline{IORQ}$ Delay From Falling Edge of Clock, $\overline{IORQ}$ Low		110	nsec	
	$t_{DH\Phi(IR)}$	$\overline{IORQ}$ Delay From Rising Edge of Clock, $\overline{IORQ}$ High		100	nsec	
	$t_{DH\overline{\Phi}(IR)}$	$\overline{IORQ}$ Delay From Falling Edge of Clock, $\overline{IORQ}$ High		110	nsec	
$\overline{RD}$	$t_{DL\Phi(RD)}$	$\overline{RD}$ Delay From Rising Edge of Clock, $\overline{RD}$ Low		100	nsec	$C_L = 50pF$
	$t_{DL\overline{\Phi}(RD)}$	$\overline{RD}$ Delay From Falling Edge of Clock, $\overline{RD}$ Low		130	nsec	
	$t_{DH\Phi(RD)}$	$\overline{RD}$ Delay From Rising Edge of Clock, $\overline{RD}$ High		100	nsec	
	$t_{DH\overline{\Phi}(RD)}$	$\overline{RD}$ Delay From Falling Edge of Clock, $\overline{RD}$ High		110	nsec	
$\overline{WR}$	$t_{DL\Phi(WR)}$	$\overline{WR}$ Delay From Rising Edge of Clock, $\overline{WR}$ Low		80	nsec	$C_L = 50pF$
	$t_{DL\overline{\Phi}(WR)}$	$\overline{WR}$ Delay From Falling Edge of Clock, $\overline{WR}$ Low		90	nsec	
	$t_{DH\Phi(WR)}$	$\overline{WR}$ Delay From Falling Edge of Clock, $\overline{WR}$ High		100	nsec	
	$t_{w(\overline{WRL})}$	Pulse Width, $\overline{WR}$ Low	[10]		nsec	
$\overline{M1}$	$t_{DL(M1)}$	$\overline{M1}$ Delay From Rising Edge of Clock, $\overline{M1}$ Low		130	nsec	$C_L = 50pF$
	$t_{DH(M1)}$	$\overline{M1}$ Delay From Rising Edge of Clock, $\overline{M1}$ High		130	nsec	
$\overline{RFSH}$	$t_{DL(RF)}$	$\overline{RFSH}$ Delay From Rising Edge of Clock, $\overline{RFSH}$ Low		180	nsec	$C_L = 50pF$
	$t_{DH(RF)}$	$\overline{RFSH}$ Delay From Rising Edge of Clock, $\overline{RFSH}$ High		150	nsec	
$\overline{WAIT}$	$t_{s(WT)}$	$\overline{WAIT}$ Setup Time to Falling Edge of Clock	70		nsec	
$\overline{HALT}$	$t_{D(HT)}$	$\overline{HALT}$ Delay Time From Falling Edge of Clock		300	nsec	$C_L = 50pF$
$\overline{INT}$	$t_{s(IT)}$	$\overline{INT}$ Setup Time to Rising Edge of Clock	80		nsec	
$\overline{NMI}$	$t_{w(\overline{NML})}$	Pulse Width, $\overline{NMI}$ Low	80		nsec	
$\overline{BUSRQ}$	$t_{s(BQ)}$	$\overline{BUSRQ}$ Setup Time to Rising Edge of Clock	80		nsec	
$\overline{BUSAK}$	$t_{DL(BA)}$	$\overline{BUSAK}$ Delay From Rising Edge of Clock, $\overline{BUSAK}$ Low		120	nsec	$C_L = 50pF$
	$t_{DH(BA)}$	$\overline{BUSAK}$ Delay From Falling Edge of Clock, $\overline{BUSAK}$ High		110	nsec	
$\overline{RESET}$	$t_{s(RS)}$	$\overline{RESET}$ Setup Time to Rising Edge of Clock	90		nsec	
	$t_{F(C)}$	Delay to Float ($\overline{MREQ}$, $\overline{IORQ}$, $\overline{RD}$ and $\overline{WR}$)		100	nsec	
	t_{mr}	$\overline{M1}$ Stable Prior to $\overline{IORQ}$ (Interrupt Ack.)	[11]		nsec	

[12] $t_c = t_{w(\Phi H)} + t_{w(\Phi L)} + t_r + t_f$

[1] $t_{acm} = t_{w(\Phi H)} + t_f - 75$

[2] $t_{aci} = t_c - 80$

[3] $t_{ca} = t_{w(\Phi L)} + t_r - 40$

[4] $t_{caf} = t_{w(\Phi L)} + t_r - 60$

[5] $t_{dcm} = t_c - 210$

[6] $t_{dci} = t_{w(\Phi L)} + t_r - 210$

[7] $t_{cdf} = t_{w(\Phi L)} + t_r - 80$

[8] $t_{w(MRL)} = t_c - 40$

[9] $t_{w(MRH)} = t_{w(\Phi H)} + t_f - 30$

[10] $t_{w(\overline{WR}L)} = t_c - 40$

[11] $t_{mr} = 2t_c + t_{w(\Phi H)} + t_f - 80$

NOTES

A. Data should be enabled onto the CPU data bus when $\overline{RD}$ is active. During interrupt acknowledge data should be enabled when $\overline{M1}$ and $\overline{IORQ}$ are both active.

B. All control signals are internally synchronized, so they may be totally asynchronous with respect to the clock.

C. The $\overline{RESET}$ signal must be active for a minimum of 3 clock cycles.

D. Output Delay vs. Loaded Capacitance
TA = 70°C   Vcc = +5V ±5%

Add 10nsec delay for each 50pf increase in load up to a maximum of 200pf for the data bus & 100pf for address & control lines

E. Although static by design, testing guarantees $t_{w(\Phi H)}$ of 200 μsec maximum

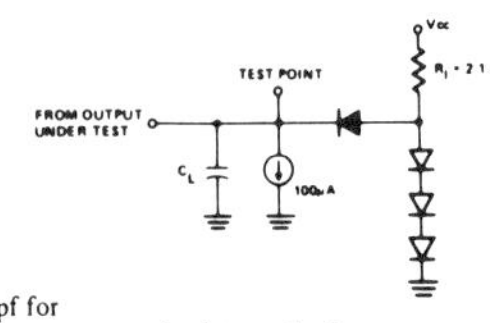

Load circuit for Output

FIGURE A-33

Glossary

Access time. The time from when memory is selected ($\overline{CE}$ goes LOW) to when stable output data is present.

Accumulator. Special-purpose register that contains the results of 8-bit arithmetic and logic instructions.

ACIA. (asynchronous communications interface adapter). A serial–interface port integrated circuit.

Active HIGH input. A circuit input that is "looking for" or "waiting for" a 1 to cause the circuit to activate or function.

Active HIGH output. A circuit output that is normally 0 and switches to a 1 when activated by the circuit.

Active LOW input. A circuit input that is "looking for" or "waiting for" a 0 to cause the circuit to activate or function.

Active LOW output. A circuit output that is normally 1 and switches to a 0 when activated by the circuit.

Address bus. A set of lines in a digital system dedicated to transmitting the address in memory or port to be used.

Address decoder. A circuit that generates chip select pulses from the address present on the address bus.

Addressing mode. Method of specifying the operands to be used in an operation.

Alternate register set. The set of registers in the Z 80 consisting of A′, F′, B′, C′, D′, E′, H′, L′.

APU (arithmetic processing unit). Integrated circuit that works in conjunction with a processor as an EPU.

ASCC (asynchronous serial communication). An IC that provides asynchronous serial communications.

ASCII (American Standard Code for Information Interchange). A 7-bit code that represents the decimal digits, letters of the alphabet, symbols, and control characters.

Assembler. A program that converts mnemonic code into op code (source code into object code).

Assembly language. A programming language composed of mnemonic codes.

Asynchronous serial communications. System of transmitting words in serial format in which the start of each word is signalled with a start bit.

Baud rate. The rate at which bits are transmitted in serial communication (bits per second).

BCD. Binary coded decimal.

BEP (burst error processor). An IC that provides error detection and correction for high-speed transfer to disk systems.

Bidirectional bus. A bus, such as the data bus, that carries information in both directions.

Bit. A contraction for binary digit. Each place in a binary number is a bit; for example 1011 is a 4-bit number.

Bit addressing. One of the modes of addressing. A 3-bit code in the op code specifies which bit is to be set, reset, or tested.

BIU (bus interface unit). Part of a processor that prefetches instructions for the EU.

Buffer. A circuit whose function is to provide greater output current drive than the input has.

Bus. A set of lines that transmits information in parallel, one line for each bit.

Bus driver. A buffer that provides sufficient current drive for the output to drive a bus line.

Byte. A binary number 8 bits long.

C (carry flag). One bit of the flag register. In operations that affect the C flag, C is set if a carry from the most significant bit occurs.

CALL instruction. An instruction that causes the CPU to begin execution of a subroutine.

CAS (column address strobe). A signal used to refresh dynamic RAM.

Central processor unit (CPU). The control unit of the microcomputer or digital system.

Chip select. A signal used to enable an integrated circuit.

CIO (counter/timer and parallel I/O). An IC that provides parallel I/O ports and counters/timers.

Clock. A continuous rectangular waveform used for timing.

Closed-loop control. A control system in which a feedback signal is used to indicate the actual condition of the system.

CMOS (complementary metal-oxide semiconductor). One of the technologies used in the manufacture of integrated circuits.

Common anode. A seven-segment display in which all the anodes are tied together internally.

Common cathode. A seven-segment display in which all the cathodes are tied together internally.

Compare. An instruction that causes the operand to be compared to the accumulator. The flags are set as if a subtraction had taken place.

Condition codes. Flags.

Conditional jump. Instruction that causes the CPU to jump to another location in the program to get the next instruction if certain conditions are met.

COP (computer operating properly). A "watchdog" system that helps protect against processor software failure.

Count-up method. One method used in analog-to-digital conversion.

CPU emulator. A circuit used to test a processor system. The CPU is replaced by the emulator for testing.

CTC (counter/timer circuit). An integrated circuit that contains programmable counter/timer channels.

D latches (data latch). A flip-flop in which one input signal is used to control both the set and reset inputs.

DART (dual asynchronous receiver/transmitter). An integrated circuit that provides two asynchronous receivers/transmitters.

Data bus. Circuits that generate, store, use, input, or output data are connected to the data bus. One line is provided for each bit of data.

DCE (data communication equipment). One of two categories of transmitting or receiving equipment referred to by the RS-232C standard (see DTE).

DCP (data ciphering processor). An IC that provides encryption and decryption for data transfer.

Debounced. Conditioned by a circuit so that contact bounce from switch closure has been eliminated.

Debug. Finding and correcting mistakes in programs.

Debugger software. A program that simulates the running of a program under test in the hardware environment in which it will actually operate.

Decrement. Decrease by 1.

Destination. Location that data is to be transferred to via a load instruction.

Digital-to-analog converter. A circuit that converts a digital signal into an equivalent analog signal.

Direct I/0. A system of handling I/0 operations whereby the I/0 ports are addressed separately from RAM or ROM (uses IN and OUT instructions).

Displacement byte. An 8-bit number in 2's complement form that specifies the direction and distance of a relative jump.

DMA (direct memory access). Transfer of data directly between memory and peripherals without passing through CPU.

DMAC (direct memory access controller). Integrated circuit that allows external devices to communicate directly with memory without passing through the CPU.

DRAM (dynamic RAM). RAM that must be refreshed periodically to maintain the data stored.

DTC (direct memory access transfer controller). An IC that manages the transfer of data from memory to peripheral or from memory to memory.

DTE (data terminating equipment). One of two categories of transmitting or receiving equipment referred to by the RS-232C standard (see DCE).

ECL (emitter-coupled logic). One of the technologies used to manufacture integrated circuits.

EEPROM (electrically erasable programmable read only memory). A ROM that can be erased electrically and reprogrammed.

EIA (Electronic Industries Association). Association that produces standards for many types of computer communication.

EPA (extended processing architecture). Has the facility to extend operations by software or hardware (see EPU).

EPROM (erasable programmable read only memory). A ROM that can be erased with ultraviolet light and reprogrammed.

EPU (extended processing unit). An integrated circuit

used in conjunction with a processor with EPA to improve speed and performance.

EU (execution unit). Part of a processor that takes instructions from the BIU and executes them.

Even duty cycle. A clock waveform that has HIGH and LOW states of equal durations.

Even parity. A system used to detect binary data transmission errors. It uses a parity bit to make the total number of 1's in a word even.

Extended addressing. One of the modes of addressing. The instruction includes two bytes that are used as an address.

Falling edge. HIGH to LOW transition of a digital signal.

FCW (flag and control word register). Special purpose internal register whose bits indicate various conditions that exist in the system.

FIFO (first-in-first-out interface unit). An asynchronous buffer that provides buffering between two CPUs or a CPU and an external device.

Firmware. A program stored in read only memory.

Flags. Bits in the flags register that indicate various conditions that result from an operation.

Flags register. Special-purpose register whose bits indicate various conditions that result from an operation.

Full decoder. A circuit that will make one output line active for a given binary number input to the circuit. Each possible binary number has its corresponding output line.

H (half-carry flag). One bit of the flags register. In operations that affect the H flag, H is set when a carry from bit 3 to bit 4 results.

H (Hexadecimal). In this text H is used to indicate that the preceding number is written in hexadecimal.

Handshaking signals. Signals used to control the transmission of data between two devices.

Hardware. The physical components of a digital system.

HCMOS (high-density CMOS). One of the technologies used to fabricate processors.

High-level language. A programming language in which a single statement translates into a series of op codes.

HMOS (high-density N-channel metal-oxide semiconductor). One of the technologies used to fabricate processors.

I (interrupt vector register). An 8-bit internal register that contains the HIGH byte of the address in memory that contains the next instruction to be used after a mode 2 interrupt.

Immediate addressing. One of the modes of addressing. The instruction contains 8 bits of data that are used as an operand.

Immediate extended addressing. One of the modes of addressing. The instruction contains 16 bits of data that are used as an operand.

Implied addressing. One of the modes of addressing. The op code implies which internal register is to be used in the operation.

Increment. Increase by 1.

Indexed addressing. One of the modes of addressing. A displacement byte in 2's complement form that is to be added to one of the index registers is included in the instruction.

Input/output read machine cycle. A group of T states used to input a byte of data to an output port.

Input/output write machine cycle. A group of T states used to output data to an output port.

Instruction fetch. M1 machine cycle. A group of T states used to load the first byte of an instruction from memory to the CPU.

Instruction set. The set of op codes that are recognized by the CPU.

Internal register. Registers contained within the CPU.

Interrupt. A signal from an external device requesting service.

Interrupt acknowledge. A signal from the system to the external device that the CPU is ready to process an interrupt.

Interrupt acknowledge machine cycle. A group of T states used to input the next instruction from an input port.

Interrupt flip-flop (IFF). A flip-flop that is set by the enable interrupt (EI) instruction to enable maskable interrupts.

IPC (intelligent peripheral controller). An integrated circuit that contains its own 8-bit CPU, parallel I/O, serial I/O, ROM, RAM, and timers for peripheral interface.

IX (index register). A 16-bit internal register that points to a "starting place" in memory. A displacement byte is added to IX to form an exact location.

IY (index register). A 16-bit internal register that points to a "starting place" in memory. A displacement byte is added to IY to form an exact location.

Large-scale integration (LSI). An integrated circuit that contains circuitry equivalent to 100 gates or more.

Leading edge. The first transition of pulse, be it LOW to HIGH or HIGH to LOW.

LIFO (last-in first-out). A memory register in which the last word written to the register is the first word read out.

Logic analyzer. A piece of text equipment that latches and stores the states of its inputs at each transition of the clock.

Long words. Words that are 32 bits in length.

Lower threshold. The lower voltage level that causes a change in output of a Schmitt trigger IC.

Machine cycle. A group of T states needed to complete a particular function.

Main register set. The set of registers in the Z 80 consisting of A, F, B, C, D, E, H, L.

Maskable interrupt. An interrupt that can be inhibited by the programmer.

Mega. Prefix meaning 10^6.

Memory. An array of cells that can store binary numbers.

Memory mapped I/O. A system of handling I/O operations, whereby the I/O ports are treated like locations in memory.

Memory read machine cycle. A group of T states used to load a byte of data from memory into the CPU.

Memory write machine cycle. A group of T states used to load a byte of data from the CPU to memory.

Minuend. The top number in a subtraction problem.

MMU (memory management unit). Integrated circuit that translates logical addresses used by the CPU into physical locations in memory.

Mnemonic. Intended to assist memory.

Mnemonic code. A code assigned to each operation code in the instruction set that facilitates programming and memory.

Mode 0 interrupt. Interrupt system in which the op code of the next instruction to be performed is input onto the data bus.

Mode 1 interrupt. Interrupt system in which the CPU takes its next instruction from memory location 0038H.

Mode 2 interrupt. Interrupt system in which the byte in the I register together with the byte input by the interrupting device points to the location in memory that contains the LOW byte of the address of the next instruction to be implemented. The following address contains the HIGH byte.

M1 machine cycle (instruction fetch machine cycle). A group of T states used to load the first byte of an instruction from memory to the CPU.

Monitor routine. The program stored in ROM that performs such duties as monitoring the keyboard.

MOS (metal-oxide semiconductor). A type of transistor used in some digital ICs.

MPCC (multiprotocol communications controller). An integrated circuit that provides for asynchronous serial data communication.

Multiple precision. Operations that involve numbers more than 1 byte long.

Multiplexer. A logic circuit that will switch one of many inputs to one output. The input that is connected to the output is selected by a binary number input to the logic circuit.

N (subtract flag [Negative]). One bit of the flags register. In operations that affect this flag, N is set if the operation is subtraction.

Nano. Prefix meaning 10^{-9}.

Nibble. Four bits.

Nonmaskable interrupt. An interrupt that cannot be inhibited by the programmer.

Nonvolatile memory. Memory whose contents are not destroyed when power is removed.

NPX (numeric processor extension). IC that executes instructions as a coprocessor.

Object code. A program written or listed in op codes.

Odd parity. A system used to detect binary data transmission errors. It uses a parity bit to make the total number of 1's in a word odd.

Op code. A binary number, usually represented in hex, that is recognized by the CPU as an instruction.

Open collector. Circuit in which the output has no internal path to the power supply. An external pull-up resistor is usually added.

Open-loop control. A control system in which no feedback signal is used to indicate the actual condition of the system.

Operand. The data, register, or memory location that is to be operated upon.

Optical coupler. An enclosed package that contains an LED and a phototransistor or equivalent device. Used to provide isolation between input and output.

Parallel interface. A circuit that provides for communication between the data bus and an external device, 8 bits at a time.

Parity. A system used to detect errors in binary data transmission.

Partial decoder. A logic circuit that will give an active signal on one output line for a given binary number input to the circuit. The circuit does not have a unique output line for each possible binary number input to it as a full decoder has.

PC (program counter). Sixteen-bit register in the Z-80 that contains the address of the next program instruction to be implemented.

Peripheral. External device.

PIA (peripheral interface adapter). A programmable parallel interface integrated circuit.

PIO (parallel input/output). An integrated circuit that provides parallel interface ports.

PI/T (parallel interface/timer). An integrated circuit used to connect peripheral devices to the 68000.

PLL (phase-locked loop). An integrated circuit used in radio-frequency applications.

PMMU (paged memory management unit). An IC that converts physical memory into pages and translates logical memory into physical memory.

Points to. Contains the address of a location in memory that is to be used in an operation.

POP. An instruction that transfers 16 bits of data from the stack to AF, BC, DE, HL, SP, IX, or IY.

Port. A circuit that can latch data on the data bus for external use or that can pass data from an external device onto the data bus when requested.

Process control. The use of a microprocessor to control a system or manufacturing process.

PROM (programmable read only memory). ROM that can be programmed only once.

Pull-up. A resistor used to provide a path to the power supply.

Pulse stretcher. A circuit used to increase the pulse width of the incoming signal.

PUSH. An instruction that loads 16 bits of data from AF, BC, DE, HL, IX, or IY onto the stack.

P/V (parity/overflow flag). A bit of the flags register that monitors overflow (V) in 2's complement arithmetic. Monitors parity (P) in logical operations.

R (memory refresh register). An 8-bit internal register that is used to refresh dynamic RAM.

RAM (random access memory). Read/write memory in which access time for any byte is constant.

RAS (row address stroke). A signal used to refresh dynamic RAM.

Reboot. To cause the computer to return to the restart of the monitor routine.

Refresh. To update the contents of DRAM.

Register. A set of read/write memory bits that work together as a unit.

Register addressing. One of the modes of addressing. A 3-bit code within the op code specifies which internal register is to be used in the operation.

Register indirect addressing. One of the modes of addressing. A register or register pair points to the operand to be used.

Relative addressing. One of the modes of addressing. The instruction contains a displacement byte to be used in a relative jump.

Relative jump. An instruction that causes the CPU to jump forward or backward from its present position in the program to get its next instruction.

Reset. An input signal that causes the CPU to fetch the next instruction from 0000H.

Restart instruction. An instruction that causes the CPU to take the next instruction from a specific location on page zero (HIGH byte = 00H).

Return. An instruction that causes the CPU to terminate the execution of a subroutine and to return to its original position in the main program.

ROM (read only memory). Memory that is read during the course of a program but not written to.

Rotate instruction. An instruction that causes the operand together with the carry flag to act as a ring counter.

RS-232C. Widely used standard for serial communication.

S (sign flag). One bit of the flags register. On operations that affect the sign flag, the sign flag follows the most significant bit (MSB) of the result.

SCC (serial communication controller). An IC that provides synchronous or asynchronous serial communication.

Schmitt trigger input. An input to a digital device that will change the output logic level at fixed upper and lower threshold voltages of the input.

SCI (serial communication interface). A serial interface integrated circuit.

SDMA (serial direct memory access). See DMA.

Shift instruction. An instruction that causes the operand together with the carry flag to function as a shift register.

Sink current. Provides a path for conventional current to flow to ground.

SIO (serial input/output controller). An integrated circuit that provides synchronous or asynchronous I/O.

Software. The program part of a digital system.

Source. Location of data to be transferred via a load instruction.

Source code. A program written in mnemonic code (assembler).

Source current. Provides a path for conventional current to flow from the power supply.

SP (stack pointer). A 16-bit register in the Z 80 that points to the location in memory to be used next as part of the stack.

SPI (serial peripheral interface). A serial interface integrated circuit.

SRAM (static RAM). RAM that retains its data without needing to be refreshed.

Stack. A section of memory where data in the registers can be stored or stacked until needed again.

Stepper motor. An electrical motor designed to rotate in definite steps.

Strobe. A signal used to enable an IC or circuit.

Subroutine. A portion of the program that performs a particular function.

Subtrahend. The second or bottom number in a subtraction problem.

Successive approximation. A method of using a digital-to-analog converter and voltage comparator to produce a binary number that is proportional to the given analog input voltage.

Synchronous serial. Communication system of transmitting words in serial format in which words are sent in blocks of 256 or 1024 bytes.

T state. One clock period.

Timing loop. Subroutine that uses up a precise amount of time.

Trap. A synchronous event that occurs when a particular condition arises during the execution of an instruction.

Tri-state gate. Gate whose output can assume any one of three states—HiZ, 0, or 1.

TTL (transistor-transistor logic). One of the popular families of digital integrated circuits.

Two's complement. The binary number formed by inverting each bit of a binary number and adding 1.

UART (universal asynchronous receiver/transmitter). An IC that provides asynchronous serial transmission.

Unconditional jump. Instruction that causes the CPU to jump to another location in the program to get the next instruction.

Unidirectional bus. A bus, such as the address bus, that transfers data one way only.

UPC (universal peripheral controllers). Microcomputer units dedicated to the control of peripheral devices.

Upper threshold. The higher of two voltage levels that causes a change in the output of a Schmitt trigger IC.

Volatile memory. Memory that loses its stored data when power is removed.

Z (zero flag). One bit of the flags register. On operations that affect the zero flag, the zero flag is set if the result of the operation is zero.

Answers to the Odd-Numbered Problems

CHAPTER 1

1. Memory, Input/Output, Central Processing Unit, Program.
3. 1024
5. Transfers addresses from the CPU to the components connected to the address bus. (one way only).
7. Data bus.
9. The CPU places an address on the address bus. After that address has become stable, the MREQ (memory request) goes low.
11. IORQ signals that an 8-bit address of an input or output device has been placed on the low byte of the address bus and is stable.
13.

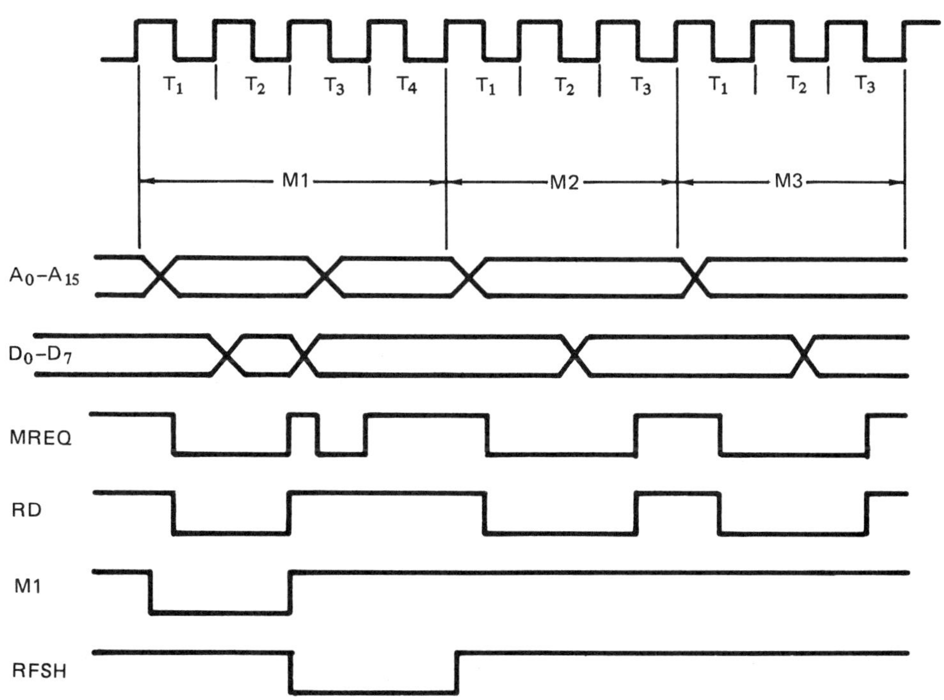

15. See Figure 1-15. A 0 on pin 19 enables each of the control gates. A 1 on pin 1 allows data to pass from pin 2 to 18, 3-27 etc. A 0 on pin 1 allows data to pass from 18 to 2, 17 to 3, etc.
17. MREQ and RD
19. The CPU holds the address on the address bus as long as wait stays low.

CHAPTER 2

1. ROM (Read Only Memory) A memory that permanently stores its bit pattern.
3. Exposure to ultraviolet light with a wavelength of 2500 Angstroms or shorter and an intensity of 15-W-sec/cm for 15 to 20 minutes.
5. Dynamic RAM
7. See Figure 2-11
9. It can store 2K (2048) bytes of data.
11. See Figure 2-5
13. during the M1 cycle.
15.

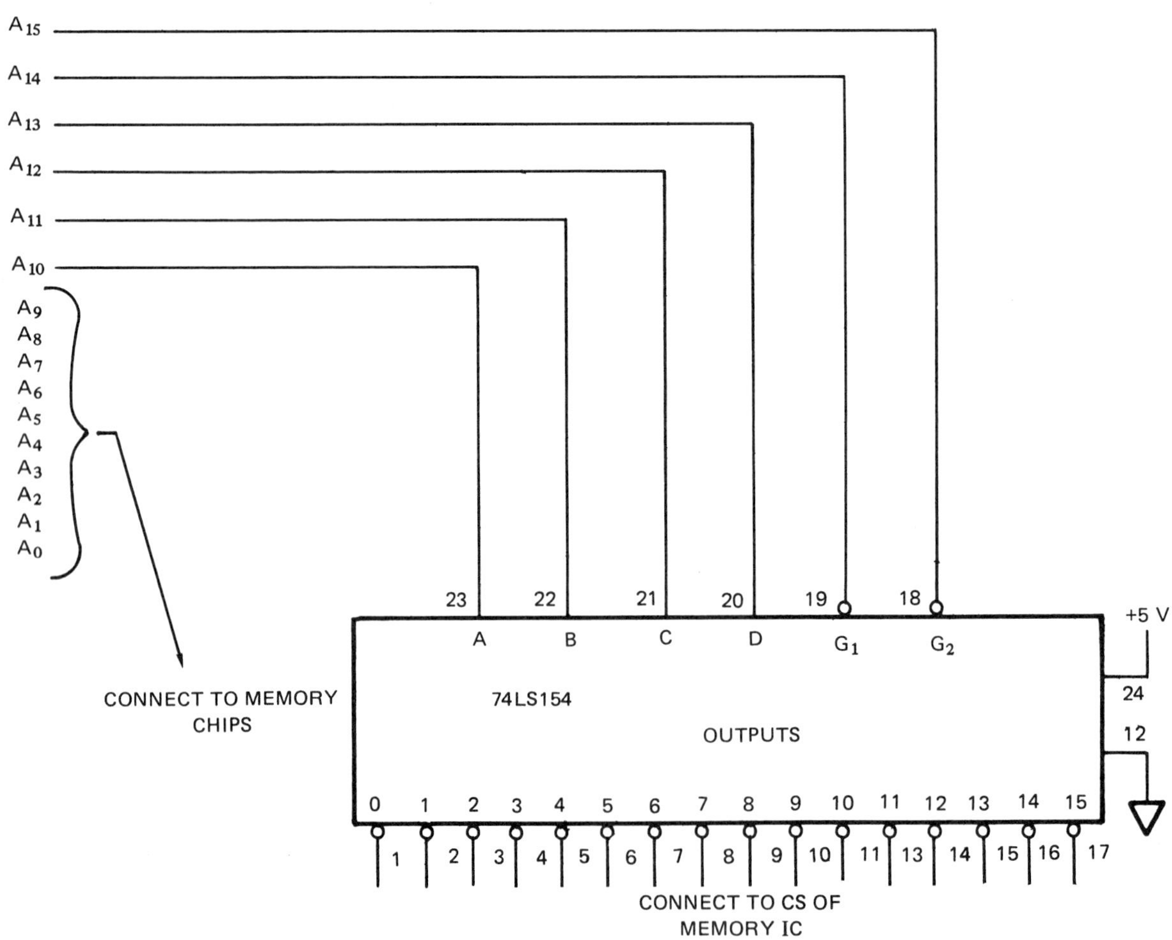

17. The 2K of ROM runs from 0000 to 07FF.
19. Core memory.

CHAPTER 3

1. 6800, 6502
3. Assuming no extra wait states 2 μs.
5. Three (0,1,2) for the user and one (port 3) for use with the keyboard.
7. Seven (1–7)
9. 03
11.

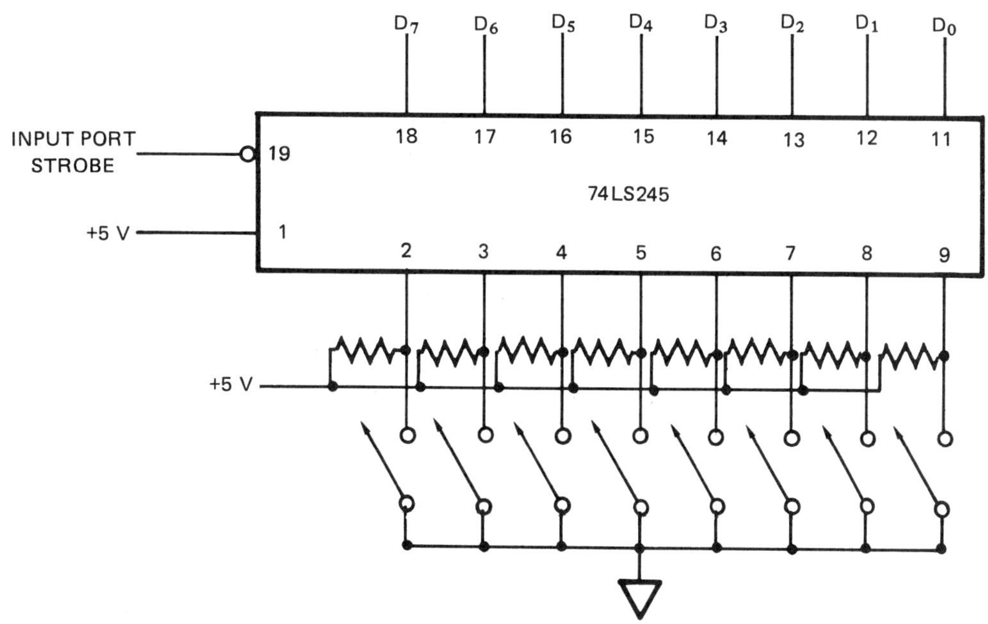

13. Falling edge of T_3.
15. It can sink more current than the Q output can source.
17. Yes
19. The decoder does not provide a unique output for each possible input combination.

CHAPTER 4

1. Program Counter—points to the location in memory that contains the next instruction to be implemented.
3. Index registers—point to locations in memory that are used as reference points.
5. 16-bit general purpose register pairs BC, DE, HL, BC′, DE′, HL′.
7. EXX

9. Register L can be output to port 2 by loading register C with 02H and then using OUT (C), L (op-code ED69H).
11. INIR (Input,Increment,Repeat) inputs the number of bytes specified by register B into memory beginning at the address pointed to by HL, via the input port specified by register C.
    INDR (Input, Decrement, Repeat) inputs the number of bytes specified by register B into memory ending at the address pointed to by HL via the input port specified by register C.
13. In a LOAD immediate instruction the operand (data to be loaded) comes from the second byte of the instruction. In a register to register load the data comes from another register.
15. DD4EA0 loads the C register with the contents of memory pointed to by IX + A0.

17a. 22H

17b. BCH

CHAPTER 5

1. P/V Flag. In two's complement arithmetic (V) it is set if the result in the Accumulator is incorrect. In logical operations (P) the flag is set if the number of 1s in the Accumulator is odd and reset if the number is even.
3. The S Flag is set if the result of an operation that affects the sign flag is negative and reset if the result is positive.
5. The N Flag is set on a subtraction type problem and reset on an addition type problem.
7. In an ADD instruction the operand is added to the Accumulator. In an ADC instruction the operand and the contents of the Carry Flag are added to the Accumulator.
9. In a subtract instruction the operand is subtracted from the Accumulator and the Accumulator changes to contain the result. In a CP (compare) instruction the Accumulator does not change. The flags are set as if a subtraction has taken place.
11. When an 8-bit register is decremented the S, Z, H, P/V and N Flags are affected. No flags are affected when a 16-bit register is decremented.
13. No.
15. a. 84
    b. C6n where n is the number to be added.
    c. 9E
    d. DDAE08
    e. FD2B
    f. ED4A
17.
```
ORG 0800H
SUB A
LD  IY,0950H
ADD A,(IY+06H)
SUB A,(IY-06H)
```

19.

	ACCUMULATOR	S	Z	H	P/V	N	C
SUB A	0 0 0 0 0 0 0 0	0	1	0	0	1	0
LD IY,0950H	0 0 0 0 0 0 0 0	0	1	0	0	1	0
ADD A,(IY + 06H)	0 1 1 1 0 0 1 0	0	0	0	0	0	0
SUB A,(IY − 06H)	0 0 1 1 1 0 1 1	0	0	1	0	1	0

(FLAGS: S Z H P/V N C)

CHAPTER 6

1. A shift instruction causes the operand along with the carry flag to function as a shift register. The bit on the end is lost. A rotate instruction causes the operand along with the carry flag to function as a ring counter. The end bit is loaded back into the other end.
3. Rotate Right Circular

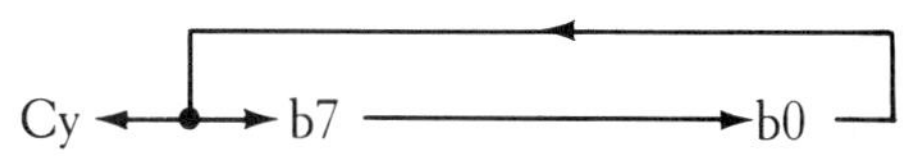

5. Rotate Right

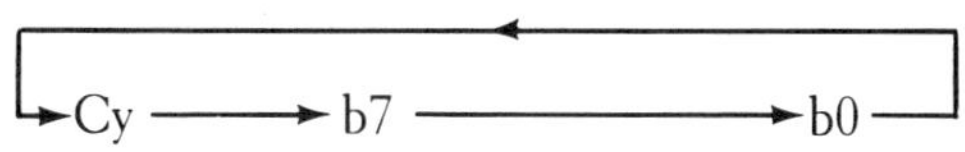

7. Shift Right Arithmetic

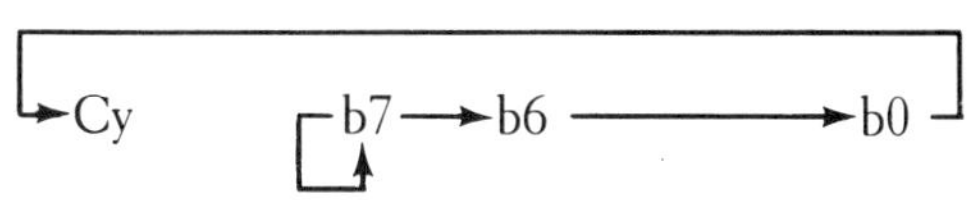

9. Rotate Digit Left

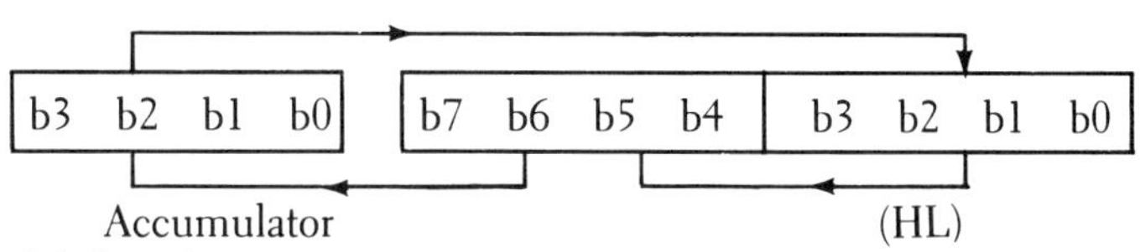

11. CB24 does a shift left arithmetic on the H register. The contents of the H register is shifted left, a zero is shifted into bit 0, and bit 7 is shifted into the Carry Flag.
13. CB21 cy ← b7 ← b0 ← 0
C register
Shift left arithmetic
15. RR A
Two byte instruction
CB1F
Flags: H = 0
N = 0
P/V = P
S = ↕
Z = ↕
C = ↕

RRA
Single byte instruction
1F
Flags: H = 0
N = 0
C = ↕
1 machine cycle
4 T-states
17. CA5009H
19. JP M (Jump on Minus) jumps to the new address if the Sign Flag is set, otherwise

the instruction is ignored. JP P (Jump on Positive) jumps to the new address if the Sign Flag is reset. Otherwise the instruction is ignored.

21. 0944 } Two byte
    0945 } instruction
    0946 contents of PC

23.
```
ORG     0800H
LD      DE,0004H
LD      B,08H
SUB     A
DJNZ    FDH
HALT
```

25. There is no jump relative on Even Parity instruction.

CHAPTER 7

1. Return
3. A subroutine that is called from within a subroutine.
5. 0BFE F — F stored at 0BFE
   0BFF A — A stored at 0BFF
   0C00
7. 09FF F — contents of 09FF into F
   0A00 A — contents of 0A00 into A
9. Mode 0,1,2
11. EI, Enable Interrupt, FBH
13. The next instruction is taken off the data bus.
15. The address formed by the I register (HI byte) and the byte placed on the data bus by the interrupting device (LO byte) points to the location in memory that contains the LO byte of the address of the next instruction to be used. The following address contains the HI byte.
17.

OP-CODE	MNEMONIC	ADDRESS
C7	RST 00H	0000H
CF	RST 08H	0008H
D7	RST 10H	0010H
DF	RST 18H	0018H
E7	RST 20H	0020H
EF	RST 28H	0028H
F7	RST 30H	0030H
FF	RST 38H	0038H

19. 0
21. INTACK must be low (IORQ, RD, M1 low) and FF 3 must be set (output of NAND gate 1 HIGH).

CHAPTER 8

1. Understand the instruction set, be able to read and write to the computer's memory, start a program at any point in memory.
3.

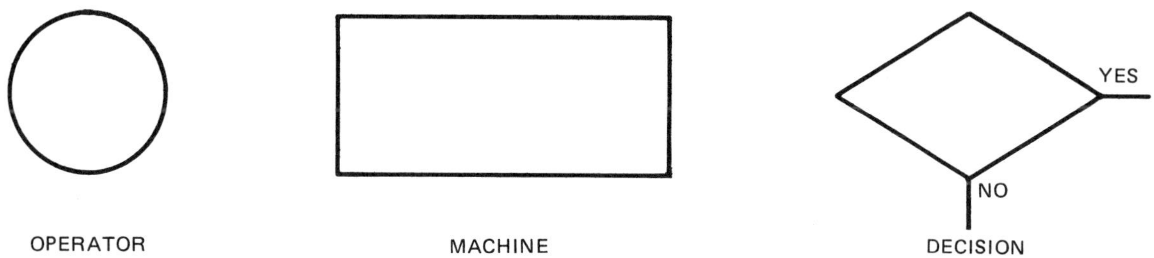

5.
```
TIME    PUSH  HL
        LD    HL,ODZAH
LOOP3   DEC   L
        JR    NZ,LOOP3
        DEC   H
        JR    NZ,LOOP3
        POP   HL
        NOP
        NOP
        NOP
        RET
```
7. A circuit that replaces the CPU during test. Switches are used to set the CPU control signals to the desired levels.
9. A logic analyzer is a piece of test equipment that latches, stores and displays the waveforms on its multiple inputs. It is used to troubleshoot digital systems.
11. 17.5 Seconds (does not include CALL instruction).
13.
```
LOOP    IN    A,(00H)
        OUT   (00H),A
        JP    LOOP
```
15. OBFFH
17.

H	01000111
L	00100111
Shift	00010111
Run	00001111

19. The first bytes of the instructions run.

CHAPTER 9

1. Memory mapped—IO—ports are treated as memory locations.
   IO mapped—uses IN and OUT instructions.
3. Two modes, 0 and 1.
5. A1 = 1 A0 = 1.
7.
```
LD  A,8BH        ;Control word
OUT (FFH),A      ;OUT control word
IN  A,(FDH)      ;IN from port B
OUT (FCH),A      ;OUT to port A
```
9. Use bit set/reset to reset PC4.
11. The A key was pressed.
13. BFH
15. 8 data bits.
17. Bit 7 1 = Active for mode control word
    0 = Active for bit set reset.
19. Not enough control lines in C.

CHAPTER 10

1. FFH
3. 6 modes
5. 00111110
7. 11111100 Counter 0
   11111101 Counter 1
   11111110 Counter 2
9. Specify the register by outputting a control word to the 8253 using D7, D6 to specify the register and D5, D4 as 00. Then read the counter desired.
11.
```
LD   A,37H
OUT  (FFH),A
LD   A,00H
OUT  (FCH),A
LD   A,20H
OUT  (FCH),A
```
13.
```
LD   A,00 H
OUT  (FFH),A
IN   A,(FCH)
OUT  (02H),A
```

15.

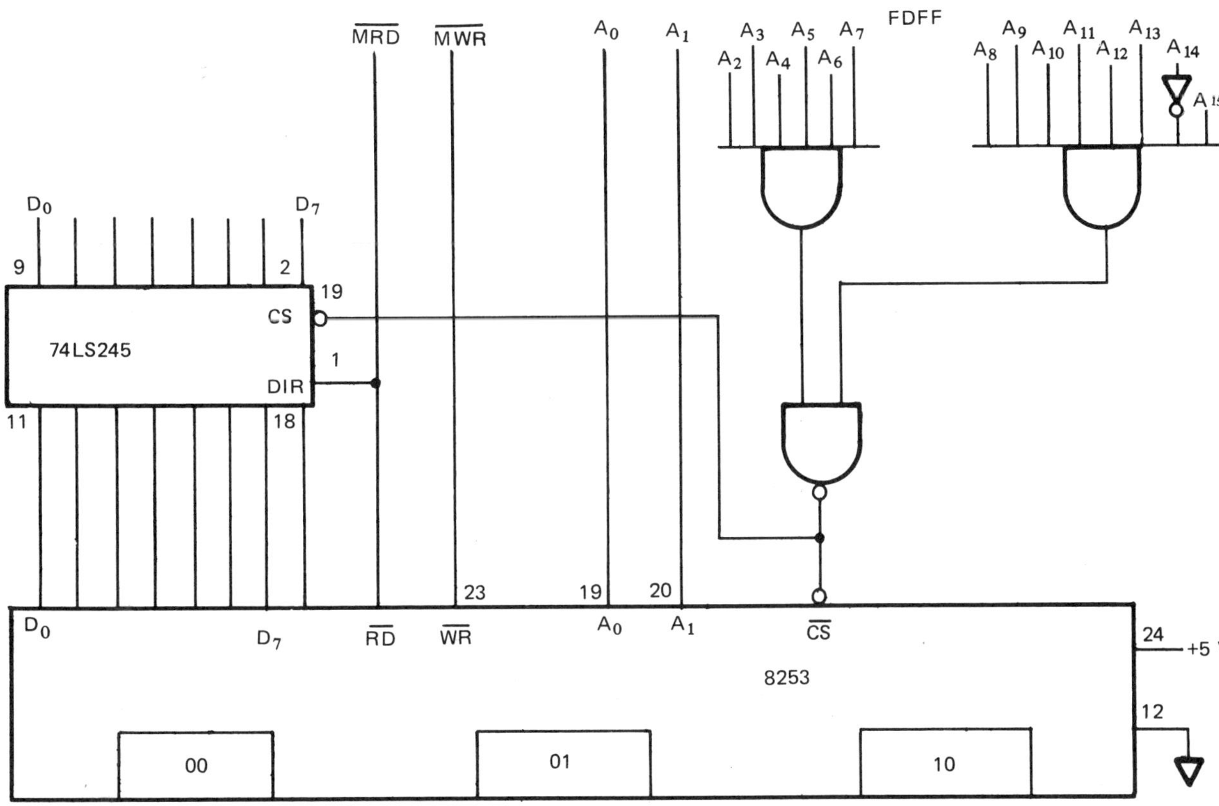

17. 10011011
19. Outputs go to HiZ—no operations take place.

CHAPTER 11

1.

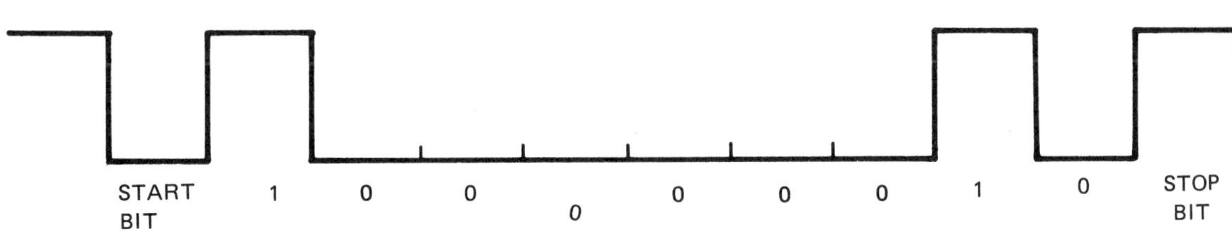

3. Data was lost because a new word was shifted in before the CPU read the previous one.
5. C/D = 1 Control register is written to
Status register is read from
C/D = 0 Transmitter buffer is written to
Receiver input buffer is read
7. To synchronize the internal operation of 8251 to the system clock of CPU.
9. External sync detect—when SYNDET goes high the receiver starts shifting in data. Internal sync detect—SYNDET goes high when the 8251 has detected sync.
11. Output logic 1 ranges from -5 V to -15 V.
13. Data communication equipment (DCE). Data terminating equipment (DTE).
15. D1
17. Pin 2
19. 1000010

CHAPTER 12

1.

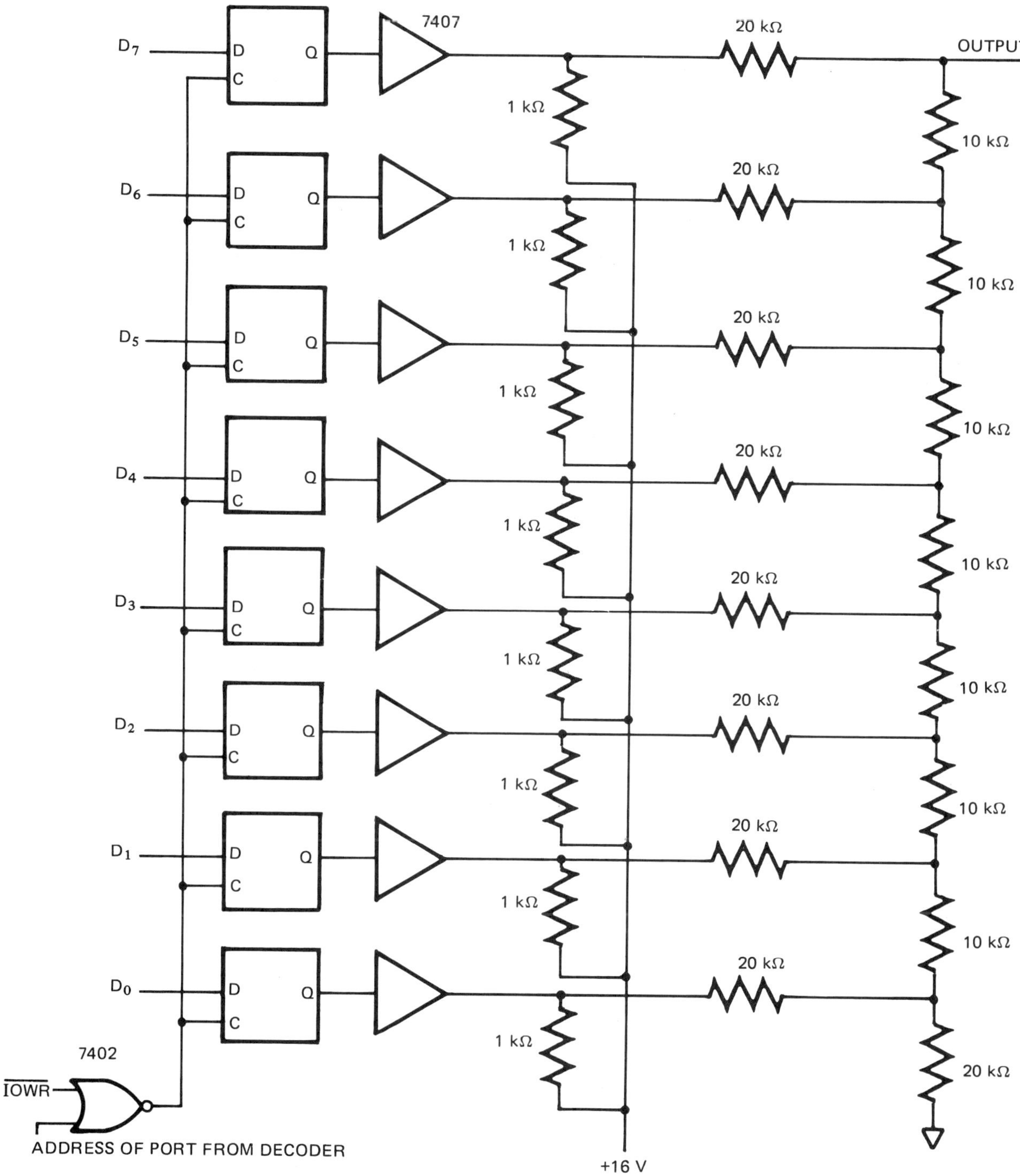
7407
20 kΩ
OUTPUT
D_7
D
C
Q
1 kΩ
10 kΩ
D_6
D_5
D_4
D_3
D_2
D_1
D_0
7402
$\overline{IOWR}$
ADDRESS OF PORT FROM DECODER
+16 V

3. The outputs of the 7406s will not go to zero. The 1 kΩ pull-ups are added to the 20 kΩ resistors.
5.

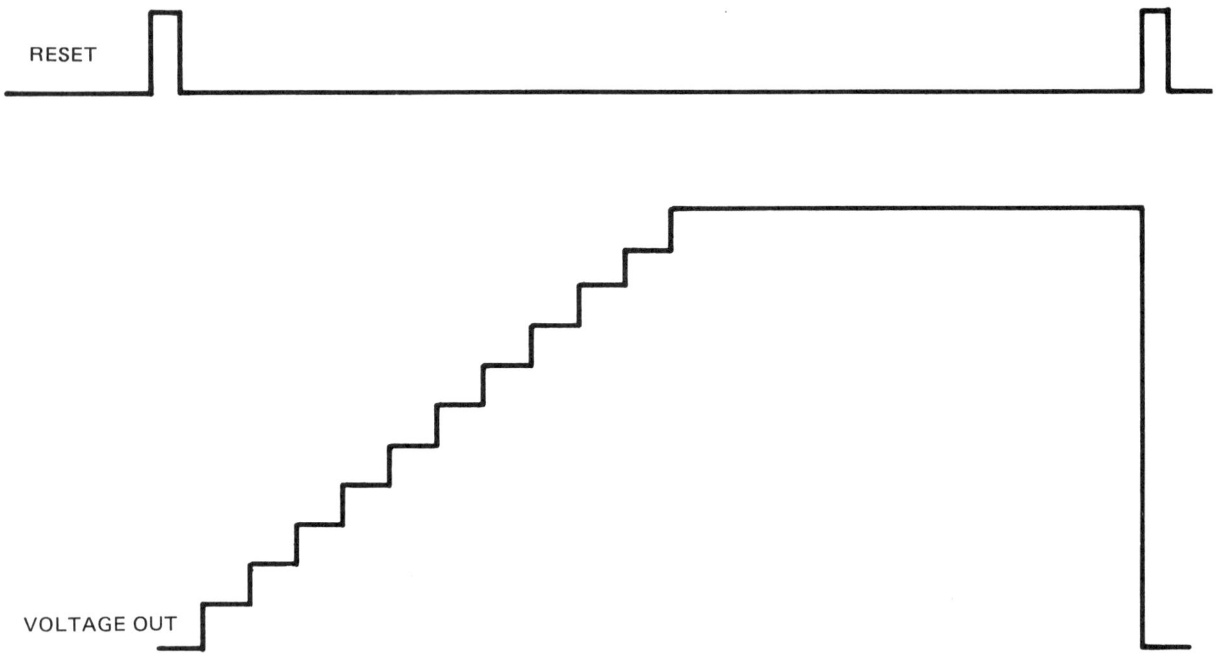

7.

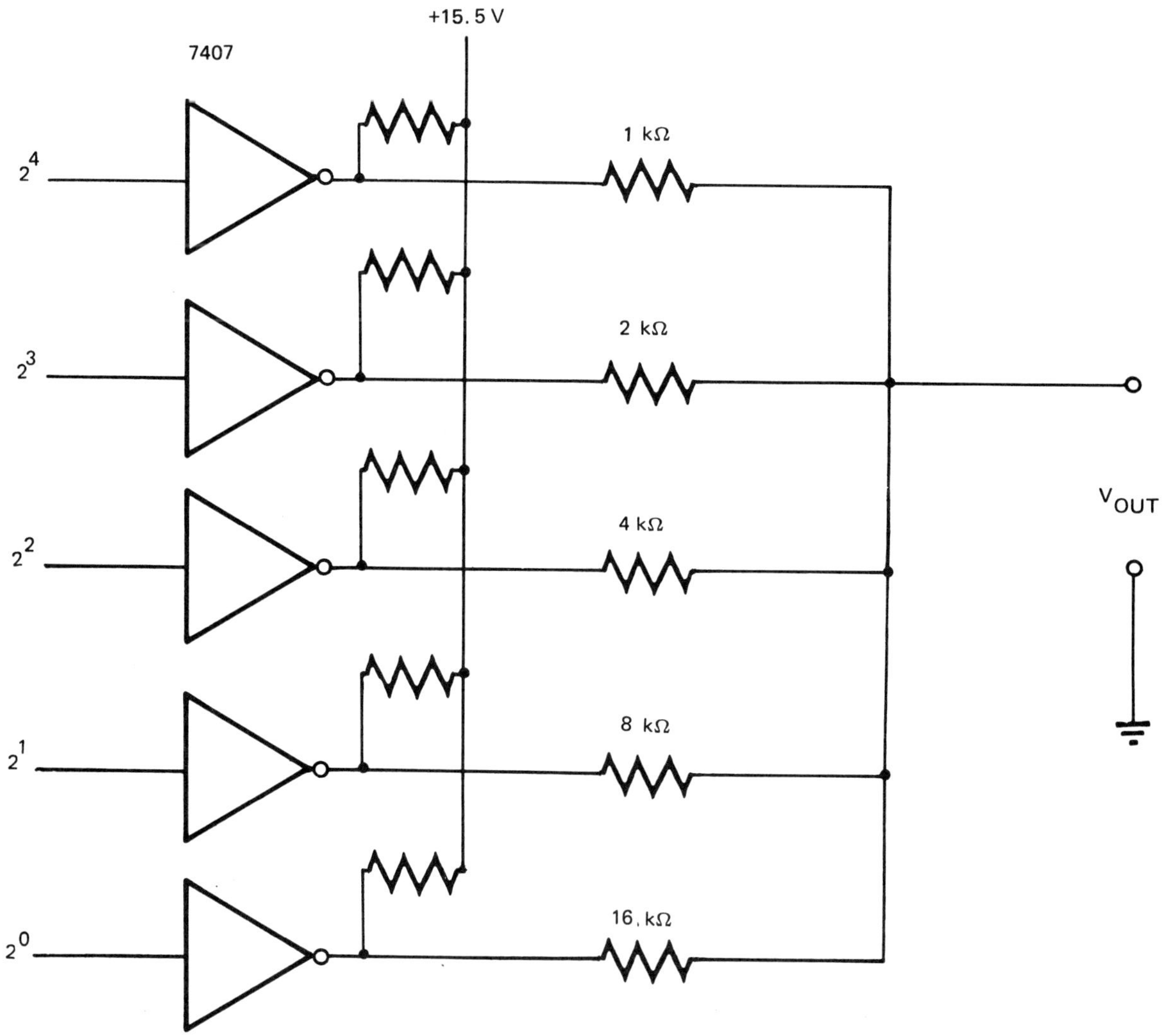

9.

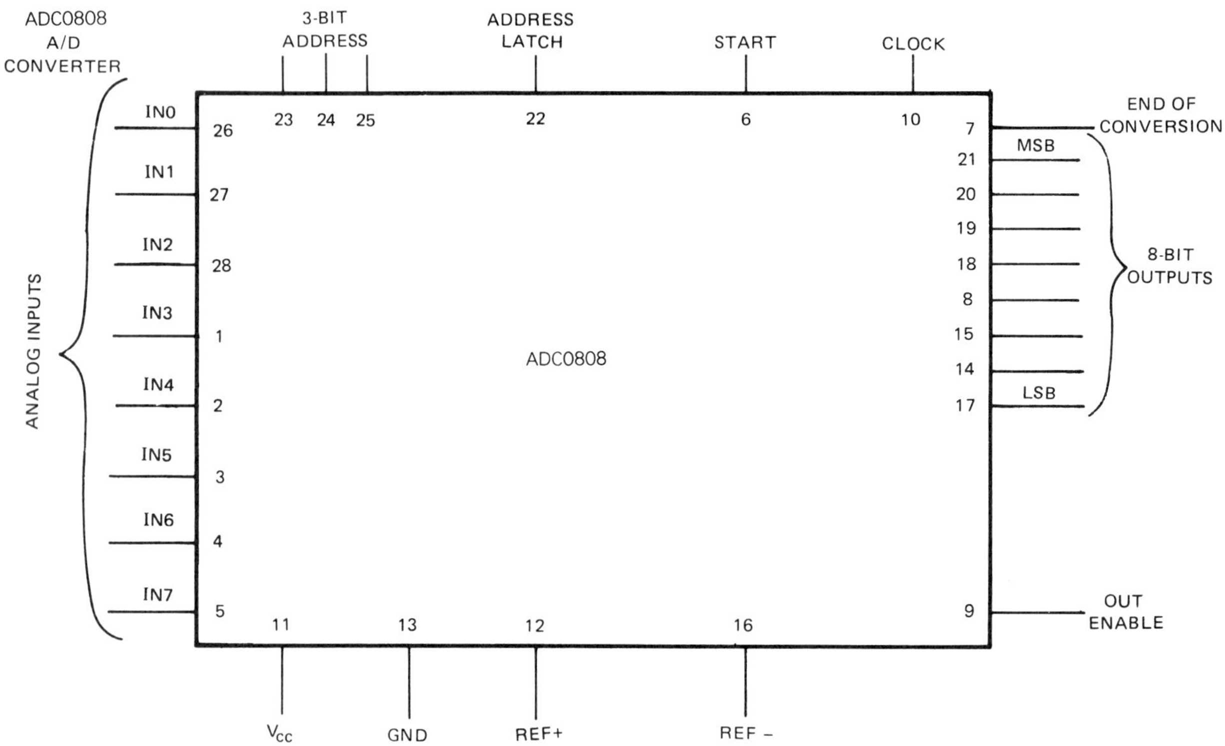

11. 256R Network
13. Stairstep with 15 steps
15. 3 V
17. See Section 12.9
19. 9 V

CHAPTER 13

1. No feedback signal is provided to indicate the effect of control signals on the system.
3. 48 mA
5. 333
7.

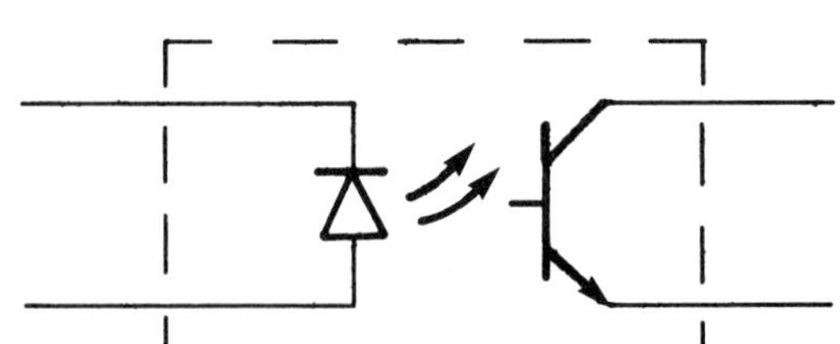

9. STOP signal
   10000000 = 80H
   10000001 = 81H
   10000010 = 82H
   10000011 = 83H
11.

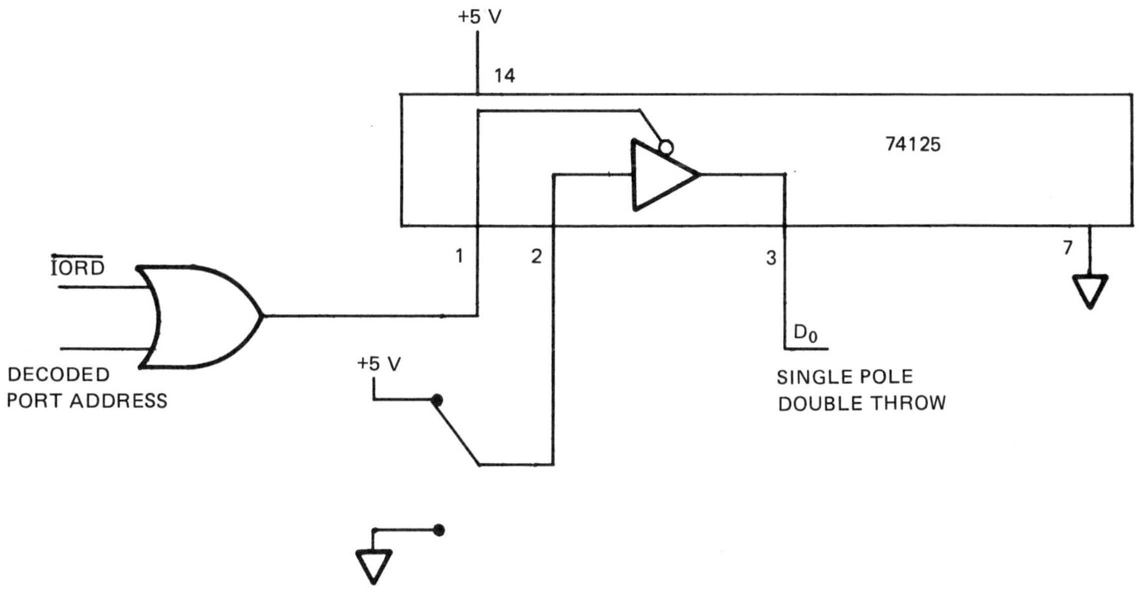

13. 466 mA
15. A feedback signal is provided to the controller to indicate the effect of the control signals on the process.
17. The current through the relay coil that will cause the armature to activate.
19.

```
        ORG     0800H
BEGIN   LD      A,7FH
        LD      B,0AH
        CALL    ROTATE      ;Subroutine Figure 13-14
        JP      BEGIN
```

CHAPTER 14

1. All load instructions to and from memory become I/O instructions, giving the programmer much flexibility.
3. Microcomputer unit.
5. The contents of DP are placed in the high byte of the address bus. The instruction being executed specifies the low byte.

7. It contains eight 32-bit data registers, seven 32-bit address registers, and a 16-bit status register.
9. 6809, 6801, 6802, 6800, 6805
11. Dual asynchronous receiver transmitter.
13. The Z8603 can be interfaced to a 2711 EPROM. The EPROM can be reprogrammed as needed to develop the system. The 8601 can be mask programmed with the resulting program.
15. A trap is an event that occurs with the clock internal to the processor. An interrupt is an external event that is asynchronous.
17. 8086
19. 64K
21. An 8087 working in conjunction with an 8086.

Index